GUNS OR BUTTER

GUNS
OR
BUTTER

The Presidency of Lyndon Johnson

IRVING BERNSTEIN

New York   Oxford
OXFORD UNIVERSITY PRESS
1996

Oxford University Press

Oxford   New York
Athens   Auckland   Bangkok   Bombay
Calcutta   Cape Town   Dar es Salaam   Delhi
Florence   Hong Kong   Istanbul   Karachi
Kuala Lumpur   Madras   Madrid   Melbourne
Mexico City   Nairobi   Paris   Singapore
Taipei   Tokyo   Toronto

and associated companies in
Berlin   Ibadan

Published by Oxford University Press, Inc.,
198 Madison Avenue, New York, New York   10016

Oxford is a registered trademark of Oxford University Press

Library of Congress Cataloging-in-Publication Data
Bernstein, Irving, 1916–
Guns or butter: The presidency of Lyndon Johnson /
Irving Bernstein.
p.   cm.
Includes bibliographical references (p.   ) and index.
ISBN 0-19-506312-0
1. Johnson, Lyndon B. (Lyndon Baines), 1908–1973.
2. Presidents—United States—Biography.
3. United States—Politics and government—1963–1969.
I. Title.   E847.B45   1996
973.923'092—dc20   [B]   94-46879

1 3 5 7 9 8 6 4 2

Printed in the United States of America
on acid-free paper

To

MIKE MANSFIELD

A superb public servant
who steered the Great Society
through the Senate and
opposed the Vietnam War

Preface

LYNDON Johnson's presidency opened with the catastrophe of the Kennedy assassination and closed in the disaster of the Vietnam War. During the intervening five years the nation was racked by turmoil—demonstrations by blacks seeking racial justice and riots in the urban ghettoes, student unrest in the colleges, and demonstrations by opponents of the war. It was an extremely trying period to be President and it is small wonder that Lyndon Johnson is ranked low among American Presidents by both the public and historians.

But there is another and very important part of his presidency: he started out brilliantly. Johnson united the country after the assassination in Dallas; he won a great landslide victory over Barry Goldwater in 1964; and, most significant, he persuaded Congress to enact a massive legislative program which greatly expanded the welfare of all Americans, rich and poor, black and white.

Lyndon Johnson has been short-changed. He has been charged with what went wrong and he has not been credited with what went right. This book seeks to redress this unfair balance.

At this time the literature on the Johnson presidency is badly skewed. There are an enormous number of studies of Vietnam; the flood of books that began in the sixties shows no sign of abating. On domestic policies there is only a respectable literature on civil rights. For the many other topics there is, at best, no more than a thin monographic literature and the searcher must dig into the primary documents. Here the great source, of course, is the Lyndon Baines Johnson Library in Austin.

Writers owe heavy debts to others who have assisted them. Three have been exceptionally helpful to me. Joseph A. Califano, Jr., who was in charge of domestic policy in the Johnson White House, was most generous with his time, his papers, and his savvy. Linda Hanson, archivist at the Johnson Library, seems to know how to locate anything in the labyrinthine recesses of that institution and led me to those documents that I needed. A. Philip Scott, the head of that library's audio-visual department, was very helpful in guiding me to the great majority of the photographs that illustrate this book.

I am also in debt to a number of kind people who took the time to read all or part of the manuscript and who between them offered many useful suggestions: Benjamin Aaron, Fritzi Bernstein, Joe Califano, Robert Dallek, Harold Horowitz, George Reedy, Murray Schwartz, Willard Wirtz, and Adam Yarmolinsky. Bonny M. McLaughlin prepared the index.

Sherman Oaks, California   *Irving Bernstein*
February 1995

Contents

III   LYNDON JOHNSON—EMBATTLED, BESIEGED, UNDERMINED

IV   CODA

PROLOGUE

THE VICE PRESIDENCY

JOHN Nance Garner said that the vice presidency "isn't worth a pitcher of warm piss." He spoke out of a rich experience, including two terms as Franklin Roosevelt's Vice President. The history of the office supported his conclusion.

The framers of the Constitution who met in Philadelphia between May 14 and September 17, 1787, were baffled by the vice presidency. They stumbled over it, were uncertain of its need and shape, and dealt with it in a clumsy manner. In fact, the issue was not resolved until the report of the Committee on Style (whose five members included Hamilton and Madison) on September 12, a few days before the convention closed. With minor changes that report became the Constitution of the United States.

Except for breaking a tie in the Senate, the Constitution dealt with the office only in the succession clause, which read: "In Case of the Removal of the President from Office, or his Death, Resignation, or Inability to discharge the Powers and Duties of the said Office, the Same shall devolve on the Vice President. . . ." Trouble came swiftly. In 1800 the Republican party nominated Thomas Jefferson for President and Aaron Burr for Vice President. While this ticket defeated the Federalists, both candidates received 73 electoral votes. The Constitution specified that the House of Representatives would break a tie. But the House that would decide had been elected in 1798 with a Federalist majority. Thus, Jefferson's enemies had the power to deny him the victory he had won, and Burr encouraged them by refusing to promise that he would not accept the presidency. Jefferson did not get the needed majority until the 36th ballot on February 17, 1801.

The controversy almost dismantled the new republic and its fledgling Constitution. But now, with the Republicans in control of both the presidency and Congress, the Twelfth Amendment was adopted in 1804, requiring separate balloting of electors for President and Vice President.

The vice presidency fared even worse as an institution than it had under the Constitution. John Adams, Washington's Vice President, referred to himself as "His Superfluous Excellency." Webster said, "I do not propose to be buried until I am dead." Clay resented offers and rejected them twice. Calhoun, who held the office under Andrew Jackson, resigned to become a senator from South Carolina.

Those who followed during the latter part of the nineteenth century were, as the Twentieth Century Fund report put it, "a virtual rogues' gallery of personal and political failures." Six suffered from old age and/or ill health and died in office. Three were tainted by financial scandal. Two were heavy drinkers. One had a penchant for slave mistresses. Three publicly attacked the Presidents under whom they served. So dismal had the reputation of the vice presidency become that the Republicans used it as a burial ground for their youthful, vigorous, and progressive Theodore Roosevelt in

1900, a scheme subverted by William McKinley's assassination the next year.

During the first third of the twentieth century the office became a national joke. Mr. Dooley said that the vice presidency is "not a crime exactly. Ye can't be sint to jail f'r it, but it's kind iv a disgrace." Woodrow Wilson's Vice President, Thomas R. Marshall, is known to history for his statement, "What this country needs is a good five-cent cigar." He described his role as "a man in a cataleptic fit; he cannot speak; he cannot move; he suffers no pain; he is perfectly conscious of all that goes on, but has no part of it." George S. Kaufman and Morrie Ryskind reached the ultimate with the invention of Vice President Alexander Throttlebottom in their smash musical *Of Thee I Sing* in the early thirties. Poor Throttlebottom was denied a library card because he could not get two references, and he took a public tour of the White House so that he could learn where the President lived.

Despite these disabilities, the vice presidency worked in the succession. Between the late eighteenth century and 1960, seven Presidents died in office and their Vice Presidents stepped up smoothly. Of the 34 Presidents from Washington to Eisenhower, 7 had come to the office from the vice presidency, about 1 in 5. During the 170 years of the presidency, almost 23 were served by former Vice Presidents, roughly 1 in 7. A candidate for Vice President, therefore, had a fair chance of becoming President merely by waiting.

More important, the office of Vice President was transformed in the middle of the century. Franklin Roosevelt enormously expanded the powers of the presidency by leading the nation through the Great Depression and World War II. This heightened the importance of the succession. Roosevelt's death on April 15, 1945, was a complete surprise to the public, and everyone asked who Harry Truman was. Henceforth presidential candidates would often select their running mates with an eye to their ability to take over the White House. Further, Presidents would arrange for their Vice Presidents to be better informed on public issues, to be accustomed to performing ceremonial functions, and, increasingly, to play legislative and administrative roles. This, in turn, led to a second succession, the development of the vice presidency as a stepping stone to the nomination for President. Richard Nixon, Eisenhower's Vice President, was the first modern figure to take this route. While Lyndon Johnson had little respect for Nixon, he must have watched that process with interest and no little admiration.[1]

Lyndon Johnson hungered after the presidency. But, as the 1960 elections approached, he was torn by ambivalence. On the one side, his record as majority leader in the Senate may have been the finest in history; his political acumen seemed unmatched; and a number of respected and prominent Democrats considered him the best qualified potential candidate. On the other, the cards were stacked against his winning the nomination. The Democratic party had not selected a southerner for a century and his style was deeply rooted in Texas and the South. The convention would be dominated by northerners—big-city bosses, liberals, organized labor, blacks, intellectuals—almost all of whom regarded him with suspicion. Moreover, his political base was tightly concentrated at the top in the Congress, really the Senate; the great majority of delegates, however, would come from the bottom and the middle, the big cities and the states.

For a year Johnson chewed over this dilemma, unable to make up his mind. Certain that he would lose, he did not enter the primaries. His hapless strategy was that John Kennedy and Hubert Humphrey would knock each other out and that a deadlocked convention would turn to him. It did not work out. Kennedy overpowered Humphrey, triumphed in the primaries, and came to the Los Angeles convention with the nomination virtually locked up. According to George Reedy, Johnson at this time was drinking very heavily, and old Washington friends Jim Rowe and Tom Corcoran, discouraged by his ambivalence, split away.

Now Johnson's options had narrowed. A Texas law tailored to fit him allowed Johnson to stand for reelection as senator while also running for President or Vice President. There was little doubt that he would be reelected and could then return to the Senate as majority leader. Or, if Kennedy offered him the second place, he could enter the race for Vice President. Which should he choose?

The debate over this question was wholly private. Johnson's public posture was that he was a candidate only for President and expected to win. Excepting his dear friend and mentor Speaker Sam Rayburn, none of his supporters imagined that he would even consider the vice presidency. His opponents, Kennedy and his entourage, were also in the dark. Nevertheless, Kennedy, convinced of his own weakness as a Catholic in the South, offered him the second spot on July 14, 1960, and Johnson accepted immediately. During the convention, while Johnson was waiting to see Kennedy, he spoke to Larry O'Brien, who would direct the campaign:

> I want to tell you something. In making this commitment, I am going to do everything humanly possible to help this man and to help this ticket. . . . And I want you and whoever else handles this campaign to tell me what I should be doing. . . . Move me everywhere and anywhere you can. I am totally committed, and you're going to find that I am everything that you would want me to be in terms of being a running mate.

O'Brien was "impressed." He now thought that Kennedy's offer to Johnson was "a stroke of genius," because it would unify the Democratic party and carry much of the South and the Southwest.

Why, everyone asked, had Johnson ignored Jack Garner's advice to take the equivalent of a pitcher of warm piss? He had good reason to do so.

If Johnson was not on the ticket and Nixon won, northern Democrats would blame him for the defeat and this would damage his chances for the presidential nomination in 1964. If Nixon was elected and Johnson was the leader of the Senate, their relations were certain to be strained, if not embittered, and Nixon would saddle him with responsibility for the stalemate. Johnson had already had a taste of this. Prior to the 1958 elections, when the Democrats were weak, he had gotten along splendidly with Eisenhower, a passive President. But those elections had brought in many new liberal Democrats who, over Johnson's objections, insisted on confronting Eisenhower. The President, his back now up, vetoed much of the liberal Democratic legislation. Johnson had been trapped in the middle. He did not look forward to a replay of the scenario of a liberal Senate battling an activist conservative Nixon in the White House.

If Kennedy won and Johnson was majority leader, the President would shape his own agenda and would get the credit for legislative successes, while Johnson would be blamed for failures. As a senator from Texas, he would remain a regional rather than become a national figure. Thus, if Kennedy were reelected in 1964, a likely event, Johnson would come to the 1968 convention with the same disability he suffered from in 1960.

In case of either a Nixon or Kennedy victory without Johnson on the ticket, he would almost certainly lose any chance for the presidency. On the other hand, if he ran for Vice President and won, he would keep that option open. Should the Kennedy-Johnson ticket succeed in 1960 and carry much of the South, including the big prize of Texas, he could claim a large share of credit for the victory.

While the notion of Lyndon Johnson, with his overpowering drive, in the vice presidency, seemed a contradiction in terms, the office was not without attractions. As he told a friend, "Power is where power goes." Through much of his career he had taken over weak offices and had infused them with authority. Perhaps as Vice President, Johnson reckoned, he could continue to run the Senate. He would certainly use the vice presidency to nationalize his base, to cease being identified as a southerner and a Texan. He could learn about foreign policy and he could speak out on national issues, particularly civil rights. And he could use the vice presidency, as Nixon had in 1960, to secure the presidential nomination in 1968, when he would still be in his prime at age 60.

Now both Kennedy and Johnson, each for his own reasons, had an enormous stake in their joint victory. While Johnson campaigned vigorously in the East and the Midwest, his main effort was in the South. With Kennedy's Catholicism on his back, he must hold part of the old Confederacy and, above all, carry Texas. Against a Protestant Democrat, Adlai Stevenson, Eisenhower had made deep inroads into the southern states in 1952 and 1956 and had swept Texas both times. Thus, Johnson faced a formidable challenge.

Always vigorous on the stump, Johnson threw himself into this campaign with passion and gusto. As Arthur Schlesinger wrote,

> Employing his whole oratorical range—first hunched over the rostrum, talking in a low, confiding, pleading voice, telling a repertory of stories unmatched since Alben Barkley, then suddenly standing erect, roaring, gesticulating, waving his arms—he carried the message of confidence with panache across the southern states.

He confronted religion at every whistle stop, attacking the bigotry of those who opposed Kennedy for his Catholicism, equating it with northern prejudice against the South. Harry Truman, who had campaigned in 1948 by train, told him, "You know, there are a lot of people in this country who don't know where the airport is, but they know where the depot is. Go out and find them." Johnson hired an eleven-car train, the "LBJ Victory Special," which reporters called the "Cornpone Special," from which he made 60 rear platform speeches across eight southern states. He talked about "mah grandpappy" and "mah great grandpappy." In Rocky Bottom, South Carolina, he said, "Ah wish ah could stay and do a little sippin' and whittlin' with you." Extremely worried about losing his home state, he covered Texas like a blanket. Fortunately, right-wing Republicans fatally played into his hands four days before the election.

Dallas was probably the most reactionary city in the nation. On November 4, Johnson and his wife crossed the street from the Baker to the Adolphus Hotel and entered the lobby. They were assaulted by an angry, shrieking gaggle of Republican women, the "Mink Coat Mob," led by right-wing Dallas Republican Bruce Alger. They spat on the Johnsons and hit Lady Bird on the head with a picket sign. While outraged, Johnson knew that the scene was being covered by television, radio, and the press. He ordered the police to leave. "If the time has come when I can't walk through the lobby of a hotel in Dallas with my lady, I want to know it." When Lady Bird started to answer a heckler, he put his hand over her mouth. He stretched the stormy voyage through the Adolphus to 30 minutes, guaranteeing that every camera would get prime shots. "Old Lyndon," Kennedy later told William S. White, "sure took his time taking himself and Bird through that lobby—and it wasn't by accident; that instinct of his just told him what to do and how to do it."

While the Kennedy-Johnson ticket carried the nation with only a razor-thin popular margin, the victory in the electoral college was more comfortable—303 to 219. They won seven southern states—Alabama, Arkansas, Georgia, Louisiana, North and South Carolina, and Texas, the last by a spare 46,000 votes. This was 81 of 128 southern electoral votes. Nixon-Lodge prevailed only in Florida, Tennessee, and Virginia, and a segregationist crowd took Mississippi. Lyndon Johnson had delivered. As George

Reedy wrote, "This may have been the only campaign in history where the vice presidential candidate made an observable difference." But on election night he was extremely depressed with the thought of becoming Vice President. Though he had now won the nation's second highest office, Leonard Baker wrote, he could not "alter the basic fact: he knew he was stepping down."[2]

The power-is-where-power-goes theory of the vice presidency never got off the launching pad. Johnson ran tests in both the Senate and the White House with equally disastrous results.

On January 3, 1961, he was sworn in as senator from Texas, 17 days before his inauguration as Vice President. A few minutes later he put his resignation before the presiding officer and walked out of the chamber.

Senator Mike Mansfield, the majority leader, called the 64 Democratic senators to an organizational caucus that afternoon. Johnson had picked him as whip in 1957 and had promoted him for the leadership. When Johnson said that he wanted to keep his huge office, known as the Taj Mahal, Mansfield quietly moved into a much smaller one. At the meeting Mansfield moved to empower Johnson to preside over the Senate Democratic caucus. Johnson and Mansfield expected this to pass easily.

There was a moment of stunned silence, followed by a strong negative reaction. Objections from a dedicated liberal like Joseph Clark or from Albert Gore, the Tennessee maverick, were hardly surprising because they nursed old grudges. But Johnson and Mansfield were shocked when Clinton Anderson of New Mexico, Olin Johnston of South Carolina, and A. Willis Robertson of Virginia joined in the attack. All were committee chairmen, pillars of the Senate establishment, and had supported Johnson's bid for the presidency. All the opponents argued the separation of powers. The Vice President was basically in the executive branch and the Senate was in the legislative and the twain must not meet. At a minimum the motion would violate the spirit of the Constitution.

While the Mansfield motion carried 46 to 17, Johnson, who had listened to the debate in numbed silence, recognized that the minority could not be managed. Humiliated, he was compelled to accept the fact that the Senate Democrats no longer wanted him to be their leader. "No other single event in those formative days of the New Frontier," Evans and Novak wrote, "cut deeper and none more influenced his conduct as Vice President after January 20. Indeed, he retired from the Senate—physically as well as legally."

Shortly after the inauguration a Johnson aide dropped off a proposed executive order for Kennedy to sign. It would have granted the Vice President general supervision over several important areas, including the new National Aeronautics and Space Administration, and would have required various departments and agencies to send him reports and policy proposals customarily sent to the President. The White House staff considered this outrageously presumptuous and spoke darkly of William H. Seward, Lincoln's Secretary of State. Kennedy seems to have been more amused by its clumsiness than concerned with its gravity. The paper was buried and forgotten. Thus, Lyndon Johnson learned very early that he was going to be Vice President and nothing else.

In fact, Kennedy was sensitive to Johnson's deep ache over his loss of power. "After all," he told Schlesinger, "I spent years of my life when I could not get consideration for a bill until I went around and begged Lyndon Johnson to let it go ahead." Sending Johnson a birthday greeting, he said, was like "drafting a state document." But he liked Johnson, respected his advice on many matters, and insisted that his own staff, including his brother, treat the Vice President with dignity. Johnson recognized the President's efforts and reciprocated by becoming a loyal Vice President.

Kennedy went out of his way to find tasks for Johnson to perform, to keep him informed ("we will not conduct meetings without the Vice President"), and to put him into the limelight. He became chairman of the Space Council, which oversaw the burgeoning space program, and mediated disputes between civilian NASA and the military. He was chairman of the Committee on Equal Employment Opportunity, which had the task of eliminating discrimination in employment in the federal service and among federal contractors. He regularly attended White House cabinet and National Security Council meetings, breakfasts with the Democratic congressional leadership, and the early morning briefing sessions prior to presidential press conferences. At the last Johnson always sat next to Walter Heller, the chairman of the Council of Economic Advisers. As Heller said, "they hit it off from the very beginning and were on a first-name basis within a couple of months." Heller gave him copies of his briefing notes and also sent him copies of many of the memoranda he wrote to the President. The economist thought it was his responsibility to keep Johnson informed and also hoped to win his support for council positions within the administration. The Vice President also had his picture taken endlessly at White House photo opportunities.

Later, Johnson told Doris Kearns about his dreams. At 15 he had dreamt that he was confined in a small cage and could not break out. When he awoke, he "escaped" from home by running away to California. When he was Vice President, he dreamt that he was seated at his desk in the Executive Office Building signing stacks of letters. At the end of the day he could see crowds hurrying home from work. He thought it would be nice to join them and, for once, have an early dinner with his family. He started to stand but could not because his legs were bound to the chair by a heavy chain. He tried to break it, but failed. He took another stack of mail and returned to work. Now, forty years later, he again escaped by running away to foreign lands.

During his vice presidency Johnson made 11 trips abroad to 33 different countries. Constrained at home, he unleashed himself overseas. He was, Kearns wrote, "once again the spoiled, demanding, and exuberant child." He carefully put together the list of his needs—an oversize bed, a needlepoint shower head, two dozen cases of Cutty Sark, 500 boxes of pens, six dozen cases of cigarette lighters. In the slums of Indian cities and the markets in Thailand he passed out pens and lighters inscribed "LBJ," shaking hands, barnstorming as he would in rural Texas. The Foreign Service did not quite know what to make of it.

There were two important incidents, one bizarre, the other significant. In a tour of Karachi before huge crowds Johnson got out of his car to shake hands and met Bashir, the camel driver. He talked with Bashir as he stood by his beast and said casually through an interpreter, "I hope some day you will have the opportunity to visit our country." The next day an imaginative columnist for a leading newspaper praised Johnson for inviting Bashir to come to the U.S. and stay at the Waldorf-Astoria in New York! The pressure built and Johnson eventually caved in. People-to-People bought Bashir an airplane ticket to America; he, indeed, stayed at the Waldorf; the State Department provided an interpreter; and the Vice President invited him to the ranch on the Pedernales. As a devout Muslim, Bashir watched what he ate and used his fingers. At a luncheon in Dallas, Liz Carpenter counted the presidents of four banks and Neiman-Marcus stuffing fried chicken, celery, and potato chips into their mouths with their fingers to make "the camel driver feel at home." As a going-away present, the Ford Motor Company gave him a pickup so that he could retire his camel.

On the other occasion he was more than an ambassador of good will. In the fall of 1961, after the East Germans had begun to build the Berlin Wall, Kennedy sent him to West Berlin. Johnson delivered a powerful speech before a crowd of at least 380,000, pledging American support for the city. As a show of good faith, the President ordered elements of the 1st Battle Group of the 8th Infantry down the Autobahn, and the Vice President greeted them emotionally as they entered West Berlin.

For the rest, his performances abroad were mixed—highly successful in the Third World and dismal in much of Europe. "His appearance," Reedy wrote, "touched off massive and exuberant demonstrations among the illiterate and poverty-stricken hordes in Vietnam, India, Pakistan, Iran. . . . The people understood him and he understood them." But Scandinavia was "a veritable disaster." He insulted the Danes by ordering the furniture removed from his room to provide space for his oversize bed. It was the work of a noted Danish craftsman. In Norway he interrupted a state banquet by blocking the pathway of the waitresses in a meaningless conversation. His persistent tardiness offended the punctiliously prompt Swedes. He shocked the Finns by walking on the graves of those who had been massacred at Rovaniemi.

In fact, Johnson was an extremely unhappy Vice President. He felt unwelcome in his former home, the Senate. His old friends, like John Connally and Robert Kerr, seemed to desert him. Kennedy and his staff were disappointed because, with a few exceptions, he declined to help on legislation. Harry McPherson, who had worked for him in the Senate, "met him on the elevator as he returned from a meeting of the Smithsonian board, where he had found a discussion of the National Zoo—the Zoo! Johnson!—fascinating." He felt culturally inferior to the Kennedys and the "Harvards," loathing the White House functions for artists and writers, where he stood in a corner with his hands in his pockets. Despite his extensive foreign travel, Kearns thought, Johnson seemed to inhabit a coccoon and learned little about the nations he visited. He was often morose about the future. Perhaps John Kennedy would not endorse him in 1968, turning instead to Johnson's nemesis, Robert Kennedy, in order to create a dynasty. He spoke vaguely about quitting in 1964 and becoming president of his alma mater, Southwest Texas Teachers College in San Marcos. The trouble was that damn vice presidency. When he was elected, he asked Norman Edwards, his chauffeur, to continue working for him. Edwards had been driving majority leaders since Joe Robinson in FDR's time. He gleamed in their reflection because they have "real power." Edwards did not want to drive for a Vice President because "he doesn't have any power at all."[3]

"It all began so beautifully," Lady Bird Johnson wrote in her diary. "After a drizzle in the morning, the sun came out bright and clear." The procession moved into Dallas. President and Mrs. Kennedy, along with Governor John and Nellie Connally, were in the lead car. The second vehicle was full of Secret Service men. "And then our car with Lyndon and me and Senator Ralph Yarborough."

The streets were lined with people and there was a festive mood, "the children all smiling, placards, confetti, people waving from windows." For years Mary Griffith had handled the alteration of the clothes Mrs. Johnson bought from Neiman-Marcus. She looked up and there was Mary, "leaning out of a window waving at me."

Lady Bird heard "a sharp, loud report," soon followed by two others. Both the President and Governor Connally had been hit. The Johnsons were driven to the Parkland Hospital. When presidential assistant Kenny O'Donnell entered the room Lady Bird knew instantly that the news was very bad. He said, "The President is dead." Shortly after, Mac Kilduff, the White House press man, came in and addressed her husband as "Mr. President."

Lyndon Baines Johnson had become the 36th President of the United States.[4]

I

CARETAKER OF JOHN F. KENNEDY'S LEGACY

1

Fifteen Days

AT approximately 1 p.m. on November 22, 1963, Father Oscar L. Huber administered last rites to John Kennedy, and Dr. W. K. Clark pronounced him dead. At that moment Lyndon Johnson became President of the United States, but he did not know it. A few minutes later presidential assistant Kenny O'Donnell came to the Johnsons and said, "He's gone." O'Donnell told the Secret Service that they should take the Johnsons to Washington immediately. Johnson asked him what Mrs. Kennedy's wishes were. O'Donnell said she would not move from the hospital without the body and was waiting for a casket. Johnson asserted that he would not leave without her, if that was her wish, but would go to Air Force One to wait for her and the body.

When Mac Kilduff addressed Johnson as "Mr. President," "I must have looked startled," Johnson wrote later. "I certainly felt strange." Kilduff wanted to announce President Kennedy's death and asked for Johnson's approval. With Secret Service assent he directed Kilduff to wait until they left the hospital. Surrounded by agents, the Johnsons were driven in separate cars to Love Field and hurried into the airplane.

Johnson immediately phoned Attorney General Robert Kennedy, who said that the FBI did not yet know whether the assassination was the act of an individual or part of a conspiracy. Johnson wanted to know whether he should take the oath of office at once and, if so, wanted the exact wording. Kennedy said he would check. He phoned back shortly to say that the oath should be taken now and that it could be administered by any judicial officer of the United States. Deputy Attorney General Nicholas Katzenbach dictated the oath to Johnson's secretary.

Johnson then phoned Irving Goldberg, a Dallas lawyer and old friend. They agreed that Judge Sarah Hughes, recently appointed by Kennedy to the district court in Dallas, should administer the oath. She was on the airplane in a few minutes.

Shortly a small plane approached. Bill Moyers, formerly on Johnson's staff and now deputy director of the Peace Corps, had been doing advance work for a big fundraiser in Austin the next day. As soon as he heard of the assassination, he chartered the plane and flew to Love Field to be at Johnson's side.

Jack Valenti, who ran an advertising agency in Houston, had worked for Johnson on political campaigns and had done the advance work that produced big crowds for Kennedy in Houston the preceding day. He had then joined Johnson on Air Force Two for the flight from Houston to Dallas. The next morning he rode in a staff bus downtown behind the motorcade and wound up at the Parkland Hospital. Overcome with grief, he stood in a stairwell and wept. Cliff Carter, who ran Johnson's office in Austin, tried to console him and said, "The Vice President is waiting for us." A Secret Service agent drove them to Love Field and they boarded Air Force One.

Liz Carpenter, also on Johnson's staff, had been on the same bus following the motorcade at the time of the shooting. A veteran newspaperwoman, she realized that Johnson would need to say something when he landed in Washington. She penciled out a brief statement and she, too, got on the airplane.

Cecil Stoughton, a White House photographer, told Carpenter, "This is a history-making moment and, while it seems tasteless, I am here to make a picture if he [the new President] cares to have it and I think he should have it." She relayed the message to Johnson and he nodded. Kilduff came aboard and told her that a press pool—Merriman Smith of United Press International, Charles Roberts of *Newsweek,* and Sid Davis of Westinghouse Broadcasting—wanted to cover the event. She asked Kilduff what he recommended and he burst into tears. She shook him and demanded an answer. He recommended the pool. They asked Johnson, who said, "Of course, put the pool on board."

Some time after 2:00 Jacqueline Kennedy entered the cabin. "I was shocked by the sight that confronted me," Johnson wrote. "There stood that beautiful lady, with her white gloves, her pink suit, and her stockings caked with her husband's blood. There was a dazed look in her eyes." The Johnsons tried to comfort her as they saw her to a bedroom. The casket, accompanied by Kennedy's devoted assistants, Larry O'Brien and Kenny O'Donnell, was taken to the rear of the airplane. Shortly, Mrs. Kennedy returned.

Lyndon Johnson, with his wife to one side and the wife of the slain President on the other, repeated the words of Judge Hughes in what Roberts described as "a low, but firm voice." "I do solemnly swear that I will faithfully execute the office of the President of the United States, and will to the best of my ability, preserve, protect and defend the Constitution of the United States." He added, "So help me God." He noticed that the Bible on which his hand rested was a Catholic missal. Larry O'Brien had found it on the plane. Stoughton stood on a couch in a corner to take the photograph.

At 2:41 p.m. the new President ordered the plane to take off. He made calls to Rose Kennedy, the dead President's mother, and to Nellie Connolly to comfort them. Johnson asked Moyers, Valenti, and Carpenter to draft a statement and they seem to have come up with something like Carpenter's note. The President made a few changes. He also instructed Kilduff to see to it that the television cameras focused on him as he read the statement.

Johnson phoned national security adviser McGeorge Bundy and his own chief of staff, Walter Jenkins, to set up meetings for that evening. He had hoped to have a cabinet meeting and was disappointed to learn that Secretary of State Dean Rusk and five other members had been on an airplane that was beyond Honolulu on its way to Tokyo, though they had now turned back.

Air Force One landed at Andrews Air Force Base near Washington at 5:59 p.m. A hastily summoned group of government officials and representatives of other nations waited on the ramp. Johnson read his statement for them and, more important, for television:

> This is a sad time for all people. We have suffered a loss that cannot be weighed. For me, it is a deep personal tragedy. I know that the world shares the sorrow that Mrs. Kennedy and her family bear. I will do my best. That is all I can do. I ask your help—and God's.

When they got to the helicopter pad, Johnson cupped his hands to Valenti's ear against the roar of the engines and shouted, "Get in the second chopper and come to my office as soon as you land." Evidently, he gave the same instructions to Moyers and Carter. In a few minutes they were on the helipad on the south grounds of the White House. The President was already talking to Secretary of Defense Robert McNamara and Under Secretary of State George Ball. Valenti, Moyers, and Carter joined them. Johnson strode through the Rose Garden to the West Wing. Valenti was surprised that Johnson did not enter the Oval Office. Rather, he walked down to the basement and took the underground passageway to the Executive Office Building and then went up by elevator to his third floor vice presidential office. The Johnsons would not occupy the White House until Mrs. Kennedy and her children moved out on December 7.

That evening the President discussed international affairs with Senator Fulbright, chairman of the Senate Foreign Relations Committee, Averell Harriman, Ball, and McNamara. The situation was, fortunately, calm and would remain so throughout his transition. He phoned former Presidents Truman and Eisenhower. He wrote letters in longhand to the dead President's children, Caroline and John. He telephoned Edward Kennedy, the President's younger brother. He met with the congressional leadership, asking for their help and counsel during this trying period. He talked to Sargent Shriver, the dead President's brother-in-law and director of the Peace Corps, who was making the funeral arrangements on behalf of the Kennedy family. Johnson had a bowl of soup, his first nourishment since breakfast in Fort Worth that morning. The President and his assistants were then driven to the Elms, the Johnson's house in northwest Washington.

After they had left Air Force One, Mrs. Johnson and Liz Carpenter went straight to the Elms. In the car Liz said, "It's a terrible thing to say, but the salvation of Texas is that the governor was hit." Lady Bird replied, "Don't think I haven't thought of that. I only wish it could have been me." When she got home, Mrs. Johnson instructed the cook to prepare a lot of fried chicken.

After the President arrived he sat in his big chair in the library and sipped orange juice. He lifted his glass to a photograph of his late great friend and mentor, Speaker Sam Rayburn. "I salute you, Mr. Sam, and how I wish you were here now, when I need you." Everyone went into the dining room for their first real meal since morning.

About midnight Johnson decided to go to bed. He led Valenti to a bedroom on the second floor and told Moyers and Carter to pick out bedrooms on the third. He told Valenti that he was going to be on the staff at the White House and that he should get some clothes from Houston and find a house for his family in Washington. He also told Moyers that he was going to work in the White House.

Valenti followed Johnson into his bedroom. The President got into his pajamas and lay down on his bed to watch TV. It was a program on himself, his background and fitness to be President. Moyers and Carter joined them. The President, Valenti wrote, "began to speak, almost as if he were talking to himself. He mused about what he ought to do and began to tick off people he needed to see and meetings he should construct in the next several days." Valenti picked up a pad and began scribbling notes, soon more than 30 pages of what was to become the agenda for the Johnson transition. It was almost 3:30 a.m. when the President said, "Good night, boys."

Moyers recalled later that Johnson had stressed three basic themes:

1. There must be continuity. There should be no hesitancy, nothing to indicate that the U.S. Government had faltered.
2. The programs of President Kennedy would be pushed.
3. The country must be united to face the crisis and the transition of power.[1]

The assassination of John Kennedy devastated the American people. Perhaps the murder of Lincoln was comparable, but there was no one about in 1865 to ask people how they felt. Among the memories of living people in

1963 there were only two vaguely similar events that were mentioned—Pearl Harbor and the death of Franklin Roosevelt—and each differed from Kennedy's assassination fundamentally.

As an historic event it made up a bundle of four days, from approximately 12:30 p.m. CST on Friday, November 22, when Lee Harvey Oswald fired the fatal shots, through the end of the day on Monday, November 25.

Many millions of Americans would remember as long as they lived exactly where they were and how they learned of the assassination of John Kennedy. The news spread faster than proverbial wildfire. Radio and newspapers gave the event enormous coverage. But it was television that had much the biggest impact. CBS started its Dallas coverage within 15 minutes of the firing of the shots; NBC was on the air only a few minutes later; and ABC soon followed. They then provided continuous live broadcasting, with neither regular programs nor commercials intruding, for the better part of four days. The networks pooled their stories.

According to the National Opinion Research Center study, by 1:00 p.m. CST on Friday, when Kennedy was pronounced dead, 68 percent of adult Americans had heard the news; by 6 p.m. it had swelled to 99.8 percent (only 2 of 1,384 respondents said that they did not hear the news till Saturday). In previous disasters at least 10 to 20 percent said they did not learn what had happened until much later.

The NORC study showed that Americans were profoundly grieved by the assassination, and were also concerned about the impact upon the United States, both at home and with regard to its relations with other nations. During the four-day period Americans exhibited many symptoms of anxiety-depression, especially African Americans.

Johnson moved quickly to overcome these troubled feelings. His task was much eased by the enormous TV viewing over the assassination weekend. Until that time Lyndon Johnson was a familiar figure in Washington and Texas, but, excepting for a minority of the politically sophisticated, was, as Vice Presidents invariably are, little known in the rest of the country. But now documentaries aired on television and he made several appearances in which he displayed compassion and dignity. By Monday night the public recognized that their new President held the reins with steady hands. A study of college students concluded that it was "possible for people fully to indulge their grief only because of the smooth, automatic succession." On Air Force One Liz Carpenter had comforted herself with the thought that "someone is in charge." She recalled Lady Bird telling her, "Lyndon's a good man to have in an emergency." But among the college students there was an undercurrent of resentment, in part because Johnson was a Texan and also because he seemed "to be somehow usurping the presidential role."

Johnson expected and understood this bitter reaction. He had not been elected President; he held the office by historical accident. He must legitimate his own presidency. A basic way to do so was by becoming the executor of the Kennedy legacy, wrapping himself in the mantle of the immensely popular fallen leader. He had, Johnson wrote,

> a deep-rooted sense of responsibility to John F. Kennedy. Rightly or wrongly, I felt from the very first day in office that I had to carry on for President Kennedy. I considered myself the caretaker of both his people and his policies. He knew when he selected me as his running mate that I would be the man required to carry on if anything happened to him. I did what I believed he would have wanted me to do. . . . I was the trustee and custodian of the Kennedy administration.

The caretaker role took several forms. As suggested, Johnson was solicitous about the Kennedy family. He deferred to Shriver on the funeral arrangements. He immediately assented to Jacqueline Kennedy's requests to remain in the White House with her children for two weeks and, by an executive order he issued on November 29, to rename the NASA launch facilities at Cape Canaveral the John F. Kennedy Space Center. In addition, Cape Canaveral with Florida's assent was designated Cape Kennedy. On January 23, 1964 he signed a bill "with great satisfaction" renaming the planned National Cultural Center in Washington the John F. Kennedy Center for the Performing Arts.

Johnson knew that Kennedy had been extremely well regarded by top officials of his own administration, of whom Secretary of Defense McNamara was an example. He greatly admired JFK and both he and his wife had become close friends of the extended Kennedy family. On the day after the assassination he instructed his aide, Joe Califano, to meet Bobby Kennedy at Arlington National Cemetery. They paced the 3.2-acre site in a heavy rain. When Califano returned to the Pentagon, McNamara said, "Joe, I want to tie up that land for President Kennedy so that no one can ever take any of it away for any other purpose." Califano pointed out that it was in the national cemetery. "I don't give a damn. Get a title search made. Write a legal opinion nailing down the title to the land. I want to sign the deed that sets this land aside forever." The papers were ready the next day and Califano took them to McNamara in the cemetery, who was checking to be sure that the site was right in the center of the view from the Arlington Bridge. He insisted on signing the order, which was not necessary. "He was so distraught," Califano wrote, "that he had to do something to relieve his sense of helplessness."

Johnson had to transfer this loyalty for the fallen President to himself. He not only invited but insisted that all members of the Kennedy administration stay on with him. This, of course, extended to the Attorney General, with whom he had a strained relationship. The White House staff, both the "Irish Mafia"—Larry O'Brien, Kenny O'Donnell, and Ralph Dungan—and the "intellectuals"—Ted Sorensen, McGeorge Bundy, Pierre Salinger, and Arthur Schlesinger—were old associates and devoted friends who were devastated by the assassination and many were expected to leave. Johnson was particularly anxious that O'Brien remain. He said, "I need you, Larry. I want you to stay and pass Jack Kennedy's program. How can you better honor Jack's memory than to stay and help to enact his program?" O'Brien agreed with him and stayed.

In inviting these people to serve, Johnson was motivated in part by the fact, as he wrote, that "by remaining on the job they helped give the government and the nation a sense of continuity during critical times." And, as he later told Doris Kearns,

> I needed that White House staff. Without them I would have lost my link to John Kennedy, and without that I would have had absolutely no chance of gaining the support of the media or the Easterners or the intellectuals. And without that support I would have had absolutely no chance of governing the country.

But there was more. Some of the Kennedy people, he noted, were "extraordinary men" and all had now had almost three years of experience in their posts. He could hardly have matched them. But he was insecure about the White House staff. Johnson did not know whether all of them would be able to transfer their loyalty to him, and in several cases, Sorensen and Schlesinger in particular, there could be little doubt that they would depart after a decent interval.

Thus, Johnson began gradually to build up his own staff, starting with the young Texans, Moyers and Valenti, recruited on the day he became President. He would increase their number. He also began consulting immediately with three notable Washington lawyers with broad government experience who were now private citizens—Abe Fortas, Clark Clifford, and Jim Rowe. In the case of Rowe, this involved repairing a breach and, something extraordinary for Lyndon Johnson, offering an apology for causing it.

A myriad of questions swirled about the assassination, challenging the continuity and legitimacy that Johnson sought. Where had the FBI been when the plan for the murder had been laid? Was it significant that the event had taken place in Texas, particularly Dallas? The arrested Oswald had said virtually nothing and his mouth was now sealed forever by Jack Ruby, the night-club operator who killed Oswald two days after the assassination. What might Oswald have said? Did he have an accomplice? Was he the hit man for an international conspiracy? What about his strange visit to the Soviet Union and his Russian wife? Why was he so interested in Castro's Cuba? These questions stirred up rumors and they, in turn, encouraged those who wanted publicity for themselves. As Chief Justice Earl Warren wrote,

> The Dallas authorities fed everything, good or bad, to the news media. The attorney general of Texas proposed having an open hearing before a justice

of the peace, which meant television, radio, and newspaper coverage, regardless of how disjointed or crisis-like this atmosphere for a trial might be. Several committees of the Congress were flirting with public hearings that would proceed in similar manner. The result would have been chaos. The world was ready to believe almost anything, and indeed it did.

A current Gallup poll showed that more than half the American people were convinced that Oswald had not acted alone.

On Sunday, November 24, Deputy Attorney General Nicholas Katzenbach sent word to Johnson through his friend, Congressman Homer Thornberry of Austin, that he was "very concerned that everyone know that Oswald was guilty of the President's assassination." He wanted to head off the gathering rumors. Katzenbach recommended an independent commission to make an investigation. He suggested two retired judges—former Supreme Court Justice Charles Whittaker and former court of appeals judge E. Barrett Prettyman—along with former Republican presidential candidate Thomas E. Dewey, "to make it non-partisan." Implicit in this group of names was that no sitting judicial officer of the United States should serve on such a commission.

The next day, Monday, Katzenbach wrote a memorandum setting forth his ideas more carefully. He urged the President to act immediately "to head off speculation or Congressional hearings of the wrong sort." Katzenbach was convinced and wanted the public "to be satisfied that Oswald was the assassin; that he did not have confederates who are still at large; and that the evidence was such that he would have been convicted at trial." Two wild theories were now being floated: the Dallas police were saying that it was a Communist plot, and the Iron Curtain press was reporting that it was a right-wing conspiracy. Both "ought to be cut off." Katzenbach was upset over the fact that the matter was being handled with "neither dignity nor conviction." "We can hardly let the world see us totally in the image of the Dallas police when our President is murdered." A "complete and thorough FBI report" might be helpful immediately. The alternative would be "the appointment of a Presidential Commission of unimpeachable personnel to review and examine the evidence and announce its conclusions."

Johnson brought in Abe Fortas. They both approved the proposal. Fortas then met with Katzenbach, who had consulted with the Attorney General, and they agreed on a seven-member commission of the following distinguished citizens: Chief Justice Earl Warren, Senator Richard Russell of Georgia, Senator John Sherman Cooper of Kentucky, Representative Hale Boggs of Louisiana, Representative Gerald Ford of Michigan, former CIA director Allen W. Dulles, and John J. McCloy, former president of the World Bank and high commissioner for Germany. Five were Republicans; only Russell and Boggs were Democrats.

Anticipating difficulty with Warren, Johnson first got the assent of the other six to serve if the Chief Justice would accept. On Friday, November 29, Katzenbach and Solicitor General Archibald Cox on behalf of the President went to the Supreme Court and asked the Chief Justice to accept the chairmanship. Warren replied that the President was acting wisely in adopting this procedure, "but that [he] was not available for service." The Court had discussed extra-judicial appointments, and, while there had never been a vote, he was certain that the justices supported his position unanimously. Warren thought that such service defied the spirit of the constitutional separation of powers. Going back to Chief Justices John Jay and Oliver Ellsworth in the early days of the republic and, more recently, with Justices Owen Roberts on the Pearl Harbor commission and Robert Jackson at the Nuremberg trials, outside activities had distracted the court. Finally, no one could predict the litigation such a commission would spawn, and, if a case reached the Supreme Court, he would have to disqualify himself. Warren told Katzenbach and Cox, "I must respectfully decline the honor."

The Chief Justice considered the matter closed, but he underestimated Lyndon Johnson. He was immediately called to the White House. The President said that he was deeply distressed over the wild rumors arising from the assassination. Because Oswald was dead, there could be no trial. He then named the other members of the commission ("all of these men . . . distinguished and honorable," Warren wrote), all willing to serve on condition that he become chairman. Nevertheless, the Chief Justice declined and repeated his reasoning.

Warren then became the object of the famous Johnson "treatment": "You were a soldier in World War I, but there was nothing you could do in that uniform comparable to what you can do for your country in this hour of trouble." Johnson went on about rumors circulating the world and the danger of nuclear war with a first strike taking the lives of 40 million people. "Mr. Chief Justice," he concluded, "you were once in the Army. . . . As your Commander-in-Chief, I'm ordering you back into service." Warren was a pigeon for an appeal to his patriotism. "Mr. President," he said, "if the situation is that serious, my personal views do not count. I will do it."

When he got home for dinner, Mrs. Warren had already heard the news on the radio. Johnson had immediately issued Executive Order No. 11130 creating the Warren Commission, officially the President's Commission on the Assassination of President John F. Kennedy.

One of the first people Johnson had called was former President Eisenhower. He drove down from Gettysburg on Saturday, the day after the assassination. They visited for the better part of an hour and then Eisenhower composed a memorandum of "the things he would do if he were in my place." Among the most important was that "you call a Joint Session of the Congress to make a speech of not over ten or twelve minutes." Johnson readily agreed on the need for such an address because he must talk directly to the American people.

But, according to Michael Amrine, there was a good deal of fussing over this speech. Several advisers urged Johnson to speak to the people over television from the Oval Office; others agreed with Eisenhower. Senator Humphrey argued that Congress "is really Lyndon's home. . . . He feels natural there and at ease." The President concurred and, indeed, said so in the address: "For 32 years Capitol Hill had been my home." He had Sorensen, John Kenneth Galbraith, Adlai Stevenson, and Horace Busby of his own staff work up drafts. On the night before the delivery Johnson invited Humphrey and Fortas for dinner and he read from these versions. Finally, he said, "Hubert, you and Abe go ahead and redraft these speeches and get me one that will be suitable for tomorrow." They worked on it till 2 a.m. and Lynda Bird, the President's daughter, typed it. Johnson made some changes the next morning.

The President addressed the joint session on November 27. He opened with a glowing tribute to President Kennedy, including the memorable opening line, "All I have I would have given gladly not to be standing here today." He, of course, stressed continuity. In his inaugural address Kennedy had said, "Let us begin." "Today," Johnson said, "in this moment of new resolve, I would say to all my fellow Americans, let us continue."

He then struck the note of unity. He urged the passage of the civil rights bill in order "to eliminate from this Nation every trace of discrimination and oppression that is based upon race or color." It was time for "Americans of all races and creeds and political beliefs to understand and to respect one another." They must turn a deaf ear to "the apostles of bitterness and bigotry." "I profoundly hope," the President concluded, "that the tragedy of these terrible days will bind us together in new fellowship, making us one people in our hour of sorrow."

He spoke slowly in a serious and dignified manner. The address, according to Amrine, was an "enormous success" with both the Congress and the American people.

In pursuit of his goal of unity, Bill Moyers said, Johnson spoke to 3000 important people in his first month in office, some alone, some in small and others in large groups. He ran his staff ragged preparing him with background information and suggested topics for discussion in these meetings. He tailored his message to those who heard him. He told businessmen how well industry was performing and how much better it would do if the tax reduction was enacted, and he told labor about declining unemployment and the prospect for even more jobs with lower taxes. But, like all the others, he stressed to both that he needed their help to pull the nation together.

Johnson made a special pitch to Republicans. Eisenhower had urged him to confer with Robert Anderson on subjects of "a fiscal and financial character." Anderson had been Secretary of the Treasury, was a rich and very conservative Texan, and shared Eisenhower's pristine views of the balanced budget. Johnson dutifully met with Anderson and, as will be noted, doffed his hat to the conservative position during the debate over the tax bill. He also spoke with the Republican leadership in both houses of Congress and particularly with the minority leader in the Senate. Lyndon Johnson and Everett Dirksen were old and close friends, understood each other perfectly, and had wheeled and dealt for years. The President wanted Republican support in the Senate for the tax bill and, more important, would depend upon it critically in the cloture vote on the civil rights bill. Dirksen was capable of supplying the votes. Johnson later wrote,

> I asked [Dirksen] to convey to his Republican colleagues, in the Senate and throughout the nation, that it was essential to forget partisan politics, so that we could weather the national crisis in which we were involved and unite our people. There was a long pause on the other end of the [telephone] line and I could hear him breathing heavily. When he finally spoke, he expressed obvious disappointment that I would even raise the question of marshaling his party behind the President.
> "Well, Mr. President," he said, "you know I will." And he did.

Johnson also moved to reunite lines to the left. Jim Rowe was a former supporter and a New Deal liberal, and the President quickly brought him back into the fold. The wooing of Joseph L. Rauh, Jr., was far more complicated. He was an ideological liberal, the leading white lobbyist for civil rights, Washington counsel for Walter Reuther's United Auto Workers, and a pillar of Americans for Democratic Action. Rauh had been at war with Johnson for years in the Senate over cloture against a southern filibuster and over the 1957 Civil Rights Act. "It was perfectly clear," Rauh said, "that Johnson was trying to appear as an all-out conservative in Texas and as a moderate in national politics." When Kennedy picked Johnson as his running mate at the convention in 1960, "nobody was any angrier about the Johnson nomination than I was." Rauh said on the floor, "the Democratic Party shouldn't have for Vice President a gas and oil, anti-civil rights senator."

Senator Herbert Lehman of New York, one of the small band of dedicated supporters of civil rights, died on December 5, 1963. Johnson invited Rauh to join him on Air Force One for the trip to the funeral in New York City. Though certain that the President was making an "appeal to the liberal forces," Rauh accepted. A few days later he was in the Oval Office. As Rauh put it, Johnson said, "Let's let bygones be bygones. If I've done anything wrong in the past, I want you to know that's nothing now. We're going to work together." They went right to work on the civil rights bill.

On the fifteenth day of his presidency, December 7, 1963, Johnson held his first press conference. He, of course, picked up his two major themes.

"We think we have made very good progress in showing the continuity in our transition. We have tried to, second, give a sense of unity in the country and in the world." This brought Lyndon Johnson's presidential transition to a close.

It had been a formidable performance. The American people, the Congress, the interest groups, and the world at large had been convinced that Lyndon Johnson had legitimated his presidency and that he would be a strong President in the twentieth-century tradition of the Democratic party. George Reedy, who worked for Johnson and whose admiration for his boss was severely restrained, wrote,

> His performance following the assassination fully justified the use of the overworked word "magnificent." He eased his fellow citizens over the shock of losing their President; he set the wheels of government in motion again; he unified the American people as they have not been unified at any point since Eisenhower stepped down.

Doris Kearns agreed. Johnson had effected a transfer of government that was "smooth and dignified" by "a brilliant display of leadership and political skill." He himself seems to have been most pleased by the fact that on Tuesday, November 26, the first day the New York Stock exchange was open after the assassination, the Dow-Jones Industrial Average staged the biggest rally in its history. The Gallup poll in interviews conducted during the week of December 12–17, 1963 confirmed the public's judgment. The way Johnson was handling his job won the approval of 79 percent; only 3 percent disapproved.

Perhaps most interesting was the letter Liz Carpenter received from her friend Tom Hatfield in Texas. He had gone south to Gonzalez, west to San Antonio, and on to Banderra and Kerrville for political sampling. "Conversation and overt concern about the assassination has subsided remarkably, as though the people have been exposed to all of the horror their minds can bear." A number of the 25 or so people he talked to said LBJ reminded them of FDR. Hatfield was "astonished" to learn that no one opposed Johnson and only one person seemed lukewarm. Kerr County was the most Republican county in Texas. A woman in Kerrville who had not voted for a Democrat since 1936 said, "I'm not just for him, I'll *fight* for him!" An elderly gentleman in San Antonio who had not voted for a Democrat since 1916 said he would vote for Johnson in 1964. As every political observer quickly realized, Lyndon Johnson himself not least among them, he would easily gain the nomination and win the election the next year.

But that lay in the future. Now the new President must confront the Kennedy legislative legacy, and he immediately set to work.[2]

2

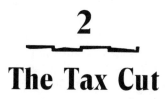

The Tax Cut

THE Keynesian tax cut came first on the unfinished Kennedy agenda. The civil rights bill had won approval only of the House Judiciary Committee; it still needed to clear the Rules Committee, gain a majority on the floor, and then confront formidable southern resistance, including a possible filibuster, in the Senate. Medicare and several federal aid for education bills had been laid over because they were snarled in complications. By contrast, the tax bill was much farther along, the opposition was fading rapidly, and passage, barring a miracle of mismanagement, seemed assured.

Kennedy had sent up a two-part tax bill on January 24, 1963. It provided for both a large reduction in tax rates for individuals and corporations and a comprehensive reform of the tax structure to restore equity by closing loopholes. Almost no one was against cutting taxes, but scores of lobbies charged up Capitol Hill to prevent reform. These vested interests dominated the hearings before the House Ways and Means Committee, and, after prolonged executive sessions, Chairman Wilbur Mills in August notified the President and the Treasury that most of the reforms must go. The administration quietly accepted the inevitable. The committee then adopted the truncated bill 17 to 8 and the House passed it on September 25, 1963, by a comfortable vote of 271 to 155. Chairman Harry Byrd of Virginia opened the Senate Finance Committee hearings on October 15, and they were expected to conclude on November 27, 1963.

Shortly before Kennedy left for Texas, Treasury Secretary Douglas Dillon met with Byrd. While the crusty Virginian had an unblemished record as a fiscal conservative and regarded the Keynesian tax cut as a dangerous disease, he seems to have become convinced that the bill would pass. According to Dillon, he was "holding out for some sort of gesture of saving money, of being careful in expenditure control, that he could tie with the bill." He told Dillon that he would not "let the bill go out of his committee

27

unless the budget for the coming year was under $100 billion." Dillon reported this to Kennedy and suggested a budget of $99.5 or $99.6 billion. The President said that "if that was necessary he'd do it."

Kermit Gordon had been a professor of economics at Williams College and a member of Kennedy's first Council of Economic Advisers, which had urged the tax cut. At the end of 1962 Kennedy had moved his budget director, David Bell, to the Agency for International Development and had put Gordon in charge of the Bureau of the Budget. The federal budget was clamped into a tight time cycle because it had to be submitted within two weeks of the opening date of the new Congress. Gordon took over in late December 1962. The fiscal 1964 budget (July 1, 1963, to June 30, 1964), therefore, had been prepared by Bell and defended by Gordon.

A year later Gordon was working up his first budget and by late November was, as he put it, "deep in the final stages." On Wednesday, November 20, he had told Kennedy that he wanted to meet with him the next week for decisions on the outstanding major problems. He got an appointment for Wednesday, November 27.

On the afternoon of Friday, November 22, Gordon and his staff were at the Pentagon meeting with McNamara and his people to lock up the department's budget. They had hardly begun when an aide entered and handed McNamara a note. He excused himself and left the room. A few minutes later he returned, ashen, and announced that the President had been shot in Dallas. "The people in the meeting," Gordon said, "just sat—just sat!" Shortly they learned that Kennedy was dead. After a while McNamara said that he did not think "there was any point in our sitting there." Gordon returned to his office and "paced the floor without knowing quite what to do." Since he wanted to be with his family, he went home.

On Saturday, Gordon said, "I began to think for the first time of my responsibilities and how this terrible thing had affected them. Of course, my first concern was with keeping the budget on the track." He would be meeting with a new President who probably did not understand the budget process, and they would have little more than six weeks to get the numbers straight. Gordon wrote a one-page memorandum briefly describing the functions and responsibilities of the Bureau of the Budget. He also wrote that if Johnson was willing "to devote a great deal of time to mastering the budget and its problems, there was still time for him to make the budget his budget." The President responded at once and met with Gordon and his deputy, Elmer Staats, on Sunday evening, November 24. Gordon elaborated on the budget process and again asked if Johnson wanted to take the time to learn it. The President most certainly did.

Gordon was puzzled. "One would assume," he said, "that a person who had been in the legislative branch for a long time would know a great deal about the way the executive branch works. That is a false assumption." Neither Kennedy nor Johnson understood the budget process when they assumed office, and both needed to be educated. In Johnson's case this was in face of the fact that he had sat on the Senate Appropriations Committee.

The Sunday night meeting, Gordon said, "began what was probably the most hectic period of my life, a solid month of meetings with the President—morning, afternoon, night, Saturdays, Sundays—reviewing the whole budget from stem to stern, and getting from him the decisions that he had to make." Johnson worked very hard and he was "a quick study." By early January 1964 "he had made the budget his budget."

From the start Johnson confronted Senator Byrd's demand that he keep the fiscal 1965 budget under $100 billion if he wanted to get the tax bill out of the Finance Committee. This created a bizarre episode. For starters, the number 100 billion, while indubitably round, had no significance. Dillon considered it a "gesture" and was confident that the budget could be brought down to that sum without "actual reductions in payments for government goods and services." Walter Heller considered $100 billion a "totally artificial administrative budget figure [that] was just a will-o-the-wisp." Gardner Ackley, also a member of the Council of Economic Advisers, said that despite Johnson's reduction, "we managed to make the tax cut several billion dollars bigger, so that we really got about the same stimulus out of the total package as we otherwise would have." Gordon thought the number entirely "symbolic," an easily recognized figure used by conservatives "to dramatize the growing size of the federal government." Charles Schultze of the Bureau of the Budget agreed. "Quite frankly," he said, "we would have had a hell of a time getting the budget up to a hundred billion . . . because, if you look at the numbers, Bob McNamara's cost reduction stuff was finally beginning to pay off."

Further, Byrd, perhaps, and Johnson, certainly, were not serious about that number. Joseph W. Barr, who worked Congress on the tax bill for the Treasury, closely followed the Finance Committee, particularly its chairman. On November 26, 1963, he wrote the White House that the vote on the House bill within the committee would be 12 for (including 3 Republicans), 4 against (Byrd among them), and 1 doubtful. The Virginian's "public" position was concern over expenditures: "Whether or not this is his real concern, the Chairman must have some reason to protect his public posture." He would probably demand a look at the preliminary budget figure, though he might be satisfied with a presidential "assurance of restraint." Barr continued: "*Privately* he has told me and others that Civil Rights *must* pass first." Thus, his "real reason" for delay might be to hold the tax cut hostage to rejection of the civil rights bill. Barr recommended that the President meet with Byrd "to explore this situation."

Byrd's $100 billion gambit energized Johnson's not inconsiderable instincts for self-dramatization, secrecy, and manipulation, the details of which will be recounted below. Kermit Gordon watched the performance from a front-row seat. The President informed the press, Gordon said later, that "it was going to be very difficult to get the budget much below 101 or 102 billion." Gordon knew this was a fiction and the White House press corps quickly reached the same conclusion. "A number of reporters said to me afterwards," Gordon said in 1969, "that they thought they were being deceived by the President . . . just . . . to build up the tension and to make the achievement of getting it below a hundred billion even more dramatic than it would have been." All Presidents engage in news management. In Johnson's case, particularly during the Vietnam War, this came to be known as the credibility gap. Gordon thought this was where it began.[1]

On Friday, November 22, 1963, Walter Heller, Chairman of the Council of Economic Advisers, and six cabinet officers—Dean Rusk, Secretary of State; Dillon, of Treasury; Orville Freeman, of Agriculture; Stewart Udall, of the Interior; Luther Hodges, of Commerce; and Willard Wirtz, of Labor—were on an airplane bound for a meeting in Tokyo of the Japan-U.S. Trade and Economic Committee. Several White House staff members, including press secretary Pierre Salinger, were also on the flight.

About an hour and 45 minutes after leaving Honolulu, Heller wrote, Rusk informed the others that the President had been shot and was "seriously wounded," and that Governor Connolly had also been hit. They canceled the Tokyo meeting and turned the plane back. There was a message from the White House from "Stranger," the code name for the communications officer with the President's party in Dallas, ordering them to return to Washington. Rusk asked, "Who is the White House under these circumstances?" They discussed "the sensitive problems of transfer and exercise of power of nuclear decision, the fear of disability if the President lived, and the awesome implications of succession if he died." About an hour later Salinger returned from the phone and said, "He's dead." Heller wrote, "The plane fell into complete grief-stricken silence."

After a brief stop in Honolulu, Heller recalled, Freeman, Udall, Hodges, Wirtz, and he had "a long, long caucus about Lyndon Johnson." No one doubted his intelligence. There was evidence that he could be either a conservative from "rich Texas" or a liberal out of the populist tradition of the Southwest. There was concern about how demanding he could be of the people who worked for him. As one put it, "He'll just suck the guts out of you." Heller was not bothered because he was already on an eighty-hour week. And there was the difference in style between "the sophisticated and polished Mr. Kennedy against the rather corny Mr. Johnson." Heller was apprehensive because he did not know whether Johnson was receiving advice from other economists. Altogether there were, Heller wrote, "a great many unknowns and a great deal of uncertainty."

When the plane landed about midnight Heller went straight to the Executive Office Building. Both other council members, Ackley and John Lewis, as well as the staff, were waiting for him, ready to go to work. They wrote two memoranda for Johnson, one describing the functions of CEA in serving the President and the other reviewing the current economy and pending issues. The latter was quite cheerful and homed in on the tax cut. The nation was enjoying its eleventh consecutive quarter of expansion since the first three months of 1961. The gross national product was rising at a good clip; the balance of payments had improved; wage increases were moderate and labor costs were quite stable; prices were moving upward only moderately. The prospect for continued expansion in the first half of 1964 was good. But unemployment was still a nagging 5.5 percent and the rate of expansion was "just keeping pace with our growing labor force and growing productivity. . . . If the tax cut failed to pass or were delayed too long, we would face a slowdown or even a downturn, in the second half of 1964." The tax bill passed by the House, if enacted, would lift the GNP by $12 billion in 1964 and by $30 billion a year when in full effect. There was no need to worry about the fiscal 1965 budget, now estimated at $101 to $102 billion. The fiscal 1964 budget deficit was about $9.2 billion and Kennedy had promised a lower deficit in fiscal 1965. That was easily achieved with the tax cut.

Heller had a long session with the new President that evening, Saturday, November 23. Johnson began by saying, Heller wrote, that "he needed my help and wanted me to stay." The economist did not disagree. While they discussed a number of important subjects, the one relevant here is what Heller called the "Troika exercise." This informal arrangement had been set up under Kennedy to coordinate revenue, budget, and economic policies by bringing the top people in the Treasury, the Budget Bureau, and the Council into a meeting with the President every month or two. The tax bill would be the topic for discussion. As Heller was about to leave, the President pushed the door shut, drew him back into the room, and said,

> Now, I want to say something about all this talk that I'm a conservative who is likely to go back to the Eisenhower ways or give in to the economy bloc in Congress. It's not so, and I want you to tell your friends—Arthur Schlesinger, Galbraith and other liberals—that it is not so. I'm no budget slasher. I understand that expenditures have to keep on rising to keep pace with the population and help the economy. If you looked at my record, you would know that I am a Roosevelt New Dealer. As a matter of fact, . . . John F. Kennedy was a little too conservative to suit my taste.

Dillon and Under Secretary Henry H. Fowler for the Treasury, Gordon and Staats for Budget, and Heller and Ackley for the Council met with the President at 9:15 p.m. on Monday, November 25. Both Dillon and Heller presented memoranda. The secretary argued for a deal with Senator Byrd. According to Ackley's notes, "a [budget] figure above $100 billion but not close enough to round up to $101 would do it—say, $100.6 or $100.7." This could be achieved easily with the savings McNamara was now getting at Defense from improved efficiency and with Gordon's gimmicks (he had become something of a budgetary wizard). McNamara had told Dillon that he could produce $500 million and Gordon thought he might push him to $700 million. Fowler, however, insisted on getting the budget under $100 billion.

Heller urged a budget of $101 to $102 billion. In real terms, he pointed out, this was a rise for 1965 of only 1.5 percent over 1964. This was less than the Eisenhower and Kennedy budget increases, smaller than the rises in state and local government expenditures, and would provide a drop in the ratio of the national debt to GNP, "the best measure of the burden of the debt."

When Johnson asked Dillon, "What about your tax bill?," he immediately answered his own question. He had been taking a head count of the Finance Committee and said, "We won't have the votes to get it to the floor unless we tell them the budget will be about $100 billion." Heller demurred, urging $101.5. Johnson said acidly, "I can defend $101.5—you take on Senator Byrd." He had talked about the budget with Eisenhower, Anderson, and members of Congress. "Unless you get that budget down around $100 billion, you won't pee one drop." He held up Heller's memo and said, "This represents my philosophy. You're writing about what's desirable; he [Dillon] is writing about what's possible." Heller insisted, "I'm writing about what's defensible." Johnson insisted, "You have to give something to buy off Byrd." Once you get the bill passed, Dillon pointed out, "you can do what you want." The President said, "Like Ike did . . . talked economy and then spent." Heller capitulated.

Gordon warned that "just the number" would not satisfy Byrd. He would demand the details and "the Committee knows how to spot the gimmicks."

Following this meeting there were, according to Gordon, "extensive direct discussions between the President and Senator Byrd." The latter "dominated the committee" and was "implacably opposed to the tax cut." The senator would never vote for it, but his "opposition to reporting out the tax cut would diminish substantially if the President was able to submit a budget which Harry Byrd thought sufficiently austere; and the magic figure . . . was . . . under a hundred billion dollars." Johnson got the message and met with the Virginian on December 5. Byrd announced that the President "assured me that the budget . . . would be presented to the Congress before the tax bill was finally enacted. . . . He would cut the cost of government in every way. . . . Before submitting the budget he would discuss it with the Finance Committee and Ways and Means Committee. . . ."

Since Johnson was meeting with Gordon daily, he pressed the Budget Director to trim. For several weeks the goal was merely to get under $100 billion and that, Gordon said, "wasn't very difficult" with the cuts in defense and his own gimmicks. "I relaxed a bit," Gordon noted. "I thought perhaps by the middle of December that we pretty much had it wound up—the budget then was significantly under a hundred billion." But the President now changed his mind; he wanted to go much lower. "He would send me back to look at this, to look at that, look at opportunities for trimming there, or for contraction there, for elimination there, and this went on into early January." Now the reductions hurt. The Department of Defense would shut down 33 military installations and would reduce the number of civilian employees by 17,000. The proposal of the Midwestern Universities Research Association (a consortium of about a dozen universities) to build a high-energy accelerator at Stoughton, Wisconsin, was killed. The space program was cut. Production of enriched uranium was reduced at both Hanford, Washington, and the Savannah River plants. When Johnson was criticized for this, he said, "I am not going to produce atomic bombs as a WPA project."

The most incredible event in this Johnsonian pseudo-drama occurred in early January, 1964. The President called Heller into the Oval Office and said, "Walter, I need a billion dollars more revenue. . . ." Heller gulped and asked, "Where am I supposed to find it?" "I don't care where you find it, just find it and report back in an hour."

Heller returned to his office. "Suddenly I remembered that Charlie Schultze [of the Budget Bureau, who was very good with numbers] had told me that moving the 15 percent withholding rate to 14 percent would shift the revenues enough to produce $800 million more . . . in the fiscal 1965 budget." The House bill provided for 15 percent in the remaining months of fiscal 1964 and 14 percent starting on July 1, 1965. If Congress shifted to 14 percent in fiscal 1964, the result would be overcollection in the final payoff on April 15, 1965. Voilà, $800 million in fiscal 1965! Heller called Gordon and said, "I need $200 million more." "Isn't that funny," Gordon said, "I was just looking at miscellaneous receipts and had . . . been on the verge of deciding that the estimates were $200 million too low!" Heller called Johnson, "Mr. President, I've got your billion dollars." Treasury approved the change in the withholding rate. Johnson wrote Byrd urging the lower rate in fiscal 1964, and it was written into the Senate bill.

The President not only cut the budget, he made economy in government a central theme of his public messages. In his address to the joint session of Congress on November 27, 1963, he said, "I pledge that the expenditures of your Government will be administered with the utmost thrift and frugality." On November 30 he instructed the heads of departments and agencies to keep their 1965 budget requests to "the barest minimum." The next day he sent personal letters to 7500 defense contractors demanding "cost reduction." In his news conference on December 7 he warmly endorsed McNamara's cost savings. On December 11 he implored the Joint Chiefs of Staff and officials of the Defense Department "to protect your country's purse." In his news conference on December 18 he said that his budget for 1965 would come in a little under "Mr. Kennedy's budget for 1964": "We are going to cut out every dime of waste." On December 26 he called for "economies" in the foreign aid program. At the news conference on December 27 he pointed with pride to a reduction in federal employment. He also said that he was conferring with former Presidents Hoover, Eisenhower, and Truman to learn how to improve efficiency. In the State of the Union message on January 8, 1964, he promised an administration which is "efficient, and honest and frugal."

What was Lyndon Johnson up to? Here was a man with a deserved reputation as a big spender in both his personal style and in his presidency. Dillon, clearly, was right in saying that Senator Byrd would have been satisfied with a budget of $100 billion. At the outset this seemed to satisfy Johnson. But in mid-December he suddenly changed course and insisted on coming in under $98 billion. Since he left almost no tracks, one must speculate about his reasons for this shift.

He seems to have been moved by two factors. The first was that, while he remained publicly very respectful of Kennedy, he had begun to compete with him. In his account of his presidency Johnson wrote, "A recent Harris poll had indicated that the most unpopular aspect of the Kennedy administration was what the public considered fiscal irresponsibility. I knew that we had to turn that feeling around." Thus, he insisted on a budget lower than Kennedy's. The second and probably more important factor was that Johnson, after an extraordinarily successful transition, was by mid-December positioning himself for the run for the presidency in 1964. His plea for national unity following the assassination had been very effective, in part by winning over Republicans, southern Democrats, and businessmen. He might retain much of that support by ringing the changes on the hoary slogans of economy in government and a balanced budget.

He went pretty far. In mid-January 1964, Johnson instructed Gordon to deliver a copy of the 1965 budget to Byrd as soon as it was printed and to brief him on it. It was an awkward occasion because the senator, "a crusty individual," as Gordon put it, "had not long prior to that demanded my dismissal." He went to Byrd's apartment at the Sheraton Park early in the morning with the still warm budget in his hand, was admitted by the senator in his bathrobe and slippers, and explained the details for half an hour. Gordon said, "I think the President's courtesy in sending the budget director to brief Senator Byrd played up to the old man's vanity and probably helped somewhat to moderate his opposition to the tax legislation that the President was determined to have."

Johnson sent the 1965 budget to Congress on January 21, 1964. His estimate of administrative budget expenditures for fiscal 1965 was $97.9 billion. This was $500 million lower than Kennedy's 1964 estimate of $98.4

billion. In the eyes of the Eisenhowers, Byrds, and most businessmen Johnson had won the race by half a billion dollars.[2]

By the fall of 1963 the tax bill had become a high-speed locomotive that could not be stopped. The American people strongly favored its passage. The campaign Heller and Kennedy had waged to educate the American public in elementary Keynesian economics had succeeded. Most well-informed citizens now agreed that the World War II–Korean War tax system was obsolete and was acting as a brake on the economy, that the achievement of economic growth and full employment demanded a reduction in both personal and corporate income taxes much like H.R. 8363, which had passed the House comfortably. Almost everyone else wanted his taxes cut. An immense number of organizations across the political spectrum had endorsed the bill: prominent business leaders in the Business Committee for Tax Reduction, the Chamber of Commerce, the National Association of Manufacturers, the Investment Bankers, the AFL-CIO, the Farmers Union, and Americans for Democratic Action, among many others.

If anything, the Senate seemed to favor the tax cut even more than the House. This was reflected in the 3 to 1 breakdown among the 17 members of the Finance Committee. The early supporters included nine Democrats—Russell Long of Louisiana, George Smathers of Florida, Clinton Anderson of New Mexico, Eugene McCarthy of Minnesota, Paul Douglas of Illinois, Herman Talmadge of Georgia, Vance Hartke of Indiana, J. W. Fulbright of Arkansas, and Abraham Ribicoff of Connecticut—and three Republicans—Everett Dirksen of Illinois, Thruston Morton of Kentucky, and Frank Carlson of Kansas. There were four opponents—two Democrats, Byrd and Albert Gore of Tennessee, and two Republicans, John Williams of Delaware and Carl Curtis of Nebraska. Republican Wallace Bennett of Utah had not made up his mind.

If Byrd seriously entertained the notion of holding the tax cut hostage to the civil rights bill, he did not mention it publicly. The only support he could have gotten was from Talmadge. Nor did he stall the committee's progress either before or after the Kennedy assassination; Johnson's budget foreclosed such a move in the later stages. Majority leader Mike Mansfield told the President on December 3, 1963, "Byrd has been cooperative. . . . We have to give Byrd credit. He is against things, but he doesn't hold them up." True, the Finance Committee held the bill from early October 1963 to January 28, 1964. But the lack of speed is explained by the flood of witnesses at the hearings, the assassination, a very large number of amendments, Byrd's insistence that every member should be allowed to speak without limit, and Albert Gore's propensity to filibuster.

Joseph Barr, who worked the Hill for the Treasury, considered Gore "hopeless," and Larry O'Brien urged Long and Smathers to ride herd on him. Gore, a maverick Tennessee populist, came out against the tax cut in 1962 before the bill was written. He wanted the government to spend more rather than tax less; he called the measure "a rich man's bill"; and he blamed the administration for allowing the House Ways and Means Committee to strip away the important reforms. Barr thought that he had "locked himself into a political posture in Tennessee that he cannot readily abandon." Since Gore was unable to stop the bill, he did whatever he could to slow it down. His tactics even annoyed Byrd.

For Johnson the tax bill offered a nostalgic reprise of his glory days as majority leader. At the Troika meeting on November 25, according to Gardner Ackley, he showed "pretty clear knowledge of every vote [in the Finance Committee]. He said that he had been checking up on it (not too directly—that would be beneath the dignity of the President!)." He seems to have been in continual touch with Senator Byrd. At the weekly congressional breakfasts he harangued the Democratic leaders, particularly Mansfield and Smathers—"give it the old college try," "get some leadership." He demanded and received a flood of memoranda on the bill's progress from those who followed it—Larry O'Brien and Mike Manatos in the White House and Dillon, Fowler, and Barr in the Treasury.

At the same time the President seized every reasonably appropriate public occasion to urge enactment of the tax cut. In his address to the joint session of Congress on November 27, 1963, he said, "No act of ours could more fittingly continue the work of President Kennedy than the early passage of the tax bill." At a meeting with the AFL-CIO Executive Council on December 4 he said that the measure should be "alive and working." At his meeting with the Business Council the same day he said, "I need it now." At his first news conference on December 7 he called for "early passage of the tax bill." He discussed it at length in the press conference on December 18. In the important papers in January 1964—the State of the Union, the Economic Report, and the Budget Message—he developed tax policy at length.

The Finance Committee, meantime, plodded along. In 32 days of hearings between October 15 and December 10, 1963, it listened to 132 witnesses. Most of January went to voting on the bill section by section and on 59 amendments. This was Gore's opportunity to toss sand into the machinery. He was absent on January 9 and the committee, Barr wrote, "plunged ahead." He returned the next day and there was "little progress." In fact, the great majority of the amendments were either minor or technical and a large proportion were acceptable to the Treasury.

Only two proposed amendments were of general interest—capital gains and the Ribicoff education credit. The former, of course, was an indestructible perennial that came up every time taxes were changed. In the original Kennedy bill in January 1963 one of the basic reforms would be a narrowing of capital gains and that had brought the lobbyists out in force. The

Ways and Means Committee actually broadened the gains. The Treasury with presidential backing tried to persuade the Finance Committee to strike the House provision and restore the old rates. The Treasury expected a very close vote because Democrats Anderson, Talmadge, and Ribicoff, along with three moderate Republicans, Dirksen, Morton, and Carlson, seemed doubtful. But in the committee vote on January 17 all six fell into line. The House was reversed 12 to 7.

The proposal to allow the parents of college students to deduct tuition from their income taxes had long been sponsored by private and opposed by public institutions. The Treasury had firmly opposed this deduction, mainly because of the loss of income, estimated at $700 million the first year and $1.3 billion by 1970. The Ribicoff amendment was artfully drawn to relate the deduction inversely to income in order to parry the charge of helping the rich. It had wide Republican support. But, Barr wrote the White House on January 13, "We have the Committee votes to beat this one." Ribicoff agreed and did not allow his amendment to reach a vote. Rather, he would take it to the floor of the Senate, where he expected stronger support.

On January 23, 1964, the Finance Committee approved H.R. 8363 as amended by a vote of 12 to 5. The majority of nine Democrats and three Republicans was exactly as anticipated. The only change was in the no vote; Senator Bennett finally made up his mind and joined the four already against the tax cut.

The Senate debated the tax bill in a rather mundane fashion for six days. The only modest sparks came from the two big amendments. The administration won handily on capital gains 56 to 25. But Ribicoff came much closer because of strong Republican support. Here Wayne Morse, the Senate's expert on education, carried the day. He stressed the fact that the Association of State Universities and Land Grant Colleges strongly objected to the amendment; that several private college presidents had told him that they would raise tuition if it passed, shifting the cost to the Treasury; and that, since many private colleges were denominational, this would raise the divisive church-state issue. Nevertheless, the administration barely won by a vote of 48 to 45. The Democratic lines were steady against the amendment 43 to 19, but a strong majority of Republicans joined Ribicoff 26 to 5.

On February 7 the Senate adopted H.R. 8363 as amended. The vote was overwhelming, 77 to 21. Heavy majorities in both parties supported the tax bill—56 to 11 Democrats and 21 to 10 Republicans.

The conference committee met between February 10 and 19 and its main task was to resolve the difference over capital gains. It pretty much accepted the Senate version and reported on February 24. The House accepted the report the next day 326 to 83. The day following the Senate approved 74 to 19. At this final stage the opposition had vanished.

The President could hardly wait to celebrate. He signed the law six hours after the Senate acted on February 26, 1964. He called it "the largest [tax reduction] in the history of the United States . . . and the single most important step we have taken to strengthen our economy since World War II." He shared the credit with "our late, beloved President John F. Kennedy" and gave the Kennedy family four pens. He expressed gratitude to Dillon, the Treasury staff, Mills, Long and even Byrd. He informed the public that their income taxes would fall almost 20 percent starting in eight days, that as consumers they would have $25 million more a day for consumption, that corporations would enjoy similar benefits and opportunities. He told everyone that, if they really loved their country, to get out there and spend. No politician could have imagined a more pleasurable task.

What had Lyndon Johnson contributed to the passage of this important piece of legislation? Dillon had been intimately involved in both shaping the bill and its legislative history. When asked whether Johnson had changed Kennedy's bill, he said, "Not at all." His only interest was in "getting the bill passed . . . and he certainly got it much quicker." Dillon canceled out the concessions to Byrd because Kennedy was also willing to bring in a budget under $100 billion. Johnson did present an even lower budget, but that was only a "gesture," not needed to satisfy Byrd.

Walter Heller, who played a pivotal role in promoting the idea of the tax bill but was not directly involved in the legislative process, was more philosophical:

> The tax cut illustrated a difference between the Kennedy and Johnson approach. Kennedy felt that the way to get the tax cut was to educate the Congress and the country and persuade them to go for it. . . . Johnson's idea was, "Let's get the damned thing passed and demonstrate to the country what it can do." That, as it happened, was probably the ideal combination, where Kennedy had done much of the educational work, and then Johnson used his incomparable technique to get the thing through.[3]

The Revenue Act of 1964 reduced nominal tax rates from a range of 20 to 91 percent in 1963 to 16 to 77 in 1964 and 14 to 70 percent in 1965. The withholding rate of 18 percent in 1963 was cut to 14 percent in March 1964. By 1965 the income tax obligations of individuals were expected to fall by $9.2 billion. The main corporation rate was reduced from 52 percent in 1963 to 50 percent in 1964 and 48 percent in 1965. On the first $25,000 of corporate income the tax rate was cut from 30 to 22 percent. By 1965 the obligations of corporations were expected to be $2.4 billion lower. Thus, the combined reduction for individuals and corporations would come to $11.6 billion by 1965.

The Keynesians had predicted that this unprecedented and radical tax change would significantly increase consumer spending and corporate investment, thereby giving the economy a big lift to an approximation of full employment. Heller had also told the President that rising incomes would increase net tax flows to the Treasury, which would create a budget surplus that he could use for new and expanded domestic programs. Publicly, of course, Johnson had fully accepted this analysis and had worked very hard to get the Revenue Act passed. Privately, he had some doubts.

Johnson would say, as Heller later recalled their conversations, "You know, Walter, I'm an old-fashioned economist, and I'm not sure I understand all these new-fashioned ideas, but I'm depending on you." He understood them all right, but he was concerned that they might not work. During the first two or three months Heller began to worry too.

In April 1964 Heller went to the White House to inform the President that he must return to the University of Minnesota. Johnson took him for a walk around the oval behind the White House. "After you leave me and go back to Minnesota," Johnson said, "I'll come out there and haul you back here and publicly horsewhip you if it doesn't come through."

The Council kept a hawk's eye on retail sales, and, Heller said, they were "absolutely dead in the water." Then John Lewis brought in a clipping from the *Washington Daily News* which read, "Waiters are reporting an enormous increase in tips since the tax cut." Lewis had written on the clipping, "Now I know what's wrong. They haven't been spending it, they haven't been saving it, they've been giving it away!" That, Heller said, "broke the tension." The American economy had been launched into a gigantic upward roll.

The indexes of economic activity moved inexorably upward month after month, quarter after quarter. It was as though the law of gravity had been repealed and the numbers had forgotten how to fall. Lyndon Johnson, particularly as his campaign for the presidency gathered steam, became obsessed by these figures. On March 21, 1964, he instructed Heller to prepare a summary of "Economic (Good) News Notes" every Monday, Wednesday, and Friday. Heller asked Secretary Wirtz to send to the Council the Labor Department statistics and other materials in the fields of "employment, wages, prices, productivity and similar economic matters." Johnson loved to rattle off these numbers. If he met with businessmen, he told them precisely how much their profits had risen. If he talked to labor leaders, he showed them the increase in employment and the decline in unemployment. His speeches and public papers were generously seasoned with good economic news. His section of the annual *Economic Report of the President* read like the annual report of a corporation that was swimming in cash.

The statistics were exhilarating. Gross national product in 1958 prices skyrocketed from $569.7 billion in the first quarter of 1964 to $631.2 billion in the last quarter of 1965. Disposable personal income shot up from $423.4 billion in the first quarter of 1964 to $486.1 in the last three months of 1965. Since the savings rate did not change, all of the gain was spent. Median annual family income in 1965 prices increased from $6,444 in 1963 to $6,882 in 1965. The number of poor families, defined as having an annual income of less than $3000 in 1965 prices, fell from 8.5 million in 1963 to 8 million in 1965.

The number of persons employed, seasonally adjusted, rocketed up from 69.6 million in January 1964 to 73.4 in December 1965, a gain of 3.8 million jobs. The number out of work dropped sharply from 4.1 million in January 1964 to 3.1 in December 1965, a decline of 1 million in the jobless. The unemployment rate, 5.6 percent in January 1964, dropped under 5 percent a year later and was down to 4.1 percent in December 1965. This virtually reached Kennedy's goal of 4 percent unemployment. Those with jobs worked longer hours. Average weekly hours in manufacturing rose from 40.5 in 1963 to 41.2 in 1965. These employment gains came in the face of an enormous inflow of jobseekers, particularly baby boomers and women, who were attracted by both their need to work and the growing availability of jobs. The labor force grew by almost 6 million between 1960 and December 1965, by just under 3 million between January 1964 and December 1965. According to the CEA, starting in 1963 GNP had to grow at a rate of 3.75 percent annually to hold unemployment constant and this was expected to rise later in the decade.

Output shot up. The industrial production index (1957–59 = 100) jumped from 127.9 in January 1964 to 148.3 in December 1965. The automobile industry broke all prior records. Business expenditures for new plant and equipment exploded from $39.2 billion in 1963 to $52 billion in 1965.

Corporate profits surged. In 1965, after taxes, they rose 67 percent over the preceding 5 years and were 20 percent above 1964.

All of this took place, until the first major military commitment in Vietnam in July 1965, in a period of virtual price stability. The all-commodities wholesale price index (1957–59 = 100) crawled up from 100.3 in 1963 to 100.5 in 1964, and to 102.5 in 1965, most of the increase taking place in the last half of the year. The all-items consumer price index (1957–59 = 100) moved from 106.7 in 1963, to 108.1 in 1964, and 109.9 in 1965.

In his Godkin Lectures at Harvard in 1966 Walter Heller could not refrain from a bit of crowing:

> The rationale of the 1964 tax-cut proposal came straight out of the country's postwar economics textbooks. And in turn the tax cut itself—recently described by Dexter Keezer as "a triumph of high-test Keynesian economic therapy"—will richly repay its debt to the textbooks by supplying the classic example of modern fiscal policy and multiplier economics at work. Careful appraisal of the tax cut's impact on GNP shows a remarkably close fit of results to expectations. And until Vietnam intervened, the tax cut *had* brought us back to "a balanced budget in a balanced economy"—in fact, by the first half of 1965, Federal receipts had already risen $7½ billion above their previous tax-cut levels, and the Federal budget (NIA basis) was in surplus. So in conception as well as in delivery, it was a textbook tax cut.

The "careful appraisal" to which Heller referred was a sophisticated analysis by Arthur M. Okun, a member of the CEA staff and later chairman, of the impact of the tax cut which was written during the summer of 1965. How, Okun asked, would the economy have performed if the Revenue Act had not been passed? There would have been modest gains in GNP, disposable income, and consumption, while profits would have slipped and investment would have leveled off. "This no-tax-cut world would have shown rising unemployment and sagging operating rates."

Tax reduction transformed this world. Consumers behaved exactly as the Keynesians had predicted and were spending almost all their tax gains. "By the second quarter of 1965, consumption expenditures had registered a remarkable rise of $45 billion from their rate in the last quarter of 1963, . . . an increase over six quarters . . . unmatched in our peacetime history." Consumption was the engine of the boom. The famous Keynesian multiplier of "close to two" proved out. Okun calculated it for 1964–65 at 1.82, that is, a reduction of $1 in taxes produced a $1.82 increase in consumption expenditures. As anticipated, the rise in consumption expenditures from higher business investment was considerably less and needed more time to make its impact.

Again as forecast, the federal government by the second quarter of 1965 was receiving $7 billion in increased receipts from the tax cut and that figure would continue to rise. State and local governments were getting $1.5 billion more. Okun estimated that ultimately the federal gain would be $10 billion annually and the state and local gains $2.2 billion, "a total that nearly matches the $13 billion of the reduction."

He reckoned that the tax cut was responsible for a $25 billion annual rise in GNP by mid-1965, that it would climb to $30 by the end of that year, and ultimately to $36 billion. Okun concluded that "the Revenue Act of 1964 lived up to the intentions and expectations of its advocates and . . . had delivered a powerful stimulus to economic expansion."

In fact, the 1964 tax cut became a legend and a sometimes misused example. Thereafter any President who wanted to reduce taxes would support his argument, regardless of conditions or timing, by citing the success of the Kennedy-Johnson tax reduction. This would be an abuse of the Keynesian analysis and a misreading of history.

John Maynard Keynes devised a system which was flexible, which offered a variety of tools of economic policy, and which was applicable to many types of economic conditions. Reducing taxes was only one of his instruments. In fact, he wrote *The General Theory* in the mid-thirties when there was business stagnation and massive unemployment and he urged increased government expenditures to lift the economy. This was certainly not the situation in 1964, when a much larger fraction of the labor force was employed and the economy was growing, albeit at a slow and inadequate rate. Nor was it the condition in the late sixties, when the expenditures for the Vietnam War imposed on an already booming economy created severe inflation.

Further, the situation in 1964 was unique in allowing for a reduction in tax rates without causing a decline in government revenues, in fact, increasing them. This was because the Revenue Act of 1964 cut the obsolete wartime tax rates which had become a drag on the economy. It was the best of all possible worlds: taxes were lower and the funds available for existing and even new government services rose. But, once the old rate structure was eliminated, that was it. Thereafter a tax reduction would reduce tax receipts and the government would need to borrow or to reduce its services, or both.

A final speculative note, an "if" of history: How would the American economy have performed if Lyndon Johnson had not taken the U.S. into the Vietnam War in July 1965? A remarkable feature of the great expansion that flowed from the Revenue Act until the latter part of 1965 was essential price stability. Preserving the balance between full employment and steady wages and prices would certainly have been the challenging policy problem in the late sixties. The probability is that the economy would have continued to expand, but that inflation would have set in.[4]

3

The Civil Rights Act of 1964

PRESIDENT Kennedy had equivocated on civil rights. But he was shocked by the violent racial confrontation in Birmingham, Alabama, in May 1963. Shortly afterward Governor George Wallace "stood in the schoolhouse door" to block the admission of black students to the University of Alabama. In a notable address to the American people on June 11 Kennedy stressed the moral imperative of civil rights for Negroes and promised to send a comprehensive bill to Congress.

The President delivered his omnibus measure on June 19, 1963. The major titles were the following:

I. Voting Rights—completion of the sixth grade of school as prima facie proof of literacy for the right to vote in federal elections.

II. Public Accommodations—persons without regard to race, color, religion, or national origin would have access to hotels, motels, places of entertainment, stores, restaurants, and similar public facilities.

III. Desegregation of Public Education—the commissioner of education would establish programs to desegregate the public schools and the Attorney General would be empowered to file suit against a school board that failed to comply.

IV. Community Relations Service—it would counsel and assist local communities in resolving disputes over discriminatory practices.

V. U.S. Commission on Civil Rights—its life would be extended by four years.

VI. Federally Assisted Programs—federal agencies which financed state and local programs would be required to withhold funds from any program which allowed for discrimination based on race, creed, color, or national origin.

VII. Commission on Equal Employment Opportunity—under the law this commission would replace the President's Committee on Equal Employment Opportunity that had been created by the Kennedy executive order.

It was clear to the Kennedy administration and the Democratic congressional leadership at the outset that such a bill would confront formidable political obstacles. This was because the Democratic party was hopelessly split: the southern Democrats solidly opposed the bill and the northern Democrats lacked a majority in either house, to say nothing of two-thirds of the Senate for a cloture vote to stop an almost certain southern filibuster. Thus, Republican support in both chambers was indispensable. Two of the key figures, therefore, became William McCulloch of Ohio, the senior Republican on the House Judiciary Committee, and Everett Dirksen, the Senate minority leader. These difficulties also called for starting in the House, where the chances of success were markedly better in part because there was nothing like the Senate's Rule 22, which allowed for unlimited debate. The administration, however, had the support of public opinion in the nation outside the South.

Many considered Title II, public accommodations, the heart of the civil rights bill. A Gallup poll for the week of June 21 to 26, 1963, showed that of those with opinions 49 percent favored a public accommodations law, while 42 percent opposed. For whites outside the South the split was 55 to 34 percent; among southern whites the opponents led 82 to 12. The majority nationally that supported the law grew to 61 percent by January 1964. Opposition in the South eroded from 82 percent in June 1963 to 72 percent by January 1964. Even more significant, southerners who opposed integration expected to lose. The Gallup poll for June 21 to 26, 1963, asked them if the day will come when both races will go to the same schools, restaurants, and so on. Some 83 percent of southerners said this would take place, 49 percent within 5 years. Significantly, after Birmingham religious organizations—Protestant, Catholic, and Jewish—increasingly put their great political weight behind civil rights.

During October and November 1963 there was a donnybrook in the House Judiciary Committee. McCulloch had helped steer a modest civil rights bill through the House in 1957 to see it gutted in the Senate by majority leader Lyndon Johnson in the face of a southern filibuster. He was determined to prevent that from happening again. McCulloch, therefore, extracted a promise from President Kennedy and the Department of Justice that they would stand by the House bill and not give pieces of it away in the Senate. The House Judiciary Committee under chairman Emanuel Celler, the New York Democrat, voted for a strong civil rights bill, called H.R. 7152, on November 20, 1963, by a vote of 20 to 14. There were a number of changes from the titles in the original administration bill: II. Public Accommodations—retail stores and personal services were excluded; III. Public Facilities—the Attorney General could intervene only after an individual had filed a complaint and had demonstrated his inability to pursue the suit; V. Community Relations—eliminated; new V. Civil Rights Commission—would become permanent; VI. Federally Assisted Programs—limited to federal grant, contract, and loan programs; and VII. Equal Employment—an Equal Employment Opportunity Commission would replace the executive order, but with restricted powers.

H.R. 7152 moved to the Rules Committee just before the Kennedy assassination. Its chairman, 81-year-old, arch-conservative, and dedicated segregationist Howard Smith of Virginia, was determined to use all of his formidable authority to prevent the issuance of a rule. If the new President wanted a civil rights law, he would have to find a way around Smith.[1]

Lyndon Johnson, despite his earlier ambivalence on civil rights, now committed himself to H.R. 7152. He had three reasons for doing so: his conviction; his constituency had widened from Texas to the nation; and his duty as the caretaker of the Kennedy legacy.

Johnson wrote, "I believed that a huge injustice had been perpetrated for hundreds of years on every black man, woman, and child in the United States. I did not think that our nation could endure much longer as a viable democracy if that injustice were allowed to continue." George Reedy worked for Johnson for years, knew him extremely well, and saw him in the round. He said,

> Mr. Johnson is one of the least prejudiced or biased or intolerant or big-oted men I have ever met. He has many shortcomings and many failings, but I don't believe there is any racial prejudice in him whatsoever; and this is the thing that became very apparent to most of the Negro leaders when they had a chance to know him personally.

Roy Wilkins of the NAACP, who dealt with Johnson over many years, agreed. "I grew to believe that the man is absolutely sincere on this question of opportunity and race. He has risen above his background." Hubert Humphrey said, "I knew he was sincere . . . [that] he was not a segregationist."

Until 1961 Lyndon Johnson had been a senator from Texas. That state was in the South and was racially segregated. No one could be elected to the Senate from Texas who spoke in favor of racial integration. During the fifties Paul Douglas had been a firmly committed member of the small band of warriors in the Senate who fought for civil rights. He regarded Johnson as the enemy. Douglas "lamented" the fact that Johnson had become President because Douglas thought he would continue to block racial progress.

He was astonished and delighted when Johnson turned completely around. "No one could have been more vigorous than he . . . on civil rights." So "I took up my courage" and asked Mrs. Johnson, who knew him best of all, to explain the change. "She said, 'The President has to take into consideration many things that a senator does not.' And that was that." George Reedy on the 1957 civil rights bill:

> LBJ didn't give a good whatever we want to use about how the southerners felt about civil rights, except to the extent that it set certain limits on what could be done with a bill. LBJ had no sympathy whatsoever for the anti-civil rights movement. If he had had the votes to do it, the legislation that would have passed would have been far more extreme than what was passed. But LBJ was not a southerner in that sense. It was rather unfortunate that the poor devil came from a Confederate state, which . . . historically was not very Confederate. Texas got tricked into the Confederacy. It did not enter very willingly, and it did not play much of a role in the Civil War.

As trustee of the slain President's legacy, Johnson had to take the same position on the bill. He did so publicly in his address to the joint session of Congress on November 27, 1963:

> No memorial oration or eulogy could more eloquently honor President Kennedy's memory than the earliest possible passage of the civil rights bill for which he fought so long. We have talked long enough in this country about equal rights. We have talked for one hundred years or more. It is time now to write the next chapter, and to write it in the books of law.

Over the next seven months, while the bill was before Congress, Johnson would return to this refrain again and again.

But the main role Johnson would play in the legislative history of H.R. 7152 would come later in the Senate. It must first clear the House and here the key figure was Howard Worth Smith of the 8th Congressional District of Virginia, widely regarded since Sam Rayburn's death as the most powerful man in the House of Representatives.

Smith was a living fossil of the post-Civil War rural South. He had been born in the family farmhouse, Cedar Hill, near Broad Run in Fauquier County in 1883, just 18 years after Appomattox, a house that somehow managed to survive the ravages of the nearby battles. He helped on the farm, was taught by a cousin, attended a local military academy, and went to the University of Virginia Law School in Charlottesville, from which he graduated in 1903. By that time his style and views had hardened and would never change. He was brilliant, extremely diligent, gracious in the Virginia manner, and soft-spoken. Carl Albert, a former Rhodes scholar who was Democratic whip in the House in 1964, knew Smith very well and much admired him:

> By birth and by choice Judge Smith, as we knew him around the Capitol, was an unreconstructed nineteenth-century Virginian. He spent his entire legislative life trying to ward off federal encroachments into the world in which he was born. He had all the attributes, including all the prejudices, of his native state. He distrusted all influences outside of his own area. He was brought up believing that Yankees, carpetbaggers, Republicans, and foreigners were enemies of his people and of the way of life they enjoyed. He was a white supremacist who fought racial integration to the bitter end. He opposed nearly all federal social reforms, including health, education, and welfare bills. He believed in the Constitution "as written." He was a strict constructionist and states' righter. He was a Tenth Amendment congressman.

In 1904 Smith opened a law office in Alexandria. He speculated in real estate and soon became rich. He entered local politics as a stalwart of the Virginia Democratic organization, later the Byrd Machine, and was elected to a number of local and state offices, including a judgeship. In 1930 the door to the 8th District fell open and Smith walked in. He would hold that seat for 36 years. Early on, in 1933, he found his home on the Rules Committee, the spigot which, turned on or off, determined whether a bill would reach the floor of the House. He seemed to have no interests save his job and worked at it extremely hard. He was a superb parliamentarian and knew more about the contents of bills than any other member of the committee. He emerged as the House leader of the southern Democratic-Republican coalition that opposed progressive legislation.

Starting with the New Deal, Smith vented his animus against organized labor and "undesirable" aliens. In 1939–40 he chaired a committee that broadsided the National Labor Relations Board. He was the author of the Smith Act, passed in 1940, which imposed many disabilities on aliens, including deportation. In 1943 he was the driving force behind the Smith-Connolly Act to prevent wartime strikes and to restrict unions. In 1947 he wrote the Hartley part of the Taft-Hartley Act, though Smith would have gone much further in punishing unions than Senator Taft allowed.

In 1954 Smith won ultimate power when he became chairman of the Rules Committee, which he came to dominate by controlling both the southern Democratic and Republican votes. He kept everything off the floor of which he disapproved. His legislative chokehold and the ruthless manner in which he exercised it became a burning issue to Speaker Rayburn and the liberal northern Democrats. Kennedy's election in 1960 and his New Frontier agenda guaranteed a showdown. Rayburn proposed enlarging the committee from 12 to 15 members, which would give the liberals and moderates a shot at an 8 to 7 majority. This led to the historic confrontation early in 1961 between Rayburn and Smith when Mr. Sam left the rostrum for a speech on the floor urging the three new members. But he barely won by a vote of 217 to 212. This did not give liberals control of the Rules Committee. Depending on the bill, it meant that they now had a chance of winning. Thus, the outcome on H.R. 7152 was much in doubt. The only certainty was that Howard Smith would fight to the finish with all his parliamentary guile to bury what he called "this nefarious bill."

The Judiciary Committee had referred the measure to the Rules Committee two days before the Kennedy assassination. Smith, when it suited him, was one of the world's great procrastinators. When what he referred to as the 1957 civil "wrongs" bill was before his committee, Smith had disappeared. The rumor was that the dairy barn on his farm had burned down and that he had to leave town to inspect the damage. A Republican on his committee said, "I knew the Judge was opposed to the civil rights bill. But I didn't think he would commit arson to beat it." Now he announced that he might have to take a trip.

In anticipation of such trouble, in early December 1963 the Democratic leadership explored the three options for prying a bill loose from the Rules Committee. Under House Rule 27, any member could file a discharge petition 30 days after a measure had been favorably reported by a standing committee. But the petition must be signed by a majority of the House—218 members. On December 9 Emanuel Celler, the chairman of the Judiciary Committee, filed the petition, But, according to Larry O'Brien, by January 6, 1964, Celler had gotten only "approximately" 173 signatures. The needed 45 Republican votes never appeared, and for good reason. McCulloch disliked discharge petitions because he thought they undermined the committee system. Halleck opposed them because he insisted that the Rules Committee hold hearings, and none had been conducted. Without McCulloch and Halleck there were no Republican votes.

Second, House Rule 24 offered calendar Wednesday. On any Wednesday the clerk could call the names of the standing committees alphabetically and, when called, the committee chairman could order his bill onto the floor. The House then became a committee of the whole and had two hours for debate. The entire procedure must take place within one day. The rule was almost never invoked because the opponents held all the trumps. In alphabetical order Judiciary ranked twelfth. Of the preceding eleven, six had southern chairmen, any one of whom could preempt Celler by calling up one of his own bills.

Finally, House Rule 11 stated that three members of a committee could ask the chairman to call a meeting. If after three days he had not done so, a majority of the committee—in the case of Judiciary, eight members—could order a meeting at a specific date and time. There were five Democrats ready to invoke Rule 11. Would the Republicans supply at least another three?

The Republican leader on Judiciary was Clarence Brown, Sr., of Blanchester, Ohio, whose district bordered McCulloch's. He was very conservative on all issues except civil rights and had worked with Smith for years to block progressive legislation. But he revered the Republican party's Lincoln tradition. Further, two black colleges, Wilberforce and Central State, were in his district, as was the town of Xenia, an important station before the Civil War on the underground railway on which runaway slaves escaped to Canada. Brown had delivered the votes for the Eisenhower civil rights bills in 1957 and 1960.

He was considerate. On December 4 he told Smith, "I don't want to run over you, Judge, but. . . ." Since Brown had the votes to force a meeting, Smith knew that the game was up. On December 18 Smith yielded, promising hearings on January 9, 1964.

The committee listened to 33 witnesses over 9 days of hearings which spread over most of the month. As was customary in Rules Committee hearings, witnesses went beyond questions of procedure to discuss the merits of H.R. 7152. There were bitter exchanges between Celler and Smith. On January 29 the chairman reached the end of the line. The Republicans wanted the bill on the floor so that debate could be concluded in time for them to deliver their traditional Lincoln's Birthday speeches on February 12. Knowing that Brown would force his hand, Smith in resignation called for the vote on January 30. The committee adopted the rule 11 to 4. All five Republicans joined five northern Democrats and one southerner in the majority. Smith won over only three other southern Democrats. H.R. 7152, gathering speed, moved to the floor of the House of Representatives.[2]

The Democratic leaders, their Republican allies, and the White House were confident. Larry O'Brien's head count for January 20, 1964, showed 220 House members, two more than a majority, pledged to support H.R. 7152. Smith was gloomy, and many southerners conceded privately that it was all over when the bill had cleared the committee. In fact, a large number did not even bother to appear on the floor. The Republicans were so hopelessly divided between those who stood for the Lincoln tradition and those with few blacks in their districts who did not want to get into a fight that Halleck refused to call a caucus. As Les Arends, the minority whip, explained, "All we would do was tear ourselves apart."

The bipartisan majority came to the debate armed with massive support. When Celler and McCulloch took their seats at the long tables on the floor, each had a large title-by-title manual prepared by the Justice Department. For every title there was an analysis of its history and need, a summary of the provisions, a review of scope and constitutionality, probable major objections, possible amendments and arguments against them, replies to the Judiciary Committee's minority report, and a summary of related state laws. There were answers to all the questions Smith had asked at the Rules Committee hearings. Eight attorneys from Justice, each a specialist in a title, stood by to help if needed. Katzenbach and Burke Marshall were seated in the gallery.

Since H.R. 7152 was long, technical, complex, and important, a large number of votes would be needed. The fact that a representative had committed himself to support the bill was interesting, but not conclusive. He must be on the floor to vote each time his name was called. The polling would take ten minutes and that was the maximum time in which to find and produce the bodies. For this operation Celler and McCulloch set up three levels of whips.

The Democratic Study Group, 120 supporters, worked the floor. Hale Boggs, the majority whip, did not participate because he was from Louisiana and would vote against the bill. Under the supervision of Frank Thompson of New Jersey, 17 DSG members were each assigned six to eight congressmen. When a vote seemed imminent, Thompson would call the DSG office, which would phone the 17 whips, and their offices would call the assigned members to get to the floor. If they did not appear when the roll was called, there would be a second call.

O'Grady's Raiders patrolled the Cannon and Longworth buildings. Jane O'Grady was the lobbyist for the Amalgamated Clothing Workers and directed 25 union volunteers who, when the vote bell rang, scurried to congressional offices to insure that members got to the floor.

The Leadership Conference on Civil Rights, a coalition of civil rights, labor, church, and women's organizations that supported H.R. 7152, had its people in the galleries. Since writing in the galleries was forbidden, each memorized the faces of several congressmen to learn who voted and who did not.

The House debate opened on January 31, 1964. Celler and McCulloch, characterized by the latter as "the Brooklyn street urchin and the Ohio plowboy," led off. Celler, describing the moment as "a golden opportunity," declared,

> What we are considering this day in effect is a bill of particulars on a petition in the language of our Constitution for a redress of grievances. The grievances are real and genuine, the proof is in, the gathering of evidence has gone on for over a century. The legislation before you seeks only to honor the constitutional guarantees of equality under the law for all. It bestows no preferences on any one group; what it does is to place into balance the scales of justice so that the living force of our Constitution shall apply to all people, not only to those who by accident of birth were born with white skins.

McCulloch continued,

> I believe in the effective separation of powers and in a workable federal system, whereby State authority is not needlessly usurped by a centralized

government. But, I also believe that an obligation rests with the national government to see that the citizens of every state are treated equally without regard to their race or color or religion or national origin. . . .

No people can gain lasting liberty and equality by riots and demonstrations. Legislation under such threat is basically not legislation at all. In the long run, behavior of this type will lead to a total undermining of society, where equality and civil rights will mean nothing. . . . Not force or fear, then, but belief in the inherent equality of man induces me to support this legislation.

On February 3 the House reached the heart of the debate—the offering of amendments. This was the supreme test for the South. Would Smith and his supporters have the votes to weaken or even gut H.R. 7152? They got off to a bad start. That day and the next the southerners offered nine amendments to Title I, Voting Rights, all defeated. Southern Republicans proposed two amendments that Celler and McCulloch accepted—granting defendants the same right to a three-judge court as the Attorney General would have and including Puerto Rico within the scope of the bill.

The amendments to Title II, Public Accommodations, consumed two days. Despite the sensitivity of the subject, the debate was conducted in good taste except for a slip by, of all people, that model gentleman from Virginia, Howard Smith. A podiatrist who practiced alone, he pointed out, would not be covered by the law, but one who had his office in a hotel would be. He could not restrain himself: "If I were cutting corns, I would want to know whose feet I would have to be monkeying around with. I would want to know whether they smelled good or bad." Upon reflection, he struck the remark from the *Congressional Record*. His motion, a restatement of the Thirteenth Amendment, was defeated 149 to 107. For a number of southerners this was decisive and they disappeared from the floor. The next afternoon, when several amendments lost, there were only about 30 of the 96 congressmen from the South in the House. All the other amendments were crushed.

On February 6, Title III, Public Facilities, came up and all the proposed amendments were defeated except for another by a southern Republican which would have the government pay the attorney's fee for a defendant who lost his suit. At first Celler objected but, when McCulloch insisted, Celler went along. Title IV, Public Education, sailed through smoothly. Six amendments were rejected and two accepted by the leaders. Celler and McCulloch, though concerned, accepted an amendment to Title V, Civil Rights Commission, offered by Ed Willis of Louisiana. It would not require the commission to investigate "the membership practices of any bona fide fraternal, religious, or civic organization which selects its membership." Another amendment was accepted which eliminated the perpetual life of the commission and limited the term to four years.

The debate on February 7 on Title VI, Federally Assisted Programs, was nasty. At a moment when McCulloch was out of the chamber, Oren Harris, Democrat of Arkansas, offered an amendment which would have drastically weakened the title and would have eliminated judicial review. Boggs spoke in support of the amendment. When McCulloch returned and learned of the speech Boggs had made, he became very suspicious. He knew that Lyndon Johnson and Hale Boggs were close friends and drew the not unreasonable, but incorrect, inference that this was another betrayal by Johnson. "Look!" McCulloch's wife, Mabel, said to Roy Wilkins of NAACP, who sat next to her in the gallery. "Bill's face is red. He's mad!" McCulloch seized a microphone and stated angrily, "If we pick up this old provision which does not provide for judicial review, I regret to say that my individual support of the legislation will come to an end." Celler had no doubt that he meant it and the House was shocked into silence. The amendment was crushed 206 to 80 with every Republican voting against it. Seven other amendments to Title VI also went down to defeat.

The climax came on Saturday, February 8, when the House debated Title VII, Equal Employment. The Labor Committee had been working on this for several years and in 1962 had reported an equal employment bill. The next year the Judiciary Committee incorporated large sections of it into Title VII. It was necessary to conform the language and Celler proposed ten technical amendments acceptable to McCulloch, which the House routinely adopted.

Now Howard Smith's moment arrived. Section 704 was the heart of Title VII. It created in five places unlawful practices for an employer, a labor organization, an employment agency, or an apprenticeship training program, forbidding them to discriminate against "any individual because of his race, color, religion, or national origin." These four factors had been used widely in prior federal executive orders and in state and local legislation. The Labor Committee in 1962 had added two new criteria, ancestry and age. On February 8 Smith dropped a bombshell. "Mr. Chairman," he said, "I offer an amendment." In the five places in the bill where the factors appeared, "after the word 'religion' insert the word 'sex.' " With this extraordinary motion Smith opened up an extremely important new issue.

Discrimination against women in the U.S. labor market was ancient and very widespread in hiring, in access to better jobs, in promotions, in wages and salaries, and in many other factors in the employment relationship. Two movements had emerged to grapple with aspects of this vast problem. The first was protective legislation enacted in the states during the Progressive Era to assist low-income female wage earners by establishing legal minimum wages, maximum hours, and adequate working conditions. At the federal level this became a basic objective of Franklin Roosevelt's New Deal, which was revived during the Kennedy administration under the leadership of Esther Peterson, who was assistant secretary of labor and head of the Women's Bureau. Such legislation won the support of the labor movement from which Peterson had come and from liberal northern Democrats. It was concerned with working women regardless of their race, color, religion, or national origin. During the Kennedy years Peterson had secured passage of the Equal Pay Act and had engineered the report of the President's Commission on the Status of Women, which recommended an even broader program.

The second movement championed the Equal Rights Amendment to the Constitution in order to guarantee women comprehensive legal equality with men. ERA was introduced into Congress in 1923. The movement was basically a one-woman crusade: Alice Paul, a former militant suffragist, and her National Woman's Party. Paul deliberately kept her party small. Its appeal was to women of means in the professions and business whose political outlook was conservative and who were likely to be Republicans unless they lived in the South. The ERA was endorsed by business organizations. Richard Nixon and Howard Smith were supporters. John Kennedy was not. Lyndon Johnson had come out for the ERA when he was a senator, but swung the other way when he became President.

In the twenties the two movements explored a merger, failed, and then developed a sour relationship. Under Kennedy, Peterson stacked the President's Commission with anti-ERA members headed by Eleanor Roosevelt and its report urged use of the Fourteenth Amendment instead of the ERA.

Martha Griffiths, the liberal Democratic congresswoman from Michigan and an ardent feminist, tried unsuccessfully to form a bridge between the movements in the sixties. But, when the civil rights bill began to work its way through the House, she quickly recognized an alternative: add "sex" to the proscribed factors in Title VII. As Griffiths wrote later,

> When I looked at the bill, I realized that the [Judiciary] committee had never really considered the rights of Negro women at all, or, if they had, they had simply believed that they would get approximately the rights of white women. I made up my mind that all women were going to take one giant step forward, so I prepared an amendment that added "sex" to the bill. Then I learned that a woman newspaper reporter had asked Howard Smith of Virginia to offer such an amendment and he had agreed. Judge Smith was the chairman of the Rules Committee and the leader of the conservative bloc, who would, if they could, have killed the bill. I realized that Mr. Smith would get more than 100 votes just because he offered the amendment. I needed, if everyone voted, 218 votes to win. Without saying anything to anyone, I decided to let him offer it, and use my powers of persuasion to get the rest of the votes.

As Griffiths put it, "I used Smith." She needed help because only ten of the 435 members of the House were women.

Smith later insisted that he was serious about proposing the amendment, that he sincerely tried to help women overcome discrimination in the labor market. This seems dubious in the extreme because his clear purpose was to defeat H.R. 7152, not to improve it. Donald Allen Robinson wrote: "His situation was desperate. Unless the civil rights coalition could be splintered, southern defenses against a broad civil rights bill appeared certain to be overwhelmed." In their definitive book the Whalens agreed: "Smith counted on the amendment passing and making H.R. 7152 so controversial that eventually it would be voted down either in the House or the Senate." Patricia Zelman wrote that Smith proposed his amendment "tongue in cheek."

This conclusion finds support in Smith's ridiculous defense of his motion. He referred to women as a "minority." Frances P. Bolton, the Republican congresswoman from Ohio, pointed out that, according to the census of 1960, there were two and a half million more females than males in the country. Nevertheless, Smith proceeded to read a letter from a female constituent who asked, in light of the "fact" that women were a minority, "what course our Government might pursue to protect our spinster friends in their 'right' to a nice husband and family?" Smith, evidently, was urging his amendment in order to provide breadwinners for aging single women!

Celler was taken completely by surprise by the Smith ploy and he did nothing to raise the level of discourse. He said he had been married for 49 years and that women were a majority in his household. Yet the sexes lived in "harmony" and this was because he had the last two words—"Yes, dear."

Martha Griffiths spoke in defense of the amendment and the level of debate rose with her. Gunnar Myrdal in *An American Dilemma,* she said, had pointed out that "white women and Negroes occupied relatively the same position in American society." The amendment would not make H.R. 7152 a comprehensive equal rights law. It would apply only to employment and, if the sex provision was rejected, the law would not even provide equality of employment. "You are going to have white men in one bracket, you are going to try to take colored men and colored women and give them employment rights, and down at the bottom of the list is going to be a white woman with no rights at all." Griffiths added, "A vote against this amendment . . . by a white man is a vote against his wife, or his widow, or his daughter, or his sister."

Katherine St. George, the conservative New York Republican, attacked the protective legislation because, by limiting the hours women could work, it denied them higher pay. "Why should women be denied equality of opportunity?" Women, St. George said, did not ask for special privileges because there was no need for them. "We outlast you—we outlive you—we nag you to death."

Edith Green, the feisty liberal Oregon Democrat, was on the spot. She, of course, agreed with Griffiths about discrimination against women. She had been an author of the Equal Pay Act and had sat on the President's

Commission on the Status of Women. But she could not support the sex amendment. She was suspicious of Howard Smith's motive and feared that the change might cause the bill to fail of passage. "For every discrimination that has been made against a woman . . . there has been 10 times the discrimination against the Negro . . . maybe 100 times as much humiliation for the Negro woman, for the Negro man and for the Negro child."

Most members of the House, clearly, regarded this as a no-win situation and did not want to be identified by a roll call. The House adopted Smith's amendment by a teller vote of 168 to 133. A lady in the gallery cried, "We've won, we've won!" and was ejected. Without a roll call it is impossible to identify conclusively the groups that composed the majority. It seems reasonable to state that they were an unlikely coalition of southern conservatives, northern liberals, and women. Martha Griffiths had shrewdly calculated the correct strategy.

The House then adopted two more amendments to Title VII. One extended coverage to retraining as well as training programs. The other created an exemption for church-controlled educational institutions to allow them to favor employees of their own faith. It was accepted in face of the argument by Celler and McCulloch that the existing exemption for religion and national origin where affiliation was a bona fide occupational qualification already dealt with the problem. That is, teaching and administrative positions in church schools were already exempt and other jobs, such as janitor, should not be. John Ashbrook, the Ohio Republican, got an amendment allowing an employer "to refuse to hire and employ any person because of said person's atheistic beliefs." It was later thrown out.

On February 10 the House defeated 22 proposed amendments and accepted four, only that of William Colmer of Mississippi being of any consequence. It would permit employers, unions, and employment agencies to discriminate against Communists and members of front organizations who refused to register. It was adopted over Celler's objection and was also later eliminated.

Titles VIII and IX attracted little attention and were quickly dispatched. Robert T. Ashmore, the South Carolina Democrat, proposed a new Title X creating a community relations service to assist localities in resolving disputes over race, color, and national origin. Lyndon Johnson had made such a proposal in 1957, which was not adopted, and it was part of the original Kennedy bill in 1963. Celler and McCulloch, by now exhausted and eager to get the Republicans out of town for Lincoln's Birthday, accepted the amendment even before Ashmore could speak for it.

The Committee of the Whole dissolved itself and the members of the House answered to the call of the roll. The amended bill passed overwhelmingly 290 to 130. It was a bipartisan victory: 152 Democrats and 138 Republicans in the majority. In opposition were 96 Democrats (86 from the

South) and 34 Republicans (10 from the South). Howard Smith had been steamrollered.

The vote was a triumph for the Brooklyn street urchin and the Ohio plowboy. Celler was unstinting in his tribute to McCulloch. For himself he said that this was the greatest accomplishment in his 41 years in the House, "like I climbed Mount Everest." McCulloch, a Scot who was spare with his words, took off at once with Mabel for a well-deserved holiday in Bermuda. Jane O'Grady stayed up all night to bake a huge quantity of "Equality Cookies," sugar cookies decorated with an equals sign. She delivered them the next day to the congressional office staffs. "We had imposed on so many people and had been so 'naggy,' " she said, "I just wanted to show our appreciation." [3]

Senate debate was scheduled to open on February 17, 1964. But the tax bill took the stage and the date was shifted to February 26. Consideration that day was brief and debate was again deferred, this time by the agriculture bill so that farmers would know its terms before the spring planting. Thus, H.R. 7152 did not reach the floor until March 9. The Democrats used the time to nail down their strategy. Their major players were Lyndon Johnson, majority leader Mike Mansfield, and whip Hubert Humphrey, who would steer the bill through the Senate.

It did not take long to resolve the issue of Senate hearings. The notorious segregationist James Eastland of Mississippi was chairman of the Judiciary Committee. President Kennedy's bill had gone to his committee in June 1963 and he had still not called hearings. The leadership could hardly place H.R. 7152 in the hands of a man whose fingers were covered with iron glue. They decided to place the bill directly on the floor. There were risks. The southern bloc would certainly scream about this unusual procedure, and some supporters, both Democrats and Republicans, would have reason to complain.

But Mansfield, and Humphrey, had a much harder time with the President over cloture. This is an opportunity to meet two of the major figures in this book.

Michael J. Mansfield was a man of remarkable achievement who had done it the hard way. His parents were poor Irish Catholic immigrants who settled in New York City, where his father was a hotel porter. Mike was born in 1903 and was three when the family moved to Great Falls, Montana. He attended both public and parochial schools and dropped out in the eighth grade. Eager to see the world, he hopped on freight trains and even did some time in jail. All his life, Harry McPherson wrote, Mansfield remained "deeply Catholic." Of his friendship with John Kennedy, Mansfield said, "We had a very, very close, very warm relationship." For the laconic Mansfield that was a fairly long speech. Ted Kennedy would say later that his favorite statements were "yep," "nope," "maybe," "could be," and "don't know." This husbanding of words along with his tall lean frame made Mansfield, McPherson noted, "manly in a Western, Gary Cooper way—taciturn and forthright, a straight shooter."

Around the time of World War I, Mansfield served in the Navy, the Army, and the Marine Corps. He enlisted in the Navy at 15 and made seven Atlantic crossings before they learned that he was under age. He then spent a year in California with the Army and two in the Philippines, Japan, Siberia, and China with the Marines. He failed to rise above private first class. But he got hooked on Asia, learned Chinese, and would become a noted authority on the region.

After military service Mansfield returned to Montana, where he met Maureen Hayes, a schoolteacher in Butte, and married her. "She put some sense into me, told me I ought to go to school and make something of myself. . . . Thank the Lord she did." He took high school subjects by correspondence while he was enrolled at Montana State University. In 1933 he got a diploma and a B.A. simultaneously. He tried to get a job as a school teacher, but two Montana towns rejected him because he was a Catholic. During the Depression he returned to MSU for an M.A., awarded in 1934. He stayed on to teach history and political science, particularly Latin America and the Far East.

Though he made full professor, Mansfield said, "There's a little bit of political blood in all the Irish." He won election to the House in Montana's first district and served five terms. Mansfield was on the Foreign Affairs Committee. In January 1945, after a visit to China, he wrote a notable report for President Roosevelt. Truman asked him to be assistant secretary of state, but Mansfield declined.

In 1952 Mansfield ran for the Senate. Though Joe McCarthy came to Montana to denounce his "Communist-coddling practices" and Eisenhower won in a landslide, Mansfield captured the seat. Thereafter he was unbeatable—76 percent of the vote in 1958, 65 in 1964, and 61 percent in 1970.

When he got to the Senate in 1953, those two canny judges of political flesh, Dick Russell and Lyndon Johnson, recognized at once that they had a Big Man from the West. Mansfield was not just extremely smart; he was, Joe Califano observed, "incredibly prescient." He soon sat on the Foreign Relations, Appropriations, Policy, and Steering committees. Everyone learned to admire and trust Mansfield. The northern liberals embraced him because he was one of them; the southern conservatives had complete faith in him; even the Republicans were unable to resist him. His dear friend, George Aiken of Vermont, said, "There isn't a Republican who would raise a finger to hurt Mike." When 20 of 28 Republicans voted against their own leader, Aiken explained that was "because that's what Mike wanted."

When he became majority leader Johnson needed a new whip in the Senate. Harry McPherson, who worked for him, urged Mansfield. Johnson had already reached the same conclusion and had asked the Montanan, who agreed to take the job. Johnson was his own "drover," McPherson wrote. "He needed a reliable man who could manage the flow of legislation."

When Johnson left to become Vice President, Mansfield was the obvious successor as majority leader, a job he did not want but which everyone insisted he take. "Johnson," McPherson wrote, "was the ideal opposition leader; Mansfield would be the perfect team player." He dismantled his predecessor's swollen machinery of leadership and retained "a handful of mechanics: [Bobby] Baker to round up votes and advise Mansfield of his chances, I to prepare the program and work the floor, Pauline Moore to keep the records."

That was typical Mansfield: all substance, no show. He was modest to a fault. Later, when asked to have his portrait painted for posterity, he declined. "When I'm gone, I want to be forgotten." He often had his eyes closed when the shutter clicked. McPherson on January 20 had been at the Kennedy inauguration. "The rhetoric, the ringing voice, the young leader coatless in January, were all images of a new myth—of a new Roland, his silver trumpet flashing in the sun, handsome, learned, witty, and brave." McPherson then walked to the Senate chamber to hand Mansfield a memorandum on the filibuster. "It was like going home to mother after a weekend with a chorus girl. Outside poetry. Inside prose." Mansfield abhorred the limelight. In the debate over H.R. 7152, which attracted enormous media attention, he gladly conceded that turf to Humphrey and Dirksen, who throve on it. He also gave Humphrey full control over day-to-day tactics, reserving strategy for himself.

Hubert Horatio Humphrey, Jr., was born on May 11, 1911, in a bedroom over his father's drug store in Wallace, South Dakota. Later, when he ran for the Senate in Minnesota, he stressed that he had been conceived in Minnesota. The area around Wallace was the setting for Ole Rolvaag's *Giants in the Earth,* the epic novel of Norwegian pioneer life. The Humphreys had migrated from Scandinavia to Britain and then to America, arriving before the Revolution. Hubert Jr.'s maternal grandfather had been a Norwegian sea captain who settled his wife and 12 children in a sod hut on 300 virgin acres in Lily, South Dakota, in the 1880s.

In 1912 Hubert's father bought a drug store in Doland, South Dakota, and the family, now with four children, moved to that larger nearby town, where Hubert Jr. spent thirteen happy years. The family was very close. Hubert Sr. was an intellectual who built a fine library and subscribed to national newspapers and magazines. He read to the children almost every night and talked politics endlessly as an implacable Democrat, one of five in Doland. Williams Jennings Bryan and Woodrow Wilson were his heroes and he regularly read the children the Cross of Gold speech and the Fourteen Points. Christine, his wife, was a strict Lutheran and a Republican and admitted that she did not understand him, "but he's brilliant." Her husband warned the children that their mother was a lovely woman, but "politically unreliable." Hubert Jr. became a Democrat.

His father had a great influence. The boy drank up the political debates when he worked the soda fountain. Papa was on the city council and became mayor and took his son to the meetings. The elder Humphrey detested idleness and considered vacations a waste of time. The boy adopted his father's work ethic.

The Great Depression battered South Dakota and the Humphreys. The massive dust storm on Armistice Day, 1932, etched itself on his memory. The sun was blacked out, the heat was oppressive, the dust penetrated every crevice, and hordes of grasshoppers descended on the region. Humphrey had to sell the house to cover his debts. The banks in Doland failed and the farmers bartered produce for goods at the drug store. Both Hubert and his brother Ralph attended the University of Minnesota, but when money ran out, Hubert went back to the store. The Depression, he said later, "left a lasting impression on me. Much of my politics has been conditioned by it." He became a devout New Dealer and worshipped Franklin Roosevelt. He went to the Denver College of Pharmacy and completed a two-year course in six months.

He met Muriel Fay Buck in 1934 and was hooked. The next year he fulfilled his dream of visiting Washington by leading a busload of Boy Scouts to the city. He wrote a "Dear Bucky" letter which became part of the Humphrey legend. "If you and I just apply ourselves. . . . I intend to set my aim at Congress. . . . I simply revel and beam with delight in this realm of politics and government."

Hubert and Muriel were married in 1936. The next year, he enrolled in political science at Minnesota and graduated in two years in 1939. With his eye on college teaching, he took an M.A. at Louisiana State. He hoped to get a Ph.D., but took a job with the WPA because he needed the money. In 1942 he ran for mayor of Minneapolis and lost. He studied the vote and concluded that the Republicans would be a minority if only the Democrats and Farmer-Laborites could unite. While teaching at Macalester College, he helped pull off the merger. He worked hard to reelect Roosevelt in 1944. The next year he ran for mayor again and won by the biggest majority in the city's history. He became a model mayor, cleaned up Minneapolis, and in 1947 was reelected even more handsomely.

In 1948 Humphrey ran for the Senate against the Republican incumbent Joseph Ball. At the Democratic National Convention that summer he delivered a celebrated address calling for a strong civil rights plank in the platform, which Paul Douglas called "the greatest speech I ever heard." He won immense applause and a huge demonstration. The vote was strongly in favor of the liberal plank and led Governor Strom Thurmond of South Carolina and a batch of southern delegates to walk out and form the States'

Rights Party. Humphrey was now a national figure, a leading voice for liberalism. After a typically strenuous campaign, he rolled up a majority of a quarter of a million votes.

Humphrey became a United States senator at 37, a member of the notable 1948 Democratic freshman class—Clinton Anderson of New Mexico, Paul Douglas of Illinois, Lyndon Johnson of Texas, Robert Kerr of Oklahoma, Estes Kefauver of Tennessee, and Russell Long of Louisiana. In the fifties he emerged both as a member of the Senate establishment and the spokesman for its liberal bloc. He was interested in a wide range of issues, international and domestic, including, of course, civil rights.

Humphrey was not so much a person as a marvel of nature. He had limitless energy, almost as much optimism, and a passion for talk. He was the fastest talker in the Senate and his tongue could not keep up with the flow of ideas. Lyndon Johnson, a big talker himself, said there was "something in the water that makes people from Minnesota talk too much." The Whalens described him as "a perpetual-motion machine, . . . long a familiar sight as he dashed down the Senate corridors, pockets bulging with scribbled, unanswered phone messages and arms filled with stacks of books and papers, talking a mile a minute, and always, to no one's surprise, arriving late." McPherson probed a bit deeper:

> Warm, open, self-amused, bursting with affirmation of life; sure that men of goodwill, with a little common sense and adventurousness, could solve any problem. A creative legislator, willing to take risks. Spectacular extemporaneous phrasemaker; when genuinely aroused, something to see and hear. Shortcoming an inability to be really cruel. . . .
>
> Humphrey's heart longed for a just and humane society; his mind told him he must accept something less, some mild improvement, or no change at all in a status quo that offended him deeply. In the pursuit of progress he politicked with his natural enemies. He was tolerant and friendly as he sought to disarm their instinctive distrust of anyone who cared deeply about remote social ills. He never preached or condemned except in public debate. . . . He was often late and disorganized, the result I thought, of an inordinate desire (which he shared with Johnson) to please his last audience *finally,* end all their doubts, answer all their questions, and convert them totally to himself and the true faith.

Humphrey was extremely ambitious and yearned to be President. He hoped to run with Adlai Stevenson in 1956, but the latter opened the vice presidential nomination to the convention. Humphrey, of course, tossed his hat into the ring, but Kefauver won, and, ominously, Kennedy was a close second. In 1960 the door was open and Humphrey could take a clean shot at the presidency. He went all out. This meant the grueling, exhausting, and extremely expensive route through the primaries, where he confronted Kennedy, who held all the cards. It was devastating to lose Wisconsin and it was fatal to get whipped in West Virginia. Sadly, Humphrey gave up.

In 1961 Humphrey was back in the Senate with his old energy and optimism, as Democratic whip working with his good friend Mike Mansfield, and pushing the Kennedy agenda hard. In early 1964, when H.R. 7152 reached the Senate, Mansfield and Johnson needed a floor leader and neither hesitated for an instant. With his long commitment to civil rights, his national stature, his knowledge of the Senate and the senators Humphrey was the only choice. He jumped at the opportunity for these reasons and hoped to be picked by Johnson for vice president that year.

McPherson wrote of the relationship between Lyndon Johnson and Hubert Humphrey: "At bottom there was mutual affection and respect." But the Johnson factor meant that it was also "extremely complex." The President could not restrain himself from badgering and lecturing the senator. This is how Humphrey told the story:

> First of all, . . . he said, "You have got this opportunity now, Hubert, but you liberals will never deliver. You don't know the rules of the Senate, and your liberals will all be off making speeches when they ought to be present. . . . I know you've got a great opportunity here, but I'm afraid it's going to fall between the boards. . . ." He knew what he was doing exactly, and I knew what he was doing.
>
> The second thing he told me was, "Now you know that the bill can't pass unless you get Ev Dirksen [still worried about those 67 votes]." And he said, "You and I are going to get Ev. . . . You make up your mind now that you've got to spend time with Ev Dirksen. You've got to play to Ev Dirksen. You've got to let him have a piece of the action. He's got to look good all the time."

Humphrey hardly needed this lecture. He had made a total commitment and was fully aware of the problems and pitfalls. As to the courtship of Dirksen, he said, "I would have kissed Dirksen's ass on the Capitol steps."

The minority leader picked Thomas H. Kuchel of California as the Republican floor leader to work with Humphrey, and they formed a close team. When Nixon became Vice President in 1953, Governor Earl Warren had named Kuchel to fill out the term. He was a California progressive in the style of Hiram Johnson and Warren and was firmly committed to civil rights. The Democrats trusted him and he was very close to Dirksen. Humphrey and Kuchel followed the Celler-McCulloch bipartisan example.

Mansfield called up H.R. 7152 on Monday, March 9, 1964. Russell convened his troops that morning and they pledged a last-ditch fight. Senate Rule 7 provided that a motion to schedule a bill must be made in the first hour of the opening two hours of the session. When Mansfield moved routinely to dispense with the reading of the previous day's Journal, Russell objected. "I trust," he said, "the clerk will read the Journal slowly and clearly. . . ." He then winked at Humphrey. It took almost an hour. Russell then proposed an amendment to the Journal and made a long speech, burning up the rest of the allotted time under Rule 7. The great filibuster had begun even before H.R. 7152 had reached the floor.[4]

Richard Brevard Russell had been born and reared in Winder, Georgia, and maintained a law office and a home there. To the people of the town, McPherson wrote, "he was leader and judge and perhaps a manifestation of God himself." He had been elected to the state legislature and the governorship and had come to the Senate in 1933. McPherson called him "a profoundly attractive man whose Roman bearing, quick mind, and unfeigned courtliness won him the deep respect of people who had little respect for his conservative views." He read widely in history and biography, the leading eastern newspapers, and the rural Georgia county seat press and was an authority on the Civil War. Later at Camp David he would enthrall Lady Bird Johnson with an account of the great battle fought nearby at Antietam.

The Georgian studied the Senate intensively, its rules, its history, the detailed content of bills, its personalities, and the distribution of power. "Russell," Reedy said, "had the most encyclopedic knowledge of the politics of the United States of any member of the Senate." He understood states as far away as Oregon and Michigan, "sometimes better than the senators from those states." By the time Lyndon Johnson arrived in 1949 Russell was almost certainly the most influential member of the Senate. He dominated two of the most powerful committees, Armed Services and Appropriations, and controlled committee assignments. He was the unquestioned leader and the strong voice of the southern bloc. As he showed repeatedly, particularly during the civil rights debates in 1957 and 1960, Russell could deliver 18 votes as a unit, nine of them committee chairmen. McPherson thought that he treasured "the generous, humane civilization" of rural Georgia built on racial segregation and he meant to preserve it against the North and even against modern Atlanta.

When Lyndon Johnson took his seat in the Senate he knew that he would get nowhere without the support of Dick Russell. He wooed the Georgian and at the same time came to admire him enormously and to treasure his counsel. He arranged to sit behind him on the floor for easy consultation. Russell, a bachelor, lived alone in an apartment downtown and was said to be lonely. He was always welcome at the Johnsons'. The display of southern charm when Dick Russell and Lady Bird Johnson got together must have been something to behold. The girls, Luci and Lynda, adored "Uncle Dick."

But now Lyndon Johnson and Richard Russell were on a collision course. The civil rights bill, Johnson wrote, would separate him from "the South, where I had been born and reared." It would also alienate him from his friends in Congress, among whom Russell came first. "One could not persuade Senator Russell by sweet talk, hard talk, or any kind of talk." Nor did the President compromise. Shortly before Senate debate began, Russell declared publicly that he expected Johnson "to throw . . . [his] full weight" behind H.R. 7152 and that the South was determined "to fight . . . to the last ditch." Johnson wrote, "It would be a fight to total victory or total defeat." And between two dear friends.

With his political sensitivity, Russell caught the bitter odor of defeat. Senator Douglas was told that Russell had said that "they could win battles, but that they were losing the war." Now there was no majority leader to cobble out a delaying compromise for him. Mansfield could not and would not play that role. In 1957 and 1960 civil rights had been a question that, excepting the South, did not much interest white America. By 1964 it was the prime issue in the country and, as the polls showed, the white North was moving inexorably toward strong support for civil rights. In the past Russell could count on conservative Republicans and western Democrats to back a filibuster. Now he might lose both. In 1964 he was 66 and suffered from emphysema. Not much of the old vigor was left.

By contrast, it took Johnson some time to catch the sweet smell of victory. In late May or early June 1963, when the Kennedy administration was drafting the civil rights bill, the President had asked Burke Marshall to talk to the Vice President. Johnson thought that providing jobs for blacks was the most important thing the government could do. Yet he was persuaded that the administration must keep fair employment out of the bill because that would kill it. In fact, Marshall said, "he was very dubious" that they could get the bill passed at all. Johnson, Katzenbach said, was convinced that an employment title was "absolutely politically impossible."

Shortly after the assassination Johnson asked Marshall how Justice expected to get the legislation through Congress. Marshall said he was sure it would pass the House; as for the Senate, he did not have "the foggiest idea." The President was interested only in the Senate, where he viewed with foreboding the possibility of a filibuster. He was obsessed with the number 67. How in the world would they ever find that many votes to close debate? Katzenbach had a hard time explaining the promise made to McCulloch: if there was no compromise in the Senate, there must be a filibuster. "President Johnson," Katzenbach said, "really felt that we were nuts in trying to think that we could get cloture."

In January 1964 the President told Attorney General Robert Kennedy:

> I'll do on the bill just what you think is best to do on the bill. We'll follow what you say we should do on the bill. We won't do anything that you don't want to do on the legislation. And I'll do everything you want me to do in order to obtain the passage of the legislation.

This was a remarkable statement. Kennedy offered the following explanation: Johnson thought the bill would fail and "he didn't want to . . . have the sole responsibility. If I worked out the strategy, . . . he could always say that he did what we suggested." Perhaps.

Johnson seemed unable to recognize that a fundamental shift in public opinion made 1964 entirely different from 1957 and 1960. The Gallup poll in early February 1964 showed 61 percent of the American people for H.R. 7152, and a Harris poll that month came in at 68 percent. By contrast, others recognized this change. In early October 1963 President Kennedy had invited Dirksen and Katzenbach to join him on Air Force One to go out to Chicago for the Army–Air Force football game. Kennedy, because of a crisis in Vietnam, canceled out. Thus, Dirksen and Katzenbach rode together and discussed the civil rights bill. As they were about to land, Dirksen said, "Don't worry. This bill will come to a vote in the Senate." Since Dirksen had the power to break a filibuster and Katzenbach had "complete confidence" in Dirksen's integrity, Katzenbach knew that the bill would pass. Manny Celler said, "The time was ripe now for civil rights." On February 11, 1964, the day after the massive House victory, Larry O'Brien told Johnson that Dirksen had to deliver the Republicans on cloture in order to protect his own party in the upcoming elections. "Ev Dirksen didn't have any alternative at all."

Johnson had another problem. He was eager to get his program through Congress before it adjourned for the Republican National Convention on July 13, 1964 (the Democratic Convention opened on August 24). There was much important legislation in the hopper, including the Big Three—the tax cut, civil rights, and poverty. Johnson sighed with relief when he signed the tax bill on February 26. But he had made a celebrated promise to launch a war against poverty and he had Sargent Shriver studying the problem and drafting a bill. The issue was extraordinarily complex and was certain to ignite controversy. Would there be enough time if the South staged a prolonged filibuster over civil rights? The President fretted and hoped to avoid or limit that battle.

About the time Senate debate opened, Katzenbach was again in the White House. The President still thought there were not enough Senate votes. Katzenbach insisted that the promise to McCulloch made a filibuster and a cloture vote necessary. He pointed out that in 1962 filibustering liberals, led by Senator Morse, had so angered conservatives, especially Republicans, on the Communications Satellite bill that they had voted for closing debate. Thus, conservatives could no longer argue that they opposed cloture on principle. The President then demanded a list of the 67 senators who would vote to stop debate. Katzenbach ticked off the 58 he had. "Now," Johnson asked, "where are you going to get the others?" Katzenbach said there were 14 possibles and they would have to get nine of them. They went over the names and Johnson was not optimistic. Katzenbach stressed that if the President indicated publicly that he doubted success, "we can't *possibly* get cloture on this bill." Johnson promised that he would not voice his doubts and he kept his word.

Finally convinced that a filibuster was inevitable, the President insisted that Mansfield enforce Rule 19 fully to require that debate go on long into the night in order to wear down the southerners and westerners. Johnson had done so in 1960. Further, he knew that the average age of those who opposed cloture was 65, that Russell was ill, and that Carl Hayden of Arizona, a long-standing foe, was 87. Mansfield refused to apply Rule 19 rigorously. He was convinced that it would not work and he would not be responsible for killing Hayden.[5]

Russell's filibuster, which began on March 9, created a gigantic snarl, wrapping the Senate's business in its coils. When Russell sat down after defeating Mansfield's motion to schedule H.R. 7152 for floor action without debate under Rule 7, the majority leader asked unanimous consent to consider the bill. Lister Hill of Alabama objected immediately. Mansfield's only recourse was to make the measure the Senate's pending business, and that motion was debatable. He and Humphrey pleaded with the southerners to allow the Senate to consider this burning national issue on its merits. Their voices fell on deaf ears. The great filibuster was now on in full force. As the Whalens wrote, it continued "that afternoon, and the next, and the next, and. . . . Their soft melodious voices resounded beautifully throughout the Senate chamber and the word around Washington was that they planned to keep on . . . until doomsday, or at least until Congress adjourned for the Republican National Convention in July." Since the legislative clock stopped at the end of the first day, it seemed as though March 9, 1964, would go on forever.

There were small signs of life. A. Willis Robertson of Virginia waved a small Confederate flag as he droned on. When done, he presented it to Humphrey. Determined to hold his temper, Humphrey praised Robertson for his "eloquence, great knowledge of history and law, and his wonderful, gracious, gentlemanly qualities." The flag, he said, was a symbol of "bravery and courage and conviction." Wayne Morse, disgusted, objected to conducting committee hearings until H.R. 7152 was passed. Russell proposed that all the black people in the U.S. should be redistributed equally among the states at federal expense.

The southerners insisted on frequent roll calls when the chamber was empty in order to kill time and to rest their vocal chords as the 100 names were called off. Russell had divided his forces into three platoons in order to get them to the floor promptly. Humphrey had six and Kuchel had a similar system for the Republicans, each connected to the other by a special telephone network.

The Department of Justice provided Humphrey and Kuchel with massive briefing books. Each morning the floor leaders, their staffs, and Justice Department experts reviewed plans for the day. On Mondays and Thursdays they were joined by Clarence Mitchell of the NAACP and other officials of the Leadership Conference on Civil Rights. The staffs held a postmortem session at the end of each day. A mimeograph machine donated by the AFL-CIO produced the "Bipartisan Civil Rights Newsletter" each morning to cover events of the preceding day and to reprint favorable editorials and statements. It went to all senators.

Several weeks into the filibuster the southerners voted 7 to 5 to allow Mansfield's motion to come to the floor. It passed easily 67 to 17 on March 26. H.R. 7152 was now the business before the Senate. Russell granted that a battle had been lost, but "we shall now begin to fight the war."

Morse moved immediately to refer the bill to the Judiciary Committee to report back not later than April 8. An excellent lawyer, Morse anticipated correctly that the Civil Rights Act would generate a flood of litigation for which committee hearings and reports would be helpful in illuminating legislative intent. Dirksen joined him because he thought it more orderly to observe Senate tradition. Mansfield strongly disagreed, stressing the perils of Eastland and the inevitable delays. He prevailed by a vote of 50 to 34.

Some businessmen and conservative senators complained that Title VII would impose racial quotas on employers, requiring them to hire specified numbers of black workers. Humphrey tried to set this concern to rest on March 20. "Contrary to the allegations of some opponents of this title, there is nothing in it that will give any power to the Commission or to any court to require hiring, firing, or promotion of employees to meet a racial 'quota' or to achieve a certain racial balance."

The filibuster frustrated the media. Their minds told them that H.R. 7152 was one of the most significant measures ever considered by the Congress, but their ears told them that virtually nothing was happening. How does one cover a nonevent? Fred Friendly, the head of CBS News, decided to bull his way forward. He said that the debate was extremely important, comparable to a space shot or a primary election. The fact that the Senate forbade coverage on the floor did not affect "our responsibility of reporting the debate and filibuster as completely as possible." CBS scheduled live TV news five times daily and radio coverage four times a day. Roger Mudd was given this miserable assignment, which he feared would turn into a "gimmicky flagpole-sitting stunt." The weather was dreadful and poor Mudd stood in the rain, snow, and cold on the Senate steps interviewing anyone with the courage to venture outdoors.

Immediately following the Easter recess "debate" commenced. Humphrey delivered a passionate three-and-a-half-hour address stressing the moral imperative of civil rights. Kuchel followed for an hour and three-quarters, explaining the bill title by title. For the better part of the week others joined in these preliminaries. On Monday, April 13, the start of the sixth week, the southerners resumed the filibuster.

Meanwhile Dirksen had been taking measurements with his experienced political eye. He agreed with the entire Democratic leadership from Presidents Kennedy and Johnson on down that Dirksen was the man, that he could deliver the Republican votes needed to end the filibuster by producing the magic 67. But there was a multitude of complications, not least among them timing. Dirksen prided himself on having the wettest finger in Washington for predicting the direction and velocity of the political wind and of positioning himself accordingly. But in 1963 he had made a grievous forecast by coming out against Kennedy's nuclear test ban treaty even before it had been signed because he was convinced that the Senate would reject it. He was horrified when it proved extremely popular and even his own Republican troops deserted their leader. Dirksen was embarrassed to have to ask his Democratic friends, Mansfield and Kennedy, to bail him out, which they happily did. At the last moment even Dirksen switched his vote. He could not afford another such mistake.

Dirksen was 68, was beset with an array of ailments including a wretched peptic ulcer, and, despite medical advice to the contrary, puffed his way through three packs of cigarettes daily. He rose very early, worked furiously for a long day, and got to bed late. His family and friends, naturally, worried about his health.

Now he faced the greatest opportunity of his political lifetime. He could be the hero of the hour by rescuing this immensely important piece of legislation. If he succeeded, children would read about him in their history books.

Dirksen was a bundle of contradictions. To much of the public he was a buffoon. He could blame no one but himself because this is the image he projected. His clothes resembled an unmade bed, his hair a weed patch. He had waged guerrilla warfare against the English language, which he loved, for decades, and was known as the Wizard of Ooze. He delighted in mispronouncing words: "missile" became "mizz-el." He was addicted to odd words like "baleful" and "felicitous." His speeches roamed about the terrain in "diversions and detours" because, he said, "I love to temporize." He could be very funny. "We must screw the inscrutable." Or, "I take my freedom straight . . . without ginger ale." On a long speech: "I learned long ago that no souls are saved after the first 20 minutes." A dedicated gardener, Dirksen recognized the arrival of spring each year with a grandiloquent speech in the Senate proposing the marigold as "the national floral emblem of our country." He and Charlie Halleck appeared on a Republican television program that was so bad that it came to be known as "The Ev and Charlie Show."

The other side of Dirksen, which he nurtured with deadly seriousness, was the professional legislator. George Reedy came from Illinois, had covered Congress as a newspaperman since the days when Dirksen was in the House, and had observed him closely when Reedy worked for Johnson. He said,

> Dirksen . . . was a very good speaker, somewhat oleaginous, but still very, very good. What was more important, Dirksen had a very subtle mind. Dirksen was probably the most—no, not the most effective. The most effective Republican Senate leader I ever knew was Charlie McNary. But after Charlie McNary, Dirksen was certainly the most effective. . . .

"Everett Dirksen," the Whalens wrote, "was a master of the legislative process." He knew the rules, observed the senators carefully, and spent long hours studying bills. Hubert Humphrey on the Johnson-Dirksen relationship:

> Johnson was able to take the measure of a man. . . . Right off the bat he sized you up. He knew with Dirksen that he had himself a match. Dirksen was clever; Dirksen was a good speaker; Dirksen was smart; Dirksen was agile; he was Machiavellian; and he was always willing to make a deal. Johnson liked that, and, even as President, Johnson worked closely with Dirksen.

In 1963, when Kennedy had sent up the civil rights bill, Dirksen had been troubled. He was uncomfortable with public accommodations because his conservative instincts were repelled by the long arm of the federal government reaching into hotels, restaurants, and movie houses to compel the proprietors to serve customers they considered undesirable. Reflecting the view of American industry, which he served faithfully, Dirksen opposed a new regulatory system to eliminate discrimination in employment. But Titles II and VII were the most important in H.R. 7152. Somebody would have to give and he hoped to get the supporters of the bill to yield.

In the early stage of the filibuster, as the Whalens put it, "he commandeered three lawyers from the Senate Judiciary Committee staff and assigned them to pick H.R. 7152 apart to see if it could be made more appetizing to the arch-conservatives in the GOP." Dirksen surprised his colleagues at the regular Tuesday luncheon of the Senate Republican Policy Committee on April 7 by presenting a bundle of 40 amendments to Title VII which would have gutted it. He said that they represented his views, not those of the party, and laid over discussion until Thursday. The 33 Senate Republicans were badly divided. There were 21 conservatives, including Dirksen (he was so slippery that he could have fitted into any of the categories), five moderates, and seven liberals, including Kuchel. On Thursday the Dirksen amendments provoked an outburst from the moderates and liberals and chairman Leverett Saltonstall of Massachusetts had difficulty keeping order. Dirksen proposed erasing Howard Smith's sex amendment. Margaret Chase Smith of Maine, the only woman Republican in the Senate, said, "I could see no reason why the Republicans should go out of their way to oppose inclusion of the word 'sex' and if such a move were made I would oppose it."

Kuchel, upset and surprised by Dirksen's move, went straight to Humphrey's office, where a group had gathered. He recounted what had taken place. Humphrey urged him not to oppose Dirksen, to allow the argument to unfold. "Dirksen," Humphrey said, "told me that if he did not get support, then he would retreat." Kuchel reckoned that "Dirksen will go through his public acting process, take a licking, and then be with us." They were right. At a press conference Dirksen said he was willing to watch his amendments "go down the drain . . . My position is negotiable."

On April 15 Humphrey cheerfully reported that he had talked Dirksen down from 40 to 15 amendments. He was hopeful that a cloture vote would take place by May 15 or 20. The next day McCulloch walked into Dirksen's office to stress to the minority leader that the framers of the Constitution had established a bicameral legislature. Two of the residual amendments were unacceptable: to deny the Equal Employment Opportunity Commission authority to file suits under Title VII and to allow a state law to preempt the federal statute (Dirksen wanted to protect the Illinois FEPC against a civil rights act).

The churches, at Humphrey's urging, now moved on Washington. Beginning in early April a prominent clergyman each day conducted a prayer service at the Lutheran Church of the Reformation on Capitol Hill. B'nai Brith Women designated April 6 as "wire for rights day." On April 19 trios of Protestant, Catholic, and Jewish seminarians began a 24-hour vigil at the Lincoln Memorial. Theology students from 75 seminaries descended upon Washington to pray in shifts around the clock. They pledged not to stop until the Senate passed H.R. 7152. The National Council of Churches, the U.S. Catholic Conference, and the Jewish community sent clergymen and lay people daily to meet with their senators. On the evening of April 28 at Georgetown University 5000 church leaders packed McDonough Gymnasium and overflowed into Gaston Hall at a big interdenominational meeting. The speakers were Humphrey, and Kuchel, New York's Republican senators Jacob Javits and Kenneth Keating, Archbishop Lawrence J. Shehan and Rabbi Uri Miller of Baltimore, and the star, the Protestant Reverend Eugene Carson Blake. Nobody in Washington had ever witnessed this kind of lobbying. Senator Russell was appalled. The opposition was taking over the nation's conscience.

On April 16 Dirksen offered his Title VII amendments, now shrunk to ten, but did not call them up. He promised a "mysterious" 11th amendment, which he introduced on April 21. There were 24 others, but none was called up.

Humphrey, as was his habit, dropped into a chair next to Dirksen's desk on the afternoon of April 21 as the southerners rambled on. Dirksen unloaded a long monologue. The time was right. H.R. 7152 was a good bill that should and would be adopted. It was his duty to put his weight behind it. He had only one more minor amendment to Title II. Humphrey could hardly restrain himself.

The two pros then got down to business. Dirksen tested the commitment of the Democrats. Perhaps, he said, a cloture vote would not be necessary. He sensed that the South was wearing out and he wanted to avoid the difficult job of producing the Republican votes. Humphrey was firm: there must be a vote on cloture. If for no other reason, this would take Senator Russell and his colleagues off the hook. They could explain that they had gone all out and had been beaten by much larger forces. Dirksen agreed. As this conversation was under way, the southerners talked their way past the 37-day record for a civil rights filibuster. Russell, weary and melancholy, told Clarence Mitchell off the record that "the jig is up." He simply could not persuade Lyndon Johnson to compromise.

On April 21, as well, the southerners momentarily changed their tactics. Herman Talmadge of Georgia introduced an amendment to Title XI, the miscellaneous provision that anyone charged with willfully disobeying a court order which required compliance in an act of antidiscrimination would be entitled to a trial by jury. He defended trial by jury as a fundamental Anglo-Saxon right dating back to Magna Carta. While everyone knew that an all-white jury in the Deep South would not vote for conviction in such a case, it put the supporters of H.R. 7152 in the embarrassing position of opposing trial by jury. But this diversion only held up the filibuster momentarily.

On April 23 Mansfield met in his office with Humphrey, Kennedy, Katzenbach, Marshall, Manatos, and Frank Valeo, the secretary of the Senate Democrats, to decide how to deal with the Talmadge amendment. They acknowledged that it would pass. Thus, the smart ploy was to counter with a bipartisan substitute. Mansfield invited Dirksen to the meeting and he promptly agreed to cosponsor the alternative with Mansfield. Katzenbach prepared the language and cleared it with Humphrey and Clifford Case, the New Jersey Republican who was in charge of Title XI. The Mansfield-Dirksen version, submitted on April 24, provided that, at a judge's discretion, a person accused of criminal contempt could be tried with or without a jury. If there was no jury, the fine could not exceed $300 or imprisonment for 30 days. Dirksen also dropped his "mysterious" 11th amendment.

The outlook in late April had much improved and even Mudd was no longer standing in the rain. Johnson and Humphrey were cheered by the smooth relationship with Dirksen and there was talk that the time might be ripe for a vote on cloture. A new Harris poll showed that 70 percent of the public supported H.R. 7152 and 63 percent favored limiting debate. At the

Republican policy luncheon on April 28 Dirksen announced that he was giving the southerners one week notice. If they did not terminate the filibuster by May 5, he would file a petition for cloture. There was, evidently, no objection from his fellow Republicans. He told the press, "This isn't a bluff. . . . The time has come to move off dead center."

But Dirksen was still playing poker. He told the reporters that the President wanted the House bill without change. He was going to the White House to tell his old buddy, "Well, in my humble opinion, you are not going to get it. Now it's your play. What do you have to say?" If Johnson agreed to compromise on his amendments, Dirksen said, he would deliver between 22 and 25 votes to stop debate.

Humphrey, anticipating such a ploy, beat Dirksen to the Oval Office. He assured Johnson that victory was near and that there was no need to make any concessions. When the outmaneuvered Dirksen got in, the President, of course, refused to bargain. As Dirksen left the White House he told the reporters that they had barely discussed civil rights.

The President had breakfast with Mansfield, Humphrey, and Hayden on May 4. Humphrey had been working over the western Democrats to abandon their historic position and vote for cloture. Johnson, frustrated by the length of the filibuster and worried about reaching 67, had decided to move on Hayden.

There had been an historic understanding in the Senate between the South and the West over closing debate. Without the West, the South would lose on civil rights; without the South, the underpopulated and semi-arid West would lose federal support for development projects, particularly access to water. Hayden had represented Arizona since it had been admitted to the Union in 1912. He prided himself on never having voted for cloture. In 1911 a filibuster had defeated President Taft's proposal to a Republican Senate to combine the Arizona and New Mexico territories into a single state. "I would never have been here," Hayden said, "but for the right to filibuster." Since 1948 he had been pushing in Congress for the massive Central Arizona Project, which would deliver Colorado River water to Phoenix and Tucson. He needed southern support. "The President suggested," the Whalens wrote, "that if Hayden voted for cloture, Johnson would help the Arizona Water Project." He did not press, but "just left the suggestion on the table." On May 7 Secretary of the Interior Stewart Udall, himself from Arizona, wrote the President that "your gambit . . . was very persuasive." He also pointed out that Hayden "will carry several other votes with him—such as the two Nevada senators." Since California and Arizona share the Colorado River border, there was a potential interstate conflict, but Kuchel worked it out. The final agreement was that Hayden would vote for cloture, if needed. If not, he would vote against it to maintain his long record.

On May 4 Dirksen, Mansfield, Humphrey, Kuchel, Warren Magnuson,

Democrat of Washington, Bourke Hickenlooper, Republican of Iowa, Kennedy, Katzenbach, and legal assistants, three for the Republicans and two for the Democrats, seated themselves at Dirksen's conference table. Their job was to draft language for the Dirksen amendments and, it was hoped, to come up with a final bill everyone could support. They spent five working days on this task, concluding on May 13. The pattern was for the whole group to meet in the mornings for "educational purposes," as Katzenbach put it. He was surprised by "the lack of real understanding of the Civil Rights Bill." The afternoon sessions that Katzenbach held with the legal technicians went off without a hitch. As he summed it up later: "The bill got completely rewritten with virtually no change of substance. . . . Just words."

It was a perfect political solution. Since much of the language was Dirksen's, he could stake a claim to authorship of the Civil Rights Act. The House of Representatives would be pleased because the new bill honored the promise to McCulloch. The Johnson administration, the northern liberals in both houses, and the civil rights movement would come away with a strong law. At a joint press conference Dirksen announced triumphantly, "We have a good agreement." The Attorney General called it "perfectly satisfactory." "And to me too," Humphrey echoed. The next day Katzenbach explained the changes in verbiage to Celler and McCulloch and both accepted them. For the Leadership Conference on Civil Rights Joe Rauh called the bill "a great victory for civil rights" and Arnold Aronson, its director, said it was "a much stronger bill than we expected."

On May 19 senators from both parties met in caucus to discuss the revised bill. Except for automatic objection from the South, Mansfield had no opposition from the Democrats. In what for him was a long speech he praised Humphrey for masterful handling of the bill.

Dirksen, however, ran into real trouble with the Republicans, particularly Hickenlooper, who called him a "softie." Through five long sessions Dirksen gradually wore Hickenlooper and his own health down. As the Whalens put it, he had now become "a crusader for civil rights." In a press conference at the close of the caucus Dirksen used a line that would go into the history books. Victor Hugo had written in his diary, he declaimed, "No army is stronger than an idea whose time has come." The time had come for civil rights and no one could stop it. At the end of the fifth day, the afternoon of May 25, Dirksen won consensus among the Republican senators to support the new bill.

Mindful of his duty to give the minority leader the spotlight, the next day Humphrey invited Dirksen to introduce the 74-page bill the press now called the "Dirksen substitute." The filibuster had gone on for a wearing 64 days. "We have now reached the point," Dirksen said, "where there must be action."

On Monday, June 1, Mansfield stated that a petition for cloture would be filed on the next Saturday and the vote would be taken on Tuesday, June 9. A reason for the delay in the vote was the California primary on June 2, which pitted Barry Goldwater against Nelson Rockefeller for the Republican nomination for President. Senator Goldwater had already announced that he would vote against cloture. Pro-Goldwater senators who intended to vote to stop debate wanted to avoid embarrassment. Another reason for delay was that Humphrey was still trying to push the number up to 67 and needed the time. On June 4 conservative Iowa Republican Jack Miller announced that he would vote for cloture in response to interdenominational church pressure in his state.

Hickenlooper was causing trouble and was trying to win over conservative Republicans. It seems to have been personal jealousy. Republican Senator Hugh Scott of Pennsylvania said that Hickenlooper was "choleric. . . . He had been in the Senate longer than Dirksen. . . . All the public attention was going to Dirksen." He demanded that the vote be set ahead a day to June 10, which Mansfield accepted. He then demanded a vote on three new amendments on June 9. This was an opening for Humphrey. In return for the agreement to provide this vote, he got four conservative Republicans to vote for cloture—Roman Hruska and Carl Curtis of Nebraska, Karl Mundt of South Dakota, and Norris Cotton of New Hampshire.

The problem which Morse had raised did not go away. The Dirksen substitute differed from the bill the House had passed in much of its language, if not in substance. There was neither a Senate committee report nor a Senate-House conference report. How could legislative intent be divined later by the Equal Employment Opportunity Commission and the federal courts? On June 4 Humphrey made a limited statement of intent.

The major provisions of Title VII, he pointed out, had not been modified, but there were three changes. The first involved EEOC authority in states and cities with effective FEPC laws. Both the House bill and the Dirksen substitute empowered the commission to make agreements with the state agencies authorizing them to handle violations of their own laws. In the absence of such an agreement a complainant without recourse to a state agency would file with the EEOC.

Under the Senate version, second, an aggrieved person could bring his own suit in federal court and need not depend entirely on EEOC. The complainant could do so through the Attorney General without cost to himself. The Attorney General could also bring suit "whenever he has reasonable cause to believe that there is a pattern or practice of discrimination in violation of Title VII."

The third change limited the record-keeping obligations of employers, employment agencies, unions, and labor-management committees.

Meanwhile, a problem had arisen in Illinois that commanded the Senate's attention. In the fall of 1963 Leon Myart, a 28-year-old black man, applied for a job checking for defects in televisions at Motorola in Chicago.

The company gave him its standard 28-question multiple-choice general ability test, which it required all applicants for such jobs to take. Myart failed the test and Motorola did not hire him. He then filed a complaint with the Illinois Fair Employment Practice Commission, alleging that the test violated the state law because it discriminated against disadvantaged blacks as a class. The examiner, Robert E. Bryant, a black lawyer, held the hearing on January 27 and issued his recommendations to the commission on March 5, 1964. Bryant ruled that the test was inherently unfair to culturally deprived groups and recommended that the FEPC order Motorola to cease giving it and to hire Myart.

Bryant's report was a sensation. Motorola, of course, appealed to the Illinois commission and was joined by employers' associations in the city and the state. The *Chicago Tribune* and Arthur Krock in the *New York Times* were outraged by this attempt to restrict an employer's right to hire qualified employees. John Tower, the conservative Texas Republican who had won Lyndon Johnson's old Senate seat, introduced an amendment to Title VII. It would make it lawful for an employer to give "any professionally developed ability test" to an individual seeking employment or to an employee applying for a transfer or promotion provided that the test was given equally to all and was administered without regard to the individual's race, color, religion, sex, or national origin.

In the debate on June 11 Tower stressed the professional character of these tests and was supported by the testimony of the psychologists who had written them. Case, the Republican manager on Title VII, while agreeing that Bryant's ruling was improper, said that the amendment was unnecessary and might actually be used to legalize discrimination. Humphrey pointed out that the experts who wrote the Dirksen substitute had given the Motorola case "the most careful attention" and had concluded that the problem could not arise under this bill. The Tower amendment was defeated 49 to 38.

But the stubborn Texan refused to yield. On June 13 he submitted a brief version, which read that an employer could lawfully "give and . . . act upon the results of any professionally developed ability test provided that such test, its administration or action upon the results thereof is not designed, intended, or used to discriminate because of race, color, religion, sex, or national origin." Humphrey, eager to move on, stated that senators on both sides of the aisle had examined and approved the amendment. It was adopted by voice vote.

On Monday, June 8, Mansfield moved to close debate on H.R. 7152 under the Senate's Rule 22. The motion was signed by 27 Democrats and 11 Republicans and called for the tally on Wednesday. The Hickenlooper amendments, none of particular importance, were disposed of on Tuesday. That evening Johnson called Humphrey to ask again about 67. "We have the votes," Humphrey crowed triumphantly. The President still expected difficulty. Later that evening two more conservative Republicans entered the fold—John Williams of Delaware and Hickenlooper. Humphrey then called three wavering Democrats—Ralph Yarborough of Texas, Howard Cannon of Nevada, and Howard Edmondson of Oklahoma. All said they would vote for cloture.

Humphrey stayed up all of Tuesday night, but on Wednesday morning, according to a friend who shared a pitcher of orange juice with him, he was his usual "exuberant, optimistic, bouncy self." On his way to the Senate chamber he passed Phil Hart, the Michigan Democrat, a slip, which read: "69." Dirksen spent the night at his Virginia farm and stayed up late working over the speech he would deliver on Wednesday. He rose at 5:00, had a light breakfast, and went to the garden to cut roses for the office.

At precisely 10:00 a.m. Lee Metcalf, the Montana Democrat who was in the chair (there was no Vice President), called the Senate to order. All the senators were present, there were 150 standees, including many members of the House, and the galleries were jammed. Mansfield, characteristically, was brief. He read a letter from a Montana woman, the mother of four, who wanted to help. "The only way I know to start is to educate my children that justice and freedom and ambition are not merely privileges, but their birthrights." Russell spoke for half an hour, mainly a constitutional attack on the bill. He appeared to lack conviction. Cecil Newman, editor of the black *St. Paul Recorder,* said, "It seemed to us as we listened to the venerable segregationist that we were witnessing the end of an era." Humphrey, with a red rose in his lapel, spoke for only two minutes. He called for making the "dream of full freedom, full justice, and full citizenship for every American a reality . . . and it will be remembered until the end of the world." Sadly, Dirksen, at his grandest moment, was suffering from his ulcer and twice needed to pop pills. He spoke quietly with no oratorical flourishes. But he did give final form to what would become his historic statement:

> It is said that on the night he died, Victor Hugo wrote in his diary substantially this sentiment: "Stronger than all the armies is an idea whose time has come." The time has come for equality of opportunity in sharing in government, in education, and in employment. It must not be stayed or denied.

As Everett Dirksen sat down with relief, Hubert Humphrey crossed the aisle and extended his hand.

At 11:00 Metcalf called for the roll. Almost all the senators kept tally sheets, and many spectators, though it was against the rules, did so as well. Roger Mudd, sweltering in 100-degree heat outside, announced each vote as it was relayed to him by telephone from the press gallery. Aiken, Allott, Anderson, Bayh, Beall—When the roll call reached Clair Engle, the California Democrat, there was a moment of silence and many wept. He sat in a wheelchair in the final stage of terminal cancer, unable to speak. He feebly raised his hand three times, pointing to his eye. Williams cast the magic 67th vote.

The final tally was 71 to 29, four more than needed. "And so," the Whalens wrote, "after 534 hours, 1 minute, and 51 seconds, the longest filibuster in the history of the United States Senate was broken." Cloture won support from 44 Democrats and 27 Republicans. The opponents consisted of 23 Democrats (20 from the South) and six Republicans.

The Kennedy-Johnson-Mansfield-Humphrey strategy had worked flawlessly, far better than they could have anticipated at the outset. To the core of liberal Democrats from the East and the Midwest, Dirksen had joined 12 liberal and moderate, and, amazingly, 15 conservative Republicans. The western bloc shattered. Bartlett and Gruening of Alaska, Engle of California, Church of Idaho, Mansfield and Metcalf of Montana, Cannon of Nevada, Anderson of New Mexico, Burdick of North Dakota, Edmondson and Monroney of Oklahoma, Morse and Neuberger of Oregon, McGovern of South Dakota, Yarborough of Texas, Moss of Utah, Jackson and Magnuson of Washington, and McGee of Wyoming, all Democrats, voted for cloture. The three negative Democrats were an odd group. Carl Hayden was told that his vote was not needed and maintained his proud consistency. Alan Bible felt that the filibuster was the best protection Nevada's gaming industry had against federal regulation. Robert Byrd of West Virginia, a former member of the Ku Klux Klan who actually conducted a mini-filibuster on June 9, many years later described his vote as the worst mistake he had made in a long and distinguished Senate career. The six Republicans who voted against cloture were all from the West—Bennett of Utah, Goldwater of Arizona, Mechem of New Mexico, Simpson of Wyoming, Tower of Texas, and Young of North Dakota.

The vote for cloture, of course, guaranteed passage of the Civil Rights Act. Excepting the segregationist press in the South, it was hailed in the U.S. as a dramatic triumph. The U.S. Information Agency made a study of the non-Communist foreign reaction with the following summary:

> Commentators viewed the passage as the most important step forward in the American Negro's struggle for equality since the Emancipation Proclamation; as a "victory" that will "shape the future of the United States"; as a "turning point" in American history; as enhancing the international influence of the United States, especially among non-white and newly-independent nations; and as reinforcing the moral authority of the United States and its dedication to freedom and social justice.

The Communist press downplayed the importance of the vote, predicting continued racial conflict. This was also a theme of non-Communist editors.

The adoption of the law would not "immediately or easily" bring equality or end strife and resistance.[6]

If the voyage of the civil rights bill through the Senate had been a five-act play, the cloture vote on June 10, 1964, was the climax at the end of the fourth act. All the drama was spent; everything else was anticlimax.

The southerners maintained a brief resistance by offering an enormous number of amendments which went down to defeat. After a few days, their vitality sapped, Russell, Stennis, and Hill were ready to quit, but Thurmond, Ervin, and Long insisted on continuing. On June 17, however, Thurmond and Ervin informed Humphrey that they were giving up. They presented a final batch of amendments two days later with the same dismal result.

On June 18 Goldwater spoke, announcing his intention to vote against the bill. "My basic objection . . . is constitutional." It would create "a federal police force of mammoth proportions." It would also foster an "informer" psychology, with "neighbors spying on neighbors." These were "hallmarks of the police state and landmarks in the destruction of a free society." If his vote was misconstrued, Goldwater said, "let me suffer its consequences." Many Republicans, Dirksen among them, feared that the worst consequences would be to their party. The minority leader had tried to turn Goldwater around by playing on his Republicanism. Such a vote, Dirksen urged, would undermine his own candidacy for President and the remainder of the Republican ticket in November. "But," Goldwater said, "he didn't convince me." Dirksen, angered, publicly denounced Goldwater's vote against the Civil Rights Act.

On June 19 Mansfield made another of his "long" speeches. He praised everyone—Dirksen—"this is his finest hour"; Humphrey—"has performed herculean feats"; and so on through the ranks. He closed with a tribute to Kennedy. "This, indeed, is his moment, as well as the Senate's." Dirksen was equally generous and stressed the "moral basis" for the bill. He closed by saying, "I am prepared to vote."

The roll was again called. Engle entered in his wheelchair and, again, pointed to his eye. The vote was 73 to 27. Four senators who had opposed cloture now voted for the bill—Bennett, Bible, Young, and, having it both ways, Carl Hayden. Two who supported cloture—Cotton and Hickenlooper—voted against the bill.

This was Humphrey's day. After the vote a large crowd gave him a thunderous send-off for his return to Minneapolis. But it was a sad moment. He was going to be with his son, Robert, who had cancer and faced surgery the next week. There were not many who now doubted that Lyndon Johnson would pick Hubert Humphrey as his running mate.

On June 19, the day of final Senate action, Celler and McCulloch issued a joint statement. While they did not approve of everything the Senate had done, none of its amendments did "serious violence" to H.R. 7152. A conference could "fatally delay enactment." They reasoned that Eastland on the conference committee could do untold damage, perhaps even opening the way for another filibuster. Further, Charlie Halleck wanted to get the Republicans out of town before the Fourth of July so they could get ready for their San Francisco convention on the 13th. These considerations called for House adoption of the Senate bill with no amendments.

But this required another rule. Howard Smith, Larry O'Brien warned the President on June 18, "will delay as long as possible . . . unless we move to cut him off." There were two possible ways to go. One was to suspend the rules, a procedure designed for noncontroversial bills, which this one certainly was not, and required a two-thirds vote, which was likely but not certain. But it was allowed only on the first and third Mondays of the month, which meant July 6. Halleck did not like that at all. The other was to force a hearing by the Rules Committee. Three members could file a request and, if the chairman ignored it for seven calendar days, eight members could compel him to comply.

The Senate bill reached the House on June 22. Celler immediately asked unanimous consent to a motion to "agree to the Senate amendment." A brigade of southern congressmen objected. Anticipating this, Celler introduced a resolution for House concurrence with the Senate bill and Speaker McCormack immediately sent it to the Rules Committee.

Smith, stalling, scheduled the hearings on the last possible day, June 30, at 10:30 a.m. At the outset Ray Madden, the Indiana Democrat, informed the chairman that a majority of the committee intended to conclude the hearings at 5:00 that afternoon. Celler and McCulloch testified that morning; four southerners in the afternoon. At precisely 5:00 Richard Bolling, the Missouri Democrat, demanded a vote on a motion to report immediately. It carried 10 to 5. Bolling now took the committee away from Smith, moving that Madden, rather than the chairman, make the report to the House. The southerners protested vehemently, but to no avail. The motion carried 8 to 7.

On July 2 in the House Madden called up the resolution for concurrence with the Senate bill. The "debate," mercifully, was brief. Smith bitterly attacked the "raw, brutal power of the majority." John Lindsay, the liberal New York Republican, lauded McCulloch and the House gave the quiet man from Ohio a standing ovation. Charles Weltner, reflecting the changing mood of his district in Atlanta, stated that he had voted against the bill originally, but now "I will add my voice . . . to a new reality." Then Celler got his standing ovation—led by Judge Smith! The roll call went 289 to 124. There were 153 Democrats and 136 Republicans in the majority; 91 Democrats (88 from the South) and 35 Republicans in the minority.

Lyndon Johnson was ready. This would be no routine bill-signing ceremony. On the evening of the day the House acted, July 2, 1964, the elegant East Room of the White House shimmered in the light from its chandeliers. That day Larry O'Brien had given the President the guest list, which ran to eight pages. There were a great many members of Congress, a large delegation from the cabinet, particularly the Department of Justice, the Civil Rights Commission, the Leadership Conference on Civil Rights, black organizations, the AFL-CIO, the churches, and women's organizations, among others.

As he signed the Civil Rights Act of 1964, the President addressed this assemblage and the nation over television and radio. "This," he said, "is a proud triumph." The law said that those who are "equal before God shall also now be equal in the polling booths, in the classrooms, in the factories, and in hotels, restaurants, movie theaters, and other places that provide service to the public." "Let us close the springs of racial poison." Johnson announced that former Florida governor LeRoy Collins, who was present, would be director of the Community Relations Service under Title X. He would soon send Congress a request for an appropriation to implement the law. That afternoon he had directed the federal agencies charged with responsibilities under the statute to get to work at once. The President then signed 72 copies of the new law, passing out that many pens.

At the close of the ceremony the President met off the record with the black civil rights leaders—Martin Luther King, Jr., Roy Wilkins, Whitney Young, James Forman, Clarence Mitchell, A. Philip Randolph, and a few others. Johnson was accompanied by the top echelon of the Justice Department—Kennedy, Katzenbach, and Marshall—Governor Collins, Secretary of Commerce Luther Hodges (whose department would house the Community Relations Service), and Lee C. White, who handled civil rights in the White House and who made the notes.

For at least a year Kennedy and Marshall had worried that these nonviolent leaders were losing control over the movement, that power was slipping to the younger, more militant black leaders who had little concern for persons and for property. During 1963 there had been serious disorders in Chicago and Philadelphia followed in early 1964 by riots in New York City and San Francisco. On April 22, 1964, demonstrators had shouted the President down when he spoke at the New York World's Fair. Now Johnson told the mainline black leaders that "the rights Negroes possessed could . . . be secured by law, making demonstrations unnecessary and possibly even self-defeating." According to David J. Garrow, King and some of the others read his statement to mean that he did not want riots during his campaign for the presidency because they "would play into the hands of Republican candidates."

The President also pointed out that there would be constitutional challenges to the Civil Rights Act. It was critical that the cases should be selected carefully for court test to guard against unfavorable decisions by the lower courts even if they were later overturned by the Supreme Court. The black leaders promised that they would cooperate with the Justice Department.[7]

The passage of the Civil Rights Act was a rare and glittering moment in the history of American democracy and of the Congress. It proclaimed the triumph of good over evil, of justice over bigotry, of the national interest over the sectional and partisan interests. It was fitting to be proud of the nation and of its leaders both at the time and in retrospect.

The Civil Rights Act was so important, so lengthy and complex, reached back so far into history, plucked at so many strings in the legislative process, and aroused so much controversy that it is impossible to narrow the credit for its passage to an individual or to a small group. Fortunately, the supply of credit is so ample that there is more than enough to spread around widely.

One must start, of course, with the civil rights movement of the late fifties and early sixties—simply put, with the black demand for the abolition of Jim Crow. This took place primarily in demonstrations at the local level in the South—on the buses, in the schools, at lunch counters, in stores, in hotels and restaurants, and so on. Here demonstrators put their bravery and their bodies on the line, often paying a heavy price. These demonstrations caught the attention of executives, legislatures, and the courts at all levels of government. Over time the civil rights movement persuaded the great majority of white people in the North (and many in the South) of the justice of their cause. More than anything else, that swelling of white public support guaranteed victory. Perhaps most important in the final critical stage was the conversion of the churches, which won over the nation's conscience.

Insofar as political leaders were concerned, John Kennedy must be first to win credit. While he took more than two years to make up his mind, once committed he went all the way. He was the bold initiator, he voiced the moral imperative, and he was the architect of the grand legislative strategy. In his gut reaction to Birmingham he must have sensed that the American people would understand, in Dirksen's words, that civil rights was an idea whose time had come.

The Department of Justice team—Robert Kennedy, Nicholas Katzenbach, and Burke Marshall—performed superbly. They were responsible for the language of the law, for extensive lobbying, for honoring the commitment to McCulloch, for helping to keep Lyndon Johnson on course, and for participating in a number of important legislative decisions.

President Johnson had trouble with the legislative strategy at the outset, but he came around firmly. He spoke out strongly and often; he refused to compromise with his old friend Senator Russell; he kept the pressure on the Senate Democratic leadership; and he helped to move up to and beyond the magic 67 by persuading doubtful senators, particularly from the West, to vote for cloture.

In the House the Brooklyn street urchin, Emanuel Celler, and the Ohio plowboy, William McCulloch, played critical but different roles. Celler insisted that the bill that cleared the House must be strong. With the help of his fellow opera buff, Peter Rodino, he was responsible for putting Title VII in the bill. McCulloch, if anything, deserves even more credit. Despite his own reservations, he accepted Celler's tough bill. More important, McCulloch dictated the legislative strategy: no compromise with the Senate. This forced a southern filibuster and, once it was broken, guaranteed passage of Celler's bill.

The performance of the Senate leaders—Mansfield, Humphrey, and Dirksen—can be summed up in one word: magnificent. Each deserved to wear in his buttonhole a freshly cut marigold from Dirksen's garden.

4

The War on Poverty

THROUGHOUT history human societies have been plagued by poverty, none more so than the subclass separated from the mainstream elements. In his magisterial history of the rise of capitalism, Fernand Braudel wrote of "the circles of hell" in European cities inhabited by the huge numbers of the "sub-proletariat" of paupers, beggars, and vagrants. Established citizens feared them and denounced them as the "scum of the earth, excrement of the cities, scourge of republics." They wanted the poor to be quiet, to be invisible, to go away. The authorities would drive them out, put them to work, keep them under lock and key, or send them overseas.

At the outset, the rise of industrialism, by widening the gap between rich and poor, made poverty worse. But the traditional features carried over: a large subclass of the poor concentrated in the towns and the propensity of prosperous citizens and governments was to deny their existence. On very rare occasions, however, intellectuals and writers interceded to speak for the poor, demanded that they be heard, insisted that their conditions be addressed. This occurred in England in the nineteenth century with the "discovery of the poor" around midcentury and their "rediscovery" at the end of that century.

There were two elements in this awakening: London and its great chroniclers—Henry Mayhew, Charles Dickens, and Charles Booth. By 1850 industrialized London contained 2.3 million people, making it the largest city in the world. Rapid growth had deformed the metropolis, leaving behind large pockets of poverty, the infamous "rookeries." Almost nowhere else was the contrast between the "two nations" that Disraeli called "the rich and the poor" more stark.

Henry Mayhew, a brilliant journalist, in 1849 launched a series of articles in the *Chronicle* on the London poor which ran for a year. He then wrote weekly pamphlets, 63 in all, between 1850 and 1852. In the earlier pieces he concentrated on the working poor and contrasted the workers' poverty with the rich of London. The later pamphlets shifted to the city's more eye-catching "street folk"—street sellers of almost anything, street performers, and street children. These people shunned steady jobs, were often in trouble with the police, were sexually promiscuous, and were sometimes members of "peculiar races"—the Irish and the Jews.

The original articles and pamphlets spawned a throng of imitators, inspired novels and plays, and stimulated parliamentary efforts to remedy the evils. Mayhew evolved the concept of a culture of poverty, an intractable problem not particularly amenable to philanthropic or economic solutions.

The discovery of the poor had a large impact upon novelists, notably Charles Dickens. Because he was a great writer and was enormously popular, Dickens did more to arouse an awareness of the poor than anyone else. Several of his novels were set in poverty—*Oliver Twist, Hard Times, Our Mutual Friend;* in many of the others there was an important "low" character. "What other reformers hoped to do by legislation," Gertrude Himmelfarb wrote, "he did by a supreme act of moral imagination. He brought the poor into the forefront of the culture. . . ."

Charles Booth, who wrote the 17-volume *Life and Labour of the People of London* (1889–1903), was a meticulous scholar who devoted many years to the study of poverty in London. He defined the poor as those who fell in income beneath the employed working class, which he described as "comfortable." His most important finding, based on careful house-to-house surveys, was that almost one-third of the city's population lived in poverty.

Concern over the poor inspired institutional changes in British society—the rise of trade unionism and the formation of the Labour Party. These developments, in turn, led to Britain's first large step toward the welfare state, which included old age pensions, labor exchanges, health insurance, unemployment insurance, and higher taxes on the rich. David Lloyd George, Chancellor of the Exchequeur, in introducing "the people's budget" in 1909, said, "This is a war budget for raising money to wage implacable warfare against poverty and squalidness." Perhaps there is a connection between Welsh and Texas hype.[1]

For a century following the English discovery of poverty no one in the U.S. studied the problem systematically. But a significant number of gifted writers, artists, and photographers, especially during the Great Depression, placed the poor on center stage.

Jacob Riis, himself a Danish immigrant, became an investigative reporter for the New York *Evening Sun* and made the tidal wave of immigration into the city his beat. His articles and books, notably *How the Other Half Lives* (1890), provided a compassionate and comprehensive portrait of the life of the poor in the city's tenements and sweatshops. Riis was drawn to Manhattan's ethnic ghettoes—the Irish on the West Side, the Germans on the East Side, the Italians way downtown and in "Little Italy" in Harlem, the Negroes uptown, and the Jews on the Lower East Side.

In the next century the massive unemployment, homelessness, and transiency created by the Great Depression stirred literary and artistic imaginations. Reginald Marsh and Raphael Soyer, both superb painters and both addicted to walking the streets of New York, concentrated on the poor—in breadlines, in flophouses, on park benches, in tenements, in missions, on the waterfront. They realistically depicted urban poverty with passion and sympathy. But the event that aroused the greatest interest was the Dust Bowl of the mid-thirties, which destroyed farms and wiped out farm families, launching the great trek of the Okies, Arkies, and Mizoos to California. John Steinbeck was inspired to write the fiction masterpiece of the era, *The Grapes of Wrath*. Woody Guthrie, himself an Okie, became the folk minstrel of the great migration. The photographers of the Farm Security Administration, notably Dorothea Lange, captured the haunting faces of the migrants on film.

Let Us Now Praise Famous Men, which ranked behind only Steinbeck's novel, was also concerned with rural poverty. James Agee, a novelist and critic, wrote the text, and Walker Evans, a luminary among the FSA photographers, provided the pictures. The book was a penetrating and heartrending portrait of the dreary lives of three poor white tenant farmer families in Alabama.

In the late fifties a new and totally different interest in poverty emerged, an effort to study it, to measure it, to analyze its characteristics, to devise policies to deal with it. This curiosity mushroomed with extraordinary speed. At the outset, when Robert Lampman, an economist at the University of Wisconsin, compiled a bibliography of poverty, it filled less than two typed pages. Dorothy Campbell Tompkins published another in 1970 which came to 442 double-column pages with 8,338 entries.

Observers have been mystified to explain this sudden impulse to confront poverty. The flood of European immigration to the U.S., which created the problems that Jacob Riis wrote about, was now little more than a trickle. The Great Depression, which explained the interest in the thirties, was now a fading bad memory. While there were recessions in the late fifties and early sixties, they were relatively brief and mild, and in 1964, when the poverty law was passed, the economy was moving up into a boom. The impulse seems to have emerged from the joining of two diverse developments—a vigorous restatement of the traditional inequity argument against capitalism, especially by economists, and the great internal migration of poor black people from the rural South to the urban ghettoes of the North. The latter was augmented by a similar but smaller movement of Puerto Ricans to New York City. Both migrations were noted by sociologists and social workers, the latter dramatized by the authors of the brilliant Broadway musical *West Side Story*.

Liberal economists, to say nothing of Marxists, had been nurtured on the inequity argument. In summary, it went as follows: capitalism had succeeded dramatically in expanding the output of goods and services. But it had failed to distribute income and wealth equitably, giving too big a share to the rich. Thus, the state must intervene with policies to shift income from the wealthy to those in need. In modern welfare states, these programs included the progressive income tax, unemployment compensation, health insurance, old age pensions, workers' compensation, a minimum wage, the encouragement of collective bargaining, the elimination of discrimination in employment, and welfare. Except for the last, the very poor were still bypassed. They enjoyed few of the fruits of either capitalism or the welfare state. Thus, the argument continued, this gap must be filled by a special poverty program for the underclass. In the early sixties the theory received a postscript. When it became clear that the Keynesian tax cut would be enacted, it also became evident that only those above the minimum income levels specified in the income tax code who paid taxes would benefit from the reduction. The really poor, who either had no or so small an income as to escape taxation, had no tax to cut. Equity, the argument ran, demanded that something else be done for them.

Relatively small numbers of blacks had lived in northern urban ghettoes prior to World War II. Their numbers swelled during and after the war. This was partly natural increase, but mainly the great migration from the rural South. A good number of these people had scratched out a marginal living as sharecroppers raising cotton. On October 2, 1944, eight of the first workable mechanical cotton pickers were tested on the Hopson plantation near Clarksdale in the Mississippi Delta. Howell Hopson kept careful books. The machines picked 62 bales that day. Hopson's figures showed that machine picking cost $5.26 a bale, picking by hand $39.41. Each machine picked as much cotton aₜ 50 people. Sharecropping no longer made economic sense and work for the croppers in the Delta petered out. A one-way ticket from Clarksdale to Chicago on the Illinois Central cost $11.50. The great migration began.

Between 1940 and 1960 the net black emigration from the rural South was almost 3 million. There were four main streams: from southern farms to southern cities—Atlanta, Birmingham, New Orleans, Houston; from Georgia, the Carolinas, and Virginia into Washington, Philadelphia, Newark, and New York; from Mississippi and Alabama via the Illinois Central to Chicago and other midwestern cities; and from the Southwest to Los Angeles and the San Francisco Bay Area, especially Oakland. By 1960, 80 percent of blacks in the North lived in segregated ghettoes.

"The circles of hell," the phrase Braudel had applied to the preindustrial urban poor in European cities, was an appropriate name for the American ghettoes. They had the oldest, most substandard, and most crowded residences. Housing was rigidly segregated by race and, flowing from that, virtually everything else. Schools, parks, garbage removal, water, and police protection were of low quality. There was a high level of illiteracy. Health was much worse than among whites. A large proportion of families was headed by women. Vice and crime flourished, particularly among teenage gangs.

Heretofore race had been an acute problem only in the South. With the emergence of the northern ghettoes the issue confronted the entire nation. The disaster of the ghettoes was forcing American cities, particularly the largest, into a state of perpetual crisis. Middle-class white citizens of these towns, like their counterparts in Braudel's Europe, wanted race to be invisible, hoped that poor blacks would either go away or become quiet segregated neighbors. That was a dream. But some sociologists, social workers, and activists worked on urban problems, recognized their gravity, and searched for remedies.[2]

John Kenneth Galbraith led the liberal economists in calling attention to poverty in 1958 in *The Affluent Society,* a book that attracted a wide audience. His basic argument, as the title suggested, was that the great majority of Americans received the benefits of a rich and growing economy. But he noted briefly that the public sector and the poor did not share adequately in the gains. The private economy received "an opulent supply" and the public sector got "a niggardly yield." In a brief chapter entitled "The New Position of Poverty" he wrote that it "does survive" as an affliction upon an uncounted number, some poor because of personal inadequacy, others because they lived on "islands" of poverty. He was disturbed because "it is not efficiently remedied by a general and tolerably well-distributed advance in income." Affluent America, if it were "both compassionate and rational," could easily move most of these people out of poverty. He offered only a first-step remedy: investment in the children of the poor in order to break the generational poverty cycle. These were well-intended and reasonably sensible observations, but Galbraith merely introduced the topic.

The entire professional career of Paul H. Douglas, both as a professor of economics at the University of Chicago and as a U.S. senator from Illinois, could be read as an attempt to redress economic inequity. In the late fifties Senator Douglas was chairman of the Joint Economic Committee and invited Robert Lampman, an authority on income distribution, to make a study of poverty. In 1959 the committee published his brief paper, *The Low Income Population and Economic Growth.* It was, evidently, the first systematic, if tentative, effort to measure poverty in the U.S., the kind of task Booth had undertaken in London.

Lampman assumed a poverty threshold annual income of $2500 for a family of four in 1957 dollars. An individual would be poor if he had an income of less than $1,157, a six-person family if below $3,236. In 1957 there were 32.2 million persons whose incomes fell beneath these levels, 19 percent of the total population. He found a clustering of poverty among the elderly, nonwhites, on farms, in the South, in families headed by women, and in families headed by a person with no more than an eighth-grade education.

This marked an improvement over the preceding decade. Between 1947 and 1957 the number in poverty had declined from 26 to 19 percent. The basic reason for the improvement was economic growth. Lampman was concerned that the process might not continue because several of the clusters of the poor were not responsive to growth. Like Galbraith, he was particularly disturbed because a fifth of the nation's children was being reared in poverty. "Probably no public program has made and can continue to make so important and fundamental a contribution to the elimination of poverty as free public education."

In 1962 Leon Keyserling's Conference on Economic Progress published *Poverty and Deprivation in the U.S.* A lawyer by training and the main draftsman of the Wagner Act in 1935, he had become a self-taught economist. He had been chairman of Truman's Council of Economic Advisers and his Conference studies were wholly economic in orientation. Using 1960 dollars and the Bureau of Labor Statistics' definitions of "modest but adequate budgets" (compared with Lampman's 1957 base and more stringent budgets), Keyserling divided Americans into five categories:

	Families	*Individuals*
Poverty	Under $4000	Under $2000
Deprivation	$4000 to 5,999	$2000 to 2,999
Deprivation-comfort	$6000 to 7,499	$3000 to 4,999
Comfort-affluence	$7500 to 14,999	$5000 to 7,499
Affluence	$15,000 and over	$7500 and over

On the basis of these categories, 38 million Americans lived in poverty in 1960, about 20 percent of the population. This compared with Lampman's 1957 estimates—32.2 million and 19 percent. In addition, according to Keyserling, another fifth of the American people, 39 million, lived in "deprivation." Combined, those in poverty and deprivation came to 77 million, about 43 percent of the population.

Poverty and deprivation clustered in these categories: the South, agriculture, personal services, the elderly, families headed by women, blacks, the deficiently educated, and those in poor health.

The interest of social scientists in the crisis of the cities seems to have begun with Leonard Duhl, a psychologist at the National Institute of Mental Health. He interpreted "mental health" broadly and in 1955 assembled a group of experts to discuss the erosion of the cities. *Sputnik* was launched in 1957 on a day when they were meeting. One said, "If they think *they're* out in space, they should see us." Henceforth they called themselves Space Cadets. Duhl funded several important urban studies mainly concerned with black ghetto life.

Paul Ylvisaker was an official at the Ford Foundation who lived in New Jersey. The bus he took to the Newark airport went through the black ghetto, which resembled the Western Front during World War I. He urged the foundation to start an action program to assist urban ghettoes, which became the Gray Areas Project.

Ylvisaker had no patience with government bureaucracies—federal, state, or local. Thus, he favored what later came to be called community action projects—locally controlled and shaped specifically to meet the needs of the town. He started a number of Gray Areas programs. New Haven, under the leadership of Mayor Richard Lee and Mitchell Sviridoff, a former UAW official, developed education and job training for recent black migrants from the South. Governor Terry Sanford of North Carolina used Ford money to develop programs across his state. The most important Gray Areas project was Mobilization for Youth, which, with the support of Mayor Robert F. Wagner, Jr., developed a broad program for the Lower East Side of New York covering law enforcement, recreation, counseling, improved education, and job training. Mobilization was unusual in having a theoretical underpinning for its program supplied by two sociologists, authorities on juvenile delinquency, at the Columbia School of Social Work— Richard A. Cloward and Lloyd E. Ohlin.

In 1960 Cloward and Ohlin published *Delinquency and Opportunity,* a theory of urban gangs. They defined three types of delinquent subcultures: the criminal, based on the pursuit of material gain by extortion, fraud, and theft; the conflict, pursuing status by the manipulation of violence; and the retreatist, persons who withdrew by dependence on drugs. These subcultures concentrated in the inner cities of large metropolitan areas and seldom appeared in the suburbs or in smaller communities. This was mainly due to the fact that big cities exposed lower-class adolescent males to a wider gap between their aspirations for material success and their realistic opportunities to achieve it. The delinquent subculture was an adaptation of escape from this trap. The criminal and conflict systems opened illegal avenues of achieving success. The retreatist, attractive to persons who had withdrawn from competition, erected a barrier against failure.

Delinquency, Cloward and Ohlin concluded, did not emerge from individuals or subcultures; it arose, rather, from "the social systems in which these individuals or groups were enmeshed." Thus, "the major effort of those who wish to eliminate delinquency should be directed to the reorgani-

zation of slum communities." That was the vision of Mobilization for
Youth.

Eunice Shriver, according to Nicholas Lemann, was the Kennedy family
"social worker" and "a world-class nagger." She had long been interested
in juvenile delinquency. In 1961 she persuaded her brother, the President,
to push through Congress the Juvenile Delinquency and Youth Offenses
Control Act, which established the President's Committee on Juvenile Delinquency and Youth Crime. She then persuaded her brother, the Attorney
General, to house the committee in the Justice Department. In prep school
Robert Kennedy had had a friend, David Hackett, who had helped out during the 1960 campaign. Kennedy made him the executive head of the committee. Hackett hired Richard Boone, who had studied parole and had
worked for the Chicago police department. This group, presumably because
of its interest in street gangs, became known as the Guerrillas. Hackett established contact with Duhl's Space Cadets and Ylvisaker's Gray Areas
Project. Hackett, who came to his job with no background in the subject,
was much taken with Lloyd Ohlin's ideas.

Hackett and Boone had $15 million to finance experimental local ac-
tion projects. They backed programs in the slums, some already supported
by NIMH and Ford; most of these projects were intended to help young
black people in the urban ghettoes.

In 1961 Oscar Lewis, an anthropologist at the University of Illinois,
published *The Children of Sanchez*. It was his sixth study of family poverty
since 1943, mainly about Mexico. He used the tape recorder for interviews
because it allowed "unskilled, uneducated, and even illiterate persons . . .
[to] talk about themselves and relate their observations and experiences in
an uninhibited, spontaneous, and natural manner." This, Lewis thought,
"made possible the beginning of a new kind of literature of social realism."
The book laid out in absorbing detail the lives of the five members of the
Sanchez family (a fictitious name), who lived in a single room in the Case
Grande *vecindad,* a one-story slum tenement in the heart of Mexico City.

By 1961, Lewis, like Henry Mayhew a century earlier, though with
much greater precision, had developed a theory of the culture of poverty,
which he set out in *The Children of Sanchez*. By this he meant "a design
for living" which parents pass on to their children. Poverty was more than
economic deprivation, "of the absence of something." It was also "positive"
in having "a structure, a rationale, and defense mechanism without which
the poor could hardly carry on. In short, it is a way of life, remarkably
stable and persistent, passed down from generation to generation along
family lines." The culture existed only among those at the very bottom, "the
poorest workers, the poorest peasants, plantation laborers and that large
heterogeneous mass of small artisans and tradesmen usually referred to as
the lumpen proletariat."

This culture of poverty had universal characteristics which transcended regional, rural-urban, and national differences. In an earlier study, *Five Families*, Lewis had found remarkable parallels in London, Glasgow, Paris, Harlem, and Mexico City. Compared with other classes, those in poverty had a high death rate, low life expectancy, more children, and, because of child labor and working women, many more gainfully employed. The culture was neighborhood-oriented and people within it were marginal in both the nation and the city.

> In Mexico City, for example, most of the poor have a very low level of education and literacy, do not belong to labor unions, are not members of a political party, do not participate in the medical care, maternity, and old-age benefits of the national welfare agency know as Seguro Social, and make very little use of the city's banks, hospitals, department stores, museums, art galleries, and airports.

Daily life was a constant struggle for survival against unemployment, low wages, child labor, the absence of savings, food shortages, pawning, and borrowing pesos at usurious interest rates. The social characteristics of the culture included lack of privacy, alcoholism, frequent resort to violence, early initiation into sex, consensual marriages, male abandonment of wives and children, mother-centered families, a time orientation toward the present, fatalism, *machismo,* and pathology. A doctor was unaffordable and a hospital was where one went to die. The poor relied on home remedies. They rarely went to church but prayed to the images of saints and made pilgrimages to popular shrines. They distrusted the government, hated the police, and were cynical about the church.

Galbraith, Lampman, and Cloward and Ohlin were concerned that poverty was not wholly responsive to economic remedies. If one accepted the Lewis definition of the culture of poverty, at least for the underclass, that worry became overpowering.

In the early sixties poverty was discovered by many more middle-class Americans than those to whom this literature was addressed. In 1960 Edward R. Murrow's television landmark, "Harvest of Shame," was shown on the CBS network. A powerful indictment of poverty among migratory farm workers, it was seen by millions of viewers then and later.

In *Night Comes to the Cumberlands,* published in 1962, Harry M. Caudill dramatically depicted the tragic human and physical conditions in Appalachia, particularly the 19 counties of eastern Kentucky known as the Cumberland Plateau. Here half a million white people lived in abject poverty, their beautiful land ravaged by a century of reckless coal mining. Secretary of the Interior Stewart L. Udall placed Caudill's book alongside Upton Sinclair's *The Jungle,* Steinbeck's *The Grapes of Wrath,* and Agee's *Let Us Now Praise Famous Men* in its power to evoke the condition of the poor.

Nature added emphasis to the book's message. In March 1963 there were immense rains and severe flooding in the Cumberlands. Kennedy, reminded of the conditions he had witnessed next door in West Virginia during the 1960 primary, declared the plateau a disaster area and sent in federal relief. On October 20, 1963, the *New York Times* carried a powerful story of poverty in the Cumberlands by Homer Bigart, one of its star reporters. Kennedy was deeply moved.

The most important book in the American discovery of poverty, Michael Harrington's *The Other America,* was published in 1962. While not immediately popular, it eventually worked its way up to the best-seller list and became a minor American classic of the stature of *Uncle Tom's Cabin.* Harrington wrote that the poor "needed an American Dickens to record the smell and texture and quality of their lives." He readily admitted that "I am not that novelist." But he did very well in describing "the faces behind the statistics." A product of the Catholic labor movement, a devoted idealist deeply committed to democracy and socialism, Harrington poured passion and compassion into his book about the poor.

He borrowed Disraeli's image of two nations: affluent America and "the other America." While he did not challenge Lampman's estimate of 32 million poor directly, his travels among those in poverty persuaded him that there were many others who slipped through the statistical cracks and he thought the number was between 40 and 50 million.

Harrington's basic finding, which Lewis had also stressed, was that the poor were invisible. "Here is a great mass of people, yet it takes an effort of the intellect and the will even to see them." One could drive the interstates in Pennsylvania and miss the gutted coal towns of the Appalachians and skip over the people in the mountain valleys. One could live in the affluent suburbs of the metropolis and avoid the slums of the inner city. One could no longer identify the poor by their clothes. "America has the best-dressed poverty the world has ever known." Many, particularly the elderly and children, could not be seen because they stayed close to home. Perhaps most important, "the poor are politically invisible. . . . They have no face; they have no voice."

Borrowing loosely from Oscar Lewis, he found many cultures of poverty. There were the "rejects," workers in "the economic underworld" of the cities. They either had no skills or the wrong skills for available jobs. Some were jobless, others had work of low skill at very low wages without protection from either unions or the minimum wage. There were marginal farmers and farm workers. There were the inhabitants of the black urban ghettoes. There were the intellectuals and artists who had opted out of the system, the alcoholics on skid row, and the urban hillbillies who had not made it. There were the aged. And there were those with mental troubles.

Harrington urged "a basic attack on poverty" to destroy "the pessimism and fatalism that flourish in the other America." He pointed particularly to housing and medical care. Since the cities were incapable of dealing with their poor, he felt that there must be a massive federal program. He closed typically on a note of optimism: "The means are at hand to fulfill the age-old dream: poverty can now be abolished."

On January 19, 1963, *The New Yorker* published an article by Dwight MacDonald, the literary critic, entitled "Our Invisible Poor," which, like Harrington's book, had a broad impact. He wrote,

> In the last year we seem to have suddenly awakened, rubbing our eyes like Rip Van Winkle, to the fact that mass poverty persists, that it is one of our two gravest social problems. (The other is related: While only eleven per cent of our population is non-white, twenty-five per cent of our poor are.)[3]

President Kennedy seems to have read *The Affluent Society, The Other America,* MacDonald's *New Yorker* article, and, perhaps, Keyserling's analysis. He was amazed that the poor were not angrier. "In England," he said, "the unemployment rate goes up two percent, and they march on Parliament. Here it moves up toward six, and no one seems to mind." Kennedy, of course, accepted the inequity argument and was much concerned that the poor would get no benefit from the tax cut. By the spring of 1963, Arthur Schlesinger wrote, "he was reaching the conclusion that tax reduction required a comprehensive structural counterpart, taking the form, not of piecemeal programs, but of a broad war against poverty itself." JFK's New Frontier program had originated in the Democratic Congress of the late fifties and others had written it into the 1960 Democratic platform. Now Kennedy wanted something that he had initiated.

Walter Heller of the Council of Economic Advisers shouldered the burden of devising such a program. He brought Robert Lampman to the Council during the spring and summer of 1963 to update his 1957 numbers on poverty. On May 1 Heller sent the President the results with a covering memorandum entitled Progress and Poverty. When Lampman varied the analysis by family size—from one person to seven or more—the number of people in poverty in 1961 was 33 million, 18.2 percent of the population. More "distressing" to Heller—"one more demonstration of the costs of economic slack"—was the historic performance of the economy in moving people out of poverty. Between 1947 and 1956 the number of families with annual incomes in 1961 dollars of less than $3000 had declined by 10 points, from 33 to 23 percent. But between 1956 and 1961 the drop was only 2 points, from 23 to 21 percent.

Before he returned to Madison for the fall term Lampman also wrote "The Problem of Poverty in America," which would become chapter 2 of the *Economic Report* published in January 1964. In that form it served two purposes—as the most comprehensive and authoritative statistical analysis of poverty in the U.S. made to that time and as the foundation for Lyndon Johnson's simultaneous call for a war on poverty in his State of the Union address.

Both the definition and the measurement of poverty, Lampman stressed, were imprecise. His general definition of the poor was "those who are not now maintaining a decent standard of living—those whose basic needs exceed their means to satisfy them." He accepted the Social Security Administration's 1962 "low-cost" budgets for a nonfarm family of four—$3,955—and "economy-plan" budget—$3,165. This led him to select conservatively an income below $3,000 in 1962 as the poverty line. For unrelated individuals, a more complicated statistical problem, he used both $1,500 and $1,000. Of the 47 million families in the U.S. in 1962, 9.3 million, over 30 million people, lived in poverty. Of unrelated individuals, 5 million had incomes below $1,500 and more than 3 million fell under $1,000. "Thus, by the measures used here, 33 to 35 million Americans were living at or below the boundaries of poverty in 1962—nearly one-fifth of our Nation."

Poverty was not homogeneous; it clustered in particular sectors. Some 22 percent of the population were nonwhite, but nearly half of all non-whites lived in poverty. A majority of the heads of poor families were not well educated; high school and college provided escape hatches from poverty. One-third of the poor were children. There was also a high incidence of poverty among the elderly. The poor were geographically everywhere—in cities, in rural nonfarm areas, and on the farm. There were many poor people in agriculture, particularly nonwhites. The South was the region which had the highest incidence of poverty by a wide margin. Nearly half the families headed by women were poor. When a family combined these disadvantages, for example, a nonwhite female family head with a limited education, 94 percent lived in poverty.

Most distressing was the fact, as Oscar Lewis had noted, that "poverty breeds poverty." It passed on from one generation to the next. Low incomes stacked the cards against the poor—high risks of illness, limited education, lack of motivation, hope, and incentive.

Lampman was convinced that an attack on poverty would be a formidable undertaking:

> Poverty . . . has many faces. It is found in the North and in the South; in the East and the West; on the farm and in the city. It is found among the young and among the old, among the employed and the unemployed. Its roots are many and its causes complex. . . . No single program can embrace all who are poor, and no single program can strike at all the sources of today's and tomorrow's poverty.[4]

During the summer of 1963 Heller assigned William Capron, formerly an economics professor at Stanford and a senior member of the CEA staff, to work on the poverty program, along with three junior economists. As Capron put it, he became Heller's "chief honcho." With Lampman, he set up a Saturday morning club with an interagency group, mainly economists, from Health, Education, and Welfare; Labor; and the Housing and Home Finance Agency. After Lampman pointed out the groups that were poor, Capron asked the economists what the government could do. HEW and Labor had a number of suggestions, but, as Capron said, they were "categorical program ideas warmed over." He drew a blank from HHFA. Capron thought he had made no progress.

In anticipation of the administration's 1964 legislative program, in September 1963 Sorensen handed out assignments and CEA received poverty. Now Capron moved his canvass up from staff to subcabinet and cabinet levels in the departments. This exposed sharp interagency differences. Secretary of Labor Willard Wirtz wanted a big program for jobs with his department in charge. Assistant Secretary of HEW Wilbur Cohen urged expansion of his department's health and education programs. HHFA seemed to have no ideas. Kermit Gordon, the Director of the Budget, set up a parallel group to CEA's under William B. Cannon to work with Capron.

On November 5, 1963, Heller addressed the "domestic cabinet"—the Secretaries of Agriculture, Commerce, Labor, HEW, the Director of the Budget, and the Administrator of HHFA—on the topic of "widening participation in prosperity." For a man with a high reputation for clarity, brevity, and precision of expression, this essay in befuddlement must have been the worst document to which Heller ever affixed his signature. The "widening" title was dreadful and he implored the recipients to help find a better one. He also urged them to make suggestions by reexamining their existing programs and by proposing "imaginative new programs."

The Council was overwhelmed by the replies, more than 100 specific proposals. The Labor Department alone submitted a 150-page document. Each department pushed its own interests: Labor suggested jobs and training; HEW, income maintenance, health, and education; Agriculture, assistance to poor farmers; and HHFA, which seems to have awakened, public housing. Capron called these suggestions "garbage." They "went into their file drawers and pulled out old programs that they had been floating around . . . , a lot of which had already been explicitly rejected by the Budget Bureau." CEA sent them to Budget and its team began the tedious job of evaluation. Both Cannon and Gordon concluded that they were "awful."

Heller worried that this unforeseen delay would cause the poverty bill to miss the January presidential deadlines. He went to see the President on November 19. Heller told him, "We were having great trouble getting a program together because of the bureaucratic infighting that was going on among his cabinet officers." Heller then asked whether poverty would be part of the 1964 legislative agenda. While Kennedy had expressed some concern about also doing something for the people in the suburbs, he responded affirmatively and asked to see the proposals in a couple of weeks.

Three days later, November 22, 1963, Heller and Wirtz were on the Tokyo-bound flight of cabinet officers when they learned of the assassination. Heller met with President Johnson at 7:40 p.m. on November 23. He reviewed the work of the Council, devoting particular attention to "the attack on poverty." They had been trying to develop "a good program," but had not yet worked it out. He informed Johnson of his last conversation with Kennedy, who, while concerned about middle-income people, "strongly urged me to move ahead on the poverty theme in the hope that we can make it an important part of the 1964 program." He then asked the new President "point blank" whether he should continue this work.

Johnson swung around in his chair and looked into Heller's eyes. This, he said, is "my kind of undertaking. I'm interested. I'm sympathetic. Go ahead. Give it the highest priority. Push ahead full tilt."

This response was in character. Lyndon Johnson's hard early years in the hill country of Texas had taught him that one paid a high price for being poor, an unpardonable price in a rich country like the U.S. As Charles Schultze put it, "He sincerely, deeply, fundamentally believed in—how do I say this?—the basic concept of providing opportunities." In addition, Johnson agreed with Kennedy that it was unfair to the poor to give them nothing while those better off got lower taxes. Finally, he became convinced that a poverty program shaped to get through Congress would help get him elected President in 1964.

But the President's commitment on November 23 put Heller in a jam. His people had gotten nowhere in setting up a poverty program and he needed one fast. Though he had not written to the Attorney General on November 5, he had received an interesting proposal from David Hackett in Justice. There were no substantive ideas, but Hackett urged an "approach," a "process." The President should establish five demonstration projects—for depressed areas, urban slums, Indians, migratory labor, and persons in institutions. These experiments would then form the basis for creating a new national poverty policy.

During December 1963 the Bureau of the Budget assumed the main responsibility for shaping the program and inherited the Hackett memorandum. A line item of $500 million was stuck into the fiscal 1965 budget, but there was no explanation of what it would be spent on. Cannon began looking seriously at Hackett's idea and became enamoured. He expanded it from 5 to 10 demonstration areas and proposed that a development corporation be responsible for each. This would leapfrog the infighting between federal departments and would pass the seemingly insoluble problem of selecting among competing programs to the new corporations. A fifth of the budget, $100 million, would be assigned to this project. Schultze endorsed Cannon's proposal, suggesting only that a new name be found for "development corporation." Hackett had also used the phrase "action program," and "community" was stuck in front of it. Thus, "community action" was born.

But Kermit Gordon was skeptical, in large part because he did not think his people or Capron knew anything about poverty. As Capron later admitted, "we didn't." More experienced advice was needed. Ylvisaker and his clients from New Haven, New York, and North Carolina descended on Washington. "Ylvisaker," Capron said, "was at his most persuasive." Hackett and Boone worked over Heller. At Hickory Hill, the Attorney General's estate in the Virginia countryside, Capron said, "Bobby pulled Walter aside . . . and made some very encouraging noises." By mid-December 1963 the council and the bureau were firmly behind community action and the whole $500 million was assigned to that program. Other projects would have to depend upon additional appropriations.

Gordon said later that he now had "a clear notion of what we were trying to do." There were many federal categorical and grant programs in education, public assistance, housing, and so on. Each was narrow in scope and independent of the others. "They did not treat the person in trouble as a person." They should, therefore, be consolidated. Poverty was "highly complex" and differed from one community to the next. "The monkey ought to be put on the back of the city itself to . . . diagnose . . . its own poverty problem . . . and to design a concerted . . . attack . . . with federal assistance." Gordon visualized local government leading with the support of private groups in the community. While he "had his doubts" whether this would work, he saw no better alternative. He thought the cities should use the first year exclusively for organizing and planning, holding back action until they knew what they wanted to do.

Budget and the Council, as James L. Sundquist put it, discovered community action "suddenly, fortuitously, and almost too late." One of its attractions was that it seemed simple but, in fact, was complicated. According to Peter Marris, it came in "three distinct and conflicting" strategies. The Ford Foundation projects were based on coordinated planning and worked through established institutions—local governments, the school system, and social agencies. This took time and required one to butt his head against local bureaucracies. Mobilization for Youth bypassed the town "power structure" to organize the poor themselves to assert their own interests. But institutions with power would not cede it without a battle. The Committee on Juvenile Delinquency and Youth Crime planned so comprehensively that it seemed to take forever to reach the action phase.

Cannon, nevertheless, patched together a memorandum with assistance from Capron and Hackett on December 14, 1963, proposing "a comprehensive community action program." Heller, Gordon, and Sorensen approved it and it was inserted into a sheaf of documents that would accompany the President to his ranch over the Christmas holiday. When Heller and Gordon got to Texas, Johnson greeted them with the news that he would not accept community action. By the next day, however, they had persuaded him to change his mind. According to his autobiography, he was now enthusiastic about community action and was recounting his own similar experiences with the Texas National Youth Administration in the thirties.

Johnson sat Heller, Gordon, Bill Moyers, and Jack Valenti down at the kitchen table in the guest house and ordered them to draft a program. The President said that there were not enough demonstration project cities and that he could not get a limited program through Congress. "It had to be big and bold and hit the whole nation with real impact." He ordered Gordon to double the budget.

Johnson wanted a fitting title. Since he wished "to rally the nation, to sound a call to arms which would stir people," he liked "The War on Poverty." But Father Theodore M. Hesburgh, the president of Notre Dame, told him that "it's just a terrible title. . . . You're looking down at people and calling them poor." Johnson called a meeting in the Cabinet Room at the White House of "his most trusted advisers," including Fortas, Clifford, several cabinet members, Larry O'Brien, and the author of the account, Gordon. This "high-powered talent" devoted "an interminable amount of time thinking up euphemisms for . . . poverty." That word was poison because it would offend the poor and would make the rich U.S. look bad abroad by admitting that it had a poverty problem. Since everything else sounded silly, they stuck with the War on Poverty.

In January 1964 the President fired his big guns. The *Economic Report* was published with Lampman's chapter on poverty. In his budget message he asked for $500 million specifically for poverty and $1 billion more under existing and proposed legislation for local community action programs. Most memorable was this passage in the State of Union address of January 8, 1964:

> Unfortunately, many Americans live on the outskirts of hope—some because of their poverty, and some because of their color, and all too many because of both. Our task is to help replace their despair with opportunity.
>
> This administration today, here and now, declares unconditional war on poverty in America. I urge this Congress and all Americans to join me in that effort.
>
> It will not be a short or easy struggle, no single weapon or strategy will suffice, but we shall not rest until that war is won. The richest Nation on earth can afford to win it. We cannot afford to lose it.

Everything about this statement was remarkable. An issue which had lain shrouded in silence for generations and only in the past few years had interested a limited group of writers and scholars was suddenly elevated to one of the most pressing questions facing the nation. When he spoke, Johnson had no proposed legislation and his advisers remained sharply divided over what such a law should provide and how it should be administered. What was he making an unconditional commitment to? Lampman had estimated that, if the government simply bought out the poor by giving all of them the cash needed to bring them up to the poverty lines, the cost would be $11 billion a year. But the President at the outside was asking for only $1.5 billion and, in fact, it turned out be less than $1 billion. This was not unconditional warfare; it was a skirmish. In fact, those who had been working on the program had already agreed that the elderly poor would be passed over, that the benefits would go to the young. The hollowness of the President's promise would plague the poverty program.

In late January the controversy within the administration intensified. Wirtz resumed his plea for jobs. Poverty, he argued, was a lack of income, and income came from work. Community action would create few jobs aside from summer and part-time work for students. While improvement in the health and education of the poor was desirable, their impact on income was indirect or remote. Moreover, the Labor Department's basic programs, like the minimum wage and manpower training, were not adaptable to the community action approach. Heller and Gordon, according to John Bibby and Roger Davidson, found it difficult to counter this argument. In addition, there was disagreement over administrative responsibility for the poverty program. HEW wanted it, but none of the other departments or agencies approved. The alternative was to create a new, independent agency with a poverty "czar" reporting directly to the President. There was another reason for putting a new boss in charge immediately. There would be, Sundquist pointed out, "an enormous lobbying job" with Congress and neither the Council nor the Budget Bureau was capable of that.[5]

It did not take Lyndon Johnson long to make his choice: his big forefinger pointed straight at R. Sargent Shriver, the Director of the Peace Corps. He was chosen, Shriver thought, primarily because "it was going to be very hard to get that program through Congress" and he had "extremely good rapport with Congress." He had gone up to the Hill every year for the Peace Corps and had enjoyed extraordinary success. He thought this was because he liked and respected the members of Congress. "I honestly believe that the principal reason why President Johnson wanted me to do it was that a large proportion of the congressmen and senators trusted me."

There could have been secondary reasons as well. At the time jurisdictional conflict between departments was bubbling up and Shriver's appointment would help prevent it from boiling over. He was a member of the Kennedy family by marriage and he was not among those who regarded Johnson as a usurper. "I came down to Washington to work for the President of the United States. I was not opposed to Lyndon Johnson; it wasn't his fault that he became President as a result of my brother-in-law's death." The fact that Bill Moyers, Johnson's fair-haired boy, had worked for Shriver in the Peace Corps and much admired him could have done his candidacy no harm.

There was another factor in Shriver's favor of which the President was probably unaware: he had a lifelong interest in poverty. His family had suffered severely during the Depression and that made "a very strong impression on me," much like being "a victim of a natural catastrophe." A Catholic, Shriver as a teenager had worked with Dorothy Day and the Catholic Worker movement with the poor in New York. He read the works of that champion of the poor, St. Francis of Assisi, and joined the Third Order of St. Francis. In Chicago he became a member of the St. Vincent de Paul Society and visited weekly those in poverty on the near North Side. As the head of that city's board of education, he worked hard to improve ghetto schools.

On January 31, 1964, Shriver came to the White House to report on "a remarkable trip" around the world that he had just concluded. The President had sent him off with many letters to heads of state and he had a good deal to say. Johnson took Shriver for a walk around the Rose Garden and the driveway. "You know," Johnson said, "we're getting this war against poverty started. I'd like you to think about that, because I'd like you to run that program for us."

Shriver had trouble thinking about it. He had a huge pile of catchup work at the Peace Corps and his wife was still in a state of shock over her brother's assassination. The next morning the phone rang at 10 o'clock. "Sarge, what do you think about that war against poverty?" Embarrassed, Shriver admitted that he had not thought about it. "Sarge, I'd like to have a press conference today at noon, and I'd like to announce you as the head of my new program." Shriver protested and said there was plenty of time. At 11 the phone rang again.

Shriver said that he needed a week to consider it; he was very happy with his job at the Peace Corps; there were more qualified people for the poverty program; and so on. Johnson said, "You think about it." At 11:30 he called back and spoke in a low voice:

> Sarge, this is your President speaking. I've interrupted a meeting going on right now in the Cabinet Room. . . . There's nobody that can see the whole picture like the President can. I need you to do this job, and I'm going to announce you as the director of the war against poverty at the news conference at twelve o'clock.

Shriver could hear the phone click.

At the news conference the President announced that Sargent Shriver had agreed to serve as his special assistant "in the organization and administration of the war on poverty program." This suggested that Shriver would draft the legislation, that a new agency would be established, and that Shriver would be its head. "Mr. Shriver," Johnson added, "will continue to serve as Director of the Peace Corps."

As Shriver started to think about his new undertaking, he realized that, as he put it, "nobody really knew how to fight poverty." He would have "to pick the brains of any qualified—and many unqualified—Americans." He would need to assemble the pickees in one place and that called for the formation of a task force.

Adam Yarmolinsky, the brilliant and acerbic special assistant to the Secretary of Defense, had worked for Shriver on the presidential campaign in 1960 and on the talent search to staff the Kennedy administration. He had been associated with Paul Ylvisaker at the Ford Foundation and was familiar with community action in its Gray Areas form. On February 2 Shriver invited Yarmolinsky to the first meeting of the task force. Shriver's plan was that he would be the outside man and Yarmolinsky would handle the inside. At the task-force stage, therefore, Yarmolinsky would be responsible for drafting the bill and Shriver's job would be to push it through Congress. Later, when the new agency was established, Shriver would play the public role and Yarmolinsky would administer the program. Since Yarmolinsky would be giving up a "permanent" job at the Pentagon for the uncertainty of becoming deputy director of the poverty agency later, he asked to be made a deputy special assistant to the President. Johnson agreed, but, shortly, Bill Moyers came by to say that the President had changed his mind. Yarmolinsky would be deputy head of the task force and, when the legislation was signed, nominated as deputy director of the administrative agency. Though annoyed, Yarmolinsky did not quit because he knew that Shriver trusted him.

Shriver's style in running the poverty task force was the same as he had used three years earlier in putting the Peace Corps together. He gathered an extraordinary group of people, 137 altogether, during the month and a half the task force existed; he gave them an electric sense of being in on the creation; and he established a mood of excitement and exhilaration that sometimes turned to exhaustion and chaos. One participant called it a "beautiful hysteria." Even the quarters in which they met were consistent with this style:

> The Task Force began its work at the Peace Corps building. Later, it was to move to the old Federal Court of Claims building; then to the basement of the unused Emergency Hospital; then to the New Colonial Hotel; and finally to the newly constructed Brown building. . . . The move from the Court of Claims was forced; one afternoon an engineer notified the planners that there was a crack in the structure (excavation was under way next door), and that everyone had to vacate within two hours. Eighty people, who had crammed into the building on an *ad hoc* basis, went streaming out, arms flowing with folders and papers. . . . The Task Force was [then] implanted in the Emergency Hospital in what had been the basement morgue.

Shriver called the first meeting, a small one, on February 2 in the Peace Corps conference room. He and Yarmolinsky knew only that the Heller-

Gordon team had developed a new approach to the poverty problem and that $500 million had been put in the budget. Schultze outlined the premises: existing government programs were too diffuse. New projects must concentrate on the "neighborhoods" and must be coordinated at the federal, state, and local levels. The primary responsibility must be state and local. Community action was the instrument for the attack on poverty. The experiences of the Committee on Juvenile Delinquency and the Ford Foundation supported these conclusions.

The participants took a break and Shriver and Yarmolinsky adjourned to the men's room. Shriver said, "It'll never fly." Yarmolinsky agreed immediately. The latter wrote later that community action was attractive, but was not sufficiently broad to encompass the many different groups in poverty. Further, it would take at least a year to develop plans, longer in rural areas. "Community action would not be able to produce the kind of concrete results in a foreseeable time period . . . to satisfy the Congress." Thus, it was necessary to make changes to the program in order to yield "visible results" during the first year.

There was another problem. Johnson had told Shriver that he would have $500 million for that year. He phoned an old friend from Yale, Dick Lee, now the mayor of New Haven, to ask how much he would have to spend on community action if he "took the rubber band off the bankroll." Projecting from that city to the nation came to half a billion dollars. Shriver concluded that he could not possibly commit so much to one program. Thus, the appropriation demanded programs beyond community action.

The operation of the task force stretched government procedures. As Shriver put it, "We didn't have any situs, any home, any authority." "If you're not authorized, it's just like being a bastard." Yarmolinsky said there was a "theoretical" budget of $10,000, which was ridiculous. "We operated by borrowing people from government agencies and nongovernment agencies and getting volunteers. We had a lot of people who just worked for free. We borrowed secretaries and we borrowed services." They even snitched stationery from the White House, which got them into trouble.

Shriver, who spent most of his time on the Hill, was present only intermittently. Yarmolinsky was in charge most of the time. They kept the President informed through Moyers, but Johnson showed almost no interest in the task force substantive proposals.

There was a group of more or less regular attendees from departments and agencies with a direct concern for the program: Heller and Capron from CEA, Gordon and Cannon from Budget, Cohen and Harold Horowitz, the associate general counsel, from HEW, Wirtz and his assistant, Daniel Patrick Moynihan, from Labor, Sundquist from Agriculture, Hackett and Boone from Justice, and Interior Secretary Udall, who was responsible for Indian affairs. From time to time experts offered advice on their specialties. Ylvisaker, Mayor Lee, and Sviridoff from New Haven, Governor Sanford of North Carolina, and Mayor John Houlihan of Oakland discussed their experiences with community action. Yarmolinsky brought in experts on logistics from Defense to deal with encampments for the Job Corps. When the thinking had crystallized, Shriver invited Assistant Attorney General Norbert A. Schlei, who was an expert on legislative drafting, to join. He put together a team consisting of Horowitz, two of his own assistants, and a lawyer from Labor. Yarmolinsky and Schlei had been friends at Yale.

Shriver was eager to get new ideas. "Shriver," Yarmolinsky said, "carries around in his head a list of interesting people whom he likes to call on." He invited input from Michael Harrington, author of *The Other America,* Paul Jacobs, a left-leaning champion of the opposite side, and Frank Mankiewicz of the Peace Corps, who had developed community action in Latin America. James Sundquist read their memoranda carefully but was convinced that the task force was reinventing Roosevelt's New Deal. "We had recreated in a single act the CCC, the NYA, the WPA, and the Resettlement Administration." The only superficially new idea was community action, and it was "a new idea only in an organizational sense, not in the program sense." One really new idea, expressed in hundreds of letters, which the task force did not know how to deal with, was to make birth control part of the poverty program.

Inevitably, the Shriver task force addressed only a small aspect of poverty. Although the final budget the President sent up was $962.5 million, it was still less than 9 percent of the estimated cost of eliminating poverty for one year. With Lampman's figures of 33 to 35 million poor people, this meant that the needs of only about 3 million would be addressed. Lyndon Johnson's promise to wage unconditional war on poverty was pie in the sky. Harrington complained to Shriver that "you've been given nickels and dimes for this program." "I don't know about you, Mr. Harrington," Shriver replied, "but this will be my first experience at spending a billion dollars, and I'm quite excited about it."

The President sought to impose another restriction on the program. He wanted to help, as Schultze put it, "the deserving poor" by improving their education, skills, and access to the growing number of jobs in the labor market. He wanted "handups," not "handouts." The government already provided about $15 billion annually in assistance to the poor, through an array of programs to supply either cash assistance or goods and services to those in need. Johnson accepted them reluctantly; for him the operative word was "opportunity." The new law would be called the Economic Opportunity Act. In his message to Congress proposing the legislation he wrote: "The war on poverty is not a struggle to support people, to make them dependent on the generosity of others. It is a struggle to give people a chance. It is an effort to allow them to develop and use their capacities. . . ."

The Shriver task force did not even seriously discuss what Yarmolinsky called "the burning sociological issue" of Oscar Lewis and his culture of poverty except for a few passing references. If Lewis was right, there was probably nothing the government could do for the underclass, those at the very bottom.

As for those the program could help, many were black and lived in urban ghettoes, even though Lampman had estimated that 78 percent of the people in poverty were white. Shriver's probings on the Hill quickly demonstrated that he would need conservative southern votes to pass the bill. Members of Congress from the South would not support heavy assistance to the black poor, particularly those concentrated in the central cities of the North. And once the bill passed, the task force predicted, the rights of poor blacks in the South to access to the program in discriminating towns, counties, and states would have to be protected.

The task force did not foresee the potential conflicts that the encouragement of "maximum feasible participation" by the poor in their cities' community action programs would cause. Shriver thought there might be battles between mayors and the poor aligned together against the "ladies bountiful," that is, the traditional social agencies. But, Yarmolinsky wrote, "the possibility of major conflict between the organized poor and the politicians in city hall was simply not one that anybody worried about."

More serious, no one anticipated that Lyndon Johnson would go into Vietnam the next year and that the real war would destroy the political base for the war on poverty. When Yarmolinsky was asked 16 years later what he would have done differently about poverty, he responded, "I would have called off the war in Vietnam. That's number one." [6]

Yarmolinsky and Schlei crafted a bill with two basic parts for the major programs and a third part consisting of the lesser programs and the administrative features. Title I was called youth programs and consisted of the Job Corps, work-training, and work-study; Title II was the community action programs (CAP); five other titles followed. Of the $962.5 million budgeted, $412.5 million (43 percent) was for youth programs, $315 million (33 percent) for community action, and $235 million (24 percent) for the others.

The Job Corps, which was allotted $190 million, was directed at males aged 16 to 21, that is, those beyond mandatory school age who had not yet found a place in the labor market. A large proportion were out of work, poor, and into drugs and crime. Young women were omitted because they remained in school longer and found jobs more readily. Secretary Wirtz pointed out that male youth unemployment in June 1963 was 21 percent, "the highest point since records have been kept." During 1963 the nation had not created "a single job" for youth. The near future could be worse because "the baby boom is just now rolling into the work force." There would be two Job Corps programs: rural camps—modeled on FDR's extremely successful Civilian Conservation Corps—in which corpsmen would receive basic education and experience in conservation work on public lands, and urban boarding schools—Shriver's idea, from his days as board of education director in Chicago—training centers in which youngsters from the ghetto would be placed into the insulated environment of a "boarding school." They would receive good housing, food, medical care, and, as Shriver put it, "an educational program, with a work component."

There was sharp disagreement within the task force about jurisdiction over the Job Corps. An insider, according to A. H. Raskin, said that "the walls dripped with blood as the empire-builders clashed with the empire-wreckers." Yarmolinsky wanted his "people" in the Department of Defense to handle the logistics. They were "best" at housing, clothing, feeding, training, and moving people, and the military was eager—if reimbursed—to take on the responsibility. But liberals objected to the possible militarization of the program; Shriver and Moyers were opposed; and Congress would not vote for it. The public lands encampments went to the Departments of the Interior and Agriculture and the urban centers were contracted to universities and corporations. Since support by the conservation lobby was considered necessary to pass the law, the proportion of Job Corps centers that would do conservation work, Yarmolinsky said, "was negotiated out very delicately." Both Wirtz and Shriver claimed the Job Corps. The secretary argued that the idea came from the Labor Department bill and that manpower training was already a departmental function. The Job Corps, however, was Shriver's darling because he was convinced that, unlike community action, it would produce quick results for which he wanted to take credit. Shriver, Sundquist said, "was running for vice president, and he wanted to do something that would get him into the limelight."

The work-training program, soon to be called the Neighborhood Youth Corps, was meant for the same age group, but without boarding. Young people would be hired for low-skilled work on projects sponsored by state and local public agencies or those run by private nonprofit organizations (not church-related). Youths would earn income, learn job discipline, and acquire minimal skills. The budget was $150 million. Again, there was a jurisdictional conflict between Labor and the Office of Economic Opportunity, the administrative arm of the poverty program, but here Wirtz won.

The final youth program was work-study in educational institutions. Francis Keppel, the Commissioner of Education, had been trying to get this program through Congress without success. He now asked Shriver to put it into the poverty bill, get it adopted, and then give it to the Office of Education for administration. Shriver readily agreed.

Students from low-income families would work for their schools or other public or nonprofit organizations, but not more than 15 hours a week while classes were in session. The $72.5 million cost would be shared: no more than 90 percent from OEO and at least 10 percent by the institution.

Title II defined a community action program as one which (1) mobilizes public and private resources for an attack on poverty; (2) provides services designed to eliminate poverty; (3) encourages the "maximum feasible partic-ipation" of residents of the poverty area; and (4) is administered by an agency which broadly represents the community. OEO could make a grant of no more than 90 percent of the cost of a program to a CAP. Projects could be in the fields of education, employment, job training, health, voca-tional rehabilitation, housing, home management, welfare, and "other fields." In making grants OEO would consider the incidence of poverty in the community. OEO would receive $315 million for community action.

Title II aroused little disagreement within the task force, perhaps be-cause of the broad language in which it was framed. As Schlei said, "The community action program can take on anything and everything. It absolves you of the necessity of picking and choosing between the problems on which you ought to focus." The origin of the phrase "maximum feasible participation" is unclear. Though it would provoke controversy later, at this stage there was none. Perhaps this was because others shared Yarmolinsky's understanding: "My conception of what it meant was that you involved poor people in the process, not that you put them in charge."

Title III established programs in rural areas that Sundquist and Secre-tary of Agriculture Orville Freeman insisted on; they would appeal politi-cally to southern legislators because rural poverty was heavily concentrated in their region. The title provided for grants of up to $1500 and loans of up to $2500 to low-income families to improve the efficiency of their farms. The grants did not survive the congressional hurdle. There was also a loan program for small agricultural cooperatives.

Title VI established the Office of Economic Opportunity. President Johnson instructed Shriver to put the OEO in the executive office of the President. Good public administration called for placing a line agency else-where and the Bureau of the Budget so argued, but to no avail. Johnson expected the program to be "very controversial" and he wanted Congress to know that he was shielding it from attack by putting it in his personal office. Shriver thought he deserved "extremely high marks" for this display of courage. The director of the OEO was authorized under Title VI to re-cruit Volunteers for America—later Volunteers in Service to America, or VISTA—to work with Indians, migratory workers, residents of the territor-ies, the mentally ill, and the developmentally disabled.[7]

Richard Rovere, Washington correspondent for the *New Yorker,* wrote the President that "he could do nothing better for himself both as a domestic and world leader" than to help the poor. Johnson replied, "I think you are probably right." No probabilities about it. He was absolutely convinced that poverty was a powerful campaign issue as long as he could convince the white middle class that its elimination could be achieved with no sacri-fice on their part. As A. H. Raskin wrote, "Every Johnson campaign speech conjured up visions of slumless cities populated by prosperous, happy, well-educated people. . . ." He not only electioneered for addressing poverty, he also lobbied Congress tirelessly to get the legislation enacted.

The political problem of the poverty bill was to win the support of southern Democrats in both chambers, but particularly the House. The vote shaped up as a standoff between northern Democrats and Republicans. Thus, the South held the balance. The congressional process, therefore, was largely one of wooing Dixie.

Lampman had written that "a politically acceptable program must avoid completely any use of the term 'inequality' or the term '*redistribution of income or wealth.*' " The President must not play Robin Hood by taking from the rich and giving to the poor. Johnson could not have agreed more. No one, he insisted, must be taxed a dime more to pay for the program. When the task force decided to increase the jobs program, it required more money, and a cigarette tax was suggested. Shriver and Yarmolinsky went to a cabinet meeting at the which the former advanced the proposal. "I have never seen a colder reception from the President," Yarmolinsky said. "He just—absolute blank stare—implied without even opening his mouth that . . . we weren't even going to discuss that one." James Reston of the *New York Times* called this Johnsonian logic "the Franklin Delano Hoover twist."

Another basic argument could not be stated directly. This was not a program intended mainly for blacks either in the rural South or in the urban ghettoes of the North. Those who thought that Negroes were shiftless and looking for a handout could sleep peacefully. Poor people would be taught to work and would be given the opportunity to find jobs. The Johnsons made highly publicized visits to the white poor, not to the black ghettoes. Lady Bird journeyed to the anthracite district of eastern Pennsylvania to talk to displaced white miners and their families. The President made a whirlwind tour of five states in Appalachia in one day and repeated it soon afterward. He liked to say that he told Tom Fletcher, an unemployed sawmill worker in eastern Kentucky, the father of eight children, "to keep those kids in school." In a later speech Fletcher's brood had grown to eleven. The poverty program, Yarmolinsky said, "was in no sense a help-the-blacks program, and not only were we saying this, but we didn't think it was."

This effort to divert attention from black poverty did not escape reply. Whitney Young of the Urban League gave the most eloquent testimony presented to the House committee by stressing the plight of the Negro, "a catastrophe, a disaster, and it is fast becoming a national disgrace." The civil rights bill, of course, was important, but it was only part of the solution. Poverty must also be addressed, particularly in the ghettoes. "The demonstrations . . . in the streets today are . . . fostered by despair and hopelessness and those of us who try to represent responsible Negro leadership in this country desperately need some tangible evidence of the intentions of this country to right a historic wrong."

The southern strategy dominated the administration's tactics on the Hill, as was evident in two key events. Shriver achieved a coup: he recruited Phil S. Landrum of Georgia to steer the poverty bill through the House of Representatives. Landrum was a mainline southern conservative; he was a certified racist; and his name was on the 1959 Landrum-Griffin law which organized labor detested. In fact, the President phoned George Meany to head off a labor denunciation of the selection of Landrum. The Georgian accepted in part because his district was becoming more liberal. Yarmolinsky thought the choice "a great stroke . . . . without it the bill might never have become law." The other event was the dumping of Yarmolinsky himself, recounted below, a sacrifice to southern conservatives.

Another tactical problem was keeping Adam Clayton Powell, chairman of both the House Committee on Education and Labor, and the Subcommittee on the War on Poverty Program, reliably at work for the bill. This handsome, expensively dressed Harlem congressman could with some understatement be described as unpredictable. But Powell wanted a $1 million community action grant for Haryou, a juvenile delinquency program for young people in Harlem. When Powell's mind wandered, the administration caught it by warning that Haryou funding depended on passage of the bill. On that the President would not tolerate delay.

The House subcommittee held 20 days of hearings between March 17 and April 28, 1964, that were dominated by supporters of the bill. The administration trotted out its heavy artillery, joined by many members of Congress as well as spokesmen for state and local governments and private organizations. The opposition was sparse—the Chamber of Commerce, the American Farm Bureau Federation, and four Republicans on the Joint Economic Committee who accused the Council of Economic Advisers of exaggerating the number of the poor.

Shriver and Heller opened with a broad justification for the bill. Secretary of Defense McNamara described the need for helping youthful males as an "urgent national problem":

> Each year we examine more than 1 million young men to determine their qualifications for military service. The medical examinations and the mental achievement tests administered to these youth are the same throughout the country. . . .
>
> Early this year an interdepartmental task force reported on the number and characteristics of the young men who were found unqualified for military service. They found that fully one out of three young men do not meet the minimum physical and mental standards. They also found that conditions resulting from poverty were closely related to their failure to qualify. Four out of five of the mentally unqualified had dropped out of school. . . . Many of those failing the medical examination were found to need medical attention but were not receiving it. . . .
>
> Unfortunately, a large proportion of the young men who knock on

our door do not have the basic educational equipment needed to function effectively as a soldier, seaman, or airman in our military forces.

McNamara also pointed out that a number of inactive military installations could be converted into most of the Job Corps conservation camps.

Wirtz, who had been the most independent member of the task force, now closed ranks. "The bill before you represents the unanimous conclusion of the cabinet officers, Mr. Shriver, and the other members of the administration." But he remained committed to jobs. "Our object is not to make poverty more endurable, but to get rid of it. We are therefore concentrating on jobs, and education and training for work. . . ."

The crusty congresswoman from Oregon, Edith Green, was the only female among the 30 members of the Education and Labor Committee. A noted spokesperson for women's rights, she loved to take on men on that issue. She cornered Shriver, demanding to know why the Job Corps was limited to young men. He said that was because males tended to be heads of families and wage earners. But she forced him to admit that many families were fatherless and were supported by women. If she wished, Shriver conceded, they could establish centers for females. She wished, and gave McNamara the same treatment. "Couldn't constructive programs be designed for young women as well as for young men?" "I think," the secretary said, "the simple answer is yes." The department could readily supply installations to permit the training of women. Wirtz and Robert Kennedy needed no prodding. Wirtz testified that the program "must include action that affects women as well as men." The Attorney General agreed. The bill was amended to allow young women to enter the Job Corps.

The church-state issue, which had torpedoed the proposals for federal aid for education, arose in the poverty debate. The administration bill for both work-training and work-study authorized payment for services to private nonprofit organizations, including churches, provided "That no such work shall involve the construction, operation, or maintenance of any facility used or to be used for sectarian instruction or as a place for religious worship." This language did not appear in Title II, community action. Representative Charles E. Goodell, the progressive New York Republican, asked the Attorney General whether it should apply to Title II. Kennedy had no objection and had no problem with a grant to a church so long as it "expended the funds . . . in a nondiscriminatory way, and, therefore, did not discriminate against anyone because of his religion."

This did not satisfy the Roman Catholic Church. Yarmolinsky, therefore, drafted an amendment to Title II which he called noncurricular education, that the subcommittee accepted. Grants could be made for community action programs which involved churches or church-related organizations, but they must be offered without discrimination and could not include sectarian instruction or religious worship. Aid to elementary and secondary schools of all types, however, was explicitly prohibited.

An issue which arose peripherally during the House hearings, not addressed by either the task force or the committee, was a program for disadvantaged preschoolers, later called Head Start. Again, Congresswoman Green was the point lady and she went after Commissioner of Education Francis Keppel. The bill, she noted, was addressed to those 16 and older. "Are we not dreaming," she asked, "that we can really change attitudes and get people motivated and equip them with employable skills if we only begin at this age 16 level?" Keppel said, "You are quite right that educationally the effort . . . must start at a younger age." But nothing was done in 1964.

The Committee on Education and Labor reported the poverty bill favorably on a straight party-line vote on June 3, 1964. Johnson held all the Democrats; the Republicans would not give him a big victory before the election without a contest.

The Senate Select Subcommittee on Poverty held brief hearings on four days between June 17 and 25. Again, the proponents were in firm control and the committee reported the bill with partisan lines holding firm.

There was a close vote in the Rules Committee on July 28. The eight who voted out a rule were all Democrats; the seven opposed consisted of five Republicans and the two southern reactionary racists, Smith of Virginia and William Colmer of Mississippi.

The Senate seemed in the bag. On July 16 Shriver had given the President a head count: "I am estimating a total of sixty-seven votes for the bill." Nevertheless, the Republicans and the very conservative southern Democrats tried to win over the other southerners. On July 22, the proponents took the ball away from them with an amendment by Democrat George Smathers of Florida which applied exclusively to the Job Corps. No camp or training center could be established in a state unless the proposal was submitted to its governor in advance and he did not disapprove of it within 30 days. The Smathers amendment was adopted without debate.

But on July 23 Republican Winston Prouty of Vermont introduced another amendment which would forbid any assistance to a community action program in any state "without the prior approval of the Governor." Russell had drafted the language in order, he said, to preserve states' rights. The amendment went down to defeat 46 to 45. The Senate then adopted the poverty bill by the overwhelming vote of 61 to 34, six votes shy of Shriver's forecast.

The House was far more complicated and its proceedings were soiled by the Yarmolinsky affair. He was certainly vulnerable to a smear campaign. If one wrote an espionage novel and named the chief Soviet spy Adam Yarmolinsky, no reader would find it amiss. A quarter of a century earlier, according to A. H. Raskin, he had attended leftist rallies as a school-boy. More recently General Edwin Walker, the right-wing extremist, had attacked him. There had been charges that his mother was a Communist poet. "His mother happened to be a poet," Norbert Schlei said, "but the charges about her politics were (a) false, and (b) amazingly irrelevant. . . ." Yarmolinsky himself was strongly anti-Communist and supported a tough anti-Soviet line in the Cold War.

Nevertheless, a group of congressmen from the Carolinas, led by Harold D. Cooley of North Carolina, chairman of the Agriculture Committee, decided to destroy Yarmolinsky as the price for their votes on the poverty bill. Several motives have been suggested. One was that he was the "architect" of the Defense Department's racial integration policy. This was partly true. While McNamara and Cyrus Vance were ultimately responsible for that policy, Yarmolinsky pushed it and had hired Alfred B. Fitt, the deputy assistant secretary (civil rights), and Fitt reported to him. Another motive, in Shriver's words, was that these congressmen were "anti-Jewish and . . . anti-liberal and . . . anti-anybody named Yarmolinsky. It was just real, lowdown racial bigotry and political venom. . . ."

The vote in the House was delayed by the Republican National Convention, which nominated Barry Goldwater for President on July 16. Judge Smith refused to issue a rule for consideration of the bill until after the close of the convention, which annoyed the President. He wanted the Democratic leadership to have a vote on July 20. But it was not to be.

O'Brien wrote the President on July 31 that he counted 195 Democrats and 8 Republicans in favor, 203 of the needed 218. Those in doubt from whom he hoped to get the other 15 votes totaled 47. But Halleck refused to concede. He was visiting every Republican in the House (with Shriver at his heels) telling "his boys" that "a vote for the poverty bill is a vote against the party."

House debate was scheduled to open on August 7. According to Evans and Novak, Shriver was called before a "kangaroo court" in Speaker McCormack's office on August 6. Aside from the speaker, those present included the House Democratic whips, Landrum, Cooley, and other Carolina congressmen. Cooley told Shriver that eight representatives from the Carolinas would not vote for the bill unless Yarmolinsky was dumped. The whips said that the bill would not pass without these southern votes.

While the President had suggested that Shriver would head the OEO, he had not agreed to do so. In fact, he did not want to be the director, much preferring to remain with the Peace Corps. He told this to Cooley and company. He also said, "Adam Yarmolinsky is an extremely competent person. I think he would be great in the program. But I do not have the right to put him in or put him out. . . .That's for the President to say."

They told him to phone Johnson. The President said, "You tell them that you won't recommend that I appoint him." Shriver said he could not do so because Yarmolinsky was his friend and was being attacked by bigots. Johnson told him to say that the President would act "in his own judgment" and that no one's recommendation would be controlling. Shriver tried it, but it was not acceptable. They wanted an "assurance" that Yarmolinsky would not be named.

Shriver phoned again and Johnson told him what to say. According to Evans and Novak, he said, "The President has no objection to my saying that if I were appointed I would not recommend Yarmolinsky." That did it.

Shriver recalled, "That was the most unpleasant experience I ever had in the government of the United States. . . . I felt . . . as if I ought to just go out and vomit." He returned to the task force office and told Yarmolinsky that he would not be deputy director of the OEO. "It was a question of whether we have this bill and the benefits which it will bring to hundreds of thousands or maybe millions of poor people, or you." In fact, Yarmolinsky learned more about what had happened from the Evans and Novak newspaper columns published on August 11 and 12, 1964.

Debate on August 7 opened innocently with a typical motion by Howard Smith to delete the enacting clause of the poverty bill. It went down to defeat 225 to 197. One wonders whether those eight southern votes were needed.

Conservative Republican W. H. Ayres of Ohio then stated that Yarmolinsky "is the man who is really running this show under Sargent Shriver." Landrum cut him off: "So far as I am concerned, this gentleman, Mr. Yarmolinsky, will have absolutely nothing to do with the program. And, second, I wish to state that not only will he not be appointed, but that he will not be considered if he is recommended for a place in this agency."

Landrum then turned to the bill and said it was "the most conservative I've ever seen." This was because it would take people off welfare and make them "taxpayers instead of taxeaters." In the vote on August 8 the House increased the margin of victory to 226 to 185. The majority consisted of 204 Democrats and 22 Republicans, the minority of 145 Republicans and 40 Democrats. The northern Democrats voted 144 to 0 for the poverty bill, the southerners 60 to 40 against. Evans and Novak wrote, "The eight votes from the Carolinas were superfluous. The sacrifice of Adam Yarmolinsky was unnecessary." On August 11 the Senate accepted the House version of the bill by voice vote.

At the President's press conference on August 8 a reporter raised the question of Yarmolinsky, starting to say that "he had been with the Department of Defense. . . ." Johnson interrupted, "He still is." The reporter thought he had been "working for the Peace Corps and working on the poverty bill." "No," the President said, "your thoughts are wrong. He is still with the Department of Defense." This was technically true in that

Yarmolinsky was not with the Peace Corps, but inferentially false in that he had been working on the poverty program.[8]

President Johnson signed the Economic Opportunity Act in the Rose Garden on August 24, 1964. His address, broadcast over television and radio, sounded like a campaign speech, which, in fact, it was. His eye was fixed on the election and he did not bother to discuss what had been accomplished. When Shriver was sworn in as director of the OEO on October 16, the President's remarks merely rambled about.

Johnson does not seem to have been much interested in his new law. Yarmolinsky said he talked about it "endlessly," "but in an impressionistic way. . . . Poverty is a bad thing, let's get rid of it, it was just about as simple as that." As Sundquist correctly perceived, administration of the program was going to be critically important. But the President thought "administration would take care of itself," and, in any case, that was Shriver's job. However, Sundquist said, "Shriver certainly had no interest," and his administrator, Yarmolinsky, had been dumped. It is unlikely that any member of Congress really understood the complications of the new law. Hackett was convinced that Shriver never did get community action straight. Kermit Gordon was persuaded that the "experts" at CEA and the Bureau of the Budget knew very little about poverty.

This general state of ignorance emerged in part from the fact that there was no consensus on the definitions of poverty and of a poor person. Lampman had done what he could with imperfect data and had been forced to make many arbitrary assumptions. Furthermore, as Lampman had stressed in the poverty chapter of the *Economic Report,* "Poverty . . . has many faces." Dealing with it would be a challenge of extraordinary complexity.

This was reflected in the administrative system set up by the Economic Opportunity Act. The OEO was not a department and was not a regular administrative agency. Rather, as the President insisted over the objection of the Bureau of the Budget, it was placed in his executive office.

Here Shriver, already encumbered by the Peace Corps, was supposed to coordinate and administer an extremely bizarre organization. Unlike other executive agencies, it had direct operating responsibilities for the urban Job Corps, the Community Action Program, VISTA, and migrant workers. The Labor Department ran the Neighborhood Youth Corps. Agriculture operated some Job Corps conservation centers and rural loans. Interior handled most of the other conservation centers. HEW was responsible for adult basic education and work experience, the Small Business Administration for small loans. There were many jurisdictional disputes between these agencies. With the stress on local control, regionalization was necessary, but a rational attempt to match the geographic boundaries used by Labor and HEW failed. The OEO established seven regional offices. Community action regionalized quickly, but the Job Corps and VISTA held back. While the framers of the statute thought the states would be of little importance, they actually became significant, in part because of the governor's veto. Community action had no choice but to function locally and this was supported by the "maximum feasible participation" standard in the law. Where blacks were involved, as in several major cities in the North as well as in the South, there was a sharp challenge by mayors. The loss of Yarmolinsky was felt keenly. In fact, the OEO did not get a "permanent" deputy director until Bertrand M. Harding took the job in June 1966.

John R. Commons at the University of Wisconsin had taught his students, including Wilbur Cohen, that a bad law well administered was better than a good law poorly administered. The conclusion Cohen had drawn was: keep it simple. He was critical of those who put together the Economic Opportunity Act. They "tried to do too much at one time." Yarmolinsky in 1980 agreed. He thought there were programs that would work with small numbers of people that could not work with large numbers. "I won't say I'm pessimistic, but I guess I am because if I were in complete charge I don't know what I'd do."

Despite these defects, President Johnson, Shriver's task force, and the Congress deserve an accolade for their accomplishment: the Economic Opportunity Act of 1964 was, truly, a noble experiment. No other nation, even Britain, had confronted the formidable problem of poverty so squarely. As Secretary Wirtz said,

> The purpose of government in a democracy must be indistinguishable from the purpose of those who are its members. To the extent that our lives as individuals find their meaning in what we can add to the lives of others, a program to fight poverty is the embodiment of the central idea of this system of government. The text for this bill could be: Inasmuch as ye have done it unto one of the least of these, my brethren, ye have done it unto me.

Henry Mayhew, Charles Booth, and Charles Dickens would have raised their glasses to wish the Office of Economic Opportunity Godspeed.[9]

II

LYNDON JOHNSON—"THE GREAT, FABULOUS 89TH CONGRESS"

5

Prelude:
The 1964 Election

THE Republican party had an identity crisis. It did not know who it was. This was caused by the unease and frustration growing out of both defeat and internal division. Jud Morhouse, the chairman of the New York State party, in 1962 referred to "the lethargic and amorphous slough of defeat and despair to which the Republican party has fallen."

Of the preceding eight presidential elections, the GOP had won two—1952 and 1956—and those Eisenhower victories from the viewpoint of the party were tarnished. No one believed that Dwight Eisenhower was both a national hero *and* a confirmed Republican. He had beaten out Robert A. Taft, "Mr. Republican," for the nomination in 1952. It was no secret that he was bored with partisan politics. Anyone with half an eye could see that Eisenhower had himself won in 1952 and 1956 and had not done very well in dragging the party after him. Nixon had then lost to Kennedy in 1960 by a razor-thin edge. "His defeat," dedicated Republican William A. Rusher wrote, "seemed to tell the world that the GOP, without some charismatic national hero like Eisenhower at its head, was still a born loser."

The congressional performance was even more dismal. Of the elections between 1932 and 1962, the Republicans had won two—1946 and 1952. In each year they captured both houses of Congress. But the Democrats took them back in 1948 and 1954. Thus, of the 30 years in this span of time, the GOP had control of Congress for four. The situation in the states was even less encouraging.

The split between the left and right wings of the Republican party could be traced back to 1912 when Teddy Roosevelt walked out to form the Progressive (Bull Moose) party, leaving the conservative shell to William Howard Taft. In the late fifties the wound bled profusely. Governor Nelson

117

Rockefeller led the liberal wing for the nomination with a progressive platform on both international and domestic issues. Senator Barry Goldwater of Arizona was the leading conservative spokesman. Nixon played the role of centrist, bridging the gap between these extremes at least long enough to insure his own nomination. But the span collapsed after his defeat.

The split had a regional dimension. The progressive East, particularly New York, confronted the conservative West, formerly led by Ohio, but later shifting farther west. New York controlled the presidential nominations between 1940 and 1956—Wendell Willkie in 1940, Thomas Dewey in 1944 and 1948, Dwight Eisenhower in 1952 (engineered by Dewey) and 1956. The losers were Ohio's Governor John Bricker in 1944 and Senator Robert Taft in 1948 and 1952. This was far more than a contest of personalities; it was a conflict over fundamental strategy. The easterners, conceding the South to the Democrats, argued that Republicans could not win with their historic base in the West. They must add New York, Pennsylvania, Massachusetts, and the smaller states of the Northeast. The western theory was that the nation had become homogenized after World War II, that the South was now ripe for the picking. Thus, an alliance between the South and the West would insure victory. Goldwater said, "Sometimes I think this country would be better off if we could just saw off the Eastern Seaboard and let it float out to sea."

The deep division within the party created splinter groups, the most important being the emergence in the fifties of a full-dress conservative movement, called the "new conservatism." Those on the right with intellectual pretensions had long suffered from an inferiority complex, the suspicion that the political theory on which they rested their case had no merit. In the nineteenth century John Stuart Mill had called conservatives the "stupid party." More relevant now, in 1950 the liberal critic Lionel Trilling had written:

> In the United States at this time liberalism is not only the dominant but even the sole intellectual tradition. For it is the plain fact that nowadays there are no conservative or reactionary ideas in general circulation. This does not mean, of course, that there is no impulse to conservatism or to reaction. Such impulses are certainly very strong, perhaps even stronger than most of us know. But the conservative impulse and the reactionary impulse do not, with some isolated and some ecclesiastical exceptions, express themselves in ideas but only in action or in irritable mental gestures which seem to resemble ideas.

The modest number of liberals who read Trilling shrugged. For the new conservatives, however, this criticism was a knife in the heart.

Thus, during the fifties they erected an intellectual edifice. A group headed by William F. Buckley, Jr., launched the *National Review,* a journal of opinion, in 1955. Buckley had a knack for attracting public attention. He did so upon his graduation from Yale by attacking his alma mater, particularly its faculty, for teaching what he considered radical ideas. With his charm, quick wit, and vaguely British accent, he became a modest celebrity as a conservative commentator on television. This did no harm to his journal's circulation. Russell Kirk started the quarterly *Modern Age: A Conservative Review* in 1957. A sometime professor, Kirk became the most obstinate of reactionaries. His style was the opposite of Buckley's: academic, highfalutin, humorless, turgid, and dour, indeed, pessimistic. Henry Regnery, the publisher in Chicago, brought out a small torrent of conservative books and tracts.

More important, the new conservatives framed an agenda of three fundamental issues, which they defined and refined to their own satisfaction, if not always to the comprehension of others. Each was keyed to an important book.

The first doctrine of the new conservatives was dedication to a free market economy cleansed of any government intervention. In September 1960, 90 approximately youthful activists met at Great Elm, the Buckley estate in Sharon, Connecticut, to form a new organization they called Young Americans for Freedom (YAFs). (Youth is relative. One of the YAFs, who felt the weight of his years, noted to several others of his vintage that they were Old Americans for Freedom, or OAFS.) The YAFs adopted the Sharon Statement, a succinct and emphatic set of principles which proved that one need not be a liberal to write well, though it probably helped. As the statement put it, the "eternal truths" that expressed the first doctrine read as follows:

> That liberty is indivisible, and that political freedom cannot long exist without economic freedom. That the market economy, allocating resources by the free play of supply and demand, is the single economic system compatible with the requirements of personal freedom and constitutional government, and that it is at the same time the most productive supplier of human needs. That when government interferes with the work of the market economy, it tends to reduce the moral and physical strength of the nation; that when it takes from one man to bestow on another, it diminishes the incentive of the first, and integrity of the second, and the moral autonomy of both.

The book which expressed these ideas most forcefully was Friedrich A. Hayek's *The Road to Serfdom* (1944). The author was a very conservative Austrian economist of the very conservative Austrian school. Hayek had left Vienna in crisis in 1931, had observed the rise of Hitler with dread from his position at the London School of Economics, and had written his tract from embattled Britain during the war. He abhorred totalitarianism and equated it with planning and collectivism. He insisted that democratic socialism was a contradiction in terms, that state control led inevitably to the destruction of freedom and ineluctably to a latter-day serfdom.

The second new conservative doctrine was to struggle against Communism both at home and abroad. The Sharon Statement's "eternal truths" put it this way:

> That we will be free only so long as the national sovereignty of the United States is secure; that history shows periods of freedom are rare and can exist only when free citizens concertedly defend their rights against all enemies, that the forces of international Communism are, at present, the greatest single threat to their liberties. That the United States should stress victory over, rather than coexistence with this menace.

A basic problem with these verities was that conservatives, old as well as new, never bothered to define Communism. If limited to the Soviet Union and the U.S. Communist party (assuming one could find it), there was little confusion. But many conservatives insisted, like Hayek, on broadening the definition. Thus, there was little difference between Soviet Communism and the British and Swedish welfare states, or, closer to home, FDR's New Deal, JFK's New Frontier, and LBJ's Great Society, on the one hand, and, on the other, the American Communist party. Even more bothersome, Robert Welch, the founder and leader of the extremely conservative John Birch Society, declared that President Eisenhower was "a conscious articulate instrument of the Soviet conspiracy." While Welch was indubitably a new conservative, this statement caused endless trouble for the official movement, not least for Buckley.

The book that spoke to this issue was the autobiography of Whittaker Chambers, *Witness,* published in 1952. Chambers was a former member of the C.P. and a courier for Soviet intelligence who had offered the decisive testimony that had led to the conviction of Alger Hiss for perjury. He was one of many former members who deserted the party, became witnesses against it, and allied themselves with new conservatism. Chambers was unusual among them in that he knew more about Communism and was an excellent writer.

The third new conservative nest of doctrines was a loose collection of historical ideas expressed by Russell Kirk in his book *The Conservative Mind,* published in 1953. It seems to have been required reading for new conservatives. Since it was pretty deep stuff, it is unlikely that many got much beyond Kirk's "six canons of conservative thought" on pages 7 and 8.

Kirk was an intellectual extremist who made Buckley look like a liberal. The richer among the new conservatives, doubtless, enjoyed driving about in expensive motor cars. Kirk, however, despite the fact that he was born and raised in Michigan, would abolish the automobile. He sometimes seemed to be a refugee from a medieval monastery. Society, he wrote, was ruled by a "divine intent," and politics was at bottom religion and morality. He adored the "mystery of traditional life." A civilized society required "orders and classes." Edmund Burke, the champion of order, was his hero. But he called himself a "Bohemian Tory," which would have caused Burke to cringe. Whether a monk or a Tory, or, for that matter, both, Russell Kirk was not the kind of man one would turn to if practical decisions were to be made.

The new conservatives spoke and wrote in two different tongues. One, used for public discourse, was heated, charged, laced with the language of struggle between the forces of good and the forces of evil as though addressed to a revival meeting. The other was a medium for transacting business, what one would expect college-educated Americans who had done well in business or the professions to use in getting through the day. It was also a way of distinguishing themselves from the "extremists" who shared many of the same ideas—right-wingers who resorted to violence and Birchers who seemed to reside on some remote planet.

The first of these languages of the new conservatives, and, even more, of Hayek, Chambers, and Kirk, was in a key not often heard in American political discourse. It was dark, morose, somber, often apocalyptic with Armageddon looming over the brow of a nearby hill. A satanic force, a sophisticated evil conspiracy, lay in the weeds ready to pounce on innocent America. The cherished liberties of a free people hung precariously in the balance. Though time was running out, there was just enough left to mobilize the patriots to attack the mortal enemy before he struck. Thus, the speaker or the writer rang the tocsin to arouse the defenders of freedom.

This sounded like political paranoia and that is exactly what Richard Hofstadter called it in a notable essay, "The Paranoid Style in American Politics." Conspiracy became the driving force of history. It might be the New Deal or the New Frontier; it certainly was Communism. "The central image," Hofstadter wrote, "is that of a vast and sinister conspiracy, a gigantic and yet subtle machinery of influence set in motion to undermine and destroy a way of life."

When three new conservatives, F. Clifton White, William A. Rusher, and John Ashbrook, met for lunch at the University Club in New York on September 7, 1961, they did not speak the language of Armageddon. Rather, they spoke the hard tongue of business and their business was to launch a real conspiracy to take over the Republican party. White was from upstate New York, had been a lead navigator on B-17s during the war, had taught briefly at Cornell, and had then been active in Republican politics and had become a skilled political mechanic. Rusher, also from New York, had served in Air Force administration in India, had attended Princeton and the Harvard Law School, had practiced law on Wall Street, and was the publisher of *National Review*. John Ashbrook had been educated at Harvard and the Ohio State Law School, had been chairman of the Young Republicans, and was now a congressman from Ohio. Methodical, he kept the Young Republican files in good shape.

These three talked all afternoon and long into the evening and agreed on the western strategy. They felt that the Republican apparatus had atrophied. As Rusher wrote, "The party had not a single leader of truly national dimensions. Eisenhower had retired; Nixon had been discredited by his defeat; Goldwater was the spokesman of what seemed a very narrow segment of opinion; and Rockefeller was the victim of the animosities his liberalism had created." A dedicated small group, they agreed, could take over the party's moribund machinery. This would require a candidate and the arrow pointed straight at the junior senator from Arizona.[1]

Michael Goldwasser, one of twenty-two children in a Polish Jewish family, fled Tsarist Russia about 1837 and settled in London, where he lived with his younger brother Joseph. The men became excited about the California gold rush and decided to try their luck, but as merchants, not as miners. The brothers reached San Francisco in November 1852, and later opened a store in Los Angeles. They anglicized their name to Goldwater.

By the late fifties the brothers operated stores in half a dozen towns with the headquarters in Prescott, the capital of the new Arizona territory. In 1877 Michael turned over management of the Arizona properties to his sons, Morris and Henry, and joined the rest of the family in San Francisco. In 1882 his son Baron moved to Prescott to work in the store. He reckoned that future growth would take place in Phoenix in the new farming area. In 1896 he opened M. Goldwater & Sons there and oversaw its development into Arizona's leading department store.

In 1903 Josephine Williams, a nurse, moved from Chicago to dry Phoenix for relief from tuberculosis. Baron married her in an Episcopal ceremony in 1907 and they had three children. They named the first, born on January 1, 1909, Barry Morris Goldwater. His education began in the Phoenix public schools, but, he wrote later, "My first year in high school . . . was not a scholastic success." The principal "diplomatically" informed Baron that his son would do better in a private school. He was shipped off to Staunton Military Academy in Virginia. Goldwater instantly fell in love with the military life, was a great success, and was encouraged to go on to West Point. But his father was ill and his mother wanted him nearby. He enrolled at the University of Arizona in Tucson in 1928, but it was not to be an enduring relationship. He quit before the year was over, he later wrote, because "I could see [that] I'd probably be the next twenty years getting out."

Goldwater went into the Phoenix store as a junior clerk and moved up to president in 1937. While he seems never to have been seduced by the romance of retailing, both he and store prospered. After the war he invented

"Antsy Pants," in Richard Rovere's immortal words, "underdrawers with red ants rampant."

He was baptized and brought up in the Episcopal Church, though he seems not to have been much of a churchgoer. He married Margaret Johnson of Muncie, Indiana, and raised four children. He was a good athlete, sat well in the saddle, loved the desert, and was devoted to the Arizona Indians. He was an addicted hobbyist—photography, sports cars, short-wave radio, and electronic devices, such as one that raised and lowered the flag outside his house by the sunrise and sunset.

But his big passion was flying, particularly military aircraft. In 1932 he had tried to get into the Air Corps, but was rejected for substandard vision. He spent much of World War II, along with other overage pilots, in the Ferry Command delivering supplies. Later he flew single engine P-47 Thunderbolts across the North Atlantic to Britain.

"Any pilot can describe the mechanics of flying," he wrote. "What it can do for the spirit of man is beyond description." This is probably the key to the real Barry Goldwater, and his bid for the presidency.

Goldwater was a very attractive person. He was stunningly handsome as a young man and aged gracefully. He was so good-looking, Hubert Humphrey said, that he got a movie contract with Eighteenth Century-Fox. He was friendly, gallant, courageous, without vanity, and had an "Aw shucks" western simplicity and integrity that were hard to resist. In thinly populated Arizona, where every voter either knew him or wished that he did, Goldwater was an unbeatable candidate. In 1952, with some help from Eisenhower, he upset Ernest McFarland, the Senate majority leader, by 7000 votes. In 1958, the year of the Democratic landslide, he again whipped McFarland, now governor, this time by 35,000 votes. Even in 1964 he would manage to hold onto Arizona by a slim margin.

But Goldwater had a serious defect: he was not very bright. "You know," he admitted to the newspaperman Stewart Alsop, "I haven't really got a first-class brain." When he got no response after reading to the Missus and a couple of her friends a speech he was going to make, "I said, what the hell is the matter, and Peggy said, look, this is a sophisticated audience, they're not a lot of lame-brains like you, they don't spend their time looking at TV westerns. You can't give them that corn." John and Robert Kennedy agreed with the Goldwaters. As RFK said, "He was not a very smart man. He's just going to destroy himself." President Kennedy was concerned that he would do so before he got the nomination and urged Walter Lippmann, who had written a column in 1963 that savaged Goldwater, to hold off. There is every reason to believe that Lyndon Johnson, who knew the members of the Senate extremely well, shared this estimate.

Though Goldwater said that he revered the framers of the Constitution and the great document they crafted, he had the odd habit of amending it to suit his own style and prejudices. He stated, for example, that the federal government could not compel white schools to admit black children because "education is one of the powers reserved to the states by the Tenth Amendment." This was a doctrine long since rejected by the Supreme Court.

Goldwater said, "My aim is not to pass laws but to repeal them." Article I of the Constitution creates a Congress with a House of Representatives and a Senate for the specific purpose of enacting laws. But as a senator Goldwater behaved as though the Senate lacked this power. He had virtually no interest in legislation except to oppose it. His name was on no law.

In fact, he spent most of his time campaigning, not so much for himself as for other Republican candidates. During the fifties he devoted an enormous amount of time and energy to his role as chairman of the Republican Senatorial Campaign Committee. He was constantly on the road making speeches to party groups. He boasted that he logged a million miles and made thousands of speeches. He preached new conservative doctrines, even invoking Edmund Burke, to the already converted and they lapped it up. In 1960 his name, followed by "the leading conservative thinker in American public life," appeared over a column published thrice weekly by the Los Angeles *Times* and soon syndicated to 162 other papers. "His" book, *The Conscience of a Conservative,* actually written by Buckley's brother-in-law, L. Brent Bozell, was published in 1960 and within a few years sold 3.5 million copies. The campaign job, Goldwater wrote, "resulted in my exposure to grass-roots Republicans, and, I believe, ultimately made me the Republican nominee in 1964."

If Goldwater was actually running for President while he did this campaigning, he was ill-advised to do so. He came from a state with only five electoral votes. "My life style," he later wrote, "is casual, informal, spontaneous." If elected, he would become a "prisoner in the White House." He did not want to surrender his privacy. He recognized his own mental shortcomings. Goldwater was "terrified" at confronting a Democratic Congress and the intransigence of the "bureaucratic overlords." He was reasonably certain that Kennedy would defeat him and, after the assassination, was convinced that he had no chance. Lyndon Johnson, whom he detested, would use every dirty trick in the pack and would campaign with "hate." While all this was probably true, there is little question that he had been bitten by the presidential bug and that the sting refused to go away. Or as Goldwater preferred to put it, millions of "dedicated Americans" demanded that he run and he felt that he could not let them down.

Rovere, who observed the senator closely over time, concluded that "there *are* two Goldwaters." It seems to have been his attitude toward the presidency: he coveted it and at the same time feared it.[2]

White, Rusher, and Ashbrook called 22 carefully selected conservatives from 16 states to a secret meeting at the Avenue Motel in Chicago on October 8, 1961. They agreed that the Republican party must become a powerful conservative force in U.S. politics in order to save the republic. Several wanted to announce for Goldwater in 1964 immediately. White said that it was too early to endorse a candidate, but he was authorized to inform the senator.

He reported to Goldwater on November 17 that the Chicago group would set up an "organizational vehicle." Goldwater said this was the "best thing I've heard of since I became active in the Republican Party on the national scene." He wished White luck and they agreed to keep in touch.

A somewhat larger group held a second meeting in Chicago on December 10. By now White was firmly in control and the movement, which had no name, was called after him. They adopted a budget, largely for an office and salary for White, divided the nation into nine regions, and devised a strategy for selecting conservative delegates to the 1964 convention. White rented Suite 3505 in the Chanin Building at the corner of Forty-second Street and Lexington Avenue in New York, and "3505" became the cover name for the group and, later, the title of his book. He stumped the country with considerable success to urge conservative Republicans to organize. He occasionally dropped into Goldwater's office to report on the new "groundswell."

Shortly after Nixon's defeat in 1960 Governor Rockefeller sought to make up to Goldwater. "Rockefeller," as White put it, "was the ardent suitor in this strange misalliance, but Goldwater was by no means the reluctant bride." They met regularly to discuss party politics. They agreed on two basic points: a strong distaste for Richard Nixon and the need to unite the party for the 1964 presidential election. Since each had the image of a party splitter, both hoped to appear as unifiers. The New Yorker also had modest success in persuading Goldwater that he was really more conservative than his reputation. The 1962 elections helped the relationship. Rockefeller was reelected governor of New York and Nixon was defeated by Pat Brown as governor of California.

With Nixon gone and Goldwater partly neutralized, Rockefeller seemed to have a clear shot at the nomination. But in late 1962 and early 1963 two events torpedoed the Rockefeller candidacy.

On October 18, 1962, White had called the next gathering of 3505 for the first weekend in December. "This meeting," he wrote, "will determine where we go—whether we are serious or dilettantes." He was now convinced that 3505 must have a candidate and that Goldwater was the man. He met the senator in the Presidential Suite at the new Americana Hotel in New York on November 12, a few days after the election. White had methodically prepared a huge briefing book containing an organizational chart by state, a budget, a timetable for state conventions and primaries in 1964, and his estimate of how many delegates they would win. This was not a paper performance; the apparatus was already in place. Goldwater was impressed. White said that he had an attractive job offer and was tempted to take it. Goldwater put his arm around White's shoulder and said, "Clif, if I didn't have to worry about anybody else I deal with in politics any more than I worry about you, I'd have a pretty pleasant life." White's conclusions: Goldwater had done nothing to discourage him and had left a "reasonably definite indication" that he would run. When White got home he told his wife that he would turn down the job offer.

The Chicago meeting was scheduled for December 2. The evening before a nervous White met those who arrived early to propose that they become a "draft Goldwater" movement provided he agreed. This group, like the larger one the next day, was extremely conservative, detested Rockefeller, and endorsed the proposal enthusiastically. White outlined an enormous organizational expansion with requisite budget. He made optimistic forecasts for both the convention and the election based on the western strategy. They agreed to come out of the closet on March 15, 1963.

But on December 3 the Associated Press unmasked 3505, reporting that the Chicago meeting aimed to draft Goldwater and stop Rockefeller. That evening CBS News was on the scene. In Phoenix Goldwater made a noncommittal remark. In fact, White was pleased to be out in the open.

His problem now was to deal with the two Goldwaters. On January 14 the senator said, "Clif, I'm not a candidate. And I'm not going to be." White replied that they planned to draft him anyway. "Draft nothin'," Goldwater snorted, "Don't paint me into a corner. It's my political neck. . . ."

White was serious. On April 8, 3505 announced formation of the National Draft Goldwater Committee. White rented P.O. Box 1964 in Washington. His group sighed with relief when an ambivalent Goldwater said, "I am not taking any position on this draft movement. It's their time and their money. But they are going to have to get along without any help from me." As the support came in, Goldwater weakened. Within a few days he told the *New York Times*, "A man would be a damn fool to predict with finality what he would do in this unpredictable world."

Thus, Rockefeller found Goldwater gaining on him in organization and in the polls. As if this were not trouble enough, he proceeded to shoot himself in the foot. In 1961 he had divorced his wife. While there were rumors of another woman, the event stirred little public interest. In April 1963 Margaretta ("Happy") Murphy divorced her husband, Dr. James S. Murphy of Philadelphia.

On May 4, according to Robert Novak, the phone rang in the Goldwater apartment in Washington. The senator was on the roof trying to fix his TV aerial. Mrs. Goldwater answered. A voice said, "Hello, this is Nelson Rockefeller." Thinking this a joke, she said, "Well, hello yourself, this is Mamie Eisenhower." He convinced her that he was really Rockefeller and she called Goldwater down. Rockefeller said he wanted the senator to know before it broke in the press: he had just married Happy Murphy. Goldwater was stunned because he realized that Rockefeller had destroyed his candidacy. He stammered out congratulations and hung up. Within a few days a Gallup poll showed that 14 points had switched from Rockefeller to Goldwater, who now led 40 to 29.

The Goldwater movement grew steadily during the summer and fall of 1963, and White concluded that the nomination was in the bag. But the Kennedy assassination on November 22 seemed to cut off the bottom. There was a widely held rumor that right-wingers had murdered the President. Since this was false, the more important fact was that Johnson's candidacy transformed the Republican strategic problem. The assumption that Goldwater would carry the South now must face up to running against a southerner who would almost certainly capture the big prize of Texas. Further, moderate Republicans who thought that Kennedy had been a shoo-in in the Northeast now felt that Rockefeller had a good chance against Johnson there.

Goldwater became certain that he would lose and fell into a mood that White described as "approaching deep depression." On December 8 he met with close friends and advisers and told them, "Our cause is lost," and that he would withdraw from the race. They refused to accept his decision and insisted he had a duty to lead the conservative cause, even if it resulted in defeat. Goldwater was deeply shaken and asked for time to think it over. He soon changed his mind.

On January 3 Goldwater, following surgery for a painful foot spur, hobbled on crutches onto the patio of his home in the Phoenix suburb of Scottsdale to face the press. He said, "I will seek the Republican Presidential nomination." The reason he gave was based on a fateful strategy: he would run on his principles. He would not curry favor with the moderates by posing as a "me-too" Republican. The resonant line was, "I will offer a choice, not an echo." Since he was sincere, he would divide rather than unite his party.

Goldwater made another early critical decision, to put management of the campaign in the hands of his home state friends, the so-called Arizona Mafia, and to freeze out the Draft Goldwater leadership, particularly Clifton White. He did this, he wrote later, because he felt "more comfortable" with his old pals—Denison Kitchel, Dean Burch, Richard Kleindienst, and others. Since these people were innocent of national campaigning and White was a genuine professional, this was, as Goldwater would admit, "a serious error on my part." "Clif White," Novak wrote, "came close to quitting more than once—mainly because he now had no authority, partly because of the confusion and uncertainty."

The fact that Goldwater's painful heel was supported by a cast was symptomatic of the wrong foot on which his campaign began. A fundamental problem that should have given any Republican candidate pause was that the polls showed that Johnson would beat any of them 70 to 30.

Goldwater's rookie managers started disastrously and got steadily worse. Kitchel seemed to have no idea of how to go about it and he alienated the Draft Committee people. The committee itself disbanded on January 14, while the field organization continued to work for Goldwater. White repeatedly urged Kitchel to file and prepare for the primaries but was talking to deaf ears. White received a stream of complaints from committee members. On February 16 they cornered an anxious Goldwater at the O'Hare Inn in Chicago and peppered him with complaints, which he did not even try to resolve.

The candidate's performance in the crucial first primary in New Hampshire, scheduled for March 10, was a catastrophe. "Barry Goldwater's ultimate defeat on November 3, 1964," White wrote, "was first etched out, indelibly and irrevocably, in the New Hampshire primary campaign." In early January he had held the high cards: leadership in the polls, the enthusiastic support of virtually all the important Republicans in the state, plenty of money, Rockefeller on the ropes, and reactionary William Loeb's Manchester *Union-Leader,* the largest and sole statewide paper fanatically for Goldwater and hardly allowing a day to pass without a nasty piece about Rocky and Happy.

The Arizona Mafia, evidently, did no research on the state, assuming that it was safely conservative and would succumb quietly to Goldwater's charms. Nothing could have been further from the truth. It was the second most industrialized state in the nation, with many new high-tech firms. While traditionally Republican because of its old Yankee citizenry, it had just elected the first Democratic governor in 40 years as industrial workers, French-Canadian, Italian, and Irish Catholics, streamed to the polls. It had a higher percentage of old folks than Florida. The Republicans were internationalist in outlook and strongly supported the United Nations.

January 5 was an exhausting day for Goldwater. He flew from Washington to Grand Rapids for a speech and then on to Concord, New Hampshire, arriving at 3 a.m. With little sleep, he faced tough questioning that morning at a press conference. He said that Social Security should be made voluntary, which experts agreed would wreck the program, and he called for another Cuban exiles' invasion of the island with U.S. air support. The banner headline in the Concord *Daily Monitor* read: "Goldwater Sets Goals: End Social Security, Hit Castro." The first, Novak wrote, was "sheer disaster" and the second fortified his image as a "trigger-happy warmonger." Thus began a long parade of goofs.

The campaign was maddening for the candidate. There were not enough New Hampshire Republicans to provide large audiences; Goldwater had to meet small groups over coffee. But his mind was not quick enough for this give-and-take. Moreover, the Rockefeller people stacked the audiences with bright Harvard Law School students who bombarded him with tough questions that embarrassed him. Lacking the stamina, he had to slog through 23 days of punishing campaigning in the snow. When it was over, he ruefully recalled his bad heel: "I remember every footstep of that campaign."

Most bizarre was the Lodge "candidacy." Henry Cabot Lodge was the ambassador to Vietnam and was not running for President. Four political amateurs, one in the mail-order business, decided to have some fun. They rented a store in Concord, got a mailing list of the 96,000 registered Republicans in New Hampshire, and sent them a letter urging that they write in "Ambassador Henry Cabot Lodge, Saigon."

The results in the New Hampshire primary were as follows: Lodge 33,521, Goldwater 21,775, Rockefeller 19,496, Nixon 15,752, and others 4,097. Lodge, who did not lift a finger, got 35 percent of the vote and, more shocking to Goldwater and Rockefeller, captured the entire slate of 14 delegates to the convention. "For mismanagement, blundering, and sheer naïveté," Theodore H. White wrote, "Goldwater's New Hampshire campaign was unique in the campaigns I have seen." In fact, "never thereafter was he to recover from it."

In the Oregon primary on May 15 Rockefeller triumphed. The results: Rockefeller 93,000, Lodge 78,000, Goldwater 50,000, and Nixon 48,000. The faltering Goldwater candidacy desperately needed a victory in giant California in June. He barely made it with 1,120,403 votes (52 percent) to Rockefeller's 1,052,053. His victory was due to an immense margin of 207,000 votes among the extremely conservative Republicans in Los Angeles and Orange counties.

The Republican National Convention that met in the Cow Palace in San Francisco from July 13 to 16 was a rogue elephant. Governor William W. Scranton of Pennsylvania, elected in 1962, had announced for the presidency on June 12. Three days later Rockefeller abandoned his quest and endorsed Scranton. On June 28 a Gallup poll of Republican voters showed, that Goldwater and Nixon each had 22 percent, Lodge 19, Scranton 18, Rockefeller 8, and others 11. Goldwater was far from having a majority. Republican voters seemed to be in a state of confusion. Nixon, Lodge, and Rockefeller together got 49 percent of the vote and none was a candidate. Scranton was only 4 points behind Goldwater. Gallup took another poll, matching Goldwater against Scranton with these results: Scranton 55 percent, Goldwater 34, and undecided 11. Scranton had picked up most of the Nixon, Lodge, and Rockefeller votes and had far outdistanced Goldwater.

But such gentle brushes with reality had no effect upon a large majority of 1,308 delegates to the convention. As a result of the masterful coup engineered by Clifton White, they were far more conservative than the party's voters. It took 655 votes to win. White predicted that they would get 884 on the first ballot, and he was off by only one vote. According to Goldwater, the Republicans had studied Larry O'Brien's manual, which described the system installed by the Kennedy people at the 1960 Democratic convention, and copied it exactly. White set up a system that allowed him through 16 walkie-talkies and 30 telephone lines to control all these delegates.

Thus, Goldwater, despite his miserable showing with Republican voters, was guaranteed a handsome first ballot victory and had total command over the convention. Everett Dirksen's wet finger was up and he knew the direction of the wind. He helped put the Illinois delegation in the Goldwater column. Though he had been appalled by the Arizonan's vote against the Civil Rights Act and had publicly upbraided him, Dirksen put Goldwater's name in nomination and lauded his "blazing courage" for voting for measures that "gained him nothing politically."

The Goldwater supporters not only dominated the floor; they also packed the galleries where they caused the most disgraceful incident of the convention. After the very conservative platform had been read, Rockefeller was given five minutes to propose a change. Much concerned about extremists, he tried to offer an amendment denouncing them by name, including the John Birch Society. Its lobbyist said that 100 delegates were members. The Cow Palace erupted in fury against Rockefeller. He taunted them and they screamed back. He said, "These things have no place in America." John Bartlow Martin wrote, "All America saw a spectacle on television that could only be described as one of savage fury."

Goldwater's victory was overwhelming and at the conclusion of the roll call Scranton moved to make it unanimous in the interest of party unity. As the senator was working over his acceptance speech, written by Karl Hess and Harry Jaffa, he learned of the latest poll: Johnson would beat him by almost 80 to 20. Nevertheless, he was furious with those who had opposed him and was totally uncompromising. Instead of picking a moderate like Scranton for Vice President to unite the party, he chose William Miller, an almost unknown conservative from Buffalo. Goldwater's speech contained two sentences that became the most famous he ever delivered. They seemed designed to drive the moderates out of the party: "Extremism in the defense of liberty is no vice. . . . Moderation in the pursuit of justice is no virtue." The nation was shocked by this language. Clifton White wrote, "I was as stunned as anyone that night by the abrasive quality of his words." The columnist Drew Pearson wrote from San Francisco, "The smell of fascism has been in the air of this convention."

Despite White's masterful performance, Goldwater nailed him. He had lobbied hard to be named chairman of the national committee so that he could run the campaign. Without discussing it with White, Goldwater picked Dean Burch. Even his good friend Kleindienst argued against Burch on grounds of inexperience. But, according to Stephen Shadegg, Goldwater wanted someone "personally loyal to him and willing to serve him without question or contradiction." Two weeks later White learned that he would become co-chairman of Citizens for Goldwater-Miller. He would form organizations with such names as Dentists for Goldwater-Miller and Mothers for a Moral America.

Barry Goldwater was a study in ambivalence. He insisted that he wanted neither the nomination nor the presidency, but at the critical junctures he always said "yes." In a sense Lyndon Johnson was possessed by a similar ambivalence. But there were differences.[3]

Lyndon Johnson did not invent the phrase "the great society." In 1776 Adam Smith had used it several times in *The Wealth of Nations*. Graham Wallas, the British economist, had made it the title of a book he published in 1914. Early in 1964 it began to pop up in Johnson's speeches, inserted there by Richard N. Goodwin. He had written speeches for Kennedy and was now doing so for his successor. Johnson liked the phrase, the press picked it up, and it began to appear in capital letters.

In early April Bill Moyers phoned Goodwin to tell him that the President wanted to see them in the swimming pool. As was his custom, he was swimming in the buff. Goodwin wrote, "The massive presidential flesh, a sun-bleached atoll breaching the placid sea, passing gently . . . . Moby Dick, I thought." Under orders from the commander-in-chief, they stripped, entered the water, and absorbed a Johnson monologue.

He said he had "two basic problems—get elected and pass legislation the country needs." Kennedy had some good programs, but they got stuck and "I had to pull them out of the ditch." There was still some legislative mucking around left—civil rights, Medicare, education. "We've got to use the Kennedy program as a springboard to take on the Congress, summon the states to new heights, and create a Johnson program, different in tone, fighting and aggressive." He told Moyers and Goodwin, "You start to put together a Johnson program." Goodwin sensed the President's "immense vitality" and was inspired.

Over the next month Goodwin talked with a number of people in order to define goals. His deadline was May 22, 1964, when Johnson would make the commencement address at the University of Michigan. The place was symbolically important because in 1960 Kennedy had proposed the formation of the Peace Corps there. Now Johnson would use the university to proclaim the philosophy of his presidency.

Goodwin conceived of his assignment to establish "a concept, an assertion of purpose, a vision, if you will, that went beyond the liberal tradition of the New Deal." This was extremely difficult to do, probably impossible. Visions, after all, are not expressed in words. The President ruled out laundry lists of grievances or programs. He wanted "a statement of national purpose, almost prophetic in dimension, that would bind citizens in a 'great experiment.' "

Goodwin finished the speech the night before its delivery. Moyers was enthusiastic. The next morning the President went over it very carefully and made a number of penciled notations. Then he said, "It ought to do just fine."

The address, delivered with many interruptions for applause, was, Goodwin wrote, "a triumph." Americans had settled and subdued a continent, Johnson declared, in order to create plenty. The challenge of the next half-century will be whether "we have the wisdom to use that wealth to enrich and elevate our national life." As they advanced in years, he told the students, "We have the opportunity to move not only toward the rich society and the powerful society, but upward to the Great Society." Johnson continued,

> The Great Society . . . demands an end to poverty and racial injustice, to which we are totally committed. . . .
> [It] is a place where every child can find knowledge to enrich his mind and to enlarge his talents. It is a place where leisure is a welcome chance to build and reflect. . . . It is a place where the city of man serves not only the needs of the body and the demands of commerce but the desire for beauty and the hunger for community.
> It is a place where man can renew contact with nature. . . . It is a place where men are more concerned with the quality of their goals than the quantity of their goods.
> But most of all, the Great Society is not a safe harbor, a resting place, a final objective, a finished work. It is a challenge constantly renewed. . . .

Goodwin, who did not accompany the President, watched the delivery of his speech from the White House basement. He was moved because his "idea had become a reality. So I clapped for the President, and for our country." The precise meaning of "Great Society" was elusive. Kermit Gordon viewed it as a "phrase," a "slogan," a "tag." Like many others who supported Johnson's domestic program, he did not care for its sound. "I remember wincing a bit when I first heard the phrase." But Johnson now at least had a name for what he was trying to accomplish which he could carry forward into the election campaign.[4]

Over the years of his quest for the presidency Lyndon Johnson had suffered from intermittent periods of self-doubt. Doris Kearns thought it was a case of what Freud had called the repetition compulsion, variations on a theme the person had neither overcome nor learned to live with. "By escaping and returning, if only in fantasy," she wrote, "Johnson could reassert his personal and political autonomy; and thereby seem to himself the determining force of his own destiny."

In May 1964 Johnson seemed to have the world eating out of his hand: he had a firm grip on the presidency; his legislative program was moving through Congress; his nomination was assured; he would pick his own running mate; and the Republicans seemed bent on self-immolation by nominating Goldwater. Nevertheless, he fell into a depression. He suffered from anxiety, he wrote, because he had reached the White House "in the cruelest way possible"; he and his family were subject to "scathing attacks" which he was certain would become worse; and he worried that his health "would not stand up." Perhaps he should retire, which, after three decades of public service, he could do in "good conscience." He discussed this with his good friend Senator Russell, with his trusted staff men Walter Jenkins and George Reedy, with several old friends in Texas, and with, "of course, Lady Bird." He asked his wife to write her views down in a memorandum and she put the pros and cons neatly down on paper. Her unsurprising conclusion: "Stay in."

While he accepted this advice, he continued to be nagged by doubt. He felt personally abused by the race riots in New York and other cities and by the crisis in the Gulf of Tonkin. His greatest worry, he wrote, was "national unity," which was of the utmost importance to him. Johnson did not believe that a southerner could unite the American people because "the metropolitan press of the Eastern seaboard would never permit it." He spoke to James Reston of the *New York Times,* the dean of Washington correspondents, who tried to reassure him. Reston got Johnson's old friend, Jim Rowe, to step in. Rowe wrote the President that as long as Scotty Reston and Walter Lippmann backed him, as they did, he was assured of eastern press support. But he remained troubled.

The Democratic Convention opened in Atlantic City on August 24, 1964. The next morning Johnson sat alone at his desk in the Oval Office writing out a statement that he told himself he would read to the convention. As Vice President and as President "I did my best":

> Our country faces grave dangers. These dangers must be faced and met by a united people under a leader they do not doubt.
>
> After 33 years in political life most men acquire enemies, as ships accumulate barnacles. The times require leadership about which there is no doubt and a voice that men of all parties, sections and color can follow. I have learned after trying very hard that I am not that voice or that leader.
>
> Therefore I shall carry forward with your help until the new President is sworn in next January and then go back home as I've wanted to since the day I took this job.

As was his custom in similar situations, Johnson showed this statement to those he most trusted. Walter Jenkins told him, "Mr. President, you just cannot do it." He walked around the White House grounds with George Reedy, his press secretary, who found the idea "absolutely incredible." As Reedy recalled later, "Naturally, I was there to talk him out of it." Lady Bird wrote in her diary that it was "the same old refrain." But this time it was much harder to persuade him. She talked to him for hours and then wrote him a shrewd and touching note, playing on his courage and his patriotism. That did it.[5]

Lyndon Johnson's depression about the presidency may well have been linked to what some called his "obsession" with "the Bobby problem," that is, with the vice presidency. For the professionals, who looked at this issue realistically, the question was: what problem? At the Gridiron Club dinner earlier that year Jenkins took Larry O'Brien into a corner and told him that the President should be free to pick his own running mate. "O'Brien listened gravely," Evans and Novak wrote, "but he was astonished at Jenkins' nervousness. O'Brien knew that the President could pick his second man by the merest flick of his finger." Clark Clifford, upon whom Johnson leaned heavily in handling this matter and who had also dealt with Kennedy, "had known from the beginning that there was simply no way that Lyndon Johnson and Bobby Kennedy could ever get along with each other."

This was fundamental: Lyndon Johnson and Robert Kennedy hated each other. It was hardly a state secret. In his newspaper column, "Washington Pipeline," John Henshaw reported (falsely) that "President Johnson and Bobby got into such a heated argument recently that the Attorney General lost his head and swung at the President, hitting him on the shoulder." While there were nasty incidents and grating differences in style, the central issue was the legitimacy of the Johnson presidency. "After Dallas," Clifford wrote, "when Bobby Kennedy looked at Lyndon Johnson, he saw a usurper in the Oval Office. . . ." If he put the Attorney General on the ticket, Johnson reasoned, his presidency would be a mere interlude between two Kennedy presidencies. He must get rid of Bobby. Early on some thought that he needed Kennedy in order to win the election, but the Goldwater candidacy buried that argument.

Kennedy, Arthur Schlesinger wrote, "saw himself as yoked with Johnson in the execution of a legacy and the preservation of a party." This implied that he would accept, and perhaps seek, the second spot on the ticket. But he said and did nothing publicly. His "friends" entered his name for Vice President in the New Hampshire primary in March and the President barely edged him out—29,600 to 25,900 votes. A Gallup poll of Democratic voters in April for Vice President showed Kennedy with 47 percent, Adlai Stevenson 18, and Hubert Humphrey 10.

Johnson was beside himself. He played with an alternative Catholic candidate—Sargent Shriver or Senator Eugene McCarthy of Minnesota. Both suffered fatal flaws. If Johnson wanted a Catholic, there was only one—Kennedy. If he wanted a Minnesotan, there was a better one—Humphrey.

In late July the Attorney General invited several of his relatives and close friends—Ted Kennedy, his brother-in-law Steve Smith, Kenny O'Donnell, Larry O'Brien, and Fred Dutton—to Hickory Hill. Goldwater's victory, Schlesinger wrote, "had extinguished any need Johnson might ever have felt for Kennedy." Now the President had a free ride in the north, where Kennedy was strong, and did not need trouble in the South and Southwest, where Kennedy would be a handicap. The Attorney General said he would forget the vice presidency, resign from the cabinet, and run for the Senate in New York. Everyone agreed that this was the proper course. His brother and Smith thought he should announce at once. "O'Donnell," Schlesinger wrote, "begged him to wait; once Kennedy was out of the running, liberal Democrats would lose their power to force Johnson to accept Humphrey." He went with O'Donnell.

The President, according to Clifford, now feared that Kennedy's appearance before the convention would be "the emotional high point" and that the delegates would "nominate him by acclamation." He must eliminate the Bobby problem before Atlantic City. On July 22 he asked Clifford to draft a talking paper for him for a meeting with the Attorney General. When they spoke together on July 29 Johnson literally read Clifford's memorandum to Kennedy.

The President, according to his own version of the encounter, said that it would be "inadvisable for you to be the Democratic nominee for Vice President." The nomination of Goldwater was the decisive factor in reaching this conclusion. The ticket must be strongest in "the Middle West and the Border States" and create as little "adverse reaction as possible upon the Southern States." Because Kennedy's public service had been "outstanding," Johnson wanted him to consider becoming ambassador to the United Nations.

O'Donnell had warned an already suspicious Kennedy that Johnson would tape the meeting and the Attorney General saw the buttons light up. Upon returning to the Justice Department, therefore, he immediately dictated his own account of what had taken place. In substance it did not differ from Johnson's, but was much fuller in detail. Among other things, Johnson had asked him to manage his campaign and Kennedy had refused.

Both had been wary and neither had been forthcoming. Johnson's stuff about the Midwest and the South had little or nothing to do with his decision, and taping the conversation was hardly likely to encourage a frank discussion. On the other side, Kennedy said nothing about his decision to resign as Attorney General and run for the Senate.

Schlesinger surmised that both men were "relieved" to put this distasteful problem behind them. But there remained a nasty question that neither had addressed: how would the public learn that Kennedy had withdrawn? Johnson did not want to be publicly accountable for dumping him. He sent McGeorge Bundy over to persuade the Attorney General to announce that he had withdrawn of his own accord. Kennedy refused. Johnson then tried to get O'Donnell to convince him to pull back, but O'Donnell declined.

On July 30 the President invited three eminent Washington correspondents to a fine luncheon that went on for four hours. He could not restrain himself from giving a self-serving account of the confrontation with embellishments from his own notable gift for mimicry. He had Bobby so upset by the news of his being dumped that "his Adam's apple [was] going up and down like a Yo-Yo." The story was soon all over Washington. Kennedy phoned Johnson to express his outrage. Incredibly, Johnson said he had not discussed the meeting with anyone! Kennedy, in effect, called him a liar. Johnson said he would check his "schedule." Kennedy's friends then released *his* version of the meeting. All in all, it was a dreadful mess and the President looked awful.

Cornered, Johnson called for help from Clifford again. As usual, the counsel came up with a formula. There had been vice presidential speculation about several high-level members of the administration—McNamara, Secretary of Agriculture Freeman, as well as Shriver. Johnson went before the television and announced that it would be "inadvisable for me to recommend to the convention any member of the Cabinet or any of those who meet regularly with the Cabinet." He specifically named Rusk, McNamara, Kennedy, Freeman, Stevenson, and Shriver. Clifford called this nonsensical creation a "cosmetic covering." It may have made Johnson feel better, but it fooled no one. Privately, Kennedy said, "I am sorry that I had to take so many nice fellows over the side with me." Stevenson, sailing in Maine and decidedly not a candidate, was informed by James Rowe that he had been dumped. He phoned an old friend in Washington and said, "Hubert, it's you." [6]

The Democratic convention met in Atlantic City during the week of August 24, 1964. The town was definitely not the first choice. John Kennedy had hoped for San Francisco, but the logistics of holding both conventions in the same city did not work out. His second city was Chicago, but local funds were insufficient. This left Miami and Atlantic City, and the former was full of rabidly anti-Castro Cuban exiles with the Bay of Pigs fresh in memory.

Atlantic City, with its long boardwalk, had once been the queen of fashionable beach resorts. But it was now dingy and threadbare. The old hotels had faded, "monuments to another era," Theodore White wrote, "a strung-out Angkor Wat entwined in salt-water taffy." Its newer motels were grungy. The plumbing did not work, the telephone system failed to connect, handles came off doors and windows. More important for hungry Democrats, the restaurants were dreadful and their stomachs were calmed only in the splendid kosher delicatessens. An added complication was that the state of New Jersey insisted on first-class rooms for the 447 police officers it sent in, including 50 at the closest good motel. The tawdriness of the town seemed to rub off on the convention.

Johnson needed, demanded, and got absolute control. Having disposed of Bobby, he was left with two serious problems. One was to resolve a potential racial crisis over the seating of the Mississippi delegation(s) that, uncontrolled, might have caused severe political damage. The other was to pick a running mate.

Despite the passage of the Civil Rights Act, race relations worsened markedly in 1964. There were vicious riots in Harlem and Bedford-Stuyvesant, in Rochester, in Philadelphia. Governor George Wallace of Alabama manipulated an emergent white backlash by invading the North to campaign for President in several Democratic primaries. Appealing to anxious ethnic working-class Democrats, he received 34 percent of the vote in Wisconsin, 30 in Indiana, and 43 in Maryland. Lake County, Indiana, with the steel towns of Gary and Hammond and a large ethnic population, Governor Matthew E. Welsh wrote Johnson, normally produced a Democratic majority of 40,000 to 50,000. Wallace won the primary by 2,527 votes.

Robert Moses, a young black man, Harlem-born and Harvard-educated, had spent three frustrating years in Mississippi trying to register Negroes to vote in the face of formidable and often violent opposition. (Three volunteers—James Chaney, Michael Schwerner, and Andrew Goodman—had been murdered.) Now Moses launched the Mississippi Educational Summer Project. Students from the North came south to assist in the registration. If white Mississippi rejected them, as it did, blacks and a few liberal whites would elect delegates from their own Freedom Democratic Party who would go to Atlantic City and demand to be seated. Humphrey had earlier warned Johnson of the dangers of Mississippi, but had been unable to get his attention.

The Mississippi Freedom Democratic Party held its convention in Jackson. Its counsel, Joe Rauh, the noted civil rights lawyer and attorney of the UAW, unveiled what he called "the magic numbers." There were 100 members of the Democratic convention's credentials committee and they needed eleven votes to file a minority report. Eight state delegations were needed to force a roll call. Rauh was certain that they had the eleven and eight. The Jackson convention had picked 68 delegates, four of whom were white. "Johnson," Rauh said, "saw this on television and he realized for the first time that this was serious."

Official Mississippi sent its own lily-white delegation, which assumed that it would be seated because it had been elected by registered voters. Many of these delegates were not loyal to the Democratic party and would support Goldwater. Many northern Democrats recognized the moral claim of blacks in the South to the right of representation.

Johnson, eager to avoid an open clash broadcast on television, devised a compromise: (1) the regular delegation would be seated on condition that it pledged support for the ticket; (2) the freedom delegation would receive the privilege of the floor, but no votes; and (3) the convention would adopt a rule making it mandatory for state Democratic parties in the South to open their rolls to blacks, thereby insuring racially mixed delegations starting in 1968. He passed this proposal to Humphrey, but did not order him to handle the problem. Johnson knew he would because of the senator's long involvement with civil rights; because he realized the effect success or failure would have on his own vice-presidential candidacy; and because Humphrey was certain from their Senate association that Johnson's style in such situations, as Evans and Novak put it, was to "stay out of sight and use leading figures on either side, whose loyalty was unquestioned, to work out the compromise." Humphrey, while willing "to do a job that had to be done," found this testing of his proven competence "aggravating."

Johnson also sent his trusted lieutenant, Walter Jenkins, to man the command post in Atlantic City and to provide the sole conduit to the President. He was assisted by Tom Finney, a member of Clark Clifford's law firm. C. D. "Deke" DeLoach, the FBI's White House liaison, headed a Bureau team of 30 men which established electronic surveillance over the telephones in the MFDP office and in the rooms of civil rights leaders Martin Luther King, Jr., and Bayard Rustin. Their main purpose, however, was to report on the activities of Robert Kennedy. DeLoach passed the substantial body of information his men collected to Jenkins.

The credentials committee hearings opened on Saturday, August 22. Rauh presented a strong brief and Fannie Lou Hamer gave a moving account of the brutalities she had suffered as a voting rights activist. This scene played on national television. King strongly endorsed the MFDP.

On Sunday Oregon Congresswoman Edith Green proposed that all members of either delegation who took a loyalty oath to the Democratic party and its ticket should be seated. An estimated 17 credentials committee members supported the proposal and it became the MFDP position. The regular Mississippi delegation would have nothing to do with it.

Humphrey then proposed Johnson's three-point plan and the administration moved in its big guns. Humphrey and Walter Reuther, who departed the General Motors-UAW negotiations, both old friends and, in Reuther's case, his client, worked over Rauh. Humphrey stressed that the President insisted upon it. According to Rauh, "Never once . . . did he ever say, 'Joe, you've got to take this settlement to help me.' " Reuther, however, was the "muscle," that is, Rauh thought he might get fired as the UAW counsel. Reuther told Rauh that the MDFP would lose the election for the Democrats—"Goldwater's going to be President." Rauh was convinced that the Republican did not have a chance. Bayard Rustin and Andrew Young of the Southern Christian Leadership Conference urged the freedom group to accept the compromise, now improved by offering two delegates in 1964. King made a thoughtful assessment of the pros and cons and suggested that acceptance was the wiser course. Meantime, the administration lobbied the state delegations who had supported MFDP and by Tuesday morning their number had shrunk below eleven. While Moses was embittered, there no longer was a rational argument against the three-point proposal. MFDP caved in and the convention adopted the settlement.

On the whole, it was a satisfactory outcome. The President had kept the party united, at least on the surface, avoiding a damaging battle on the floor of the convention and a walkout by the Mississippi regulars perhaps joined by other southerners. Humphrey had emerged as the triumphant mediator, thereby soldifying his quest for the vice presidency. The mainline civil rights organizations, for whom Rustin and King spoke, much preferred in the long run a grateful President and representation at future conventions to a symbolic losing fight for MFDP in 1964. But Moses and many other young militants were convinced that they had been sold out by the joining of the white and black power structures to destroy them. They would exact a price in return.

Lyndon Johnson's remaining task was to pick a Vice President. Here he would diddle Humphrey mercilessly. This served two purposes: to demean the senator in order to exact a pledge of absolute loyalty and to add a note of uncertainty to a convention that seemed otherwise to create no excitement.

Johnson insisted that *his* Vice President must be *his* man. As Arthur Schlesinger reported, he put it in ways that left no room for doubt. "Whoever he is, I want his pecker to be in my pocket." And he wanted men around him "who were loyal enough to kiss his ass in Macy's window and say it smelled like a rose."

Hubert Humphrey desperately wanted to be Vice President and was forthright about his ambition. His people started a campaign in December 1963 but remained discreet as long as Robert Kennedy was a contender. Johnson began saying nice things about Humphrey in March 1964 and in a private conversation remarked, "If I just had my choice, I'd like to have you as my Vice President." He insisted, however, that this was not a promise and the ever-patient Humphrey understood. But there was trouble in Texas. Governor Connally argued that Humphrey's long championship of civil rights (he was then steering the civil rights bill through the Senate) would damage the ticket in the South and on the border. The governor, who was very conservative, also worried about a possible liberal Humphrey presidency. Walter Jenkins agreed with this analysis. Lady Bird Johnson, a close friend of Abigail McCarthy's, was charmed by her husband, Senator Eugene McCarthy of Minnesota, for his wit and intelligence. Johnson explored the political value of McCarthy's Catholicism as a substitute for Kennedy's and began to toy with him.

On July 30, 1964, just before he went on television to announce his "final solution" to the Bobby problem, Johnson directed Rowe to make two points to Humphrey, which he did that evening. The first was that, if he won the vice presidency, he must be totally loyal to the President. Humphrey said that was no problem. The second, as Rowe put it, was, "If you've got any strength, show it." Humphrey, already in the starting blocks, could hardly wait for the gun. At the same time, Johnson instructed Jenkins to notify McCarthy that he was still in the running. A week later Rowe sat Humphrey down on his front porch in the Cleveland Park section of Washington to examine virtually every aspect of his political and personal life to determine whether there was a skeleton in a closet. There was none.

Humphrey now cashed in the chips he had spent years accumulating. He showed his support among liberal organizations, the labor movement, the civil rights movement, and prominent Democratic politicians. A Gallup poll of 3000 Democratic county chairmen in June showed him ahead of Kennedy by almost two to one. He was endorsed by 40 Democratic senators, nearly all significant party leaders in 26 states and a majority in six others. His greatest strength was in the Midwest, where Johnson might be weakest. A Harris survey demonstrated that Humphrey was preferred over Miller by a margin of seven to three. Robert Kennedy endorsed him. He went on television to court the South.

On Sunday, August 23, the day before the convention opened, Humphrey and McCarthy were both on national TV. Immediately afterward, Johnson phoned each to tell him that he had given him an A-plus. But Lady Bird stuck with McCarthy.

In one sense Humphrey was lucky in being responsible for the crisis over seating the Mississippi delegations. Over the weekend and during the first two days of the convention he was so busy that he had little time to fret over the vice presidency. This was in the face of well-founded rumors that Johnson was now making advances to Mike Mansfield while courting McCarthy.

The astonishing aspect of this unfolding melodrama was that it was produced and staged by the President of the United States. "It was," Theodore White wrote, "a mixture of comedy, tension and teasing, it was a work of art; it was as if, said someone, Caligula were directing *I've Got a Secret*." On August 22 Johnson had told Kenny O'Donnell to set the wheels in motion for a last-minute switch to Mansfield. O'Donnell, who was a close friend of the majority leader, said that Mansfield would not accept for all the copper in Montana. The President then ordered Jenkins to instruct Rowe, as the latter put it, "to take a reading on who would be better, Mansfield or Humphrey." Rowe was from Montana, had been Mansfield's campaign manager, and was his close friend. "Oh, come on, Walter," Rowe said, "I am too old to be playing these games." Jenkins said, "He means it." Rowe retorted, "The hell he does." Nevertheless, Rowe dutifully asked Mansfield whether he would accept the vice presidential nomination. The answer might have come from General Sherman. "No possible chance. I would not have the slightest interest in it."

Rowe had now become Johnson's point man in Atlantic city. The President dictated detailed instructions to Jenkins, who took them down in shorthand and then typed them up for Rowe. On Monday Johnson had given correspondents from the Washington *Post* and *Star* the elaborate qualifications he expected his Vice President to have. Among others, they included no public disagreement with the President, speeches cleared by the White House, acceptance of all administration policies, and no breach of secrecy, even with his wife. They were published on Tuesday. Jenkins then transmitted the final instructions for Humphrey that Rowe would deliver: he would be nominated; the seconding speech was to be from Georgia and other seconders were named; Humphrey must read and accept the qualifications listed in the *Star;* he and his wife Muriel were to stand by for a special flight to Washington.

Rowe could not find a copy of the *Star* in Atlantic City, but he did locate a *Post.* He called Humphrey to his suite at the Colony Motel. The senator arrived with his wife, William Connell, his executive assistant, and Max Kampelman, his close friend and adviser. Rowe took him into the bedroom and gave him the President's instructions. The senator was delighted and relieved and started to open the door to inform Muriel. Rowe quickly closed it, telling him that Johnson forbade the sharing of secrets with his wife. By now the weather was bad and all flights had been canceled. Kampelman suggested that they drive to Washington. But the President had said *fly.* They waited for the weather to lift.

Rowe now told Humphrey that he must come without Muriel; he would be accompanied by another senator, Thomas J. Dodd of Connecticut, which led, as Johnson intended, to press speculation over another vice presidential candidate. Jack Valenti met them in Washington and took them on a tour of the sights. This was because Lady Bird Johnson was landing in a helicopter in Atlantic City at that moment and the President did not want to divert TV attention from her. Eventually they made it to the White House.

Johnson now engaged Humphrey in a long chat. He stressed the "thanklessness" of the vice presidency and that "most Presidents and Vice Presidents just don't hit it off." Again, "this is like a marriage with no chance of divorce. I need complete and unswerving loyalty." Humphrey assured him. Then Johnson said something that moved the senator, that he was "the most capable of all the men [he knew] to take on the duties of the presidency if anything should happen." They exuberantly phoned a number of Democratic leaders to share the good news. The President took Humphrey into the Cabinet Room, where he found Rusk, McNamara, and McGeorge Bundy. All of them, Johnson said, had supported his candidacy. Impulsively, Johnson phoned Muriel. "How would you like to have your boy be my Vice President?" Then on to meet the press and spread the news.

On the flight to Atlantic City they watched a jittery television broadcast of Governors John Connally of Texas and Pat Brown of California putting Lyndon Johnson's name into nomination. The demonstration followed.

Johnson made his entrance and Humphrey was also nominated. The Democrats had their ticket.

By midnight Tuesday McCarthy realized that he had been left out to dry. As Albert Eisele wrote, he had been "humiliated" and he was "deeply offended by Johnson's playing with him like a puppet on a string, and he never forgave Johnson for it." He sent a telegram withdrawing his name so that the President's "choice would be a free one" and urging Humphrey as the man best fitted to Johnson's qualifications. His assistant read it over the phone to Jenkins the next morning after it had been released to the press. He correctly assumed that Johnson would forbid its publication; in fact, Jenkins exploded. Later Jenkins phoned to ask McCarthy to nominate Humphrey. Having just heard that Dodd was on the airplane, McCarthy caustically recommended Dodd. Jenkins insisted and, after consideration, McCarthy agreed to make the speech.

As Johnson had dominated the choice of the Vice President, so he dominated the shaping of the Democratic platform. It had two basic themes, opening with the first: "America is *One Nation, One People.*" The "survival of each of us resides in the common good—the sharing of responsibilities as well as benefits by all our people." The platform was "a covenant of unity." Republicans who were offended by Goldwater were urged not to go astray by "narrow partisanship."

The second theme was the Kennedy-Johnson linkage. Together they had carried the tremendous burden placed upon them. The platform pointed to the "towering achievement" of the legislation that had already been enacted. "We are proud to have been part of this history. . . . Let us continue."

None of this moved the delegates and the convention crowd. But there was one exhilarating moment: Robert Kennedy introduced a film about President Kennedy. It had been scheduled for Tuesday night, the evening before the Johnson-Humphrey ticket was nominated. But, as noted, Johnson feared that the Attorney General would stampede the delegates and be nominated for Vice President by acclamation. This, in fact, was not Kennedy's intention. Nevertheless, the presentation was switched to Thursday night.

Senator Henry "Scoop" Jackson of Washington introduced Kennedy. He was greeted by an immense ovation that rolled on and on and on. Schlesinger, who was on the floor, wrote, "I had never seen anything like it." On several occasions Kennedy tried to stop the demonstration without success. Jackson leaned over and said, "Let it go on. . . . Just let them do it, Bob. . . . Let them get it out of their system." It continued for 22 minutes. Finally, Kennedy spoke briefly, concluding with the lines from *Romeo and Juliet* that Jacqueline Kennedy had given him.

When he shall die
Take him and cut him out in little stars,

> And he will make the face of heaven so fine
> That all the world will be in love with Night,
> And pay no worship to the garish sun.

Theodore White wrote that the film closed with "the sense of the joy of life and youth and the dead President teaching his baby boy how to tickle his chin with a buttercup. And we all wept."[7]

If history can be said to have an Aristotelian logic, that is, a story with a beginning, a middle, and an end, the 1964 presidential campaign was not history. The calendar, mercifully, imposed a beginning and an end, but neither had any particular relevance to the middle. The campaign was all middle, a series of disconnected episodes. In fact, there were two campaigns, Goldwater's and Johnson's, and they hardly intersected. "Looking back," Goldwater said, "I see the campaign as less of a debate than two monologues." The more important episodes were the following:

Goldwater's (Dis)Organization. Barry Goldwater, whatever his virtues, was born totally devoid of any sense of organization. Worse, the people he installed to run his campaign were genetically programmed to produce disorganization. The result must have been the most mismanaged and the funniest campaign in the history of the republic.

Despite the western strategy propounded by the new conservatives, the campaign seemed to have no strategy. There was the shadow of one at the outset, but it quickly expired. Since Gallup showed him behind 65 to 29, Goldwater decided to clinch the three midwestern states which were the Republican bedrock—Ohio, Indiana, and Illinois—in September as a base for turning the country around in October. He hired a 22-car train to whistle-stop through the small towns and rural areas and drew quite good crowds. In Hammond, Indiana, the Yugoslav steel workers came out to demand that the U.S. overthrow Tito. Swinging into the mood, Goldwater made a bellicose speech with references to "holocaust," "push the button," and "atomic weapons." This reinforced his image as trigger-happy, as not hesitating to use The Bomb. Almost everyone was terrified. In university towns the placards read, "STAMP OUT PEACE—VOTE GOLDWATER." His crowds were also concerned about race. His answer: "Part of that civil rights law is nuts. It's okay to say you'll give a fellow civil rights, but once you tell him who can come into my restaurant and who can't—then, boy, there's trouble." Some did not think this was carefully thought through.

The organizers in Washington spent five weeks setting up their own quarters—new partitions, painting, and so on. But the folders, buttons, and bumper stickers that should have been ready in July did not go out till September.

Ralph Cordiner, the former president of General Electric, was in charge of finance and tried to run the campaign like a business—in the black. But political cash flow does not fit that accounting theory. In September, when there was little money, he canceled TV time booked for late October, and later, when there was plenty of cash, the spots needed had been preempted by other advertisers. Cordiner got into an awful fight with Burch because the latter was spending too much. He tried to appeal to Goldwater, but he refused to see Cordiner. He even flew on the candidate's airplane from Washington to Phoenix and was unable to breach the wall erected by the Arizona Mafia.

Goldwater did make one wild stab at creative policy formulation. In a speech at Dodger Stadium in Los Angeles he slipped in an idea proposed by Milton Friedman, the conservative monetarist economist from the University of Chicago: "I shall ask Congress to enact a regular and considered program of tax reduction of five per cent per year in all income taxes, both individual and corporate." Aside from the fact that such a perpetual system would bankrupt both the government and the country, Goldwater had voted against the much more modest Kennedy-Johnson tax cut for exactly that reason. Friedman's idea never left the ball park.

The time of the kickoff speech in Prescott, Arizona, was suddenly changed from 4:00 to 2:00 p.m. Instead of a big out-of-town crowd, only local residents showed up. Somebody forgot to arrange for TV and radio coverage. The Boise appearances ignored an intra-party dispute that left the Republican governor, according to Stephen Shadegg, doing "a slow burn which rivaled the magnificence of the Idaho sunset." The farm speech at the plowing contest in Fargo, North Dakota, seemed to advocate immediate abandonment of price supports, which frightened farmers and shocked conservative Republican senators from the Dakotas. Milwaukee, Shadegg wrote, was "the most incredible foul-up of the Goldwater campaign." Elaborate publicized arrangements were made for live national TV coverage. On Kitchel's orders at the last moment an earlier taped speech was substituted without informing the locals. The Milwaukee station threatened to sue for fraudulent advertising. Good Republicans stopped payment on campaign contributions. The advance man resigned. Further insult: Two nights later Humphrey spoke on television in the same arena to a big crowd from precisely 8:30 to 9:00.

Richard Rovere spent a week in September "behind" Goldwater in seven southern states. The candidate had chartered a Boeing 727 jet which he christened *Yai Bi Ken,* Navajo for House in the Sky. It carried Goldwater, the missus and her hairdresser, half a dozen advisers, and about 50 representatives of what the Goldwaterites called "the rat-fink Eastern press." The journalistic overflow, up to a dozen, including Rovere, followed in a slow propeller plane which they called the *Enola Gay.* It was, he wrote, like "giving hot pursuit to an Alfa Romeo on a tricycle." Missing about half of Goldwater's speeches was not all bad. "On the whole, I was more relieved than distressed by the news that our group would be unable to make

Shreveport, Louisiana, where, according to one authority in our entourage, 'there are more haters per square mile than anywhere else in the country.' " But he was sorry to be absent in Knoxville, where, under a rippling Confederate flag, Goldwater called for the sale of TVA to private interests, and Orlando, where he made a speech to senior citizens attacking Medicare. Rovere's fellow traveler, Mary McGrory of the Washington *Star*, cheered him by pointing out the world records they had established: flying from New Orleans to Springfield, Missouri, for lunch and from Memphis to Macon for a cup of coffee.

An embittered Goldwaterite later asked Theodore White about the new conservatives. "Where were they when we made our charge up San Juan Hill? They blew the trumpets—but when we charged, nobody followed." Where were Bill Buckley and his stable of *National Review* writers? Where was Kirk? Bozell? "At least you got to say this for a liberal s.o.b. like Schlesinger—when his candidates go into action, he's there writing speeches for them." In fact, the Arizona Mafia considered using the new conservatives, but decided they were "too arrogant, too cold, too intolerant."

Johnson's Organization. Theodore White wrote that it was "as bizarre as the organizational chart of the old China-Burma-India theater during the war." But it worked. Johnson ran everything himself except for Jim Rowe's citizens' committees, which were exceptionally successful. "Until about the last week," Rowe said, "he was perfectly happy, then he had everything so well organized, he started to come over and organize me." The President, according to White, grouped everyone into teams.

Team A, the Household Guard, was his immediate staff—Walter Jenkins (until his troubles), Bill Moyers, and Jack Valenti. Moyers handled speeches and the media. Secretary of Labor Willard Wirtz, a noted wordsmith and speech writer for Adlai Stevenson, moved into the Executive Office Building, where he worked up material coming in from the government agencies. He passed drafts to the speech-writing group—Richard Goodwin, Horace Busby, and Douglass Cater. They delivered to Moyers and the President. Moyers and Goodwin dealt with the advertising agency, Doyle Dane Bernbach, which played a critical role in the campaign.

Team B consisted of the three lawyers in whom Johnson reposed the greatest trust—Clifford, Fortas, and Rowe. They reviewed major decisions and dealt with crises, notably the Jenkins affair, which is discussed below.

Team C was composed of the two superb professionals inherited from Kennedy—Larry O'Brien and Kenny O'Donnell. If anyone other than Johnson had been the candidate, O'Brien would have managed the campaign. Instead he ran a masterful intelligence operation. He took to the road for 23 meetings with 43 state Democratic organizations at which progress in the election was examined comprehensively, including problems and remedies. The President had never seen such political intelligence before and insisted that O'Brien dictate his analyses speedily over the telephone. Sample:

A ten-page report on October 4 of eight regional meetings covering 19 states of key campaign leaders. O'Brien summarized Johnson's standing and that of Democrats in every Senate and House race with a forecast of the probable outcome of each. The key to the election: "The bomb is the biggest issue by far. Voters are frightened of Goldwater and don't want him in the same room with the nuclear trigger." West of Chicago three hate books distributed by the Republicans and the Birch Society hurt. O'Brien urged putting $200,000 immediately into the close congressional races he identified.

O'Donnell scheduled the President's campaign trips, a complex undertaking. Efficiency note: As of October 3, every stop planned through October 17 had been fully worked out and advance people were in the field; the stops for the last two weeks of October were 80 percent finished, leaving details only in California and Pennsylvania. Significant O'Donnell observation: A serious problem was a "sense of overconfidence, which leads to apathy." This was due to the polls and the fact that Republicans outside the South "have given up totally on the Presidential election." This gloom spilled over onto the Democrats. O'Donnell's was one of many reports to the White House in late September and early October of a Goldwater collapse. It was not confined to Democrats. Clifton White, after talking to Goldwater in early October, wrote that it was "obvious that the Senator had given up, though the election was then a month away."

Team D called itself the "Five O'Clock Club" or the "Anti-Goldwater Program," specializing in the quick counterpunch. Myer Feldman and Fred Dutton, two Kennedy holdovers, were in charge and more than a dozen smart people contributed, including Wilbur Cohen, Tom Finney, James Sundquist, and Adam Yarmolinsky. The team met daily at 9:30 a.m. and 6:00 p.m. According to Theodore White, they had Goldwater's schedule and even the texts of his speeches in advance. Thus, the Democratic mayor, governor, or congressman was supplied with a refutation that would appear in the same issue of the local paper with the story on Goldwater's speech. Rockefeller turned over his files, which saved Team D time. It also published books—*You Can Die Laughing, Goldwater vs. Republicans,* a book of cartoons, a picture book. They prepared questions for reporters who were at Goldwater press conferences and suggested topics for columnists. They wrote letters to advice columnists Ann Landers and Mary Hayworth. When Goldwater attacked Kennedy in Seattle, they prepared a sentimental newspaper reply.

Team E was the Democratic National Committee chaired by John Bailey of Connecticut. Johnson had a low regard for the committee and Baily realistically described its role as "housekeeping." It concentrated on voter registration and, along with AFL-CIO's COPE, probably added 2 million Democratic voters in 1964.

The masterpiece was Jim Rowe's citizens' committees for businessmen, labor, farmers, women, youth, scientists and engineers, artists and writers, and others. They served two main purposes: to provide a home for disaffected Republicans and to offer prominent citizens an opportunity to voice their concerns over Goldwater, particularly on The Bomb.

Goldwater, of course, had divided his party decisively in San Francisco. Shortly thereafter a dozen top Republicans, including Eisenhower, Nixon, Goldwater, Rockefeller, Scranton, and Governor Romney of Michigan, had met in Hershey, Pennsylvania, hoping to reunite the party. Theodore White, who read a copy of the transcript, wrote that "no more dreary document has turned up in American political history." Goldwater made no effort to stanch the flow of blood.

The result was a massive Republican defection to the Johnson-Humphrey ticket, including some very important people. The former showed up in the polls. Alf Landon, the presidential candidate in 1936, had worked for a year to stop Goldwater. He pointed to the "terrible destruction of a Goldwater candidacy to the good Republican candidates at all levels, as well as to the party institution, and the damage Goldwater's candidacy does to maintaining a responsible foreign policy." Rockefeller, of course, detested Goldwater and helped Johnson. Lewis Douglas of Arizona, who had been FDR's first budget director and had resigned over the unbalanced budget, had not supported a Democrat since 1932 and had backed Goldwater in both of his Senate races. Now he thought his fellow Arizonan's nomination a "tragic mistake" and publicly backed Johnson. He was one of many prominent bankers and businessmen to do so. Ed Mennis of the Wellington Fund had attended a luncheon of eleven top business executives. One "confessed" that he would vote for Johnson. Eight others made the same confession. Only two had ever voted for a Democrat before—for Al Smith in 1928! One was undecided. Goldwater got one vote.

Former undersecretary of the treasury Henry H. Fowler had created the highly successful Business Committee for Tax Reduction to push the tax cut. Rowe got Fowler to repeat this performance with the National Independent Committee for Johnson and Humphrey, whose members consisted of many of the industrial and financial leaders in the U.S.

Writers and artists, already heavily Democratic, could hardly be restrained from showing their distaste for Goldwater. Rowe installed Roger L. Stevens, the theatrical producer, as head of that committee, which included many of the brightest minds in the country.

The Bomb. Goldwater made nuclear war the fundamental issue and it vaporized him. Following the new conservatives, he had long argued that the U.S. must not negotiate with the Soviets but must defeat them. No one had any idea of how this could be done without the use of nuclear weapons. His name appeared on the spine of a book called *Why Not Victory?*. In September 1963 he had made an impassioned speech against the test ban treaty and had then voted against ratification. It was hardly the first time, but in October he told the press that the U.S. could reduce its forces in Europe if "commanders" were empowered to use tactical nuclear weapons on their own initiative. During the primaries Rockefeller and Scranton had attacked him mercilessly on this issue. But Goldwater did not know how to keep his mouth shut. He insisted that he was misunderstood and repeatedly "explained" his position to a puzzled and increasingly fearful public.

Thus, the Democrats got free an issue that in itself guaranteed their victory. Larry O'Brien said later, "The overriding issue in 1964 was, very simply, in one word, Goldwater." Rovere asked a matron in Atlanta covered with Goldwater-Miller buttons if her candidate's views on nuclear warfare troubled her. "Certainly not," she replied. "We're not cowards down here." There were very few who shared this view.

The Democrats exploited the issue relentlessly. Television expert Tony Schwartz created two extraordinary TV commercials. The first opened with a little girl, her hair tossing in the wind, picking daisies. She then plucked the petals of a flower, counting up. A doomsday male voice joined hers at 10, but counted in reverse. When he reached zero, there was an immense explosion and a mushroom cloud rose slowly into the sky. President Johnson said, "These are the stakes. . . . We must either love each other, or we must die." The voice of doom returned: Vote for Johnson. "The stakes are too high for you to stay home."

The second showed a little girl licking an ice cream cone. A woman's voice told her that atomic bombs used to be exploded in the air and that the fallout made children die. A treaty now forbade testing in the atmosphere. But Goldwater had voted against it. A Geiger counter clicked in crescendo. The announcer repeated the voting message.

These spots ran on television in mid-September and created a sensation. Goldwater and many others, including many Democrats, were outraged and the first ad was withdrawn. But it was too late; the damage had been done. "It is my candid opinion," O'Brien wrote the President, "that this ad did more to crystallize public opinion against Goldwater than any other single tool we are using."

The Republicans agreed. Their headquarters team desperately tried to think of an answer without success. Kitchel said, "I would lie awake asking myself at night, how do you get at the bomb issue? My candidate had been branded as a bomb-dropper—and I couldn't figure out how to lick it." He called in experts on selling toothpaste and cars, but they, too, were helpless.

Johnson would not allow Goldwater to self-destruct and insisted on presenting himself as the only candidate who advocated peace, especially in Vietnam. According to his *Public Papers*, he reassured mothers several times that he would not send Americans to die in a war in Vietnam that should be fought by Asians:

I want to be very cautious and careful . . . when I start dropping bombs around that are likely to involve American boys in a war in Asia with 700 million Chinese.

. . . for the moment I have not thought that we were ready for American boys to do the fighting for Asian boys. What I have been trying to do . . . was to get the boys in Viet-Nam to do their own fighting with our advice and our equipment.

Goldwater as Radical. The bomb issue fed into an extraordinary transformation: the nation's leading conservative became a radical in the public mind. A Harris poll released in July 1964 forecast this result. It asked how Americans stood on ten basic foreign and domestic issues. On eight, Harris wrote, "The American people feel they are in sharp disagreement with the Arizona senator." Conclusion: "Barry Goldwater has a massive communications problem." While the logic may be strained, it followed that a politician who failed to communicate with the American people must be a "radical."

By September the Democratic polls showed that folks were afraid of Goldwater because he was a "kind of radical." Stephen Shadegg, the manager of the Arizonan's earlier senatorial campaigns, wrote that "Lyndon Johnson and Barry Goldwater had changed places. The Republican candidate was now the dangerous radical."

Goldwater and Race. Though he had voted against the Civil Rights Act, Goldwater insisted that he was not a racist and bristled when he was called one. But, excepting his home state, the only region from which he won any support was the Deep South and there because he was perceived as a racist.

Goldwater prided himself on being for states' rights. Yet, in his law and order speech in St. Petersburg, Rovere wrote, he asserted that crime was so rampant that the *federal* government must stamp it out. He allowed himself to become the centerpiece for "great numbers of unapologetic white supremacists to hold great carnivals of white supremacy." This was certainly the case in the lily-white rally in Crampton Bowl outside Birmingham. The football field was strewn with living lilies—700 white Alabama girls in long white dresses. Rovere concluded that the large Goldwater movement in the South "appears to be a racist movement and very little else."

Ronald Reagan's Appearance. The former movie actor and General Electric luncheon speaker was testing the right-wing political waters in 1964. He had supported Goldwater against Rockefeller in the California primary. Now, basing his remarks on his G.E. speech, he taped an address, "A Time for Choosing," scheduled for network TV on October 27. But Kitchel tried to cancel it because Reagan attacked Social Security and he thought his man had suffered enough on that issue. A distressed Reagan appealed to Goldwater to overrule Kitchel and, when the candidate made no decision, interpreted this as assent. The speech went on the air. While it had no impact on the election, Republican conservatives lapped it up, and, according to Clifton White, Reagan's performance "catapulted him into the political limelight."

Johnson's Campaign. There was some talk at the outset, particularly by John Connally, that he should be "presidential," tending to the nation's business in the Oval Office, going out to the country only on ceremonial and nonpolitical missions. If this was, in fact, the plan, it belied Lyndon Johnson's nature and his Texas origin. He loved to say on the stump, "Y'all come down to the speakin'." He throve on a political contest, was exhilarated by the crowds, and loved to press the flesh.

On September 28 the real Johnson emerged. He ventured into Kennedy country for six stops in one day—Providence to Hartford to Burlington to Portland to Manchester and on into Boston at 2 a.m. If he had any doubts about the reception he would receive, Providence put them to rest. The Rhode Island capital had a population of 208,000; Theodore White estimated the turnout as "perhaps half a million." Richard Goodwin had campaigned with Kennedy in 1960 and had been impressed by the number of people on the streets. Now there were "unprecedented crowds, dwarfing the Kennedy receptions." Despite the fact that the Warren Commission report had been published that day, Johnson gave the Secret Service fits. He yelled at the crowds through a bullhorn, encouraged them to climb on the car, and shook so many hands that his right paw became swollen, bruised, and bled. He was 70 minutes late for the convocation at Brown University. So it went at every stop he made.

On October 9 Larry O'Brien met with the campaign managers, along with Speaker McCormack and Chairman Bailey, at the Parker House in Boston for a five-hour review of New England. He reported to the President:

> You are about to make history in New England. You should become the first Democratic candidate for President in history to win all six New England states. It seems certain you will win Massachusetts, Connecticut, and Rhode Island; it is highly likely that you will win New Hampshire; and the chances of your winning Maine and Vermont are much brighter than I would have believed at the start of this campaign. As you know, Vermont never has gone Democratic in a Presidential election, but our people there firmly believe you will win the state.

O'Brien was confident that the four Democratic senators up for reelection would win. The Republican in New Hampshire looked safe, but his opponent had an outside chance. He thought it fairly likely that the House delegation, already heavily Democratic, would add another Democrat in each of Connecticut, Maine, and New Hampshire.

After the smashing success in New England, Johnson poured it on across the country. Since the polls showed him victorious by a landslide and his crowds were enormous and enthusiastic, he no longer seemed satisfied with merely winning. He seemed to want, Rovere wrote, "about seventy million [votes] and five hundred and thirty-eight in the Electoral College." Someone observed that, if he lost ten states, "he might decline to serve, saying that he just didn't want to be President unless he could be President of *all* the people." Johnson wanted to win by the biggest margin in history and received a staff memorandum on that topic.

"Biggest margin" presented a problem. If one measured by the *number* of electoral votes, FDR in 1936 held the record with 515. If by the *percentage* of electoral votes, Washington was supreme with 100 percent in 1789 and 1792. During the Era of Good Feelings Monroe would have reached the same level except that William Plumer of New Hampshire wanted only Washington to be perfect. Thus, Monroe received 99.006 percent. In modern times Roosevelt in 1936 was at the top with 98.5. He was also first in his *winning margin* of 11,072,014 votes. For the *percentage of the total vote* Harding in 1920 led with 60.4 and FDR in 1936 was second with 60.2 percent.

The Jenkins Affair. Johnson's supreme confidence in his campaign was temporarily shattered on October 14. Walter Jenkins was the most trusted and loyal member of his staff. He had worked for Johnson, excepting military service and an unsuccessful campaign for Congress, since 1939, and made himself available at any hour. He was dedicated, thorough, and precise. Listeners knew that he spoke for the President. He was treasurer of the Johnson family corporation, handled sensitive tax papers, and dealt confidentially with the FBI. He was married, the father of six children, and a devout Catholic.

Jenkins had been arrested and booked by the Washington police in 1959 on a morals charge. Then and in 1964 homosexuality was illegal in most states and the District of Columbia. On October 7, 1964, he left work at the White House for a party celebrating the opening of the new offices of *Newsweek,* where he had several drinks. He then went to the basement of the YMCA, a rendezvous for homosexuals, which had been staked out by the police. Shortly, Jenkins and an elderly Army veteran were arrested and booked on charges of disorderly conduct. Jenkins posted a $50 bond and was released. He went back to work at the White House.

The FBI, according to Theodore White, leaked the story to the Republican National Committee and the committee's investigator examined the police blotter. Goldwater learned of the arrest and chose to remain silent. The Chicago *Tribune* and Cincinnati *Enquirer* (two of the few Republican papers that remained loyal to Goldwater) received the story and decided not to publish. On October 14 the President was in New York campaigning jointly with Robert Kennedy and was staying at the Waldorf Astoria. George Reedy, his press officer, was with him.

That morning Charles Seib, the assistant managing editor of the Washington *Star,* called the White House, White wrote, "with heavy heart," to seek confirmation of the story. The call was relayed to Walter Jenkins. When he hung up, he went straight to Abe Fortas at his home.

Jenkins was so distraught that, Fortas said, he "could not at that moment put one word consecutively after another." The lawyer slowly drew the outline of the story from him. He then phoned Clark Clifford. "Walter Jenkins is here with me. He needs our help." He told Clifford to meet him outside the latter's office in ten minutes.

Fortas recounted to Clifford what he knew as they drove to the *Star*. "It had to be a mistake," Clifford said. "It couldn't be the same Walter Jenkins we both knew." They agreed to tell no one at the White House or the President.

They met with Newbold Noyes, Jr., the editor of the *Star,* and told him what they knew. They asked him not to publish the story. Noyes asked whether they knew all the facts. They did not. He told them two of his reporters had examined the police blotter on October 8, had confirmed the arrest, and had learned of the 1959 incident. Noyes said this was a human tragedy as well as a news story. Normally the *Star* did not print such stories and would hold back if the other papers also did so. The *News* also had the story and agreed not to publish. The *Post* did not know about the event and its editor said that he wanted time to consider the question.

Fortas went to his home where Jenkins was resting with his doctor. When the attorney told him what he had learned, Jenkins, Clifford wrote, "came apart completely." The doctor gave him a sedative and took him to the George Washington University Hospital.

Clifford went to the White House where he talked to Moyers and, later, Fortas. They decided to ask the President for the authority for Fortas to obtain Jenkins's resignation. They talked to Johnson in New York, who, according to Clifford, was "struck dumb" by the news. He reluctantly granted the authorization and Fortas persuaded Jenkins to resign.

By late afternoon the news was all over Washington and, soon, the entire country. Reedy, weeping openly for an old friend, confirmed the story in New York. Dean Burch, chairman of the Republican National Committee, issued what Clifford called "a cruel and cryptic statement." "There is a report sweeping Washington that the White House is desperately trying to suppress a major news story affecting the national security."

Lady Bird Johnson sent out the following statement:

> My heart is aching today for someone who has reached the end point of exhaustion in dedicated service to his country. Walter Jenkins has been carrying incredible hours and burdens since President Kennedy's assassination. He is now receiving the medical attention which he needs. I know our family—and all of our friends—and I hope all others—pray for his recovery. I know that the love of his wife and six fine children and his profound religious faith will sustain him through this period of anguish.

The President remained silent. He ordered an FBI investigation into the possibility of a breach of national security. None was found. He directed his pollster, Oliver Quayle, to make an instant survey. The next day Quayle reported no significant shift in voting intentions and suggested that the President proceed with his campaign plans. The results were confirmed by other polls.

The next day, suffering from a cold and fever, Johnson campaigned with Kennedy before immense crowds in Buffalo and Brooklyn. They were a tonic for his ailments, physical and emotional. His luck turned in the next few days as public attention shifted to larger matters: the deposition of Khrushchev in the Soviet Union, the detonation of China's first atomic bomb, the defeat of the Tory government in Britain, and the victory of the St. Louis Cardinals in the World Series. The Jenkins affair was forgotten.

Miller and Humphrey. William Miller was convinced from the outset that he did not have the slightest chance of becoming Vice President. After the convention he seems to have slipped into a black hole and was never heard from again.

Humphrey was his usual optimistic, ebullient, and energetic self. His four-engine Electra, called the *Happy Warrior,* hardly ever came to rest. Sample for September 27 to October 2: four stops in Georgia, including Atlanta, two in Detroit, two in Iowa, including Des Moines, one each in North Dakota and Montana, three in Washington, including Seattle, and a day touring Los Angeles with speeches at the University of Southern California and the Shrine Auditorium.

The Polls. The major polls—Gallup, Harris, and Roper—showed a massive landslide from start to finish. Gallup consistently gave Johnson 5 points more than Harris, in late October 67 percent as against 62. On October 29 Moyers's office put together a composite of all the state polls and state estimates from *Congressional Quarterly, Newsweek,* and *Time.* The total for the U.S. gave Johnson a 60–40 sweep, a plurality of 14 million, and the electoral votes of 46 states, including Arizona, closely. Goldwater would carry only Alabama, Louisiana, Mississippi, and South Carolina. The International Institute of Public Opinion Research made two national polls for Rockefeller on September 31 and October 30. With a bit of diddling with the undecided and the margin of error, the Institute's final prediction was 61–39.

John Bailey, like a ball player, was superstitious and placed great confidence in high school polls in small towns near Hartford. He sent the results to the President on October 22. Wethersfield was a Republican town. In 1960 Kennedy's run had been "outstanding," but he still lost to Nixon in the election by 800 votes. Now Johnson-Humphrey carried the high school in Wethersfield 888 to 146. Avon was another Republican community where Nixon had won easily in 1960. Now the Democrats were ahead

301 to 115. East Hartford was heavily Democratic. Kennedy won overwhelmingly and Johnson had about the same margin.

The Democrats swept the Ivy League: Harvard 84-16, Yale 69-20, Princeton 67-23, Columbia 81-19. The nationwide popcorn poll taken in the lobbies of movie houses (how unscientific can you get?) came out about the same—77-23. The Virginia barber shop poll was a bit lower—65-25.

Fact magazine made the most original and controversial poll. It asked 12,350 psychiatrists the question: Do you believe that Barry Goldwater is psychologically fit to serve as President of the United States? There were 2,417 replies of which 1,189 held him unfit and 657 voted him fit. This was not far from the outcome of the other polls. The others who responded did not take a position.

The Press. Until 1964 the newspapers had always been overwhelmingly Republican. Now this was completely reversed. In fact, only three important Republican papers stayed with Goldwater—the Los Angeles *Times,* the Chicago *Tribune,* and the Cincinnati *Enquirer.* The list of desertions was enormous and included the New York *Herald-Tribune,* the Hearst papers, the Detroit *Free Press,* the Philadelphia *Bulletin,* and the Baltimore *Sun.* For some it was a first Democratic endorsement, such as the Binghampton *Sun-Bulletin,* a first since 1822. Equally remarkable, the *Saturday Evening Post, Life, Time,* and the *Atlantic Monthly* endorsed Johnson.

Protestant Religious Journals. Historically church papers had maintained strict political neutrality. This changed dramatically in 1964. *The Christian Century* editorialized "Goldwater? No!" Later it declared, "Johnson? Yes!" The Arizonan was a member of the Episcopal Church. *The Witness,* the church's magazine, published a stinging editorial signed by eleven ministers denouncing him. Bishop William Scarlett, who had baptized Goldwater and had great affection for him, was compelled to disagree with his social and political views. Of his foreign policy proposals, he wrote, "Frankly, he scares me." *The Churchman,* another Episcopal paper, printed an editorial called "The Goldwater Threat to America." [8]

For those accustomed to the interpretation of early returns the election was over by 4 p.m. eastern time on November 3. People were still eating lunch in California and breakfast in Hawaii. The Republicans had to deliver heavy majorities in New England villages no one had heard of in order to make it close. They failed. Johnson was ahead in New Hampshire 35 to 29 and in Massachusetts 28 to 18. Kansas had been the most Republican state in the U.S. in 1960. By 5:30 Johnson was leading in Kansas 65,000 to 62,000. Thereafter he piled on the votes.

A total of 70,621,479 people went to the polls. The Johnson-Humphrey ticket received 43,126,218 votes to 27,174,898 for Goldwater-Miller. This was a plurality of 16,162,052, or 61 percent. The Democrats swept 44 states with 486 electoral votes. The Republicans carried 6 with

52: Arizona, Mississippi, Alabama, Louisiana, South Carolina, and Georgia. The damage Goldwater did to the rest of the Republican ticket was devastating. Robert Taft, Jr., running for the Senate in Ohio, polled 400,000 more than Goldwater and still lost. Charles Percy, the Republican candidate for governor in Illinois, ran 300,000 ahead of Goldwater and went down to defeat. Kenneth Keating, the incumbent senator from New York, outpolled Goldwater by 860,000 and lost his seat.

Johnson's plurality was the greatest in history, exceeding FDR in 1936 by 5 million votes. In the electoral college he ran behind Roosevelt, who lost only Maine and Vermont. But Johnson's percentage of the total vote was slightly higher—61 to 60 percent.

Frank Cormier, a White House correspondent, bet the President $5 that Goldwater would carry no more than two states. When he paid off, he wrote "with much regret that Goldwater got four states more than I bet he would and six more than he deserved."

Johnson had long coattails. Some 28 Democratic senators and 295 Democratic representatives were elected. The Democrats gained two seats in the Senate, their number rising from 66 to 68, as against 32 Republicans. The entire "Class of '58," those liberal Democrats elected for the first time in 1958, was reelected in 1964. The House would have 295 Democrats, an enormous gain of 37, as against 140 Republicans. Some said the United States would have a one-and-a-half party system in the 89th Congress.

Some thought the Republican party had been so savaged that it would not recover for a generation, if ever. Johnson was not among them; he expected a quick return. This was because the Republicans would not soon repeat the mistake of nominating a divider and loser like Goldwater and because the Democrats could not possibly keep those gigantic majorities. In 1964 the Democrats won 61 seats in the House with less than 55 percent of the vote, 37 of them with below 53 percent. Many of those closely-contested seats would move back into the Republican column in 1966.

Thus, Johnson had the two years of the 89th Congress to put over his Great Society. The old southern Democratic-Republican coalition that had dominated the Congress since 1938 was temporarily disabled. He could get whatever he wanted, but he would have to hurry.

James Reston of the *New York Times* called the 89th the "Goldwater Congress":

> The record of the 89th Congress shows what can happen in this country under the leadership of Lyndon Johnson and Barry Goldwater. They did not intend to cooperate, but they have. Apart they are insupportable; together, invincible. In combination, their unintended alliance has produced a torrent of social and economic legislation. . . .
>
> The irony of the Goldwater challenge to the welfare state and planned economy is that, by losing so overwhelmingly, he brought in a Congress that enacted precisely the legislation he ran for the Presidency to oppose.[9]

6

Medicare: The Jewel in the Crown

TWO Wilburs starred in the leading roles, Wilbur Cohen as the supreme advocate, Wilbur Mills as the master legislator. Cohen was the assistant secretary of Health, Education, and Welfare responsible for legislation, Mills the chairman of the House Ways and Means Committee, which handled Social Security.

Medicare, no matter how measured, was enormous and enormously important. During 1966, the first year it was in effect, the number of persons 65 and older enrolled in the hospital insurance program was 19.1 million, in supplementary medical insurance 17.7 million. In fiscal 1967, the first full year of operation, it paid over 7.1 million hospital bills for a total of $3.1 billion, and 24.4 million doctor bills with total charges of $7.5 billion. Since the number of old people would grow steadily, the program would inevitably become much larger. It would have a great impact upon the structure of the nation's health care delivery system. Organized medicine, that is, the American Medical Association, feared and opposed the establishment of Medicare with passion. The AMA waged what was probably the biggest and costliest lobbying campaign in history to prevent the passage of the law. It had 70 publicists at work in its Chicago headquarters and 23 at its lobby in Washington. The AMA spent $50 million on this unsuccessful battle. When the bill passed in 1965, Richard Harris wrote, "members of both political parties in both houses of Congress agreed that their votes on the measure were the most important ones they had ever cast."

The nation was fortunate to have these very large stakes in the hands of such gifted professionals as Cohen and Mills. Wilbur J. Cohen was born in Milwaukee in 1913 and attended the experimental college of the University of Wisconsin in Madison. He was a brilliant student and was profoundly influenced by three distinguished labor economists—John R. Commons, Selig Perlman, and Edwin E. Witte. He graduated in 1934.

That year President Roosevelt committed himself to an omnibus economic security law and instructed Secretary of Labor Frances Perkins to chair the committee to draft a bill. She appointed Arthur J. Altmeyer assistant secretary of labor and put him in charge. He was from Wisconsin and had taken his doctorate with Commons. Altmeyer asked his friend Witte to become executive director of the committee. Witte brought his student, Wilbur Cohen, with him.

This experience, which led to passage of the Social Security Act in 1935, hooked Cohen on two interests that would dominate his life: Social Security and the ways of Congress. After the law was passed Altmeyer, a dedicated public servant and brilliant administrator, became the key figure in directing the administration and expansion of the Social Security system. Cohen was at his side, working on legislation with the House Ways and Means Committee and the Senate Finance Committee.

Every industrialized nation in the world except the U.S. had either a nationalized health system or national health insurance. In 1934 FDR had wanted to put a national system into the Social Security Act, but had backed off in the face of powerful opposition from the AMA. In 1939 liberal Democrats proposed the Wagner-Murray-Dingell bill to establish national health insurance, but it got nowhere. By 1950 the expert backers, including Cohen, concluded that the AMA had made the prospect hopeless for the foreseeable future. They decided to narrow their target to those who needed help most, the elderly, and to coordinate what they called Medicare with Social Security. In 1951 Cohen and his good friend I. S. Falk, the head of Social Security's bureau of research and statistics, wrote the first Medicare bill.

But Eisenhower's victory and the election of a Republican Congress in 1952 not only prevented any action on Medicare but got Cohen and Falk in trouble. The Republican National Committee decided to throw out the top team at Social Security and instructed HEW Secretary Oveta Culp Hobby to get their resignations. Altmeyer and Falk were among those who left quietly. But Cohen refused to resign. "It was extremely humiliating to me," he said, "but I made up my mind that I was not going to get kicked around for political reasons by the Republican National Committee." He was a career civil servant who thought political reprisal was "unsound, and undesirable, and unfair, and inequitable, and inconsistent with our career service." The new commissioner of Social Security, John Tramburg, was a friend and declined to fire him. Next best, the Republicans demoted him one grade into Falk's old job and cut his pay. Cohen swallowed this arrangement briefly. Satisfied that he had established his principle, he departed for the University of Michigan in 1955.

By this time Cohen was the nation's leading authority on Social Security. As Senator Paul Douglas said, "An expert on Social Security was any-one with Wilbur Cohen's phone number." Nelson Cruikshank did not know him when he took over the Social Security department at AFL-CIO. "I guess that, if there was one, there were 50 people who told me that the first thing I should do was get acquainted with Wilbur Cohen."

Cohen knew Theodore Sorensen and Myer Feldman, who worked for Senator Kennedy, and they sought his advice. Elizabeth Wickenden was also a good friend and got him to counsel her old friend Senator Lyndon Johnson. He helped write a new Medicare bill which Representative Aimé Forand of Rhode Island introduced in 1957 and which quickly gathered wide support. In fact, it became one of the hottest issues in the 1960 presidential campaign. After his victory Kennedy asked Cohen to chair the task force on health and Social Security and Cohen brought Wickenden on board. To no one's surprise, the task force strongly endorsed Medicare under Social Security. At the request of Senator Robert Kerr of Oklahoma, Cohen wrote the Kerr-Mills bill for medical assistance to the poor. Despite the objections of supporters of Medicare, he insisted that Medicare and Kerr-Mills were complementary rather than alternatives, that both were necessary because each addressed a different group of the elderly who needed help. He added, "I felt this developed the principle of public financial responsibility for medical care."

In 1961 Kennedy gave Cohen the job he hungered for, assistant secretary of HEW responsible for legislation, a base for shaping national policy. It must have been the most important congressional relations position in the executive branch, covering, among other important matters, Social Security, including Medicare, and the enormous complex of legislation embraced by federal aid for education.

Cohen had a staff of two deputies, two special assistants, a program planning group of four, and he coopted anyone in HEW when the need arose, which was often. He may well have been born with a sense of history. If not, he certainly acquired it from his mentors in Madison—Commons, Perlman, and Witte. Cohen recognized that the sixties constituted, as his assistant Michael L. Parker put it, a "singular moment in history." He instructed Parker several times "to push the people I was working with as hard as I could, whether they protested or not; that we were to work any day, any hour, to do whatever was necessary to pass the legislation." His administrative style fitted this tempo. He chose good people, insisted that they take responsibility for important decisions, backed them up, and maintained a flexible, informal shop. Cohen himself seemed tireless and worked extremely long hours.

Douglass Cater, the White House staff member with whom Cohen worked on both Medicare and education, thought he was "the ideal public servant, in that he had great ideals and great freshness of approach." Moreover, he was "very shrewd and very skilled in how to maneuver programs through Congress." Most amazing, Cater thought, was that "he showed no sign, up until the very day he left office, of ever getting bureaucratic battle fatigue."

There were two extremely important people with whom Cohen enjoyed a special relationship—the President of the United States and the chairman of the Ways and Means Committee. Lyndon Johnson was hardly among the first politicians to see the significance of Medicare, but by the time he became President his commitment was total. Cohen thought he felt so strongly because of "the biblical injunction of honoring thy father and thy mother." He was concerned about "people who became old and indigent and sick and disabled and he wanted to do something for them." Further, as Johnson told Richard Goodwin, doctors had "too much money already . . . Hell, if I were a young man today, I'd get myself a medical diploma and then find an investment broker to handle the profits."

The Medicare bill, which ultimately reached 400 pages in length, had the appeal of an insurance policy, which, in a sense, it was. Johnson had only a general notion of what was in it. But he held Franklin Roosevelt in awe and he thought Social Security was his greatest domestic achievement. He associated Wilbur Cohen with Social Security and his good friend Elizabeth Wickenden assured him that he was correct. Cohen said that Medicare would help the old folks in need and that was good enough.

Cohen understood the President very well, and, by and large, they got along swimmingly. He could always count on Johnson on the big issues and the President never snarled at him. The only problem he had was with the White House staff. There had been no difficulty with Kennedy. "When you dealt with Ted Sorensen and you agreed on something, you were 9,999 times [out of 10,000] agreeing with the President." But Johnson bred uncertainty. Neither Cater nor, later, Joe Califano, knew how the President would react and they were cautious. "And the President would reverse them many times, or delay, or the President would consult with someone else."

Cohen had studied Wilbur D. Mills for years and found him endlessly fascinating. He had been born and raised in Kensett, Arkansas, a town with a population of 2500. His father was a country banker. As a "small town boy," Mills's view of life, said Cohen, was "uncomplicated . . . based on mutual respect and integrity and understanding." At age ten he decided to become a congressman. After attending Harvard Law School, he practiced law for a few years and in 1938 ran successfully in the Second Congressional District. Thereafter he was reelected endlessly, usually with no opposition. Mills became a member of the Ways and Means Committee in 1943 and its chairman in 1957.

Mills, Cohen said, had an "incisive mind." Good lawyer that he was, he briefed both sides of an issue before he reached a conclusion. He was by a wide margin the hardest worker on the committee, if not in all of Congress. In Cohen's judgment, he was one of five members of Congress who understood how Social Security was financed and was probably the only member "who completely understands the actuarial basis of Social Security."

Prior to 1961 Mills had served in the House under Speaker Rayburn, whom he revered. Nobody understood the House of Representatives so well and Mills learned his lessons from Mr. Sam. The House, with 435 members, was too big and unwieldy to perform legislative work efficiently. Thus, it depended almost totally upon its committees, of which Ways and Means ranked first. "I was always taught by Mr. Rayburn," Mills said, "that our whole system was to settle disputes within the committees. It's a waste of time to bring out a bill if you can't pass it. I just don't like to have a record vote for the sake of having a vote." Nelson Cruikshank said he never observed a significant vote on the floor. "When you got it settled in the Ways and Means Committee, it was settled."

Article I, Section 7, of the Constitution declares, "All bills for raising Revenue shall originate in the House of Representatives." Social Security was a revenue bill. This meant that Medicare must start in Ways and Means. Prior to the 89th Congress, the committee, consisting of 15 Democrats and 10 Republicans, was very conservative. Before 1961 a decisive majority of Republicans and southern Democrats, including Mills, rendered the prospects for Medicare hopeless. Mills had reluctantly allowed a vote in 1960 that went negative 17 to 8. As a result of the 1960 elections the majority was shaved by one vote; there remained 10 Republicans and 6 southern Democrats against 9 northern Democrats. By 1962 there was a further erosion to 14 to 11.

Mills, reflecting the mood of his committee and the House, gradually moved toward Medicare. The pressure from Kennedy was difficult to resist. On the morning of the assassination, November 22, 1963, Mills reached agreement with the administration on a financing formula and appeared to have joined the supporters. But this guaranteed nothing because the chairman would not act without a large majority on Ways and Means.

He was obsessed with overwhelming majorities and was remarkably ingenious and patient in devising compromises in order to get them. John F. Manley wrote, "If Chairman Mills's idea of going on the offensive is to lean forward in his foxhole, there is a second reason behind it. Majorities are built in the House, not elected to it; therefore House politics is coalition politics." In the game of coalition politics partisanship played a secondary role. Mills was very close to John W. Byrnes of Wisconsin, the minority leader, and he courted other Republicans on his committee.

In the chairman's mind a 13 to 12 victory was a defeat in disguise because it undermined his own and his committee's credibility and could split the House. That was exactly the way the committee divided in 1964. There were two very conservative Democrats, A. Sydney Herlong of Florida and John Watts of Kentucky, who joined the 10 Republicans in opposition to 12 liberal Democrats. Mills held the swing vote, a power that made him extremely nervous.

Thus, the prospects for Medicare in the House in 1964 were gloomy. Kennedy had expected its passage in 1965. The likelihood of a Democratic landslide in the elections must have made Mills even less inclined to force a close vote in 1964. A bit of patience and all would fall into place the next year.[1]

But President Johnson was not patient. He was eager to secure passage of Medicare in 1964, that is, during the second session of the 88th Congress. He wanted to go into the presidential campaign with that major triumph added to his already impressive list of legislative victories.

The Senate seemed safe. In 1962 Senator Robert Kerr of Oklahoma, who led the opposition, had tricked the supporters and had won by the close margin of 52 to 48. By 1964, however, the lineup was reversed. As a result of deaths (including Kerr's), defeat in the 1962 elections, retirements, and changes of position, the opponents had lost 10 votes and had gained 4 for a net loss of 6. The proponents of Medicare for the same reasons had lost 6 votes and had gained 12, for a net advance of 6. By this simplest method of calculation Medicare would pass the Senate 54 to 46. Further, Senators Russell of Georgia and Sparkman and Hill of Alabama had voted with Kerr for reasons that were now moot and Senator Monroney of Oklahoma had done the same as a courtesy to his fellow Sooner. Mike Manatos, who covered the Senate for the White House, thought it likely that these and other southern gains could push the majority to 60-40.

The House was another matter. On February 17, 1964, Henry Hall Wilson, who handled the House for O'Brien, thought it impossible to get the bill onto the floor, "if it can be got out of committee at all." This was because Mills would avoid breaking a tie at almost any cost. Further, the committee division probably reflected an extremely close vote in the House which might easily go against Medicare. As Mills saw it, this was no time to lean forward in his foxhole.

Shortly after becoming President, Johnson had invited the chairman and Mrs. Mills to dinner at the White House for an evening of persuasion. In the State of the Union message in January he declared, "We must provide hospital insurance for our older citizens financed by every worker and his family under Social Security." He sent Congress a special message on health on February 10 which covered six major topics. He placed Medicare first and he strongly urged its passage. This was all very well, but it changed the minds of none of the 10 Republicans or 2 opposition Democrats on Ways and Means.

Mills had begun hearings on November 18, 1963. His plan was to listen to testimony for nine days and to be finished in the latter part of the month. November 22, the day Kennedy was assassinated, was the fifth day, and Mills promptly stopped the hearings. They reopened on January 20 and ran for five consecutive days. A spectacular number of witnesses representing an extraordinary range of interest groups testified. The hearings filled five volumes, a total of 2,502 pages.

The subject was broadly defined as "Medical Care for the Aged." While there were many bills, three were most important. The administration proposal, introduced by Representative Cecil King of California and Senator Clinton Anderson of New Mexico, had been before Congress in 1962 and was the real Medicare. It would cover persons under Social Security and Railroad Retirement 65 and older and some of the elderly who were not entitled to pensions. They would be insured for hospital, nursing home, home health, and outpatient diagnostic services, but *not* for doctor bills. These benefits would be financed mainly by an increase in the Social Security tax. Benefits for the uninsured would be paid out of general revenues. The estimate was that 18 million people would be eligible in January 1965, 2.25 million of them uninsured.

The Health Care Insurance Act, also known for its sponsor, Senator Jacob Javits, was the progressive Republican alternative to Medicare. The New Yorker had a political problem: he was up for reelection in 1964 and in his liberal state he dared not vote against Medicare. He told Cruikshank, "I've got to have something here that has a Javits element in it or a Javits label."

His cosponsors constituted the little band of Republican liberals—Clifford Case of New Jersey, John Sherman Cooper of Kentucky, Kenneth Keating of New York, Thomas Kuchel of California, and Margaret Chase Smith of Maine. The National Committee on Health Care of the Aged, a distinguished group of experts, Democrats and Republicans, chaired by Arthur S. Flemming, president of the University of Oregon and former secretary of HEW, drafted the bill. It offered a choice either of Medicare under Social Security or essentially the same benefits provided by a private carrier who would be reimbursed by the government. But Javits went beyond Medicare. His private insurance policy would pay for physicians' services at an estimated cost of $2 a week. The AFL-CIO liked the Javits bill. "It is significant," Cohen wrote, "that not a single Republican on the Ways and Means Committee has introduced . . . the Javits bill. Nor has Mr. Mills in our discussions with him indicated any interest. . . ." But Mills had taken careful note of the feature providing for the payment of doctor bills.

The final important proposal was Kerr-Mills, technically Medical Assistance for the Aged. It had nothing to do with Social Security. Rather, it was a welfare program with a means test for persons 65 or older who did not receive old-age assistance and who could not afford health care. The federal government made grants to the states which must share between 20 and 50 percent of the costs. The states determined the services that would be covered. In 1964 10 million people were potentially eligible; in fact, only about

500,000 were covered, one in 20. The AMA strongly supported Kerr-Mills as an *alternative* to Medicare and sought to strengthen it. The fact that the beneficiaries were by definition too poor to pay doctor bills and the government would pay for them must have been an attraction.

Of the great number of organizations which testified before the Ways and Means Committee, only four were significant: the American Medical Association, AFL-CIO, the American Hospital Association, and the insurance industry.

As it had been for many years, AMA was *the* opposition to Medicare. Its leading spokesman, Dr. Edward A. Annis of Miami, became the president of the association in 1963. "Our objections to this bill are manifold," he said. " 'We disagree with its basic philosophy. We oppose its method. We are deeply concerned over the effects it would have upon the Nation's standards of health care." Medicare would lock the practice of medicine into an iron girdle, "socialized medicine." This would destroy the doctor-patient relationship and undermine the present high quality of medical care. The AMA also charged that the proponents falsely advertised the program by calling it a form of "insurance."

Many critics of the AMA were convinced that these arguments were window dressing, that the doctors really sought to protect their already very high incomes. Cohen disagreed. Under Medicare "they're going to make more money, and they know that their incomes are going to rise." Rather, the doctors had swallowed their own propaganda and had concluded "on a very high ethical plane" that the central issue was the "quality of medical care." They honestly believed that Social Security would destroy American medicine.

The labor movement was the counterweight to organized medicine. AFL-CIO had supported Medicare from its inception and, because of growing numbers of retired union members with health needs, had stepped up its lobbying. Health insurance under Social Security was its aim. While it also backed private health programs, including those collectively bargained, and the Kerr-Mills welfare law, labor considered them supplementary. The unions provided the foot soldiers in the battle for Medicare.

The American Hospital Association had gone through a sea change in viewpoint. In the forties the hospitals had opposed the Wagner-Murray-Dingell health insurance bill. Now, according to Cohen, AHA said, "There ought to be something," and "something" might include Medicare. He had asked Kenneth Williamson, who represented AHA in Washington, "If it passes, don't you want it to be the best kind of a bill?" Williamson did indeed and helped Cohen make the bill workable and protect the autonomy of the hospitals.

The insurance industry did not hear the whistle and missed the boat. It might have sailed into a sea of new business, as Javits proposed. But it spent all its time denouncing Medicare, allegedly because it was not insurance.

Javits said he made "great efforts" to persuade the health and life insurance companies to support his bill, but "ran into the problem of their being against anything." As a result, he said, "they ended up having no influence." Thus, as noted above, neither the Republicans nor Mills on Ways and Means had any interest in the Javits bill.[2]

The second session of the 88th Congress, that is, 1964, was not a happy year for Wilbur Mills. While he did not receive the famous Johnson "treatment" until later, he was under continuous pressure from Cohen, O'Brien, and Wilson. Supporters of Medicare accused him of "single-handedly" preventing its passage, and, even worse, some charged that he had been captured by the AMA. The AFL-CIO denounced his big majority strategy and made muffled noises about running someone against him in Arkansas.

The more Mills studied the Medicare problems, the more complicated and intractable they seemed to become. King-Anderson covered only hospital bills. This made little sense in a measure supposedly providing health care for the aged, who, of course, must pay their doctors as well as their hospitals. In fact, a very large fraction of those who supported Medicare incorrectly assumed that physicians' bills would be insured. Both the Javits bill and Kerr-Mills provided payment for doctors. But this added benefit would require a higher tax, which raised another serious problem.

Old-age pension benefits had not kept pace with the rise in the cost of living. A powerful congressional movement emerged in 1964 to increase pensions fueled by the fact that almost no member of Congress, Republican or Democrat, wanted to face his elderly constituents without having voted for fatter benefits. A rule of thumb had emerged that the Social Security tax rate should not exceed 10 percent of covered earnings. A combined increase in the pension tax and a new levy for King-Anderson could easily push through this arbitrary ceiling. In an election year no Democrat, starting with the President, was eager to impose *two* tax increases simultaneously.

During 1964 several Democratic members of Ways and Means whose votes seemed certain began to waffle. Clark W. Thompson of Texas publicly refused to say where he stood on Medicare. The President reminded him that Johnson had written to 2500 of Thompson's constituents to support him in the 1962 primary. The congressman was reconverted.

Mills, hoping to break the thirteenth vote deadlock, had persuaded John C. Watts of Kentucky to give him his proxy. But Dr. Annis outsmarted the chairman. The district Watts represented in western Kentucky was tobacco country. In early January 1964 Annis addressed the Kentucky legislature, noting that the Surgeon General would issue a report in a few days asserting that cigarette smoking caused cancer. "The A.M.A.," he told the legislators, "is not opposed to smoking and tobacco, but it is opposed to disease." On February 7 six leading cigarette companies gave the AMA $10 million to study smoking and health. Watts withdrew his proxy and lined up against Medicare.

During the spring Mills proposed a number of amendments in the hope of shaping a firm majority. These included using Blue Shield to administer hospital insurance; raising the earnings base, that is, income subject to Social Security tax, from $4800 annually to $5800; amending Kerr-Mills to make it more attractive to the states; allowing the beneficiary the option of either hospital coverage or a monthly cash sum; and exploring about a dozen combinations of reduced benefits in order to narrow the costs. None worked.

The votes were simply not there. The Ways and Means Committee was locked into a 12 to 12 split. Even worse, the House itself was against Medicare. Mills had a list of 220 congressmen who opposed the bill. A head count on September 4 showed that representatives who were "reasonably certain" of their position would vote against King-Anderson 222 to 180. Even if all "probable/possibles" were considered in favor of the bill, it would be defeated 222 to 209.

On June 24 Mills called the committee to vote. Cecil King, certain that his beloved bill would go down to defeat, withdrew it at the last moment. Mills then offered a 5 percent increase in pension benefits, which would raise the contribution rate to almost 9.5 percent. John Byrnes, the Republican leader, then moved to raise the pensions to 6 percent. This would push the tax rate to the ceiling and allow no room for Medicare.

The voting was dramatic. The northern Democrats, because one was absent, had only 11 votes. The 9 Republicans were joined by Mills, Herlong, and Watts for a total of 12. But Bruce Alger, the extremely conservative Republican from Dallas, dumbfounded everyone by voting against the Byrnes motion, defeating it by a tie vote. He explained that he opposed Social Security on principle and consistency demanded that he vote against its extension.

On July 7 the Ways and Means Committee reported a 5 percent increase in pensions to offset in part the 7 percent rise in the cost of living. On July 29 the House adopted this proposal by a massive majority of 388 to 8. Neither the committee nor the House had acted on Medicare.

These discouraging developments created what Henry Hall Wilson called the "Medicare dilemma," a euphemism for defeat. But the President on the eve of his nomination was in no mood to accept a defeat. The House would automatically forward its bill, H.R. 11865, to the Senate. There the administration would load Medicare onto the increase in pensions.

Cohen had anticipated this problem. On July 13 he had proposed to his boss, HEW Secretary Celebrezze, a substitute for the House bill. All retired and disabled workers would receive a flat $7 increase in the benefit per month. He/she would then have the option of either taking it in cash or using $5 to buy insurance, 45 days of hospitalization without a deductible. A modest increase of 0.2 percent in the contribution rate for both the employer and the employee would finance this program.

On July 20 Senator Abraham Ribicoff, former HEW secretary, wrote the President that the Senate would easily vote for higher pensions and would then be reluctant to vote for "the big tax increase that would be needed to add hospital insurance." Thus, the House bill "may well foreclose all hope of a medicare bill for a long time." The solution was to offer the worker "a *choice* at age 65 of whether he wanted an increased cash benefit or hospital insurance instead." Ribicoff then laid out Cohen's plan with the added options of 90 days of hospitalization with a small deductible or home nursing care. The senator was convinced that it would pass both the Finance Committee and the Senate and that it would be "a hard one for Wilbur Mills to reject after Senate passage."

The Senate Democratic leadership coalesced around the Ribicoff strategy. Manatos reported that majority leader Mansfield, vice presidential candidate Humphrey, and Medicare sponsor Anderson agreed that it was the "*only*" approach." Ribicoff and Anderson would have the bill printed and Mansfield and Humphrey would cosponsor it. They urged the President to persuade the southern Democrats on the Finance Committee—George Smathers of Florida, Russell Long of Louisiana, Herman Talmadge of Georgia, and William Fulbright of Arkansas, along with Wilbur Mills—to accept the strategy. Anderson felt that if Mills did not go along they should allow the pension proposal to die. If it took effect, he said, "Medical Care is lost for all time."

But there were many problems. If both measures were enacted, Democratic senators from rural states might be compelled to vote against an increase in the tax which could reach $500 on a self-employed farmer. Dr. Annis had controlled the Smathers's vote since 1950 when the AMA ran him successfully against Claude Pepper, "Mr. Social Security," in the Democratic primary. While the immigration of oldsters into Florida was tilting the state toward Medicare and he was considering a declaration of independence in 1965, he was committed to the AMA in 1964. Russell Long had also been captured by organized medicine. His father Huey, the Louisiana Kingfish, had taught his boy that benefits to constituents should be distributed by the Long machine. The well-informed clerk of the Senate Finance Committee said that the pension bill could move to the floor "with dispatch." If the President insisted on adding on Medicare, the committee would hold hearings which "would last until October," that is, the middle of the presidential campaign.

These difficulties paled alongside those raised by Mills. On July 20 Wilson informed the chairman that the administration was considering the Ribicoff strategy. He "obviously, was surprised." He strongly opposed a conference between the houses to reconcile the bills in which pressure would be put on him to accept Medicare. He wanted to know no details of the Ribicoff bill, Wilson wrote, "lest the word get out that he was trying to dictate the Senate bill." On August 13, Cohen wrote O'Brien, "I now have three reports that Wilbur Mills has said that under no circumstances will he accept a hospital insurance proposal in conference." Cohen feared that "Mills had so staked himself out to so many people that he cannot possibly back track."

The Senate Finance Committee held hearings on seven consecutive work days between August 6 and 14, 1964. It considered three bills: H.R. 11865, the House-passed increase in old-age benefits, and two amendments to it—King-Anderson, which because of Senator Anderson's illness was introduced by Senator Gore of Tennessee and was called the Gore amendment, and the Javits bill. The Ribicoff version was not even before the committee.

Celebrezze spoke for the administration. "H.R. 11865," he said, "is seriously lacking in the area of highest priority need . . . , hospital insurance for the aged . . . under social security." Thus, he strongly urged the Gore amendment. At the same time, Celebrezze asked for enactment of the increase in pension benefits. But, Byrd pointed out, the rule was that the payroll tax should not exceed 10 percent. "If you take both of these bills, it will be 10.4." Celebrezze explained that the combined tax would remain under 10 percent if the taxable wage base was raised from $5400 to $6600. "If I had to make a choice," he said, ". . . hospital care for the aged is much more important . . . than a small increase in benefits."

This argument fell on deaf ears; the Finance Committee strongly opposed Medicare. The six liberal Democrats—Anderson, Gore, Ribicoff, Paul Douglas of Illinois, Eugene McCarthy of Minnesota, and Vance Hartke of Indiana—faced a solid phalanx of six Republicans led by minority leader Everett Dirksen and four southern Democrats—Byrd, Smathers, Long, and Fulbright. The Gore amendment went down 11 to 6. Ribicoff then offered his substitute, which was whipped 12 to 5 (Hartke switched). The Javits bill lost by voice vote. The committee then unanimously reported H.R. 11865 on August 20 and took no action on Medicare.

But the political situation in the Senate differed from that in the House. In the latter the split in Ways and Means reflected the division in the House. The Senate, however, was much more liberal than its Finance Committee. The voting on the floor on the Gore amendment on September 2 was confused. At the outset several liberal Democrats were absent, and the vote was 42 to 42. With great publicity Barry Goldwater arrived dramatically from Arizona to cast his vote against Medicare, calling it "an insult to the intelligence of the American people." (That afternoon Bill Moyers had the Democratic National Committee pushing the news to organizations of the elderly, particularly in Florida and southern California). On the third ballot, still with a few absent, the Senate adopted the Gore amendment 49 to 46. This was the first time either house had voted for Medicare. On September 3, 1964, the Senate passed the combined bill—higher pensions and Medicare—by a vote of 60 to 28.

The worst fears of Wilbur Mills had come to pass: he must attend a conference on Medicare. The Senate named seven conferees: five Democrats—Byrd, Anderson, Gore, Smathers, and Long—and two Republicans—John Williams of Delaware and Frank Carlson of Kansas. In fact, only Anderson and Gore had voted for Medicare. Byrd, who opposed Social Security in any form, felt constrained to uphold the Senate at least by abstaining. That made four to two. The House designated five conferees: three Democrats—Mills, King, and whip Hale Boggs—and two Republicans—Byrnes and Thomas Curtis of Missouri. King and Boggs had voted for Medicare; Mills, Byrnes, and Curtis against.

The conference sat for two tortured weeks in the latter part of September. Cohen sent in a stream of possible compromises which were exhaustively debated. O'Brien, Manatos, and Wilson suggested a variety of parliamentary moves. They included a metaphysical debate with the House parliamentarian over whether the bill was properly "in conference" because of an uncertain relationship between the hospital insurance trust fund and the Social Security Act. There was great pressure on the President to intervene in order to turn several of the conferees around and he came on with flags flying, but with only middling success. Smathers was persuaded to desert the AMA earlier than he had intended. Long, who hoped to inherit the position of majority whip from Humphrey, received the needed assurances. This meant that the Senate conferees were now four to two for Medicare with one abstention.

But nothing could move Mills. He said that he was concerned about the financial soundness of Medicare and that was true. But that could hardly have justified the pressure and bad press to which he was subjected. Some thought he was protecting his friends in the House who did not want to alienate either the oldsters or the doctors by voting on the eve of the election. More likely, he must have expected the bill to fail in the House and inviting that result would violate his longstanding objection to meaningless ceremonies.

The decisive conference vote on the Senate Medicare bill took place on October 1, 1964. Senators Long, Smathers, Anderson, and Gore were in favor; Williams and Carlson were opposed; and Byrd abstained. But only King and Boggs joined them from the House. Byrnes, Curtis, and Mills voted against Medicare.

As a consequence, the 88th Congress did not enact hospital insurance. Wilbur Mills became the public villain. Lyndon Johnson, as *Congressional Quarterly* pointed out, suffered his "worst legislative defeat in an otherwise impressive record." At his press conference on October 3, the President said, "We regret that we could never get . . . Mills . . . , Byrnes . . . , and

Curtis to yield or to moderate their views. . . ." But now Johnson and Humphrey had a powerful campaign issue which they could exploit with elderly voters.

The loss, in fact, was only a passing incident. "From day one on Medicare," Larry O'Brien said, "never did I envision ultimate, final failure. It was only a matter of time. Because the guts of it . . . demanded favorable action." Wholly aside from the anticipated electoral landslide, Medicare by the fall of 1964 was unstoppable. Four years of hammering by Kennedy and Johnson had made an impact in both Congress and the country. The polls showed about two-thirds of the voters favored Medicare. The health needs of the elderly were increasing in both numbers and costs. Neither of the alternatives—Kerr-Mills or Javits—was feasible. The increasingly shrill, often false, and costly AMA campaign was losing effect, as defections among its own members and among politicians like Smathers and Long demonstrated. The competence of the Social Security Administration enjoyed universal confidence. The Senate had now voted for King-Anderson. Thus, Wilbur Mills in a speech in Little Rock on September 28 said, "I am acutely aware of the fact that there is a problem here which must be met."

If there were any residual doubts, the election results laid them to rest. The Goldwater-Republican opposition to Medicare took a fearful drubbing. One estimate was that 22 percent of those who voted were over 60 and that 2 million of them switched from Republican to Democratic. Among the 10 states with the highest percentage of elderly voters, seven were traditionally Republican; all 10 went Democratic. Of the 14 doctors who ran for Congress, 11 were defeated. The three who won included one supporter of Medicare, a long-time incumbent, and one who ran in a safe district against a weak opponent. The AMA lost three sure votes on Ways and Means. Most important, both the Senate and the House would have large pro-Medicare majorities in the 89th Congress. Manatos estimated the Senate margin very conservatively as 55 to 45.

No one ever accused Wilbur Mills of indifference to the direction of the political wind. Soon after the election he made another speech in Little Rock in which he said, "I can support a payroll tax for financing health benefits just as I have supported a payroll tax for cash benefits." He stated that he would be pleased to present a Medicare bill to the Ways and Means Committee if the President asked him to. The President said he would ask.[3]

The massive Democratic victory struck the committees of the House of Representatives like an earthquake. Judge Smith and his Rules Committee were decisively unblocked by reinstatement of the 21-day rule. Now a committee majority could dislodge a bill from Rules after a minimum delay of three weeks. More relevant to Medicare, the House abandoned the 3 to 2 ratio for committee membership, 15 Democrats to 10 Republicans, for the actual distribution between the parties, 2 to 1. Thus, Ways and Means was now composed of 17 Democrats and 8 Republicans, the ratio that prevailed after Roosevelt's landslide in 1936. This guaranteed a pro-Medicare majority.

The Republicans were also affected. Representative Frank T. Bow, a prominent conservative from Ohio, wrote all the House members of his party, "Social Security and medical care were primary issues in 1964, and the Republican response on these issues was a major factor in the disaster that befell us." Minority leader Charles Halleck had led the opposition to Medicare. The House Republicans voted to replace him with Gerald Ford of Michigan, who promised "positive opposition." While Ford's views were virtually identical with Halleck's, they seemed different because he was more attractive and genial.

Johnson was implacable. In the State of Union message on January 4, 1965, he called for assistance to the elderly "by providing hospital care under social security and by raising benefit payments to those struggling to maintain the dignity of their later years." The top priority attached to Medicare was reflected in the bill numbers: H.R. 1 and S. 1. On January 7 the President sent Congress a special message—"Advancing the Nation's Health." The first proposal in this comprehensive program was hospital insurance for the aged. "I consider this measure to be of utmost urgency."

The President called the departmental people handling legislation to the Fish Room in the White House, and Wilbur Cohen was among them. Johnson said that he had just won an overwhelming victory, but "every day while I'm in office, I'm going to lose votes. I'm going to alienate somebody." This had happened to Wilson and to Roosevelt. Thus, "We've got to get this legislation fast. You've got to get it during my honeymoon."

Cohen had worked up the bill to be submitted to Congress during the fall of 1964 and had a draft ready by November 15. "We are considering a 7% increase" in old-age benefits. In 1964 the Senate amount was $7 and the House adopted 5 percent. This would be retroactive to January 1, 1965. The earnings base would rise from $4800 to $5600. The combined employer-employee payroll tax rate would increase from 8.8 percent in 1966 to 10.4 in 1971. The hospital insurance draft closely followed the bill that passed the Senate in 1964. Javits was pressing again for his version. While the leadership seemed to have little objection, complementary private health insurance had aroused no interest. Neither the committee nor the conference had supported it. "Nor," Cohen wrote, "do I see anything in it which will help us obtain support from Mr. Mills."

The AMA, stumbling politically, decided that it must appear "affirmative" and trotted out what it called Eldercare. In essence an extension of Kerr-Mills, federal and state grants would subsidize private health insurance for old people who chose the plan voluntarily. The main feature was the coverage of both doctor and hospital bills. Herlong and Curtis, who were members of the Ways and Means Committee, introduced the Eldercare bill on January 27. The AMA then launched a massive and expensive advertising campaign to persuade the public that Medicare would cheat the elderly by failing to pay their doctor bills. But no one took Eldercare seriously. Representative Frank Thompson of New Jersey suggested an alternative, which he called "Doctorcare":

> It was to be financed by a two-per-cent federal tax on applesauce, and the funds were to be used to provide special therapy for any physician who felt himself suffering from an urge to make house calls; if he didn't respond satisfactorily to the arguments of his colleagues over the phone, he would be rushed to the nearest Cadillac showroom.

On January 28, Byrnes introduced the Republican bill. It had been written by an insurance company and represented the views of House minority leader Ford. The federal government would administer and finance private health insurance for those who chose it. The attraction of the Byrnes bill was that its coverage was much broader than Medicare, including physicians' services, drugs, private duty nursing, and care in mental hospitals. Byrnes called his bill Bettercare. Both Mills and Cohen worried that the Republicans could claim that they offered, as Cohen put it, "a more comprehensive and a better package" than Medicare.

From late January to early March 1965 the Ways and Means Committee took expert testimony in executive session from Blue Cross, the American Hospital Association, the Kaiser Health Plan, Group Health, state health officials, the Council of Economic Advisers, and the Treasury. The committee also discussed technical aspects of the bills before it. Cohen was continuously present and made regular reports to the White House.

The developments on March 2, 1965, Cohen wrote the President, were of "major significance." In the morning Mills asked Cohen to review the bills before the committee. He finished with the Byrnes bill about 3 p.m. "You know, John," Mills said to Byrnes, "I like that idea of yours." He proceeded to speak out loud about the ideas that had been turning over in his mind. Everyone in the room studied each word with care because they realized that he was laying out what would become the national policy.

Mills viewed the Republican bill not as an *alternative* to Medicare, but as a *supplement* to it. He then proposed what he called a "three-layer cake." An expanded Kerr-Mills would be the bottom layer, to take comprehensive care of those without means. Medicare would be the middle layer to provide hospital care for those under Social Security. The Byrnes bill would be the top layer, a voluntary system to cover doctor bills.

"Like everyone else in the room," Cohen recalled later, "I was stunned by Mills's strategy. It was the most brilliant legislative move I'd seen in thirty years. . . . Mills had taken the A.M.A.'s ammunition, put it in the Republicans' gun, and blown both of them off the map." Byrnes "just sat there with his mouth open." The beauty of the Mills strategy was that it disposed of *all* the substantive issues and guaranteed that the legislation would clear Ways and Means, the House, and the Senate with overwhelming majorities. No wonder Cohen was stunned.

When he finished Mills asked Cohen whether he could weave the Byrnes bill into King-Anderson that night. Cohen said that he could. Mills told him to do so, to have Robert Myers, Social Security's chief actuary, estimate the added costs, and to have everything ready the next morning. On March 3 Cohen presented the amended bill. Myers would fund medical coverage by having each individual pay a $50 deductible, along with a contribution of $6 a month, $3 by the covered person and $3 from the Treasury. "O.K." Mills said, "it sounds fine." He adjourned the meeting.

That afternoon Cohen was in the Oval Office with his written report. "Mr. Mills has become very much concerned—as I am—over the fact that the Republican proposal . . . provides for medical benefits much broader in scope than our proposal." If the administration enacted King-Anderson, the GOP could attack it for being narrower than Bettercare. The Mills strategy was "unassailable politically." But it would require $400 to $500 million from the Treasury to pay the $3 for doctor bills.

Johnson was dazzled by the chairman's master stroke. He asked what he could do to help. Cohen, puzzled, asked about the $500 million. The President said, "I'm going to run and get my brother." More puzzled, Cohen said he did not understand. Johnson said the railroad gave a prospective switchman an intelligence test. "What would you do if a train was coming from the east going 60 miles an hour and another one was coming from the west going 60 miles an hour, and they were heading for each other at just a mile separate?" "I'd go get my brother." "Why?" "Because he hasn't ever seen a train wreck." The President gave Cohen the $500 million and told him to watch out for trains.

Mills had a deserved reputation for being a world-class staller, but now he was all business. He told the White House that he intended to have the bill ready for voting in the week of March 15. Since the version before the committee came to 253 pages and it was read page by page, this was a formidable task. And there were complications. Gardner Ackley, chairman of the Council of Economic Advisers, pointed out that the increase in payroll taxes would create a "large fiscal drag on the economy in the first half of 1966." This led to extended discussions between the Council, the Treasury, HEW, and Mills to shift the timing of collections and disbursements in order to reduce the drag. There was also a sharp disagreement over whether the bills of radiologists, anaesthesiologists, pathologists, and those in physical medicine should be paid under the hospital or the medical program. The administration, concerned about rising costs, urged the hospital route. But Mills, Cohen wrote, was "absolutely adamant . . . He wants to be able to say on the House floor that physicians are *not* covered under the social security part." At this time the chairman was in complete control and he overrode the opposition. The revised bill, now grown to 296 pages, was completed on March 19, 1965.

Mills called the Ways and Means Committee to vote on H.R. 6675 on March 23. It went 17 to 8. All the Democrats, including those from the South, followed the chairman and all the Republicans opposed him. Mills had always insisted that important legislative work be performed in committee and he demanded large majorities. This action fitted his preferences snugly.

The "debate" on H.R. 6675 was desultory and took only one day. In fact, it was Wilbur Mills Day. When he walked to the rostrum in the well of the House he received a standing ovation from both sides of the aisle. Mills presented a masterful summary and analysis of H.R. 6675, only rarely glancing at his notes. There was nothing left but the voting and it was overwhelming—313 to 115. The bill gained the support of 248 Democrats and 65 Republicans; it was opposed by 42 Democrats and 73 Republicans. The northern Democrats were solid—189 to 2. Mills carried with him a majority of the southern Democrats—59 to 40. The President immediately phoned congratulations to the House leadership and to Mills, King, and John Dingell, the son of one of the authors of the Wagner-Murray-Dingell bill of the forties. He was unable to reach Aimé Forand, who first introduced Medicare and who would have been extremely pleased.

The Senate, without strong leadership, dragged its way through H.R. 6675. The President wanted no trouble from Senator Byrd and gave the crusty Virginian a big shove. On March 26 he called a group of leaders of both houses to the White House for a televised press conference. All those who attended except Byrd, who was installed in a chair on Johnson's left, strongly supported Medicare. The President started at his right and asked each individual what he thought of the bill. Everyone thought that it was great and that it would soon be enacted. He then asked the embarrassed Byrd to "make an observation." He said he had none to make because the bill had not yet reached the Senate, but there would be hearings. "And you have nothing that you know of that would prevent that coming about in reasonable time, not anything ahead of it in the committee?" Byrd gulped, "Nothing." Johnson summarized: "You will arrange for prompt hearings and thorough hearings?" "Yes." Carl Albert said, "That was the best example of 'The Treatment' in public that anyone ever got."

In return, the Virginian used an opening to embarrass the administration. The Civil Rights Leadership Conference wanted to be certain that hospitals which participated in Medicare would administer their programs without discrimination based on race, creed, color, or national origin. The question was whether Title VI of the Civil Rights Act of 1964 would apply to Medicare. If it did, they would not jeopardize the bill by offering an amendment. If it did not, they would insist upon one. On April 13 Byrd wrote Secretary Celebrezze to ask whether Title VI would apply to H.R. 6675.

The problem was legally complicated and was turned over to Lee White, the President's counsel on civil rights. Celebrezze's instinctive reaction was to say that Title VI was inapplicable because the law expressly excluded insurance and Medicare was an insurance program. But the Department of Justice wrote a memorandum concluding the opposite. On the other hand, White wrote the President, "They could support a theory that the Title does not apply if it is desirable to do so." Larry O'Brien reckoned that the addition of a nondiscrimination amendment would cause trouble in the Finance Committee and would reduce the majority on the floor to a shaky 51 votes. White, supported by Moyers, strongly urged that Celebrezze write Byrd that Title VI applied to Medicare and should so testify before the committee. He did both.

The hearings before the Finance Committee took place from April 29 to May 18, 1965. Old spokesmen went over old ground and no one seemed to pay attention. But in the deliberations of the committee hell broke loose. In part this was due to the enormous pressure on the committee and on the Senate itself in May and June from Lyndon Johnson's gigantic legislative program. Manatos wrote on June 16:

> The Senate this week has passed Foreign Aid, Excise Tax Repeal, Saline Water, Debt Limit, Wheat Agreement Extension, Grand Coullee Powerhouse, and Cigaret Labeling (7 bills). It takes up Silver Coinage tomorrow, and could probably clear the decks the balance of the week to make ready for Community Mental Health Centers Staffing, Drug Abuse Control, Health Research Facilities, and Regional Medical Complex (Heart, Cancer and Stroke) next week.

While this was an immense burden, its main effect on Medicare was to cause delay (the President typically insisted on having it both ways—a huge program and speedy action). The much nastier problem was Russell Long.

The senator from Louisiana, with Clinton Anderson's support, had, indeed, become majority whip and, after Kerr's death, was the ranking Democrat on the Finance Committee. Further, the leadership with the approval of both the New Mexican and the White House had installed Long as floor leader on Medicare because Anderson's energy had been sapped by illness.

But Long had his own game to play, by his own rules. Under strong presidential pressure, he had cast his ballot for the contemporaneous Voting Rights bill, which had damaged him politically with the rednecks in Louisiana. He used H.R. 6675 to demonstrate back home that he was not Lyndon Johnson's errand boy. Whether he intended it or not, the AMA accepted his ploy as a means of creating a deadlock in the Senate-House conference and so supported his proposals despite the fact that they were substantively anathema to organized medicine.

Long offered an omnibus amendment that would kick out King-Anderson and would (1) combine the hospital and medical programs; (2) broaden the benefits to provide longer hospital stay, payment for drugs, and payment for many additional medical services; (3) eliminate the $3 monthly charge on individuals and stick the Treasury with the whole cost; and (4) change the $40 and $50 deductibles to 10 percent of the individual's income up to a maximum of $1000. Wilbur Cohen was appalled and had an extended session with Long on May 5, but was unable to change his mind.

Long, of course, grabbed the spotlight and was delighted with the publicity he aroused. He enjoyed himself by telling key people that he was only putting on a show or that he was in dead earnest. He certainly made suckers out of the innocent liberals.

For a long time Long did not have his proposals printed in order to prevent other senators from seeing them. He explained them orally to liberal Democrats, assuring them that they were modest. Since he represented the administration, they assumed that he had the President's approval. As the committee was adjourning for lunch on June 17, he appeared suddenly and orally set forth his amendments. He said the present bill was a political time bomb and that he would save them from defeat. There were a few minutes of discussion, which Richard Harris described as perhaps "the most casual treatment of a major piece of legislation in Senate history," and Long called for the vote. He won 7 to 6! Anderson then cast Fulbright's proxy, making it a tie, which was defeat. Long said Fulbright had changed his mind and that he had a later proxy. The clerk verified the date on the paper. The vote was 8 to 6 in favor and the committee adjourned for lunch. Anderson, puzzled, got the proxy and while the date was indeed later, discovered that it was for *another* bill. That afternoon, Anderson and Fulbright, both incensed, confronted Long and demanded a new vote. Mansfield later denounced him at a Democratic policy meeting. Paul Douglas had voted for Long's bill. When he got back to his office, he figured out what it meant and was staggered. Aside from busting the bank and being administratively unworkable, it would turn the nation's hospitals into warehouses for the senile. He joined the ranks of the outraged. The President by telephone on June 18 demanded that Long withdraw his amendments. He refused. Johnson called him to the White House on June 21. But the Texas Treatment did not work in Louisiana.

By June 30, when the final vote was taken, everyone knew what Long was up to. It went 12 to 5 in favor of H.R. 6675. There were several amendments, all of which, Cohen wrote, could be "satisfactorily adjusted in Conference." The majority consisted of six liberal Democrats—Anderson, Douglas, Gore, McCarthy, Hartke, and Ribicoff—four southern Democrats—Smathers, Talmadge, Fulbright, and Long (!)—and two Republicans—Dirksen and Carlson. This was, Manatos wrote, "the first Medicare bill to come out of Finance." Six of those in the majority—Long, Smathers, Talmadge, Fulbright, Carlson, and Dirksen—"had never before voted for Medicare."

When the committee bill reached the floor, Long's disease had become catching. Some liberal senators, certain that Mills would tolerate no nonsense in conference, played to their constituents and won majorities. As floor manager, Long welcomed these amendments. Anderson, completely out of patience, wrote the President imploring him to impose discipline on the Democrats. The White House feared that Long was deliberately making H.R. 6675 unacceptable to the House and the President instructed him to halt. Long immediately called for more amendments! Hartke introduced one that would have defined blindness so broadly that anyone with poor eyesight would qualify. Ribicoff's amendment would offer unlimited hospitalization. Another was a laugher. The AMA, which opposed coverage for doctors, had refused to poll its members on whether they wanted Medicare for themselves. Thus, they were left out. But state medical society polls showed that they wanted to be included and an amendment was proposed. Gore said, "The A.M.A. has made such a fine contribution to the enactment of Medicare that I think it has earned the right to come under its benefits." It passed.

On July 6 Manatos made a head count which showed a minimum of 58 senators for H.R. 6675. In addition, there were a number of uncertain southerners, Democrat Frank Lausche of Ohio, and a group of Republicans who might join the majority. Obviously, he expected a handsome victory. He was right.

H.R. 6675 laden with amendments passed the Senate on July 9, 1965, by a vote of 68 to 21. Fourteen Democrats, mainly from the South, and Lausche switched their votes from 1964. A fat group of Republicans joined them.

Mills totally dominated the six meetings of the conference committee and he swung a meat cleaver. He said with satisfaction that he chopped away at least 95 percent of the Senate amendments. Long, who stood by helpless, said that Mills would have opposed the framing of the Constitution that "created the U.S. Senate." Thus, the final bill was essentially the one that the House had adopted. On July 27, 1965, that body accepted it by a vote of 307 to 116. The Senate followed the next day 70 to 24. The President quietly signed Public Law 89–97 on June 30, 1965, in order to protect $30 million in benefits for widows and orphans which would have been lost in the new fiscal year. He would have his big party a month later.[4]

The Voting Rights Act and Medicare were passed at virtually the same time. The President wanted to have a Texas-style ceremony to celebrate the passage of H.R. 6675. On July 16 he instructed six members of his staff to choose appropriate locations for the signings. They recommended the Capitol for voting rights. "Sign Medicare in Independence, Missouri in the presence of President Truman. Signifying the relationship between the first call for Medicare and its final passage. We would carry with us in the President's plane the Congressmen and Senators who ought to be at the signing." Johnson approved both. Horace Busby was in charge of arrangements.

Busby soon convinced himself that Independence was "inadvisable." Truman in 1945 had urged health care for the *entire* population, not just the elderly. Meeting in Independence would suggest that Johnson wanted to extend Medicare to all Americans. The AMA might respond with a boycott. Truman, known for his tart tongue, might make some "distasteful remarks . . . about the medical profession." Cohen noted that August 15 would be the thirtieth anniversary of the Social Security Act. Why not honor FDR with a ceremony at Hyde Park? But Busby thought Johnson should not play Roosevelt because that would enhance his image of "vanity, self-centeredness." He preferred the White House. Cohen was talking of a guest list which might reach 700, and they could be accommodated at the executive mansion. "A quest for publicity" in Independence "might unhappily coincide with somber decisions or news relative to Viet Nam." But the President insisted and Independence it would be.

On the sunny afternoon of July 30, 1965, the two Presidents stood on the steps of the Truman Library before a large crowd. The old man was delighted, used his tongue graciously, and was a splendid host. In a brief speech Johnson managed to mention almost everybody from the old-timers like FDR, Wagner, Murray, Dingell, and Forand to the current Democratic leadership, including Russell Long for his "effective and able work"! He merely listed Wilbur Cohen (this was mainly legislators' day) while he spoke of the "legislative genius" of Wilbur Mills. "But it all started really with the man from Independence." It was quite a party.

Public Law 89–97, officially the Social Security Amendments of 1965, now grown to 400 pages, was comprehensive and, as Cohen and Robert M. Ball, the Commissioner of Social Security, wrote, "embod[ied] the most far-reaching social security legislation to be enacted since the original Social Security Act was passed 30 years earlier."

The most important change, of course, was the introduction of health insurance for the aged, both hospital and medical, which became the new title XVIII of the Social Security Act. Present and future recipients of old-age pensions at age 65 (most of those presently uncovered would be brought in by 1968) would be automatically covered by hospital insurance. It would provide care for up to 90 days for each illness. The patient would pay a $40 deductible for 60 days and $10 a day thereafter. It would also provide posthospital extended care, outpatient diagnostic services, and posthospital home health services with similar payment arrangements. The worker and his employer would contribute throughout the former's working life to the Hospital Insurance Trust Fund at the combined social security rate of 7 percent in 1966 (rising thereafter to 11 percent in 1973–75) of the first $6600 of annual earnings. Social Security would contract with "providers of service" (Blue Shield, insurance companies, Kaiser, etc.) for hospital care at prices based on "reasonable costs."

Medical insurance was voluntary and available to anyone 65 or over. The individual would pay $3 a month and the Treasury would pay a like amount from general revenues. The money would be banked in the Supplementary Medical Insurance Trust Fund. Enrollment would take place between September 1, 1965, and March 31, 1966; benefits would start on July 1, 1966. They would cover physicians' services, home health services, and numerous other medical and health services. The plan would cover 80 percent of the doctor's bill. HEW would contract with insurance carriers to administer the program. The charges must be "reasonable," defined as those no higher than others were charged and those prevailing in the locality.

Old-age, survivors', and disability insurance benefits were raised 7 percent across the board, retroactive to January 1, 1965, with a minimum of $4 a month for retirees. This would require part of the increased contributions by employers and employees noted above.

A new title XIX of the law would replace Kerr-Mills for the aged medically needy, defined to include as well the blind, the disabled, and families with dependent children. The states would administer the program with federal matching funds ranging from 55 to 83 percent, the states supplying the remainder.

There were a great number of amendments of lesser importance, many relating to children. Among them, of course, and with a certain irony, was Medicare coverage for self-employed doctors of medicine.[5]

On July 27, 1965, just before the party at the Truman Library, the President appointed Anthony Celebrezze to the Court of Appeals for the Sixth Circuit and John W. Gardner as Secretary of the Department of Health, Education, and Welfare. Celebrezze had long held the ambition of becoming a federal judge. Gardner, the president of the Carnegie Corporation and a distinguished authority on education, would be in general charge of launching Medicare. There were two immediate and formidable problems: winning the cooperation of the AMA and erecting a massive administrative structure for the program.

Cohen set out the complicated situation with organized medicine, an analysis the President fully shared:

> I knew that the only way that you could provide medical care in this country is through doctors. Government people don't give Medicare; it's an individual doctor. The doctors . . . were feeling a sense of complete frus-

tration and complete betrayal by the Congress. They could not understand what happened to them because their indignation was self-righteous. They had been led to believe that they were right and everybody else was wrong. . . . With their defeat they expected to be kicked around by the government as if they were a vanquished enemy in a great battle. . . . I . . . sent notice to Chicago that . . . we would be glad to meet with them. . . . "You fellows can be on the inside."

But this was only one of AMA's problems. The Ohio Medical Association, representing 10,000 doctors, had already adopted a resolution to boycott Medicare. Some 25,000 physicians gathered in New York on June 20, 1965, for the AMA convention and there was widespread support for a boycott, including the outgoing president. Nine state delegations introduced boycott resolutions. But cooler heads prevailed. Dr. James Z. Appel, the incoming president, warned against "unethical tactics such as boycott, strike, or sabotage." The trustees, concerned about pushing Congress to take even more drastic action, put together the votes to elect Dr. Charles L. Hudson of Ohio as president. Though a strong Goldwaterite, he was a moderate on Medicare and had opposed his state's boycott proposal. The House of Delegates then adopted a resolution authorizing its officers to meet with the President to discuss legislation with "a view to safeguarding the continued provision of the highest quality and availability of medical care to the people of the United States."

The meeting took place at the White House at noon on June 29. AMA sent its eleven top officers: Dr. Appel, Dr. Hudson, four members of the board of trustees, the chairman of its committees on legislation and medical service, the executive vice president, and his assistant. On July 26 Cohen had submitted a memorandum listing the ten important points that he urged the President to make. The meeting was memorable. "I'd never seen anything like it," an administration official said. He gave this account:

The President made a powerful, moving appeal to the doctors to accept the new law. . . . He went on in that way for some time, and then he began talking about what wonderful men doctors were, and how when his daddy was sick the doctor would come over and sit up all night with him, and charge a pittance. . . . Then, suddenly, he got up and stretched. Of course, when the President of the United States stands up, everybody stands up. They jumped to their feet, and then he sat down, so they sat down, too. He started off again, with another moving statement about this great nation and its obligation to those who had helped make it great and who were now old and sick and helpless through no fault of their own. Gradually, he moved back to the cornfield, and then he stood up again, and again they jumped to their feet. He did that a couple more times—until they were fully aware of who was President—and then he turned to a memorandum on his desk. He read the statement in the bill prohibiting any government interference in any kind of medical practice at any time, and also the statement guaranteeing freedom of choice for both doctors and patients, and assured them there would be no government meddling in these matters. Next, he explained that Blue Cross and private insurance carriers, who are the administrative middlemen under the law, would determine the bill's definition of "reasonable charges" on the basis of what was customary for a given area. Naturally, the doctors went for this, because they have great influence with most of those outfits. Toward the end, he asked for their help in drawing up regulations to implement the law. Then he got up one more time, and said that he had to leave. Before he went, he turned to Cohen, who is the A.M.A.'s idea of an archfiend, and, shaking a huge forefinger in his face, he said, "Wilbur, I want you to stay here with these gentlemen, and work things out according to my instructions—no matter how long it takes you." Afterward, I heard one A.M.A. man say to another, "Boy, did you hear how he talked to Cohen." Of course, Wilbur had written the memorandum.

The demands for a boycott within the AMA continued to resonate, but gradually died out by July 1, 1966, when Medicare took effect. The formerly irate doctors learned that they would, indeed, continue to deal with familiar intermediaries and that no bureaucrats would tell them how to practice medicine. Moreover, they would enjoy a flood of new business at higher fees. Medical heartburn subsided.

"The application of Medicare to twenty million people on July 1," Wilbur Cohen said, "was perhaps the biggest single governmental operation since D-Day in Europe during World War II." Robert M. Ball, the Commissioner of Social Security, was a superb administrator and this was his master performance. He started planning eleven months before the program went into operation. At the suggestion of I. S. Falk, Cohen and Ball chose to begin on July 1 rather than January 1, 1966. Hospitals admit 10 to 20 percent more patients in January because of winter ailments and the first week in July includes the holiday of the Fourth, when many people are on vacation. "So," Cohen observed, "we started at a point where the congestion is the least."

Social Security, using special funds appropriated by Congress, created a new Bureau of Health Insurance. It took on 9000 permanent employees and 3000 temporaries, the latter to handle the initial load. Beyond the regular field system of 622 offices and 3500 itinerant service points, 100 new offices and 21 service centers were opened. Massive computers were installed to keep the records.

An immense mail, press, radio, and TV barrage notified eligible persons of their benefits and the enrollment procedure before March 31, 1966. It was remarkably successful. Prior to the deadline, Ball wrote, "we had reached individually . . . just about all of the 19.1 million people who will be 65 or over on July 1 of this year." By early May 1966, 16.8 million, 88 percent, had voluntarily enrolled for medical insurance. "I doubt," Ball wrote, "if ever in history nearly 17 million people, in the course of 7 months, signed up to pay $3 a month for anything." Old-age pension recipients were automatically covered for hospital insurance, over 20 million people. By early May over 90 percent of the nation's accredited hospitals and more than 80 percent of the nonaccredited had applied for participation in the program. Agreements were quickly negotiated with Blue Cross, Blue Shield, and the insurance companies to act as intermediaries. The American Medical and American Hospital associations were cooperating fully.

Social Security anticipated that Medicare would increase the hospital load by about 5 percent nationally, but with an uneven distribution, thereby creating local shortages of hospitals, doctors, and nurses. Congress was asked to enact comprehensive legislation to push up supply. During 1965, 30,000 hospital beds and 40,000 nursing home beds were added, and the numbers went up in 1966. The systems of nursing homes and home health services were expanded to ease the load on hospitals. Eight new medical schools opened their doors and the number of graduate nurses rose sharply.

Responding to careful planning and outstanding organization, Medicare opened its doors to the public on July 1, 1966, without a hitch. The newspapers put reporters on the steps of hospitals all over the country to report, in Kermit Gordon's words, "the inevitable bungling confusion and chaos." They expected a "massive surge of old people . . . jamming the hospitals, paralyzing the hospitals. . . . It never happened." Social Security immediately began to pay off millions of hospital and medical bills routinely.

Gordon was Director of the Budget, was intimately familiar with federal agencies, and looked on their efficiency with a skeptical eye. The Medicare law created a Health Insurance Benefits Advisory Council to track the new operation and make recommendations to the secretary of HEW. Gordon, who was chairman of the council, had an insider's view of the administrative performance. "The cunning of Wilbur Mills," he said, had created a program that was "twice as difficul. to administer as it needed to be." Nevertheless, Gordon concluded,

This was one of the most brilliant administrative performances I have ever seen in the United States government or anywhere else—*the* most brilliant. Social Security, which happens to be one of the tightest and smoothest operations in the federal government, was ready for this. . . . It went off with almost astonishing smoothness. . . .

With a mere nine months to prepare, administratively this was the largest and most complicated thing the . . . government had ever done outside the military field. . . . It turned out to be a real jewel in the crown of the federal government.[6]

Medicare stands alongside the Civil Rights Act as the two most significant and enduring legislative monuments of the Kennedy-Johnson era. It would help to transform the status of old people in American society from a majority who lived in or near poverty and could not afford health care to a majority who were comfortably off and were able to qualify for hospital and medical care under this program.

Who deserves the credit for this triumph? Lyndon Johnson comes first. He won the indispensible electoral landslide and he waged an unrelenting campaign to push the legislation through Congress. President Kennedy also played an important role by introducing the original bill in 1961 and by educating the public to accept the idea. The two Wilburs made formidable contributions. Wilbur Mills closed the loop by providing the formula for consolidating the significant bills, most important by adding medical to hospital coverage. Wilbur Cohen was the supreme advocate, tireless in his command of both ideas and technical details at every step of the legislative process. Robert Ball's careful planning and administrative skills were critical in erecting the administrative structure for Medicare. The AFL-CIO and its shock troops provided the necessary counterforce to the AMA. Finally, in a backhanded way Barry Goldwater deserves credit for guaranteeing the Johnson landslide and the massive Democratic majorities in Congress.

7

Breakthrough in Education

NO President prior to John Kennedy had exercised leadership on federal aid for education. By the sixties the need was clear. The huge baby boom generation was rolling into the schools and straining the capacity of the states and cities to bear the costs. Kennedy perceived this and staked out a strong position. Theodore Sorensen wrote, "The one domestic issue that mattered most to John Kennedy: education." If faith in education was a passion for Kennedy, it was an obsession with Lyndon Johnson. He said to Francis Keppel, his commissioner of education, "I want to see this coon-skin on the wall."

For a boy from the hardscrabble hill country of Texas schooling was the escape route to the large world, to the promise of American life. It offered equality of opportunity, a level playing field, to young people who lived in poverty, to blacks, to Mexican-Americans, and to women, an appealing concept to a democratic populist. He had attended Southwest Texas State Teachers College in San Marcos. He had devoted a year to teaching Spanish-speaking fifth, sixth, and seventh graders in God-forsaken Cotulla in the South Texas brush country. He had taught speech and debate for fifteen months at Sam Houston High School in Houston. In both schools he had thrown himself into teaching with passion and had enjoyed striking results. He knew what education could accomplish.

In addition, Johnson seems to have been moved by the need to compensate for his shame over the inadequacies of his own education. As a child he hated to go to school, was a discipline problem, and had academic difficulties. A record of his attendance for 1920 showed that of 180 days of school he was absent for 50 and tardy on 30. He resisted his parents' insistence that he go to college and ran away to California. "My daddy always told me," he told Doris Kearns, "that if I brushed up against the grindstone of life, I'd come away with far more polish than I could ever get at Harvard or Yale. I wanted to believe him, but somehow I never could." Southwest Texas State Teachers College, Robert Dallek wrote, was "a small provincial school with little standing in the world of higher education." It had won accreditation only two years before he entered. By contrast, Lady Bird was a graduate of the University of Texas. Johnson would always feel uncomfortable with the people he called "the Harvards," who included John and Robert Kennedy and many of his own White House advisers. He did not want others to feel his shame.[1]

In the interregnum between his election and taking power, Kennedy had appointed a task force on education of which Frederick L. Hovde, the president of Purdue, was chairman. Other members included John Gardner, president of the Carnegie Foundation, and Francis Keppel, dean of Harvard's School of Education. Among its key recommendations were financial support for public, but not private, schools with the amounts skewed in favor of low-income states with poor school systems and ghetto schools in the big cities. Keppel was proud of the fact that this was the first concrete proposal to give special assistance to inner-city education. Another important recommendation was for grants and loans to colleges to construct academic facilities.

In 1961 Kennedy sent up bills incorporating these ideas and many others. The key primary and secondary education bill foundered on the church-state issue. While there were many private schools, the Catholic Church operated 85 percent of them for its more than 5 million pupils. The National Catholic Welfare Conference insisted that, if Congress was going to support education, the parochial school pupils must get their fair share. Two powerful lobbies, the National Education Association, representing close to a million teachers, and the National Council of Churches, speaking for 31 Protestant denominations, opposed any support for parochial schools. The bill cleared the Senate but sank on the church-state reef in the House Rules Committee.

In 1962 the President tried again, but with no better result. The parochial school issue had not cooled and the House declined even to consider the basic bill.

Kennedy realized that something must be done to move the legislation and in late 1962 persuaded Keppel to become commissioner of education. He put together about two dozen proposals in a single bill, which he expected Congress would break up. By the fall of 1963 the individual bills began to clear both houses. The most important was the Higher Education Facilities Act; there were five others. Kennedy lived to sign one; Johnson put his name on the others shortly after the assassination.

Except for progress on some of the secondary legislation, the year 1964 was a time for regrouping. Keppel was convinced that another expert study was needed and, along with everyone else, felt that nothing could be done on basic primary and secondary education until the religious issue was resolved.

The President agreed with Keppel on both counts. A new, hard look in 1964 could take account of recent developments, among them the relationship of the Civil Rights Act and the poverty program to federal aid for education. Further, Johnson was confident that he would win the election handsomely and bring in large Democratic majorities in both houses in 1965. This would allow him to accomplish far more in 1965 than either Kennedy or he had been able to do so far.

In his commencement address at the University of Michigan on May 22, 1964, the President had both announced his Great Society and had suggested how he would go about reaching it:

> We are going to assemble the best thought and the broadest knowledge.
> . . . I intend to establish working groups to prepare a series of White
> House conferences and meetings—on the cities, on natural beauty, on the
> quality of education, and on other emerging challenges. And from these
> meetings and from this inspiration and from these studies we will begin to
> set our course toward the Great Society.

On May 30 Walter Heller and Kermit Gordon proposed 14 task forces on policy issues, including education. They suggested that the members should be experts who "possess the gift of originality and imagination." They insisted that the task forces should be small, that they work "quietly," and that their reports should be submitted immediately after the presidential election in November. That is, they would form the basis for the Great Society's legislative program that would be submitted to Congress in January 1965.

The President was enthusiastic and announced the plan to his cabinet on July 2. Since the task forces would be encouraged "to think in bold terms" and "to strike out in new directions," they must function "without publicity":

> I attach great importance to this effort. I believe you share my desire that
> this be an activist Administration, not a caretaker of past gains. I want to
> get the advice of the best brains in the country . . . and I want their help
> in devising the best approach. . . . I want these task forces to question
> what we are now doing and to suggest better ways of doing it. You and I
> will still have the final task of accepting or rejecting, of making the judg-
> ments of what is feasible and what is not. But I want to start with no
> holds barred.

Johnson felt that some of Kennedy's task force reports had been undermined by their release to the press. Joseph Pechman's task force on intergovernmental fiscal cooperation in 1964 became a front-page story in the *New York Times* before the President had seen the report. Thereafter the White House insisted on secrecy. The education study would not be released until 1972.

Bill Moyers was in charge of launching the task forces and he devised a common formula. Education was probably its most notable and successful example. The task force consisted of 14 experts drawn from the various levels of education, public and private, secular and sectarian, white and black. Keppel was a member. Richard Goodwin was the White House liaison and William B. Cannon was the Bureau of the Budget expert on education financing. Moyers sent instructions to 13 task forces on July 6 (Shriver had already created his own and the poverty law was enacted on July 2, 1964). The deadline for the report was November 10.

Moyers also sent Goodwin a big think issue paper on education policy written by the Bureau of the Budget. The statutes enacted between September 1963 and February 1964 had a combined financial impact of only $750 million, less than the subsidy to universities for research alone. The defects in the educational system demanded much greater support—$2 billion at the start and $6 to $8 billion annually by the fourth year.

In the past, Budget noted, legislative proposals had come from the educational establishment and reflected the aims of the interest groups—teacher salaries, classroom construction, vocational education, state departments of education. Such programs were too particular and too small to do much good. Thus, the task force must think big. The education program should follow the example of the poverty program by stressing the "value of developing human resources" which met the "needs of people." "A single comprehensive education program can serve as a rallying point for all pressure groups."

Keppel had selected the members of the task force, starting with John Gardner, its gifted chairman. They were close friends, greatly admired each other, and looked at educational problems through the same lens. In fact, Keppel's father had headed the Carnegie Foundation before Gardner took over.

John Gardner had been born in Los Angeles in 1912 and raised in then pastoral Beverly Hills. After an M.A. at Stanford, he then got a Ph.D. in psychology at Berkeley. He taught at the Connecticut College for Women and Mt. Holyoke. During the war he worked with noted Harvard psychologist Henry Murray. Afterward Murray helped him get a job at Carnegie, where he rose rapidly to become president in 1955. With the position he held and his impressive writings in a style *Current Biography* called "clear, distilled, and aphoristic," he emerged as one of the nation's leading authorities on education. He had a "patrician bearing and calm manner [that] exudes an air of quiet strength and integrity." He was a progressive Republican, but had edited a volume of Kennedy's speeches. He made a very big impression in Washington, not least with Lyndon Johnson.

The President told Gardner that "he wanted our ideas, he wanted our best thinking, he wanted our most innovative thinking. And he wanted us to forget politics." Johnson added, "I'll figure out how to do it." Keppel played a decisive role on the task force. He was, Gardner said, at "every meeting, he knew everything that was going on, he contributed ideas, he took ideas out of the meeting. There was a complete exchange. . . . So some of the ideas went into the pot immediately." The task force scoured the country for suggestions. For example, it paid heed to a seminar the Office of Education held in 1963 for improving the education of the poor and for dealing with segregated schools.

The other members of the task force were James E. Allen, Jr., New York State Commissioner of Education; Hedley W. Donovan, editor of *Time;* Harold B. Gores, president of Educational Facilities Laboratory; Clark Kerr, president of the University of California; Edwin H. Land, president of Polaroid; Sidney P. Marland, Pittsburgh's superintendent of schools; Professor David Riesman of Harvard; the Reverend Paul C. Reinert, of St. Louis University; Raymond R. Tucker, the mayor of St. Louis; Ralph W. Tyler, director of the Center for Advanced Study in the Behavioral Sciences in Palo Alto; Stephen J. Wright, president of Fisk; and Professor Jerrold R. Zacharias, of MIT.

This was, Gardner wrote in the report, "a fateful moment in the history of American education." The system needed basic overhaul. If the U.S. was to build a "Great Society," education must be its heart. The key was "access." Millions of students were denied a proper education because they lived in states too poor to provide one, or in central cities in which the schools were beggared, or suffered from physical or emotional handicaps in localities which offered no or, at best, inadequate special education, or could not find the money to pay for a college education.

Thus, the thrust of the report was to raise the federal share of financial support for primary and secondary education from its current 3.5 percent, compared with 96.5 percent from state and local sources. This would be done with equalization formulas skewed to give poor states and ghetto schools a bigger share. Special education for the mentally retarded, the deaf, the speech impaired, the emotionally disturbed, the blind, and the crippled required additional funding. For college students loans, scholarships, and work-study should assist the academically qualified to pay for the costs of higher education.

The task force recommended a number of categorical programs: preschool teaching run by Head Start under the Office of Economic Opportunity; supplementary educational centers to assist local school systems in broadening their offerings; national laboratories to gather and develop technologically innovative methods of teaching; vigorous enforcement of Title VI of the Civil Rights Act to overcome school segregation; and expansion of university extension programs to include courses concerned with community problems.

When President Johnson read the Gardner report in mid-November, he pounced on its recommendations for a legislative strategy. In the week following Thanksgiving he met at his ranch with Secretaries Celebrezze and Wirtz, along with Moyers, Cohen, Keppel, and Cannon. There would be two bills, one to be called the Elementary and Secondary Education Act (ESEA), the other the Higher Education Act. The schedule for the major messages was laid out. Johnson had hired Douglass Cater, formerly on the staff of *The Reporter* magazine, as a White House assistant to write speeches and coordinate programs, including education. Cater and Keppel wrote the education message.

Meanwhile, Keppel was working on the major hurdle ESEA must overcome, the church-state controversy. When President Kennedy had brought Keppel on board in 1962, he had insisted that he establish immediate contact with the National Catholic Welfare Conference (NCWC). Over the preceding two years Keppel, an Episcopalian, had developed trusting relations with the Catholics as well as with their opponents, the National Education Association and the National Council of Churches. This positioned him to act as mediator. His first task was to clear away each side's adherence to hallowed principles. For Catholics this was that Congress must treat parochial schools equally. NEA and the National Council, along with many Jews, insisted on a rigorous separation of church and state, that is, no assistance to parochial schools. Keppel's burden was to move the argument from these principles to practicality.

In retrospect, the formula that emerged seems ridiculously obvious, but it struck everyone at the time like a bolt of lightning. It was to provide aid not to *schools* but to *pupils*, which was known as the child benefit theory. After its dramatic success many claimed pride of authorship.

"With all humility," Wilbur Cohen admitted, "I worked out this device which I think broke the log jam." His boss, Secretary Celebrezze, also a humble man, took a different position. "I presented it. . . . They agreed to it. What I was trying to do was help the student." Kermit Gordon was more detached: "The strategy and the conceptual brilliance—the political brilliance—of the legislation, I think, was almost wholly attributable to Larry O'Brien's work." Cater was convinced that the idea came from the Gardner task force. Gardner personally, however, credited Keppel and Senator Wayne Morse.

In fact, the child benefit theory was invented many years earlier. It first found expression in *Cochran v. Board of Education* in 1930. Governor Huey Long had gotten the Louisiana legislature to enact a law to provide every school child in the state, including those in parochial schools, with free textbooks. The statute was challenged on several grounds in the state court, one as an establishment of religion in defiance of the First Amendment. Long himself argued the defense before the Supreme Court. In an opinion for a unanimous court, Chief Justice Charles Evans Hughes cited with approval the Louisiana court's holding: "The schools . . . are not the beneficiaries of these appropriations. They obtain nothing from them, nor are they relieved of a single obligation because of them. The school children and the state alone are the beneficiaries."

In 1947 the Supreme Court on a closer question voted five to four in *Everson v. Board of Education* to extend the child benefit theory to transporting children to and from school. The court sustained a local ordinance in New Jersey which allowed a town to reimburse parents for the cost of bus trips to both public and parochial schools.

In 1964 Title II of the Economic Opportunity Act provided for "special remedial and other noncurricular educational assistance for the benefit of low-income individuals and families," presumably attendees of both public and private schools. That same year Senator Morse had introduced a bill to amend the impacted areas program to allow the inclusion of children in families suffering from economic hardship as measured by unemployment and welfare assistance, again without reference to public or parochial schools.

Keppel, perhaps better informed than the others, was more statesmanlike. When asked where the idea came from, he said, "Oh, from a bunch of people. Since it worked politically, there are a lot of fathers of this bill."

The conditions for mediation on church-state were bright for the first time. All the parties knew that the President would insist on the enactment of legislation and that he would not permit a religious conflict to block the way. "Don't come out with something that's going to get me right in the middle of this religious controversy," he told Cohen. "I don't want the Baptists attacking me from one hand and the Catholics from another."

The elementary and secondary education bill sidestepped teacher salaries, the issue that had divided the NEA and the NCWC. NEA had long asked for federal support for the pay of its members. The baby boom had sharply increased the cost of running the Catholic schools. In fact, enrollment in their elementary schools had risen during the past 20 years by 129 percent compared with 69 percent for public schools. Average class size in parochial schools was 42 pupils. There were not enough nuns to do the teaching and the Catholics had been forced to enter the teacher labor market, where salaries for unionizing teachers were now rising rapidly. The church recognized that for constitutional and political reasons it could not get the government to pay its teachers. ESEA would do nothing for teacher salaries.

By 1965, both NEA and NCWC were weary of their historic conflict.

The result had been to block the passage of any legislation. They were ready to move from principle to practicality. "Now," Cater wrote, "they both accepted the fact that the other side had to be given something."

In the latter part of 1964 Keppel met regularly for dinner with the education lobbies, particularly the NEA and the NCWC, to explore areas of agreement. Sometimes Celebrezze and Cohen joined them, and, more important, so did John Brademas, who represented the Third Congressional District in northern Indiana and sat on the House Education Subcommittee.

His father was a Greek immigrant who ran a restaurant. "John," he said, "I'll never leave much money to my children but I will leave you all a first-class education." His mother was a Hoosier schoolteacher of Scots-English-Irish-Pennsylvania Dutch ancestry. Her father had been a high school superintendent and college professor who had accumulated a huge library. Brademas was an educator almost from birth (he would become president of New York University). He also developed a keen interest in politics. He went to Harvard, was a Rhodes scholar, and took a Ph.D. in government.

Brademas had been widely exposed to religious teaching. As he told the House,

> I am the Methodist nephew of a hard-shell Baptist preacher. My mother belongs to the Disciples of Christ Church. My father is Greek Orthodox, and before coming to the Congress of the United States, I taught at a Roman Catholic college. If I can find myself a Jewish bride, I would represent the finest example of the ecumenical movement.

One of his largest constituents was the University of Notre Dame in South Bend. Robert Wyatt, the current president of NEA, had headed its Indiana affiliate and was a friend. So was Monsignor Frederick Hochwalt, who represented the NCWC.

The *Monsignori,* as Keppel called them, were a "convivial gathering" and his relations with them were on a "good footing." But they knew the weaknesses in their bargaining position. In a meeting in mid-December they left Keppel with two strong impressions. They did not want aid that would provoke a court test. This would cause delay and create acrimony. Though they did not say so, obviously, they might lose. They also stressed that they did not want federal money as a *substitute* for their own costs, but as a *supplement.* Monsignors Hochwalt and Hurley, however, visited him privately to emphasize their need for help with teacher salaries. It would not be part of the legislative package and it would certainly cause a court challenge that the Catholics could easily lose.

Wiser heads prevailed. In February 1965 Jack Valenti of the President's staff met with Archbishop Egidio Vagnozzi, the Apostolic Delegate. He was,

Valenti wrote, an "extremely able man" who spoke flawless English and had worked in Portugal, Paris, India, the Philippines, and Washington. He strongly favored ESEA as it was and said the "great majority" of the bishops shared his view. Even crusty Cardinal Spellman of New York agreed. He expected that Cardinal McIntyre of Los Angeles would be alone in opposition. The bishops seemed to have accepted the view that their main aim should be to establish the principle of federal aid for their schools.

The parochial schools would gain only limited assistance under ESEA. The basic Title I program of aid to low-income families would provide payments only to *public* agencies. But "shared services" would be encouraged, that is, resources in public schools would be available to private schools that served the poor. Under Title II library resources, textbooks, and instructional materials would be provided only to a state public agency, but it could pass them on to pupils in *all* the schools in the state, including those enrolled in private schools. This would be the main assistance to parochial schools. The Justice Department thought that constitutionality would hinge upon the mechanism used by the state. Title III would create supplementary educational centers to provide physical education, music, languages, advanced science, remedial reading, television equipment, and teaching innovations for both public and private schools. Justice was optimistic about constitutionality. Title VI would finance laboratories at universities for research and development of methods of education, which would be available to parochial schools. But there was a prohibition on the teaching of religion. Title VI would forbid "any payment under this Act . . . for religious worship or instruction."

Keppel estimated that nonpublic schools could receive between 10.1 and 13.5 percent of the dollars appropriated under ESEA. Parochial schools had about 15 percent of the enrollment. The President wanted to know why they did not get 15 percent of the benefits. Cater explained that the parochial schools had been expanding twice as fast as the public. The law should "not encourage continued growth of the parochial school system at a faster rate than the public system."

Chester Relyea of the general counsel's office of HEW drafted the elementary and secondary education bill, with important help from Samuel Halperin, acting deputy commissioner in the Office of Education.

The President delivered a special message, "Toward Full Educational Opportunity," to Congress on January 12, 1965. Youngsters from poor families, he pointed out, suffered a serious handicap. Almost half the nation's school districts offered kindergarten, but only about 100 of the 26,000 districts provided nursery schools. In the summer of 1965 the OEO would offer a community action preschool program called Head Start to begin in the fall.

Elementary and secondary education were the bedrock of the U.S. system. They now enrolled 48 million students and soaked up 71 percent of educational expenditures. They were in bad shape and the President advanced a program to help them.

Most important was major assistance to public schools that served children from low-income families, for which he asked $1 billion, two-thirds of the total. Differences in income distribution significantly influenced school quality. The five states with the lowest incomes and the poorest schools spent less than half as much per pupil as the five with the highest incomes and the best schools. Big cities spent only two-thirds as much as their suburbs. In the 15 largest cities 60 percent of tenth graders from poor neighborhoods dropped out before finishing high school. The President urged equalization formulas that would assist low-income states and the urban slums.

School libraries were a national disgrace. Almost 70 percent of public elementary schools had no libraries at all and 84 percent were without librarians. Many schools averaged less than half a book per child. The President wanted federal assistance to allow both public and private schools to buy books and hire librarians.

There had recently been dramatic advances in teaching the "new" math, the sciences, foreign languages, remedial reading, and the physically and mentally handicapped. But these methods had hardly penetrated the school system. The President proposed the creation of federally funded supplementary education centers and services to bring these and other techniques to the schools.

The National Science Foundation had developed new instructional materials for teaching science. Johnson proposed institutionalizing this program by creating a system of regional laboratories to undertake research in teaching and to train teachers.

State departments of education were notoriously bureaucratized and sleepy. The President, with Keppel pushing, thought that a little extra federal money would wake them up. "The last thing in the world I wanted," Keppel said, "was all those 25,000 school districts coming in with plans with my bureaucrats deciding whether to approve them or not. I wanted that stuff done out in the states."

Finally, Johnson outlined the higher education program: scholarships, loans, and work-study for qualified students to attend college; aid to "less developed" institutions; support for college libraries; and increased funding for university extension programs that addressed the problems of the local community.

The reaction to the President's message was enthusiastic. NEA declared that it was "one of the strongest commitments to meeting the urgent needs of the public schools ever to come from the White House." Monsignor Hochwalt stated, "This emphasis on the child, the student, I applaud." The *New York Times* called the message "a skillful effort to fix national priorities while avoiding paralyzing controversies." The *Washington Post* agreed.

"Lyndon Johnson's genius for finding a way out of blind alleys is brilliantly exemplified in his message to Congress on education." Protestants and Other Americans United for Separation of Church and State disagreed. "This is federal aid to parochial schools by a method which attempts to circumvent the constitutional issue." Cater found that telegrams to the White House ran three to one in favor and that "opposition is exclusively directed at aid to parochial schools." The U.S. Conference of Mayors unanimously endorsed the education proposals.[2]

The administration bill was introduced on January 12, 1965, in the House as H.R. 2362 by Carl Perkins of Kentucky, chairman of the General Education Subcommittee, and in the Senate as S. 600, by Wayne Morse of Oregon, chairman of the Education Subcommittee. Because of the delicate compromises upon which the bill rested politically, the administration and the congressional leadership devised an unusual legislative strategy in the crafting of which Morse played the central role.

Historically the Senate had been much more favorable to federal aid for education than the House. H.R. 2362, therefore, moved first to the House. The instructions Perkins received were to push his bill through his committee and onto the floor as swiftly as possible, to avoid any significant amendment, and to concede as few minor ones as possible. Thus, Perkins would lead with his hearings and Morse would follow at a more leisurely pace. The objective was to avoid a conference at all costs since that would require action by the still dangerous Rules Committee and, more important, would risk unravelling the strategy. It could be accomplished if the Senate adopted exactly the same bill the House had passed. Morse's plan was bold and risky and was certain to arouse opposition.

Wayne Morse was the Senate maverick, its hair shirt. Brilliant and courageous, he spoke his mind—sometimes at length, holding the record for the longest speech in Senate history. He could, however, change his mind, having been a Republican, an Independent, and, now, a Democrat. He was a proud teacher, a former professor and dean at the University of Oregon Law School.

Morse was totally committed to federal aid. In fact, he and Charles Lee, the Senate subcommittee staff director, had been advocating the linkage of school aid to poverty since 1954. The country was now catching up with him. Morse had done a superb job on education for Kennedy in 1963 and he intended to do even better for Johnson in 1965. This was despite Vietnam. Morse recoiled before the President's growing commitment in Southeast Asia and had been, with Senator Ernest Gruening of Alaska, one of the two members of both houses who had voted against the Tonkin Gulf resolution. But Lyndon Johnson was right on education and Wayne Morse, to Keppel's astonishment, would stand by the President.

Perkins held the House Subcommittee hearings on eight days between

January 22 and February 2, 1965. He took his commitment to speed seriously and was a tough taskmaster. He shunted witnesses in and out like railroad cars and, since a large number lined up to testify, filled two fat volumes with their testimony. Perkins proudly reported to the White House that every witness who wanted to appear was heard and that the Republicans were allowed to examine them without time limits. The great majority favored H.R. 2362. There was a slight tremor when Wilbur Cohen's tongue slipped and he said that library materials would go *directly* to private schools. This, in fact, was the most troubling issue raised by several other witnesses.

Perkins, Larry O'Brien wrote the President, "pushed the committee night and day and did a tremendous job of achieving a markup on Monday, February 8." There were nine amendments, all but one of secondary significance. The important one addressed title to library books and textbooks. Indicative of the Catholic commitment to the bill, Hugh Carey of New York, recognized as the spokesman for the Church, sponsored the amendment. Title would vest in a "public agency" and a "public authority" would have sole administrative control over their use. Students in parochial schools, therefore, would be loaned these books. All six Democrats voted for the amended H.R. 2362. The three Republicans boycotted the meeting at which the ballots were cast. According to one, Charles Goodell of New York, they did so to protest the subcommittee's "hasty and superficial" action.

Perkins was eager to have the full committee act prior to Lincoln's birthday on the 12th. He did not take account of its chairman, Adam Clayton Powell. Cater reported to Johnson on the 16th that, despite the support of all the important lobbies, he had received "plaintive calls" from committee members that Powell would not move.

This flamboyant headline-grabbing Harlem preacher could not restrain himself from exploiting the situation. His committee, the Democratic leadership, and the White House were extremely anxious to get swift action. He would stop them in their tracks.

Powell, according to O'Brien, made "firm commitments" to Speaker McCormack and himself that the committee would take up the bill on February 8. He canceled the meeting, left for Puerto Rico, and refused to return calls. The Rules Committee was scheduled to decide on a request for funds from Education and Labor on February 17. Powell's staff alerted the members of his committee that they would meet on the 18th. Rules had gone 9 to 1 and 9 to 2 against Powell on preliminary votes. As a result of "total pressure" from the leadership, Powell was given the money. But he still did not show up. The Republicans, O'Brien wrote, now understood what was going on and were "backing Powell to the hilt."

The Speaker and O'Brien, at the end of their rope, decided to take the committee away from Powell. The method they chose was to have a workable majority and a quorum present on the next regular meeting day, February 25, to adopt a resolution keeping the committee in continuous session till the education bill was voted out. On February 24 the Administration Committee and the House itself reversed Rules and denied the funds to Powell. The next day the majority and the quorum were present with the resolution, and the chairman decided that the jig was up. As O'Brien put it, "Powell had to rush to get in front of the troops."

The committee meetings provoked a donnybrook over the distribution of funds under Title I. If the formula had been based strictly on pupil population, one could have argued that it was equitable. But by skewing to favor the poor states heavily concentrated in the South and the ghettoes in the big cities a host of apparent inequities appeared. The formula was as follows: average state expenditure per pupil was divided by 2, and the result was multiplied by the number of children aged 5 to 17 in families with annual incomes under $2000; that became the number of dollars payable to the local school district.

The South with many poor school districts liked the results. Texas beat out California, Mississippi got more than Missouri, Georgia surpassed Michigan, Alabama almost reached Ohio and beat Massachusetts by two and a half to one. The problem in the cities was even more glaring, as an illustration from Detroit and its suburbs demonstrates. James O'Hara represented Macomb County, Michigan, a bedroom suburb of Detroit. There were very few pupils in its schools from families with incomes below $2000. But the schools were desperately overcrowded and were on half-day schedules. Enrollment in the county had risen 72 percent in the preceding seven years and two school districts had grown by 177 and 360 percent. Macomb and its sister in the Detroit area came in last among Michigan's 83 counties for Title I funds. O'Hara screamed. O'Brien pointed out that accommodating O'Hara would have "destroyed the whole theory of the bill and have completely unzipped the religious consensus. . . . The Catholic spokesmen, we were amply notified, would have shot the whole bill down in mid-air."

The managers decided that they must put more money into the cities and suburbs. They proposed $50 million, but, as things worked out, it became $63 million. In addition, Roman Pucinski of Mayor Daley's Chicago machine put over an addendum to the formula to count as poor children those under Aid to Families with Dependent Children whose family incomes were $2000 or *more*.

By the afternoon of Friday, February 26, action on amendments was concluded and the committee would be ready to vote the next day. But now Edith Green of Oregon made her appearance, or, more precisely, nonappearance. A key member of the Education Subcommittee, she was in Florida and had gotten an advance promise that the vote would be delayed until she returned. She told the speaker that she was making a speech in San

Francisco Monday evening and would be out of town that day and Tuesday. McCormack, with difficulty, persuaded her to cancel the speech.

On Monday morning Mrs. Green, put out, made a stormy entrance. In fact, nobody knew how to deal with Edith Green. In Kennedy's time she had terrified the President, Sorensen, Cohen, and Keppel. Moyers and Cater, both innocents, took her to lunch and into the Oval Office to talk to the President and receive a signed portrait. As Cater put it, "He tried very hard to keep her from jumping off the reservation." But Green was in one of her world-class jumping moods.

According to O'Brien, "She argued passionately . . . for a delay of several weeks." She negotiated with the Republicans to work out a substitute. She called Protestant leaders to her office and told them that H.R. 2362 would "put Catholic priests in the public schools." Green demanded and won a caucus motion to amend the Appalachia bill. She delayed the Public Works Committee's consideration of the water pollution bill by threatening to vote against Appalachia unless they put northwest flood control ahead of water pollution. She got her way and still voted against Appalachia.

Nevertheless, the House Education and Labor Committee reported the bill on March 2, by a vote of 23 to 8. All 21 Democrats (including Edith Green!) voted in favor and were joined by two Republicans, Ogden Reid of New York and Alphonzo Bell of California. But O'Brien wrote with foreboding, "Mrs. Green's industry continues." He considered the administration fortunate to have weathered the storm so successfully thus far and remained concerned about religion and race.

On March 22 Speaker McCormack convened the Democratic leadership to plan floor strategy. Eugene Eidenberg and Roy D. Morey reported an "undercurrent of tension" attesting to the uneasiness of the bill's supporters on the eve of debate. O'Brien caught the mood:

> In many ways this bill is the cornerstone to the entire Administration legislative program for the Eighty-ninth Congress. It contains so many different fundamental issues—church-state, rural-urban, north-south—that affect Congressmen so deeply that it could easily fall apart. If we can hold the troops together on this one it will surely make things much easier during the remainder of the session.

The House debated H.R. 2362 for three days, March 24 to 26. The head counts were encouraging. On March 2 the NEA had reported that those with "positive commitments" split 242 for to 68 against. Gerald Ford, it was said, would announce no GOP position on the bill, but would allow Republicans to vote their districts. This suggested a substantial favorable Republican vote, and already two from Kansas had announced support. On

March 23 Celebrezze came up with 200 to 18. On the next day he reported 248, and O'Brien, always cautious, turned up 229.

At the outset of the debate the Republicans attacked the way the Democrats had rammed the "railroad bill" through the subcommittee, the allocation formula, and the distribution of library materials to parochial schools. Perkins, who had been a good subcommittee chairman, was an ineffective debater. Brademas, as usual, stepped in to defend the bill against these charges with skill and wit.

There were two important issues: the allocation formula under Title I and aid to parochial school children. Edith Green was the leader in both fights and she was formidable. Of March 24, O'Brien reported, "It's been hell today."

Green proposed replacing the present formula with a straight $200 grant for every child from a low-income family. New Jersey under the administration bill would receive $283 per child, Mississippi only $120. How, she asked, could liberals feign concern for the troubles in Mississippi? "Are you really shedding crocodile tears?" There were two answers: it was much more expensive to educate a child in the North than in the Deep South and the South would get much bigger percentage increases. The Green amendment was rejected 202 to 136.

Green's attack on assistance to Catholic pupils was more serious because it played to the ambivalence among Jews. "Mrs. Green," Valenti wrote the President, "is trying to pick off the Jewish vote." The Jewish community was very well organized, but hopelessly divided. Twelve groups had testified on H.R. 2362. While all but three had supported the bill "generally," they did so with varying reservations. Views ranged from strong support from the National Society for Hebrew Day Schools, which wanted federal funds for its own parochial school system, to sharp opposition from the American Jewish Congress.

Historically Jews had attached critical importance to the establishment clause of the First Amendment and had insisted upon a sharp separation of church and state. As a small minority with a wretched history of persecution in nations with established churches, Jews had good reason to oppose state support for religion. At the same time, most Jews strongly backed education and approved of federal assistance to the public schools. They also favored government help for blacks, who would be among the main beneficiaries under the bill. Two aspects of H.R. 2362 bothered them: providing library materials and textbooks for Catholic schools and the absence of an explicit judicial review provision in the bill.

The Atlanta attorney Morris Abram was a good example of Jewish ambivalence. He was playing a key role in the desegregation of Atlanta, including its schools. At the same time Abram, as president of the American Jewish Committee, was asking for insertion of judicial review in H.R. 2362.

The library issue had already been substantially resolved by Carey's amendment establishing public title to printed materials. Thus, Green concentrated on judicial review and gained support from the American Jewish Committee, the American Jewish Congress, the Lutheran Church, the Christian Church, and the American Civil Liberties Union, among others. There were actually two proposed amendments, one by Howard Smith of Virginia, making any part of the law subject to court review, and the other by John B. Anderson, the Illinois Republican, authorizing a state, its instrumentalities, and nonprofit institutions to bring suit.

In fact, this was all sound and fury. The Department of Justice was convinced that there was no constitutional question and that the right to judicial review was constitutionally based, requiring no statutory authorization. Emanuel Celler, the chairman of the Judiciary Committee, himself a Jew and a constitutional authority, strongly emphasized the inherent right to judicial review. His reassurance on the floor caused the National Council of Churches to send a telegram to Carl Albert undercutting Mrs. Green. Nor was she consistent. In 1963, when she was handling the Kennedy higher education bill, she had opposed judicial review over the Catholic warning that they would vote the bill down in the Rules Committee. They were still as strongly opposed, as O'Brien had emphasized. The Smith amendment was defeated by voice vote, Anderson's by a 204 to 154 teller vote.

On March 26 the House of Representatives passed H.R. 2362 by a vote of 263 to 153. The northern Democrats were solid—187 to 3, including Edith Green. The southern Democrats split 54 to 41 against and the Republicans divided 96 to 35 opposed.

Edith Green had an unusual critic. Adam Clayton Powell, Cater wrote the President, "is burning mad over Edith Green's behavior." He threatened reprisals: (1) remove vocational education from her subcommittee's jurisdiction; (2) fire her sister from the committee staff; and (3) shift sponsorship of the higher education bill to John Brademas. "Brademas is uncertain about No. 3, but is willing to undertake the job if it will serve the good of the bill." [3]

Fellow Oregonian Wayne Morse detested Edith Green and had derived great satisfaction from the bashing she had taken. But he had more important matters to be pleased about. His legislative strategy was unfolding according to plan. H.R. 2362 as enacted by the House was acceptable to him and to the Johnson administration. The House of Representatives, the historical burying ground of education bills, had passed the big one with a majority of 110. His Subcommittee on Education had ten members, seven Democrats and three Republicans, and he already had a majority. All the Democrats except Lister Hill of Alabama, the chairman of the full Labor and Public Welfare Committee, had sponsored H.R. 2362. The hearings, held between January 26 and February 11, 1965, had gone very well. Especially gratifying had been support from three top officials of the Eisenhower administration—Dr. James R. Killian, Jr., of MIT, former science adviser to the President; Marion B. Folsom of Eastman Kodak, former secretary of HEW; and Arthur S. Flemming, president of the University of Oregon, first vice president of the National Council of Churches, and also former HEW secretary. The testimony of 103 witnesses and 42 statements filled six volumes totaling 3200 pages. Morse anticipated no serious trouble from the Republicans; he could afford to treat them generously. His strategic goal seemed within easy reach. The White House and the Democratic leadership agreed with this analysis. While they had monitored the House very closely, their policy in the Senate was: leave it to Wayne.

Morse's main problem during the subcommittee stage came from two important Democrats, the new senator from New York, Bobby Kennedy, and his younger brother from Massachusetts, Teddy. When Keppel testified RFK asked whether educationally deprived children were found only in low-income families. The response was that deprivation could arise from "a host of reasons." Kennedy urged a broader definition. With Celebrezze the senator noted that many school boards and state commissioners refused to deal with deprivation. The secretary replied that so long as education was managed locally "that was the price of democracy." Some newsmen interpreted this as another rift between Bobby and Lyndon Johnson.

When, following the 1954 *Brown* decision, Prince Edward County, Virginia, had abandoned its public schools, RFK and Keppel had reopened them in order to provide education for black children. This included bringing in outside teachers who formed a kind of teacher corps. John Kenneth Galbraith in 1964 suggested the formation of a national corps to work in impoverished areas. Now Teddy Kennedy and Wisconsin Democrat Gaylord Nelson formally proposed a teacher corps as an amendment to H.R. 2362. Morse strongly favored the idea but, given his no amendment policy, was strapped. He met privately with Kennedy and Nelson and persuaded them to hold back in return for his promise to attach the teacher corps to the higher education bill.

The House had passed H.R. 2362 on Friday, March 26. Morse called his subcommittee into session the following Tuesday, determined to get a unanimous vote. There was, in fact, only one proposed amendment. Ralph Yarborough, the Texas Democrat, and Peter Dominick, the Colorado Republican, asked to increase Title I allocations to the poor states by taking the money from the rich. Yarborough argued that H.R. 2362 did not recognize the equalization principle. Cater pointed out to him that the bill went further toward equalization than any prior legislation. The eleven southern states would receive 40 percent of the funds. Texas would get $74.6 million under the administration's bill and $76.7 from Yarborough's, hardly enough difference to justify the risk of defeat.

Dominick and Winston Prouty, the Vermont Republican, would probably have voted against H.R. 2362 had they not known that Morse eagerly sought unanimity. The members of his subcommittee, including the Republicans, held the chairman in high esteem, and, Eidenberg and Morey wrote, "The time-honored canon of politics applied in this case was that one should not go out of his way to make enemies if it is obvious that his side is going to lose anyway." They would put out IOUs that could be cashed in later. The vote was 10 to 0.

The full committee on Labor and Public Welfare was even easier. Dominick went through the motions of proposing amendments on allocations, library materials, and private schools. The first was defeated 6 to 4, the others by voice vote. The committee then balloted, again unanimously, for H.R. 2362 on April 5, 1965.

It would be an exaggeration to call the Senate's consideration a "debate" or even to add the adjective "desultory." It began on April 6 and ended on the 9th. On the first day Morse explained the bill to two senators who were talking to each other. On the second Dominick and Company went through their amendment routine to no avail. On the third Sam Ervin, the North Carolina Democrat who had proposed judicial review for Kennedy's higher education bill in 1963, renewed the amendment. He was defeated 53 to 32. On April 9, H.R. 2362 passed the Senate by a vote of 73 to 18. The Democrats voted for it 55 to 4 and even a majority of Republicans backed it 18 to 14.

Wayne Morse had pushed the House bill through the subcommittee unanimously, the full committee unanimously, and the Senate overwhelmingly. All within two weeks!

Douglas Cater suggested to the President that he hold the signing ceremony in "the little schoolhouse which you attended near the ranch." Johnson embraced the idea.

On Palm Sunday, April 11, 1965, Lyndon Johnson was on the lawn of the Junction Elementary School in Johnson City, where he had started his education at age four. His teacher, Kate Deadrich Loney, who handled eight grades in one room, came back from California. "Come over here, Miss Katie, and sit by me, will you? . . . They tell me, Miss Kate, that I recited my first lessons while sitting on your lap." Hugo Kline had also sat on her knee. Now a barber in Fredricksburg, he had come down for the ceremony. There were other former schoolmates and pupils from San Marcos, Cotulla, and Houston. Senator Eugene McCarthy had lectured at the University of Texas in Austin the day before. Carl Albert, who had helped put the bill through the House, was spending the day in his district in McAlester, Oklahoma. Both came over to Johnson City.

The Attorney General, Johnson said, had told him that it was constitutional to sign the Elementary and Secondary Education Act on Palm Sunday and his minister said that he would not violate the Lord's day by doing so to "bring mental and moral benefits to millions of our young people." He did not want to miss a day in putting this wonderful law into effect. And "I felt a very strong desire to go back to the beginnings of my own education—to be reminded and to remind others of that magic time when the world of learning began to open before our eyes." It was a warm and joyous event.

On Tuesday, April 13, the President held another ceremony in the East Room of the White House. He wished that President Kennedy and Senator Robert A. Taft were alive to see this "dream come true." He expressed gratitude to the Democratic leadership in both houses and, of course, to Carl Perkins and Wayne Morse. "With all the differences I have with Wayne Morse on Viet-Nam, we don't differ on education." And he noted the contributions of John Gardner, Francis Keppel, and Anthony Celebrezze.[4]

Francis Keppel observed the rapid march of ESEA through Congress with the Higher Education Act not far behind with pleasure alloyed by distress. Stephen Bailey and Edith Mosher summed up his ambivalence neatly:

> Whatever skills Keppel had as a forceful and brilliant policy strategist and external negotiator, he was not a tidy administrator. The mundane details of internal structure and process bored his restless and creative mind. . . . Furthermore, Keppel's essential command from Presidents Kennedy and Johnson had been to catalyze new legislative breakthroughs. This role Keppel performed with distinction, but it was a role that precluded the pouring of extensive energies into solving difficult problems of organization and methods inside USOE [U.S. Office of Education] itself.

The Office of Education was a very old and very stodgy bureaucracy which had spent most of its energies in the collection of statistics. The average age of the professional staff was over 50, and it was distinguished, Bailey and Mosher wrote, by neither "energy [n]or imagination." The operating bureaus put "sand in the personnel machinery." The financial and management systems were "decentralized, disparate, and ineffective." The structure of the agency was hopelessly obsolete. Its personnel, conditioned to the "theology" of local control, avoided national leadership as if it were a fatal disease. Its elderly civil servants isolated themselves from other federal agencies concerned with education, and they harbored an "almost pathological suspicion" of parent HEW.

The 1963 legislation, particularly the Higher Education Facilities Act, had imposed an immense increase in workload of an unfamiliar kind, program administration, including supervision of construction contracts. Now the new ESEA and Higher Education Act programs would raise the budget of USOE by 526 percent over 1961. The staff would grow during fiscal 1966 alone by 50 percent, over 800 jobs, many at top levels. As if that were not enough, the agency was already responsible for the formidable task of desegregating the nation's schools under Title VI of the 1964 Civil Rights Act.

Keppel, who recognized his own limitations, began searching for a tough administrator in 1964 and had trouble finding one. Finally, in March 1965 he located a new deputy commissioner of education. Henry Loomis had a broad background in science, defense, and foreign policy and the reputation of an outstanding administrator. He was leaving as director at Voice of America and made an unfortunate farewell address to the staff.

Loomis said he was fed up with the "inept leadership" of VOA chief Carl Rowan and that he resented "political interference" in the agency's operations. Mary McGrory carried his statement in the Washington *Star*. What Loomis did not know was that the nation's most omnivorous reader of Washington political news was Lyndon Johnson. Loomis said later that he was pointing at the State Department. But Johnson read the statement as an attack on the White House. He considered it both bad judgment and disloyalty. The fact that Loomis was an Eisenhower Republican and proudly kept a picture of Ike on his office wall probably did not help.

Johnson, enraged, broke into a phone conversation that Keppel was having with a southern governor, chewed him out, and demanded that he rescind the appointment of Loomis. Keppel refused, insisting on his right to choose his own deputy. Thereafter, whenever he saw the President he was asked, "Have you fired that son-of-a-bitch yet?" Johnson insisted now that all supergrade appointments in USOE must be approved by presidential assistant Marvin Watson, a man Keppel grew to detest.

Loomis brought over his personal hatchetman, Walter Mylecraine, who became known at USOE as "the terrible Turk." But he had to delay the wielding of his axe because Cater was concerned about the Department of Health, Education, and Welfare.

Cater got an old newspaper friend, Mike O'Neill, who covered HEW for the New York *Daily News* and *Medical World News*, to assess the department. Its high command, O'Neill wrote, was an "administrative mess which has been inadequate to the Department's mission for more than 10 years and will collapse completely under the weight of its new Great Society responsibilities." Excluding education, O'Neill went on in this vein for ten pages of detail. On April 2, 1965, Cater sent O'Neill's letter to the President and proposed that a small group consisting of Kermit Gordon, John Macy of the Civil Service Commission, and himself make plans to reorganize HEW. The President approved and the results would be given to John Gardner when he became secretary in July.

Cater then addressed the "urgent" problem of the Office of Education. Celebrezze and Keppel recommended formation of a "working task force" to study the agency's reorganization. Gordon and Elmer Staats of the Bureau of the Budget strongly recommended that Dwight A. Ink be placed in charge. Perhaps the federal government's top administrator, Ink was now assistant general manager of the Atomic Energy Commission. He was constantly being "borrowed" for tough jobs, most notably for the rebuilding of Alaska after the immense earthquake of 1964. Ink's availability for the education study delighted Keppel. The other members of the task force were Herbert Jasper of Budget and Gilbert Schulkind of Civil Service. The comprehensive recommendations of the White House Task Force on Education were delivered on June 14, 1965.

Bailey and Mosher considered the Ink report a "grand design." Hardly any part of the agency would escape reorganization. "Sweeping in scope, it represented a massive attack upon the traditional shortcomings of the United States Office of Education and an attempt to develop an organizational structure and a management philosophy that would equip this office for the new burdens it was about to assume."

Keppel and Loomis accepted the Ink recommendations as gospel and Loomis persuaded Keppel to launch the reorganization swiftly, that is, in late June 1965. The agency was stood on its head. Of 36 divisions only two escaped major surgery; of 25 supergrade personnel only eight held onto their jobs. Bailey and Mosher wrote, "The ensuing, if temporary, administrative chaos was shattering. For days and weeks, people could not find each other's offices—sometimes not even their own." Morale declined sharply as the volume of business shot upward. A new crisis emerged over the enforcement of Title VI of the Civil Rights Act in the North, namely, Chicago. The summer months at the Office of Education, therefore, were traumatic. But, by September, while there was still much to accomplish, the foundations of a new agency were in place.

Ink was later asked whether the reorganization was carried out. "It was carried out, but not to my satisfaction." Within a few months Keppel and Loomis were gone and the "momentum had been lost." The combined impact of Johnson's attack on Loomis and the catastrophe in Chicago severely damaged the Office of Education.[5]

The Higher Education Act of 1965 was in substantial part a holdover from Kennedy's 1963 agenda. He had made two basic proposals—federal support for the construction of college buildings and financial aid for students. Congress gave him the former in the facilities act, but declined student assistance in 1963. The Gardner task force the next year urged loans, scholarships, and a work-study program for students. This became the heart of the 1965 bill, but there were many other features.

In fact, the content of the bill was a more difficult problem than its politics. There was no doubt whatever that a higher education bill would pass both houses, probably with handsome majorities. There were a number of reasons for this.

Keppel did not have to deal with the *monsignori* or the Protestant churches because there was no church-state issue. In 1961, when the first Kennedy education program was submitted, Alanson W. Willcox, general counsel of HEW, had, after consultation with the Department of Justice, written a memorandum on constitutionality under the First Amendment of federal aid to education, including higher education. One could argue, as many did, that federal assistance to parochial lower schools raised a serious question under the establishment clause. But, Willcox contended, no such argument could be made with regard to colleges.

This was a difference rooted in history. The states had opted for compulsory public education for lower schools where the teaching of religion was prohibited. Higher education had an opposite history. At the outset most colleges were private and had a religious origin. Even now 41 percent of college students were in private institutions. Attendance at lower schools was mandatory, at colleges voluntary. It would be ridiculous for the federal government to offer financial aid exclusively to public institutions in the current context of strain on the colleges to admit all those clamoring at the gates. The nation needed private institutions, even if church-related. No opponent of federal aid to the colleges bothered to raise the establishment clause issue during the legislative history, nor, evidently, was a suit filed later to challenge the law.

The structure of the Congress made aid to colleges inherently popular. There were about 2300 higher education institutions in the country located basically in accordance with the distribution of population. All were eager to receive the funds that would become available under the new law. Thus, every senator was well supplied with constituents who wanted him to vote for the bill. Even low-density states were stocked with colleges. Alaska, for example, had nine, and Wyoming had eight. The number of institutions per district in the House was similar. Thus, any member of either house who opposed the bill would be voting against the interests of important constituents.

The colleges, now reeling under the impact of the baby boom, were in obvious need of financial assistance. A Congress which had voted overwhelmingly for ESEA could hardly fail to do as well, and probably better, with a politically more acceptable higher education bill.

The measure introduced by the administration, S. 600, had four substantive provisions. Title I addressed community problems—housing, poverty, government, recreation, health, and so on. The funds would go to university extension departments to develop programs to deal with these questions.

Title II would improve inadequate library resources. The libraries of half the four-year and 82 percent of the two-year institutions failed to meet minimum standards of books per student. The skimpy libraries of many research universities called for a very large increase in acquisitions. There was also a severe shortage of librarians, estimated at 125,000. Grants would be made to colleges and universities to address the book shortage and to expand or establish schools for librarians.

The 2300 institutions of higher education in the U.S. were of extremely varied quality. Almost 10 percent were unaccredited; several hundred lacked research facilities and qualified instructors; professor salaries in many were extremely low. Title III would strengthen "developing institutions" by providing funds to improve their academic programs.

Title IV, the heart of S. 600, would help meet the financial needs of low- and middle-income young people to obtain a college education. There would be three new programs—scholarships, insured reduced-interest loans, and work-study. In addition, the existing National Defense Student Loan Program would be extended for three years.

There was little controversy over the first three titles and scholarships and work-study. The key issue in the legislative history was student loans. If one assumed that national policy should encourage young people to attend college, the need for financial assistance, including loans, was obvious. In 1960, 78 percent of high school graduates from families with incomes over $12,000 attended college; only 33 percent from families with incomes under $3000 did so. In a study of 1,860,000 high school graduates who went to college, 22 percent dropped out during the first year. The most important reason for doing so was financial difficulty. The average annual direct cost of college in 1962–63 was $1,480 in public and $2,240 in private institutions. Median family income was $6000. Thus, keeping a son or daughter in college was a heavy burden on most families, exceeded only by the cost of a home. Most students did not qualify for loans under the restrictions of the National Defense Education Act.

The Citizens National Committee for Higher Education opposed all forms of federal aid for education, including low-interest guaranteed loans. It strongly urged the tuition tax credit which would allow deductions from the income tax for tuition payments, not just for students and their parents, but also for other persons. A similar conservative position which many Republicans had long supported was voluntary college attendance. Federal financial assistance to students was not acceptable. Students, their families, private donors, cities, and states must bear the costs. But the massive force of the baby boomers marching onto campuses overwhelmed these conservative arguments. In fact, the Citizens Committee did not even testify on S. 600.

The student loan idea was in the air. The launching of the *Sputnik* in 1957 had alarmed the nation and had raised questions about the adequacy of the educational system. The next year the Congress enacted the National Defense Education Act in order to strengthen programs related to defense. It provided fellowships, grants, and *loans* to students to encourage the study of science, engineering, mathematics, and foreign languages. As noted, Title IV of the higher education bill would extend the life of NDEA.

By the end of 1964, 14 states had established loan guaranty programs and had 78,595 loans outstanding. Massachusetts and Maine had led the way in 1957 and New York came on the next year. They concentrated in the East where there were many private institutions with high tuitions, but there were two in the Midwest and two in the South. Excepting New York, with 50,820 loans outstanding, and Massachusetts, with 4,468, they were very small programs. By July 1965, five other states had established programs. Senator Javits proposed an amendment to S. 600 to protect the state and private arrangements with a 50-50 matching formula with federal funds.

United Student Aid Fund, a nonprofit corporation, started in 1960 to guarantee loans to college students. By 1965, 5,522 banks and 685 colleges were participating; the 68,379 outstanding loans totaled almost $49 million. Sophomores, juniors, and seniors could borrow $1000 annually up to a maximum of $4000, graduate students $2000 a year to the same ceiling. United Students Aid Fund was concerned that S. 600 might put it out of business. It proposed amendments to protect itself and that was one purpose of the Javits amendment.

Secretary of Labor Wirtz on December 12, 1964, put into the pot a proposal by the labor economist Charles C. Killingsworth of Michigan State to establish a Higher Education Loan Pool (HELP) from which students could borrow the cost of tuition and subsistence for four years to a maximum of $12,000. The interest rate would be 2 percent for 15 years and would be repaid through the income tax. Assistant Secretary of the Treasury Stanley S. Surrey thought the idea "highly ingenious" but felt it should not be adopted because "we just don't know how it will eventually score out."

Politically the most important proposal was the Ribicoff income tax credit for tuition, fees, and books for the families of students. It was popular in states with high-tuition colleges, like Connecticut, and among Republicans who liked to cut taxes. Senator Ribicoff, Kennedy's first secretary of HEW, had proposed it as an amendment to the big tax cut in early 1964 and it was barely defeated in the Senate. He reintroduced his bill on January 6, 1965, and it would become a proposed amendment to S. 600. The Treasury strongly opposed the Ribicoff credit because it would create a very large revenue loss, four times that of the administration bill; it would help high-income families whose children could go to college in any case and not assist those with lower incomes whose children could not afford to go; it would encourage the colleges to raise tuition; it would, when combined with the 1964 tax cut, provide double relief to the beneficiaries; and there were better ways to aid needy students. Nevertheless, the idea had great political appeal. "The hard-core support," Surrey wrote, ". . . comes from well-to-do . . . taxpayers who already have children in college and can see a tax windfall for themselves."

The initial administration loan plan was worked up by the Office of

Education. It became the basis for the final agreement reached by Surrey, deputy undersecretary for monetary affairs Paul Volcker of the Treasury, and Cohen and Keppel for HEW on January 12, 1965, which went into the bill.

Any student enrolled full-time in an accredited post-secondary institution would be eligible to borrow without regard to need up to $1500 per academic year to a limit of $7500. Any financial institution subject to federal or state supervision would be eligible to lend. The loans would be fully insured but interest would not be. Repayment would begin a year after the borrower left college and must be completed within ten years. If the interest rate was 6 percent, the student would pay 4 and the Treasury would subsidize 2 percent. The cost to the government would be $14 million per $100 million over nine years. In 1966 there would be $700 million in insured loans, in 1967 $1 billion, and for the next three years $1.4 billion a year. All a college had to do was to certify that the student was enrolled.[6]

The House Special Education Subcommittee held hearings on 15 days in February and March of 1965. Celebrezze and Keppel led off and were followed by a parade of witnesses who either supported the bill or asked for amendments, all but one of little consequence. There was no general opposition; those who were against federal aid to higher education did not show up. Even the negative testimony was mixed with approval.

The American Bankers Association strongly favored government assistance to improve education and to assure that "access . . . [was] open to all qualified young people, regardless of circumstances." It stood behind three of the four programs to provide student aid—scholarships, work-study, and NDEA loans. But the bankers could not support "federally insured loans coupled with an interest-cost subsidy." There were two reasons: lack of need for the program and the risk that state and private plans would be "impaired." The evidence consisted of the rapid increase recently of alternative systems. These arguments made little sense; the bankers really opposed a cap on interest rates. Nevertheless, many Republicans supported the ABA position.

The Special Subcommittee, chaired by Edith Green, reported on May 18. While it increased funds for a number of programs, it eliminated subsidized loans. Green accepted the bankers' argument that there was no need for loans and was concerned about the high incidence of defaults under the NDEA program. At the same time, the subcommittee unanimously improved scholarships. The Republicans had abandoned their traditional opposition to scholarships in return for a stipulation that the student must obtain half his support from another source, which would encourage borrowing under the state and private programs.

On May 18 Green informed Cater that her subcommittee had eliminated loans. He was concerned about the indirect effect. "This . . . ," he wrote the President, "could increase the possibility of a Ribicoff Tax Credit Amendment, which would be very costly."

On May 21 the full committee reversed its subcommittee and restored loans by a vote of 13 to 12. This, evidently, was the result of White House intervention. Johnson as a senator had sponsored insured loan programs and was disturbed about the Ribicoff amendment.

By June 8 the administration, working through John Brademas, had brought Green around. They had devised a new student loan program, the main features of which were the following: grants to the states of $25,000 to help them establish loan programs which met federal standards; federal loans would not be available in states with their own plans; maxima of $1000 annually for undergraduates and $2000 for graduate students with aggregate tops of $5000 and $7500; repayment within 5 to 10 years; a maximum interest rate of 6 percent (7 in exceptional circumstances); and an interest subsidy for a student from a family with an income under $10,000.

On June 23 the House Republican Conference unanimously endorsed tax credits for college expenses. Within a few days, 64 Republicans had signed on. The next day the full House Education and Labor Committee reported the bill out by a vote of 21 to 2. It included the Waggoner-Dirksen amendment, introduced by Joe D. Waggoner of Louisiana. The administration bill contained a provision prohibiting the government to "exercise any control" over the operations of any college or university. The amendment would extend the ban to fraternities, sororities, private clubs, and religious organizations. But it also changed the opening sentence from "nothing contained in this Act" by adding "or any other Act." No one caught this sleeper before it was adopted. In fact, Cohen wrote Cater that the House version was "superior to the original Administration proposal. The American Bankers Association and many Republicans will oppose no matter which version is adopted but the House Committee version is much more viable."

It would be a long summer for the higher education bill. This was partly due to the fact that the administration, which had brought great pressure for passage of ESEA, was now applying very little. There seems to have been an emotional letdown, a feeling of anticlimax. There were extended meetings with the bankers to work out a compromise loan program. Adam Clayton Powell disappeared early in August. McCormack, Albert, and O'Brien searched everywhere for him, with no luck. He, of course, suddenly appeared and demanded immediate action. McCormack and Albert were so enraged that they refused to put the bill on the weekly calendar. "They are totally disturbed with Powell," O'Brien wrote, "and are not going to allow him to dictate their procedures." O'Brien implored them to give in and feared that he was incurring "the wrath of the Leadership." Judge Smith came to life on the Rules Committee and made trouble about scheduling a rule. In the latter part of August Morse reported that the Senate Republicans were stalling both bills, higher education and the amendment to the

Taft-Hartley Act. The administration wanted education first, but AFL-CIO, though it strongly supported S. 600, put its own interest first. Everyone knew that education would pass, but that would come only after a run on the patience bank.

Cater, Treasury, the Budget Bureau, and the Office of Education tried to reassure the bankers that the bill would not kill the state and private programs. "But," Cater wrote the President, "the bankers are still trying to get us to eliminate the federal loan guarantee . . . altogether, while retaining the subsidy for student loans." The government people, including O'Brien's staff, agreed that "we must not yield . . . and that we will be able to make it stick in Congress." Johnson instructed Cater to enlist the help of his old Texas banker friend, Robert B. Anderson, who had been Eisenhower's Secretary of the Treasury.

On July 11 the ABA conceded, entering into an agreement with United Student Aid Funds and the government to accept an amendment protecting state and private loan funds. They would "give every assistance to the Office of Education in an earnest effort to make this program effectively serve the Nation's college students." The bankers would give primary support to the state and private plans, but, if there was none in any one state, they would "support and promote" federal insurance.

House debate took place on August 26. Green offered the administration amendment on loans and it was adopted by voice vote. The House then passed the higher education bill 368 to 22. Republicans, instead of fighting for the tax exemption for college expenses, voted overwhelmingly for the bill.[7]

Morse's Subcommittee on Education held leisurely hearings over 12 days in March and June, which filled three volumes of 1500 pages. The testimony was overwhelmingly favorable and it was formidably detailed. Five members of the subcommittee, including Morse, offered an amendment for matching grants to colleges for the acquisition of laboratory equipment and for training instructors to use it.

More important, on July 17 the President proposed the teaching professions bill, an expansion of the Kennedy-Nelson proposal. It would create a national teacher corps for work in poverty areas, fellowships to prepare superior students for careers in elementary and secondary teaching and to improve the skills of present teachers, and financial aid to colleges to enhance teaching programs. Johnson sent his bill to both houses. Morse, as he had promised Kennedy and Nelson, incorporated it into S. 600. The House, after holding separate hearings, also stuck it into the higher education bill.

On September 1 the Senate Labor and Public Welfare Committee, now working with the House bill, H.R. 9567, made a number of amendments and reported the measure out. Once again, the vote was unanimous. Even

Senator Dominick, still yearning for the Ribicoff amendment, called it "excellent." The very next day the Senate voted for an amended H.R. 9567 by an incredible 79 to 3. Only the two Mississippians, John Stennis and James Eastland, along with Willis Robertson of Virginia, voted against it, probably for reasons that had more to do with race than with higher education.

On September 10, Wilbur Cohen, now undersecretary of HEW, sent Larry O'Brien an alarmed memorandum over the Waggoner-Dirksen amendment. HEW's general counsel, Alanson Willcox, had concluded that there was a "great danger that the . . . amendment . . . will be held by the courts to exempt *all* educational institutions (elementary, secondary, and higher) from the provisions of Title VI of the Civil Rights Act of 1964, which forbids discrimination in federally assisted programs." H.R. 9567 would soon go to conference. *"If it passes in its present form,"* Cohen wrote, *"we intend to recommend that it be vetoed."* He attached a long Willcox memorandum carefully pointing out the offensive character of the words "or any other Act."

A few days later Morse sat down in conference with Powell, Green, and the technical staffs of both committees. Though the two Oregonians disliked each other intensely, both were civil and constructive. They seemed to get along extremely well on higher education, as they had demonstrated with the facilities bill in 1963. Morse had narrowed the differences to four or five items, the spadework was done, and he expected no "philosophical differences." He anticipated a "speedy conclusion" and, as usual, he was right. The differences between the houses were eliminated and the language of Waggoner-Dirksen was cleaned up.

Both houses accepted the conference report on October 20, 1965, the House by a vote of 313 to 63, the Senate by voice vote with no opposition.

President Johnson signed the Higher Education Act in the Strahan Gymnasium at Southwest Texas State College in San Marcos on November 8, 1965. It was, he said, "a proud moment in my life," because "a great deal began for me some 38 years ago on this campus." He recalled living in a tiny room over Dr. Evans's garage, shaving and showering in the gym, and working at a dozen odd jobs to support himself. He spoke warmly of his first real position at that "little Welhausen Mexican school" in Cotulla. "I shall never forget the faces of the boys and girls . . . and the pain of . . . knowing then that college was closed to practically every one of those children because they were too poor."

"The great, fabulous 89th Congress," Johnson called it, had enacted the "keystones," ESEA and the Higher Education Act. Now all young people who had been unable to pay for college had a way to do so. "For them and for this entire land of ours, it is the most important door that will ever open—the door to education."

The titles of the statute as enacted were as follows (appropriations in parentheses):

   I. Matching grants to the states for universities for research and extension programs to help solve community problems ($25 million for the first year, $50 million the second and third).

  II. Grants to college libraries for acquisitions ($50 million for each of three years). Grants for training librarians ($15 million for each of three years). Grant to the Library of Congress for cataloguing ($5 million for the first year, $6.315 million the second, $7.77 million the third).

 III. Grants to "developing institutions" to raise their academic quality. Grants to encourage agreements between developed and developing institutions to assist the latter. Teaching fellowships for graduate students and junior faculty to teach at developing institutions ($55 million for the first year).

  IV. Grants to graduating high school students to attend college who otherwise would be unable to do so ($70 million for each of three years). Encouragement of state and private insured loan programs, a federal program where access was unavailable, and payment of part of the interest ($1 million or more to establish the fund, $17.5 million to state and private programs for reserve funds). $1000 per year for undergraduates, $1500 for graduates and professionals, total ceiling of $7500. College work-study transferred from the Office of Economic Opportunity to the Commissioner of Education ($129 million for the first year, $165 million the second, and $200 million the third).

   V. National Teacher Corps for schools in low-income districts ($36.1 million for the first year, $64,715,000 the second and third). Fellowships for training teachers in elementary and secondary schools ($160 million for the first year, $275 million the second).

  VI. Financial assistance for purchasing equipment useful for college instruction programs ($35 million for the first year, $50 million the second, $60 million the third). Faculty training for use of equipment ($5 million for each of three years).

 VII. Broadened authority for colleges to finance buildings under Higher Education Facilities Act beyond natural sciences, mathematics, languages, engineering, and libraries ($190 million).

VIII. No federal control of fraternal organizations with a sterilized Waggoner-Dirksen amendment.

The cost of the bill had grown dramatically as it had advanced through the Congress. The original administration bill, including the teacher corps, had provided $330 million. The House version almost doubled to $618 million. The final statute topped out at $785.3 million.[8]

The 1965 education legislation was a grand breakthrough in public policy. After decades of effort the right of the federal government to give financial assistance to the nation's schools and colleges was conclusively established. The religious bottleneck had been removed. These new programs would make an important contribution to the educational system's ability to accommodate the baby boomers and to improve its quality.

But this must be placed in context. While the appropriation seemed like a lot of money, it was very little measured against the immense cost of operating the entire educational system. No individual school or college would receive very much. The federal share of support for lower education as a result of ESEA would rise from 3.5 percent to 8 percent. On the impact of the legislation, one should note the words of Francis Keppel:

> I don't know how one measures this, to tell you the truth. I don't know what standard one uses. We got the money out. None of the people I appointed with one possible exception were crooks. The money didn't stick to people's fingers. Some things got done, money got spent. Whether the obvious fact that these various bills scarcely reformed American education in three years is to be regarded as a failure of the act is a question in part of what you think 8-percent leverage means on a huge enterprise, and that's about the leverage. About 8-percent federal money was going into primary and secondary schools. Well, that's not an awfully long crowbar, and there are an awful lot of big boulders around. So I don't know how you measure it.

Lyndon Johnson was neither as well informed nor as detached as Francis Keppel. In his mind the enactment of ESEA and the Higher Education Act was the crowning achievement of his presidency. It recalled his childhood and his parents and his experiences as a schoolboy and a teacher. He felt, and properly so, that he was doing a great deal for those he treasured most, the young people of America. He worked extremely hard to deploy his troops and to push the House of Representatives to pass ESEA. There can be no doubt that he would have done the same in the Senate for ESEA and in both houses for higher education. But the easy victory in the House broke the back of opposition and there was no need to do so, except to police Adam Clayton Powell. One must place Johnson first in awarding credit for this accomplishment.

But it is necessary to strike a sour note. He wanted trophies to mount on his walls, that is, bills enacted by Congress. He seems to have had very little interest, if any, in the administration of those laws. This was evident in the Loomis affair here as it had been in the Yarmolinsky affair and the passage of the Economic Opportunity Act. He almost certainly misread Loomis's intention and he demonstrated no understanding of the immense administrative problems with which Keppel was wrestling.

President Kennedy had launched the quest in 1961, had persevered in the face of defeat, and had made significant gains in 1963. For this he deserves important recognition. But the assassination left much to be done. One may note that the passage of ESEA and the Higher Education Act represented President Johnson's final discharge of the Kennedy legacy. Henceforth whatever he did was his, was exclusively part of his Great Society.

Wayne Morse, as Keppel pointed out, was "magnificent." His management of two very important, very controversial, and very complex bills in the Senate may have been without match in the history of that venerable body. He was a master of legislative management.

Finally, Francis Keppel, who, like his favorite President, John Kennedy, was noted for intelligence, detachment, grace, civility, and dry wit, brought his formidable knowledge of the American educational system, including its weaknesses, to bear in creating the Gardner task force, drafting the legislation, and, most important, resolving the politically critical religious controversy.[9]

8

Selma and the Voting Rights Act

SELMA rested on the west bank of the Alabama River, which flowed south to Mobile on the Gulf of Mexico. Highway 80 crossed the river by the Edmund Pettus Bridge, named for the town's most prominent historic figure, a Confederate general. The road led east 54 miles to Montgomery, the capital of Alabama.

Selma had been founded in 1817 in the rich Black Belt of Dallas County. Before the Civil War the town flourished as the center of a slave-based cotton economy, surrounded by large plantations with columned white mansions, their grounds graced by magnolias dripping with Spanish moss. Selma shipped the cotton down river to Mobile. The town did not fall to Union forces until the closing days of the war and Reconstruction seems to have treated it gently. Nor did General Pettus allow the Ku Klux Klan to operate locally because of his contempt for the low social status of its members.

Time hardly moved in Selma. The relations between the races, except for the abolition of slavery, barely changed over a century and a half. By 1960 the population was 29,000, slightly more than half black. Everything was segregated: jobs, housing, government, police, firemen, churches, schools, buses, hotels and restaurants, the library, playgrounds, swimming pool, public toilets, and drinking fountains. In 1965 median family income for whites was $5,150, for blacks $1,393. In Dallas County median school years completed for both races was 9, for blacks 5.8. The streets were paved in white neighborhoods; dirt roads turned to mud when it rained in black ones. Even the *Times-Journal* segregated the white and the black news.

While virtually all whites there wanted segregation, they split into two schools. One, led by Sheriff Jim Clark, did not hesitate to use violence. "A heavy-set lawman with a sizable temper and paunch," Stephen L. Longenecker wrote, "[Clark] fit the northern stereotype of a southern sheriff. . . .

He wore a military-style outfit with a gold-braided officer's cap, and he dangled a billy club and an electric cattle prod from his belt." In addition to his paid deputies, Clark had volunteer posses of poor whites—mounted, water, and on foot. They were available to put down civil rights demonstrations anywhere in Alabama. His strongest supporter was Circuit Judge James Hare. The judge fancied himself an amateur anthropologist. Selma's blacks, he insisted, were of low intelligence because they descended mainly from the inferior Ibo tribe of Nigeria and had no Berber blood.

The other segregationist faction preferred order to violence. The new mayor, Joe T. Smitherman, spoke for them. He thought the town was decaying economically and hoped to persuade northern firms to locate in Selma. Scenes of black people being beaten by local police shown on national television would hardly help. Distrustful of Clark, the mayor named Wilson Baker director of public safety, supervising both the police and fire departments. The trouble was that Baker never learned how to control Clark. Baker was a professional lawman and had taught police science at the University of Alabama. He wanted to preserve segregation as long as possible without turning to force.

Ralph Smeltzer, a minister of the Church of the Brethren, spent several years in Selma out of public view trying to establish a dialogue between the races. He searched in vain for whites who would be willing to talk privately to blacks. Smeltzer did turn up two white men who strongly opposed segregation. Father Maurice Ouellet supervised the Catholic St. Elizabeth's Mission, which provided schools and a hospital for blacks. The dominant fundamentalist Baptist preachers, who equated Romanism with Satan, refused even to speak to him. His archbishop moved him out of town to another post in 1965. Art and Muriel Lewis, who were Jewish, also spoke out against segregation. He had been a businessman in Florida and they had retired to Selma. They were subjected to abuse and harassment and Muriel was convinced that this was the cause of Art's fatal heart attack.

Despite the Fifteenth Amendment and a voting rights campaign waged by the Student Nonviolent Coordinating Committee in 1963–64, almost all the black citizens of Dallas County, Alabama, were denied the right to vote. In 1961 the county had a voting-age population of 29,515, 14,400 whites and 15,115 blacks. The number of blacks registered was 156—1 percent. Attorney General Nicholas Katzenbach explained, "The history of Negro voting rights in Dallas County, Ala., of which Selma is the seat . . . in three words: 'intimidation,' 'discouragement,' and 'delay.' " The Department of Justice had fired off a battery of suits, four against intimidation alone, all still dragging their way through the courts. Few people in the North knew about it, but Selma was a national disgrace.[1]

In the winter of 1964–65 the mood of Martin Luther King, Jr., changed from exaltation to despair. In October 1964, while in the hospital in Atlanta overcoming exhaustion, he learned that he had been awarded the Nobel Peace Prize. At 35 he was the youngest person ever to win it. "This was not simply a personal award," David J. Garrow wrote, "but the most significant international endorsement possible of the civil rights struggle." It meant that he could never retreat to a quiet life. "More than anything else, the prize made the cross loom larger."

A big King party—immediate family, parents, close friends, and colleagues from the Southern Christian Leadership Conference—left New York for Europe on December 4. Outwardly the voyage was an immense triumph. On December 6 in London King preached to thousands in St. Paul's Cathedral and had many meetings with Anglican church leaders, Indian dignitaries, and spokesmen for the peace movement. Oslo was the capstone. He received the prize at a magnificent ceremony at Oslo University on December 10 in the presence of the Nobel officials and the royal family. The next day he delivered his address on the theme of nonviolence in domestic civil rights demonstrations and in international disarmament. The party moved on to Stockholm where King preached a sermon at the cathedral and was received by Gunnar and Alva Myrdal, he the author of the pathbreaking study of racism in the U.S., *An American Dilemma,* and she to become herself a winner of the Nobel Prize. Returning to New York, King was given a hero's welcome. Governor Nelson Rockefeller loaned his private jet to the King family for the flight to Washington where President Johnson offered his congratulations.

But all was not well. His close friend and leading assistant, Ralph Abernathy, backed by his wife, was extremely jealous of the acclaim King had received and demanded equal recognition. In the hotel in Oslo two members of the party, including King's brother, were picked up in the lobby naked chasing two women who were almost as sparely clad. Far more important, King was very depressed to learn that he had become a prime target of the FBI.

The Bureau had been bugging his rooms and tapping his phone conversations and had acquired much damaging information. Stanley Levison, one of his closest advisers and personal friends, had been involved with the finances of the Communist party. More telling, the FBI tapes revealed that King had an insatiable sexual appetite. Constantly on the road and often propositioned by attractive women, he indulged himself freely. This was common knowledge in the civil rights movement. When a friend warned him to take care, King said, "I'm away from home twenty-five to twenty-seven days a month. Fucking's a form of anxiety reduction." The FBI machines faithfully recorded these often athletic events.

J. Edgar Hoover had set out to destroy King. He hated blacks and considered King the worst of the lot. On November 18, 1964, at a press conference with women journalists the director called him "the most notorious liar" in the U.S. and added, off the record, that he was "one of the lowest characters in the country." King replied politely that Hoover must be "under extreme pressure." He offered to meet with the director. This made news headlines.

At the urging of Katzenbach, a meeting took place at the end of November. King brought along Abernathy, Andrew Young, and Walter Fauntroy; C. D. DeLoach sat beside Hoover. King spoke of his high regard for the FBI and Hoover rambled on about the bureau's civil rights activities in the South. The affair was wholly ceremonial; no one broached the real issues. On November 24 the director sharpened his attack in a speech in Chicago, referring to "pressure groups" which were led by "Communists and moral degenerates." There were leaks to journalists and churchmen.

In mid-November assistant FBI director William C. Sullivan instructed the lab to compile a tape of "highlights" of King's sexual adventures collected over the preceding ten months. Sullivan then added an anonymous letter. An agent took the tape and letter to Miami and mailed the package to King at SCLC headquarters in Atlanta. The staff assumed that it was a recording of one of his speeches and saved it for Coretta, his wife, who collected them. She picked it up after New Year's and played it. As Garrow wrote, she was "surprised and shocked" and immediately turned it over to her husband.

The letter was both insulting and threatening. "I will not dignify your name with either a Mr. or a Reverend or a Dr. . . . You are a complete fraud and a great liability to all of us Negroes. . . . You . . . turned out to be . . . a dissolute, abnormal moral imbecile. . . . King you are done.

"King, there is only one thing left for you to do. You know what this is. You have just 34 days. . . . There is but one way out for you. You better take it before your filthy, abnormal fraudulent self is bared to the nation."

King immediately called his advise.rs—Abernathy, Young, Joseph Lowery, and Chicago lawyer Chauncey Eskridge—together to listen to the tape. They concluded that it had come from the FBI and that the invitation to suicide in 34 days had expired on Christmas Day.

King became despondent and seemed to lose his bearings. But on January 8 he and his advisers in a meeting at the Park Sheraton in New York decided that he must confront the FBI. Agents tracked them to the hotel and bugged the room. King seems not to have been up to another meeting himself with Hoover or even DeLoach. Young and Abernathy, therefore, met with the latter. Young said he had heard that the FBI was interested in Communists, SCLC's finances, and King's personal life. DeLoach said that the Bureau was not at liberty to discuss Communists and that the agency had no interest in the organization's finances or its leader's private activities.

As Young reported to King, "There wasn't any honest conversation." The leaks continued.

King remained extremely depressed. It was in this mood that he launched the campaign for voter registration in Selma.[2]

Selma's blacks had hoped that the passage of the Civil Rights Act in 1964 would bring improvement, but they were bitterly disappointed. Modest attempts to enter the white section of a movie theater and to be served in a drive-in restaurant led Judge Hare to issue an injunction forbidding 15 named organizations and 50 individuals to hold meetings of more than three people. The Holiday Inn, linked to a national chain, quietly rented rooms to blacks and then, doubtless under local pressure, became all-white again. When Smitherman became mayor in October, Smeltzer urged him to meet secretly with black leaders, but he refused. The SNCC's voter registration drive was almost totally ineffective. Only 353 Negroes, 2.1 percent of eligible black voters, were enrolled in Dallas County. As King pointed out, "It would take about 103 years to register the adult Negroes." The Dallas County Board of Registrars was open for business only two days a month and the members had a taste for long lunch hours. On a good day they processed 15 applications, including rejections.

When King was at the White House in December, the President pointed out to him that the poverty program would help blacks and urged that they seek leadership roles. But, King countered, there was still a serious voting rights problem in the South. Later he recalled Johnson's reply: "Martin, you're right about that. I'm going to do it eventually, but I can't get a voting rights bill through in this session of Congress." He needed southern votes for other Great Society programs and 1965 was just not the right year. Though he did not say so, King disagreed.

In late 1964 SCLC representatives were in Selma making connections with local black leaders, and the Reverend James Bevel, based in Montgomery, was put in charge of the Alabama voting project. King held a meeting of about 100 SCLC officials, local people, and SNCC leaders in Montgomery, which adopted a plan to attack segregation in Alabama, starting with a voting rights campaign in Selma. Large numbers of blacks would appear at the courthouse on registration days and King would make widely publicized appearances in defiance of the Hare injunction. He would be put in jail. The Birmingham experience in 1963 was the example. Just as Selma-born Bull Connor's police brutality had aroused the nation and the world two years before, Jim Clark's force would behave the same way with the same results.

On January 2 King delivered a fiery address to a crowd of 700, including state and local lawmen and reporters, at the Brown Chapel of the African Methodist Episcopal Church in Selma. "Today," he declared, "marks the beginning of a determined, organized, mobilized campaign to get the right to vote everywhere in Alabama. . . . We must be ready to march; we must be willing to go to jail by the thousands. . . . *Give us the ballot!*" There was no police intervention. Wilson Baker had kept Jim Clark's men away from Brown Chapel.

On January 14 King was again in Selma. He announced that he would lead a march to the courthouse on registration day, Monday, January 18, and that he would test the antebellum Hotel Albert by trying to become its first black guest.

On Monday morning King headed about 400 blacks who, at Baker's suggestion, walked in groups of three or four, from the chapel to the courthouse. There was quite a welcoming committee: Baker, Clark, about 80 media people, as well as George Lincoln Rockwell of the American Nazi Party, and Jimmy George Robinson of the National States Rights Party. Clark herded the marchers into a roped-off area in the alley behind the building and gave them numbered cards ostensibly for registration. But he admitted only 40 whites. The blacks stood in the bitter cold all day.

There was no incident or violence. Similarly, the manager of the Albert simply registered King and ten members of his party. Robinson had followed King into the lobby and hit him with his fist on the temple and tried to kick him in the groin. Baker immediately seized Robinson, put him under arrest, and tossed him into a police car.

On Tuesday morning the marchers repeated their walk, this time stopping at the front door of the courthouse in order to avoid the alley. Clark immediately arrested them. Amelia Boynton was a dignified lady, a dedicated civil rights activist, and a registered voter, present, as the law required, to vouch for the applicants. She did not walk as fast as Clark liked. He grabbed her by the collar and shoved her stumbling half a block to the sheriff's car in full view of the press. He took in a total of 67 people. But the NAACP Legal Defense Fund had them out of jail before supper. SCLC was pleased that Clark had bitten the bait; Baker, however, was appalled.

On Wednesday morning three successive waves of about 50 marchers walked to the front entrance. Clark, boiling, was waiting for them. He ordered the first group, led by John Lewis of SNCC, into the alley. They refused. "You are an agitator," he said to Lewis, "and that is the lowest form of humanity. If you do not disperse in one minute . . . as I have directed you, you will be under arrest for unlawful assembly." He ticked off the seconds. No one moved. He put them in the county jail in city hall. He treated the second wave the same way. When the third arrived, Baker told them to line up by another entrance so as not to obstruct the sidewalk. Clark demanded that Baker arrest them and he refused. Clark grabbed a bullhorn, gave the crowd a minute to disperse, and then arrested them himself.

On Friday afternoon Selma's black school teachers, led by the Reverend Frederick D. Reese and the teachers' association president, A. J. Durgan, joined the demonstration on their own initiative. SCLC staffers said, "Brother, we got a *move*-ment goin' on in Selma!" The teachers were dressed in their Sunday best, had toothbrushes in their pockets, and assumed they would be out of jail by the time school opened on Monday. In pairs, 100 teachers marched to the courthouse after classes ended on Friday. Clark, his posses, and the media were waiting for them. Reese said they only wanted to walk by the closed registration office. Clark, trembling with anger, would not let them enter the building. Reese led them away.

On Saturday, on the motion of the Justice Department, District Judge David Thomas vacated the Hare injunction. He ordered an end to intimidation and harassment of citizens of Dallas County legitimately attempting to register to vote. But white Selma was in no mood to bend to the will of any judge.

The next week the blacks resumed their daily marches. On Monday Clark shoved Mrs. Annie Lee Cooper. A sturdy woman, she hit him in the face and, as he staggered, slugged him twice more, knocking him to his knees. The deputies wrestled her to the ground, Clark jumped on her, and he hit her in the head with his baton. The next morning the *New York Times* had a picture of Clark sitting on Mrs. Cooper on its front page. Governor Wallace sent Colonel Al Lingo and his feared Alabama State Police into Selma.

From the outset SCLC had planned that King should be arrested and write a letter from jail, as he had from Birmingham in 1963. The staff chose Monday, February 1, the next regular registration day, when there would be a big crowd and the media present, with shutters cocked.

The authorities soon learned the plan. They agreed that the blacks should be arrested, but Baker and Clark each wanted the other to do the arresting. Further, Mayor Smitherman had convinced the Hammermill Paper Company of Erie, Pennsylvania, to announce its plan to build a large plant in Selma on February 3. It would not do to have the glad news published while the town's jail was filled with demonstrators, including the Nobel Prize-winner. The SCLC staff preferred that Baker be the arrester because they feared that Clark would bash King if he got him away from the cameras.

Baker, in fact, did arrest King along with 260 marchers and jailed them. King kept very busy. He sent detailed instructions to Andrew Young to try various devices to involve the federal government, to get public support from notable politicians and show business stars, and to publicize the Selma struggle. Lee White, the President's adviser on civil rights, took Young's call and urged a moderate response. "I assume," he wrote Johnson, "that the basic reason for King's call is to have a reply that he can publicize and indicate Presidential support for his position." Thus, he should be told that John Doar of the Civil Rights Division was in Selma and was already reporting to the President through the Attorney General; if Johnson needed to make a statement, it should say blandly that he was committed to the right to vote and was working on legislation.

At his press conference on February 12 the President went beyond White's recommendation:

> All Americans should be indignant when one American is denied the right to vote. The loss of that right to a single citizen undermines the freedom of every citizen. This is why all of us should be concerned with the efforts of our fellow Americans to register to vote in Alabama.

King's letter from jail was written for a purpose: it appeared as an advertisement in the *New York Times* on February 5 in an appeal for money for the SCLC.

King then asked for a meeting with the President. This made the White House skittish, excepting the President's commitment to the right to vote. Johnson did not want to appear to be taking sides in the Selma imbroglio and King had a history of squeezing publicity out of presidential appointments. White worked out an arrangement to protect the President. He told King that he could announce only that he was conferring with the Vice President and the Attorney General. Then the President would *try* to see him for a few minutes. "I told his lawyer . . . ," White wrote, "that if word of this got out in advance, all bets were off."

On the afternoon of February 9 Humphrey and Katzenbach in the former's office in the Executive Office Building briefed King and his aides on the voting rights bill. King was little interested, waiting anxiously for a call from the White House. It seemed forever, but finally came. Humphrey led them across the street. Johnson greeted them and then spoke privately with King for ten minutes. They talked only about the bill, nothing about Selma. King was told that he must limit his press statement to the bill. He did so dutifully.

The tension in Selma was rising. Differences over strategy between SCLC and both the local leaders and SNCC had sharpened. The Reverend Bevel was in jail. Malcolm X came to Selma and, to everyone's relief, spoke with restraint, urging support for King.

The conflict spilled over into nearby Perry County, where the registrars defied a federal injunction by denying blacks the vote. There were rallies and marches to the courthouse in the village of Marion. On February 18 the police arrested James Orange, the SCLC leader, and the mayor asked the governor to send in Lingo's troopers. A number of reporters and photographers in Selma, smelling a story, drove to Marion.

That evening hundreds of blacks gathered at Zion Chapel to hear the Reverend C. T. Vivian of the SCLC. Earlier that day he had been punched in the mouth and jailed in Selma, but was released after a few hours. Jimmy Lee Jackson, his mother, his sister, Emma Jean, and their 82-year-old grandfather, Cager Lee, were among those present. Vivian called for a march to the jail to protest the arrest of Orange.

As they started down the street, the police chief declared an unlawful assembly, the street lights went out, and the troopers, joined by local toughs, attacked. Many blacks were knocked to the ground and bloodied. Pete Fisher of United Press International was clubbed and his camera smashed. Richard Valeriani of NBC suffered a head wound that required six stitches.

The Jacksons were separated. Cager, behind the church, was beaten and kicked by local whites until they recognized him. Jimmy Lee, the women, and Cager made their way to Mack's Cafe, but the troopers invaded, swinging their clubs indiscriminately. When his mother was knocked to the floor, Jimmy Lee lunged at the trooper and was hit in the face. As he tried to rise, a trooper shoved him against the cigarette machine and another fired a gun into his stomach from five feet. It was several hours before he was taken to the Catholic hospital in Selma and an infection had set in. He died on February 16.

On the morning of March 3 a crowd of 3000 attended a memorial service for Jimmy Lee at Brown Chapel in Selma. That afternoon 400 crowded into the Zion Chapel in Marion, while 600 stood in the rain outside. King delivered a powerful eulogy. As Jackson's body was lowered into his grave, the Reverend Bevel announced that there would be a march along the 54 miles of Highway 80 from Selma to Montgomery led by King on Sunday, March 7.

By now the leaders on both sides were wearing out. King, who both led the Selma marches and flew around the country making speeches to raise money, was exhausted and had to take to his bed. Sheriff Clark moved into the hospital, complaining of chest pains: "The niggers are givin' me a heart attack." The venom in his system, however, soon had his heart beating steadily and he was back on the streets. Baker sneaked off to Louisiana for a respite from the tension.

The issue was no longer Selma. The announcement of the march to Montgomery would create a series of new crises—for the civil rights movement, for the state of Alabama, and for the federal government.[3]

The Fifteenth Amendment to the Constitution, ratified in 1870, declared, "The right of citizens of the United States to vote shall not be denied or abridged by the United States or by any State on account of race, color, or previous condition of servitude." After Reconstruction, when whites reestablished political control over the states of the former Confederacy, they systematically denied blacks the franchise with devices such as the grandfather clause, the all-white primary, the poll tax, literacy tests, and educational achievement requirements.

In the twentieth century the National Association for the Advancement of Colored People challenged these bars to voting and gradually convinced the Supreme Court to hold them unconstitutional. Congress in the Civil Rights Acts of 1957 and 1960 made modest efforts at the federal level to open registration. In 1962 President Kennedy urged Congress to enact and the states to ratify what in 1964 became the Twenty-fourth Amendment, which forbade the denial to any citizen of the right to vote in federal elections "by reason of failure to pay any poll tax." The 1964 Civil Rights Act restricted the use of literacy tests in voting rights cases. The U.S. Civil Rights Commission maintained a steady drumbeat of demands for the elimination of bars to voting.

The consequence of these gains was a gradual extension of the suffrage to black voters. By 1964 the poll tax was still used discriminatorily in only five states—Alabama, Arkansas, Mississippi, Texas, and Virginia. In the presidential election that year there were only seven states left with extremely low voter participation rates, six of them in the South—Alabama, Georgia, Louisiana, Mississippi, South Carolina, and Virginia. The seventh was Alaska and no one seemed able to explain it or to address it. All of these states had literacy and/or educational attainment tests for registration. Thus, by 1965 the remaining problems still not reached by existing law were confined to the South.

While these residual issues were narrowly confined geographically, they were extremely troublesome legally. This was because, as Katzenbach pointed out, "it was just an impossible system of law enforcement":

> The courts had been very, very slow on this; people obviously were qualified to vote who were being turned down; then we had to bring a lawsuit; then we had to go through all the appeals and another election would go by. . . . it just took forever . . . in terms of personnel and work and everything else.

President Johnson, as he had told King, was deeply concerned about discriminatory denial of the suffrage. In his State of Union message on January 4, 1965, he declared, "I propose that we eliminate every remaining obstacle to the right and the opportunity to vote." In fact, he had already directed Katzenbach, Lee White, and Bill Moyers to move ahead with preparation of a bill. Whether he intended to introduce legislation in 1965 is doubtful. He had already told King that it should wait and White also had misgivings about timing, though not about the merits. But the conflict in Selma would overwhelm the arguments for delay.

Some, like Senate majority leader Mike Mansfield, thought that writing a voting rights bill based on the Fifteenth Amendment was "simplicity itself." The top lawyers in the Department of Justice were not among them. Katzenbach himself, Deputy Attorney General Ramsey Clark, Solicitor General Archibald Cox, and the head of the Civil Rights Division, Burke Marshall, worked on the drafting, assisted by attorneys from Marshall's staff and the Office of Legal Counsel. It took these luminaries well over two months to complete a short bill that would have a chance of passing a constitutional challenge.

This was because many questions demanded answers. A memorandum of "issues to be resolved" written after the work was well under way raised some thirty queries. Two were of great importance. The first was whether there should be a constitutional amendment or a statute. Justice was of both minds and prepared drafts of an amendment as well as of a bill. The former would read as follows:

> The right of citizens of the United States to vote shall not be denied or abridged by the United States or by any State for any cause except (1) inability to meet residence requirements not exceeding sixty days or minimum age requirements, imposed by State law; (2) conviction of a felony for which no pardon or amnesty has been granted; (3) mental incompetency adjudicated by a court of record; or (4) confinement pursuant to the judgment or warrant of a court of record at the time of registration or election.

The attraction of amendment, the Attorney General argued, was that it was both the "most drastic and the most effective" of the alternatives. The bar to black voting, the literacy test, would become unconstitutional by exclusion from the list of exceptions. The drawback, Katzenbach wrote, was that it was "much more cumbersome to amend the Constitution than to enact simple legislation." The Twenty-fourth Amendment had cleared in less than two years, but that was unusually fast, and the poll tax was much more unpopular than the literacy test. Only 13 states were needed to block adoption, and, while the South could not supply quite that large a number, Katzenbach pointed out, "There may be opposition from sources genuinely concerned about federal interference with a fundamental matter traditionally left to the States."

Legislation could take one of two forms. The first would empower a federal commission to conduct registration for federal elections, perhaps by using postmasters or appointees of the Civil Service Commission as registrars. The appeal was that there was no constitutional problem because Congress would be exercising its constitutional power to regulate the "manner" of holding federal elections. But there were two serious deficiencies. One was that state and local elections were not reached; the other that conservatives would consider this "an unwarranted interference with a state function."

The other legislative formula was to empower the federal government to control registration in all elections in counties in which the percentage of black registrants was abnormally low. But, Katzenbach pointed out, "its constitutionality is more dubious than that of the preceding suggestion."

The civil rights movement, of course, strongly opposed the amendment process because of the time required. Further, the mounting crisis in Selma required swifter action. This left the legislative alternative. But it was not until early March before the President decided in favor of federal control over registration for all elections, hoping to surmount the constitutional hurdle by hooking the bill to the Fifteenth Amendment.

The other difficult question was the literacy test. For the civil rights leaders this was a non-issue. Joseph L. Rauh, Jr., counsel to the Leadership Conference on Civil Rights, submitted a draft bill to the Attorney General on February 12, 1965, which stated that "any literacy . . . or other educational requirement for voting necessarily denies the right to vote on grounds of race and color." Aside from being untrue, this language suffered from intellectual myopia. Many fair-minded Americans who strongly disapproved of the discriminatory use of literacy tests, as in Dallas County, Alabama, believed that citizens of the U.S. who voted should be able to read and write. More than 30 states which did not discriminate against blacks used these tests. They usually required the ability to read English and often to write one's own name.

The Justice Department consulted with Richard Scammon, who had been Director of the Census and chairman of the President's Committee on Registration and Voting Participation. While he had himself voted to abolish the tests, it was, he said, "a difficult political judgment." It involved balancing the risk of misuse in order to discriminate as against the views of "many honest and fair-minded men who feel that a literacy requirement is reasonable and beneficial." Four such members of his committee had voted against abolition. In Hawaii, where there was no question of racial discrimination, a 1964 referendum to eliminate the test was defeated 77,200 to 72,500.

The bill the President submitted to Congress heeded Scammon's advice by zeroing in on the discriminating areas. The federal government would be empowered to take over registration only in those states and counties in which less than half of the persons of voting age were registered in 1964 and in which less than half voted in the 1964 presidential election. This limited the reach of the bill to the six states noted above, Alaska, 28 counties in eastern North Carolina, three in Arizona, and one in Idaho. No qualification for voting based on race or color would be lawful. In the affected areas registrants would not be required to demonstrate literacy, a level of educational achievement, good moral character, or to submit the voucher of a registered voter.[4]

Bevel's announcement of the march from Selma to Montgomery created division, uncertainty, and confusion on both sides. A number of the SNCC staff members thought it a waste of energy and resources. Its executive committee voted to oppose the march but to allow any individual to take part on his own. Young wondered whether it might be better to get a court order in advance. On the evening before the demonstration word came from Governor Wallace that his troopers would "use whatever measures were necessary to prevent a march." There were death threats to King. Bevel and Hosea Williams phoned King in Atlanta to advise him that it was too dangerous to come to Selma. He agreed to stay away.

The governor did not seem to know how to grasp the handle on the Selma crisis. When a number of aides argued on Saturday that the troopers should not stop the demonstration, that the marchers could not possibly walk 54 miles, that King would become a laughing stock, Wallace changed his mind. Word went out that the demonstration could go forward without hindrance. But now there was another hitch. Route 80 narrowed from four to two lanes as it crossed Lowndes County, a sparsely populated area that was well stocked with heavily armed members of the Klan. The county's representative warned that there could be murders on that desolate road. Wallace switched back. Lingo would halt the column before it crossed the Pettus Bridge.

Baker was convinced that the troopers would use force. He told Mayor Smitherman on Saturday night that he would not allow his men to take part and was resigning. But on Sunday morning several members of the city council hammered out a compromise. Baker's men would not assist Lingo and Clark and Baker would stay on.

On the eve of the march the SCLC leadership was at a loss. Although the demonstration was scheduled for 10 a.m. on Sunday, King was still in Atlanta on Saturday night. Late Sunday morning Bevel, Williams, and Young, who were in charge, did not know what to do. Some 500 prospective marchers were milling about the Brown Chapel. Williams phoned Atlanta but was unable to reach King, who was preaching at his church. He got Abernathy and asked him if he and King wanted the march to proceed. King reluctantly approved and Abernathy agreed.

Bevel, Williams, and Young split the group into three waves. They flipped coins to decide which of them would lead the first group and Williams "won." John Lewis of SNCC would be beside him.

Meantime Lingo had closed Route 80 on the far side of the Pettus Bridge and a line of cars backed up. The troopers stood shoulder-to-shoulder across the four lanes. Their clubs were at the ready and gas masks hung from their belts. Clark's mounted posse was in reserve behind them.

Williams led his wave, now quiet, in double file down Sylvan Street, turned right along the river on Water Avenue, and then left on Broad Street, which led up onto the arching bridge. The troopers came into view when they reached the crest of the arch. Williams and Lewis asked each other if he could swim. Neither could.

As the wave came down the far side of the bridge, Major John Cloud, who was in command, ordered his men to don their masks. He directed the marchers to halt and to disperse within two minutes. Williams asked to speak with him. Cloud said, "There is no word to be had. Troopers, advance!" In Selma May 7, 1965, became known as "Bloody Sunday." Roy Reed's front-page account in Monday's *New York Times:*

> The troopers rushed forward, their blue uniforms and white helmets blurring into a flying wedge as they moved. . . .
>
> The first 10 or 20 Negroes were swept to the ground, screaming, arms and legs flying, and packs and bags went skittering across the grassy divider strip and on to the pavement on both sides.
>
> Those still on their feet retreated.
>
> The troopers continued pushing, using both the force of their bodies and the prodding of their nightsticks.
>
> A cheer went up from the white spectators lining the south side of the highway.
>
> The mounted possemen spurred their horses and rode at a run into the retreating mass. The Negroes cried out as they crowded together for protection, and the whites on the sidelines whooped and cheered.
>
> The Negroes paused in their retreat for perhaps a minute, still screaming and huddling together.
>
> Suddenly there was a report like a gunshot and a grey cloud spewed over the troopers and the Negroes.
>
> "Tear gas!" someone yelled.
>
> The cloud began covering the highway. Newsmen, who were confined by four troopers to a corner 100 yards away, began to lose sight of the action.
>
> But before the cloud finally hid it all, there were several seconds of unobstructed view. Fifteen or twenty nightsticks could be seen through the gas, flailing at the heads of the marchers.
>
> The Negroes broke and ran. Scores of them streamed across the parking lot of the Selma Tractor Company. Troopers and possemen, mounted and unmounted, went after them.

The *Times* reported that 57 individuals were injured. Other estimates ran as high as 90 to 100. A volunteer group of doctors and nurses from New York City treated many of them at the Brown Chapel; others received care at the Good Samaritan Hospital and the Burwell Infirmary.

That evening Young spoke to King in Atlanta for over an hour, and they agreed to take two steps. On Monday SCLC would ask federal Judge Frank M. Johnson, Jr., in Montgomery for an injunction prohibiting interference with the demonstration. King would lead a second march from Selma to Montgomery on Tuesday, March 9. King sent telegrams to 200 religious leaders across the country urging them to walk with him.

Selma was now a news sensation. ABC interrupted its Sunday night movie, *Judgment at Nuremberg,* for a long televised report on the assault. Every major newspaper in the country carried a front-page story under a big headline on Monday. Senators Javits of New York, Yarborough of

Texas, and Mondale of Minnesota denounced the attack on the floor of the Senate. It was said that even Governor Wallace was outraged by the lack of control and blamed Jim Clark.

The White House remained silent because the President was torn. "The most obvious step," he later wrote, "and the one most passionately desired by citizens in the North who supported equal rights for Negroes was to send federal troops to Alabama." He heard that advice close by. His aide Harry McPherson wrote him on March 12, "What the public felt on Monday, in my opinion, was the deepest sense of outrage it has ever felt on the civil rights question. I had dinner with Abe Fortas Monday night. That reasonable man was for sending troops at once." But others disagreed. Humphrey reviewed the options with the Equal Employment Opportunity Commission. "With but minor dissent, the group indicated a strong belief that federal troops should not be used under present circumstances." The President concurred. A military display might "destroy" the voting rights bill, would make Wallace a martyr, and would undermine southern moderates. "We had to have a real victory for the black people, not a psychological victory for the North."

On Monday the civil rights lawyers met with Judge Johnson to ask for an immediate injunction. He refused to issue one without a hearing. He wanted the Tuesday march canceled and would open his hearings on Thursday.

On Monday night in Selma the civil rights leadership met for 12 hours—King, Abernathy, Young, Williams, the lawyers, James Farmer of the Committee on Racial Equality, and James Forman of SNCC. The initial decision, reached about midnight, with Williams and Forman dissenting, called for accepting the judge's postponement till Thursday. But they had not counted on the impact of the news, particularly the television footage of the attack at the Pettus Bridge, along with King's call for volunteers. Hundreds of sympathizers had dropped what they had been doing, hopped on airplanes, and were now reaching Montgomery and Selma.

James J. Reeb was a Unitarian minister working for the American Friends Service Committee on housing for low-income blacks in the Roxbury ghetto in Boston. He learned of King's plea about noon on Monday. That afternoon he arranged to leave his job and his family (over the protest of his wife). He was on an Eastern Airlines flight to Atlanta at 11 p.m. and caught another to Montgomery, arriving around 8:00 Tuesday morning. A rental car had him in Selma about 9:00. Reeb was one of scores of clergymen arriving from all corners of the country. Their presence created enormous pressure on King to go forward with the march that day.

On Monday night and early Tuesday morning the Johnson administration pushed King to comply with Judge Johnson's request for delay. John Doar of the Civil Rights Division and Fred Miller and James Laue of the new Community Relations Service urged him to wait. At 4 a.m., however, the leaders decided to proceed. Within the hour Katzenbach phoned to press King to reverse the decision. LeRoy Collins, the former governor of Florida and now head of the Community Relations Service, joined the meeting and was also unsuccessful.

Collins, as good mediators with tough cases must, had an inspiration. He went to Lingo and Clark and told them that King was determined to march. They said they would not allow him to go beyond the Pettus Bridge. Collins asked whether they would forgo force if the marchers stopped before they reached the line of troopers and then turned back. Lingo and Clark said they would not attack. Collins returned to King and explained the ploy. Collins and his staff were convinced that King agreed, though others said that he merely smiled.

In mid-morning Judge Johnson converted his request for delay into a formal restraining order. It was served on the SCLC staff members. Now a march would be in defiance of a federal court order. Shortly before 3 p.m., as the lines were forming, Collins approached King, told him "everything would be all right," and handed him a piece of paper.

The march moved down Sylvan to Water and then onto Broad to the foot of the bridge. There a U.S. marshal read the restraining order to King. The marshal stepped aside and the marchers proceeded up onto the bridge and down the other side where the troopers at the ready were in full view. When only 50 feet separated them, King halted. Prayers were recited and the marchers sang "We Shall Overcome." Simultaneously King turned the march around and led it back across the bridge as the troopers, evidently on telephoned orders from the governor, withdrew from the roadway, leaving the road to Montgomery seemingly open. But King continued back through Selma to Brown Chapel. SNCC was outraged by this "sell-out" and its already strained relations with SCLC snapped.

That afternoon the President finally spoke out. He deplored Sunday's "brutality," denying citizens the "precious right to vote." He promised that the voting rights bill would be ready by the next weekend. The government, he said, was following events in Selma closely and was trying to lessen the tension. In Washington hundreds protested outside the White House and the Department of Justice.

There were about 50 Unitarian Universalist clergymen who had walked in the aborted march. A friend of Reeb's said he was driving to Atlanta that evening and offered to take him to the airport; Reeb accepted. But another friend urged him to stay another day and he changed his plan. Reeb and two others walked into town to find a place to eat supper. They stopped at the SNCC office to get advice. A tall Negro asked, "Would you prefer a place of your own?" They said they preferred a black restaurant and were told to go to Walker's Cafe. It was crowded with civil rights marchers and they had to wait. By the time they left it was 7:30 and dark.

As they started down the street Reeb was on the outside near the curb.

Almost immediately four white men, shouting, "Hey you niggers!" moved in on them. One with a three-foot club, swinging with all his might, struck Reeb in the head above the left ear and he went down. The two others were assaulted by fists and also fell to the pavement.

Reeb was taken to Burwell Infirmary. But the doctors were unable to handle so serious a case and suggested the Birmingham University Hospital. It was four hours before he arrived there. He had sustained a massive skull fracture which had shattered his brain and had caused cardiac arrest. He died at 6:55 p.m. on Thursday. The preceding day Wilson Baker had arrested four white men for the murder. Three were indicted and were tried in December. Despite firm identifications by the ministers, they were acquitted by an all-white jury.

The Johnsons were hosting a congressional reception at the White House when the President was handed a note informing him that Reeb had been clubbed. He excused himself and phoned Mrs. Reeb. "No matter what I could find to say to her," he wrote later, "I had no answer to the one question that kept turning over and over in my mind. How many Jim Reebs will die before our country is truly free?" He did provide Mrs. Reeb with an airplane, which allowed her to be with her husband when he died.

People in the North, already enraged, became enflamed by the murder. It was, of course, the top story in the media. Thousands marched in sympathy in Boston, New York, Chicago, Los Angeles, and many other cities. In Detroit, Michigan's governor, George Romney, and Mayor Jerome Cavanaugh led 10,000 people through the downtown area.

Judge Johnson's hearings opened in Montgomery on Thursday, March 12, and continued on Friday, Saturday, and the following Monday. On Wednesday he issued his decision, a total victory for the SCLC: Governor Wallace's prohibition of a march was unconstitutional; the judge gave the SCLC an injunction against either the state or the county interfering; and he approved a detailed plan for the 54-mile walk. Hosea Williams announced that it would begin on Sunday, March 21.

Wallace must have sensed that this was coming. After all, Frank Johnson was a firm supporter of civil rights and the governor had repeatedly called him "a low-down, carpetbaggin', scallawagin', race-mixin' liar." Wallace's options were closing. He could not order Lingo's troopers to beat up King's marchers again, this time with many white people involved. This would defy a federal court order and he himself might wind up in jail. It would also wipe out the already severely tarnished reputation of the state of Alabama. But, if he complied with the injunction, he would sell out his rabid redneck constituents. His only way out was to dump the problem on the federal government.

On Friday afternoon, March 12, the governor held a strategy session with his key advisers. They agreed that he should ask the President for a meeting to discuss Selma, and he immediately sent a telegram to the White

House. Johnson, who was anxiously trying to avoid sending troops to Alabama in the face of growing public demand, wrote that his "hopes were realized."

They met the next day in the Oval Office for three hours. The President considered Wallace a "runty little bastard" and "just about the most dangerous person around." He kept his eyes on Wallace's face the whole time. He saw "a nervous aggressive man; a rough, shrewd politician who had managed to touch the deepest chords of pride as well as prejudice among his people." Burke Marshall said,

> The President handled Wallace very well, very well. He really had Wallace impressed, sort of cowed and pliable. . . . He kept telling him we have to view ourselves and view this problem as history will view it in the future. Wallace ate all that stuff up, and it was very effective. It didn't last, but it was very effective for the time being.

The governor complained, the President told a press conference immediately afterward, that the demonstrations constituted a threat to the peace and security of the people of Alabama. Johnson answered, "I am firmly convinced . . . that when all the eligible Negroes of Alabama have been registered, . . . the demonstrations . . . will stop." He asked Wallace to support universal suffrage, to assure the right of peaceful assembly, and to call a biracial conference to improve relations between whites and blacks. When asked Wallace's reaction, he said, "We are not in agreement on a good many things." A reporter inquired whether he intended to send troops; Johnson deflected the question. Lee White had warned him against giving Wallace the press after the meeting. Johnson handled it alone. Thus, the governor returned to Alabama empty-handed. As politicians do in such situations, he attacked the press.

Monday, March 15, was a notable day. During the morning Wilcox and Lowndes counties registered a total of 12 black voters, their first in the twentieth century. After a battle led by LeRoy Collins and Wilson Baker, Selma that afternoon allowed a memorial service for James Reeb on the courthouse steps before a crowd of 2000. King preached and a number of national figures were present. Most important, that evening President Johnson presented the voting rights bill to a joint session of Congress before an enormous television audience, which will be recounted shortly.

But on Tuesday there was a vicious incident in Montgomery. About 600 demonstrators, mostly white and from the North, gathered near the state capitol. Some of the officers supposedly maintaining order—city, county, and state police—suddenly rode their mounts into the crowd and beat the marchers mercilessly with their batons.

Late Tuesday afternoon the President met with Moyers, Katzenbach, Clark, Marshall, and Buford Ellington, former governor of Tennessee and director of the Office of Emergency Preparedness. Cyrus Vance, Secretary of the Army, was also consulted. The President insisted that he wanted an "adequate" troop level: "if you haven't enough you will wish you had." He added, "I want professionals there, not drugstore cowboys." Vance proposed putting a military police battalion into the Selma area and another near Birmingham, along with federalization of the Alabama National Guard. He also suggested "a good man" for the command, Brigadier General Henry V. Graham of the 31st Infantry (Dixie) Division. He had led a similar force in 1963 when George Wallace had tried to prevent black students from enrolling at the University of Alabama.

Katzenbach pointed out that, according to the Constitution, the President could not act on his own: "The only way to get federal troops in is for the Governor to say that he is unable to maintain law and order." Ellington phoned Wallace to tell him to request federal assistance and he immediately agreed to do so. The President asked, "How do you explain the change in Wallace's attitude?" Ellington replied, "He had confidence in you. He needs help. He has been an entirely different person." Wallace, of course, had no choice.

Thus, the governor did as he was told, but in his own way to save his political face in Alabama. On March 18 he wired the President that the state was unable to provide security for the "so-called march" from Selma to Montgomery. This would require "6,171 men; 489 vehicles; 15 busses, not including support units." The state had only 300 troopers and 150 alcohol control officers. "I respectfully request that the United States provide sufficient federal civil authorities or officers to provide for the safety and welfare of citizens in and along the proposed march routes and to provide for the safety and welfare of the marchers." The governor then got his legislature to pass a resolution declaring that Alabama was asking for federal help because it did not have the funds to pay for the mission.

Lyndon Johnson could also play at the game of dissembling. He sent the following telegram to Wallace on March 20:

> Responsibility for maintaining law and order in our federal system properly rests with state and local governments. On the basis of your public statements and your discussions with me, I thought that you felt strongly about this and had indicated you would take all necessary action in this regard. I was surprised, therefore, when . . . you requested federal assistance. . . . Even more surprising was [the statement] . . . that both you and the Alabama legislature, because of monetary considerations, believed that the state is unable to protect American citizens and to maintain peace and order . . . without federal forces.
>
> Because the court order must be obeyed and the rights of American citizens protected, I intend to meet your request by providing federal assistance to perform normal police functions. . . .

The President issued Executive Order 11207 nationalizing the Alabama National Guard on March 20. General Graham was placed in command of the initial forces, consisting of an infantry battalion (1,837 men) from his division in Alabama along with the 503rd military police battalion from Fort Bragg, North Carolina, (500 men) and the 720th military police battalion from Fort Hood, Texas (509 men). An infantry battalion of the 20th Infantry Division at Fort Benning, Georgia, was put on alert.

In addition, the Department of Justice established its own emergency organization in Alabama with Ramsey Clark in charge. He would be in a radio car between Selma and Montgomery. John Doar was assigned to General Graham and was also in a radio car. Burke Marshall was in Selma. Almost 100 U.S. marshals were brought into the area.

On the eve of the march Bill Moyers phoned the substance of a long memorandum, obviously from the FBI, to the President at his ranch. King, deeply disturbed, had called his advisers, Bayard Rustin and Harry Wachtel, to report a serious rift with SNCC. Forman at a recent church meeting had called for violent overthrow of the government. SNCC, King understood, was going to provoke a race riot in Montgomery in order to "get a martyr in Alabama." They wanted to have "somebody from SNCC killed." Rustin told him that he must "divorce himself from SNCC publicly" when the march was over. The Bureau reported that people from all over the country were pouring into Alabama and expected more than 5000 by March 21. King estimated that 9000 marchers would leave Selma and that 25,000 would enter Montgomery.

In fact, the numbers at the outset were much smaller and the march itself was a bit of an anti-climax. Joe Califano, the aide to Secretary McNamara, transmitted the Army counts for the four days of the march to the White House and the Department of Justice. The first day, as they left Selma, there were 392 marchers, approximately 45 white. On the last day, as the procession entered Montgomery, the numbers swelled dramatically to 1200 and that evening to 5000. The next day in the city there were about 10,000.

The problems were routine. At the start the cold brought frost. Later it rained heavily and one of the bivouac areas became a sea of mud. The marchers, with General Graham's permission, slept on the highway to try to keep dry. Sixteen black women worked furiously in the kitchen at the Green Street Baptist Church in Selma to prepare hot meals of pork and beans and spaghetti which were delivered in new garbage cans in a rented Hertz truck. Professor Elwyn Allan Smith, who taught ecumenics at the Pittsburgh Theological Seminary, commanded the delivery crew. The San Francisco Theological Seminary provided portable toilets. The narrow highway through Lowndes County was negotiated without incident. There were protecting soldiers on the ground and helicopters overhead. The only incidents were minor. A guardsman spat on a priest, for which he was relieved of his post and reprimanded. A latrine truck got stuck in the mud in a bivouac area and the Army took quite a while to get it back on the road. A black driver of a "logistical support vehicle" (could that be Armyese for the Hertz truck loaded with spaghetti in garbage cans?) stopped for gas and the owner of the station punched him in the nose. The military police moved in until the local cop arrived. So it went.

King headed the march intermittently the first three days. He seemed extremely tired and his feet blistered. He spent the nights in a mobile home. On Wednesday morning he rested and at midday took a flight to Cleveland for a fund-raising rally. Many marchers called him "De Lawd."

On the outskirts of Montgomery the marchers, triumphantly singing "We *Have* Overcome," reached their last campsite, the Catholic City of St. Jude. As the Army figures indicate, they were joined by many others from Selma and from across the nation who had reached Montgomery. They turned the St. Jude field into churned mud. Entertainment was scheduled for 9 p.m., but was two hours late and did not end until 2 a.m. Show business descended en masse—Shelley Winters, Sammy Davis, Jr., Tony Perkins, Tony Bennett, Dick Gregory, Mike Nichols and Elaine May, Harry Belafonte, Joan Baez, and many others. Renata Adler wrote that the performance looked like a "football rally, then like a carnival and a hootenanny, and finally like something dangerously close to a hysterical mob."

On Thursday morning King, exhausted but triumphant, with Coretta and the Abernathys beside him and followed by many dignitaries and the marchers, led the way to the capitol. Memories were stirred when he passed the Dexter Avenue Baptist Church, where he had been the pastor at the time of the Montgomery bus boycott. The platform was on the steps of the capitol and a crowd estimated at 25,000 filled the plaza below. King delivered a powerful oration on this "shining moment in the conscience of man."

But the day was marred by tragedy. Viola Gregg Liuzzo, a white woman, was a housewife, the mother of five, and married to a business agent of Teamsters Local 247 in Detroit. In her early years she lived in Georgia and Tennessee. An activist and committed to civil rights, she had been deeply moved by the television coverage of the carnage at the Edmund Pettus Bridge. She took off in the family Oldsmobile and three days later was in Selma. She stayed with a black family in a public housing project and became a chauffeur, ferrying people between Selma and Montgomery. At St. Jude's at the end of the march she said to Father Tim Deasy, "I feel it. Somebody is going to get killed."

After the ceremonies at the capitol she drove several marchers to Selma. She and LeRoy Moton, a young black man, then set off on Highway 80 for Montgomery. In Lowndes County a car drew alongside and its occupants opened fire. A bullet to the head killed Viola Liuzzo instantly.

The next day President Johnson announced that four Klansmen suspected of the murder had been apprehended by the FBI. One of them, Gary Thomas Rowe, Jr., was an FBI undercover agent and had notified the Bureau. But the others went free because all-white juries refused to convict them. King, with the FBI still on his mind, sent Hoover a telegram congratulating him for the Bureau's good work.

After the march to Montgomery Selma became quiet. The focus of decision had now shifted to Washington.[5]

Lyndon Johnson took no chances. The massive Democratic majorities in both houses and equally great public support in the North seemed to assure Senate passage of the voting rights bill. There were even inroads into the South. On March 11 Senator Russell Long of Louisiana said privately that he was for the bill and that he planned to carry the votes of 11 of the 22 southern senators with him. Nevertheless, Johnson wanted to be sure that two-thirds of the senators would vote to shut off debate if the southerners filibustered. This required Republican support. Late Sunday afternoon on March 14 he met with the congressional leadership in the Cabinet Room. Senate minority leader Everett Dirksen, whip Thomas Kuchel, and House civil rights leader William McCulloch were the Republicans present. Vice President Humphrey, Speaker McCormack, and Senate majority leader Mansfield were the Democrats. Also present were several White House aides along with Attorney General Katzenbach and his assistants. Johnson reviewed the events in Selma and the provisions of the bill. The main issue was how these matters should be presented to the Congress and the country. The leaders of both parties decided to invite the President to address a joint session of Congress at 9 p.m. the next day.

This speech, called "The American Promise," was said to have been viewed by an audience of 70 million and, because he spoke from the heart, may have been the finest Lyndon Johnson ever delivered. Richard Goodwin drafted it and the President himself worked it over very carefully. On Monday afternoon, Lady Bird wrote, "the tension began to mount." By 6:00, Jack Valenti was feeding Johnson a page at a time. "He was going over it, scratching out lines. . . . I could very nearly hear [Jack] groan whenever Lyndon marked out a line and wrote in something else." That evening in the House chamber the President spoke:

> At times history and fate meet at a single time in a single place to shape a turning point in man's unending search for freedom. So it was at Lexington and Concord. So it was a century ago at Appomattox. So it was last week in Selma, Alabama.
>
> There, long-suffering men and women peacefully protested the denial of their rights as Americans. Many were brutally assaulted. One good man, a man of God, was killed. . . .

Our lives have been marked with debate about great issues. . . . But rarely in any time does an issue . . . challenge . . . the values and the purposes and the meaning of our beloved Nation. . . .

"All men are created equal"—"government by consent of the governed"—"give me liberty or give me death. . . ."

These words are a promise to every citizen that he shall share in the dignity of man. . . .

The most basic right of all . . . [is] to choose your own leaders. . . .

Yet the harsh fact is that in many places in this country men and women are kept from voting simply because they are Negroes. . . .

So I ask you to join me in working long hours . . . to pass this bill. . . . Outside this chamber is the outraged conscience of a nation, the grave concern of many nations, and the harsh judgment of history on our acts.

At this point the President paused and pronounced the title of the anthem of the civil rights movement: "WE SHALL OVERCOME!" There was a standing ovation. He continued,

As a man whose roots go deeply into Southern soil I know how difficult it is to reshape the attitudes and the structure of our society.

But a century has passed, more than a hundred years, since the Negro was freed. And he is not fully free tonight. . . .

These are the enemies: poverty, ignorance, disease. They are the enemies and not our fellow man, not our neighbor. . . .

In Selma as elsewhere we seek and pray for peace. We seek order. We seek unity. But we will not accept the peace of stifled rights, or the order imposed by fear, or the unity that stifles protest. For peace cannot be purchased at the cost of liberty.

Lady Bird, good wife that she was, was both proud and critical. "It was a magnificent speech." But it was "too long. It ran forty-two minutes and would have been better at twenty-five."

The country, however, did not quibble about length. The civil rights movement, of course, was ecstatic. The press was overwhelming in its support, even in the South.

The President sent up the voting rights bill on March 17, 1965, and it became S. 1564 and H.R. 6400. While, as already noted, it raised difficult questions, the bill itself was short and simple. Section 2 forbade the denial of the right to vote on account of race or color. Section 3 invalidated "any test or device" employed to deny the right to vote in any federal, state, or local election in effect on November 1, 1964, in which less than 50 percent of the persons of voting age were not registered and did not vote in the presidential election. Sections 4 and 5 constituted the "triggering" mechanism. Twenty or more residents of a jurisdiction could petition the Attorney General alleging that they had been denied the right to vote on the basis of race. If he certified the complaint, the Civil Service Commission would appoint examiners to consider the applicants' qualifications and, if qualified, would certify them to vote. No one could be denied the right to vote for failure to pay a poll tax. Under Section 9, violations of the law would be criminal acts.

The Senate Judiciary Committee presented a modest problem. Its chairman, James Eastland of Mississippi, had allowed only one of 121 civil rights bills out of his committee and the exception had been a fluke. But in 1965 there were at least nine firm votes for the bill among the 15 members of the committee. Taking no chances, Mansfield and Dirksen jointly got the Senate by a 63 to 13 vote to instruct the committee to report no later than April 9, 1965. An outraged Eastland howled that a deadline was "unheard of."

The Senate committee conducted hearings between March 23 and April 5, 1965. Attorney General Katzenbach carried the entire burden, testified for three days, and performed in masterly fashion. General opposition was almost nonexistent and some of it was ridiculous. Leander H. Perez of Plaquemines Parish, Louisiana, claimed that he spoke for Governor John J. McKeithen and denounced the bill as a Communist conspiracy to establish Negro rule in the South. Dirksen, who had himself participated in drafting the bill, said this was "stupid." McKeithin announced that he had authorized Perez only to say that he thought voter qualification should be left to the states.

Senator Sam Ervin of North Carolina, an authority on the Constitution, argued that the bill contravened the prohibition on ex post facto laws of Article I, Section 4. S. 1564 presumed "rascality" and punished states and localities for acts that took place before the law was enacted. Katzenbach replied that there was no "punishment." Rather, the bill sought to effectuate the Fifteenth Amendment by redressing a century of discriminatory administration.

Ervin also contended that Congress had no power to set aside the constitutional authority of the states to establish qualifications for voting. Katzenbach responded that the Fifteenth Amendment had superseded Article I, Section 2, and that this theory had won judicial approval.

Finally, Ervin attacked the 50 percent formulas because they picked up counties in which there was no discrimination against blacks, such as Aroostook County, Maine, several in Alaska, and, most important to him, allegedly 28 counties in eastern North Carolina. He stressed that four of those areas contained large military installations whose personnel either voted in their home states or did not bother to vote. The trouble with the argument was that only one, Onslow County with Camp Lejeune, had more than 50 percent of the voting age population registered in 1964. The chairman of the North Carolina Board of Elections stated that pending legislation in the state, if enacted, would remedy low figures in the 27 deficient counties.

Solicitor General Archibald Cox, like Senator Ervin, was much concerned about S. 1564's constitutionality, particularly the argument just made. He wrote Katzenbach on March 23 that the bill "goes far to demonstrate the lack of any but a coincidental relationship between racial discrimination and the facts. . . . One might equally well make the Act applicable to any State whose name begins with Vi or Mi or Lo or Al or Ge or So." He proposed language to remedy this problem. In fact, the administration and Senator Dirksen agreed on three amendments to take care of this and other problems.

Another issue was the demand by Puerto Ricans in New York City to be covered under the bill by an amendment establishing a "conclusive presumption of literacy" for anyone with a fourth-grade education without taking a test. Irma Vidal Santaella, chair of the Legion of Voters, wrote Lee White on March 9 to ask for the amendment. Puerto Ricans were "American citizens by birth" who attended federally subsidized bilingual schools. Yet they were ignored by both the New York legislature and the Congress. White submitted her letter to Clifford L. Alexander, Jr., who was close to the civil rights movement. He advised that "we ignore this letter . . . until our voter legislation is through the Congress." Anything else would "only serve to muddy the waters."

But Mayor Robert F. Wagner, Jr., of New York City and both New York senators, Javits and Robert Kennedy, took up the Puerto Rican cause. Katzenbach and White agreed. "The real problem," the former wrote, "is that Dirksen simply does not look kindly on adding 500,000 to 600,000 Democratic votes in New York City and, therefore, opposes this feature." The Puerto Ricans asked to see the President. Despite the urging of White, Johnson declined to do so. If cloture came up, he would need Dirksen's support.

The Leadership Conference on Civil Rights, Senator Edward Kennedy, and the House Judiciary Committee urged a permanent national prohibition of the poll tax. Katzenbach thought it a bad idea. King, Larry O'Brien informed the President, "may find it necessary to demonstrate," and James Farmer of CORE demanded a "complete ban" on the poll tax. In fact, the House added such an amendment.

On May 21 Katzenbach sent the President a formidable argument in support of his opposition. In *Breedlove v. Suttles* in 1937 the Supreme Court had unanimously sustained the Virginia poll tax. This and other cases had compelled Congress to abolish the poll tax in federal elections by constitutional amendment in 1962. A flat ban would cause trouble. Vermont, for example, which did not discriminate based on race, would be forced to abandon a poll tax that exempted the poor. Vermont, certainly, would challenge the constitutionality of such a law.

A prohibition would be an "invitation to persons not to pay these taxes." Thus, first-time voters in the Deep South who did not pay the tax might lose the suffrage in state elections if the law was later held unconstitutional. Further, this constitutionally vulnerable part of the law could put the remainder at risk.

Finally, Katzenbach pointed out, opposition to "the flat ban also appeared advisable as the best means of assuring the necessary votes for cloture." He noted that Senator Dirksen "has strongly opposed the ban, questioned its constitutionality and indicated to the press that its adoption would make cloture very difficult. If we had not opposed the flat ban, I believe Senator Dirksen, Senators Aiken and Prouty of Vermont, and other Republicans would probably be lost for cloture. With only 45 Democratic votes, we could not prevail without these Republicans."

In the light of these arguments, Mansfield and Dirksen jointly proposed a narrower substitute. The Attorney General would be obliged to file action against any poll tax which, as a condition of voting, had the purpose or effect of abridging the right to vote in violation of the Constitution. "The Mansfield-Dirksen approach," Katzenbach wrote the President, "is clearly constitutional." Nevertheless, the Judiciary Committee adopted the ban on the poll tax in state and local elections by a vote of 9 to 7. The majority consisted of 6 liberal Democrats and 3 moderate Republicans.

The Judiciary Committee reported the amended voting rights bill on April 9 by a vote of 12 to 4. The majority consisted of 7 northern Democrats and all 5 Republicans. Only the 4 conservative southern Democrats voted against S. 1564. This vote shredded the historic southern Democratic-Republican coalition. It also met the Mansfield-Dirksen requirement of a report by April 9.

Action on the Senate floor dragged on from April 22 to May 26 because of a sharp conflict over the ban on the poll tax. In 1965, 27 states imposed a poll tax, but only 4 used it as a qualification for voting in state and local elections—Alabama, Mississippi, Texas, and Virginia. The other southern states, led by North Carolina in the 1920s, had dropped their levies. Movements were under way in May 1965 to take similar action in Virginia and Texas.

Despite the narrowing of the problem and the constitutional questions Katzenbach had raised, the civil rights movement and its supporters in Congress pressed for a flat ban. On May 11 Mansfield and Dirksen substituted their court test amendment. Senator Edward Kennedy immediately moved to put the ban back and lost by the close margin of 49 to 45. On May 19 two poll tax amendments were adopted. One, offered by the leaders with the Attorney General's endorsement, declared this levy an unconstitutional infringement of the right to vote. It was adopted 69 to 20. The other, proposed by Hiram Fong, the Hawaii Republican, authorized poll watchers in counties in which federal registrars were named. It passed 56 to 20.

On May 20 the Senate by a vote of 48 to 19 accepted the "American Flag" amendment offered by Robert Kennedy and Javits. A person who was illiterate in English could not be denied the right to vote if he had an equiva-

lent sixth-grade education in a school located under the American flag conducted in another language. This would cover the New York City Puerto
Ricans.

On May 4, 12, and 19 Mansfield asked for unanimous consent to close
debate. The South had decided to force cloture, and each time Senator Allen
Ellender of Louisiana objected. There would be a reprise of the 1964 maneuver over the Civil Rights Act, but without the prolonged debate. On
May 25 the Senate voted for cloture 70 to 30, a winning margin of 3. The
majority consisted of 47 Democrats and 23 Republicans, the minority of 21
Democrats and 9 Republicans. The bill was passed the next day 77 to 19.
The winners consisted of 47 Democrats and 30 Republicans, including 5
southern and border state Democrats.

A House Judiciary Subcommittee had held hearings between March 18
and April 1, 1965, and reported an amended H.R. 6400 by a vote of 10 to
1 (the latter not identified) on April 9. Several amendments were important:
a flat ban on the poll tax in state and local elections; a new Title I of the
Civil Rights Act of 1964 to cover state and local elections; a sixth-grade
education in English as a "rebuttable presumption" of literacy; and a congressional finding that payment of a poll tax violated the Fourteenth and
Fifteenth amendments.

The Judiciary Committee split three ways on June 1, 1965. The majority, consisting of the northern Democrats and three liberal Republicans, approved the bill with the amendments just noted. The other eight Republicans called the bill "hastily contrived, [a] patchwork response to the
nation's demand for social justice." They offered a substitute bill. The three
southern Democrats denounced the bill and the substitute as unconstitutional.

Emanuel Celler, the chairman, was in command. The committee bill
sailed through the House on July 9 by a vote of 333 to 85. The majority
consisted of 221 Democrats and 112 Republicans, among them 33 Democrats and 3 Republicans from the South. The opposition was made up of
61 Democrats and 24 Republicans, all but 9 from the South.

The conference faced two central issues—the ban on the poll tax and
the Puerto Ricans. The civil rights organizations, concerned about the long
delay, reversed themselves and urged the House conferees to give up on the
poll tax. Katzenbach suggested compromise language resembling the Senate
version. The key negotiators, Dirksen and Celler, both professionals,
quickly reached agreement on new language for the ban and on inclusion
of the Kennedy-Javits American flag provision.

The House adopted the conference report on August 3 by a vote of 328
to 74, and the Senate followed the next day 79 to 18. In the House the
favorable vote included all 180 northern Democrats, 37 southern Democrats, and 111 Republicans; the opponents consisted of 54 southern Democrats and 20 Republicans. Those in favor in the Senate were 43 Democrats

from the North, 6 from the South, and 30 Republicans. The opponents were 1 northern Democrat, 16 southerners, and 1 Republican.

President Johnson on August 6 held a televised ceremony for the signing of the Voting Rights Act of 1965 in the Capitol rotunda. He then moved to the President's Room off the Senate chamber for the actual signing, the room President Lincoln had used on August 6, 1861, to sign a bill freeing slaves who had been pressed into service by the Confederacy. "Today," Johnson said, "what is perhaps the last of the legal barriers is tumbling."[6]

The implementation of the Voting Rights Act required the cooperation of the Department of Justice, the Civil Service Commission, and the Bureau of the Census. Planning began in June 1965, two months before the act was passed, and everything was in place when it was signed.

The role of Census was rudimentary. The Attorney General would suspend literacy tests in counties in which less than 50 percent of persons of voting age were registered on November 1, 1964, and less than 50 percent voted in the presidential election in November. Since the Bureau already had these data in its files, it could supply them quickly and at no cost. Prior to August 6, the Attorney General formally asked the Director of the Census to specify the states with literacy tests used to prevent the registration of blacks, and the director provided the voting age and election statistics by county. This allowed the machinery to move immediately on August 6.

In fact, by July 14 the agencies had identified the tough counties—eight each in Alabama, Mississippi, and Louisiana, along with four in Georgia, plus two urban counties in each of these states. These counties were listed in the *Federal Register* when the law was signed.

The problems with Civil Service were complex and required extended meetings. The Commission insisted that its examiners should make no policy decisions; they would "exercise a ministerial function only." Civil Service needed to know where examiners would be located, how many were needed, the grounds for challenging the examiner's decision, and whether to employ blacks as examiners. They also needed forms and insurance of safety in rural counties with a reputation for violence. All these questions were answered.

At the outset Civil Service supplied and trained 68 of its own employees drawn from the affected areas wherever possible to serve as examiners. While a number of blacks were invited to participate, only two agreed to become examiners. Supervision operated out of regional Civil Service offices in Atlanta and Dallas. The local offices opened on August 10 and were available six days a week from 9 a.m. to 5:30 p.m. A citizen interested in registering would go to an office, obtain a form, and fill it out. The examiner would assist him when needed. If the applicant was unable to read or write, the examiner would record the information on the form. If the applicant met the requirements, the examiner would give him a certificate of eligibility to vote and put his name on lists submitted to state and local election officials. In states that still imposed a poll tax, the examiner would receive the payment and provide a receipt.

Aside from placing notices on post office billboards, the government could assume no responsibility for bringing people to the examiners. That burden rested on the civil rights organizations and they were not enthusiastic about carrying it. It was a thankless task and they complained of lack of money and the difficulty of recruiting volunteers, particularly in bad weather. This created an undercurrent of criticism. After viewing an NBC broadcast, Harry McPherson wrote the President that "there still seems to be among Negro leaders more interest in discovering fresh fields for conquest than in making use of the franchise."

Nevertheless, the impact of the program was dramatic. It went into operation quickly, smoothly, and with almost no controversy. In Alabama, Mississippi, and Louisiana 17 offices had opened by early November, and the program had been extended to two counties in South Carolina.

John Macy, the chairman of the commission, made an inspection of his operation in late October and passed on his observations to the President. The examiners were performing with "skill and efficiency" and had won the respect and cooperation of community leaders, black and white. Excepting Montgomery, the number of applicants had dropped to a "very low level." The reasons seemed to be the cotton picking season, the loss of students who had returned to college, apathy, and fear. Legal uncertainty was a problem—challenges to the constitutionality of the statute and, in Montgomery, to the legality under Alabama law of registering illiterates. A significant portion of those registered were illiterate; in Greenwood and Belzoni, Mississippi, for example, between a fifth and a third. In rural areas those who registered were relatively old because young people had migrated. While there was fear in tough rural counties and charges of intimidation, none had been substantiated.

By the end of January 1966 the program had listed 93,778 new voters, 91,212 Negro and 2,566 white, in the four states. Of the 310,641 potential black voters, 30 percent had been registered. The numbers grew slowly thereafter. By March 31, 1968, the total registered in these states plus a few counties in Georgia reached 159,378, of whom 152,046 were nonwhite. In Dallas County, Alabama, where the crisis had arisen in Selma, only 320 blacks had been registered in 1964. By 1969 federal examiners had added 8,992, more than half of the total number of voting age. In neighboring Lowndes County no blacks were registered in 1964; in 1968 there were 2,792.

The gains under the statute were accompanied by a sharp increase in voluntary compliance by local officials. The Department of Justice reported that more than a quarter of a million Negroes were registered this way by June 1966.

The progress under the Voting Rights Act was due in substantial part to what Katzenbach called "the magnificent cooperation between the Department of Justice and the Civil Service Commission. I think this joint program was . . . an excellent example of how the total . . . can be greater than the sum of the parts." But Justice also had to confront the constitutionality of the statute and of the poll tax. On August 6, 1965, the day the President signed the law, Katzenbach determined that South Carolina had maintained a literacy test on November 1, 1964, and the Director of Census held that fewer than 50 percent of the persons in the state had registered and had voted in the 1964 presidential election. The law was invoked against South Carolina. On September 29 the state asked the U.S. Supreme Court for leave to file an original action against the Attorney General challenging the constitutionality of the Voting Rights Act. The court accepted the case. The other states affected filed briefs *amici curiae*.

On March 7, 1966, Chief Justice Warren for a unanimous court, excepting a partial dissent by Justice Black, held the central provisions of the Voting Rights Act constitutional. The Congress enjoyed a broad power under the Fifteenth Amendment to enact laws to prevent denial of the right to vote based on race. It might prohibit a literacy test, otherwise constitutional, when it was used to discriminate on account of race. While the 50 percent rule was subject to abuse, none had yet occurred and the administration of the law thus far had been fair and reasonable. "We here hold," Warren wrote, "that the portions of the Voting Rights Act properly before us are a valid means for carrying out the commands of the Fifteenth Amendment. Hopefully, millions of non-white Americans will now be able to participate for the first time on an equal basis in the government under which they live."

The American Flag provision of the law, unrelated to the Fifteenth Amendment, was not reached by the *South Carolina* decision. The Morgans, a husband and wife who were registered voters in Kings County (New York City), brought suit to enjoin enforcement. Puerto Ricans who were literate in Spanish but not in English, they argued, could not vote meaningfully because most political information was published in English. If they were given the franchise, the votes of the Morgans and others like them would be diluted. A three-judge district court held the provision unconstitutional on the ground that the qualifications for voting were reserved to the states and Congress had no power to act for New York. The Supreme Court reversed in 1966 in an opinion for the court by Justice Brennan with Justice Harlan dissenting. It was decided entirely under the equal protection clause of the Fourteenth Amendment. The American Flag provision, Brennan wrote, is "appropriate legislation to enforce the Equal Protection Clause."

The Department of Justice filed suits against Texas and Alabama and a brief *amicus curiae* against Virginia to invalidate their poll taxes. Three-judge district courts set aside the Texas and Alabama levies and the Supreme Court joined them in the Virginia case.[7]

The Voting Rights Act of 1965 closed the gap that the Civil Rights Act of 1964 had left open. The voting law, Lee White said, "may well prove to be one of the most significant pieces of civil rights legislation ever put on the books." Now under both laws the rights of blacks, along with those of others discriminated against because of their race, creed, color, or national origin, were legally protected by federal law over a wide range of day-to-day activities, including political participation. This was an extremely important advance. But it did not mean that blacks had won full integration into American society.

Several years later Burke Marshall was asked whether he still believed that laws *can* change men's minds. He replied,

> I said that, and it was correct. . . . That remark . . . [was] directed at eliminating the official legal caste system in the South. Now the official legal caste system, segregation in schools and all of that business, has basically been eliminated. I don't mean it doesn't still exist, but it doesn't exist officially, and . . . it's no longer . . . a viable constitutionally-protected system of state government. . . . We changed that and I think that change has basically been accepted. And that just doesn't happen to be very much of the problem any more.

In identifying those primarily responsible for the passage of the Voting Rights Act one must start with the civil rights movement, particularly the Southern Christian Leadership Conference and its formidable leader, Martin Luther King, Jr. They launched the voting rights drive in Selma and carried it through with determination and courage in the face of ruthless opposition. And there were the martyrs—Jimmie Lee Jackson, James J. Reeb, and Viola Liuzzo—who gave their lives for this cause.

Lyndon Johnson made the decisive political commitment to pass a voting rights law in 1965 and he pushed it through Congress. This sprang from moral conviction. Like President Kennedy in 1963, he knew that civil rights legislation would exact a heavy price from the Democratic party. The Solid South would be smashed. Henceforth a white backlash, already evident in 1964, would provide a base for Republican control of the South, primarily in presidential elections. Nevertheless, Johnson believed that giving blacks the vote was his most important achievement.

Nicholas Katzenbach and his colleagues in the Department of Justice performed in masterful fashion. They drafted the bill, they guided it through the Congress, they established an efficient administrative system, and they brought and argued the cases that confirmed the law's constitutionality.[8]

Flanked by his wife and Jacqueline Kennedy, Lyndon Johnson being sworn in as President by Judge Sarah T. Hughes on Air Force One, November 22, 1963, the day of the Kennedy assassination. Cecil Stoughton, LBJ Library Collection.

LBJ proclaiming the Great Society at the University of Michigan, May 22, 1964. Cecil Stoughton, LBJ Library Collection.

Delivering the Warren Commission report on the Kennedy assassination to the President, September 24, 1964. From left: John McCloy, Lee Rankin (counsel), Richard Russell, Gerald Ford, Earl Warren, LBJ, Allen Dulles, John Sherman Cooper. The other member of the commission, Hale Boggs, seems not to have been present. UPI/Bettmann.

LBJ campaigning for President in 1964. Cecil Stoughton, LBJ Library Collection.

LBJ inauguration, January 20, 1965. Cecil Stoughton, LBJ Library Collection.

Senate Majority Leader Mike Mansfield, who steered the Great Society bills through the Senate and strongly opposed the Vietnam War. August 23, 1968. Yoichi R. Okamoto, LBJ Library Collection.

Two old pros and close friends—Senate Minority Leader Everett Dirksen and LBJ. January 20, 1965. Yoichi R. Okamoto, LBJ Library Collection.

Clark Clifford, LBJ's trusted adviser and Secretary of Defense. Yoichi R. Okamoto, LBJ Library Collection.

Maverick Senator Wayne Morse, who supported LBJ on education and labor and opposed him on Vietnam. Yoichi R. Okamoto, LBJ Library Collection.

LBJ's mentor and dear friend, the leader of the southern bloc, Senator Richard Russell. Yoichi R. Okamoto, LBJ Library Collection.

LBJ with John Gardner, Secretary of Health, Education, and Welfare, who was deeply concerned about educational reform. Yoichi R. Okamoto, LBJ Library Collection.

Larry O'Brien, the political expert who handled congressional relations for the White House. Yoichi R. Okamoto, LBJ Library Collection.

Wilbur Cohen of HEW nursed Medicare through Congress. Yoichi R. Okamoto, LBJ Library Collection.

Labor Secretary Willard Wirtz and Interior Secretary Stewart Udall. Yoichi R. Okamoto, LBJ Library Collection.

LBJ *with the chairmen of his Council of Economic Advisers. Above:* Walter Heller. Below: *Gardner Ackley, with Joe Califano listening. Both Yoichi R. Okamoto, LBJ Library Collection.*

Treasury Secretary Henry Fowler. Yoichi R. Okamoto, LBJ Library Collection.

Sargent Shriver, director of the poverty program. Yoichi R. Okamoto, LBJ Library Collection.

Secretary of State Dean Rusk, LBJ, and Secretary of Defense Robert McNamara.
Rusk accepted and McNamara urged Johnson's decision to go to war in Vietnam.
Yoichi R. Okamoto, LBJ Library Collection.

National Security Adviser McGeorge Bundy also strongly recommended that Johnson go into Vietnam. Yoichi R. Okamoto, LBJ Library Collection.

Undersecretary of State George Ball strongly opposed the Vietnam War. Yoichi R. Okamoto, LBJ Library Collection.

Wilbur Mills, chairman of the House Ways and Means Committee, was the key to passage of Medicare but later became an enemy of the Great Society. Frank Wolfe, LBJ Library Collection.

Martin Luther King, Jr., with LBJ, a troubled relationship. Yoichi R. Okamoto, LBJ Library Collection.

King leads the civil rights march across the Pettus Bridge over the Alabama River in Selma on the way to Montgomery. March 21, 1965. UPI/ UPIBettmann.

Three-year-old Thomas Allen stands in the ruins of his home that burned down in the great Detroit riot in July 1967. UPI/Bettmann.

The National Guard restores order on "Charcoal Alley," 103d Street in Watts, during the great riot of August 1965. John Malmin, Los Angeles Times.

9

Immigration: Righting the National Origins Wrong

IMMIGRANTS, like blacks, were the victims of ethnic prejudice. At the end of the nineteenth century the great majority of Americans was descended from people from the British Isles, including Ireland, or from Germany, Holland, or Scandinavia. The large wave of "new" immigrants who arrived between 1890 and 1914 was primarily from southern and eastern Europe. Many of northwestern European stock did not know Italians, Greeks, Slavs, or Jews, to say nothing of the Chinese and Japanese, and found their languages, religions, customs, and cuisines alien and, sometimes, offensive.

More serious, in the early twentieth century racism acquired a façade of scientific validation from the eugenics movement. Francis Galton, the cousin of Charles Darwin and a noted scientist himself, coined the word "eugenics" in 1883 from Greek, meaning "noble in heredity." He sought to establish a science that would improve the human stock by giving "the more suitable races or strains of blood a better chance of prevailing speedily over the less suitable." He would better the "race" by having gifted mates produce children who would inherit their intelligence. A eugenics movement (some called it a cult) blossomed in England and soon emigrated to the United States. Charles B. Davenport, a distinguished biologist at the University of Chicago, was a notable convert. He persuaded the new Carnegie Institution to fund an experiment station at Cold Spring Harbor on Long Island. Davenport believed that "race," which he equated with nationality, determined behavior. Thus, Poles, Italians, the Irish, and Jews were biologically different from the English and the Scots, as well as from each other. None was "superior" or "inferior." In 1910 Davenport induced the widow of E. H. Harriman, the railroad magnate, to support a Eugenics Record

Office on her land near the experiment station. It would collect data on those imprisoned and disabled. Dr. Harry H. Laughlin became the superintendent of the Eugenics Record Office.

Laughlin was convinced that the science of eugenics dictated racism. In other words, he took the step that Davenport had refused to take, that some races were superior and others were inferior. This led him inexorably to immigration policy. He became a consultant to New York's Chamber of Commerce, which was a staunch advocate of the national origins quota system, and to the House Committee on Immigration and Naturalization, which drafted the legislation of the twenties. One may note that, while Laughlin's ideas were finding policy expression in the U.S., an obscure German political figure named Adolf Hitler was writing a book, *Mein Kampf,* which voiced the same racist views. The most committed spokesman against the racist legislation in the U.S. was a young liberal Democratic congressman from Brooklyn, Emanuel Celler. Franz Boas, the great anthropologist at Columbia, considered these race and blood ideas pernicious nonsense and fed Celler arguments against them.

Laughlin was obsessed by immigration and wrote extensively about it. A nation, he argued, could be conquered either by military force or by the immigration of inferior races. The latter was the great threat to the U.S. He found a lesson in the house rat, which had spread all over the world via commercial shipping vessels.

The American race, he wrote, had been shaped by more than 300 years of history. It consisted of "white people who have fused into a national mosaic composed originally of European stocks." In origin it was British, Irish, German, Scandinavian, French, and Dutch. This American race, Laughlin asserted, "must protect its own interests by filtering the incoming stream of immigrants as thoroughly and as many times as may be necessary, in order to admit only the number and quality of immigrants whom it desires." Above all, the nation must protect itself biologically.

This race, Laughlin contended, had been reasonably pure until about 1890 because the "American people are derived basically from the people of Great Britain." But the new immigrants had introduced debased blood lines which were undermining its quality. Laughlin believed immigration should be abolished or, at the very least, that strict standards should be imposed on any immigrants.[1]

During the colonial period and most of the first century of the Republic the door for immigrants was wide open. Land was plentiful and cheap and the great majority became farmers. In the mid-nineteenth century unskilled immigrants, Vernon Briggs pointed out, were in demand to "staff the emerging factories, to work the mines, and to build the railroads and the public works infrastructures associated with a nation on the verge of entering the industrial revolution."

The importation of Chinese coolie labor to work in the California gold mines and to build the western railroads created a powerful backlash, particularly by organized labor in California. Thus, the Burlingame Treaty of 1868 between China and the U.S. prohibited the forced migration of these workers. But this did not still the clamor on the Pacific Coast. In 1882 Congress passed the Chinese Exclusion Act, the first immigration law to discriminate on the basis of race or nationality. In effect, it forbade the Chinese to enter the country and denied persons of Chinese extraction citizenship.

A similar problem arose with the far more sensitive Japanese after the turn of the century. President Theodore Roosevelt negotiated the face-saving Gentlemen's Agreement with Japan in 1907. The U.S. would not exclude Japanese immigrants, but the Japanese government would forbid its citizens to emigrate to America.

In the years before World War I the flow of immigrants from southern and eastern Europe was enormous, with over a million persons entering the country annually. The peak was reached in 1907—1,285,349. The historic ethnic composition of the American population was changing. There was an outcry from xenophobes and more reasonable people, including scholars, who felt that some restriction on numbers was needed. In 1907, therefore, Congress created the Joint Commission on Immigration to study the problem and to recommend a policy. Senator William P. Dillingham of Vermont was chairman and his investigation yielded 42 fat volumes published in 1911.

Although the commission was, unlike Laughlin, circumspect in its use of nouns, it swallowed the eugenics analysis. The U.S., it held, was a nation of northwestern Europeans. The new immigrants from southern and eastern Europe posed formidable, if not insurmountable, problems of assimilation. To drive this point home, the commission issued a *Dictionary of Races or Peoples*. Thus, the Dillingham Commission recommended immigration restriction based on a discriminatory national origins quota system.

The Immigration Act of 1917, passed over President Wilson's veto, was the first statute to express this theory against Europeans. At that moment it was not necessary because World War I prevented southern and eastern Europeans from emigrating. The authors of the law assumed that northwestern Europeans were literate and southern and eastern Europeans were illiterate. Thus, they imposed a literacy test. A new Asiatic Barred Zone, skirting the Japanese Gentlemen's Agreement, banned immigration from Asia. Because American farmers and ranchers were beginning to suffer a wartime shortage of labor, an exception was made for the temporary importation of Mexican workers if the Secretary of Labor certified their need.

But the literacy test did not work because many southern and eastern Europeans could read and write. The Italians established special schools to teach peasants how to pass. In 1921 the number of immigrants mounted to

805,228 and it seemed that the prewar flood had resumed. Thus, Congress passed and President Harding signed the temporary Immigration Act of 1921. It limited entry by national origins quotas based on the distribution of the U.S. population by nationality shown in the census of 1910. It was in effect for three years. The Western Hemisphere, which produced few U.S. immigrants, was excluded from the system.

The National Origins Act of 1924 was signed by President Coolidge and established a very restrictive system. It took effect incrementally and became permanent in 1929. At the outset the entire Eastern Hemisphere received an annual ceiling of 164,000. But the distribution by nationality would be based on the percentages shown in the census of 1890, thereby substantially eliminating the new immigration. The results were dramatic: the Italian quota fell from 42,000 to 4000, the Polish from 31,000 to 6000, the Greek from 3000 to 100. In 1929 the Eastern Hemisphere total dropped to 154,277. The British quota alone was 65,000. Every nation received at least a token quota of 100. The law was also known as the Japanese Exclusion Act. Many Japanese-American residents of Hawaii were emigrating to the mainland and there was a renewed demand from the West Coast to keep Asiatics out. The Supreme Court had held that persons of Japanese ancestry were ineligible for naturalization as American citizens. The Gentlemen's Agreement, of course, was repudiated and the Japanese were humiliated. The day the law took effect became a day of national mourning in Japan.

This quota system remained on the books until 1965. But its extreme restrictiveness proved unworkable and required many exceptions. A preference for family reunification, at first of wives and children and later of husbands, was adopted. Nazi Germany, Fascist Italy, and Stalin's Soviet Union created an enormous number of refugees in the late thirties and forties. The U.S. insisted that they must be admitted under quota restrictions. The issue arose dramatically in 1939 when Congress refused the entry of 20,000 German refugee children with U.S. families as sponsors because the quota was full. World War II created an immense European population of refugees. The Displaced Persons Act of 1948 allowed 205,000 to enter the U.S. But this was done under the quota system by allowing each nation to mortgage up to 50 percent of its future quotas. Estonia, Latvia, and Lithuania, for example, took the maxima for 67, 76, and 65 years respectively.

The Refugee Relief Act of 1953 widened the holes in the system. Now Communist China had also created many displaced persons and they were added to the Europeans. A total of 215,000 would be admitted outside the quotas on condition that each person was sponsored by an American citizen who became responsible for finding the refugee a job and a home and guaranteed that the refugee would not become a public charge. The Soviet invasion of Hungary in 1956 caused the flight of 200,000. President Eisenhower admitted 6,150 under unused quotas and others under the parole authority given the Attorney General by the McCarran-Walter Act of 1952. Similarly, after Castro came to power in 1959, many Cubans fled to Miami and President Kennedy used the parole power to exempt them.

At the end of World War II opponents of the national origins system and those concerned about refugees urged Congress to overhaul the immigration system. But the Cold War bred a powerful opposition to Communism, expressed as McCarthyism. It made the abolition of national origins politically impossible. The McCarran-Walter Act in 1952 reaffirmed the old quota system, converted the Asiatic Barred Zone into the Asia Pacific Triangle (excluding Australia and New Zealand), and made the control of Communism an immigration issue, barring Communists, along with Fascists, from entry and requiring their deportation. President Truman vetoed the bill on the grounds that national origins was racist and insulted many American citizens. He was overridden.

Wholly aside from its discriminatory character, the national origins system was grossly inefficient. Between 1955 and 1964 Great Britain used only 25,000 of its annual quota of over 65,000, Ireland but 7000 of almost 18,000. On the other hand, China, with an annual quota of 105, contributed 4,209; Greece, with 308, supplied 5000; Hungary, whose quota was 865, sent 5,721; Italy, with 5,666, contributed close to 22,000; Japan, with 185, produced 4,973; and so on.[2]

Legislatively considered, immigration reform suffered from an almost fatal defect of narrow public focus. It had a great appeal to such organizations as the American Jewish Committee, the Lithuanian Immigration Service, Catholic Relief Services, the Church World Service, the Sons of Italy, United Ukrainian Relief, the Greek Archdiocese, the Japanese-American Organization, the Chinese Welfare Council, and several industrial unions with memberships drawn heavily from the more recent immigrants. But in the aggregate they represented only a small minority of the American people. *Congressional Quarterly* pointed out, "Many of the immigration bill's most ardent supporters . . . believed the public at large was not greatly interested in immigration reform or especially concerned about the national origins quota system." This was most evident in the South, which had the fewest new immigrants. Southerners were overwhelmingly descended from old immigrants and members of Congress from the region voted for McCarran-Walter and liked the quotas. Even Secretary of State Dean Rusk, a moderately liberal Georgian who supported civil rights for blacks, told Abba Schwartz, "After all, we are an Anglo-Saxon country."

The Irish immigrants of the mid-nineteenth century, while technically old immigrants, were, as John Fitzgerald Kennedy, himself a descendant, wrote, "the first to endure the scorn and discrimination later to be inflicted, to some degree at least, on each successive wave of immigrants by already settled 'Americans.' " The Fitzgerald and Kennedy offspring in Boston received this message with their mothers' milk. This, doubtless, contributed to John Kennedy's sense that the world was unfair and the pleasure he took in making it a little more fair. In the fifties when he was a senator from Massachusetts, that state had a higher percentage of recent immigrants than any other.

Thus, Kennedy became a leading spokesman for immigration reform. He voted against McCarran-Walter and to sustain President Truman's veto. He sponsored the Displaced Persons Act, the Refugee Relief Act, and the 1957 bill to unite families. In 1958 he published a little book, *A Nation of Immigrants,* in which he argued that the population of the U.S. consisted almost entirely of peoples from overseas, each of whom had made an important contribution to American life. During the 1960 presidential campaign Kennedy spoke out for immigration reform, though it was hardly an important issue.

But when he became President in 1961, he was unable to move immigration reform. It was near the bottom of his agenda and Congress showed little interest. Francis E. Walter, the aged Pennsylvania Democrat who had authored the 1952 law, was still chairman of the House Judiciary Subcommittee on Immigration and Nationality and had blocked every previous attempt at reform. James O. Eastland of Mississippi was chairman of the Senate Judiciary Committee and strongly opposed change. As if this were not enough, the President bumped into an obstruction in the State Department's Bureau of Security and Consular Affairs.

This monstrosity, a monument of the McCarthy era, had been created by the McCarran-Walter Act. Abba Schwartz described the bureau as it took shape in the fifties under Secretary of State John Foster Dulles as follows:

> The Bureau was given the responsibility for investigating the loyalty, the manhood and the morality of the twenty-five thousand employees of State in Washington, and its embassies and consulates throughout the world. It was also charged by Dulles with the physical security of the Department's property at home and abroad and with the protection of visiting foreign dignitaries.
>
> At the same time, it had the statutory responsibility for administering the immigration and nationality laws which had themselves become part of the McCarthy problem in the 1950's. In those years, there was great concern over both the admission of subversives and other undesirables to the United States and of communists who were not entitled to passports under the Internal Security Act of 1950.
>
> To a considerable extent, in other words, the Bureau assumed in those years the negative functions of a police agency.

The first administrator, Scott McLeod, was, in fact, a policeman. He had been an FBI agent and an investigator and had a close relationship with Joe

McCarthy. When he left, one of his main assistants, Frances Knight, stayed on as head of the passport office. She saw her function as that of preventing communists, very broadly defined, from entering the country and of compelling them to leave. She was especially close to the Senate Internal Security Subcommittee and two of its key members, Eastland and Thomas Dodd, the Connecticut Democrat, who gave her political clout.

Schwartz was an authority on refugees and the related questions of visas, passports, and immigration. His interest started at the Harvard Law School, where he joined other students in a committee to assist German student refugees from Hitler. While practicing law in Washington after the war, he worked with several international organizations on refugee matters. He also counseled Senator Kennedy on immigration.

In January 1961 the new President asked Schwartz if he would be interested in taking over the Bureau of Security and Consular Affairs. He said he would if changes could be made in its operations. The next month Kennedy told him he had run into a problem of "ethnic politics." The Italian-American members of Congress had complained to Larry O'Brien that Italians had not been adequately recognized in appointments. Peter Rodino, the New Jersey Democrat, who represented Italian-Americans in Newark, lobbied for Salvatore Bontempo for the job at State. In July 1961 Secretary of State Rusk named this New Jersey politician head of the bureau.

But Bontempo hardly got his feet under the desk. He resigned in December. Kennedy went back to Schwartz. He said he would accept if he became a presidential appointee and if security matters were removed from the bureau, which required a change in the law. Walter said he wanted to help that "fine young man," as he referred to the President, and he and Senator J. William Fulbright proposed legislation which was enacted in June 1962.

Kennedy told Schwartz that he wanted America to become an "open society," a term they had often discussed and which both understood to embrace the end of the national origins quota system, freedom of aliens to visit the U.S. even if they held hostile views, the right of Americans to travel anywhere in the world except in wartime, and a revival of the full traditional policy of welcoming refugees from oppression. The President submitted the Schwartz appointment to the Senate, which approved with only one vote in dissent, and he became Assistant Secretary of State on October 5, 1962.

In effect, more than two years had been lost in Kennedy's plan to reform the immigration law. His Immigration Message to the Congress did not go up until July 23, 1963.

The quota system, he declared, is "without basis in either logic or reason" and should be abolished. It was heavily weighted in favor of northern Europe. On the other hand, "an American citizen with a Greek father or mother must wait at least 18 months to bring his parents here to join him."

The use of the 1890 census to determine quotas was "arbitrary" and intended to discriminate.

He proposed that the shift to the new system take place over a five-year period. Each year 20 percent of the quota would be placed in a reserve pool to be allocated by the new formula. During the transition no country would have a quota in excess of 10 percent of the total. The President also asked for a new immigration board to advise him and to set standards for the admission of those with skills.

Since 1952 Jamaica and Trinidad and Tobago had won their independence from Great Britain; their citizens should enjoy free entry like other nations of the Western Hemisphere. Under McCarran-Walter no person with a mental problem was admissible except by enactment of a private bill. Kennedy recommended that such individuals should be allowed to enter if they were close relatives of U.S. citizens or resident aliens.

The President hoped for early hearings on the bill. But Eastland remained adamantly opposed. Michael A. Feighan of Ohio had replaced Walter as chairman of the House subcommittee. While the administration hoped that he would be open-minded, he refused to hold hearings in 1963. On November 22 Kennedy was assassinated.

Since Schwartz had a close personal relationship with Kennedy, he was deeply concerned. He had barely met Lyndon Johnson, merely shaking hands in a White House receiving line. The little he knew about him was discouraging. In 1952 then Senator Johnson, like other southerners, had voted for McCarran-Walter and to override Truman's veto. But there was much about Johnson that Schwartz did not know. He was very sensitive to ethnic discrimination and in 1938 and 1939, when he was in the House, had helped Jews to escape from Hitler. The most notable case involved the Austrian conductor Erich Leinsdorf, for whom he got a temporary visa; when it expired, he sent him to Cuba from which he could return to the U.S. under the Austrian quota. He had also arranged for 42 German and Polish Jews to enter the country, many of whom settled in Austin.

When he became President, Johnson was uninformed about immigration reform. Myer Feldman, who had worked on the issue for Kennedy since his Senate days, said, "I had to educate both President Johnson and [his assistant] Jack Valenti." Once briefed, Johnson became an unwavering supporter. In early 1964, for example, he phoned Celler to congratulate him on passage of the Civil Rights Act and, characteristically, told him to get busy on the immigration bill.

Schwartz felt that he had everything riding on the immigration measure. "If strong backing were not to be forthcoming, I . . . decided there was no use in my remaining in the administration." He talked to Bill Moyers in the White House, who assured him that the President was fully committed.

In the State of the Union message on January 8, Johnson declared,

We must . . . lift by legislation the bars of discrimination against those who seek entry into our country, particularly those who have much needed skills and those joining their families.

In establishing preferences, a nation that was built by immigrants of all lands can ask those who now seek admission: "What can you do for our country?" But we should not be asking: "In what country were you born?"

On January 13 the President met in the Cabinet Room with 60 representatives of church, nationality, and labor groups that supported the Kennedy bill, along with involved members of Congress. Johnson told them that he was for immigration reform and would work hard for the bill. He asked Eastland if he would hold hearings and the senator said he was always ready to do so. Johnson then asked Feighan the same question. He said that the McCarran-Walter Act provided for a joint committee and that hearings should be held under that provision, an observation that almost no one present understood. Walter had thought the device useless and had never invoked it.

This was the start of the administration's education into the ways of Michael Feighan. He was a slippery character capable of making endless trouble. The son of a banker, he had attended Princeton and then Harvard Law School. He then joined a Cleveland law firm with his four brothers, all lawyers, which was called Feighan, Feighan, Feighan, Feighan and Feighan. In the House he represented part of that city and its suburbs. While his district contained many voters descended from southern and eastern Europeans, he was a strong supporter of McCarran-Walter. According to Assistant Attorney General Norbert Schlei, who dealt with him extensively, Feighan viewed his constituency as "the traditional supporters of the national origins system (veterans groups, patriotic societies, conservative nationality groups, etc.)."

Feighan's superior, Celler, thoroughly distrusted him, including his plan to invoke the McCarran-Walter committee. Celler was convinced that this would be "the end of any immigration legislation" and, with Larry O'Brien's help, got the appropriations subcommittee to deny Feighan the funds he had asked for.

Celler introduced the administration bill, H.R. 7700. It had been written by a team in the Department of Justice headed by Schlei, by another from the State Department led by Schwartz, and by Feldman of the White House staff. It was proposed in the form of amendments to the Immigration and Nationality (McCarran-Walter) Act. The main provisions were the following: All quotas would fall 20 percent a year for five years. These reduced numbers would be placed in a quota reserve from which qualified applicants would be allowed to enter the U.S. The minimum quota for each nation would become 200. Persons from independent nations in the Western Hemisphere, including adjacent islands, would be admitted with their spouses and children outside the quota system. Individuals with special skills not available in the U.S. would receive preference. So would persons part of whose families were already legally within the country.

Thus, these amendments would eliminate the historic national origins quota system. But the bill proposed no annual total number of immigrants. The assumption was that the number allowed in each year would differ little from those in recent years under McCarran-Walter. Schlei estimated an increase from 157,000 to 165,000 because of the rise in the minimum from 100 to 200, not counting special cases. But they would now come from all over the world without being weighted in favor of northwestern Europe. The anti-Communist provisions of the 1952 law would be unchanged.

Feighan's subcommittee held hearings on H.R. 7700 between June and September 1964. He worked over Schwartz. Feighan compelled him to admit that there was "nothing in the administration proposal which in any way alters or changes security safeguards spelled out in the present law." He attacked Schwartz for helping to arrange for the entry into the U.S. from Turkey of 200 Russians of the Old Believer sect who had fled religious persecution in the Soviet Union. While the hearings were quite thorough, it was obvious that no legislation would be enacted in 1964. Great Society bills congested both congressional calendars and everyone in Washington had his eye on the election.

Further, the outlook in both the subcommittee and the parent Judiciary Committee was dismal. Henry Hall Wilson, who covered the House, wrote O'Brien on July 11, 1964: "As a practical matter I think we have to call it about an impossibility to get this out of subcommittee." Three of the five members were "clearly and decisively wrong," and one was "absolutely frantic." Of Feighan, "we must suspect both his good faith and his capacity." If a "miracle" occurred in the subcommittee, the committee would also be "tough." The Senate was little better since Eastland's committee was hopeless.

Feighan promised the administration that his subcommittee would report out "a good immigration bill." But he did not mean H.R. 7700. The measure he introduced was entirely different. It would admit 10,000 people presently on the waiting list and would establish a board to examine the distribution of 100,000 unused quota numbers over the next two and a half years. His bill did not abolish the national origins system, did not eliminate the Asia-Pacific Triangle, and did not require the mandatory distribution of unused quota numbers. Even this was too much for Eastland and there was talk that the American Legion was lining up senators to filibuster. On August 12, Feldman wrote Valenti that "time is so short that I doubt that much can be done." He was right. Nothing happened in 1964.[3]

The 1964 elections transformed the political prospect. Though public interest in immigration reform did not rise, the immense Democratic majorities in both houses virtually guaranteed that Johnson would get what he wanted. The House Judiciary Committee changed from 21 Democrats and 14 Republicans to 24 and 11. The immigration subcommittee was increased from 5 to 9 members, thereby assuring the administration a majority. Two of the new Democrats were Jacob Gilbert of New York and Harold Donohue of Massachusetts, both from immigrant-heavy districts, as well as Jack Brooks of Texas, who was close to Johnson. While Feighan had hardly changed his mind and he had a nasty public fight with Celler, he could read the political signs and made friendly noises. Even Eastland told Mike Manatos of O'Brien's staff that "Ted Kennedy is in charge of immigration."

Johnson sent up a special message on immigration on January 13, calling for elimination of national origins. "That system is incompatible with our basic American tradition." He proposed a bill virtually identical to the one Kennedy had offered in 1963. Celler introduced it in the House as H.R. 2580, Philip Hart of Michigan in the Senate as S. 500. Administration strategy was to move the bill through the House first.

The subcommittee hearings consumed 12 days between March and June 1965. Attorney General Katzenbach, whose department had led in drafting the bill and which included the Immigration and Naturalization Service, was the main spokesman for the administration. The primary purpose of H.R. 2580, he said, was to "abolish the national origins quota system and in its place . . . establish a standard for the selection of quota immigrants which is clear and fair." They would be chosen on a first come, first served basis "within a total limit." Otherwise, McCarran-Walter sanctions against Communists would carry over. The total admitted would rise only slightly.

The lobbies that had supported the elimination of national origins— nationality groups, churches, and organized labor—reaffirmed their positions. But a significant change occurred among some who had opposed— patriotic organizations like the American Legion. Now Daniel J. O'Connor of the Legion testified that his organization was "not unaware of the strength and direction of the current political winds" and was impressed with the fact that the quota system had "not worked in practice as in theory." While he did not endorse reversal explicitly, he left no doubt that the Legion would not stand in the way.

Though Feighan also felt the new winds, he insisted on a last stand. In early May he made a proposal to the White House and the Justice Department in which he conceded on national origins. "Every trace of a system under which eligibility for immigration shall be based upon . . . place of birth, race or . . . nationality is removed immediately." But he wanted something in return from the administration: a *worldwide* (including the Western Hemisphere) fixed ceiling of 325,000 persons admitted annually. This would not only eliminate discrimination among nations in Europe, Asia and Africa, but between continents as well.

Schlei, who negotiated with Feighan, concluded that he had fallen into a political trap. He needed an explanation for his acceptance of the elimination of national origins that would appeal to his constituency. "He wants to be able to say that in return for scrapping the national origins system . . . he has gotten . . . for the first time in our history a limit on *all* immigration."

The problem was the Western Hemisphere, which had always been outside the quota system. The average annual immigration from the New World in the five most recent years was 125,014, including averages of 33,496 from Canada and 43,565 from Mexico. About one-fourth of the total consisted of close relatives of persons already in the U.S. and, therefore, automatically admissible, about one-third in the case of Mexico. Any tampering with the historic open border between Canada and the U.S. and the resulting intermingling of the Canadian and American peoples was out of the question. The problem in Latin America, including Mexico, differed, but was hardly amenable to quotas.

Johnson said he would accept a worldwide ceiling including Latin America only if Secretary of State Rusk approved. The secretary said that he "absolutely could not live with a numerical ceiling on the Western Hemisphere." The Latin nations were extremely sensitive to insults from their North American neighbor. Further, Johnson had sent the Marines into the Dominican Republic on April 28 to the extreme displeasure of the Latin countries. If the U.S. now imposed immigration quotas, Rusk told Valenti, "we will vex and dumbfound our Latin American friends, who will now be sure we are in final retreat from Pan Americanism." Moreover, Schlei pointed out, the Feighan proposal would serve no immigration purpose because "existing restrictions on non-quota immigration in reality control immigration from the Western Hemisphere adequately."

To placate Feighan, the administration offered a worldwide maximum of 350,000 annually, 25,000 above his limit. But he had no bargaining power. There were five solid votes against him on the subcommittee and he had only three, including his own.

Celler thought this bargaining with Feighan was demeaning and unnecessary. He was now battling publicly with Feighan over the McCarran-Walter joint committee. While it was ostensibly over funding the committee, Celler was convinced that Feighan wanted to delay the immigration bill until 1966 and to smear alleged security risks.

There was some delay in getting the bill out of the subcommittee by the question of whose name should go on it. Celler was the obvious choice, but both Feighan and Peter Rodino wanted at least part of the credit. Speaker McCormack "suggested" to Feighan that it be called the Celler-Feighan Act, and, according to O'Brien, Celler and Feighan had a "love feast," a rather improbable notion. But Rodino resented being left out and Valenti was called upon to bring his fellow Italian-American around. There were, Valenti wrote, "interminable conversations," and he told Rodino that "we were counting on him in a very vital way and he simply could not let us down. He agreed to go along." The irrepressible Feighan still would not give up the Western Hemisphere. "But we got it out," Valenti wrote with relief, "and then Feighan stayed hitched."

On July 22 the subcommittee voted out the administration bill 8 to 0, with one Republican counted as present. The Judiciary Committee followed on August 3 by a 27 to 4 vote, though the Republicans, wanting to have it both ways, filed minority reports complaining about the Western Hemisphere exemption. The House debate was low-key on H.R. 2580 on August 25. The only significant amendment was a proposal to limit entries from the Western Hemisphere to 115,000 annually, which was defeated 218 to 189. The House then adopted the bill 318 to 95. The northern Democrats were overwhelmingly in favor, 179 to 8, and the Republicans joined them 109 to 29. The southern Democrats alone opposed H.R. 2580, 62 to 30. All of the 92 Catholics in the House except 3 of the 9 southerners and all 15 Jews voted for the bill.

The Senate subcommittee took no action until the House had moved, but held 29 days of hearings between February and August. Eastland, the chairman of both the subcommittee and the Judiciary Committee, removed himself from the proceedings. But he was not "guided by Ted Kennedy's wishes." In fact, Senator Sam Ervin, Jr., of North Carolina chaired the hearings and handled S. 500. While, like other southerners, Ervin preferred McCarran-Walter, he was somewhat more liberal about immigration and had a particular respect for Greeks. The difference from the House subcommittee was that Ervin, unlike Feighan, had a majority and was, therefore, tougher on the Western Hemisphere.

On August 20 Ervin told Manatos that he insisted on a total quota of 300,000, including 120,000 from the Americas. O'Brien informed the President on August 24, "It is clear that some sort of compromise involving a worldwide quota may be necessary to spring a bill from the Senate Judiciary Committee." Johnson, who wanted quick action, conceded at once. That same day Katzenbach notified Ervin and minority leader Dirksen that the administration would accept 120,000 on condition that a select commission on Western Hemisphere immigration should be established to examine the question and report within three years. If it recommended a figure other than 120,000, Congress would consider its proposal; otherwise, a 120,000 ceiling would take effect on July 1, 1968. The senators agreed and the subcommittee amended the bill on August 26 by a vote of 5 to 3. The Judiciary Committee accepted the report on September 15. The vote was 15 to 2, the latter both conservative southerners.

The Senate debated H.R. 2580 with the Ervin amendment for four days and on September 22 adopted it 76 to 18. The northern Democrats were for it 43 to 2, the Republicans 24 to 3. The southern Democrats voted against it 13 to 9. All the Catholics and Jews in the Senate favored the bill.

The conference report came down on September 29 for the Senate bill. The Senate adopted it by voice vote the next day. In the House that day Democrat Henry Gonzalez of Texas proposed rejection of the Latin American limitation to no avail. The House then accepted the report 320 to 69.

The Select Commission on Western Hemisphere Immigration consisted of 15 members, five named by the Senate, including Dirksen, Eastland, and Ted Kennedy, five by the House, including Celler, Feighan, and Rodino, and five chosen by the President with Richard M. Scammon, former Director of the Census, as chairman. Its report, issued in January 1968, was divided. The more liberal majority recommended postponement of the ceiling to July 1, 1969, to allow more time for study, while the conservative minority urged that the law should go into effect as passed. Congress took no action on the majority recommendation and the 120,000 maximum became effective in 1968.

The signing of the new immigration law called for a special celebration and, as several people pointed out, there was no better place for it than Statue of Liberty Island. Secretary of the Interior Steward Udall, who was responsible for its administration, called it a "dramatic setting for the signing." Ellis Island, the only alternative, lacked landing facilities and was in a state of disrepair. Statue of Liberty Island had open terraces above the museum which afforded a superb view of New York Harbor.

At the foot of the statue on October 3, 1965, President Johnson hailed the immigration law for eliminating "a very deep and painful flaw in the fabric of American justice." The days of unlimited immigration were over, he said, but "those who do come will come because of what they are, and not because of the land from which they spring." The U.S. had just concluded a treaty with Castro's Cuba to allow for the emigration of Cubans to Miami in order to reunite families. "The lamp of this grand old lady is brighter today—and the golden door that she guards gleams more brilliantly in the light of an increased liberty for the people from all the countries of the globe." [4]

The 1965 immigration law contained these basic provisions:

> The national origins system, the central feature of U.S. immigration policy for 40 years, was abolished by July 1, 1968. Thereafter immigrants would be admitted by preference categories—family relationships to American citizens and resident aliens and occupational qualifications—on a first come, first served basis without reference to country of birth. During the three-year interim period unused portions of national quotas would be placed in a pool from which preference immigrants from oversubscribed nations might draw.

The Asia Pacific Triangle was abolished immediately. Under that system a person who was at least half-Asian was classified not by nation of birth but by Asiatic ancestry.

Immigration from the Western Hemisphere would be limited to 120,000 annually starting on July 1, 1968.

The number of Eastern Hemisphere immigrants would be 170,000 annually with a 20,000 limit per country. Neither restriction would apply to immediate relatives of U.S. citizens.

The old list of four preference criteria was increased to seven with reliance on family relationships over occupational skills. A new quota of 10,200 annually was established for refugees from Communism, the Middle East, and natural disasters. Individuals suffering from mental illness would be admissible if they were close relatives of U.S. citizens or resident aliens.

While the new law generated little public interest, it was to be of enormous significance in several ways. Both those who supported and those who opposed its passage looked to the past. At a time when the government was intervening to eliminate discrimination based on race and sex, it was hardly surprising that it should seek the eradication of discrimination stemming from national origin. The idea that America must preserve historic northern European domination in the distribution of its population was eradicated. Henceforth all the peoples of the world who wished to settle in the United States would be treated equally.

Neither members of Congress nor of the administration spoke of the future. The Immigration and Naturalization Service issued estimates only for the three-year interim period, which projected a decline to 310,000. No one anticipated the dramatic changes that would soon take place. In particular, Charles Reimers wrote, "Congress did not foresee exactly how the 1965 act would work, especially in the case of Asian workers."

Between 1966 and 1980 the average number of legal immigrants admitted annually was 435,000; from 1978 to 1980 it was 547,000. This did not count a heavy illegal flow from Mexico, Central America, and the Caribbean islands. In the 1920 census the foreign-born numbered 13.9 million, 13.2 percent of the population. Thereafter through 1970 each successive census showed a decline in both of these figures. The 1980 census, however, produced the first reversal. The number of foreign-born returned to 13.9 million, 6.2 percent of the population. In the 1970s immigration accounted for 40 percent of population growth. The new migrants poured into California, Hawaii, New York, Florida, and New Jersey, overwhelmingly into large metropolitan areas.

Immigrants from the Western Hemisphere were free to enter prior to 1968. Those who came sent for their relatives under the new law. The Vietnam War created a large flow from Southeast Asia. Legal immigrants could now enter from the Philippines, China-Taiwan, Korea, India, and Hong Kong. Those who came earlier from the Philippines and China-Taiwan brought their families. Professionals from Korea and India qualified under the occupational preference. As a result, by the late seventies 42 percent of the immigrants were from Latin America, 39 percent from Asia, and only 13 percent from Europe (5 from the northwest and 8 percent from the south). By 1980 the five leading nations of origin in descending order were Mexico, Vietnam, the Philippines, Korea, and China-Taiwan. The 1965 law, Briggs wrote, is "contributing to an ethnic pluralism of the population to a degree that has never truly existed before."

The credit for passage of the immigration reform law is clear. Both Presidents Kennedy and Johnson played central roles. The Department of Justice team, particularly Nicholas Katzenbach and Norbert Schlei, was extremely effective. On the Hill the accolade must go to Emanuel Celler, after whom the law was called. His maiden speech in the House four decades earlier had been an attack on the national origins quota system. Now he proudly presided over its demise.

Politics, one might say, is sometimes the art of the implausible. Michael Feighan, who was extremely well stocked with both chutzpah and monkey wrenches, insisted after the law was passed that he was its author and that he deserved credit for eliminating discrimination based on national origin. He seems to have had some success in foisting this fiction off on the public. The headline over his obit in the *New York Times* in 1992 called him "Architect of '65 Immigration Law."[5]

10

The Environment: From Conservation to Pollution

THE Carsons lived on 65 acres outside Springdale in the lower Allegheny Valley of western Pennsylvania when Rachel was born on May 27, 1907. While they kept a few cows, horses, and chickens, most of the property remained wooded. Her mother, who had a great influence on Rachel, gave her a passionate love for nature and for books. "I was rather a solitary child," she wrote, "and spent a great deal of time in woods and beside streams, learning the birds and the insects and flowers." She was read to and read widely herself "almost from infancy." She assumed that she would become a writer. At 10 a story she wrote won a prize from the children's magazine *St. Nicholas*.

At the Pennsylvania College for Women she had two inspiring teachers, one in English composition and the other in biology. The latter led her to major in zoology. She then took a masters degree in that field at Johns Hopkins and taught there and at the University of Maryland. She had always dreamt of the sea and studied during the summers at the Woods Hole Marine Biological Laboratory.

While in college Rachel Carson wrote poetry, which she submitted to magazines. After her death a number of rejection notices were found among her papers. While many of the readers of her books considered her a poet and she was often compared to Emily Dickinson, she seems to have written no verse later in life. Rather, she folded poetry into her prose style.

When her father died in 1935 she took a job at the Bureau of Fisheries writing scripts called familiarly "Seven Minute Fish Tales" for the radio series "Romance under the Waters." When that ended her boss told her to do something general about the sea. He read it and said, "I don't think it

261

will do. . . . But send this one to the *Atlantic*." The magazine took "Undersea."

Hendrick Willem van Loon, then a famous author, thought it superb and urged Quincy Howe, an editor at Simon and Schuster, to get Carson to expand the article into a book. It became her first, *Under the Sea-Wind*, published in 1941. It was not a success at first, but after she became famous it was reissued, became a best-seller, and was widely translated abroad.

During the war her job as chief editor at the Fish and Wildlife Service gave her the opportunity to learn about oceanography and meet with specialists. She decided to do a general book about the sea, and completed the manuscript of *The Sea Around Us* in July 1950.

Her agent submitted chapters to a long list of magazines, virtually all of which rejected them. Edith Oliver of *The New Yorker* was enthusiastic and the editor, William Shawn, saw at once that this was a great book. He did the condensation himself and published half the book in a three-part series. The response was the greatest the periodical had ever received.

The Sea Around Us was published on July 2, 1951, and took off at once for the stratosphere. The advance printing immediately sold out, with enthusiastic reviews. It was a Book-of-the-Month alternate, and the *Reader's Digest* did an abridgment. By early November sales passed 100,000 and before Christmas it went out at the rate of 4000 a day. The *New York Times* poll picked it as the outstanding book of the year; it won the John Burroughs Medal and the National Book Award. It remained on the best-seller list for 86 weeks, a record for nonfiction, and displaced Thor Heyerdahl's *Kon-Tiki*. By March 1, 1952, sales pushed over 200,000. RKO made a documentary film based on the book which won an Academy Award. Carson had become an instant celebrity, a mixed blessing for someone who treasured her privacy. She no longer had financial problems. She built a cottage on the Maine coast at West Southport, overlooking Sheepscot Bay. She quit her job at Fish and Wildlife and returned a Guggenheim Fellowship to the foundation.

For the next seven years Carson searched for the subject of her next book. She wrote a short volume, *The Edge of the Sea*, and several magazine pieces. During the war, when the powerful insecticide DDT was introduced, she had been concerned about its unintended side effects upon nature. In 1957 she became involved when the state of Massachusetts sprayed around Duxbury and wiped out a private bird sanctuary and when the authorities on Long Island sprayed to exterminate the gypsy moth, leading to a lawsuit. She busily collected material on the chemical menace. E. B. White wrote her that pollution "starts in the kitchen and extends to Jupiter and Mars." In 1958 she signed a contract to publish what she thought would be a short book.

In fact, it proved a formidable undertaking that consumed four years. She tracked down the published sources, corresponded with experts all over the U.S. and Europe, and scrupulously checked the accuracy of everything she wrote. Her health deteriorated—sinus trouble, strep throat, an ulcer, and the breast cancer that would eventually kill her. Both her mother, at age 87, and her niece, Marjorie, died, the latter leaving a small son whom she adopted.

Exhausted, Rachel Carson sent off the manuscript early in 1962. She had always been enchanted with the alternation of the seasons, one of the "great earth rhythms," and spring was her favorite, the "vernal blooming." Her editor had suggested a new title for one of the chapters, "Silent Spring," and she decided that it should be the title of the book. A friend sent her the lines from Keats that became part of the epigraph:

> The sedge is wither'd from the lake,
> And no birds sing.

Unlike anything Rachel Carson had written earlier, *Silent Spring* was a polemic, a cry of rage and a call to arms. It seemed out of character for a woman of gentle manner with a strong taste for privacy. But she was furious because she felt that her deepest values were in danger. Powerfully composed, *Silent Spring* immediately took its place alongside the great American polemical works—Tom Paine's *Common Sense,* Harriet Beecher Stowe's *Uncle Tom's Cabin,* and Upton Sinclair's *The Jungle.*

The enemies were "the elixirs of death," synthetic chemicals employed as insecticides which were recently being sold in prodigious quantities.

> For the first time in the history of the world, every human being is now subjected to contact with dangerous chemicals, from the moment of conception until death. In the less than two decades of their use, the synthetic pesticides have been so thoroughly distributed throughout the animate and inanimate world that they occur virtually everywhere. They have been recovered from most of the major river systems and even from streams of groundwater flowing unseen through the earth. Residues of these chemicals linger in soil to which they have been applied a dozen years before. They have entered and lodged in the bodies of fish, birds, reptiles, and domestic and wild animals so universally that scientists carrying on animal experiments find it almost impossible to locate subjects free from such contamination. They have been found in fish in remote mountain lakes, in earthworms burrowing in soil, in the eggs of birds—and in man himself. For these chemicals are now stored in the bodies of the vast majority of human beings regardless of age. They occur in the mother's milk, and probably in the tissues of the unborn child.

Ingenious chemists in laboratories had produced the toxic chlorinated hydrocarbons—DDT, chlordane, heptachlor, dieldrin, aldrin, and endrin—and the even more poisonous organic phosphates—malathion and parathion.

Carson traced carefully the penetration of these toxic chemicals into the land, the sea, and rivers and lakes. "Over increasingly large areas of the United States, spring now comes unheralded by the return of the birds, and the early mornings are strangely silent where once they were filled with the beauty of bird song." Rachel Carson pointed out that nature was fighting back. Through genetic selection insects developed strains that were resistant to the toxins. The chemicals upset the balance of nature. By eliminating one species, they breached the environment's defenses, thereby allowing other species to take over.

Most infuriating to her was the fact that this was unnecessary. There was, she wrote, "a truly extraordinary variety of alternatives," all biological rather than synthetic. Natural enemies could be introduced to keep undesirable insects under control. Sterilization of the male often produced this result. Other methods of biotic control, such as reactions to scents and sounds, were in the early research stage.

Silent Spring was serialized in *The New Yorker* in June and was published in September 1962. The book was a sensation. It enjoyed enormous notice, critical acclaim, heavy sales (over 100,000 by Christmas), selection by the Book-of-the-Month Club, condensation in *Reader's Digest,* and translation into 18 languages. The author received a large number of honors. Perhaps the one she treasured most came from Lewis Mumford, president of the American Academy of Arts and Letters, announcing her election. There were 50 members, and only three were women. Mumford's citation described her as "a scientist in the grand literary style of Galileo and Buffon."

The chemical industry, as the author had anticipated, mounted a massive campaign against her and her book. "Perhaps," Paul Brooks wrote, "not since the classic controversy over Charles Darwin's *The Origin of Species* just over a century earlier had a single book been more bitterly attacked by those who felt their interests threatened." But this onslaught failed because Rachel Carson had her facts straight.

Silent Spring had a political impact. President Kennedy, evidently, read the *New Yorker* articles and promptly instructed his science adviser, Dr. Jerome B. Wiesner, to investigate. The White House established a Panel on the Use of Pesticides. Professor Colin M. MacLeod of the NYU School of Medicine was chairman and the other members were mainly academic experts in chemistry and health. At his press conference on August 29 the President was asked about the "growing concern among scientists as to the possibility of long-range side effects from the widespread use of DDT and other pesticides." He stated that "since Miss Carson's book" the government was looking into the question.

The panel submitted its report, *Use of Pesticides,* on May 15, 1963. It pointed both to the gains—the improved quantity and quality of foods and fibers—and to the hazards—those *Silent Spring* had addressed. Since little research had been done on the latter, it urged more study of the risks of these dangerous chemicals to all forms of life, including man, and of the use of biological controls. Rachel Carson regarded the report as an endorsement of her position. But she added, "It must now be translated into action."

Both Secretary of the Interior Stewart L. Udall and Senator Abraham Ribicoff of Connecticut were enormously impressed with *Silent Spring*. Udall determined to push Interior to the forefront in dealing with environmental pollution, and Ribicoff, a member of the Committee on Reorganization, held hearings on the coordination of all federal activities in this field. Rachel Carson was a witness.

Rachel Carson died at home in Silver Spring, Maryland, on April 14, 1964, at the age of 56. At the funeral service in the National Cathedral Udall and Ribicoff were pallbearers. Prince Philip sent a large wreath. Ribicoff on the floor of the Senate paid glowing tribute to "this gentle lady."

While the author could hardly have anticipated this, *Silent Spring* led to the dramatic broadening of the conservation ethic and movement that took place in the sixties. Historically the word "conservation" had meant the preservation of America's natural treasures in national parks, national forests, and wilderness. Its heroes were John Muir, Theodore Roosevelt, Gifford Pinchot, Franklin Roosevelt, and Harold Ickes. Now that stream became wider, encompassing a new concern for the protection of the environment against pollution. And now there was a new heroine, Rachel Carson.[1]

The national treasures for which the Department of the Interior was caretaker were located overwhelmingly in the trans-Mississippi West. Thus, Presidents traditionally named a westerner as secretary. When he campaigned in the West in 1960, Kennedy pointed out that the two greatest conservation Presidents—Theodore and Franklin Roosevelt—were from New York. Nevertheless, he conformed to the custom and chose Stewart Udall of Arizona, who would serve for the entire Kennedy-Johnson era. He was not just from the West. He had the lean athletic look of a movie cowboy hero. He loved the wilderness and spent his spare time hunting, fishing, hiking, and shooting rapids.

The Udall family was prominent in Arizona. David King Udall had moved from Salt Lake City to St. Johns in the eastern part of the territory as a Mormon missionary in 1880. His son, Levi Stewart Udall, had served on the Arizona Supreme Court for 13 years. He had four children, two of whom became members of Congress—Stewart, born in 1920, and Morris ("Mo"), who was noted for his brilliant wit. Stewart attended the University of Arizona and its law school. He spent two years as a missionary for his church. During the war he served with the 15th Air Force in Italy as a gunner on a B-24 bomber.

Arizona had two seats in the House—Maricopa County (Phoenix) and all the other counties in the state. Udall ran for the latter as a Democrat in

1954 and easily defeated Senator Goldwater's administrative assistant. He was reelected handsomely in 1956 and 1958. He was a stalwart of the northern liberal bloc. He served on the Committee on Interior and Insular Affairs and came to understand its prickly chairman, Wayne N. Aspinall of Colorado. He also got to know John Kennedy, was an early supporter, and turned the Arizona delegation away from Lyndon Johnson to Kennedy at the 1960 convention. Kennedy named him Secretary of the Interior. When Johnson became President, Udall wondered whether he would remember and dump him. There can be no doubt that Johnson remembered, but he never raised the question.

Udall said later, "I had the best job in the cabinet . . . and . . . I could see the significant accomplishment [that] was taking place." "We were breaking new ground . . . coming up with new ideas." Udall wanted the country to "reshape its goals" on the environment. On conservation, Philip S. Hughes of the Bureau of the Budget said, Udall "was the key figure. He is a guy of vast energy. He gave us all kinds of trouble but had lots of energy and lots of dedication and lots of courage."

Udall transformed the Department of the Interior. It would cease being just western and acquire, he said, a "national image and a national role." He welcomed the views of conservationists from east of the Mississippi, set up national parks and a seashore in the East, helped provide outdoor recreation facilities for those in the cities and the suburbs, and, of course, was concerned about the national problems of pollution. His aspiration was to convert the Department of the Interior into a department of natural resources.

Udall was full of ideas and was constantly proposing new legislation. Both Kennedy and Johnson, he said, "seemed to have a great deal of confidence in me and therefore I had pretty much of a free hand." In fact, the only brake he ever felt was in the latter years of the Johnson administration when the war in Vietnam squeezed his budget, a victim of guns over butter. In fact, he would have preferred more attention from the White House. No staff member oversaw Interior as Douglass Cater monitored Health, Education and Welfare. While he personally wrote the weekly activity reports, he was not sure that Kennedy read them and Johnson seems only to have skimmed them.

Most important, Udall could do pretty much as he pleased legislatively. He was the only cabinet member with congressional experience. "I was able to formulate, initiate and carry out the programs." He developed his own congressional relations staff and did not go through Larry O'Brien.

Udall hired Robert McCone from New Mexico, who knew the chairmen of both Interior Committees, Senator Clinton Anderson of New Mexico and Aspinall. McCone and his staff knew their way around the Capitol and started the day there each morning. "I think," Udall said, "ours was one of the most efficient and effective liaison operations that was run." He got Johnson to name Aspinall's son the governor of Samoa. He needed the President's help for a call to the Hill only once or twice.

Udall's relations with Kennedy had been excellent, but the results were limited. While the President philosophically favored conservation, it was certainly not a priority issue for him. He depended on Udall. At the outset the secretary was busy reorganizing his department and was feeling his way programmatically. There was, however, one conservation issue about which Kennedy felt strongly: Cape Cod. He had sailed his boat for years out of Hyannis Port and, like everyone else, was enraptured by the Cape. After the war it was surrendering rapidly to unplanned development. Kennedy wanted to save what was left and while in the Senate had proposed turning part of the great outer beach into a protected national park. When he became President, he moved with Udall at his side. Until that time no seashore was part of the park system. Udall suggested a new form: the national seashore. On August 7, 1961, Kennedy signed the bill creating the Cape Cod National Seashore Park, noting that "this is a matter of great interest to me." Udall followed in 1962 with national seashores on Padre Island in Texas and at Point Reyes in California.

Udall's relationship with the Johnsons, both Lyndon and Lady Bird, was much closer. The President seems to have approved of every proposal he made. If Udall said, " 'This is good for the land and good for the people,' he bought it." Udall thought this was because of Johnson's rural upbringing and because it was a project his idol, Franklin Roosevelt, would have favored. He seemed to have an "instinctive feeling" for the land.

Lady Bird shared her husband's outlook and, in fact, developed her own beautification program and came to rely on Udall. He helped get her bill through Congress and with others from Interior drafted her speeches. The first lady, of course, generated great interest in the media and Udall often had her photographed with the national treasures—Big Bend Park in Texas, Point Reyes, the Adams House in Quincy, Massachusetts, and Padre Island—and he even got the noted conservationist, Laurance Rockefeller, to arrange for a ride in a 1911 Stanley Steamer in Woodstock, Vermont. Udall was careful in using the first lady and, excepting the tough fight over the Redwoods National Park, did not make her into a "battering ram." [2]

In 1958 Congress had created the Outdoor Recreation Resources Review Commission to "inventory and evaluate the outdoor recreation resources and opportunities . . . which will be required by present and future generations" in order to guide the federal government and the states in meeting these goals. The commission consisted of 15 members, four from the Committees on Interior and Insular Affairs of each house and seven informed citizens named by the President. It received an appropriation of $2.5 million.

President Eisenhower chose Laurance Rockefeller as chairman. He headed the Rockefeller Brothers Fund and had inherited from his father, John D. Rockefeller, Jr., a dedication to conservation on behalf of the nation. He had developed the Jackson Hole Preserve in Wyoming and was establishing the Rocresorts there and in the Virgin Islands. ORRRC had a large staff, an assortment of expert advisory bodies, research contractors, and liaison arrangements with federal agencies and the states. A total of 27 specialized reports were written. All this consumed more than three years and the commission submitted its report, *Outdoor Recreation for America,* to the President (then Kennedy) on January 31, 1962.

Participation in outdoor recreation, the commission calculated, had been growing at a prodigious rate since the end of World War II. This was the result of a sharp increase in population, rising prosperity, greater leisure time, and improved transportation, particularly cars, among other factors. The commission anticipated that this trend would not only continue but accelerate. It estimated that about 90 percent of Americans engaged in such activity in the summer of 1960 on 4.4 billion occasions. By 1976 this number would grow to 6.9 and by 2000 to 12.4 billion. The physical facilities to meet this demand were not available presently (the strains on Yosemite and Yellowstone National Parks were already notorious). There must be a great and planned expansion of the lands and waters for parks to meet the need.

A long-term program would require the cooperation of federal, state, and local governments, along with the private sector. The commission identified six classes of recreation areas:

   I. High density areas designed for mass use in and near urban centers
  II. General areas for a variety of specific uses
 III. Natural environments that lent themselves to specific uses
  IV. Unique areas of natural wonder, scenic splendor, or scientific interest that should be available for limited use
   V. Primitive (wilderness) areas that should be severely restricted
  IV. Historic and cultural sites, such as Mount Vernon, Civil War battlefields, and the Indian dwellings in Mesa Verde, for very limited use

A program of this magnitude required central leadership. Thus, the commission recommended establishment of a new bureau of outdoor recreation in the Department of the Interior to coordinate about 20 existing federal programs, stimulate and assist state planning, administer grants-in-aid to the states and localities, conduct research, encourage regional and interstate cooperation, and formulate a national recreation plan.

While ORRRC placed no price tag on its proposals, it stated that "substantial additional funds would be needed at all levels of government for planning, acquiring, developing, operating, and maintaining facilities." It recommended a variety of financial devices: general obligation and revenue bonds, user fees, federal matching grants to the states, general funds from the Treasury, and federal loans to the states.

Both Udall and Kennedy welcomed the ORRRC report with open arms and the former was spurred into action. On February 7, 1962, only a week after receiving the study, the secretary submitted to the White House the draft of a presidential message to Congress on conservation along with bills to effectuate the commissions's recommendations, a reorganization plan to create the bureau of outdoor recreation, and a proposal for a White House conference on conservation in April.

The message went to the Hill on March 1 and outdoor recreation was its centerpiece. The President enthusiastically endorsed the proposals for the new bureau, for matching grants to the states to finance land acquisition for parks, and for a sharp increase in the federal system of national parks, forests, and wildlife refuges. He would present a bill to finance this program from user fees in federal facilities, user charges on boats, diversion of taxes paid on boat fuel from the Highway Trust Fund, and receipts from the sale of federal nonmilitary real property. To encourage the prompt acquisition of land, the President asked for immediate Treasury loans to a total of $500 million for eight years to be repaid from the anticipated income.

On April 2 Udall established the Bureau of Outdoor Recreation. It would work with federal departments in formulating policies and with the states in developing their programs, but it would not itself administer any programs. He chose Edward C. Crafts as head of the bureau. He had graduated from the University of Michigan School of Forestry and had a Ph.D. from the University of California School of Forestry at Berkeley. He had worked for the Forest Service for 29 years, the last dozen as assistant chief forester, where, among other duties, he was responsible for congressional relations. Crafts had assisted in creating the Rockefeller commission. He knew the members of the Agriculture and Interior committees in both houses, and considered Stewart Udall a good friend.

On April 27 the President issued Executive Order 11017 creating the Outdoor Recreation Advisory Council of the heads of departments and agencies involved in recreation. "It is essential," Kennedy stated, "that there be close coordination among these different groups and that all plans be fitted into a basic national policy." "Coordination" was a code word for the avoidance of jurisdictional disputes. Everyone involved with conservation knew of the titanic brawls that had been waged between Agriculture and Interior over the Forest Service in the Progressive and New Deal eras. Fortunately, the relations between Agriculture Secretary Orville Freeman and Udall were excellent and there would not be a third bloodbath.

The White House Conference on Conservation met at the end of May. Key committee members of Congress, governors of many states, and conservation organizations were urged to support the administration program.

The legislation proved far more daunting. This was not due to disagreement over the basic proposal; almost everyone accepted the idea that a great expansion of outdoor recreation facilities was desirable. Rather, the controversy was over funding, and there were two basic complaints.

Udall hoped to establish a kind of Interior Department conservation bank account that would have a continuing source of income from user fees on parks and boats, the recapture of fuel taxes on motor boats, and the sale of surplus federal lands. The funds would be used to acquire land, which was rapidly appreciating in price, and to administer the system. "It was clear," he said, "that we had to have a new policy. . . . Some kind of conservation fund . . . like the highway trust fund." But he soon ran into roadblocks within the government and from those with an interest in the free use of waterways.

On February 12 Udall had circulated four bills and quickly met a stone wall. The Bureau of the Budget objected to earmarking revenues by removing them from budget review and control, for it made budget balancing difficult, and it objected to "backdoor" borrowing from the Treasury without an appropriation. The Treasury agreed. The Council of Economic Advisers, despite strong support for the expansion of parks, also considered the financing arrangements improper. Walter Heller thought there should be "a new breed of fiscal animal—perhaps called a capital fund—which would take its place beside the trust fund as a type of expenditure outside of the normal budgetary process."

The water user objections came from two sources. The barging industry on the Mississippi and Ohio river systems, according to Crafts, was determined to protect its free use of these watery roadbeds, which provided a competitive advantage over the railroads and trucking. The bargers opposed any precedent of a fee or tax on the use of waterways. Recreational boating also objected. The Army Corps of Engineers had built dams in Oklahoma, east Texas, southwest Missouri, and northwest Arkansas which formed backup lakes that boaters used without charge, and the same was true in the Tennessee Valley. Both the Corps and TVA opposed user fees.

There were abortive House hearings in July which served as a forum for these objections. Later that year Interior searched for a different solution. The original bill had stressed federal land acquisition; now the emphasis would be on grants to the states for planning, acquiring, and developing state parks. This would prove more popular in Congress and the Bureau of the Budget approved. The Senate committee held hearings in March and the House followed in May and July.

Aspinall held the bill up for more than a year. On November 4, 1963, President Kennedy wrote him to urge that this "most significant legislation" should be enacted in the current session. By now virtually every conservation organization and 46 states had endorsed the measure. The Interior Committee reported out the Land and Water Conservation Fund bill, H.R. 3846, on November 14 in essentially the form the final statute would take. It would create a self-sustaining trust fund for 25 years. Sixty percent of the money would be distributed to the states in matching grants that would cover up to 50 percent of the cost of both land acquisition and the development of parks. The remaining 40 percent would be used by the federal government, but only for land acquisition. The fund's income would be received from the sale of federal surplus property (estimated at $50 million annually), the motor boat fuel tax presently going into the Highway Trust Fund ($30 million), and new entrance and recreation user fees at national parks, national forests, and other federal properties, including Corps of Engineers and TVA sites ($60 to $65 million). Fees for water navigation by commercial vessels were prohibited. Congress would make a supplemental appropriation of $60 million annually. Udall wrote President Johnson: "The House Committee has reported an excellent bill. Outlook is favorable."

The bill sailed through Congress. On July 22, 1964, a test roll call on the rule for debate in the House passed 338 to 8. The next day the body adopted it by voice vote. There was even less trouble in the Senate. The amendments were picky, such as entrance fees to Great Smoky Mountains National Park only with the consent of North Carolina and Tennessee. The Senate passed H.R. 3846 on August 12 by a vote of 91 to 1. The conference committee had little to do and its report was adopted by both chambers by voice vote on September 1, 1964.

By early August Udall realized that his one-armed bandit was about to give him a huge legislative payoff. He and presidential aide Lee White thought there ought to be "a very big to-do" at the White House over the signings. Udall wrote President Johnson on August 13, "It now appears that by a strange quirk nearly all major conservation bills will reach your desk jackpot-fashion in the final days of the session." There were two landmark measures—Land and Water Conservation Fund and Wilderness (to be treated next)—along with many of regional significance. Johnson selected three of the latter for the occasion—Ozark National Scenic Riverways, Fire Island National Seashore, and Canyonlands National Park, the first new national park in North America in 17 years.

The ceremony was held in the Rose Garden on September 3, 1964. The President delivered a glowing message on conservation. The nation was now in what Udall liked to call the third wave of conservation. TR had led the first, FDR the second. Now, as Johnson put it, the 88th Congress, the "conservation Congress," was launching the third. It was far more than the laws he was now signing. "Action has been taken to keep our air pure and our water safe and our food free from pesticides; to protect our wildlife; to conserve our precious water resources." He stressed the overwhelming votes in both houses (Wilderness passed 73 to 12 and 373 to 1) as evidence of broad bipartisan support. He expressed special gratitude to Udall, Clinton Anderson (and Senator Henry Jackson of Washington, who succeeded to the committee chairmanship), and to Congressman Aspinall. His only regret was that Laurance Rockefeller was unable to be present. The President wrote him: "You may well take pride in your contribution . . . , not only in your part in the ORRRC Report and the results so far accomplished, but for the many other personal contributions that you, and your father before you, have made to the field of conservation."

Crafts gradually built up the Bureau of Outdoor Recreation to handle its responsibilities. When fully operational, it had almost 500 employees in Washington and in regional offices in Philadelphia, Atlanta, Denver, Seattle, and San Francisco. BOR undertook the drafting of a national recreation plan. It required the states to prepare their own detailed plans as a condition of federal aid. It worked with the National Park Service, the Forest Service, and the Bureau of Sport Fisheries and Wildlife to promote land acquisition and the development of federal recreational facilities. It helped produce several new concepts—national recreation areas, wild and scenic rivers, both interstate and local trails, miniparks in the cities, and coastal and freshwater islands.

By 1968 BOR had approved assistance to states and cities for more than 3000 projects, 1500 in the last year. By 1967 the National Parks, the Forest Service, and Sport Fisheries and Wildlife had acquired 313,000 acres of land with help from the conservation fund.

The consequences were dramatic. The growth of state and municipal parks was unprecedented. At the federal level the accomplishments exceeded those of Franklin Roosevelt and Harold Ickes during the New Deal. For the Johnson period, 1963–68, that is, excluding the Kennedy administration, the national park system grew by 46 new areas, including several novel forms that differed from the traditional national park:

	Number	*Notable Examples*
National historic sites	16	Saint Gaudens (New Hampshire) Golden Spike (Utah)
National recreation areas	6	Delaware Water Gap (Pennsylvania-New Jersey)
National monuments	4	Biscayne (Florida)
National parks	4	Redwoods (California) North Cascades (Washington)
National historical parks	3	Nez Perce (Idaho)
National memorials	3	Johnstown Flood (Pennsylvania)
National seashores	3	Fire Island (New York) Assateague Island (Maryland-Virginia)

National lakeshores	2	Indiana Dunes (Indiana)
Farm park	1	Wolf Trap (Virginia)
International park	1	Roosevelt Campobello (U.S.-Canada)
National scenic riverway	1	Ozark (Missouri)
National scenic trail	1	Appalachian (Maine to Georgia)

By the latter part of the decade it became clear that the funding system was not working, mainly for three reasons. The first was that income was low due to failure of the Golden Eagle Passport. It was a pass which entitled the occupants of a car to enter all the national parks for a year for $7. Most visitors preferred to pay $2 for the day. Anticipated to produce $50 million, the Golden Eagle actually raised only $3.8 million in 1967. The second was that land prices, pushed up by the inflation of the Vietnam War, were appreciating at a rate of 10 percent a year. Finally, as Udall said, "The one really major disappointment to me was when the Vietnam War really began to be felt. The last three years were essentially tightening down. . . . It became a kind of hold-the-line operation. . . ." On January 3, 1967, he informed the Bureau of the Budget that the shortfall for the next decade could be $2.5 billion.

During 1967 Interior, Budget, and both Interior committees worked on a solution. For 1969 through 1973 they set a level of $200 million annually, a total of $1 billion. The income would be split evenly between the federal government and states, $100 million annually for each. Permits, admissions, and user fees would produce $12 million a year, the motorboat fuel tax about $35 million, and the sale of federal lands just under $50 million, a total around $97 million. The remaining $103 million would come from a new source, receipts from oil and gas leases on the outer continental shelf. But neither house acted until 1968, when the bill was easily passed and signed by the President on July 15. Thus, the solvency of the Land and Water Conservation Fund was assured for at least the next five years.[3]

Wilderness has been the beating heart of the conservation impulse. "Everybody," John Muir wrote, "needs beauty as well as bread, places to play in and pray in, where Nature may heal and cheer and give strength to body and soul alike." Michael Frome wrote, "One cannot be lonesome, as John Muir once said, when everything is wild and beautiful and busy and steeped with God." No movement could match wilderness preservation in attracting so many gifted writers, painters, and photographers to its ranks, among them: John James Audubon, George Catlin, Henry David Thoreau, Muir, Ansel Adams, Rachel Carson.

Aldo Leopold, called by some the "Father of the National Forest Wilderness system," defined wilderness as an area big enough to provide a two-week pack trip without having to backtrack or cross one's own trail. The main draftsman of the Wilderness Act, Howard Zahniser, was more specific in the statute:

> A wilderness, in contrast with those areas where man and his own works dominate the landscape, is hereby recognized as an area where the earth and its community of life are untrammeled by man, where man himself is a visitor who does not remain. An area of wilderness is further defined to mean in this Act an area of undeveloped Federal land retaining its primeval character and influence, without permanent improvements or human habitation, which is protected and managed so as to preserve its natural conditions and which (1) generally appears to have been affected primarily by the forces of nature, with the imprint of man's work substantially unnoticeable; (2) has outstanding opportunities for solitude or a primitive and unconfined type of recreation; (3) has at least five thousand acres of land or is of sufficient size as to make practicable its preservation and use in an unimpaired condition; and (4) may also contain ecological, geological, scenic, or historical value.

The primary object of wilderness legislation was the 9,139,721 acres controlled by the Forest Service of the Department of Agriculture in the lower 48 states which it classified as "wilderness," "wild," or "canoe." Alaska was its own problem which would be confronted later. In addition, the Forest Service was responsible for 5,477,740 acres classified as "wild," some of which might be brought into a wilderness system. All of these lands were in the West except for small tracts in North Carolina and New Hampshire. The canoe area was in northern Minnesota in the chain of lakes and streams shared with Canada along the international border.

In addition, the Department of the Interior administered two programs which contained wilderness areas. The Bureau of Sport Fisheries and Wildlife was responsible for bird and animal sanctuaries, refuges, and ranges from which commercial activities were excluded by regulation. The bureau estimated that up to 24.4 million of its 28 million acres might be considered wilderness. The National Park Service produced similar numbers—22.2 million of 26.5 million acres. The national parks were protected from private exploitation by statute. There was, finally, an unknown acreage of wilderness that was privately owned and never considered for inclusion in the system.

Thus, the focus of attention was the Forest Service. From its inception in 1905 under Chief Forester Gifford Pinchot, the service had relied on policies of multiple use and sustained yield to resolve the conflict between development and conservation. Using timber as an illustration: Lumber companies were permitted to cut trees in the national forests on condition that they planted new trees to provide the same yield in the next generation. Since minerals and oil and gas were not renewable, sustained yield could not apply. In 1960 Congress converted Forest Service policy into law in the Multiple Use and Sustained Yield Act, authorizing the "most judicious use" for recreation, soil, range, timber, watershed, wildlife, fishing, and mining. The Wilderness Society feared that this broad language would lead inevitably to the death of wilderness in the national forests.

A few individuals in the Forest Service believed in wilderness and urged the abandonment of multiple use. Arthur H. Carhart, who surveyed for a request to convert the Trapper's Lake region of the White River National Forest in Colorado in 1919 for roads and homesites, recommended rejection of the petition.

When he was a forester in Albuquerque, Aldo Leopold, concerned about the preservation of wildlife, argued for the maintenance of wilderness habitats. He succeeded in having 574,000 acres in New Mexico's Gila National Forest set aside from development. Leopold was an outstanding writer and published his views widely, particularly in the celebrated collection of essays, *A Sand County Almanac*.

Bob Marshall was the most dedicated of the early advocates of wilderness. Independently wealthy and the holder of a Ph.D. from Johns Hopkins, he worked for the Forest Service and as chief forester in Interior's Bureau of Indian Affairs. At the outset of the New Deal he convinced Secretary Ickes, who headed the Public Works Administration, not to build roads in wilderness areas. Marshall, more than anyone else, developed a comprehensive philosophy of wilderness, notably in his book *The People's Forests*. He urged a network of primeval reservations in all sections of the country.

In 1934 Marshall and several other wilderness enthusiasts hiked into what would become Great Smoky Mountains National Park and there agreed to form an organization to unite the friends of wilderness. The next year Marshall left the government and with several others, including Howard Zahniser, created the Wilderness Society. A young man, he died in 1939 and left the society $400,000.

In 1954 James P. Gilligan received a Ph.D. from the University of Michigan School of Natural Resources after writing a dissertation on Forest Service administration of wilderness areas. The picture was bleak. That fall he addressed the Society of American Foresters to summarize his findings and urge the passage of a new law. In 1955 the Wilderness Society published Gilligan's paper in its journal, *The Living Wilderness*. Zahniser, who had become the society's executive secretary, pursued Gilligan's ideas in a speech of his own. Senator Humphrey read it and inserted the text in the *Congressional Record*. The Wilderness Society, the Sierra Club, the National Wildlife Federation, the National Parks Association, and other conservation organizations joined to draft the bill Gilligan had urged. In fact, Zahniser was the main author, which may explain the oddity of the Wilderness Act among federal statutes for its lucid and graceful prose. He was, indeed, special. Michael Frome found Zahniser to be "studious, soft-spoken, and patient, both persuasive and persistent, a man of love for his fellow men, and highly principled."

Humphrey introduced the first wilderness bill on June 7, 1956, with bipartisan sponsorship. In the Eisenhower era Humphrey did not expect quick action. In fact, there would be four Humphrey bills over the next eight years. The opposition from industry was formidable and there was, of course, no administration support. But the ever-cheerful Humphrey was neither surprised nor daunted.

The political situation changed dramatically for the better with Kennedy's election in 1960. In his special message on natural resources on February 23, 1961, the new President urged Congress to enact the wilderness bill. It had the strong backing of both Freeman and Udall, along with a solid phalanx of conservation groups. Opposition came from the lumber, livestock, mining, and oil and gas industries, joined by the Chamber of Commerce and the National Association of Manufacturers.

The bill, S. 174, would place all areas classified as wilderness, wild, or canoe in a National Wilderness System immediately. The construction of roads and commercial activities, except those already in operation, would be prohibited. Mining presently under way could continue, but there would be no new mines unless the President certified that they were necessary in the national interest. Other lands in the National Forests, in the National Parks, and under the jurisdiction of Sport Fisheries and Wildlife would be reviewed over the next decade for inclusion in the system. The President could add these lands, but must notify Congress. Unless both houses voted to override him, these lands would be designated as wilderness. The responsible agency would be obliged to administer the selected areas in order to preserve their primitive character.

In the early sixties large majorities in both houses and in both parties favored a strong wilderness bill. Clinton Anderson, chairman of the Senate Interior Committee, was a protagonist and held in his pocket 12 of the 16 votes in his committee. Years before, Anderson and Aldo Leopold had been intimate friends and had hiked the New Mexico wilderness together. The problem was Aspinall, the slippery chairman of the House committee. At times he seemed to be for wilderness and at others opposed. In early 1964, Mike Manatos found him "precariously balanced." Manatos, Larry O'Brien, and Lee White thought it a mistake to bring him to the White House for persuasion with President Johnson because he would resent the pressure. Aspinall, Manatos wrote, is a "very difficult individual." While he lacked the power to prevent passage of the bill, he might be able to weaken it with amendments and he certainly could delay its passage.

On January 5, 1961, Anderson had introduced the Humphrey bill as S. 174 with 13 cosponsors. He held prompt hearings and the committee reported the bill on July 17 by a vote of 12 to 4. It reached the floor on

September 1 and several delaying or debilitating amendments were defeated comfortably. The Senate adopted S. 174 on September 6 by a vote to 78 to 8.

Aspinall, bowing to pressure by opponents, delayed his hearings until the Outdoor Recreation Commission published its Study Report No. 3, "Wilderness and Recreation." But the report, issued on April 16, 1962, strongly supported legislation to create a wilderness system.

The Subcommittee on Public Lands held hearings during the spring of 1962. At its executive session on June 29 Aspinall offered an "amendment." It would have gutted the bill, and both Interior and Agriculture strongly opposed it. Nevertheless, the subcommittee followed Aspinall. The full committee went even further, allowing mining in wilderness until 1987 and authorizing a ski resort on 3500 acres of the San Gorgonio Wild Area in Southern California. While the committee reported on August 30, Aspinall did not file the report until October 3, 1962, the eve of adjournment. Thus, the wilderness bill died with the expiring 87th Congress.

Anderson cheerfully started over on January 14, 1963, in the 88th Congress, introducing the bill the Senate had passed in 1962, this time as S. 4 with 21 cosponsors. President Kennedy endorsed it in his Budget Message on January 21. Anderson held brief hearings and the Interior Committee reported the bill on April 2 by a vote of 11 to 5. After cursory debate, the Senate adopted it 73 to 12.

During the summer of 1963 Aspinall negotiated with Interior and Agriculture and they agreed on a new version of the bill. He abandoned his substitute and received only a few minor concessions for commercial interests. The conservation groups, including the Wilderness Society, endorsed the revised bill.

Aspinall held extended hearings in Olympia, Washington, Denver, Las Vegas, and Washington, D.C., between January and May 1964. The Wilderness Society noted, "Excellent hearings, fairly and expeditiously conducted, once again demonstrated the g.eat public support . . . for wilderness preservation—and also revealed a new willingness on the part of former opponents to accept recently revised bills." Zahniser testified on the last day. "It may seem presumptuous," he said, "for men and women who live only 40, 50, 60, 70, or 80 years, to dare to undertake a program for perpetuity, but that surely is our challenge." Six days later he was dead of a heart attack.

Aspinall now became the champion of wilderness. In a speech on the floor of the House he paid tribute to Zahniser and promised that his great goal would be reached. And so it was. The Interior Committee adopted the measure almost unanimously. On July 30 the House passed the bill by the incredible vote of 374 to 1. Udall wrote the White House that after "nearly six years of agonizing frustration," history was being made "due in part to the leadership efforts of Rep. Aspinall." The modest differences between the versions were quickly resolved in conference. Both houses adopted the final bill on August 20, 1964.

Vice presidential candidate Hubert Humphrey wrote Larry O'Brien to suggest that the President at the signing ceremony "pay his respects and his tribute to the late Howard Zahniser . . . , the father of the wilderness bill." He continued,

> I would also like to add that yours truly, Hubert Humphrey, was the original sponsor . . . and turned it over to Clint Anderson here in the Senate when he was chairman of the Interior Committee. I have been the main co-sponsor ever since the early 1950s. This bill was highly controversial in the beginning and I had to take most of the brickbats at the early stages [from the commercial interests in the northern Minnesota canoe district]. Like many other things, some of the controversy is dissipated in proper time and the bill passes. In the meantime, a few of us come out with the battle scars.

In his remarks at the mass signing on September 3, 1964, Johnson mentioned neither Zahniser nor Humphrey. The former, evidently, meant nothing to him and he did not hesitate to ignore or even humiliate Hubert Humphrey. Rather, he gave credit to his "distinguished and able Secretary of Interior," along with Clinton Anderson, Henry Jackson, and Wayne Aspinall. Udall, Anderson, and Aspinall, the last in a bizarre way, fully deserved the accolade. One must certainly add the conservation organizations, particularly the Wilderness Society and its leader, Howard Zahniser. While Presidents Kennedy and Johnson both endorsed the bill, neither did much to get it through the Congress.

The statute created the National Wilderness Preservation System "to secure for the American people of present and future generations the benefits of an enduring resource of wilderness." All National Forest areas classified as wilderness, wild, and canoe were immediately placed in the system. Within the next ten years the Secretaries of Agriculture and Interior could recommend to the President the addition of other lands under their jurisdiction. Each agency must administer system lands so as to preserve their wilderness character. Commercial activities already under way could continue, but new exploitation was severely restricted.

The National Wilderness Preservation System started with 9.1 million acres of Forest Service lands. By 1980 the service had contributed another 4.4 million in the lower 48 states and 5.3 million in Alaska. In his study Craig Allin anticipated the later addition of about 8 million acres. Thus, between 17 and 18 percent of Forest Service lands would become protected wilderness. Fittingly, this included the Bob Marshall National Forest in western Montana just south of Glacier National Park.

The National Park Service supplied less than 3 million acres in the lower 48, but added 32.4 million for wilderness in Alaska. The Bureau of Sport Fisheries and Wildlife holdings, including Alaska, had 19 million acres of wilderness, but very few were so designated because of differences over policy. The Bureau of Land Management had large holdings of which 10 to 20 million might eventually become wilderness.

Thus, Allin concluded, the nation could eventually look forward to a system with 100 to 130 million acres in wilderness, about 5 percent of the land area of the U.S. While conservationists wanted more, he wrote,

> The magnitude of the victory for preservation will be greater than preservationists could have imagined as recently as 1964. That victory will come none too soon, for the time is now within our comprehension when the only wilderness that will remain is the wilderness that has been purposefully preserved.[4]

"Of all our natural resources," Rachel Carson wrote in *Silent Spring*, "water has become our most precious." Yet the U.S. was squandering this critical asset by polluting its rivers, lakes, streams, wetlands, and seashores. Collectively they had become the nation's dump. They received the chemical garbage from industry, the human, household, and commercial wastes from the cities, agricultural runoff from farms and feedlots, radioactive wastes from nuclear reactors, and, now, the residues of chemical pesticides.

By 1965 all of the nation's significant rivers were polluted. The lower Great Lakes—Michigan, Erie, and Ontario—were in dreadful shape and it was often said that Lake Erie was "dead." A very large number of other waterways were either already cesspools or well on their way to becoming them.

The White House Task Force on the Quality of the Environment informed the President of the damage. The 1966 report stated that the most abundant wastes consisted of sediment from erosion and organic materials. Some organic chemicals—phosphates, nitrates, and other minerals—removed oxygen from the water and destroyed aquatic life. They were potentially toxic to humans and so prevented the use of polluted waters for recreation: "Children have become ill swimming in rivers temporarily saturated with toxic pollutants." The 1967 report stressed agricultural waste. A beef feedlot which held 10,000 head of cattle produced daily 260 tons of solid waste and 100 tons of liquids. A dairy barn with 500 cows had the waste equivalent of 8000 people. Fertilizer and pesticide consumption was growing exponentially, much finding its way as drainage into bodies of water with the resulting growth of algae.

The Savannah River rises from clear mountain streams in the Blue Ridge of the Carolinas and upper Georgia and races for 300 miles to the Atlantic, forming the boundary between South Carolina and Georgia. Flowing through an area which receives 46 inches of annual rainfall, second only to the Pacific Northwest, it is a mighty river with an average daily flow of

7.2 million gallons of water. For most of man's history along its banks, it seemed big enough to withstand any abuse.

But in the twentieth century the twin forces of population growth and industrialization overpowered the river. Savannah, a city of 135,000, poured raw sewage into the stream. The stench was unbearable, swimming and boating became impossible, and the fishing grounds and oyster beds were declared off-limits. Bad as this was, the industrial effluents were worse. The main culprit was the huge kraft paper mill opened in 1935 by Union Bag, later Union Camp, which pushed a torrent of coffee-colored waste into the river. Combined with the outfall from the town's sewage system, James M. Fallows wrote, "At times the water in front of City Hall literally boils as pockets of hydrogen sulfide and methane gas rise from the wastes on the river bed." The final insult was delivered by American Cyanimid, which poured sulfuric acid into the Savannah. Oxygen-consuming wastes killed the fish.

Gallinée, a missionary, was on the northeastern shore of Lake Erie during the winter of 1669–70, an area he called "the earthly Paradise of Canada." "The woods are open," he wrote, "interspersed with beautiful meadows, watered by rivers and rivulets, filled with fish and beaver, an abundance of fruits, and . . . full of game." The men had more meat than they could eat, picked wild walnuts, chestnuts, apples, plums, cranberries, and grapes. They made 25 or 30 hogsheads of red wine "as good as vin de Grave." Lake Erie and its region retained these pristine qualities for a century and a half.

In the middle of the nineteenth century the south shore of the lake became critically important to the iron and steel industry. Coal was readily available by rail from the mines in western Pennsylvania, southeastern Ohio, West Virginia, and Kentucky. After the building of canals and locks, iron ore was shipped cheaply by ore carriers from the great northern Minnesota deposits through the Great Lakes to Lake Erie. Steel mills, metalworking industries, and, later, the auto industry grew in the large cities on the U.S. side of the lake—Buffalo, Cleveland, Toledo, and Detroit—and in smaller towns like Huron, Sandusky, Lorain, Ashtabula, Conneaut, and Erie. The St. Lawrence Seaway in the mid-twentieth century connected the lake to the Atlantic and so to the world. By the 1960s, 10.4 million people lived on the south shore of Lake Erie and it had become one of the world's greatest concentrations of heavy industry.

The Canadian north shore, excepting Windsor, did not develop industrially, in part because of the virtual absence of coal in Ontario. Windsor, which is just across the river from Detroit, became an auto town. But the entire Canadian population along the lake was only 1.4 million.

As with the Savannah River, the dumping of untreated human excrement and industrial wastes into rivers that drained into the lake and directly into the lake itself created massive pollution. Cholera epidemics in the late nineteenth century had been an unheeded omen. The pollution became progressively worse and by the 1960s was desperate. Noel M. Burns, an authority on Lake Erie, identified seven major problems which demanded "serious attention:" soil erosion, creating siltation; loss of shoreline marshes; destruction of one of the world's great fisheries for herring, lake trout, sturgeon, whitefish, sauger, and walleye, along with the accidental introduction of new parasitic species; a great increase in pathogenic bacteria and refuse; an immense increase in the water's phosphorous content, causing rapid algae growth; an enormous rise in the number and amounts of toxics, especially the dangerous heavy metals; and the killing of fish at electrical stations and water works, aggravated by the recent development of nuclear generating plants.

By the early sixties, Democratic Senator Edmund S. Muskie of Maine had emerged as the leading congressional authority on both water and air pollution and became known as "Mr. Clean." Muskie's father had come to the U.S. from Poland in 1903 and settled in the small town of Rumford, Maine, where he ran a tailor shop. Edmund was born in 1914, the second of six children. He was educated at the local public schools, at Bates College, and at the Cornell Law School. He was an outstanding student and a natural leader. During World War II he served on destroyer escorts in both the Atlantic and the Pacific.

The state of Maine, with dense woods, myriad lakes and streams, spare industry, and low population density, was hardly a leading polluter. But Muskie learned about "public concern and indignation" in Rumford, where he was raised. "Our river," he wrote, "the Androscoggin, . . . begins its run to the ocean in the high, clear mountain streams in the northwestern corner of Maine. It flows into New Hampshire, then back into Maine, picking up pulp and paper wastes in Berlin, New Hampshire, Rumford and Livermore Falls-Jay, Maine." As David Nevin wrote, "Nature made [the river] one of the most beautiful and a whole series of pulp and paper mills have made it one of the filthiest rivers in America. A pall of smoke and a sour odor seeping from the single mill that dominates Rumford hangs overhead like a rich uncle's foul breath which everyone resolutely ignores."

After the war Muskie practiced law in Waterville. Moved by FDR and the New Deal, he became a Democrat. This was a problem in Maine, which was overwhelmingly Republican. Muskie pretty much created a viable Democratic party so that he could have a political career. He won several elections to the state legislature. He then challenged the dominant Republicans by running for governor. He was elected narrowly in 1954 and then handsomely in 1956. In 1958 he ran for the Senate and in the Democratic sweep defeated the Republican incumbent by a wide margin, a victory that attracted national attention.

Early in 1959 he ran into trouble with his majority leader, Lyndon Johnson. Their first conversation began pleasantly enough, and the Texan gave him some avuncular advice. "There will be times, Ed, when you won't know how you're going to vote until they start calling the M's." The key issue of the moment was an amendment to Rule 22, limiting filibusters on civil rights. The liberals wanted restriction and Johnson had advanced a compromise that he explained. Muskie, who had lined up with the liberals, was silent. "Well, Ed," Johnson said, "you haven't much to say on Rule 22." Putting on the laconic style of the Maine farmer, Nevin wrote, Muskie "took the straw out of his mouth, hooked a thumb in his overalls and said, 'Well, Lyndon, we haven't gotten to the M's yet.' " Johnson did not like that crack.

He punished Muskie by giving him his fourth, fifth, and sixth choices of committees—Banking and Currency, Government Operations, and Public Works. While Muskie was disappointed at the outset, as things worked out, Johnson had done him a favor. Fate did him another: two powerful senior Democrats on the Public Works Committee died—chairman Dennis Chavez of New Mexico and the formidable Robert Kerr of Oklahoma. Liberal Pat McNamara of Michigan became chairman. He created a new special Subcommittee on Air and Water Pollution and installed Muskie as chairman. A quick study, he soon was an acknowledged expert and his dedication and intelligence won the admiration of his fellow senators as well as Lyndon Johnson. He would play the central congressional role in shaping the water and air pollution legislation of the sixties.[5]

The first federal statute that addressed degraded water was the Water Pollution Control Act of 1948. It provided for abatement procedures against industrial and public polluters as well as federal financial assistance to localities for the building of sewage treatment plants. The Justice Department, with the consent of the state, could bring action against a polluter before a board. It would issue recommendations to end the pollution. If the state did not comply, the government would seek an injunction. The law applied only to interstate waterways. Until 1956 it was virtually unenforced. It also provided $27.8 million for loans to the states for construction of treatment plants, a token amount. The Public Health Service was responsible for administration and its performance was dismal. Amendments in 1956 mildly strengthened enforcement and in the next five years 13 abatement actions were filed, none brought to conclusion. There was another round of amendments for enforcement in 1961. By 1965, a total of 21 actions had been started, only one of which reached a court, where it was settled by a consent agreement.

Thus, by the mid-sixties the nation confronted an immense water pollution problem which was rapidly growing worse as a result of rising population, industrial growth, and the obsolescence of treatment facilities. But there was virtually no program to deal with it. On January 31, 1963, Senator Muskie introduced his pollution control bill. The states would be required to establish water quality standards for all interstate waterways. Failing to do so, the federal government would step in. Recently introduced laundry detergents, which formed great mounds of suds in rivers and lakes and brought water out of taps with heads, would be banned unless the detergents met standards of biodegradability. Grants for treatment plants would be significantly increased. Pollution by federal agencies would be regulated. A new Water Pollution Control Administration in the Department of Health, Education and Welfare, replacing the Public Health Service, would administer the program.

Muskie held hearings and pushed his bill through the Public Works Committee and the Senate, the latter on October 16, 1963, by a vote of 69 to 11. As usual, the lobbies made their stand in the House. The committee stalled for more than a year and the measure it reported on September 4, 1964, made a shambles of Muskie's bill. HEW would recommend, not set, water quality standards. The provisions covering detergents and federal installations were removed. A new gimmick, certain to cause trouble, forbade construction of an interceptor drain in northern California. The Rules Committee dutifully objected and denied a rule. Muskie had to start over.

He introduced S.4 on January 6, 1965, his 1963 bill with two deletions. The federal installation provision was eliminated because the President had taken care of that problem by executive order. On May 21, 1965, the Soap and Detergent Association announced that the industry had licked the sudsing problem and that all the large firms would switch to the new formula by July 1, 1965. The detergent provision was removed. But the heart of the bill remained: the establishment of state water quality standards under federal supervision.

Senate hearings were held in January 1965 and the committee reported favorably on the 27th of that month by a vote of 16 to 1. The next day the Senate went along 68 to 8; 3 Republicans who had voted against the 1963 bill now switched.

The speed with which Muskie had moved caught the Johnson administration by surprise. In mid-February Bill Moyers held a White House meeting of representatives from HEW, the Bureau of the Budget, and the Office of Science and Technology to figure out what the President should do. They agreed to accept Muskie's S.4 except for strengthening enforcement. But they were worried about what the House Public Works Committee might do.

In his message to Congress on conservation and beauty on February 8, 1965, the President spoke at length on water quality. He noted that "every major river is now polluted," that in the summer of 1964 over a fourth of Lake Erie had been almost wholly without oxygen, that waterborne viruses constituted a "significant health hazard," and so on. He urged passage of the Senate bill with stronger enforcement. Clearly, he was nudging the House.

While the new House elected in 1964 viewed water quality more sympathetically than its predecessor, it remained more obstinate than the Senate. The powerful polluting industries were determined to strip authority over state standards from the federal government, with the oil industry, a massive polluter, leading the way.

Democratic Representative John A. Blatnik of Minnesota introduced H.R. 3988, a bill much like S. 4. Hearings were held in February 1965, highlighted by the testimony of Governor Nelson A. Rockefeller of New York calling for substantially larger grants to the states for treatment plants.

In its March 31 report the Public Works Committee radically changed the standards provision. HEW's final authority was abandoned. Now each state would be required to file notice of intent to accept standards. If it failed to do so, it would lose eligibility for federal construction awards. The committee added $50 million for these grants. On April 28, 1965, the House accepted this version 396 to 0.

The developments in the House caused great concern in the White House. Philip S. Hughes of the Bureau of the Budget wrote that the committee report "threatens the President's objectives by deleting authority to establish Federal water quality and by increasing the waste treatment authorization carrot without adding the enforcement improvement stick," a view shared by Budget Director Kermit Gordon. Wilbur Cohen of HEW called the result a *"very weak ineffectual* bill which carries with it none of the President's recommendations."

Since the houses differed so fundamentally, it took the conference nearly five months to reach a compromise. Muskie and the administration held out for a restoration of federal authority and won. The state would have the first crack at fixing quality standards for its interstate waterways. If it failed to act or set inadequate standards by June 30, 1967, HEW would determine its standards. The conference also increased the appropriation for sewage treatment plants from $100 to $150 million. A Water Pollution Control Administration under a new assistant secretary of HEW would administer the program.

Both houses approved the conference report on September 21, the House 379 to 0 and the Senate by voice vote. The President signed the Water Quality Act of 1965 in the White House on October 2, 1965. He pointed out that two centuries earlier George Washington had stood on his lawn at Mt. Vernon and had looked down on a Potomac that was "clean and sweet and pure." Theodore Roosevelt swam in the river. "But today the Potomac is a river of decaying sewage and rotten algae. . . . All the swimmers are gone." He promised that "we are going to reopen the Potomac for swimming by 1975." Not so. Larry O'Brien observed in 1986: "As we sit here that hasn't been fulfilled."

Stewart Udall, no mean bureaucratic infighter, had watched these legislative developments with keen interest. While Congress, the administration, and HEW saw water and air pollution as a public health question, he viewed them as natural resource issues. He wanted to take over the new water agency and the small HEW air program that would soon be expanded. Water was a big issue in the currently dry Northeast and he already had a small desalinization program in Interior. Both Udall and the President were interested in a river basin program which would treat water as a resource, including cleaning up the basins.

Udall moved a month and a half before the water bill was signed. He discussed reorganization with Joe Califano, who handled domestic issues in the White House, and with Charles Schultze, the new director of the budget. On September 2, 1965, he wrote the President, "Our Great Society goals will be achieved by new laws, by appropriations, by reorganization, and by crusading leadership." Water and air pollution required the last two. They demanded *a reorganization to put the various programs under a single Cabinet officer, prepared to give crusading leadership on this issue.* Secretary John Gardner of HEW provided this leadership on Medicare and education. Water and air, however, are at the "heart of our paramount program interests here." Udall suggested a trade: he might agree to transfer to HEW the Bureau of Indian Affairs' jurisdiction over education on the reservations.

Califano suggested that the President wait until HEW had picked the new assistant secretary. Udall, he wrote, was the "most enthusiastic" member of the cabinet, and that has "advantages." He asked the President for authorization to discuss the matter with Udall. Johnson approved and scribbled, "I think without any info Udall is right."

Udall told Gardner of his plan to convert Interior into a department of natural resources in which water pollution would be a central feature in the proposed federal-state river basin system. Gardner had no interest in releasing the new water agency or in getting the Indian education jurisdiction. Udall went ahead with a bill to launch the river basin plan, including transfer of the water agency.

In response to a request from Califano, Gardner set forth his objections. Interior had "close working relationships" with the oil and mining industries, which were "major" polluters. This could be a "built-in conflict of interest." By contrast, HEW's "only clientele is people rather than interest groups." Interior's Bureau of Reclamation was the "major governmental polluter of water." Water pollution had a significant health side and the water agency should be close to others responsible for public health. HEW was where water pollution "grew up." The Indian transfer, Gardner wrote, "deserves more careful study than I can give it at this time."

Schultze had a laundry list of six "reservations" about the reorganization. But, as Califano privately informed the President, his "main problem is that he thinks John Gardner is more competent than Stew Udall." On this Califano disagreed.

Lee White of the White House staff and Udall went to see Muskie, the former to sound him out, the latter to win his support. But the senator, after very serious consideration, opposed the reorganization. Perhaps it would work out in the long run, but it should not be undertaken now.

Getting the Water Quality Act through Congress, Muskie wrote, had been a "long and sometimes bitter struggle." Now, only a few months later, the President is asked to "dismantle and transfer" the program "before it has been fully established." During the debate he had to "reassure the critics" that a move to Interior was not contemplated. State and county officials, mayors, and business would oppose the transfer. It would disrupt administration and prevent the development of new ideas. "The important thing is for us to maintain the momentum of existing public interest while we move toward those changes. . . ." Muskie told Califano, "The Interior Department is western oriented and the most serious pollution problems are in the east." He said he would hold hearings on the question. Califano warned the President that Muskie "is not a demagoging Senator and will oppose it with a great deal of intelligence and experience in this field."

Nevertheless, Johnson came down on Udall's side. Califano may have been speaking for the President when he wrote:

> My own personal view—which may be an oversimplified one—is that the Water Pollution Administration should be moved to Interior. It is similar to the views of the vast majority of Senators and Congressmen [including the leadership in both houses] contacted have expressed—namely, that all water functions eventually are going to go to one place, and that Udall would obviously give much more time and energy to this problem, which is an urgent one, than Secretary Gardner, who has staggering problems in administering billions of dollars of new money and getting HEW in shape.

The water pollution control reorganization was prepared by the Bureau of the Budget, edited by Califano, and certified for legality by the Department of Justice. The President submitted it to the Congress on March 1, 1966. It would become effective after 60 days unless a majority of either house disapproved. Neither acted and the transfer took effect automatically. Udall, delighted, wrote Johnson, *"This is the most significant action taken by any President to enlarge Interior's mission since the Department was created in 1849."*

Senator Muskie became convinced that the $150 million for matching grants for sewage treatment plants was grossly inadequate. He held hearings during 1965 to determine the needs and in January 1966 came up with a figure of $6 billion over five years. The President, concerned about the rising cost of the Vietnam War, was alarmed and offered $50 million a year. Muskie then reduced his figure to $3.35 billion over five years and won approval of both houses. Johnson, after considering a veto, signed the Clean Water Reclamation Act on November 3, 1966.

As Muskie had predicted, the trauma over the transfer of the water agency and the battle over construction funds impaired the administration of the Water Quality Act. But it was only one of several reasons for a miserable performance.

Uniformed officers of the Public Health Service form a career service rather like the Coast Guard. By the time the water agency was transferred to Interior, all had resigned to stay with Public Health. Thus, Interior had to recruit a whole new staff. James Quigley, the man HEW chose to head the new program and who remained in charge at Interior, was incompetent. He was a lame duck congressman from Pennsylvania who spent much of his time with his old cronies on the Hill and who knew nothing about water and cared less. He is said never to have spoken to his most dedicated subordinate, Murray Stein, who headed enforcement. Quigley hung on till 1968 when Udall replaced him with Joe Moore, the head of the Texas Water Quality Board, a water expert and an accomplished administrator. Moore said that when he came in "the entire organization was demoralized, the staff was shell-shocked." Almost three years had been wasted.

Setting standards, the heart of the law, was extremely complex. A decision had to be made on the number of parts per million of a particular chemical that was dangerous to health. There was virtually no prior research and there were thousands of chemicals, making the process slow, laborious, and costly. Industries and municipalities often challenged the standards, thereby drawing out the process. By the demise of the Johnson administration, only the standards of Georgia and Indiana had been fully approved, while those of Oregon, New York, Alabama, South Dakota, and Ohio had gained partial acceptance. This was not because the standards were high. They rarely called for secondary sewage treatment and there were no criteria for salinity and thermal pollution.

Enforcement was a disaster. For the 20 years of the abatement program only one case had gone to court, an action requiring St. Joseph, Missouri, to stop dumping raw sewage into the Missouri River and to build a treatment plant with connecting sewers. The city defied the federal court and the citizens twice voted down the issuance of bonds. By 1973 it had built only a primary, but not a necessary secondary treatment plant and an inadequate sewage system.

The risks were dramatically highlighted by the *Torrey Canyon* disaster in March 1967. The tanker split open in the English Channel and poured oil on the French coast, with American television viewers watching in gruesome horror. In fact, oil spills were common. In 1966 an unloading tanker had dropped from 500 to 1200 barrels of crude into the York River in Virginia, fouling the stream for ten miles. In the summer of 1967 about 30 miles of the Cape Cod coast was contaminated by oil slicks from an unknown source. The 1967 presidential task force reported, "The potential pollution sources include tankers, barges and water transport in general; offshore oil operations; pipelines; and waste oils from gasoline service stations and other sources." The Water Quality Act did not even cover such events, a tribute to the lobbying muscle of Big Oil.

Another loophole was intrastate waterways, which were exempted from the law. Many were as polluted as their interstate sisters. The 1966 task force recommended drafting a model state law with encouragement to the states to adopt it. Nothing happened.

Another problem that neither the administration nor Congress had even addressed was the effluent fee, that is, the requirement that the polluter pay for the damage he caused rather than saddling the cost on the taxpayer. The effluent fee was widely used in Europe, notably in Germany, France, and the Netherlands, and Canada was moving in the same direction. The 1965 task force headed by Gardner Ackley, the chairman of CEA, had made a special report urging an effluent fee for the U.S. and had even outlined a legislative proposal. The polluter would have to pay both for the costs of cleanup and for administration. The income would be used for pollution abatement. A case study of the Delaware River showed that it would produce "considerably lower total costs of treatment than conventional approaches." Yet no proposal for an effluent fee was made.

Senator Muskie, concerned about enforcement problems, submitted a list of 13 improvements and, as Terry Davies of the Bureau of the Budget wrote, "clobbered us." Davies selected three of the 13 for possible action: extending federal jurisdiction to all navigable rivers, authorizing the Attorney General to seek an injunction when there was a threat to public health, and requiring the registration of effluents. His memorandum found its way into a White House file, where its slumber was undisturbed.

Nevertheless, there was a fair amount of voluntary compliance by both industry and municipalities, for the latter especially in New York state. Lake Erie was slowly being cleaned up, in part because the Canadians insisted. Industry, particularly, steel and pulp and paper, made investments in cleanup equipment. The federal matching grant system gradually increased the number of municipalities with treatment facilities. But because of the war, only a fraction of the authorized federal funds was actually appropriated. In fiscal 1968 only $203 million of $450 million was appropriated and in 1969 just $225 of $700 million.

Thus, the Water Quality Act of 1965 was little more than a halting first step. It would require repeated amendment to improve its scope and effectiveness. The credit for its passage goes primarily to Edmund Muskie. The White House helped, but not much. Stewart Udall's dream of a department of natural resources was frustrated. In fact, after he left office in January 1969, the Nixon administration's new Environmental Protection Agency took the water program away from Interior.[6]

The Los Angeles basin is rimmed on the north and the east by a semicircle of mountains and is open to the sea on the west and the south. The prevailing winds during the day are off the Pacific, usually gentle, and they push the air slowly up against the mountain barrier. The basin is often subjected to temperature inversion, that, is, the lower layer of air, from 600 to 1200 feet in height, is cooler than the air above it. Since the lower stratum contains gases, smoke, fumes, and particulates, it is more dense than the higher and, therefore, cannot escape by rising. Thus, the lower layer sits at the foot of the San Gabriel Mountains waiting for the reverse winds of night to move it out to sea.

The towns at the base of the San Gabriels, including Pasadena, suffered a severe deterioration in the quality of their air after World War II. Because it was thought to be a combination of smoke and fog, it came to be called "smog." Dramatic episodes of true smog, including sulphur, in 1948 had attracted wide attention. A six-day siege in Donora, Pennsylvania, caused 20 deaths and 6000 cases of illness, followed shortly by a massive event in London that killed 800 people. Even after it became clear that smoke and fog, though present over Los Angeles, were not the main cause of its air problem, the word smog stuck.

One of Pasadena's proudest monuments is the California Institute of Technology, a world-renowned center for science and engineering. In the late forties A. J. Haagen-Smit was a professor of biochemistry at Caltech who worked on food flavors. Like other residents of Pasadena, he observed and was irritated by the ambient smog and grew curious about its chemical makeup and its effects upon life forms. He began to use his sophisticated laboratory equipment to determine the constituents of smog, an extremely complex undertaking.

In 1950 Haagen-Smit reported his preliminary findings, followed by a technical analysis of smog in 1952. The air above the Los Angeles basin on a bad day was a huge chemical garbage can full of numerous chemicals and their reaction products, many harmful to life. The symptoms he investigated were a decrease in visibility, crop damage, eye irritation, objectionable odor, and rubber deterioration. The key problem was the very large quantities of hydrocarbons and nitrogen oxides in the atmosphere. Sunlight caused the oxides to react with the hydrocarbons to produce ozone. Haagen-Smit's experiments demonstrated that these chemicals accounted for all the symptoms. Hydrocarbons in petroleum products, harmless themselves, when transformed into new compounds by photochemical action triggered by sunlight, "should be considered toxic materials." He also found a number of metal compounds which evaporated from oil refineries, service stations, and cars, which burned only part of the contents of their fuel tanks. This fitted the historic fact that smog in the basin had become much worse as the number of cars and trucks had mushroomed after the war.

Haagen-Smit's findings had no immediate impact upon policy in either California or the U.S. The oil industry and car manufacturers did their best to deflect regulation, and the prevailing view at the federal level was that air pollution was a local problem. The 1955 law enacted by Congress provided $5 million annually for research by the Public Health Service and explicitly passed by regulation. Some of the research money was farmed out to California institutions. During the fifties it became evident that Los Angeles, while the worst case, was hardly unique, that every city with a heavy concentration of cars suffered from smog.

The public health studies confirmed Haagen-Smit's findings and were summarized by Secretary of HEW Abraham Ribicoff on August 7, 1961: "Adverse effects from motor vehicle air pollution have been specifically identified in approximately half of the States and the District of Columbia." They had been identified in "all metropolitan areas" and in many rural districts within more than 100 miles of major cities. The incriminated pollutants were those Haagen-Smit had identified a decade earlier: hydrocarbons, oxides of nitrogen, carbon monoxide, lead, and sulfur dioxide. In sunlight hydrocarbons and oxides of nitrogen formed a number of "toxic and irritating substances," including ozone. "Unless corrected, . . . air pollution will inevitably increase." The auto population was 70 million in 1961 and was expected to grow to 90 to 100 million by 1970.

These cars ran on extremely inefficient gasoline engines which emitted unburned gasoline in large quantities at three points: the tailpipe exhaust supplied 50 to 60 percent of the effluents, crankcase ventilation (blowby) constituted 30 to 40 percent, and evaporation from fuel tanks and carburetors provided 15 to 25 percent. The quantity of lead in fuel additives had not been determined.

The end of the fifties witnessed a significant political shift in California and the nation. Under Republican Governor Goodwin Knight, California had supported research but had left action to local governments, which did nothing. Despite opposition from the Public Health Service, HEW Secretary Arthur Flemming urged some movement toward regulation. But President Eisenhower insisted that there was no federal problem. In January 1959 Democrat Pat Brown became the governor of California and in January 1961 Kennedy became President. Brown moved quickly, while Kennedy hesitated until 1963. Meantime, Flemming and the American Medical Association proposed federal abatement authority over interstate air pollution. In December 1962 Wilbur Cohen, HEW's assistant secretary over legislation, convinced Kennedy that he could not stand to the right of Republican Flemming and the AMA. The President finally offered legislation in February 1963. Thus, California led the nation.

In 1959 the state Department of Public Health had established three levels of uniform standards throughout the state: "adverse," "serious," and "emergency." They were set for the worst case, Los Angeles County, and would apply only to blowby. In 1960 the legislature enacted the Motor Vehicle Pollution Control Act. A new board would fix criteria for blowby devices, test them, and issue certificates of approval for those that passed.

In 1961 new cars sold in California were fitted with blowby systems. Though hardly a comprehensive system of controls, the state had taken a significant first step.

The Clean Air Act of 1963, proposed by Kennedy and signed by Johnson, was, in the words of James E. Krier and Edmund Ursin, "more bark than bite." It was a compromise between the mayors and the conservationists urging the exercise of federal power and industry and the states opposing it. The research program was expanded and HEW was to develop air quality standards. But the abatement authority could not be taken seriously because it was patterned after that in the hapless water program. HEW was instructed, as well, to encourage the auto and oil industries to develop emission devices to recapture escaping gasoline.

No one was more aware of the deficiencies in the Clean Air Act than Senator Muskie. Between January and June 1964 his subcommittee went on a highly publicized nationwide tour, holding hearings in Los Angeles, Denver, Chicago, Boston, New York, Tampa, and Washington. The subcommittee listened to governors, mayors, pollution officials, industry, and conservationists on a broad range of air pollution problems. In October 1964 it published a masterful report, *Steps Toward Clean Air,* which would provide the basis for Muskie's 1965 bill.

There were two fundamental findings: the problem of the nation's degraded air was of the utmost gravity, and, while it occurred locally, it was nationwide in scope and demanded uniformity of treatment. The report identified five problems that called for legislation—exhaust emissions from gasoline-powered motor vehicles, exhaust emissions from diesel-powered vehicles, solid waste disposal, establishment of a federal air pollution control laboratory, and the combustion of coal and fuel oil, which emitted oxides of sulfur. In addition, the subcommittee recommended that HEW draft model state laws and municipal ordinances and that the President name a committee to examine pollution from jet aircraft, rocket and missile testing, and experimental fuels.

The exhausts from gasoline engines on 82.5 million cars, trucks, and buses accounted for half the air pollution in the U.S., annually more than 14 million tons of hydrocarbons, 4 million of oxides of nitrogen, and in excess of 75 million of carbon monoxide. Measured by auto density per square mile, Los Angeles at 1,350 was surpassed by Chicago at 1,541, Detroit 1,580, New York 2,220, Philadelphia 3,730, and Washington 4,100. Los Angeles, the only city with a moderately serious abatement program, did nothing yet to reduce exhaust emissions. California law stated that new cars must have exhaust devices for the 1966 model year. Used cars would be fitted with them when registered. The subcommittee urged federal legislation to impose California standards on the nation for exhaust controls and blowby devices as well as state inspection of emission devices.

There were many fewer diesel engines on trucks, buses, and utility vehicles. While they could be made to burn cleanly, operators increased power by feeding more fuel, creating characteristic black diesel smoke. The subcommittee proposed that HEW issue diesel standards.

Growing population and ballooning consumption were producing immense quantities of solid waste, in the cities 500 million pounds daily. It was either burned, creating air pollution, or dumped into unsanitary open pits, which required a huge expanding area for landfills. Almost none of the cities had modern disposal systems. The subcommittee proposed federal financial assistance for municipalities for clean incinerators and sanitary landfills.

Since so little was yet known about air pollution, the subcommittee urged the establishment of a research laboratory in HEW that would be devoted exclusively to that problem.

Much of the coal and fuel oil burned in the U.S. for power generation and heating had a high sulfur content, releasing gases over the entire country that were both a danger to health and an economic burden. Methods of removing sulfur, sometimes converting it into salable sulfuric acid, were available, but the coal, oil, and power industries had shown no interest. The subcommittee urged HEW to draft model laws for states and cities to deal with this problem.

On January 7, 1965, Muskie introduced S. 306 with 20 cosponsors incorporating these recommendations. Once again he caught the Johnson administration by surprise. In his special message on conservation and beauty on February 8, the President referred vaguely to solid waste, but stressed junk cars because of Lady Bird's interest in beautification. He continued, "I intend to institute discussions with industry officials and other interested groups leading to an effective elimination or substantial reduction of pollution from liquid fueled motor vehicles." This seems to have been a rekindling of his old senatorial preference for bargaining by "reasoning together." It may also have reflected his debt to Henry Ford II, the most obstinate of the car manufacturers, for having supported the tax cut and his 1964 presidential campaign.

Muskie held hearings April 6 to 9, 1965, which exposed administration confusion. New HEW Assistant Secretary Quigley led off by saying that S. 306 was premature, that there already was adequate federal authority, and that legislation should await the completion of research. Muskie gasped in amazement and some of the nation's leading newspapers denounced the "love affair" between Johnson and the auto industry. Quigley returned shortly with new marching orders. He now testified that both the administration and HEW agreed that new legislation was "appropriate" and that they wanted to work "hand and glove" with the subcommittee.

Despite his promise, Johnson did not meet with the auto executives. Rather, the administration moved in on the Senate Public Works Committee, which on May 14, 1965, reported out a watered-down S. 306. Explicit crankcase and exhaust emission standards were replaced with discretionary authority for HEW to set standards. The deadline for their issuance was moved from November 1, 1966, to September 1, 1967, that is, on 1968 rather than on 1967 models. But HEW meant business. According to R. W. Markley, Jr., the Ford lobbyist, Wilbur Cohen had written to Muskie that HEW had "every intention of requiring the exhaust controls on 1968 model cars." But grants to municipalities for construction of solid waste disposal facilities were converted into a research program. Mandatory state inspection of cars was abandoned as was the modest proposal to deal with sulfur. The Senate on May 18 passed this truncated S. 306 by voice vote.

Now that the knives were unsheathed, the House Interstate and Foreign Commerce Committee continued cutting away in its report on August 31, 1965. The 1967 emissions deadline was removed and the secretary was authorized to issue standards "as soon as practicable" after allowing the industry time to comply voluntarily. The research laboratory was eliminated. What little was left of S. 306 passed the House on September 24 by a 294 to 4 vote. The Senate accepted the House version by voice vote on October 1. The auto pollution provisions became Title II of the 1963 Clean Air Act and the others went into a new Solid Waste Disposal Act. The President signed this "hopeful beginning" on October 20, 1965. He said, "This act will require all 1968 model automobiles—including foreign models that are sold here—to meet Federal control standards for exhaust."

The original Muskie bill had been stripped of all its teeth except for one: the discretionary authority of Secretary Gardner to fix emission standards. He told the industry flatly that he would act on 1968 models. General Motors, Chrysler, and several smaller firms accepted the inevitable, but Ford balked. Markley proposed a "compromise" to Henry Hall Wilson in the White House on December 17, 1965. California already had standards and New York and New Jersey were moving "aggressively" in the same direction. Ford would supply cars with emission devices in those states alone on 1968 models. It would add them to all its cars in model year 1969, assuming HEW's testing showed that "control devices will be effective on a national basis and will not impair vehicle performance." The compromise was not accepted. Cohen said that "Ford was complaining because its device was more costly than [those of] the other manufacturers."

The HEW standards, patterned after those of California, were published in the *Federal Register* on March 29, 1966. They required that all 1968 model standard cars be equipped with both blowby and exhaust devices. Vehicles with very small engines, motorcycles, and commercial automobiles under half a ton were exempted. The standards applied to only two important pollutants—hydrocarbons and carbon monoxide.

For Senator Muskie this was a significant gain for which he had paid a heavy price. By 1965 it was clear to him that the regulation of air pollution, if it came at all, would progress in stages, a gradual advance with a new law whenever the politics allowed. In one sense Muskie had time on his side because air conditions were growing worse and the public's patience was wearing thin. But with the next law, the President and his men vowed, they would not be beaten off the starting blocks by the senator from Maine.[7]

In 1966 Joe Califano established a high-level administration Task Force on the Quality of the Environment, with Gardner Ackley in charge. Califano suggested several broad environmental issues, starting with air pollution. He wrote Ackley, "We hope to develop, with your help, a vigorous and imaginative program for consideration by the first session of the 90th Congress."

Between 1963 and 1966 the public had become much more concerned about air pollution. An earlier impression that smog was just another nutty problem confined to Los Angeles was displaced by recognition that it was of national scope and demanded federal action. Thomas J. Watson, Jr., the head of IBM, wrote the President that he did a great deal of flying and was appalled by the contaminated air that enveloped the cities. Johnson agreed. Over the Thanksgiving holiday in 1966 New York City suffered a four-day catastrophe.

"The atmosphere of New York," John C. Esposito wrote, "was bombarded with more man-made contaminants than any other big city in the country—almost two pounds of soot and noxious gases for every man, woman, and child. So great is the burden of pollution that were it not for the prevailing wind, New York City might have gone the way of Sodom and Gomorrah." Hospitals reported a dramatic increase in deaths from pulmonary emphysema and chronic bronchitis. During the episode an air inversion trapped 16 million people inside a blanket of foul air. An estimated 80 persons died and thousands of others became severely ill.

Both the Johnson administration and Congress recognized that existing legislation was grossly inadequate and that a new policy was needed. The task force in its report on November 21, 1966, defined six major problems:

1. The new exhaust devices, unless maintained, lost their effectiveness within a short period. The requirements for 1968 models did not apply to older models, much the larger part of the nation's fleet. The states should be required and assisted to inspect all vehicles annually.
2. Motor fuel additives, particularly lead, should be registered with HEW and the secretary should be authorized to forbid any "found to be harmful to health."
3. In the case of an episode that presents "a clear and present danger to public health" the Attorney General should seek an injunction allowing entry and inspection of any facility emitting contaminants. HEW should have the authority to shut it down by "summary order."

4. HEW should establish "minimum standards of pollution control for selected classes of industries." The states should be required to meet those standards and, if they failed to do so, the federal criteria should apply automatically.
5. "Air pollution does not recognize nor respect political boundaries." Big cities exported their foul air to adjoining states: New York City to Connecticut and New Jersey, Chicago to Indiana and Wisconsin, and so on. The Clean Air Act had offered a financial incentive for interstate compacts, but there had been no takers. The task force recommended that HEW establish "air sheds" with mixed federal-state commissions to impose federal standards.
6. Finally, there were several presently intractable problems that required intensive research: exhaust devices for diesel engines, alternative propulsion systems (electric cars) that made no pollution, and a sulfur-free fuel for generating electricity and for space heating. The task force urged a sharp increase in funding for this research.

The estimates for all six programs over five years would rise from $18.5 million in fiscal 1968 to $156 million in 1972. The total would be $500 million.

This was pretty strong stuff. Would Lyndon Johnson and the Congress accept these heavy remedies?

On January 17, 1967, Califano wrote the President that he had "a very constructive talk with Senator Muskie . . . . He will support our clean air program vigorously and would like to hold hearings in Washington on February 8. . . ." Muskie gave him a "feeling stone," evidently a good-luck charm, that he wanted Califano to present to Johnson. By 1967 Lyndon Johnson needed all the luck he could get.

On January 30, 1967, the President sent a special message to Congress, "Protecting Our National Heritage," with air pollution leading off. He pointed to the New York disaster and noted that smaller cities, like Weirton, West Virginia, and Gary, Indiana, both steel towns, were also afflicted. "This situation does not exist because it was inevitable, nor because it cannot be controlled. Air pollution is the inevitable consequence of neglect. It can be controlled when that neglect is no longer tolerated." He proposed a bill that followed the task force recommendations with two significant omissions. HEW would register fuel additives, but it would have no authority to ban those harmful to health; the Attorney General would have no power to seek an injunction and the secretary would not be allowed to shut down a polluting facility. Muskie introduced the administration bill, S. 780, on January 31.

His subcommittee held hearings between February 8 and May 18 in Los Angeles, Detroit, Denver, and St. Louis. In Los Angeles he learned that exhaust controls supposed to be effective for 50,000 miles failed after 5,000. The auto industry in Detroit said that it now accepted federal regulation and Muskie sighed with relief. Surgeon General W. H. Stewart testified that Public Health studies demonstrated a direct connection between air pollution and health in general as well as with particular diseases. He painted, in his words, "a disturbing portrait of a major health menace." It was "imperative to clean the air." But Democratic Senator Jennings Randolph of West Virginia, whose state lived off coal, worried about the regulation of sulfur in the burning of bituminous. The coal, oil, and steel industries backed him.

Meantime, Secretary Gardner imposed fuel tank and carburetor standards on 1969 model cars. Over strong opposition from the coal industry, he published the first report on sulfur oxides, which pointed a finger straight at coal and oil. He imposed restrictions on sulfur dioxide emissions at federal installations in New York, Chicago, and Philadelphia. Secretary Udall changed oil import policy to make low-sulfur crude available. Oil coming in from Venezuela was hopelessly high in sulfur content.

Muskie's hearings and these policy changes caused deep concern, if not fear, among the captains of American industry. The chief executives of the Pennsylvania Railroad, Standard Oil of New Jersey and California, Continental Oil, General Motors, Ford, Chrysler, U.S. Steel, the Iron and Steel Institute, Union Carbide, Du Pont, American Electric Power, and Consolidation Coal banded together. They wanted to join with the government in a vast research and demonstration project on air pollution. They engaged Leon Jaworski, a prominent Texas attorney, to represent them.

He met with Gardner, who rather favored the idea, and with Califano, who was more cautious and asked the Department of Justice for an antitrust opinion. On May 31, 1967, Edwin M. Zimmerman of the Antitrust Division sent over a negative report. "Technological breakthroughs are best achieved by having several independent sources of innovation." When a whole industry works cooperatively, the most progressive member will be held back until the least was ready. A joint venture of this size would inhibit smaller players from entering the game. Finally, there was "no conceivable justification" for blessing a venture of this magnitude. "There can be no scale economies, no need for funds, no need for complementary technologies, etc. which warrants anything like a pooling together of the research activities of the companies here involved."

Nevertheless, Califano was of two minds. While there were serious obstacles, he wrote the President on May 31, "I believe there is a way to work out the problems." But Johnson did not want to get involved. He wrote, "Keep this away from W.H. [White House]. Let Udall do this if he and [Attorney General] Clark agree it is desirable." In effect that killed the Jaworski proposal. Gardner and Cohen did meet with the industry leaders on August 17, and, after a pep talk from the secretary, Cohen wrote the President, the executives "pledged their cooperation to work with the Government," whatever that might mean.

When Muskie's subcommittee met on April 6 to draw up its report, Chairman Randolph of the parent Public Works Committee was ready with a laundry list of amendments. Muskie and Randolph argued for more than three months before they reached agreement on July 15 and put the amended S. 780 through the full committee. Randolph had significantly weakened the bill: Authority for HEW to fix national standards for industry was replaced by state control with federal intervention only if a state after 15 months had declined to set criteria. HEW was empowered to seek an injunction only in the case of an emergency which created an "imminent and substantial" danger to public health. Research on fuel combustion would be encouraged by an appropriation of $375 million over five years. California, which had higher automobile standards than the federal government, was exempted from the controls. Once again the administration had lost control over the legislation.

The Senate adopted the amended S. 780 on July 18, 1967, by an amazing roll-call vote of 88 to 0. No senator from either party proposed an amendment. Randolph was lavish in his praise for Muskie and called the bill the most significant pollution abatement measure in the nation's history, which, clearly, it was. Republican John Sherman Cooper of Kentucky said he had "never seen . . . a better demonstration of the Committee legislative process." He commended Muskie, Randolph, and the ranking minority member of the subcommittee, J. Caleb Boggs of Delaware. Majority Leader Mansfield was pleased by the nonpartisanship.

The House Interstate and Foreign Commerce Committee, of which Harley Staggers of West Virginia was chairman, held hearings between August 15 and 24 and listened to substantially the same testimony the Senate subcommittee had heard. The committee adopted the Senate bill with these changes: elimination of the research program on fuel combustion, reduction of the total appropriation, and removal of the California exemption. This last was proposed by John D. Dingell of Michigan on behalf of the car industry, which wanted all autos sold in the U.S. to be identically equipped. The two California members issued a stinging dissent.

In the floor debate on November 2 the Californians reinserted the exemption for their state. Unanimity now ruled. Not to be outdone, the House adopted S. 780 by a vote of 362 to 0.

In the conference Muskie restored $125 million for fuel combustion research with what he described as "mathematical gyrations." In fact, Secretary Gardner had already gained Budget Bureau approval for a $17.7 million appropriation for sulfur research on removal of the chemical prior to combustion as well as on cleaning up smokestack gases. Gardner thought this would help him with Muskie, Randolph, and Staggers. On November 14 both houses accepted the conference report without debate.

The signing ceremony for the Air Quality Act of 1967 took place at the White House on November 21, 1967. The President gave a weather report: " 'Dirty water and black snow pour from the dismal air to . . . the putrid slush that waits for them below.' Now that is not a description of Boston, Chicago, New York, or even Washington, D.C. It is from Dante's Inferno." He doffed his hat to the man from Maine. "Senator Muskie has been shoving me as no other person has, all these years, to do something in the pollution field." Muskie had kept reminding him that until now we had taken only "baby steps." Now "we grow up to our responsibilities." The President also praised Secretary Gardner. He might have added Ackley's task force for its splendid report.

While the Air Quality Act of 1967 was certainly a large step forward compared with its predecessors, there was still an enormous distance to go. The law proved cumbersome, slow, difficult to administer, and, like the earlier statutes, required amendment within a few years. On the day before the President signed it the population of the U.S. reached 200 million. This rapid increase in the number of people was accompanied by a sharp rise in the number of factories, mines, and automobiles spewing contaminants into the atmosphere. Thus, clean air was a game of continuous elusive catchup. So long as industry, with its great political power, resisted abatement controls, the goal of clean air would never be reached.[8]

As a child in Karnack in east Texas the girl who became Lady Bird Johnson fell in love with nature, a passion she would never abandon. "Some of the most memorable hours I've ever spent," she said many years later, "have been in the out-of-doors, communing with nature and reveling in the scenic beauty which abounds." On her seventieth birthday in 1982 she would give 60 acres of land east of Austin and $125,000 to launch the National Wildflower Research Center.

First Lady is not a federal office described in the Constitution. But it is a position of great prominence and its incumbent and her husband, the President, can make of it whatever they like. As Lyndon Johnson idolized Franklin Roosevelt, Lady Bird Johnson revered Eleanor Roosevelt. But their styles differed so markedly that she could hardly emulate her illustrious predecessor. In her careful and cautious manner, Lady Bird pursued a role as First Lady.

In August 1964 she and Stewart Udall made a tour of the Rocky Mountain West. She dedicated the Flaming Gorge Dam, visited several Indian reservations, and made speeches supporting the reelection of Democratic Senators Gale McGee of Wyoming and Frank Moss of Utah. James Reston, Jr., of Udall's staff, wrote the speeches and they stressed conservation. Best of all, she had long easy talks with Udall in which they shared an enthusiasm for the natural beauty of the country and the need to preserve it. She found him a mother lode of information about the West.

Lady Bird was moving toward "beautification," a word nobody liked. She and Udall found it distasteful. Carpenter wrote that it was "too dainty." Critics used it derisively to imply superficiality, cosmetics, and, worst of all, femininization, that is, something that was all right only for women. The word raised unpleasant memories of the City Beautiful movement at the turn of the century, which had been drummed out of existence by the criticism of architects and city planners. But the search for a better word came up empty.

In November 1964 the Task Force on Natural Beauty urged the President to launch a national program for beautification—highway landscaping, regulation of billboards, rehabilitation of parks, and so on. It recommended a White House conference on "America the Beautiful." Mrs. Johnson read the report with enthusiasm. In fact, she had already been planning to work on the beautification of the city of Washington and the nation's highways.

The President was her staunchest supporter. In his State of the Union message on January 4, 1965, he asked for a "substantial effort . . . to landscape highways." He called for the beauty conference a month later.

Laurance Rockefeller was chairman and his staff worked out the program. While these people meant well, according to Elizabeth Drew, they "lacked the savvy to deal with the politics of beauty." Their main accomplishment was to publish an almost unreadable 782 pages of proceedings. Eight hundred delegates gathered in Washington on May 24–25, 1965, and 15 panels discussed a wide variety of topics, mainly in unmemorable generalities. One participant told Drew that it was a "kind of shambles" and many left "mad." The panel on roadside control, however, was significant.

In 1956 Congress had authorized construction of the immense 41,000 mile Interstate Highway System. Though prior road laws had provided for a 50–50 split of the cost between the federal government and the states, now the federal share jumped to 90 percent. The new Highway Trust Fund provided the program with an assured source of income. All federal taxes on cars, trucks, buses, gasoline, diesel fuel, motor oil, tires, and automotive equipment poured into the trust fund.

Because of its size, long life, and guaranteed income, the system was called by some the biggest pork barrel in the history of the Republic, a prize that was guarded by an extraordinary interconnected series of powerful lobbies. The interstates would cross all 50 states and 406 of the 435 congressional districts. The Public Works Committees of both houses were so solicitous of the system that they were said to be willing to authorize pouring concrete over the entire land surface of the nation, including Alaska, if asked to do so. In 1965 Jennings Randolph of West Virginia was chairman of both the Senate committee and its subcommittee on roads. He had been treasurer of the American Road Builders Association for ten years before being elected to the Senate. On the House side committee chairman George H. Fallon of Maryland was the author of the Highway Trust Fund and he,

John C. Kluczynski of Illinois, chairman of the roads subcommittee, and William C. Cramer of Florida, the ranking Republican on both committees, were very close to the road builders. The American Association of State Highway Departments and the National Association of Counties opposed the use of trust fund money for anything but road construction.

The private lobbies were formidable: the contractors, the road builders, the asphalt and concrete industries, the auto, truck, bus, petroleum, and tire industries, hotels, motels, filling stations, and other roadside businesses. At the end of the list came the notorious debeautifiers—the billboard industry represented by the Outdoor Advertising Association and its clever lobbyist, Philip Tocker, along with the auto junkyard and scrap metal industries.

The groups that supported beautification could hardly be called lobbies: Road Councils in a few states and the Garden Clubs, both dominated by women. The mainline conservation organizations, like the Sierra Club and the Wilderness Society, did not consider beautification a conservation issue. Further weakening support was the fact that the Commerce Department rather than Interior was in charge of legislation because it included the Bureau of Public Roads.

Since Lyndon Johnson had been majority leader at the birth of the interstates and the Highway Trust Fund, he was fully aware of this grotesque imbalance of political forces. He must have known that pushing an effective highway beautification bill through Congress was virtually impossible. Nevertheless, he waded in. He wanted to present his wife with what came to be called "Lady Bird's bill." He derived great pleasure from giving the people he loved large showy gifts. In his legislative world the biggest present he could bestow upon anyone was a statute. "You know," he told his staff, "I love that woman and she wants that highway beauty bill. By God, we're going to get it for her."

Outdoor advertising along roads preceded the invention of the automobile, and objections to the clutter went back almost as far. When Congress launched the interstates in 1958, it offered the states bonuses to ban billboards within 660 feet of the highway (90.5 instead of 90 percent of the cost paid by the federal government) and 3 percent of their allotments in the trust fund to buy roadside land to improve scenic beauty. But the incentives flopped. By 1965 only 209 miles of the 41,000 mile system restricted billboards, and the scenic provision was not used at all.

In 1963–64 the Johnson administration and the Outdoor Advertising Association negotiated over the roadsides. The Bureau of Public Roads got nowhere with Tocker. The President put Bill Moyers in charge. Both he and Tocker were Texans, the latter from Waco. Tocker hired Donald S. Thomas, a prominent Austin lawyer who was the personal attorney and friend of both Lyndon and Lady Bird Johnson. It was no contest. While highly intelligent, Moyers was no match for them in expertise or lobbying skill. On the eve of the May 25 meeting of the panel on roadside control the administration caved in.

The panel, except for Tocker, consisted entirely of people who favored the mandatory prohibition of billboards on the interstates. Mrs. Cyril Fox of the Pennsylvania Roadside Council, who had been battling Tocker for years, told the Rockefeller people that he was the "camel's nose in the tent." He proposed what he called an "agreeable surprise," a ban on billboards if industrial and commercial zones were exempted. This, in fact, would have *increased* the number of billboards. The majority preferred not to be surprised and voted for a prohibition on both the interstates and primary roads.

That afternoon members of the majority were startled to hear President Johnson state that both the billboard and junkyard provisions of the bills he was sending up the next day would not apply to commercial or industrial areas. They would have been even more shocked if they had known that Tocker was listening to the President's speech in the White House office of Bill Moyers.

The President proposed four bills on May 26, 1965. The first two would require the states after January 1, 1968, to eliminate billboards and junkyards within 1000 feet of an interstate or primary highway except in industrial and commercial zones. While the states would determine the exempted areas, they must be approved by the Secretary of Commerce. Existing signs and junkyards would have to be removed by July 1, 1970. A state that did not comply would lose its federal aid grant. A state without adequate police power could ask the federal government to pay the cost of purchase or condemnation.

The third bill would require a state to use 3 percent of its allocation from the trust fund for landscaping and rest and recreation sites along the highways. The fourth would compel the state to use one-third of the funds it received for secondary roads for improved access to scenic and recreational areas.

Though these measures were modest, the lobbies immediately opposed them. The Highway Trust Fund, they argued, was a sacred commitment to construction and there must be no alternative use of funds. With more power in the states, the lobbies resisted mandatory federal controls. They wanted the federal government to bear the entire cost of removing signs and junkyards.

These arguments dominated the hearings before the roads subcommittees of both houses in the summer of 1965, and the voices of the ladies of the Roadside Councils and Garden Clubs were barely audible. It seemed that no bill could pass. The committees were ready to fold their tents in late August, when, according to Drew, "word came from the White House that the highway beauty bill was one . . . the President wanted this year, that he had to have this one, it was reported, 'for Lady Bird.' "

The Senate committee proceeded to treat the beautification bill (the four had been consolidated) as though it was peeling an onion layer by layer until little was left except a bad smell. A state rather than the Secretary of

Commerce would determine zoning. If a state had once been eligible for a bonus, it would continue to enjoy it even after relaxing controls. The Highway Trust Fund would pay nothing; all costs would be assessed against the Treasury. The federal government, not the states, would pay compensation. If a state was suspended for noncompliance, there would be no penalty. The use of secondary road funds for scenic improvement was deleted. So much for beautification.

The Senate Public Works Committee adopted this shadow of the bill on September 14, 1965. The administration restored a few minor provisions on the floor and the Senate adopted the bill on September 16 by a vote of 63 to 14. The House bill closely resembled the Senate's.

By late August, Johnson had become frantic over the measure. He told Califano: "Take over the highway beautification bill." Califano soon learned that he had given the same order to Moyers, Valenti, Busby, White, O'Brien, and Commerce Secretary John Conner. Both Johnsons worked the phones relentlessly. "Everyone was involved," O'Brien recalled later. "But I don't know as we involved the fellows in the White House mess." By September 12 chaos reigned and Califano urged Johnson to put O'Brien in charge. The latter informed the President about "our confusion, about our unnecessary harassment of friendly members, and about irritations which can prove damaging with other bills." He pointed his finger at the President, but to no avail.

House debate opened on Thursday afternoon, October 7, a special day. That evening members of the House had been invited to a reception at the Chinese Embassy for Madame Chiang Kai-shek and then to a White House party to celebrate the legislative achievements of the 89th Congress. The representatives' wives that afternoon were seated in the galleries in their evening finery, fuming over the delay. The President demanded a vote that evening on the beautification bill and the Republicans could not resist holding it up until after midnight.

The "debate" is not noted as one of the finest hours in the history of the House. Cramer, a master filibusterer, said, "I resent, and I say it with just as much strength of purpose as I can," the refusal by the Democrats to cross a "t" or dot an "i." "I am for beauty. As a matter of fact, I married one of the most beautiful girls in the world." Cramer intimated that Johnson had voted in 1958 to strike the billboard control provision from the earlier bill because he would have had to take a sign down on Route 290 near Austin advertising the family TV station, KTBC. Was the President twisting arms? "My arm is real sore."

House minority leader Gerald Ford insisted on the Republican right to offer "constructive amendments." Sample by Representative Bob Dole of Kansas, a man who never hesitated to rise in order to deliver a low blow: "Strike out the word 'Secretary' wherever it appears . . . and insert the words 'Lady Bird.' "

The Republicans had their fun and made their point. It was 12:07 a.m. before they finished, by which time the guests at the White House salute had departed. The Democrats then passed the bill 245 to 138, and the Highway Beautification Act was signed on October 22, 1965. The President made the only defense possible: "It is a first step." It would also be the last.

"Much of the fault," Califano wrote, "lay with the President for the one inept legislative experience I witnessed and participated in as a member of his staff." Johnson wished this disaster upon himself by uncharacteristically ignoring the political realities. The committees would gladly have allowed the bill to die. The Bureau of Public Roads had no stomach for the brawl. The White House staff considered the exercise ridiculous and O'Brien thought it politically damaging. Moyers, according to Lewis Gould, "distanced himself from his connection with the billboard organizations and particularly the president of the OAAA, Philip Tocker."

But the troubles had only begun. The administration of the Highway Beautification Act was a disaster. The Outdoor Advertising Association and the Republicans declared war on improving the statute. Regulations proposed by the Department of Commerce on January 28 and July 1, 1966, and on January 16, 1967, were rejected by Congress. Except for compensation for firms that took down signs, it was virtually impossible to obtain funds. By 1978 over $107 million had been paid for billboard removal and the General Accounting Office estimated the ultimate cost at $823 million. Tocker's success in exempting industrial and commercial zones was a master stroke. As Charles F. Floyd and Peter J. Shedd pointed out, "The practical effect of the provision has been to allow billboards in commercial areas where they are totally inharmonious, and also in areas which are almost totally rural in character." The billboard firms cut down trees that blocked the views of their signs. The Highway Beautification Act, Senator Robert T. Stafford of Vermont wrote, became the "Billboard Protection and Compensation Act."

The junkyard program, by contrast, was a modest success. By 1979, some 2,345 noncomplying yards had either been removed or screened and 1,055 illegal yards had been shut down. But there were still 10,608 nonconforming junkyards in operation. Scenic improvements along highways may have done as well.[9]

There was a dramatic change in environmental policies during the sixties. The historic conservation programs—national parks, monuments, rivers, and wilderness—were broadly expanded and improved by the Land and Water Conservation Fund and the Wilderness Act. And now there were also the first efforts to establish controls over the new problems of water and air pollution in the face of formidable industry opposition. "From beginning to end," Krier and Ursin wrote, "pollution policy in the years up to 1970 was made by a process of least steps taken down the path of least resistance—

steps, that is, quite consciously designed to disturb the existing situation as little as possible." How far the nation must still travel was evident in the report of the President's Task Force on the Quality of the Environment of October 1, 1967: "We are just beginning to marshall our forces. No one who has breathed the air in one of our leading cities, dared to swim in one of our great rivers, or been assailed by jet noise overhead, can be complacent about the future." The Highway Beautification Act, which might be called Lyndon Johnson's Folly, is best forgotten.

Another stain fell on Lyndon Johnson's record as conservationist. With Theodore Roosevelt leading the way, most Presidents in the waning days of their terms, as Udall put it, "take lands from the public domain and enlarge the national park system and enlarge the national wildlife refuge system." T.R. in 1905 had established the national forests. Even Herbert Hoover in 1933 had set aside 4 million acres, including Death Valley National Monument.

Udall, acting on this tradition, raised the issue with the President in July 1968. Johnson said, "Go ahead." Udall then got his people at Interior to put together a big package of 7 million acres—three areas in Alaska and two each in Arizona and Utah. Udall himself had authority to sign off on a few of the minor units set aside for Alaskan wildlife refuges, but the President must be responsible for the major ones. Udall assembled an impressive presentation with magnificent photographs. He cleared the idea with a few members of Congress, swearing them to secrecy, but avoided those he knew would oppose, including Wayne Aspinall. He recognized that Johnson liked to touch base in Congress, but warned him "this is the one instance, as you go out the door, you shouldn't care whether congressmen like it or not. The issue is what's good for the country, and . . . they will accept it."

In mid-November Udall made the presentation at the White House. The President had invited Clark Clifford, Charles Murphy, who had been Truman's counsel, and Lady Bird Johnson, who was enthusiastic. Udall said he "came away with the impression that the President wanted to do the whole thing, [but] that he wanted to be satisfied on legal questions." There were none. He began working up the orders and the press releases. His idea was to break the story before Christmas so "the President could . . . announce it as his parting Christmas gift to the American people." But the White House lawyer, DeVier Pierson, kept raising questions about political clearances and the decision was delayed. Since the secretary's own actions required thirty-day notice, he signed the Alaskan refuge orders on December 19.

In early January, Pierson raised a question of Venezuelan oil and mixed it with the public lands proposal. Udall began to feel that he was finished. In the State of the Union message on January 14, 1969, Johnson, after reading that lands had earlier been set aside for the American people, ad-libbed, "and there is more that will be set aside before this administration ends." Udall had required total secrecy and now the President himself had "let the cat out of the bag." Meantime, Nixon had selected Governor Walter J. Hickel of Alaska as his Secretary of the Interior; Hickel was testifying before the congressional committees and was certain to oppose the set-asides; and smart reporters now knew that a big plan was in the works. Congressmen were raising hell and Johnson notified Udall indirectly that he was upset because the secretary had not done his "homework with the members of Congress."

On Friday, January 17, the press broke the story. Johnson phoned immediately and Udall said, "was very unhappy and bawled me out good that he hadn't made a decision and we turned it loose. And I pointed out that he had let the cat out of the bag himself and that we just couldn't hold it all back." Johnson snapped, "Hell of a way to run a department." That was the last time Stewart Udall spoke to Lyndon Johnson.

A few moments later Pierson called Udall and said he knew about his "rough conversation" with the President. He then got down to business. "If you get this Venezuela oil thing worked out, maybe that would get the President back in the right frame of mind and we can get it done this afternoon." Udall blew up and then reluctantly agreed to sign off on oil.

On Inauguration Day, January 20, 1969, the President signed the three smallest orders, a combined total of 300 acres in the Sonoran Desert in Arizona and an enlargement of Mt. McKinley National Park and a new park above the Arctic Circle in Alaska. He stated publicly that the big proposals would "strain" the law and would transgress the right of Congress to review these actions. Among those killed was an order for a million-acre park in southern Arizona in the congressional district Stewart Udall had once represented and the representative for which now was his brother Morris. "The President," Stewart said, "was trying to show me who was boss the last day he was in office. And he did!"

How does one explain Lyndon Johnson's aberrant behavior in this incident? His concerns for "straining" the law, here the obscure Antiquities Act, and congressional prerogatives, make no sense and were, obviously, window-dressing. It is unlikely that he would have soiled an otherwise impeccable record on oil at the last moment by bending to pressure. Much more likely, as Califano thought, it was Udall's decision to name the new District of Columbia Stadium after Bobby Kennedy that "soured everything."

The Secretary of the Interior and the D.C. Stadium Board shared the authority to name the stadium. David Black, the Undersecretary of Interior, came up with RFK. Udall, thought it was "a pretty good idea." Since the Stadium Board had stalled, Udall thought it would not act before January 20 and he did not bother to clear the new name with the White House. To his surprise, the Board issued a press release approving the name on January 17 during his phone conversations with Johnson and Pierson, too late to head it off.

The President, evidently, was outraged both because he was not notified and because an honor was bestowed upon his arch-enemy. It defies reason to believe that he would carry on this grudge even after Kennedy's murder, when RFK was no longer a challenge to his dying presidency. But Lyndon Johnson had a deep reservoir of bitter and irrational resentment.[10]

11

Failure: The Repeal of Right-to-Work

LYNDON Johnson enjoyed extraordinary success in 1965 in persuading the first session of the 89th Congress to enact the legislation he wanted. It would be the triumph of his presidency. But he had a notable failure that can be read as a harbinger of others to follow. It was the refusal of Congress to repeal Section 14(b) of the Taft-Hartley amendments to the Wagner Act. At the same time he suffered a similar defeat over his proposal to grant home rule to the District of Columbia.

For the century and a half prior to the New Deal American labor unions had maintained a precarious existence in a hostile environment. The majority of employers refused to recognize or bargain with them, often aggressively, including resorting to violence. Government—local, state, and federal, particularly the courts—usually lined up on the side of the employer. In a society that touted individualism, workers hesitated to act collectively through unions, especially resisting the payment of dues. In a labor movement that treasured jurisdiction, rival unions vied with each other to assert bargaining claims.

As a result, American unions were insecure. Themselves helpless to change the environment, they sought security through collective bargaining. They persuaded or pressured employers who could hire and fire to engage only members of the union (the closed shop) or to require the employees they did hire to join the union (the union shop). In either form, if the employee failed to maintain his membership in the union, including the payment of dues, the employer would be obliged to fire him. Closed shops were common in industries with intermittent employment, such as construction, longshoring, maritime, and entertainment, where they were usually administered through union hiring halls. Union shops were more frequent in industries with longer-term employment, like manufacturing, transportation, and utilities.

The National Labor Relations Act of 1935, called the Wagner Act after its author, Senator Robert F. Wagner of New York, made union security provisions lawful under federal law. Section 8 forbade the employer to engage in five unfair labor practices, the third of which, intended to eliminate the company-dominated union, was to discriminate among his employees for the purpose of encouraging or discouraging membership in the union. But a proviso to Section 8(3) said that a closed or union shop contract was not illegal if made with a union representing a majority of the employees in an appropriate bargaining unit without illegal assistance from the employer. As a result both the number of collective bargaining agreements with the closed or union shop and the number of employees covered by these provisions grew dramatically.

But the Wagner Act and the National Labor Relations Board came under heavy attack from employers and their sympathizers in Congress, and the proviso to 8(3) became a prime target. In the closing days of World War II a movement emerged to persuade the states to make union security illegal, which called itself right-to-work. It quickly won support from the American Farm Bureau Federation, which feared the unionization of agricultural workers. This movement won its first victory in Florida in 1944 with a constitutional amendment.

By mid-1947, when Section 8(3) was gutted, a total of 25 states had either enacted statutes or adopted constitutional amendments outlawing all forms of union security. Excepting Wyoming, which acted in 1963, the great majority of right-to-work gains took place in the forties, with a handful following in the fifties. By the late fifties, in fact, the movement was on the defensive. Six states repealed their earlier enactments. More important, in 1958 right-to-work suffered overwhelming defeats in three industrial states—California, Ohio, and Indiana. Thus, by 1965 the following 19 states had laws or constitutional amendments: Alabama, Arizona, Arkansas, Florida, Georgia, Iowa, Kansas, Louisiana (limited to farm workers), Mississippi, Nebraska, North and South Carolina, North and South Dakota, Tennessee, Texas, Utah, Virginia, and Wyoming. These states were overwhelmingly in the South and Southwest or in the agricultural Midwest. None was a significant industrial state. Politically right-to-work was a combination of the old southern Democratic–midwestern Republican coalition which had dominated Congress before Lyndon Johnson had become President.

A great wave of strikes in late 1945 and early 1946 aroused public resentment against unions and the Wagner Act and helped the Republicans capture both houses of Congress in the 1946 elections. The first order of business in the new Congress in 1947 was to amend the NLRA comprehensively. It took shape as the Labor-Management Relations Act, known after its authors as Taft-Hartley, which was passed over President Truman's veto in 1947. It made the closed shop, but not the union shop, illegal in federal law. In addition, a provision was added to protect and encourage the right-to-work movement.

Section 14(b) read as follows: "Nothing in this Act shall be construed as authorizing the execution or application of agreements requiring membership in a labor organization as a condition of employment in any State or Territory in which such execution or application is prohibited by State or Territorial law." This meant that a state right-to-work law or amendment took precedence over federal law within the state. Thus, despite the fact that Taft-Hartley permitted union shop agreements, they remained illegal in, for example, Florida, because that state's amendment took precedence over Taft-Hartley.

The labor movement, which detested the 1947 law as a whole, reserved its harshest criticism for 14(b). Politically, however, it was helpless until 1965 because of the southern Democratic–Republican domination of Congress. In 1965 there seemed a chance to eliminate the right-to-work provision. AFL-CIO had gone all out with money and manpower to help Lyndon Johnson during the 1964 election; it was the most reliable and effective interest group backing Great Society legislation; and it was now supporting Johnson's decision to send U.S. troops to Vietnam. For a generation there had been no Congress as friendly to labor as the 89th. To be sure, as a Texas congressman in 1947, Johnson had voted both for Taft-Hartley and to override Truman's veto. But by 1965 he had changed his mind. When AFL-CIO president George Meany asked him to support the repeal of Section 14(b), the President readily agreed.[1]

In his State of the Union message on January 4, 1965, the President stated, "As pledged in our 1960 and 1964 Democratic platforms, I will propose to Congress changes in the Taft-Hartley Act, including Section 14(b)." Since this would inevitably be controversial, the administration delayed action to allow for passage of the education, Appalachia, and Medicare bills. An AFL-CIO spokesman said, "The measures he wants are things we want too, and we are willing to wait." By mid-May education and Appalachia had been enacted and Medicare had passed the House.

On May 18, therefore, Johnson sent Congress a special message on labor dealing with the minimum wage, unemployment insurance, and the repeal of 14(b). Chairman Frank Thompson of New Jersey of the House Special Labor Subcommittee introduced H.R. 77, and Pat McNamara of Michigan, chairman of the Senate Labor Subcommittee, submitted the same bill as S. 256.

Thompson held hearings between May 24 and June 8, 1965. Secretary of Labor Willard Wirtz pointed out that "right-to-work" had nothing to do with the right to a job, that repeal would not make the union shop mandatory, and that the state laws created disruptive and unfair competition for lower wages between states. AFL-CIO, the Teamsters, the civil rights movement, the Central Conference of American Rabbis, and a small group of employers joined in urging repeal. Reed E. Larson of the National Right to Work Committee argued that the state laws protected the worker against corrupt and Communist-dominated unions that used his dues for political campaigning. Leading employer organizations and the Farm Bureau Federation joined the opposition.

On June 3, 1965, the House subcommittee reported the bill by a 6 to 3 vote. The next day the full Education and Labor Committee agreed 21 to 10. Of the 21 Democrats only two from southern right-to-work states opposed repeal. Of the ten Republicans, two, Ogden Reid of New York and William Ayres of Ohio, voted against right-to-work. Ayres, who was from Akron, told Henry Hall Wilson that "any Republican who failed to learn a lesson from the disasters of 1958 in Ohio, Indiana, and California is completely stupid." His constituents, the big rubber companies with southern plants, had problems operating partly nonunion.

The administration and AFL-CIO worried about getting a majority in the House. This was because many Democrats from conservative midwestern districts feared that farmers would vote against them in the 1966 elections. The administration, therefore, created a farm-labor coalition. Urban northern Democrats, who would have voted against the farm bill because it would raise the price of wheat and so of bread, supported the farm bill in return for the promise that Democrats from midwestern farm districts would vote for repeal of 14(b). The Farmers Union and AFL-CIO worked hard on this political bargain and they got a big boost from Vice President Humphrey.

On July 28, 1965, the House passed H.R. 77 by the close vote of 221 to 203. The majority consisted of 182 northern Democrats, 18 southern Democrats, and 21 Republicans. The minority was made up of 117 Republicans, 78 southern Democrats, and 8 northern Democrats. Humphrey seems to have been decisive. He was assigned 42 Democratic members of the House from rural districts in Colorado, Indiana, Iowa, Michigan, Minnesota, Montana, Nebraska, North Dakota, Utah, Wisconsin, and Wyoming. He succeeded with 40; only the irascible Wayne Aspinall of Colorado and Clair Callan of Nebraska voted against repeal. His performance with the seven-member Iowa delegation was brilliant, all six Democrats.

The Senate subcommittee conducted hearings on June 22–25, 1965. The same witnesses repeated the arguments they had made earlier. The subcommittee adopted H.R. 77 with an amendment proposed by Wayne Morse of Oregon on August 12 by a vote of 7 to 1. Several small churches forbade their members to join any nonreligious organizations. The Morse amendment would permit anyone who opposed union membership because of his faith to substitute payment of the equivalent of union dues to a charity. The Labor and Public Welfare Committee approved H.R. 77 by a vote of 12 to 3 on September 1.

While the bill was before the committee word spread that the opponents of repeal would filibuster in the Senate, and everyone turned to Everett Dirksen. In fact, the minority leader had been turning over this question in his mind for months, and now the House action forced him to a decision. "Senator Dirksen," Neil MacNeil wrote, "who never forgot his special relationship to Robert Taft, automatically opposed repeal of any provision of the law that Senator Taft regarded as his legislative monument." Could he win? Both the Democrats and the Republicans knew that repeal would carry on a straight vote because 52 senators had already committed themselves. In mid-August Dirksen met with two of the most conservative Republicans in the Senate, Carl Curtis of Nebraska and Paul Fannin of Arizona. They gave him a list of 18 senators who had agreed to filibuster.

Dirksen visited his old friend, Lyndon Johnson, to see whether there was any give in his position. There was none. "I'm committed," Johnson said. Dirksen replied, "Mr. President, I am also committed."

When George Meany of AFL-CIO came to see him, Dirksen said, "George, I'm glad to see you. How's Mrs. Meany?" "Everett, you know why I'm here." "Oh sure, I can guess." "All we want is a straight up-and-down vote." 'George, you're not going to get a straight up-and-down vote. I am no spring chicken, but so long as there is any breath and energy in this carcass, we will go ahead. We mean business."

Meany appealed to Majority Leader Mansfield to hold the Senate in around-the-clock session in order to wear out the filibusterers. But this was not Mansfield's style; he would not break any elderly or frail member of the Senate. He stated publicly that he would not allow a vote based on "physical endurance." There would be "no pajama sessions of the Senate." "Why," Lyndon Johnson asked, "do I have to have a saint for Majority Leader? Why can't I have a politician?"

The President informed Meany and Andy Biemiller, AFL-CIO's lobbyist, that they would have the main responsibility for getting the senators to vote for repeal, and they accepted the burden. They spent a week in mid-September meeting with five groups of Democratic senators, all of whom agreed to work to break the filibuster. They doubted Dirksen's claim that he had 26 filibusterers lined up. But, Biemiller wrote ominously, "They felt that round-the-clock sessions would probably be needed."

On October 1, 1965, Mansfield moved to make H.R. 77 the business of the Senate and "debate" on the motion opened on October 4. That is, the coalition of Republicans and southern Democrats under Dirksen's leadership started their filibuster. In a maneuver on October 8 Mansfield moved to table his own motion. He urged those who were for repeal to vote against tabling. Dirksen countered by instructing his followers also to vote down the tabling motion. The vote was 94 to 0 to defeat Mansfield's motion. The filibuster continued.

Mansfield then petitioned with 21 signatures, five more than required, to invoke cloture with the purpose to *begin* rather than to *limit* debate. The roll call took place on October 11 and the Mansfield motion was defeated 47 to 45. While Dirksen had needed only a third of the senators, he got more than half. The majority consisted of 26 Republicans, 16 southern Democrats, and 5 northern Democrats. The minority was made up of 36 northern Democrats, 4 southern Democrats, and 5 Republicans. Dirksen had breathed life back into the Republican–southern Democratic coalition. But everyone agreed that, if the vote had been strictly on repeal of 14(b), Mansfield would have won by a fairly comfortable margin.[2]

The vote on October 11 to defeat cloture in order to begin debate left a narrow escape hatch. There had been no vote on the question of *limiting* debate. On November 18 the President promised the AFL-CIO to "finish the unfinished battle." In his State of the Union message on January 12, 1966, he renewed the pledge.

On January 24 the Senate resumed consideration of H.R. 77. The following morning Mansfield tried to get the bill before the chamber by a special maneuver to avoid a filibuster, but Dirksen was ready for him. For the next two weeks there was perfunctory discussion of the merits, mainly by opponents. On February 8 Mansfield moved for a roll call on cloture, which required 66 votes. The vote was 51 to 48 in favor, 15 votes short. On February 10 he tried again, this time losing 50 to 49. The main change from 1965 was that all 99 senators voted in 1966 (Pat McNamara of Michigan had died). If Mansfield had any hope of increasing his support, it had been wiped out by a two-week strike of subway and bus workers in New York City in January. Mayor John V. Lindsay, who had been in the House for the earlier vote and had cast his ballot for repeal of 14(b), said the stoppage was the "death warrant." Secretary Wirtz agreed. "It left a very bad taste in people's mouths about organized labor."

George Meany was extremely angry over the defeat and seemed to blame the Democratic party for failing to deliver the vote. The President replied that he did his best and had talked to 61 senators.

In the 1966 congressional elections the Republicans gained 47 seats in the House and three in the Senate. Wirtz reviewed the effect of these changes and concluded: "*In general,* the prospects for 14(b) repeal . . . are clearly reduced sharply by the election results." There would be no other opportunity.

Larry O'Brien later reflected on the failure of repeal, which he called "a rare defeat, but it was anticipated, . . . an effort pretty much doomed to failure." The time was right to try, "the high-water mark of recent history in terms of the strength of the President and, in turn, his strength with the Congress." It was a "Democratic Party commitment." O'Brien's view was that "it just wasn't going to happen. . . . The cold reality was that it was extremely difficult and, I felt, an impossible task. . . . We didn't have the muscle to repeal 14(b)." Labor never was able to give the administration a favorable head count. Biemiller was fully aware of the real situation. Mike Mansfield knew that he would lose and said that he would "shoulder the blame for not having the round-the-clock sessions."[3]

Since 1878 a three-member board of commissioners appointed by the President had governed the District of Columbia. In 1964 residents of the district won the right to vote, but only for President and Vice President. The problem was that Washington was primarily black, 60 percent in 1965 and growing steadily more so. Many southern Democrats did not want them to vote on racial grounds and many Republicans because they would elect Democrats.

On February 2, 1965, the President sent a special message to Congress urging home rule. His justification was simple: "Our Federal, State and local governments rest on the principle of democratic representation—the people elect those who govern them." The residents of the District of Columbia were denied this fundamental right. Presidents Truman, Eisenhower, and Kennedy had supported home rule and the Senate had passed bills in 1949, 1952, 1955, 1958, and 1959. But the House District of Columbia Committee, dominated by southerners, had refused to report out these bills.

Johnson proposed a Charter Act to create a representative local government. The mayor, a 15-member city council, and a nonvoting member of the House of Representatives would be elected by the citizens. Both Congress and the President would retain the power to overrule the local council. Once again the Senate acted favorably, approving the bill by a vote of 63 to 29 on July 22, 1965. But the House committee did not change; it sat on the bill.

On August 4, the President wrote to Speaker McCormack: "The House . . . must be given the opportunity, and promptly, to restore the basic rights of democracy at the very heart of the greatest constitutional system in the world." The committee was not moved. On August 11 New York Democrat Abraham J. Multer filed a discharge petition. If a majority of the House, 218 members, signed the petition, the bill would be taken from the District of Columbia Committee and placed on the floor for debate and vote. The next day the committee announced that hearings would open on August 18. Johnson, aroused, launched a strong campaign to get signatures for the petition and it reached 218 on September 3—169 northern Democrats, 23 southern Democrats, and 26 Republicans. But a number of the signers said that they would not vote for the bill in its present form.

Moreover, that same day the committee reported a substitute bill: the federal government would retain jurisdiction over the old Federal City of Washington as it existed between 1791 and 1871; the remainder of the district, a majority of the residents, would be offered to Maryland. If the state rejected the offer, the residents would hold a referendum on the issue of creating a board to draft a home rule charter. Either house of Congress would have the power to reject the charter.

Chaos reigned when both bills and many amendments reached the floor on September 29. Ultimately a bill was passed 227 to 174 calling for two memoranda, one on whether to have a charter, and, if adopted, the other on its terms.

Everett Dirksen said he would "stand in a state of marvel and wonderment at the wisdom" of a conference committee that could resolve the differences. Wayne Morse called the House action "a parliamentary exercise in avoiding an issue." House Majority Leader Carl Albert said that home rule was a "dead duck" and he was right.

In addition to losing a good bill and inflicting a nasty defeat to President Johnson, the failure of the home rule bill seems to have marked the virtual end of congressional support for civil rights. The white backlash so evident later in the decade first appeared here over home rule for the District of Columbia.[4]

III

LYNDON JOHNSON—EMBATTLED, BESIEGED, UNDERMINED

12

Unhinging the State of the Union

AMONG the years of Lyndon Johnson's presidency 1965 stood alone at the top in both domestic and foreign policy. Exploiting his massive victory in the 1964 elections, the President rammed through the Congress the next year a broad array of domestic legislation: Medicare, the Elementary and Secondary Education Act, the Higher Education Act, the Voting Rights Act, the immigration law, the Water Quality Act, the Solid Waste Disposal Act, along with other statutes of lesser consequence. In 1965, as well, Johnson fatefully led the nation into the Vietnam War.

In the early part of the year the White House was not organized to handle the immense flow of domestic legislation. While Bill Moyers was ostensibly in charge, he seemed to have little interest in the responsibility and discharged it indifferently. In July 1965 George Reedy resigned as White House press officer and the President replaced him with Moyers. He then installed Joseph A. Califano, Jr., as his special assistant on domestic affairs. Califano would remain in that position until the end of the administration and would play a decisive role in shaping domestic policy.

He had been born and was raised in Brooklyn. He attended Jesuit schools, including Holy Cross College. He then went to the Harvard Law School, from which he graduated in 1955. Califano would later explain his sensitivity to social needs as arising from his Jesuit schooling and Paul Freund's analysis of the Constitution in law school. He then spent three years in the Navy in the Judge Advocate General's office in the Pentagon. In 1958 he joined Dewey Ballantine, a big Wall Street law firm. At this time he had no political commitment, leaning, if anything, toward the Republicans.

Califano spent the Washington's birthday weekend in 1960 at home sick. He read *John Kennedy: A Political Profile* by James MacGregor Burns and sat in on a couple of meetings his wife held in their apartment on

Democratic reform politics. Califano was hooked. He became a Democrat and a vigorous supporter of JFK, throwing himself into the campaign at the "lowest imaginable level."

After the election, because he was impressed by the new President's appointments and was hopelessly saddled at the law firm with an "enormously boring but complicated stock-split transaction," Califano began to think about going to Washington. He learned that McNamara had named Cyrus Vance, a very good lawyer, general counsel at Defense. Though he did not know Vance, on Wednesday before the inauguration Califano wrote him saying that he would like to work for him and enclosed a resumé. Vance phoned on Friday asking him to come down for an interview the next day. On Monday Vance offered him a job as his special assistant. Califano would have jumped at once but could not shed the stock-split albatross until April. In 1962 Vance became Secretary of the Army and brought Califano along. Within a few months he became general counsel of the Army, "a wonderful opportunity," he said, "for a 31-year old lawyer."

In April 1964 McNamara asked him to succeed Adam Yarmolinsky as his special assistant. This was on the assumption that Yarmolinsky would leave to become deputy director of the poverty program, which did not work out. Califano got the job and worked on a great variety of important assignments, many involving contacts with the White House staff.

On the day after the 1964 election Mac Bundy and Bill Moyers invited Califano to become a special assistant to President Johnson to head the talent hunt and to work on Latin America. Califano said he had to talk to McNamara. They told him not to because the President had not yet spoken to him. Califano insisted. But Moyers called McNamara before Califano could get back. The secretary told Moyers that he was out of his mind and ought to take a vacation. He then told Califano that there were only two jobs at the White House better than the one he now had—Bundy's and Moyers's, if it could be pumped up as domestic adviser. McNamara then talked to the President and told Califano that "he'd gotten me [Califano] about six months of grace time, but that the President would make another pass."

On the day Moyers was named press secretary he told Califano that the President wanted him to handle domestic programs. Califano then had a long talk with McNamara about what the job should cover, which he summarized as

the preparation of domestic programs, first, that is, in terms of legislation and administration; second, the coordination of the operation of the domestic programs once they were begun; third, the handling of domestic crises; and fourth, heavy involvement in the economic area. [If this was an accurate job description, McNamara said,] you could probably make something out of the domestic part of the government.

The secretary presented these points to the President and stressed that Califano must report directly to him. Johnson agreed. That weekend Califano and his wife were at the ranch. He went to work as special assistant to the President for domestic affairs in late July 1965. He soon put together a small, extremely competent staff and, with a big shove from Johnson, waded into the heavy seas of the Great Society.

A young man who could win the high esteem of Cyrus Vance, Robert McNamara, and Lyndon Johnson was, obviously, special. Joe Califano had the essential qualities: high intelligence, loyalty, probity, command of language, an easy manner that made friends quickly, enormous energy and diligence, great curiosity, and management skills. Like the President, he believed that government could be used to broaden democracy in order to raise those at the bottom of the social order. At the same time, Califano was a political pragmatist. As with his boss and the best kids on the streets of Brooklyn, he held no prejudices based on ethnicity or religion. While it is difficult to imagine two people more different than Lyndon Johnson and Joe Califano, they meshed almost perfectly. The President came to rely on him heavily and put him in charge of major crises. Further, at moments when Johnson was under great strain he would turn to Califano for personal support.

In 1966 when the President was about to leave for Southeast Asia he brought Califano to his bedroom. As Califano recounted, Johnson said,

> "You're going to be the President. . . . We have to get all this legislation passed. We have to do this, we have to do that." And then he proceeded to load me up. He gave me cufflinks. He gave me an electric toothbrush with the Presidential seal on it. He gave me a tie clasp, he gave me cigarette lighters and I ended up walking with my arms full of all these presents, to say goodbye to him. . . . I don't think I slept . . . for all the time he was away. I worked so hard because all these bills were on the Hill. [His] calls were always at . . . three in the morning.

By the fall of 1965 it was clear that the war would not be over soon, more likely not for many years. This raised acutely the question of guns or butter. For those concerned about the economy, piling the costs of the war upon a system presently fully employed guaranteed rapid inflation. The Federal Reserve was about to raise interest rates and the Council of Economic Advisers was considering higher taxes. Conservatives who believed in the war as a fight against Communism urged the abandonment of the Great Society. Liberals who supported Johnson's domestic policies feared that their programs would be washed down the drain in Vietnam. The guns or butter issue could tear the social fabric of the nation as well as the Johnson presidency to pieces.

The President was compelled to confront the problem and he did so by making it the theme of the State of the Union message to Congress on January 12, 1966. The composition of that speech became an ordeal of exceptional messiness.

The original scheme seemed sensible—Bundy would handle the part on the war, Califano would submit the legislative program, and Jack Valenti would pull the pieces together for final editing by the President. Califano thought that Johnson was "a very good editor once he got down to the nitty-gritty." He had a "way of making things clear, easily understood by the American people." But the plan did not work out. On November 27 Valenti, supported by Califano, asked the President for permission to bring in Dick Goodwin, who had resigned during the summer. This opened a can of worms.

Valenti's suggestion had a certain logic. Goodwin had written three of LBJ's "most memorable speeches"—the Great Society address at the University of Michigan on May 22, 1964, the We Shall Overcome speech to a joint session of Congress on March 15, 1965, and the Howard University address on race on June 4, 1965. "At his best," Valenti wrote, "[Goodwin is] incandescent and possibly a near-genius in his field. For when Goodwin is collaborating with his muses, he is the most skilled practitioner of an arcane and dying art form, the political speech." But he had a bad side. Goodwin was "a prickly chap," as "lovable as a sullen porcupine." He held on to a speech until the last moment to prevent the speaker from messing around with it. Nor did he care for anyone else's prose. In this case Valenti got John Steinbeck to submit some chiseled lines. Example: "The Great Society is not the ordered, changeless, and sterile battalion of the ants." Johnson loved it; Goodwin tossed the Nobel Prizewinner's phrasemaking into the trash bin. The President, moreover, disliked and distrusted Goodwin and told Valenti he did not want him around.

But a month later there was still no progress. Johnson, at the urging of Valenti, Califano, and Moyers, authorized a call to Goodwin. But he himself would edit Goodwin's drafts and he absolutely refused to meet with him directly. Shortly after the new year Goodwin checked into the Mayflower and worked out of his hotel room.

While Johnson drew immense pride from the enormous legislative achievements of the first session of the 89th Congress, he would not tolerate any resting on the oars. He demanded that the second session be even bigger, to fix in law his vision of the Great Society. Thus, he drove Califano and his team relentlessly to scour the universities, the federal agencies, and any other source they could think of for legislative ideas.

On December 29, 1965, Califano was in Johnson's office at the ranch with a huge loose-leaf notebook entitled "The Great Society—A Second Year Legislative Program." Califano slowly turned the pages as the President chose the proposals he wanted and discarded the rest. The number that went through the screen was enormous. "We were serving up plenty of butter to go with the guns," Califano wrote, "a grand design. . . . It was an extraordinary experience. In less than two hours, this President had blessed a massive second-year program that would astound the Congress and the country when he unveiled it in his State of the Union message on January 12, 1966."

Between January 5 and 11 the White House and its Mayflower annex became a madhouse as the President sent draft after draft back for revision. A basic problem was that Johnson and Bundy found Goodwin's dovishness intolerable.

The night of January 11 was unreal. Califano, Valenti, and Moyers had a "final meeting" with the President in which he gave them "his last round of comments." Califano said later, "I remember essentially being up all night writing. So I slept on the couch in my office." Goodwin wrote that he approached the end of what he called the "guns and butter" speech at dawn. He had worked, "without respite, for almost thirty-six consecutive hours." He could barely make out the keys on the typewriter and was unable to formulate coherent sentences. Desperate, he phoned the White House doctor to give him a few more hours. The M.D. arrived quickly, "draw a hypodermic partially filled with an unnamed red liquid from his bag, and, as I continued to jab haltingly at the typewriter keys, . . . injected the chemical into my shoulder." The doctor said, "Don't tell anyone." It worked. Goodwin finished his draft.

By 7:15 a.m. on January 12 Johnson had read the "final" draft and had rejected it. At a conference with his exhausted staff in his bedroom he demanded a rewrite. He worked on it throughout the day and got many revisions. In the afternoon he got Fortas and Clifford to go over it. "Lunch" was at 6:17. Califano got a call from him at 7:32 "on this damn message that he's going to deliver at nine o'clock." With his usual fussiness Johnson arranged for counting and measuring the applause and for Marvin Watson and Larry O'Brien to start clapping if it lagged. Finally, he got a haircut, dressed, and left for the Capitol.

At the end of the afternoon Johnson's secretary had awakened Goodwin at the hotel. "The President would like you to ride up to the Hill with him for the speech." Goodwin was tempted but decided not to accept and went back to sleep. "I was never to see or talk to Lyndon Johnson again."

In the House chamber at 9:04 that evening the President opened the State of the Union message by joining guns *and* butter:

> We will not permit those who fire upon us in Vietnam to win a victory over the desires and intentions of all the American people. This Nation is mighty enough, its society is healthy enough, its people are strong enough, to pursue our goals in the rest of the world while still building a Great Society here at home.
>
> And that is what I have come here to ask of you tonight.

He laid out his demands for a massive second round for the Great Society. "I recommend," he said repeatedly, and rattled off the items like a machine gun: financing for the recently enacted health, education, and poverty programs; a "daring" foreign aid program to attack hunger, disease, and ignorance and to control population; the complete rebuilding of central and slum areas in the cities (to be called Model Cities); the cleanup of rivers and their basins; an attack on crime; the elimination of racial discrimination in jury selection, in the obstruction of efforts to secure civil rights, and in the sale and rental of housing; creation of a new Department of Transportation; increasing the term of members of the House to four years served concurrently with the President; a special set of programs for the rural poor; an increase in the minimum wage and an extension of coverage; the repeal of Section 14(b) of the Taft-Hartley Act; control of strikes which threaten the national interest; a new G.I. Bill of Rights for Vietnam veterans; a Teacher Corps; rent assistance; home rule for the District of Columbia; a highway safety law; the elimination of deception in lending and in the sale of drugs and cosmetics; a new supersonic transport plane; and full disclosure of political contributions. The plate would overflow for the second session of the 89th.

Now Vietnam. The Communists of the North had mounted an assault on the South. "We could leave," he said, "abandoning South Vietnam to its attackers and to certain conquest, or we could stay and fight beside the people of South Vietnam. We stayed." The U.S. was totally committed. "We will give our fighting men what they must have: every gun, and every dollar, and every decision—whatever the cost or whatever the challenge. . . . And let me be absolutely clear: The days may become months, and the months may become years, but we will stay as long as aggression commands us to battle."

Despite this huge and open-ended commitment, the U.S. could wage this war and still finance the Great Society at virtually no cost. In part this was because the U.S. was extremely rich and its economy was growing at a rapid rate. "If you approve every program that I recommend tonight, our total budget deficit will be one of the lowest in many years. It will be only $1.8 billion next year." On a cash basis it will "actually show a surplus."

It was a magic show, all smoke and mirrors. Twenty-two years later Joe Califano, who was standing in the chamber, recalled the reaction of the Congress. Johnson, he said,

> was really like a purring cat. . . . He had really wowed them. . . . I could feel guys—they were just stunned—that he could go forward with a program like this. And then you'd have guys come up to you and say, "Is he really serious? Are we really going to do this?" And then the bills started coming up. . . . I remember . . . [Congressman] Bill Barrett . . . on Model Cities. . . . He was saying, "Joe, you can't be serious. How can you push this program? Where are we going to get the money?"

Despite the presidential purring, it was a bad speech, really a very bad speech. It reads as though it had been composed by a harried committee, which, of course, was the fact. It was too long, repetitious, disorganized, and impossible to believe. Far more serious, Johnson completely avoided the fundamental question Bill Barrett raised: "Where are we going to get the money?"

In this address Lyndon Johnson was speaking in the realm of fantasy; he refused to leave it for the painful world of reality. His motives were pure and noble. He desperately wanted to bring the poor, particularly blacks in poverty, into the mainstream of American society. Thus, he was eager to pour funds into the basic programs he had already launched—poverty, education, health—and to add new programs, especially model cities and an end of discrimination in housing. This would require an immense increase in the expenditure of public money. Even without Vietnam, he would have confronted formidable opposition. The war made it impossible.

The numbers Johnson used were false and intended to mislead. As will be pointed out in Chapter 14, he had ordered McNamara to cook the books. In its first year the war actually cost $20 billion. Thus, the deficit was not $1.8 billion, but $9 billion. As the conflict dragged on, the costs and the deficit rose. In the second half of 1965 the White House launched a massive and unsuccessful campaign to persuade corporations and unions not to raise prices and wages. On December 3, 1965, the Fed raised the discount rate from 4 to 4.5 percent and about that time both the Bureau of the Budget and the Council of Economic Advisers became convinced that a tax increase was necessary. The President, trying to preserve an image of the costless war, rejected the idea instantly. The Great Inflation took off. In the contest with the Great Society the Vietnam War was the certain victor.[1]

13

Vietnam: Sliding into the Quagmire

UNTIL 1964 few Americans recognized the name Vietnam or could locate it on a map. They were mainly adult males who had collected postage stamps as boys, and they knew it as French Indo-China. Daniel Ellsberg wrote, "There has never been an official of Deputy Assistant Secretary rank or higher (including myself) who could have passed in office a midterm freshman exam in modern Vietnamese history, if such a course existed in this country."

The French in 1887 had imposed military control over the Indochinese Union, the three territories that would become Vietnam—Cochin-China, Annam, and Tonkin—along with Cambodia; Laos would be added six years later. French rule was repressive and was based on economic exploitation. Indochina became an exclusive source of raw materials for French industry and a protected market for French goods. Monopolies over alcohol, salt, and opium financed the colonial government. Rice, which should have been consumed by the peasantry, was exported.

The Vietnamese, a proud and ancient people, resented this system and some became revolutionaries who dreamed of overthrowing colonialism. Among them was Nguyen Sinh Cung, born in 1890 in Nghe An province in central Vietnam. Over a long life he used many names, the one known to history being Ho Chi Minh. In 1911 in Saigon he signed on as a stoker and galley boy aboard a French freighter bound for Marseilles. It would be 30 years before he returned.

Ho traveled widely in Europe and North America, living for six years in Paris after World War I, where he became a Marxist. He wrote for left-wing newspapers, denouncing French colonialism. In Moscow he met the Soviet leaders and attended a school for oriental revolutionaries. He was in

China for the struggle between the nationalists and the Communists and mobilized Vietnamese students. Then on to Paris, to Bangkok, a center for Vietnamese dissidents, to Hong Kong, and to London. In 1941-42 the Japanese swept through Southeast Asia—the U.S.-protected Philippines, British Malaya, the Dutch East Indies, and French Indochina. The next year Ho slipped across the Chinese border into Vietnam and joined confederates in a cave in the north. The time had come, he told them, to act. He formed the Vietnam Independence League, the Vietminh, to fight both the Japanese and their French collaborators. During the war the movement grew in both size and guerilla capability. On August 16, 1945, as Japan was collapsing, Ho proclaimed the provisional government of Vietnam with himself as president.

But General Charles DeGaulle, who was in command in liberated France, determined to preserve the French empire, including Indochina, and he gained both British and American support. Ho was trapped. After prolonged negotiations, he agreed in 1946 to split the country, giving France the south and hopefully retaining the north. But the French did not abide by the agreement.

This led to the "first" Vietnam War, which lasted for the better part of a decade and bled France white. It reached a climax in 1954 in the great battle of Dienbienphu west of Hanoi with the victory of the Vietminh under the brilliant generalship of Vo Nguyen Giap. Ho thought he had driven the French out of Vietnam and had united his country, but it was not to be.

The Chinese dominated the Geneva conference of 1954. Zhou Enlai wanted to deny the U.S. a reason to intervene in Vietnam, which might threaten China; further, the Chinese and the Vietnamese had quarreled for 2000 years and he preferred a weak and divided Vietnam. Zhou told Ho that he must accept half the country and stay out of Cambodia and Laos. The Soviets supported Zhou and Vietnam was split at the 17th parallel. But the closing documents basically proclaimed a cease-fire and did not constitute a political settlement. The agreement between France and the Democratic Republic of Vietnam, as the Vietminh now called itself, provided for a *temporary* division of the country. A nationwide election would be held in the summer of 1956 to create a united Vietnam. But, as events worked out, Ho had won the war and lost the peace.

The playboy Vietnamese emperor, Bao Dai, who resided in a chateau on the French Riviera, selected Ngo Dinh Diem, who came down from Paris, as prime minister of the new South Vietnam. Bao Dai made Diem swear to defend the country against both the Communists and the French. Diem arrived in Saigon on June 28, 1954. While patriotic, he could hardly have been less fitted to govern his restless country. He was almost totally indifferent to the realities of Vietnam and this was, Neil Sheehan wrote, "willful." "He lived in a mental cocoon spun out of a nostalgic reverie for Vietnam's imperial past." Diem was a militant Catholic in a country that was overwhelmingly Buddhist. He distrusted everyone except his brother, Ngo Dinh Nhu, and the latter's wife. They were even more paranoid than Diem and some considered them mad. Stanley Karnow thought them a cross between the Borgias and the Bourbons. Diem accepted endemic corruption as a national way of life.

He flouted the Geneva accords by assuming that South Vietnam was already a permanent nation. He refused to allow elections in 1956 and he demanded American support. The Eisenhower administration, while dismayed by Diem personally, found no alternative but to back his war against Ho. About $30 million a year of U.S. money propped up his regime and American experts created and trained the South Vietnamese armed forces.

Determined to unite the country, Ho had no option but to resume the war. He gradually built up an underground revolutionary cadre in the South, the Vietcong, but it made slow progress. In 1959 he began converting the Ho Chi Minh Trail, which ran from North Vietnam through Laos and Cambodia to South Vietnam, into a military highway to infiltrate the South.

In the late fifties South Vietnam was ravaged by civil war. As the U.S. supplied Diem, the Soviet Union and China looked after Ho. There was a rough equilibrium: the government more or less controlled the cities and the Vietcong dominated most of the countryside. Neither was winning and it appeared that the war would go on for many years.

Eisenhower's top advisers urged him to break the deadlock by sending in U.S. combat forces, but he refused. He simply passed the problem on to Kennedy in 1961.

The new President was baffled, enraged, and scarred by Vietnam. Accustomed to making decisions on a reasonable approximation of the facts, he could make no sense of the conflicting flow of information into the White House. He sent a stream of representatives to Vietnam, who brought back reports that piled up the confusion. In December 1962 the President sent out his dear friend, Mike Mansfield, an authority on Asia. His report was realistic and extremely gloomy. On reading it, Kennedy became so depressed that he spoke unkindly to Mansfield. He later told Kenny O'Donnell, "I got angry with Mike for disagreeing with our policy so completely, and I got angry with myself because I felt myself agreeing with him." In September 1963 Marine General Victor H. Krulack and Joseph A. Mendenhall, director of the State Department's Far East Planning Office, went on a four-day inspection. Krulack reported that Diem's problems had no effect upon military operations and that we were winning the war. Mendenhall said the civilian government was collapsing and that there was danger of a religious war or a major defection to the Vietcong. "Were you two gentlemen," Kennedy asked icily, "in the same country?"

While the American public was kept almost totally in the dark, a deep and bitter struggle between hawks and doves was already evident under

Kennedy. The big raptors were the armed forces speaking through the Joint Chiefs of Staff and the civilian leaders of the Department of Defense, Secretary McNamara and his top aides, John McNaughton and William Bundy. In the State Department, Secretary Rusk, though reluctant to express his views openly, was a hawk, and many in the department shared his outlook. McGeorge Bundy and Walt Rostow in the White House were also cold warriors. The doves were less numerous and less influential—Averell Harriman, George Ball, Roger Hilsman, and Paul Kattenburg at State, Arthur Schlesinger in the White House, J. K. Galbraith, the ambassador to India, and Mansfield and Wayne Morse in the Senate.

A similar division also arose in Saigon, but not within the government. Rather it was between the U.S. military command and the embassy, both unrelentingly hawkish, and the dovish press. At this time there were few reporters in Vietnam, a handful from the large dailies, the newsmagazines, and the press associations. But they included some exceptionally gifted newsmen—David Halberstam of the *New York Times,* Stanley Karnow of the Washington *Post,* Neil Sheehan of United Press International, and Malcolm Browne of the Associated Press.

Pierre Salinger noted that Kennedy (and Johnson later) "pushed hard . . . to tighten the rules under which correspondents could observe field operations." But neither dared to impose censorship. Diem was also restrained from throwing the reporters out for fear of an outcry in Congress. But there were other methods. The Saigon police and the Sûreté plainclothesmen cornered Peter Arnett of the AP, Halberstam, Browne, and Sheehan in a narrow alley in Saigon. The Sûreté men threw Arnett to the ground and were about to attack his kidneys with their pointy-toed shoes when Halberstam, a very large man, charged with fists ready, and shouted, "Get back, get back, you sons of bitches, or I'll beat the shit out of you." They backed away. Kennedy tried to pressure Arthur Ochs Sulzberger, the new publisher of the *Times,* to transfer Halberstam out of Saigon, to no avail.

The crisis Washington had dreaded began on May 8, 1963. The Buddhists in Hué gathered to celebrate the 2,527th birthday of the Buddha. The Catholic provincial officer forbade them to display their flag. The Buddhists, outraged by another act of discrimination, gathered at the radio station. Two armored cars from Nhu's special forces opened fire, killing nine and wounding fourteen. In the following weeks there were Buddhist demonstrations in many towns, often suppressed brutally. On June 11 an elderly bonze sat down on the pavement at a busy Saigon intersection and was doused with gasoline and set afire. Browne, tipped off in advance, carried a camera. His photograph of the immolation appeared the next day on the front pages of many of the world's newspapers. This grisly spectacle was repeated. Despite strong U.S. criticism, the Nhus admitted no responsibility and blamed the demonstrations on the Vietcong.

On June 27, 1963, Kennedy named his old political rival, Henry Cabot

Lodge, his ambassador to Saigon. He had been in Vietnam and was fluent in French. More important, he held Diem in low regard and was tough. Kennedy must also have thought that, if South Vietnam collapsed, it would be politically convenient to have a Republican to share the blame.

During the fall of 1963 the South Vietnamese generals in Saigon and the U.S. government in Washington began to talk separately about a coup to overthrow Diem. While both were eager to get rid of him and his family, neither wanted to take responsibility. The only one who was firm was Lodge, who pressed Washington for authorization to proceed.

On October 5 General Duong Van ("Big") Minh, the leading plotter, told Lieut-Col. Lucien Conein, the CIA agent, that, while Minh's group expected American support, they needed "assurances" that the U.S. would "not attempt to thwart this plan." Lodge urged Kennedy to give the assurances. On October 5 he received a cable from Washington with this language:

> While we do not wish to stimulate coup, we also do not wish to leave impression that U.S. would thwart a change of government or deny economic and military assistance to a new regime if it appeared capable of increasing effectiveness of military effort, ensuring popular support to win war and improve working relations with U.S.

Conein on October 10 conveyed this assurance to Minh.

But the plotters hardly leapt at the news. The Vietnamese, though they lived in the tropics, moved at glacial speed. As Lodge put it, "The U.S. is trying to bring this medieval country into the 20th century."

They did move on the afternoon of November 1, when their troops captured the presidential palace, police headquarters, and the radio station in Saigon. Diem and Nhu fled to the air-conditioned cellar of the palace. Diem learned that the officers upon whom he had counted had deserted. Lodge offered the brothers a safe conduct out of the country. Diem did not respond. Then the mutineers made the same proposal and he rejected it. During the evening the brothers drove to Cholon, the Chinese section, and entered a safe house. The following morning Diem informed the plotters that they were at St. Francis Xavier, a French church.

Minh sent an armored personnel carrier and four jeeps. He signaled the officer in charge by raising two fingers of his right hand, that is, to murder both brothers. At the church the officer put them in the carrier and climbed into the gun turret. At a railroad crossing he shot them with an automatic weapon and stabbed them with a knife. President Kennedy was in a meeting when the grisly news arrived. General Maxwell Taylor said that he "rushed from the room with a look of shock and dismay on his face." Schlesinger, who saw him shortly, wrote that he was "somber and shaken. I had not seen him so depressed since the Bay of Pigs."

Kennedy had tried to construct a policy for Vietnam: the preservation of the South as a non-Communist haven in Southeast Asia, hopefully, along with the North, neutralized. As Theodore Sorensen put it, he sought "both to raise our commitment and to keep it limited." In 1961 he had been urged to send in combat troops and to increase the number of advisers. He rejected troops but increased the advisers to 15,500 by the end of 1963. He hoped to democratize the country, but found Diem impossible to deal with. The attack on the Buddhists deeply offended Kennedy. At the United Nations General Assembly on September 20, 1963, he said that essential human rights were not respected "when a Buddhist priest is driven from his pagoda."

Thus, the Kennedy policy was a failure. Ho Chi Minh would not stop the war until Vietnam was unified under his control. Diem, counting on American support, refused to fight seriously or give up his tyranny. But Kennedy held back on committing U.S. combat forces. Doubtless, as he told O'Donnell, he hoped to get through the 1964 election before confronting that issue. But he was assassinated only three weeks after Diem met the same fate.[1]

Clark Clifford, who knew both well, wrote that John Kennedy and Lyndon Johnson viewed Vietnam through entirely different eyes. Kennedy considered it "an international problem—not something aimed at him personally." Johnson, by contrast, would "personalize the actions of the Vietcong, interpreting them as somehow aimed personally at him." Thus, the sources of Johnson's decisions to commit U.S. forces in Vietnam and to refuse to pull them out are found in his personality and in his personal history.

Johnson's greatest fear, Doris Kearns wrote, was that he should display "unmanliness" publicly. He proudly thought of himself as a "patriot" and he bestowed that honorable title upon those who shared his love for country and his pride in its great military strength. He came from the South, the region with the strongest military tradition, and from Texas, with its own special memory, the Battle of the Alamo. In a super-patriotic speech to the troops in Korea in 1966 he said, "My great-great-grandfather died at the Alamo." While a lie, it certainly demonstrated his need to identify with the past military glory of Texas. In an emotional speech to senior officers at Cam Ranh Bay on October 26, 1966, Johnson said, "Go out there and nail that coonskin to the wall." He took pride in his naval air service during World War II and wore a rosette in his buttonhole for the Silver Star he received. He had been a member of the Senate Armed Services Committee and had voted to build up the armed forces. He had worked to locate military installations and defense plants in Texas. He was not about to allow North Vietnam, which he sometimes called "that damn little pissant country" or "that raggety-ass little fourth-rate country," to push the United States of America around.

But Johnson and his military advisers did not seem to understand that Vietnam posed formidable military problems. Anyone with even a rudimentary knowledge of the country could see that Ho Chi Minh enjoyed great advantages. Thomas Powers, a recent Yale graduate, was inducted into the Army as the bombing of the North began in 1965 and was sent to Fort Gordon, Georgia, to train as a switchboard operator. Curious, he read books in the base library on guerilla warfare and quickly became convinced that the U.S. was in trouble because it was "breaking all the rules."

The essential conditions were these: Much of Vietnam was covered with jungle, an ideal terrain for guerillas. Ho's army was skilled in guerilla warfare and U.S. troops were not. The North Vietnamese had endless patience and the Americans had very little. Ho could count on large troop levies. His soldiers were willing to die in a war they saw as national liberation against a colonial western power. The South Vietnamese had almost no stomach for combat. North Vietnam had little industry to destroy from the air and the Chinese and Soviets would supply arms. The U.S. would be reluctant to attack along the Chinese border for fear of dragging China into the war, as had happened in Korea. It was impossible to use atomic weapons for fear of retaliation.

George Ball wrote that Vietnam constricted the American government's vision, like a camera focussed on a near object with little depth of field. "I knew from experience with my French friends, there was something about Vietnam that seduced the toughest military minds into fantasy." DeGaulle told Ball that France had learned to her sorrow that Vietnam was "rotten country." He strongly urged the U.S. not to repeat his nation's mistake, but his warning fell on deaf ears.[2]

During 1965 America began to divide sharply between doves and hawks. Like the birds themselves, the groups shared some characteristics but differed in others. This may be visualized by placing a neutral on the war at zero, with doves ranging in intensity of their dovishness from −1 to −10, and hawks spreading out in commitment from +1 to +10.

At one extreme Jeannette Rankin was a −10, a pure-as-driven-snow pacifist. In the House she had voted against declarations of war in both 1917 and 1941. Now she led the Jeannette Rankin Brigade, 5000 women, in a march on Congress to protest the Vietnam War. Other doves may be ranked as follows: Mike Mansfield −6, George Ball −5, Clark Clifford −2.

At the other extreme as +10s were Barry Goldwater and General Curtis LeMay. During his 1964 presidential campaign the senator seemed to favor dropping nuclear bombs on North Vietnam and the head of the Strategic Air Command appeared to want to nuke anyone he did not like. Bellicose Admiral U. S. Grant Sharp, who commanded the Pacific fleet, was a +9. The Joint Chiefs of Staff came in at +8. Secretary of State Dean Rusk was a wavering +6. The three critically important people were President

Johnson, National Security Adviser McGeorge Bundy, and Secretary of Defense Robert McNamara. The President, his macho-Alamo streak much outweighing his doubts, was a solid +6. Bundy, who seemed to suffer doubts about nothing, including Vietnam, but who had not lost his senses like Sharp, LeMay, and Goldwater, came in at +8. McNamara, whose mind was more open than Bundy's though less clouded than Johnson's, was a +7.

Since Bundy was a paradigm of the American Establishment, one must explain that very important, though ill-defined, institution in order to understand him. The core of the Establishment consisted of gentlemen of breeding, privileged education, wealth, and power, who concentrated at the foot of Manhattan Island in investment banking and corporate law with tentacles reaching out to Washington and Boston. Overwhelmingly Republican, they included several notable Democrats and they willingly served Democratic Presidents, usually at substantial financial cost to themselves.

The mission of the Establishment was to shape and execute American foreign and defense policy to fit the goals of peace and international stability as well as the free flow of capital and trade between nations. During the nineteenth century Britain had maintained a balance of power in Europe and the Royal Navy had kept the seas open. With the decline of Britain in the twentieth century, the Establishment saw America as heir to these policies by maintaining peace in Europe and by resisting aggression, notably by Germany in both World Wars, by Imperial Japan in the second, and by Soviet and Chinese Communism after World War II. Such a role required massive military forces.

Throughout its history the Establishment had been led by men of unusual ability and character. This started with Elihu Root, the foremost corporate lawyer of his time, who served as Secretary of War for McKinley and Secretary of State for Theodore Roosevelt. His heir and the most notable of them all was another distinguished New York lawyer, Henry L. Stimson, who was Taft's Secretary of War, Hoover's Secretary of State, and Franklin Roosevelt's Secretary of War. Stimson was followed by two men—the Wall Street banker Robert A. Lovett and the Wall Street lawyer John J. McCloy—both of whom had held prominent positions under Stimson in the War Department during World War II. Another important Stimson associate both at State and at War was the noted Boston lawyer Harvey Bundy.

Bundy had not been born into the Establishment; rather, he came from Grand Rapids. But aside from his close association with Stimson, he had attended Yale and the Harvard Law School (first in his class followed by a clerkship with Justice Holmes). More important, he married Katherine Lawrence Putnam, who was both a Putnam, which was important, and a Lowell, which was extremely important. The first member of the family arrived in Massachusetts in 1639. In the nineteenth century the Lowells became extremely wealthy in textiles. John Amory Lowell selected six presidents of Harvard. His son, Augustus, increased the family fortune dramatically and fathered Amy Lowell, the poetess, A. Lawrence Lowell, the educator, Percival Lowell, the astronomer, and Elizabeth, who married William Putnam and gave birth to Katherine, who married Harvey Bundy.

McGeorge, "Mac," born in 1919, was a *Wunderkind.* When David Halberstam wrote a book called *The Best and the Brightest,* he could have stopped after finishing the chapter on Bundy. At Groton he was first in everything except athletics, though Halberstam wrote that "he could have been a good second-team quarterback—excellent play calling—but he thought athletics took too much time." He won the Franklin D. Roosevelt Debating Trophy three times. The novelist Louis Auchincloss, who was at Groton with him, said that Bundy was fit to be dean at age 12. Richard Irons, the top history teacher, said Bundy's essays were better than the books he based them on. He graduated at 16, *summa cum laude.* Yale was more of the same. He was the first applicant to receive three perfect scores on the entrance exams. As a freshman he wrote an essay entitled "Is Lenin a Marxist?" The historian David Owen said there were not two members of the Yale faculty who could have written it. He was, of course, Phi Beta Kappa. The yearbook called him "Mahatma" Bundy.

He was then selected as a Junior Fellow at Harvard. The Society of Fellows had been established by a large gift from his great uncle, A. Lawrence Lowell. It allowed individuals of extraordinary intellectual talent to exercise their own curiosity outside the rigorous discipline of a doctoral program. Bundy used his time to write Stimson's memoirs. The title page of *On Active Service in Peace and War* cited two authors—Stimson and Bundy. But "the writing of the book," the great man noted in the introduction, "has been the work of Mr. McGeorge Bundy."

During the war Bundy's draft board rejected him for bad eyes. He memorized the eye charts and made it into the Army on the second try. He became an aide to Admiral Alan Kirk, a friend of the family, and he helped General Omar Bradley plan the D-Day landings on Kirk's flagship *Augusta.* Characteristically, Captain Bundy corrected the general on several matters.

After the war he taught in the government department at Harvard and gave an extremely popular course, "The U.S. in World Affairs." He stressed the virtue of force in the conduct of international relations and argued the point with J. K. Galbraith, who was deeply attached to peaceful means. He did a little discreet recruiting for the CIA. Director Allen Dulles was a fellow Establishmentarian as well as a family friend, and his brother, Bill Bundy, worked for the agency.

When President Conant left Harvard to become U.S. High Commissioner to Germany in 1953, there was talk of Bundy, at 34, as his successor. But Nathan Pusey was chosen as president and Bundy became dean of the college. A cautious leader, Pusey soon lost the respect of the faculty. By contrast, Halberstam wrote, "Bundy was dashing, bright, brittle, the antibureaucratic man, the unconventional man," who was "enormously sure of himself." He filled the vacuum that Pusey left. Despite departmental opposition, he made several spectacular appointments—David Riesman (social sciences), Erik Eriksen (psychiatry), Laurence Wylie (French civilization), Lillian Hellman (English).

Though a Republican (his brother was a Democrat), Bundy through Arthur Schlesinger got to know John Kennedy and they soon grew to like and respect each other. Bundy studied important people carefully. As Halberstam wrote, he soon came to "sense Kennedy's moves, his whims, his nuances." He, of course, shared the "Establishment's conviction that it knew what was right and what was wrong for the country." Thus, Bundy took a "hard-line attitude which was very much a product of the fifties and the Cold War, the ultrarealist view," which he had been teaching Harvard students. The Communists used force; the free world must respond with force.

Kennedy invited Bundy to become Special Assistant for National Security Affairs and he accepted enthusiastically. He recruited a brilliant staff— Walt Rostow, Carl Kaysen, Robert Komer, Michael Forrestal, and Bromley Smith. Kennedy, Schlesinger wrote, "saw the White House and the Department [of State] as intimate partners in the enterprise of foreign policy." Bundy provided the link. "Bundy saw his function as that of the clarification of alternatives set before the President and the recording and follow-up of presidential decisions."

When Johnson took over there was a certain tension. He distrusted fancy Establishment types and he bridled to learn that Bundy had mocked him. But McNamara, whom Johnson held in awe, spoke well of Bundy and the President soon realized that he could not operate without him. While the relationship never became easy, it worked and Johnson listened closely to Bundy on Vietnam.

Robert McNamara came from an entirely different background. He was born, raised, and educated at the other end of the continent. His family was lower middle class (his father sold shoes) and enjoyed neither wealth nor connections. With help only from public educational institutions, including the University of California, he was entirely self-made.

McNamara was born in San Francisco in 1916 and spent his youth across the Bay in Oakland. His mother soon realized that she had a gifted child and arranged for him to get a quality education in nearby suburban Piedmont High School. He then moved a few miles north to Berkeley. There McNamara learned that he was obsessed with quantification, studied mathematics, and learned to think and speak in the language of numbers. Because of the Depression, like many others, he majored in economics. Upon graduating in 1937 and eager for a good job, he moved on to the Harvard Business School. He made an outstanding record and found his specialization, control accounting. He then returned to San Francisco to a drudge accounting job with Price Waterhouse. He married Margy Craig and they seemed ideally suited to each other.

In 1940 he was invited to join the faculty of the Harvard Business School to teach accounting. But the war soon interrupted his academic career. In 1942 he was introduced to the American Establishment.

Henry Stimson had installed Robert Lovett as Assistant Secretary of War for Air. Lovett and Army Air Force chief General H. H. Arnold needed a system of statistical control for a service that was growing exponentially and would soon operate around the globe. They wanted to track planes, engines, crews, and spare parts to manage the Air Force in an orderly manner. Lovett placed Charles Bates "Tex" Thornton in charge and he went to the Business School for help, acquiring several instructors, including McNamara. This group became known as Lovett's Whiz Kids, and McNamara had the most whiz. Once the system was established they could tell, for example, whether the B-17 was a more efficient fighting machine than a B-24. It was. The operation became legendary in business operations annals.

When the war was over McNamara wanted to go back to teaching in Cambridge. But Margy came down with severe polio and the medical bills were staggering. Tex Thornton, a great hustler, had the idea of selling the Stat Control group as a unit to a large corporation. Henry Ford II had just taken over his grandfather's almost bankrupt car company and desperately needed help. He hired three top executives from General Motors headed by Ernie Breech and the Stat Control unit. McNamara worked in finance and introduced many efficiencies. He rose quickly and by by 1960 became president of the Ford Motor Company.

But the McNamaras were uncomfortable in the auto culture of Detroit and the Ford Motor Company. He did not like to play golf, get drunk, and talk cars, especially fast cars. The auto executives were Republicans. While McNamara was not a Democrat, he had voted for FDR in 1940 and JFK in 1960. Neither he nor his wife wanted to live in a Detroit suburb with auto executives. Rather, they settled in Ann Arbor to hobnob with the University of Michigan faculty. While the wives of other Ford big shots liked style shows featuring mink coats, Margy showed them the University of Michigan cyclotron. Most important, McNamara did not believe in fashionable and profitable frills on cars. He wanted to provide basic utilitarian transportation like Henry's Model T and his pet project was the Ford Falcon. He also tried to keep prices low. Thus, he alienated other Ford executives, to say nothing of dealers. As Halberstam put it, "It is not easy being a puritan in Babylon."

When Kennedy was getting together a cabinet in late 1960 he talked to Lovett. He was so taken with the Republican banker that he offered him his choice of State, Defense, or Treasury. Lovett said his ulcers made federal service impossible. Was there anyone else? Kennedy asked. Lovett mentioned the fellow out at Ford who had worked for him during the war and had been outstanding. Kennedy invited McNamara to take either Defense or Treasury. He did not know what the Secretary of the Treasury did, and, furthermore, finance was boring. McNamara became Secretary of Defense.

In a cabinet of stars McNamara's shone brightest. Defense was notorious for its waste, inefficiency, politicization, and service rivalries. McNamara brought in a team of exceptionally talented people—Cyrus Vance, John McNaughton, and Roswell Gilpatric on policy, Charles Hitch on budgeting, Alain Enthoven in systems control, and the administrative whiz kid Joe Califano, among others. He studied the operations intensively and quantified everything possible. He then introduced a great many efficiencies, which reduced costs significantly. They also led to a wholesale loss of jobs and much annoyance to the brass. But they impressed both Kennedy and Johnson. Further, he was a formidable witness before congressional committees and enjoyed a great press.

McNamara had become a cold warrior in 1949 when he read an article in *Foreign Affairs* that laid out Stalin's imperial acquisitions. In 1961 he sided with the Joint Chiefs in a memorandum to Kennedy arguing that South Vietnam was crucial to the U.S. in its conflict with Communism and that its fall would have a domino impact in Southeast Asia along with worldwide effects. He urged a limited military commitment to defend South Vietnam. He told Kennedy that he would "look after" a war in Vietnam. Also in 1961 he and James Webb, administrator of NASA, supported Vice President Johnson's recommendation to the President for a program to place a man on the moon before the USSR did so. It would, they wrote, enhance "national prestige" and become "part of the battle along the fluid front of the cold war." Thus, as early as 1961 Robert McNamara was a very cold warrior.[3]

Some who opposed intervention in Vietnam charged that a war without congressional approval was unconstitutional. In early 1964, at Rostow's urging, the State Department started to draft a joint resolution to authorize the President to take action unilaterally. By June Johnson had become interested. But he soon changed his mind, reckoning it would not be politic to present himself as a warmonger in the campaign against Goldwater.

For a decade the CIA had sent clandestine South Vietnamese teams to the North to plant guerrillas, abduct or assassinate officials, disrupt installations, and so on, much as the Vietcong did in the South. Almost all the operatives were killed or captured. The South Vietnamese paratroopers failed to report for their missions, and officers arrived in drunken stupors. In late 1963 the Joint Chiefs revived and expanded the raids with presidential approval as OPLAN 34-A. The North Vietnamese had modern Soviet anti-aircraft missiles and radars around their cities and along the Gulf of Tonkin. To locate the sites, the U.S. ran U-2 overflights and put naval ships with electronic eavesdropping monitors in the gulf. Extremely fast Norwegian patrol boats with South Vietnamese crews, called DeSoto missions, moved into the gulf to activate the radar transmitters.

The first mission sailed on July 30, 1964, when four boats from Danang attacked the radars. On August 2 three North Vietnamese torpedo boats went after the U.S. destroyer *Maddox*. The skipper, John J. Herrick, radioed the carrier *Ticonderoga* for air cover. The North Vietnamese launched their torpedoes, two of which missed, and the third proved a dud. Only one machine-gun bullet struck the *Maddox*, harmlessly. The aircraft sank one boat and crippled the others.

Johnson played down the incident. But the Joint Chiefs demanded retaliation. Another carrier, the *Constellation*, moved into the South China Sea and a second destroyer, the *C. Turner Joy*, joined the *Maddox*.

On August 3 both ships were in Tonkin Gulf as the South Vietnamese boats sped toward the radars. There were summer storms and heavy seas and the visibility was poor. That evening the sonar on the *Maddox* was erratic and the skilled operator, who doubled as a gunner, was manning a turret. His job was turned over to an inexperienced sailor. During the evening radio signals were intercepted that gave Herrick the "impression" that the North Vietnamese were preparing an attack. He radioed the *Ticonderoga* for support and eight aircraft arrived, led by Commander James B. Stockdale, an outstanding pilot. His earphones crackled with radio traffic between the destroyers alerting each other to imaginary approaching patrol boats. He wrote later, "The *Joy* was firing at 'targets' the *Maddox* couldn't track on radar and the *Maddox* was dodging 'torpedoes' the *Joy* couldn't hear on its sonar." In his first report Herrick counted 22 torpedoes, none of which scored a hit, along with two or three patrol boats, all sunk. As he left the site of the "action," Herrick began to have doubts. A questioning of crews on both destroyers revealed that no sailor had seen or heard enemy gunfire. The radar blips could have been due to bad weather or the bad judgment of the rookie sonar technician. Stockdale later wrote that he had "the best seat in the house" over the alleged battle for an hour and a half. The debriefing officer asked whether he had seen enemy boats. "Not a one. No boats, no boat wakes, no ricochets off boats, no boat gunfire, no torpedo wakes—nothing but black sea and American firepower."

Herrick sent his first message at 7:40 p.m. Saigon time on August 4 and it moved up the chain of command to the Pentagon. The North Vietnamese appeared to be preparing an attack on the destroyers. The President was in a breakfast meeting with the congressional Democrats at 9:12 a.m. Washington time when McNamara relayed this news. Johnson informed the leaders. They agreed that, if they struck, he should seek a congressional resolution and retaliate. He asked House Majority Leader Carl Albert to stay. McNamara called to report that the North Vietnamese had attacked, which was not true. Albert heard Johnson say, "They have? Now, I'll tell you what I want. I not only want those patrol boats that attacked the *Maddox* destroyed, I want everything at that harbor destroyed; I want the whole works destroyed. I want to give them a real dose."

Kenny O'Donnell walked out with Johnson immediately afterward and they "agreed as politicians that the President's leadership was being tested under these circumstances and that he must respond decisively. His opponent was Senator Goldwater and the attack on Lyndon Johnson was going to come from the right and the hawks and he must not allow them to accuse him of vacillating or being an indecisive leader."

McNamara spent a frantic afternoon seeking confirmation of the attack. Herrick, under enormous pressure, gradually became more affirmative. By 4:49 p.m. the Joint Chiefs and McNamara concluded that there was enough evidence to confirm and Johnson was notified. McNamara proposed reinforcements for the destroyers and an air strike at the bases.

The President met with the congressional leadership of both parties that evening and, excepting Mansfield, got approval for both the attack and the resolution. He then spoke to Goldwater, who concurred. The President ordered the Navy to retaliate "against gunboats and certain supporting facilities in North Vietnam." He made a television statement at 11:36 p.m. on August 4, hardly a time to attract an audience. Ironically, Stockdale was ordered to lead the reprisal. His reaction: "Reprisal for what? . . . How do I get in touch with the President? He's going off half-cocked." As he dropped his bombs on Vinh, Stockdale said to himself, "America has just been locked into the Vietnam War." Later he would be shot down and would spend almost eight years as a prisoner-of-war, in addition to losing a leg.

On August 4 Abram Chayes, the State Department legal adviser, worked over the resolution which was approved by, of all people, George Ball. The next morning Bundy convened a small group, including Douglass Cater, the new White House adviser on domestic issues, to discuss the resolution. "Isn't this a little precipitous?" Cater asked. "Do we have all the information?" "The President," Bundy said, "has decided and that's what we're doing." "Gee, Mac," Cater said, "I haven't really thought it through." Bundy said, "Don't."

The President sent the Tonkin Gulf Resolution to Congress on August 5, 1964. The timing was perfect politically. The Republicans had already nominated Goldwater and the Democratic convention would open the following week in Atlantic City. Thus, the GOP was already committed to a hawkish position and members of the party in Congress must vote for the resolution. Most dovish Democrats, of whom there were a fair number, had no alternative but to support their President, who was certain of nomination, rather than open themselves to the charge of deserting him during a military "crisis."

The heart of the resolution, Section 2, read as follows:

The United States regards as vital to its national interest and to world peace the maintenance of international peace and security in Southeast Asia. Consonant with the Constitution of the United States and the Charter of the United Nations and in accordance with its obligations under the Southeast Asia Collective Defense Treaty, the United States is, therefore, prepared, as the President determines, to take all necessary steps, including the use of armed force, to assist any member or protocol state of the Southeast Asia Collective Defense Treaty requesting assistance in defense of its freedom.

The resolution sped through Congress. The hearings were held on August 6, those before the House Foreign Affairs Committee for 40 minutes, those before the joint Senate Foreign Relations and Armed Services Committees for 1 hour and 40 minutes. The House committee was unanimous as was the House itself, 416 to 0. The Senate committees voted 31 to 1, with Morse dissenting. The Senate split 88 to 2, Ernest Gruening of Alaska joining Morse. President Johnson had what Ball called his "blank check." It was based on what David Wise called "the most crucial and disgraceful episode in the modern history of government lying."[4]

Johnson distanced himself from major action on Vietnam prior to his assumption of the presidency on January 20, 1965. "In 1964," Califano said, "he took the position that he wasn't going to make major decisions in an election year on war and peace and life and death. He just wasn't going to do it." Having spent his professional lifetime as an elected official in a representative government, in his mind election by the people legitimated political power. As an accidental President, he had authority to execute Kennedy's legacy. But he would not make a fundamental military decision on Vietnam until he had been elected and inaugurated as President himself.

The U.S. had established an air base at Bienhoa 12 miles north of Saigon to train South Vietnamese pilots on B-57 bombers. Before dawn on November 1, 1964, a hundred Vietcong dressed in black peasant pajamas silently invaded the compound to shell the airplanes and buildings. Six B-57s were destroyed, 20 other aircraft were damaged, five Americans and two South Vietnamese were killed, and nearly a hundred were injured. Search parties found no one. All had melted into the friendly countryside.

The Joint Chiefs demanded retaliatory air strikes against North Vietnam and Laos. Johnson, who was campaigning, declined to act and remained silent. He did, however, order Mac Bundy to establish the National Security Council Working Group to make a comprehensive study of Vietnam and to propose policy options. Officials just below the secretary level headed teams from Defense, State, the CIA, and the Joint Chiefs—John McNaughton from Defense, William Bundy from State, and Admiral Lloyd Mustin from the chiefs. None had ever heard the cooing of doves. William Bundy and McNaughton wrote the report. The Working Group spent an intensive three weeks on the study and produced three presidential options.

The report is significant both for paving the road to war and for establishing the assumptions on which the Johnson administration acted. There is no doubt whatever that these premises were fully accepted by the principals—Mac Bundy, obviously, McNamara and Rusk, Director of Central Intelligence John A. McCone, and Chairman of the Joint Chiefs General Earle Wheeler. The President accepted their analysis and chose from their policy options. In determining and assessing how the U.S. got into the Vietnam War, therefore, one must start with these assumptions and examine their validity.

The premise of the study was that the preservation of an anti-Communist South Vietnam was the linchpin to the U.S. "overall policy of resisting Communist expansion world-wide." Both the major Communist powers, the Soviet Union and China, were assumed to seek territorial aggrandizement, in part by taking over movements for national liberation, as in Vietnam. China by proximity was the greater threat in Southeast Asia. The group argued that the fall of South Vietnam would drag along Laos, Cambodia, Thailand, Malaysia, and the Philippines. While they shied away from using Eisenhower's term "domino theory," evidently because of differences over its definition, this was what they meant: push one and all would fall. Further, if the U.S. withdrew from or was forced out of Vietnam, that would, they predicted, shake the resolve of the American people and their European allies to resist Communism elsewhere. This would pose an additional threat to South Korea, Taiwan, India, and Iran, and might even cause trouble in Japan. As Admiral Mustin put it, we would be forced to "accept world-wide humiliation." America's "national prestige, credibility, and honor" were at stake.

One of the many problems with this geopolitical analysis was that the linchpin was made of loose sand and kept falling apart. South Vietnam was not a nation; the North and South together were the Vietnamese nation. South Vietnam was a great power concoction to deny Ho Chi Minh control over half the country. The prodigious American effort to create what the Working Group called a "viable effective government in SVN based on the broadest possible consensus" had failed. A large part of the population in the South, perhaps a majority, supported the Vietcong and even Buddhist bonzes expressed their opposition to military governments by immolating themselves on the streets of Saigon.

The tyranny of Diem had ended in a military coup and his assassination in November 1963. The junta which followed could not stick together and its leader, General "Big" Minh, preferred to raise orchids and play tennis. General Nguyen Khanh took over by coup in January 1964. In August student and Buddhist demonstrations overthrew him and he was followed by a weak triumvirate—himself, Minh, and Khiem. Riots by Catholics and Buddhists disposed of them. Another coup restored Khanh in September, but he lasted only till November when a civilian, Huong, stepped forward. Khanh overthrew him in January 1965 and installed General Oanh. Maxwell Taylor, the American ambassador, wrote wistfully, "Only the emergence of an exceptional leader could improve the situation, and no George Washington is in sight."

As the options proposed to the President disclosed, the authors of the study strongly and unanimously favored a sharp escalation in the U.S. military commitment to South Vietnam, particularly the bombing of the North. Their most powerful argument was the ineffectiveness of the Saigon government, and they painted it in the starkest colors. It was, they charged, incapable of governing in either the civilian or military spheres. "Government ministries in Saigon are close to a standstill." Administration was "plagued by confusion, apathy, and poor morale." McNaughton thought progress unlikely "despite our best ideas and efforts." Even with a major U.S. military commitment, South Vietnam "might still come apart." Was this sorry mess a proper linchpin of American foreign policy?

Because of South Vietnamese weakness, the U.S. had no bargaining power in negotiating a peaceful settlement with Hanoi. Thus, there must be no negotiations until the Vietcong and the North Vietnamese were battered into submission. Likewise, there must be no coalition government because the Communists would quickly assert their dominance. But the prospect of ultimate negotiations, when Hanoi would capitulate to American terms, was a key feature of the options. The group perceived a scenario culminating in an international "Geneva format" setting. At that point both North Vietnam and the U.S. would withdraw from South Vietnam.

For the Working Group the prospects were extremely grim. The United States, therefore, must take great risks. They did not hesitate to urge President Johnson to assume them:

> We cannot guarantee to maintain a non-Communist South Vietnam short of committing ourselves to whatever degree of military action would be required to defeat North Vietnam and probably Communist China militarily. Such a commitment would involve high risks of a major conflict in Asia, which could not be confined to air and naval action but would almost inevitably involve a Korean-style ground action and possibly even the use of nuclear weapons at some point.

In the options it proposed, however, the Working Group did not discuss ground forces, to say nothing of nuclear bombs. They offered the President three choices: Option A would continue present covert military and naval operations, would add bombing reprisals for attacks on U.S. facilities, and would reject negotiations unless the North accepted the American interpretation of the Geneva accords. Option B would continue present operations, add a progressively heavier bombing campaign, and negotiations during the bombing. McNaughton called this a "fast/full squeeze." Option C was like B except that the onset of negotiations would trigger a halt in the bombing.

George Ball described these choices as an exercise in the "Goldilocks Principle": A was too soft; B was too hard; and C, the Working Group's favorite, was "just right." By the latter part of 1964, Ball, who was undersecretary of state, was the only dove who remained in a high position in the administration and, though very well informed, had no direct responsibility for Vietnam. When Chester Bowles became ambassador to India, Averell Harriman left the far eastern desk to succeed him as undersecretary. William Bundy replaced Harriman. Roger Hilsman and Paul Kattenburg were relieved of responsibility for Vietnam. Rusk pretty much ceded control over Southeast Asian policy to McNamara. In the White House Schlesinger resigned to write a biography of Kennedy. Galbraith returned to Harvard. McGeorge Bundy had been "gatekeeper" for Kennedy as National Security Adviser, presenting the facts and options without expressing his own views. Now with Johnson he made recommendations, which were invariably hawkish.

In late September 1964 Ball became alarmed by the drift to war. "An unmistakable smell of escalation [was] in the air." While virtually certain that he could not stop the slide, he felt morally obligated to launch a "rearguard action." Fully occupied with Cyprus, Europe, and other areas during the day, he dictated into a machine at home late at night. On October 5, 1964, he finished a massive memorandum and on June 29, 1965, as Johnson was about to commit ground troops, he submitted another. Together they presented a devastating analysis of the Working Group report. Mike Mansfield shared Ball's views and wrote four letters to the President which meticulously expressed his deep misgivings over the prospect of war. In addition, the French government was con.inced that an American war in Vietnam would be a grievous error. Foreign Minister Couve de Murville told this to Bundy and Johnson in February 1965. According to Bundy, he believed that "there is not, and cannot be, any workable government in a situation of 'American occupation.' " The U.S., he said, cannot "avoid defeat in South Vietnam," a potential danger to Europe and so to France.

On one point these critics and the Working Group were in full agreement: the bankruptcy of the government of South Vietnam. "From the point of view of legitimacy, effective representation of the major elements of opinion and social and economic progressiveness," Ball wrote, "the present government seems even worse than its predecessors." Mansfield was convinced that this regime was incompetent even for "negotiating a bona fide settlement, let alone for going ahead into North Vietnam." Diem and "Big" Minh had more legitimacy. "We are now in the process of putting together makeshift regimes in much the same way that the French were compelled to operate in 1952–54."

The notion that the worldwide struggle between the free nations and the Communist bloc turned on South Vietnam struck the critics as ridiculous. Ball, who had worked on the rebuilding of Europe after World War II, was convinced that the U.S. had a far higher security and economic stake in Europe; among our friends in Asia, South Vietnam was near the bottom of his list. With all this talk about prestige and humiliation, Ball wrote, "we have tended to give the Vietnamese struggle an exaggerated and symbolic significance. (*Mea culpa,* since I personally participated in this effort)." Mansfield was appalled by the idea that South Vietnam was the linchpin of a world struggle. In his mind it was the outcome of misguided great power policy and he would do everything possible to isolate it. "American interests are served not by United States domination of the Indo-China area at whatever the cost and by total exclusion of Chinese influence, which is, in any event, culturally impossible and, in the long run, economically improbable."

The Working Group's corollary, that the fall of South Vietnam would bring many other dominoes down, made no sense to these critics. Each of the neighbors had unique interests. Communism was not a monolith. The Soviet Union and China had sharp differences; China and Vietnam were historic enemies. North Vietnam, an extremely poor and war-torn nation, lacked the power to engage in imperial conquests. Finally, a guerrilla war cannot be exported.

Despite the fact that the Working Group urged U.S. entry into an important and dangerous war, its report, amazingly, failed to address military questions except for a cursory treatment of bombing. There was no discussion of the ground forces needed, none of how to deal with guerrilla warfare, none of the potential costs in lives and dollars, none of the duration of the conflict. Ball and Mansfield, neither a military expert, addressed these questions as best they could.

Ball had been on the Strategic Bombing Survey which evaluated U.S. and RAF bombing of Germany during World War II. The study nurtured a healthy skepticism of the capacity of saturation bombing to destroy an industrialized nation's economy and its will to fight. Skepticism turned to cynicism in the case of a basically peasant society. Bombing the Vietcong in South Vietnam was virtually useless because they could not be located in the jungle. Very heavy bombing of the North could cause severe damage, but essentially to civilians and the buildings they occupied. The military and its supporting infrastructure was diffused and the Soviet Union and China would quickly replace losses. Since Ho was determined to unite Vietnam, there was no chance that bombing would compel him to sue for peace. The most important result of bombing the North, Ball argued, would be the shift of veteran North Vietnamese combat divisions to the South, which would much stiffen the Vietcong. The U.S. would then be compelled to build up its ground forces in the South. This would prolong a guerrilla war of stalemate, hardly an attractive prospect for the U.S. A major worry: "If we do expand the deployment of United States forces in South Viet-Nam and find that this does not do the trick, we shall be under enormous pressures to extend the territorial scope of the bombing offensive and widen the war." Does anyone in his right mind want a war with China?

Mansfield, who made a similar analysis, was deeply worried about expanding the war. "If a significant extension of the conflict beyond South Vietnam should occur then the prospects are appalling. Even short of nuclear war, an extension of the war may well saddle us with enormous burdens and costs in Cambodia, Laos and elsewhere in Asia, along with those in Vietnam." When the military asked for authorization to bomb the Hanoi-Haiphong area in early June 1965, Mansfield opposed strenuously, not least because he expected it would lead to greater Chinese involvement.[5]

Since Johnson respected both Ball and Mansfield for their experience, intelligence, loyalty, and integrity, he was deeply troubled by their opposition. Nor were they alone. The President's old friend and mentor, Dick Russell, according to Halberstam, warned him "not to go ahead, that it would never work; Russell had an intuitive sense that it was all going to be more difficult and complicated than the experts were saying." Johnson's trusted adviser Clark Clifford wrote him, "This could be a quagmire. It could turn into an open end commitment on our part that would take more and more ground troops, without a realistic hope of ultimate victory."

Johnson, Halberstam wrote, became "restless, irritable, frustrated, more and more frenetic, and more difficult to work with." Richard Goodwin and Bill Moyers went further; they questioned his mental stability. The President was trapped in the guns or butter dilemma. He was pushing the Great Society and the Vietnam War at the same time. "He knew," Halberstam wrote, "he would not have the resources for both the domestic programs and a real war."

In December 1964 the President invited three newsmen, including David Wise of the *Herald Tribune,* to a three-hour backgrounder in which he talked about Vietnam. Wise wrote:

> He likened his situation to standing on a copy of a newspaper in the middle of the Atlantic Ocean. "If I go this way," he said, tilting his hand to the right, "I'll topple over, and if I go this way"—he tilted his hand to the left—"I'll topple over, and if I stay where I am, the paper will be soaked up and I'll sink slowly to the bottom of the sea." As he said this, he lowered his hand slowly to the floor.

Johnson liked this kind of image. In July 1965, as he was making the ground force commitment in Vietnam, he interrupted a meeting at the

White House to say, "Vietnam is like being in a plane without a parachute when all the engines go out. If you jump, you'll probably be killed, and if you stay in you'll crash and probably burn."

Johnson, obsessed, talked incessantly about Vietnam. In June 1965 Moyers and Goodwin held a dinner for task force chairmen, and Charles Haar of the Harvard Law School, who had headed the beautification group, was a guest in the mess hall in the west wing of the White House.

About 10:30 the President walked in. Having missed dinner, he put away "huge portions" of steak and lobster tails capped by "enormous gobs" of vanilla ice cream. After 11:00 Humphrey entered and Johnson left. Around midnight when everyone was a "little tired and sleepy" Johnson returned and launched into a monologue on Vietnam, a subject Haar knew nothing about. He cited the prominent people who urged him to send in ground forces, spoke movingly of the mothers who would lose their sons, and talked of Wilson and FDR forfeiting the New Freedom and the New Deal to wars. "I don't want that to happen to the Great Society. . . . I don't want to get involved in a war." It was, Haar said, a "virtuoso performance."

About 2:00 Moyers said to the President that they ought to call it a night. A number of the chairmen were so shaken that they repaired to an all-night hamburger stand and talked till 4:00. Later Haar returned to work on model cities and he wondered about guns or butter. He remembered LBJ saying Vietnam would not stop him. "He would not let it happen to the Great Society. Of course, it sure as hell happened."

Despite his doubts and fears, Johnson agreed with the Working Group analysis and the pressure from Bundy and McNamara was unrelenting. "Both of us," Bundy wrote on January 27, 1965, "are now pretty well convinced that our current policy can lead only to disastrous defeat." The U.S. was waiting vainly for "a stable government" in South Vietnam. Our Vietnamese friends were becoming convinced that the Vietcong would win and were "covering their flanks." This mood was evident among some Americans. "The worst course of action is to continue in this essentially passive role which can only lead to eventual defeat and an invitation to get out in humiliating circumstances."

Bundy, who had never been to Vietnam, went out in early February for an assessment. By coincidence, Aleksei Kosygin, the new Soviet premier, was in Hanoi at the same time to persuade the North Vietnamese to discuss peace. They angrily denounced his proposal and instead demanded more arms, which they got.

American special forces and advisers were billeted at Camp Holloway, three miles from Pleiku in the central highlands. A large fleet of airplanes and helicopters was parked on a nearby airstrip. In the darkness of February 6–7, 1965, the Vietcong carried out a massive surprise attack. Eight Americans were killed, a hundred were wounded, and ten aircraft were destroyed.

Virtually all the Vietcong escaped. In the clothing of one of the few who were shot was an accurate map of the camp.

Bundy was packing to leave when he learned of the attack. He met immediately with Taylor and Westmoreland. They agreed that the "streetcar" had arrived and Bundy phoned the White House to urge strongly immediate retaliatory air raids against North Vietnam. Westmoreland thought Bundy behaved like a civilian field marshal who had smelled gunpowder for the first time.

That same day Bundy wrote a chilling memo to the President on "The Situation in Viet Nam." "Defeat appears inevitable." There was just enough time to turn it around, "but not much." The "prestige" and "influence" of the U.S. were at stake. "The energy and persistence of the Viet Cong are astonishing." The attack on Pleiku demanded "sustained reprisal."

Johnson reacted strongly to the taking of American lives. After easily obtaining the approval of the National Security Council, he launched Flaming Dart, which soon became a program of gradually broadened air attacks against North Vietnam with certain areas, including Hanoi-Haiphong and the Chinese border, out of bounds. In March the air attacks were significantly expanded into Rolling Thunder, that is, massive raids on infiltration routes and military installations in the North, including for the first time the use of B-52s with carpet bombing and napalm.

In his February 7 memo Bundy made a suggestion that the President rejected at once:

> At its best the struggle in Vietnam will be long. . . . This fundamental fact [must] be made clear . . . to our own people and to the people of Vietnam. . . . No early solution is possible. . . . The people of the United States have the necessary will to accept and to execute a policy that rests upon the reality that there is no short cut to success in South Vietnam.

While he was unable wholly to conceal the fact that he was taking the U.S. into war, Johnson made every effort to carry it off in secrecy. As the truth filtered out, of course, his credibility gap widened and deepened. In February 1965 James Reston of the *New York Times* wrote, "It is time to call a spade a bloody shovel. This country is in an undeclared and unexplained war in Vietnam." By February 9, the telegrams reaching the White House on the air strikes were running almost 12 to 1 against.

But the bombing created its own irresistible momentum. The American airfield at coastal Danang was vulnerable to Vietcong guerrilla attack. On February 22 Westmoreland asked Johnson for two marine battalions, 3500 men, to protect the base. On March 8 they splashed ashore in full battle dress on the beach at Danang, cheered on by pretty Vietnamese girls.

Early returns on the bombing were not encouraging. Between February 7 and April 4, 1965, the U.S. had conducted 34 strikes and the South Vietnamese 10 more on military installations in North Vietnam using bombs up to 1000 pounds and napalm. The U.S. had lost 25 planes, the South Vietnamese 6. Until almost the end of the period all had been shot down by antiaircraft guns; now, ominously, MIGs were also bringing them down. The North Vietnamese were taking many measures to minimize the damage. "The air strikes," General Wheeler wrote, "have not reduced in any major way the over-all military capabilities of the DRV." The economic effects seemed "minimal." "Outwardly, the North Vietnamese government appears to be uninfluenced by our air strikes." Director John McCone of the CIA was worried. "The strikes to date have not caused a change in the North Vietnamese policy of directing Viet Cong insurgency, infiltrating cadres and supplying materiel. In anything, the strikes . . . have hardened their attitude." This meant inevitably that there would be pressure on the U.S. to commit ground troops. "We will find ourselves mired down in combat in a military effort that we cannot win, and from which we will have extreme difficulty in extracting ourselves." Neither Johnson nor his advisers seem to have paid any attention to this warning.

On April 6, 1965, the President signed the critically important National Security Action Memorandum No. 328. He approved a wide range of stepped-up military decisions: 12 covert actions by the CIA; 21 actions by the Army; an 18,000 to 20,000 man increase in support troops; deployment of two marine battalions and one marine air squadron; a broadening of the mission of all marine battalions; "urgent exploration" with the governments of South Korea, Australia, and New Zealand of their deployment of "significant combat elements" to South Vietnam; an "ascending tempo" of Rolling Thunder strikes; and the bombing of Laos.

The extraordinary concluding paragraph of No. 328 read as follows:

> The President desires that with respect to the actions in paragraphs 5 through 7 [increases in ground forces], premature publicity be avoided by all possible precautions. The actions themselves should be taken as rapidly as practicable, but in ways that should minimize any appearance of sudden changes in policy, and official statements on these troop movements will be made only with the direct approval of the Secretary of Defense, in consultation with the Secretary of State. The President's desire is that these movements and changes should be understood as being gradual and wholly consistent with existing policy.

No. 328, David Wise pointed out, "ordered that the commitment of American combat troops in Vietnam be kept secret." This was "not designed to fool Hanoi or the Viet Cong, who would find out quickly enough who was shooting at them; it was designed to conceal the facts from the American electorate." Westmoreland agreed. "To my mind the American people had a right to know forthrightly . . . what we were calling on their sons to do."

No. 328, Wise concluded, "must surely be one of the most shameful official documents of a shameful time in American history."

In May the Vietcong attacked the South Vietnamese army. They overran Songbe, the capital of Phuoc Long province north of Saigon. They destroyed two South Vietnamese battalions near Quangngai in central Vietnam. They then returned to Phuoc Long to raid government headquarters at Dong Xoai and struck at U.S. special forces nearby. Several South Vietnamese units disintegrated and their officers fled. In June Catholic militants overthrew the government. General Nguyen Van Thieu became chief of state and Air Vice Marshal Nguyen Cao Ky became prime minister. Westmoreland was appalled by these events and informed Johnson that only U.S. combat troops could prevent the collapse of South Vietnam.

On July 20, 1965, McNamara sent the President a key memorandum entitled "Recommendations of Additional Deployments to Vietnam." He was joined by Westmoreland, the Joint Chiefs, Admiral Sharp, and the embassy in Saigon.

"The situation in South Vietnam," he wrote, "is worse than a year ago (when it was worse than the year before that)." The Vietcong was mauling the South Vietnamese army, which had been forced to abandon five district capitals. "The government is able to provide security to fewer and fewer people in less and less territory as terrorism increases." Roads, railroads, power lines, and communications links had been knocked out. The economy was breaking down; peasants were displaced; and inflation was rampant. The odds were against the Ky government surviving for a year. At the same time, the Vietcong was receiving a steady flow of supplies. The bombing of the North had no visible impact on Hanoi.

The only option McNamara could see was to "expand promptly and substantially . . . U.S. military pressure," which should come in stages. The present 75,000 men would increase to 200,000 by October. He would call up another 235,000 by the end of the year from the Reserve and the National Guard. In the first half of 1966 another 375,000 would follow, making a total of 600,000. He urged a request to Congress for an appropriation to finance these massive troop levies. If his recommendations were adopted, McNamara observed with very guarded optimism, the U.S. could expect an "acceptable outcome within a reasonable time."

McNamara offered a vague and conventional plan for victory. "The strategy for winning this stage of the war will be to take the offensive—to take and hold the initiative." This would be accomplished by "aggressive exploitation of superior military forces," by "pressing the fight against VC/DRV main force units in South Vietnam to run them to ground and destroy them." It did not seem to occur to McNamara or to the others who signed on that they were dealing with guerrilla warfare.

Bundy recommended that only the proposals for the period until the fall of 1965 should be approved now. Johnson strongly agreed; he opposed calling out the Reserves and the Guard and would not make an appeal to Congress. On July 27 the President approved the short-term McNamara troop recommendations. This was a momentous step: a decisive U.S. military ground commitment to Vietnam. Now there would be no turning back.

The next day, July 28, at noon, when the TV audience was very small, President Johnson in a press conference sort of informed the American people that their nation was at war. He justified his action with a barebones summary of the Working Group's reasoning: the great stake in Vietnam in the contest between Communism and the free world and the domino theory. He argued that his policy flowed from that of Eisenhower and Kennedy.

This was, in Arthur Schlesinger's phrase, the "imperial presidency" run wild. Here Lyndon Johnson acted alone to put the nation into a major war. He did not seek the approval of Congress or of the American people, which, in any case, could not have given it because the public was almost totally uninformed.

The President said that he had asked Westmoreland what he needed, had been told, and gave it to him:

> I have today ordered to Viet-Nam the Air Mobile Division and certain other forces which will raise our fighting strength from 75,000 to 125,000 men almost immediately. Additional forces will be needed later, and they will be sent as requested.
>
> This will make it necessary to increase our active fighting forces by raising the monthly draft call from 17,000 over a period of time to 35,000 per month, and for us to step up our campaign for voluntary enlistments.

This was an opportunity for the President to announce the nation's war aims, to give the American people and the troops the justifications for the war. He did nothing of the sort. His brief allusions to the struggle with Communism and the domino theory had little or no meaning to Americans. His claim that Eisenhower and Kennedy had made "most solemn pledges" to defend South Vietnam was untrue. Neither Eisenhower nor Kennedy had pledged, solemnly or otherwise, to go to war to preserve South Vietnam. Johnson said nothing about a strategy for victory because he had none.

A reporter pointed out that the National Commander of the American Legion had recently returned from Vietnam and had predicted that the war would go on for "5, 6, or 7 years." Was that possible? Johnson replied that there was "no quick solution," but he would not predict "the months or years or decades." Another reporter asked whether the "American people may have to face the problem of guns or butter." Answer: "I have not the slightest doubt but whatever it is necessary to face, the American people will face." Not very illuminating.

Given the enormous importance of the occasion, the President's performance was disgraceful. The reporters sensed that something was wrong. The columnist Joseph Alsop, himself an extreme hawk, watched with dismay. "It must be said," he wrote, "there is a genuine element of pathos (and pray God the pathos does not turn into tragedy) in the spectacle of this extraordinary man in the White House wrestling with the Vietnamese problem, which is so distasteful to him, and all the while visibly longing to go back to the domestic miracle-working he so much enjoys."[6]

General William C. Westmoreland had come to Vietnam in January 1964, had taken over the advisory group in June, and became commander when the great military build-up started in July 1965. He was, Stanley Karnow wrote, "nearly fifty years old, and he looked like the model of a modern American general. A tall, erect, handsome West Pointer with hooded eyes and a chiseled chin, he had earned a chestful of ribbons during World War II and Korea, and he exuded the same virtuous resolve he had displayed as an eagle scout during his boyhood in South Carolina." He viewed generalship as an exercise in management and was extremely well organized. Under his watchful eye the Americanization of the war between 1965 and 1967 was conducted masterfully. He demanded enormous numbers of troops and immense quantities of equipment and supplies. He got everything he asked for. U.S. troops in Vietnam (end of year numbers) rose from 23,000 in 1964 to 184,000 in 1965, 385,000 in 1966, and 486,000 in 1967.

Karnow recalled the Vietnam he knew in the late fifties. Saigon could have been a provincial French city—"its acacia-shaded streets lined with quiet shops and sleepy sidewalk cafes, its residential district of handsome villas wallowing in lush tropical gardens of jasmine, mimosa and brilliant red and purple bougainvillea." Danang, Nhatrang, and Vung Tau were "lovely little seaside towns." Those in the Mekong Delta awakened only once a week when the peasants brought their produce to market. Michael Herr, who covered the war with the grunts, their faces in the mud, came in low over Saigon on a chopper at dawn on a day in late 1967. He saw something "beautiful for once, and only once." He saw the city as it had once been. "Paris of the East, Pearl of the Orient, long open avenues, lined and bowered over by trees running into spacious parks, precisioned scale, all under the soft shell from a million breakfast fires, camphor smoke rising and diffusing, covering Saigon and the shining veins of the river with a warmth like the return of better times."

Karnow was astonished by the "convulsive transformation" of the country:

> American army engineers and private contractors labored around the clock, often accomplishing stupendous tasks in a matter of months. Their giant tractors and bulldozers and cranes carved out roads and put up bridges, and at one place in the Mekong Delta they dredged the river to create a

six-hundred-acre island as a secure campsite. They erected mammoth fuel depots and warehouses, some refrigerated. They constructed hundreds of helicopter pads and scores of airfields, including huge jet strips at Danang and Bienhoa. Until their arrival, Saigon had been South Vietnam's only major port, and its antiquated facilities were able to handle only modest ships. Now, almost overnight, they built six new deep-water harbors, among them a gigantic complex at Camranh Bay, which they completed at breakneck speed by towing prefabricated floating piers across the Pacific. They connected remote parts of the country with an intricate communications grid, and they linked Saigon to Washington with submarine cables and radio networks so efficient that U.S. embassy officials could dial the White House in seconds—and President Johnson could, as he did frequently, call to check on progress.

By 1967, a million tons of supplies a month were pouring into Vietnam to sustain the U.S. force—an average of a hundred pounds a day for every American there. An American infantryman could rely on the latest hardware. He was transported to the battle scene by helicopter, and, if wounded, flown out aboard medical evacuation choppers known as dust-offs because of the dust they kicked up by their rotors as they landed. His targets had usually been "softened" by air strikes and artillery bombardments, and he could summon additional air and artillery assistance during a fight. Tanks and other armored vehicles often flanked him in action, and his unit carried the most up-to-date arms—mortars, machine guns, grenade and rocket launchers, and the M-16, a fully automatic rifle.

With the exception of the nuclear weapon, nearly every piece of equipment in America's mighty arsenal was sooner or later used in Vietnam. The skies were clogged with bombers, fighters, helicopters and other airplanes, among them high-altitude B-52s and such contrivances as "Puff the Magic Dragon," a converted DC-3 transport outfitted with rapid-fire machine guns capable of raking targets at the rate of eighteen thousand rounds per minute. So dense was the air traffic, in fact, that South Vietnam's airports became the world's busiest. In addition to flying from bases inside the country, the air armada operated out of Guam and Thailand and from carriers in the South China Sea. And the U.S. flotilla deployed off Vietnam also included destroyers, patrol boats, tankers, hospital ships and light craft to penetrate the rivers and canals of the Mekong Delta. Every service sought to be represented in Vietnam because, as American officers explained at the time, "it's the only war we got."

John P. Roche, a presidential aide, spent six or eight weeks in South Vietnam in 1966. He was appalled by "this incredible input of Americans and American stuff just piling into this little country and literally tearing its social fabric. . . . We should have cut two-thirds on the size, and we might have increased the efficiency 50 per cent."

Westmoreland quickly developed a strategy for victory, which he expected to have in hand by 1967. He visualized a two-sided enemy. "Guerillas, local forces, and political cadres at the hamlet and village level continued their small-unit war, seeking to terrorize and control the population and knock off small government outposts." In the wings the enemy kept larger regiments and divisions "to seize and retain territory and to destroy the government's troops and eliminate all vestiges of government control."

Westmoreland visualized three strategic phases: First, American troops would develop and secure their logistical bases. Second, South Vietnamese and American forces would eliminate enemy base camps and sanctuaries. A final major ground attack would destroy their main forces or drive them out of South Vietnam.

Meantime, Rolling Thunder would destroy Hanoi's capability to prosecute the war by wiping out its industry, transport, and oil supplies. South Vietnam would win over the hearts and minds of its peasants in the countryside, a program called "pacification" and, later, "Vietnamization." American officers described it this way: "Grab 'em by the balls, and their hearts and minds will follow."

It is said of failed generals that they insist on fighting the last war. This may have been Westmoreland's problem. In any case, he misread the topography of the country, the intelligence and perseverance of the enemy, the limits of his own forces, and the competence of the government and armed forces of South Vietnam.

Thomas C. Thayer, who spent 13 years analyzing the conflict, concluded that it was "a war without fronts or battle lines, different from the wars we fought in Europe or Korea." In those conventional struggles, "a commander needs to know only two items to monitor his progress. First, he has to know where the front is and which way it is moving. Second, he needs to know the strengths of friendly and enemy forces." Both vanish when there is no front and the enemy cannot be seen. General Lewis Walt, who commanded the Marines, said, "Soon after I arrived in Vietnam it became obvious to me that I had neither a real understanding of the nature of the war nor any clear idea as to how to win it."

The North Vietnamese, in fact, wrangled in 1965 over how to respond to the immense American build-up, whether to infiltrate big units quickly or to pursue a more modest and slower course. The Chinese for their own interests urged the latter. The North Vietnamese rejected their advice and decided to annihilate the South Vietnamese army swiftly in order, they hoped, to produce a U.S. withdrawal. They placed a few large units in the South. But U.S. firepower was decisive in a series of battles during 1966 in which these units suffered devastating casualties. In 1967 General Giap, the hero of Dienbienphu, took over and changed the strategy. The war should be fought by squads, not regiments; it might take 15 or 20 years to gain the victory. The number of battalion or larger attacks declined from 73 in 1965 to 44 in 1966 and 54 in 1967; smaller unit attacks for the same years rose from 612 to 862 to 1,484.

All the studies concluded that Rolling Thunder was a failure. The magnitude of the bombing strains credulity. Thayer counted 3.4 million combat sorties between 1965 and 1973. "In five years, 1965–1969, the U.S. dropped nine times the tonnage it dropped in the Pacific during World War II. This averages out to 70 tons of bombs for every square mile of Vietnam and about 500 pounds of explosives for every man, woman and child in the country."

The *Pentagon Papers* summarized a careful study for 1966. The preceding year there were 55,000 sorties and 33,000 tons of bombs. In 1966 these numbers rose to 148,000 and 128,000. By now most of North Vietnam, excluding part of the Hanoi/Haiphong sanctuary and the Chinese buffer zone, was open to attack. The cost was formidable. In 1965, 171 aircraft were lost; in 1966, 318. A CIA study estimated that it cost $6.60 to inflict $1.00 in damage in 1965, $9.60 in 1966. Estimated casualties in the North, 80 percent civilian, went up from 13,000 to almost 24,000.

But these massive attacks had accomplished little. One study found that they had "not eliminated any important sector of the NVN economy or the military establishment." The Ho Chi Minh Trail through Laos and Cambodia, which Neil Sheehan called "one of the engineering marvels of modern military history," remained open. A concentrated attack on the petroleum supply achieved nothing. Nor had there been any adverse impact on morale, if anything, the opposite. Stepped-up supplies from China and the Soviet Union quickly relieved shortages.

The pacification program to protect South Vietnamese peasants to win their support for the war and the government faced insuperable odds. The Vietcong controlled or contested the countryside. The war disrupted farming and about 4 million people—a quarter of the population—were refugees, and they streamed into the cities, particularly Saigon. Karnow wrote: "They were shunted into makeshift camps of squalid shanties, where primitive sewers bred dysentery, malaria, and other diseases." The cities acquired "an almost mediaeval cast as beggars and hawkers roamed the streets, whining and tugging at Americans for money."

Thus, Vietnam was a guerrilla war on the ground, an agonizingly ruthless war of attrition. When Westmoreland realized that his strategy was irrelevant, he substituted "search and destroy." This was, he argued, "nothing more than the infantry's traditional attack mission: locate the enemy, try to bring him to battle, and either destroy him or force his surrender." As a result, American infantrymen carried the murderous responsibility for finding an enemy who was usually invisible and engaging him in small unit fire, M-16 versus AK-47. This was the war that Michael Herr discovered when he came to Vietnam in 1967:

> Search and Destroy, more a gestalt than a tactic, brought up alive and steaming from the Command psyche. . . . The VC had an ostensibly similar tactic called Find and Kill. Either way, it was us looking for him looking

for us looking for him, war on a Cracker Jack box, repeated to diminishing returns.

Westmoreland talked about "the light at the end of the tunnel." Herr again:

> Outside of Tay Ninh City a man whose work kept him "up to fucking here" in tunnels, lobbing grenades into them, shooting his gun into them, popping CS smoke into them, crawling down into them himself to bring the bad guys out dead or alive, he almost smiled when he heard that one and said, "What does that asshole know about tunnels?"

Herr's apartment in Saigon had an archaic map on the wall, showing Tonkin, Annam, Cochin China. But a new one told you no more about Vietnam. "That was like trying to read the faces of the Vietnamese, and that was like trying to read the wind."

In the jungle you had to keep a cigarette going all the time to fend off the mosquitoes. "War under water, swamp fever and instant involuntary weight control, malarias that could burn you out and cave you in. . . ." Herr:

> Every day people were dying there because of some small detail that they couldn't be bothered to observe. Imagine being too tired to snap a flak jacket closed, too tired to clean your rifle, too tired to guard a light, too tired to deal with the half-inch margins of safety that moving through the war often demanded, just too tired to give a fuck and then dying behind that exhaustion.
>
> The roads were ruined, the trails booby-trapped, satchel charges and grenades blew up jeeps and movie theaters, the VC got work inside all the camps as shoeshine boys and laundresses and honey-dippers, they'd starch your fatigues and burn your shit and then go home and mortar your area. . . . Choppers fell out of the sky like fat poisoned birds a hundred times a day. After a while I couldn't get on one without thinking that I must be out of my fucking mind.
>
> There wasn't a day when someone didn't ask me what I was doing there. . . . Blah, blah, blah cover the war. . . . Not that you didn't hear some overripe bullshit about it: Hearts and Minds, Peoples of the Republic, tumbling dominoes, maintaining the equilibrium of the Dingdong by containing the ever encroaching Doodah. . . . Some young soldiers speaking in all bloody innocence, saying, "All that's just a *load,* man. We're here to kill gooks. Period." That wasn't at all true of me. I was there to watch. . . . I went to cover the war and the war covered me.

"In Vietnam," Jonathan Shay wrote, "the enemy struck not only at the body, but also at the most basic functions of the soldier's mind, attacking his perceptions by concealment; his cognitions by camouflage and deception; his intentions by surprise, anticipation, and ambush." Deception was as old as warfare, but in American experience it had always been directed at commanders. In Vietnam, however, deception was aimed at the infantryman. "Americans soldiers literally felt tortured by their Vietnamese enemy. Prolonged patrolling in Vietnam led to a decomposition of the normal, the familiar, the safe." Worse, the attacks came around the clock, but especially at night.

By the end of 1967 this war had killed 15,755 Americans. During that year the President and his advisers knew that the war could not be won. Some, like McNamara, knew earlier. This transformed the way they looked at it. In memoranda written in the spring of 1967 John McNaughton wrote that victory was no longer an option. The best hope was a prolonged stalemate. That meant attrition, and in a war of attrition Hanoi held the winning cards. Ho would certainly not negotiate unless the U.S. stopped the bombing and he probably would not go to the table in any case until after the 1968 presidential election. On the American side, McNaughton wrote, the war had become

> increasingly unpopular as it escalates—causing more American casualties, more fear of its growing into a wider war, more privation of the domestic sector, and more distress at the amount of suffering being visited upon the non-combatants in Vietnam, South and North. Most Americans do not know how we got where we are, and most, without knowing why, but taking advantage of hindsight, are convinced that somehow we should not have gotten this deeply in. All want the war ended and expect their President to end it. Successfully or else.[7]

During 1967 the Vietnam War destroyed Robert McNamara. His intimate relationship with the President collapsed. Johnson wrote later,

> When I met with him . . . on the night of November 22 [1963], I told him that if he ever tried to quit I would send the White House police after him. Brilliant, intensely energetic, publicly tough but privately sensitive, a man with great love for his country, McNamara carried more information around in his head than the average encyclopedia.

But now Johnson was deeply troubled about his Defense Secretary on several counts. McNamara was the bearer of the bad news he did not want to hear: the war could not be won; it was tearing the country to pieces; the U.S. should seek peace with North Vietnam. Equally, and perhaps more important, McNamara and his wife were extremely close to the Robert Kennedys and, during 1967, on many occasions the secretary would be in the White House during the day and with his wife at Hickory Hill in the evening. Johnson detested Kennedy and must have regarded McNamara's behavior as disloyalty. Johnson could hardly fail to observe the terrible toll the war was inflicting on McNamara's mind and body. During the summer of 1967 McNamara's private phone line to the Oval Office stopped ringing. When both McNamara and Johnson were approached separately about McNamara's leaving the Pentagon to become president of the World Bank, neither spoke to the other about the proposal.

Further, the secretary was now at war with the armed forces. According to his biographer Deborah Shapley, "almost anyone in the military who expressed admiration for McNamara jeopardized his chances for promotion." The "senior brass were embittered by the endless fights and mutual accusations of dishonesty. . . . A still uglier notion percolating in some quarters of the Building was that McNamara's quantitative management techniques had not only hurt the armed forces but had caused the inconclusiveness of the war in Vietnam."

McNamara felt very much alone. George Ball and McGeorge Bundy were gone. While visiting his wife at the Johns Hopkins University Hospital in Baltimore, McNamara got the awful news that John McNaughton, his close friend and key adviser in the Pentagon, had been killed in a plane crash. He and his wife grieved together in the bare hospital room.

Twenty-two years earlier Margy McNamara had been at the Hopkins Hospital for polio. Now in July 1967 she returned for several ulcer operations, doubtless induced by the enormous stress the McNamaras were bearing. She said, "Bob has all the problems and I have the ulcer." He said, "Margy got my ulcer." She entered under an assumed name so the press would not accuse him of deserting her for a visit to Vietnam that the President had ordered. Thereafter he made the 40-mile trip to Baltimore each night and arrived at his office the next morning unshaven and haggard.

Shapley examined the old photos and listened to the old tapes to determine the physical impact of the strains on McNamara. They were shocking. A close-up on February 16 showed "the ragged, spotty pallor of the skin, the sleek hair flecked with gray. One eye only is visible; it is shadowed, catlike, rolled sideways. . . . His hand conceals his mouth in an uncharacteristic pose of doubt." In the briefings he gave on the war he would put his hand to his mouth "to catch the confused tide of emotions surging within." In a speech at Millsaps College on February 24 when he came to a line which upset him, "his face can be seen in a terrible convulsion—mouth open, eyes shut, grimacing as though a knife were twisting through him."

McNamara received regular CIA briefings from George Carver, an extreme hawk. One day Carver was unable to come and George Allen, an old realistic Vietnam hand, arrived instead. Under agency policy he was required to give Carver's line. McNamara said he was not interested; just let's talk about the war. Allen said he must leave, otherwise he would have trouble with Director Helms. McNamara said he would take care of Helms. He asked, "What would you do if you were sitting here?" This led to a free discussion on the war for an hour.

William Brehm was in Systems Analysis in Defense and was talking to the secretary about an ammunition order for Vietnam. On the wall of the huge office hung a portrait of James Forrestal, the first Secretary of Defense, the highest official of the U.S. government in history to commit suicide. McNamara was pacing the floor and calculating the ammunition order. He looked up at Forrestal and shuddered violently. Brehm realized that he was weeping as though he could never stop.

On March 27, 1967, General Westmoreland asked for 210,000 more troops to bring his forces to 665,000, along with 10 tactical air squadrons for attacks in Cambodia and Laos. The Joint Chiefs supported the request. McNamara insisted on a careful review in the Pentagon. Both Systems Analysis and McNaughton (who would shortly be dead) strongly opposed the proposal and McNamara, of course, agreed. After many months of internal debate the President gave Westmoreland a total of 525,000. McNamara had pretty much prevailed. But his already frayed standing with the armed services was destroyed.

On June 17, 1967, McNamara made a remarkable decision. He called in a youthful Pentagon employee, Leslie H. Gelb, a recent Harvard Ph.D., and named him director of the Study Task Force. His assignment, as Gelb wrote later, was "to study the history of United States involvement in Vietnam from World War II to the present." The report was to be "encyclopedic and objective." Gelb received full access to the secretary's files as well as to some CIA and State Department sources. He was assisted by six full-time researchers and thirty who worked intermittently. Gelb expected to be done in three months, but it took a year and a half. He submitted the massive report to Secretary Clark Clifford on January 15, 1969. There were 37 studies and 15 collections of documents in 43 volumes. "The result," Gelb wrote, "was not so much a documentary history as a history based solely on documents—checked and rechecked with ant-like diligence." Thus, the origin of what would come to be known as the Pentagon Papers.

Gelb never talked to McNamara during the course of the study. When it was done and 15 copies had been prepared, Gelb and a military officer carried one set to the World Bank and placed the boxes on a low table in McNamara's office. Gelb pulled out one volume with a light blue binding and passed it to McNamara. He merely glanced at it and pushed it back. He said he did not want the documents in the bank and told Gelb to return them to the Pentagon. He did so.

On August 9 Senator John Stennis of Mississippi, an unrelenting hawk, opened hearings on the bombing of Vietnam. He called the military commanders first, who testified behind closed doors. They blamed Johnson and McNamara for tying their hands behind their backs, creating the military stalemate. The way to achieve quick victory, they argued, was with a massive strategic bombing campaign with no restrictions on targets. Johnson, worried, opened the door a crack. The next day the big bridge over the Red River in Hanoi was attacked and a few days later American planes bombed the buffer zone along the Chinese border.

McNamara testified in public and was subjected to grueling examination for seven hours on August 25. He argued forcefully against a widening of the air war. The bombing of the North had always been a supplement to the combined ground and air war in the South. The volume of bombs dropped on the North was now approaching the amount that fell on Europe during World War II. But Ho could keep his operation going on only 15 tons of imports daily. There were just 57 targets left that had not been attacked and they were trivial—a tire plant producing 30 units daily, fuel sites holding less than 6 percent of the country's energy, a small repair shop. The bombing had already knocked out 85 percent of electric generating capacity. Haiphong's port supplied little of military value, and there was the danger that a bomb might hit a Soviet vessel.

While McNamara's analysis was correct, it damaged him severely. The President was angry and disavowed him. The Joint Chiefs met in secrecy the night he had testified and agreed that they would resign en masse the next morning at a press conference. General Earle Wheeler, the chairman, said the U.S. should "make an unambiguous stance in Vietnam—or get out." He had suffered chest pains during the prior week and during the night was torn by the conflict between resignation and his military oath of obedience. He called off the press conference.

Under its charter the president of the World Bank was an American nominated by the President of the U.S. George Woods's term would end in August 1967. He asked McNamara about becoming his successor, and McNamara said he would remain at Defense as long as the President wanted him. Johnson was extremely interested. But, as noted, neither spoke to the other. In November the President instructed Treasury Secretary Fowler to clear McNamara's name with the other member nations. Shortly, the *Financial Times* of London reported that Britain had been asked to approve the nomination. McNamara rushed to the White House to speak to the President. When he returned to the Pentagon, he found Robert Kennedy, who had raced over to urge him to resign with a blast at the administration over the war. McNamara refused to make such a statement, but he accepted the presidency of the bank. He would prepare the next Defense budget and leave on February 29, 1968. When he departed Johnson presented him with the Medal of Freedom in, Joe Califano wrote, "a moving ceremony during which both men struggled to maintain their composure." Clark Clifford succeeded Robert McNamara as Secretary of Defense.[8]

14

Launching the Great Inflation

ARTHUR Okun, who sat on the Council of Economic Advisers and was its chairman in the Johnson years, wrote in 1969 of "the agonizing balance between growth and price stability." The Great Inflation began on Okun's watch and its birth can be pinpointed to President Johnson's decision to commit American forces to Vietnam in July 1965. It would continue for 17 distressing years. "The initial impact of the Vietnam escalation in the second half of 1965," Okun wrote, "both directly and through its stimulus to business investment, generated a disruptive boom." Real output leapt from 5.5 percent in the first half of 1965 to 8.5 percent in the following three quarters. "Our price performance was unhinged. . . . The economy had especial difficulty adapting to the breakneck advance."

The writing of history viewed as a path is strewn with pitfalls. Perhaps the most common may be called the hindsight syndrome. Every policy maker who has blown his assignment, or his apologist, hastens to point to the obvious, that it is easier to make a sound decision after the event than before it. A large number of those who write about the past ignore this truism. Another common pitfall is that, because a mistake was made, it must have been deliberate. This is the devil theory of history. The writer, therefore, must identify Satan and condemn him. While inflation has some beneficiaries, it has no friends. Johnson's failure to confront inflation immediately, particularly with higher taxes to pay for the war, has drawn a number of hindsight authorities, and they have identified two devils—LBJ and McNamara.

During his years reporting from Saigon David Halberstam helped to invent the credibility gap and was pleasantly surprised whenever he discovered Lyndon Johnson telling the truth. Thus, he had no trouble identifying the devil.

Johnson, according to Halberstam, treated the cost of the war as a "public relations problem." The true numbers were "kept partially secret from the press and the Congress and the allies." The Joint Chiefs knew those costs and at the outset asked that the nation be put on a wartime footing with the necessary higher taxes. "Lyndon Johnson would not give accurate economic projections, would not ask for a necessary tax raise, and would in fact have *his own* military planners be less than candid with *his own* economic advisers." The President's reasons for this duplicity, Halberstam wrote, were familiar:

> He was hoping that the worst would not come true, that it would remain a short war, and he feared that if the true economic cost of the war became visible to the naked eye, he would lose his Great Society programs. The result was that his economic planning was a living lie, and his Administration took us into economic chaos: the Great Society programs were passed but never funded on any large scale; the war itself ran into severe budgetary problems . . . ; and the most important, the failure to finance the war honestly, would inspire a virulent inflationary spiral.

Wilbur Mills made the same point another way. He told the President that it was impossible to have both guns and butter. "I talked to him about it, but it didn't appear to make a lot of difference to him. Lyndon Johnson always was a spender."

The President waited two critical years before he asked Congress for a tax increase to pay for the war. When his economic advisers urged him to move, he refused. The reason he gave was that the public would not stand for it and Congress would not enact it. While his economic advisers had no choice but to defer to his political judgment, they questioned it. CEA chairman Gardner Ackley said he did not know how much the war was going to cost, but that did not matter. "What it was doing to the economy now was about all we needed to know, and it was clear that what it was doing to the economy at the end of 1965 already spelled trouble, and that it was time for policies to adjust to it."

Charles Schultze, the Director of the Budget, favored a tax boost at the end of 1965, but, he later recalled, "I feel much more strongly about this from hindsight than I did from foresight." Schultze observed that "deep down inside and intuitively, Johnson recognized the problem of fighting a limited war." It would have been as "easy as the devil to sell an all-out war." Play on hate, wave the flag, nothing too good for our boys. But it was very hard to "fight a limited war for limited objectives with limited means." If he had wanted to go all-out, he could have whipped up the American people and slapped on a war economy, even wage and price controls. But that ran the risk of letting the hawks take over and that would be the end of the Great Society.

Deborah Shapley, his biographer, pointed her finger at McNamara for doing Johnson's bidding. The secretary promised that the war would be financed by open and honest accounting and that it would be the "most economically fought war in history." Both proved false. At the outset Westmoreland demanded an immense build-up of men and arms and McNamara and Johnson gave him everything he asked for.

McNamara hid and falsified the costs from the Council of Economic Advisers, the Treasury, the Congress, and the public. He ordered the Defense Department controller, Robert N. Anthony, to assume that the war would end on June 30, 1967. He raided other parts of his budget to pay for the war. In early September 1965 there were rumors of 500,000 troops and $10 billion. Ackley, who was making a speech on September 9, checked the cost with McNamara. He said that the figure was not even close to $10 billion. Ackley made the wrong speech and soon was told that the real number was $12 billion! Even this was not correct. At a meeting at the Johnson Ranch on November 22, 1966, McNamara admitted that the actual cost was $20 billion. The federal deficit, instead of being $1.8 billion, was $9 billion. Shapley summed it up this way:

> Through 1966 McNamara was the President's hard nosed servant. He deflected questions and speculation about the future scale of the war and its cost. He displayed an amazing ignorance of whether the war would get larger or smaller, whether it was likely to end sooner or later. Since he didn't know, it would be "irresponsible" to name a figure. He answered questions on future troop numbers artfully, steering clear of any hint of a wider war. He avoided lending any credence to those who suspected—rightly—that Johnson was in deeper than he said and was going deeper still.[1]

The Kennedy administration had adopted a loose incomes policy to deal with mild peacetime inflation. The January 1962 *Economic Report* in the Council's section, not the President's, contained this sentence: "The general guide for noninflationary wage behavior is that the rate of increase in wage rates (including fringe benefits) in each industry be equal to the trend rate of over-all productivity increase." Since man-hour output had been rising at approximately 3.2 percent annually, that number became the "guidepost" for wage advance. If the employer kept his wage increases within that figure, he would have little reason to raise his prices. Since there were no sanctions to enforce the guidepost, this was wage-price restraint by exhortation, or, as it was popularly known, "jawboning." In 1965 the Council, consisting of Chairman Ackley and members Okun and Otto Eckstein, was generally responsible for informal administration of the system. But after the troops went to Vietnam they received extraordinary help from the President. The early problems arose in the metals—steel, aluminum, and copper.

In 1965 the Steelworkers insisted on a handsome wage increase. They had not had one since 1961 and during the spring I. W. Abel had defeated the high-living David McDonald for the presidency of the union. He wanted to show his members that they had made the right choice. USW had historically compared itself to the UAW and Walter Reuther had negotiated guidepost busting settlements with the auto companies in 1964. The steel industry was losing its export markets and imports were now pouring in. It insisted that profit margins were too low. The steel contracts had opened on January 1 and the ensuing bargaining had been fruitless. The deadline was pushed forward to August 1 for notice and September 1 for a strike.

On August 17 the President met with Abel, who demanded a big boost. Califano checked it with Eckstein, who specialized in the guideposts, and he said the demands were way out of line and would cause a big increase in prices. Johnson rejected the union's demand. LBJ's formula: no strike, a wage increase of not more than 3.2 percent, and no increase in prices.

The President distrusted Secretary of Commerce Jack Connor and Secretary of Labor Willard Wirtz because, he thought, they were prejudiced in favor of their constituents. He informed each of the deal he insisted upon. He then bypassed them by naming a mediation team consisting of LeRoy Collins, the conciliator of racial disputes, and Wayne Morse, an expert on labor relations. While the senator had bitterly opposed the President on Tonkin Gulf, he was a professional who did not hesitate to support him on wages and prices. But the team failed to produce an agreement.

On August 30 Johnson gave the negotiators an ultimatum: accept his deal or postpone the strike. He sent them to Room 275 in the Executive Office Building, which he had occupied as Vice President. He then named a new team, which he kept secret from Connor and Wirtz: Arthur Goldberg, who had long represented the Steelworkers, and Clark Clifford, who presently represented Republic Steel. "He indicated . . . ," Califano wrote, "that he had no confidence in Connor and Wirtz, and at the same time told the secretaries that he was depending solely on them to settle the strike on his terms." The parties extended the deadline for eight days.

After intense negotiations Clifford reported that the companies would improve the wage offer if LBJ would permit price increases in products that had no Japanese competition; Wirtz said the union believed it could get a better deal if the President "winked" at modest price increases. Johnson: "None. Zero."

Connor and Wirtz then got into an argument over the cost of the fringe benefits. Johnson insisted that they agree and ordered Califano to mediate a settlement. After a number of exhausting sessions Connor and Wirtz on behalf of their constituents signed an agreement. Johnson, triumphant, called the negotiators into the Oval Office, congratulated them, and announced the agreement on national television. He sent word "to our soldiers out tonight in the jungles of Viet-Nam [that] it means a continued uninterrupted flow of the goods that are so essential to freedom and to his life, and even more, the assurance that those at home will never forget his sacrifice in the pursuit of their selfish ends." CEA costed out the wage and fringe benefits at 3.2 percent, right on the nose.

"Johnson's decision to hold off a tax increase," Califano wrote, ". . . set us on a scavenger hunt to find money for the federal treasury." A prime source was the sale of government stockpiles of strategic materials built up after World War II. "The big bucks were in aluminum: 1.4 million tons of excess aluminum could be sold for close to $700 million."

In November 1964 the price was set at 24.5 cents per pound. While there were eight firms which produced aluminum, the Big Three—Alcoa, Reynolds, and Kaiser—dominated ingot output and in mid-1965 were operating at 100 percent of capacity. Fabrication was more competitive. On October 29 Ormet, a small firm, raised the ingot price half a cent. Reynolds and Kaiser followed immediately and Alcoa was studying the action. Eckstein informed the President that the increase was unjustified, that the industry should *reduce* prices.

If Eckstein was upset, Johnson was enraged. In fact, he was in a dreadful mood, recovering slowly from gall bladder surgery, publicly ridiculed for exposing his big scar to news photographers, on a tight diet restricting his huge appetite. Califano found him almost impossible to deal with:

> What I didn't know at the time was that this had been a terrible day for LBJ: as a result of a map-plotting error two American pilots had destroyed a friendly village of Vietnamese civilians; his daughter, Luci, who was eighteen, had told him she was going to marry Patrick Nugent and the President and Mrs. Johnson thought their youngest daughter was too young to get married and was making a serious mistake; and Johnson had seen Peter Hurd's portrait of himself, which he hated. He called it "the ugliest thing I ever saw." Mrs. Johnson said afterward that she didn't expect to endure an encounter so grim if she "lived to be a thousand."

To top it all, the *New York Times* reported that he was "sputtering mad." He roared at Califano, "Do you hear me? I am not now, never in my life have been, and never will be 'sputtering mad!' " Califano had to bite his hand to restrain his laughter. The poor aluminum industry did not have a chance.

When Alcoa also raised its price, McNamara on November 6 released 200,000 tons of virgin aluminum from the stockpile. It was not enough. Johnson told him to add another 100,000. On November 10 Alcoa rescinded its action and within hours the rest of the industry followed.

At that moment Anaconda, the leading copper firm, raised its price. But U.S. copper, unlike aluminum, followed the world price and Chile was the price leader. Johnson sent Averell Harriman to Santiago to demand that President Eduardo Frei roll back his price, and 200,000 tons of copper were marketed from the government stockpile. Anaconda surrendered.

Lyndon Johnson's virtuoso performance in the metals in the latter part of 1965 made him the world's greatest guideposter. Ackley was a witness to what he described as an "awesome" performance when he brought Roger Blough, the chairman of U.S. Steel, to the Oval Office to discuss steel prices.

> Roger started to explain what it was that he wanted to do and why it was a reasonable thing to do. And the President just started working him over. . . . I have never seen a human being reduced to such a quivering lump of flesh. Roger was unable to speak at the end of that interview. LBJ just took him apart, spread him out on the rug, and when he left, Roger was just shaking his head.

But the massive force of the Great Inflation would soon wipe out Johnson's role and the guideposts themselves.[2]

In mid-1965 the Keynesian economists at the Council of Economic Advisers could look on the nation's economy with great satisfaction. They had guided the country, particularly with the 1964 tax cut, into an extraordinary controlled boom. This was the fifth consecutive year of economic growth. The Industrial Production Index (1957–59 = 100) had stood at 109.7 in 1961. In June 1965 it reached 143.1. The Council had persuaded Kennedy to fix an "interim" unemployment goal of 4 percent. In 1961 the rate had been 6.7. In June 1965 it had fallen to 4.7 percent. In fact, it would break the 4 percent barrier at 3.7 in February 1966. And, *mirabile dictu,* there was virtually no inflation. In June 1965 on the base of 1957–59 = 100 the Consumer Price Index stood at 102.8.

Walter Heller later reflected on this triumph, of which he had been the main architect. There was "very little price inflation" and that was almost entirely due to farm prices which have a "certain life of their own" unrelated to aggregate demand. "So . . . there was no real inflation." He had not anticipated both full employment and stable prices. No industrial economy had ever achieved that utopia. But "the Vietnam escalation just knocked things into a cocked hat."

For most of the rest of 1965 the economists were led astray because the impact of the war was masked by two factors. The first was the duplicity of Johnson and McNamara in concealing the real cost. Ackley, depending on McNamara, assumed the maximum increase in the defense budget at $3 to $5 billion. He did not learn the actual figure until January 1966—$12.8 billion! The other factor was the lag between the letting of a defense contract and the payment for the goods when they were delivered. In the case of ammunition the delay was about six months; for a military airplane it was 18 months. Robert Warren Stevens wrote:

> In the second half of 1965, companies that were already almost fully occupied with meeting the booming civilian demand for capital goods and automobiles suddenly received new high priority orders from the Pentagon.

These new orders immediately set off inflationary developments in the private sector of the economy as employers began to expand their plants and to raise wages in order to attract more workers into defense production.

They also trooped to the banks for loans to finance their interim costs.

Thus, in the latter part of 1965 the economists at CEA, lovingly caressing their cheerful economic indicators, were oblivious to the gathering storm. In fact, economists generally groped in the dark. Seymour E. Harris, who was a consultant to the Treasury, set up a meeting of 20 top economists with high officials of the interested departments on November 23, 1965. They agreed that the economy would grow in 1966 at 4 percent in real terms, somewhat less than 1965. "With a few dissenters, there was no great concern that the economy was overheated and would require restrictive monetary policy."

William McChesney Martin, the chairman of the Federal Reserve Board, invariably opened a conversation with an economist by saying, "I am not an economist," to which the under-the-breath reply was, "Amen!" He believed that inflation of any magnitude was a variety of the bubonic plague. Lyndon Johnson, by contrast, was a Texas populist on high interest rates: He hated them. The Keynesians, preoccupied with overcoming unemployment by stimulating growth, much preferred fiscal to monetary policy. Both, therefore, looked at Martin with deep suspicion. A brawl was inevitable.

The news rose within the banking system to the Fed that businessmen were lining up at their banks for bridge loans to finance their defense orders. Martin got worried and in the early fall of 1965 began to hint that the time was approaching when interest rates must go up. Ackley, Schultze, and Treasury Secretary Henry Fowler warned the President and he called a meeting of the Quadriad—Martin, Ackley, Fowler, and Schultze—for October 6, 1965.

Fowler pointed out that Morgan Guaranty was considering a rise in rates. Johnson wondered whether he should issue a statement about keeping interest rates low. Martin wanted to know how much the government was going to spend, "particularly by McNamara on the war." Johnson mentioned $3 to $5 billion. Martin said he was leaning toward higher rates. Johnson opposed an increase, saying it would hurt small farmers and businessmen. Ackley and Schultze agreed. Martin looked the President in the eye and said, "If we thought you were right we'd all do the same thing. But the question is, whose crystal ball is right?" Johnson had gotten nowhere. On December 3, with Martin leading the way, the Fed voted 4 to 3 to raise the discount rate from 4 to 4.5 percent.

In fact, the administration was ambivalent about the Fed's action. Privately the President was angry and inspired congressional hearings on the independence of the central bank without consultation with the White

House. But he issued a mild public statement, which opened, "The Federal Reserve Board is an independent agency." It would have been better, he said, for the Fed to have waited till January, when the new budget would be ready and policies could have been coordinated.

Johnson called Martin and his economic advisers, including Heller, to a meeting at his ranch on December 6. "Sitting on the lawn in front of the ranch house," Califano wrote, "LBJ at first probed for any way of turning Martin around. He quickly saw that there was none." The President, moreover, recognized that the Fed's action was not all bad because it seemed to make a tax increase unnecessary. As Kermit Gordon pointed out, there "wasn't nearly as much of a conflict as it appeared on the surface. There was a good deal of covert support within the Executive Branch for that act."

By the end of 1965 the economists had grasped reality. They now realized that McNamara's numbers were much too low, that a big inflation was coming, and that a tax hike was necessary. The President asked CEA whether a federal budget of $115 or $110 billion would require a tax increase. Ackley replied on December 17 that a $115 billion budget would require a "significant tax increase" and $110 would "probably call for one." Heller told Johnson, "What we really need is a surtax on the individual income tax." He suggested 5 percent. Undersecretary of the Treasury Joseph Barr, who had been in Southeast Asia in November and had talked to many military experts, came back convinced that "we really had a bear by the tail. I recommended to Secretary Fowler . . . that we consider getting our taxes up and do it quickly." Budget Director Schultze agreed. But the President would not budge.[3]

Robert Warren Stevens called 1966 the "year of reckoning," a "traumatic" time for the American economy. James L. Cochrane described it as "a vintage year" when "events overran policies," which "began badly and then deteriorated." If one is searching for the year during which the Great Inflation began, the choice is manifest: 1966.

The Fed, deserted to face the storm, squeezed the supply of money and shoved up interest rates. Soaring interest took a toll. Savings and loans and mutual savings banks, locked into low returns on long-term mortgages, were unable to borrow. By midyear the commercial banks felt a similar pressure: their large holdings of municipal bonds could not be sold because they paid too low an interest. Bond houses were threatened with failure. The stock market, which had been falling since February 9, suffered a sharp drop in August. The reason, Ackley explained to the President, was because an investor could earn only 3.5 percent on corporate dividends, compared with 6 percent on government guaranteed federal bonds. Rising interest on mortgages severely retarded the housing industry. Imports increased sharply; exporters lost foreign markets; and the balance of payments soured. Holders of life insurance borrowed from their policies, which paid 5 percent, and received better rates elsewhere.

At the same time, manufacturing and construction boomed. Many of the firms in these industries either financed themselves or borrowed at risky high rates. On August 10, 1966, Ackley wrote Johnson, "I was told . . . that Morgan Guaranty's loan demand for September and October is absolutely unbelievable." A week later the Fed squeezed large banks, as Ackley put it, to "ration their loans to their big customers." On September 17 he sent Johnson a three-page list of price increases on everything from eggs to electrical transformers that rose in the preceding week. November 8, he reported, "has been a bad day for prices." Nor did corporations hesitate to raise wages either in collective bargaining or voluntarily in order to hold on to their skilled workers as unemployment held quite consistently under 4 percent.

The wage-price guideposts were swept into oblivion, carrying with them that great mediator, Lyndon Johnson. People asked, "Where did 3.2 go?" In January 1966 the new Republican mayor of New York, John V. Lindsay, settled the city's transit wages for an increase of 6.3 percent. The construction unions vied with each other to see which could kick the guideposts farther. The unsavory Peter Weber of the Operating Engineers, Local 825, in New Jersey highway construction seems to have become champion. The most explosive case involved the Machinists and five large airlines— Eastern, National, Northwest, TWA, and United. A presidential board consisting of Wayne Morse, David Ginsburg, and Richard Neustadt recommended 3.5 percent plus a clever reopener that came into play only after a very big rise in the cost of living. But the IAM rejected the deal and struck. The President caved in and on July 29, 1966 accepted 4.3 percent. But the membership even rejected that. The union eventually got 4.9.

The White House was shaken and Califano asked CEA for comments on creation of a commission on price stability and the collapse of the guideposts. The Council thought the commission a good idea. "I certainly agree," Ackley wrote, "that it is useful to put the recent guidepost defeats into perspective, and I have long agreed that we will need to retreat from the 3.2 percent guidepost figure." He opposed abandonment and urged getting something in return from labor for giving up 3.2. In August Representative Henry Reuss of Wisconsin held ceremonial hearings on the extinct guideposts.

In December 1966 the President threw in the towel on taxes. His advisers had pressed him all year. In May both Ackley and Schultze had called for a 10 percent surtax. A prominent group of Harvard and MIT economists led by Otto Eckstein met for three months and brought in Ackley, Ginsburg, Fowler, and Califano. On August 23 they made their recommendation: "A personal and corporate tax increase was absolutely essential, and the sooner the better." Schultze, and Ackley concurred. On September 2

Fowler, McNamara, Katzenbach, O'Brien, Schultze, Ackley, Ginsburg, and Califano agreed.

In his State of the Union message on January 10, 1967, the President said, "I recommend to the Congress a surcharge of 6 percent on both corporate and individual income taxes—to last for 2 years or for so long as the unusual expenditures associated with our efforts in Vietnam continue."[4]

It would be a year and a half—all of 1967 and the first half of 1968—before Congress gave Johnson the surtax. During that period economic conditions were much as they had been in 1966: heavy price pressures and distortions with no wage-price policy and the whole burden of restraint falling upon the Federal Reserve.

Though the Fed's governors followed interest rates very carefully and intervened frequently, their limited powers were hardly up to the task. Okun, who had succeeded Ackley as chairman of CEA, summed up the disaster for the President on May 23, 1968: "Many *interest rates* are now at *their highest level in nearly fifty years.* Rates have jumped *1 1/2 to 2 percentage points* since late 1965." Mortgages averaged 7 percent and in many areas were 8. They might soon go to 10. The annual rate of price increase was 4 percent, *"the worst performance in 17 years."* The international trade deficit hit a record in March 1968. There was talk of a flight from the dollar and even of a world financial crisis.

On June 9, 1967, the President had met with his top economic advisers and Fowler said he found the money market "disturbing." Corporations, anticipating a large federal deficit and no tax increase, were borrowing long-term funds heavily and interest rates were rising sharply. On present, not projected, facts, "Fowler urged strongly that it was necessary to go forward now on the tax surcharge." He thought the banking and business communities would understand and back the hike. He expected a budget deficit of $23 to 28 billion. The President, shocked, said he "refused to run a deficit of the magnitude projected." He was ready to cut spending "drastically" on domestic programs. "The country, and Democratic Congressmen in particular, would have to choose between the domestic programs and the tax increase." He ordered Schultze to work out a curtailed budget and he suggested that the surcharge might to go 10 percent rather than 6 percent.

CEA explained the significance of a 1 percent rise in interest rates. The cost to the federal budget would be $3.6 billion annually, $29 billion to the national debt, and $4.5 billion to private, state, and local government costs. Johnson asked for a comparison of price inflation between the U.S. and the European democracies. Writing in January 1968, Ackley pointed out that the U.S. had much the best performance since 1960. But for the period of the Vietnam War, that is, since June 1965, Germany, France, and the Netherlands had a better record and the U.K. and Italy had done as well.

Private investment in plant and equipment continued to be the great engine driving the boom. Inflation aside, this had its attractive aspect—high output and high employment. On October 23, 1967, Ackley wrote George Christian, the White House press secretary:

> On November 1, we will have gone 81 months without encountering an economic recession. This will break all records for the duration of an expansion; the previous high of 80 months was set from 1938 to 1945 (including World War II). The average length of expansions (since 1854) is 30 months, and the last three prior to the present one were 45, 35, and 25 months, respectively.

But very high employment in the absence of an incomes policy drove up wages. In the first quarter of 1967, excluding construction, union contract increases averaged 4.9 percent compared with 4.5 in 1966. The Teamsters' national agreement in the second quarter of 1967 came to 5.5 percent plus a cost of living escalator. Ackley's memorandum on construction was titled "The Disaster Toll." In Chicago the carpenters and painters settled for 6.6 percent. In Cleveland the plumbers got an "incredible" 40 percent over 3 years and the carpenters and bricklayers surpassed them. In Connecticut the operating engineers received 7.4 to 9.2 percent. "Many contractors," Ackley wrote, "seem to be offering nothing more than token resistance to this union assault."

In September 1967 Walter Reuther negotiated a pathbreaking agreement for the UAW with Ford: 6.2 percent, a cost of living escalator, and a new guaranteed annual wage. After a strike in the spring of 1968 the telephone contract came to about 6.5 percent a year for three years.

On February 23, 1968, the President created the Cabinet Committee on Price Stability, consisting of the Secretaries of Treasury, Commerce, and Labor, the Director of the Budget, and the Chairman of the Council of Economic Advisers. The basic recommendation in its report, delivered on December 27, 1968, was hardly earthshaking: "Voluntary restraint by business and labor in wage and price decisions is an essential element in the overall program to achieve full prosperity and reasonable price stability." Amen.[5]

When he announced the proposal for a 6 percent surcharge on January 10, 1967, the President said, "I will very soon forward all of my recommendations to the Congress." Very soon became a very long time. He did not send up a tax bill. Without his vigorous leadership, the Democrats remained silent and the Republicans called for reductions in Great Society programs. In late February even liberal Democrat William Proxmire of Wisconsin, the chairman of the Joint Economic Committee, was inclined to "take a solid position against a tax increase" until Ackley persuaded him to soften his language. The Business Council's committee on the CEA unanimously voted down the surcharge in its Hot Springs meeting in May. Constituent mail to Congress, according to *Congressional Quarterly*, was "extraordinarily heavy" against the levy. During the spring, as the CEA put it, the economy was "schizophrenic—a case for psychiatric rather than fiscal or monetary help." Higher interest rates had slowed the sale of houses and big-ticket items. "We have taken a slowdown without stalling." Califano informed Johnson in June that Fowler, Ackley, Schultze, Trowbridge (Commerce), Wirtz, McNamara, and he agreed that "your tax proposal should not go to the Congress until after the recess."

By late July the doldrums were history and the boom was again in command. Martin of the Fed came out publicly for a 10 percent surtax. On July 22 the cabinet committee urged the President to ask for the same amount on corporations effective July 1 and on individuals effective September 1. Reuther told Ackley that he agreed, though he preferred a January 1, 1968, starting date. Without higher taxes, he argued, "domestic social programs would be under very heavy pressure."

By mid-1967 Lyndon Johnson's scheme to finance the war painlessly had been torpedoed. He could no longer hide the high cost or the devastating impact upon the federal budget. The Defense Department estimates of expenditures to support U.S. obligations in Southeast Asia by fiscal year were as follows: 1965, $103 million; 1966, $5,812 million; 1967, $20,133 million; 1968, $26,547 million; and 1969, $28,805 million. By mid-1967, the start of fiscal 1968, the number of troops in Vietnam peaked at 525,000; the cost topped out at $28.8 billion in 1969. Thereafter both counts went into decline.

On August 3, 1967, Johnson sent a special message to Congress, called the State of the Budget and the Economy, and held a painful press conference. At the start of the year his estimated budget came to $135 billion with revenues of $127 billion, including income from a 6 percent surtax. Thus, he had estimated the deficit at $8 billion.

LBJ now pointed out with alarm, "Since then much has happened to change these prospects." These were the "hard and inescapable" facts: Expenditures might go $8.5 billion higher to $143.5 billion, while revenues, even with the tax increase, would be $7 billion lower. "Without a tax increase and tight expenditure control, the deficit could exceed $28 billion."

"A deficit of that size," he said, "poses a clear and present danger to America's security and economic health." It would bring with it "a spiral of ruinous inflation, . . . brutally higher interest rates, . . . an unequal and unjust distribution of the costs of supporting our men in Vietnam, and . . . a deterioration in our balance-of-payments. . . ." This crisis demanded both a reduction in civilian expenditures and a tax increase, not of 6 percent, but of 10 percent, effective for corporations on July 1 and for individuals on October 1, 1967.

The broad implications of this analysis were clear: the hope for both guns and butter had vanished and the Great Society programs would be seriously underfunded. Johnson, Califano wrote, had told him that, if he asked for higher taxes, " 'All hell will break loose on our domestic program.' He was more right than he feared." Johnson wrote later, "My willingness to compromise had sharpened the appetites of those who saw in this struggle a long-awaited chance to slash the Great Society programs."

At the press conference a reporter asked whether Wilbur Mills supported the surcharge. The President said he had talked to Mills and his committee several times, but he did not know "what Mr. Mills will do, or what the Ways and Means Committee will do, or what Congress will do." He had good reason to be concerned about Mills. The tax increase had no appeal to him; never one to proceed unless his majorities were safe, Mills was convinced that both Ways and Means and the House would vote it down; and his relations with Lyndon Johnson were cool, if not strained. (Schultze said they did not speak to each other during 1967.)

Mills did hold hearings in August and September. Aside from its own witnesses, the administration received support from the Federal Reserve, the banking and insurance industries, many economists, and the AFL-CIO. But there was strong opposition from industry. The economists split in an interesting way. Joseph Pechman of Brookings submitted a petition signed by 320 academic economists who supported the surtax. The opposition consisted mainly of those who opposed the war and considered it immoral to support it financially. Even some business economists took this position.

On October 3, 1967, Ways and Means, confirming Mills's hunch, voted 20 to 5 to lay the tax bill aside until "the President and Congress reach an understanding on a means of implementing more effective expenditure reductions and controls." Mills defended this action and other recent cuts in appropriations. "These actions are not irresponsible, bullheaded, or spiteful, nor are they maneuvers for partisan advantage." Rather, they represented an "uneasiness" among citizens about the rise in federal expenditures. The bill, Mills said, was "dead" unless the President mended his ways.

Immediately afterward Fowler and Schultze met with Mills and Chairman George H. Mahon of the House Appropriations Committee. Mills insisted on a firm commitment that there would be no new domestic programs in fiscal 1969, a commitment the President refused to make. On October 7 an administration group worked up a lesser set of concessions: (1) a $2 billion cut in defense, (2) Mahon's "line item" listing of 700 specific reductions, and (3) a program evaluation commission to propose cuts in federal programs after the 1968 elections. Califano pointed out that this package was "fragile." Fowler seemed willing to take the losses; McNamara was concerned about preserving the Great Society; Schultze did not like the commission; and Barefoot Sanders, who now worked the Hill for the White

House, as well as Larry O'Brien, were pretty much convinced that the tax bill was dead. "Both O'Brien and Barefoot," Califano wrote, "are concerned about the hundred or so Democrats in the House that stand ready to join with the two Kennedys and others in the Senate and jump the Administration for any association it has with spending cuts."

Johnson was enraged and vented his anger against Mills and minority leader Gerald Ford at a press conference on November 17. "I think one of the great mistakes that the Congress will make is that Mr. Ford and Mr. Mills have taken this position that they cannot have any tax bill now. They will live to rue the day when they made that decision." This made headlines across the nation. Mills and the Republicans were furious and there were congressional predictions that LBJ would "rue the day" he made the statement because it had killed his chance to get a tax bill.

The situation seemed out of control. McNamara, Fowler, Schultze, Ackley, and O'Brien urged a resumption of pressure for the tax hike. Democratic bankers from Wall Street lectured Democratic senators: if the economy disintegrated, there would be disasters in the stock and bond markets. Business economists strongly urged a tax increase. CEA's top advisory team was unanimous in its support.

On November 18, 1967, the British government devalued the pound from $2.80 to $2.40 and raised the discount rate from 6.5 to 8 percent. This threatened more inflation in the U.S. Thus, Fowler argued, the tax increase was "more important than ever." The Fed raised the U.S. discount rate on November 19.

Mills, disturbed by British devaluation, resumed hearings on November 29 and 30. Fowler presented a two-headed proposal: the 10 percent surcharge and a specific statutory expenditure reduction plan to reduce the deficit by $11.4 billion. To the reasons for the program he now added defense of the dollar. But Mills was not impressed. He said the administration exaggerated the danger of inflation and should concentrate on reducing expenditures on domestic programs. He told reporters that it was too late in the session to consider the tax increase. Thus, the surtax died in the Ways and Means Committee. Wilbur Mills had pinned Lyndon Johnson's shoulders to the mat.[6]

When the new Congress opened in January 1968 Johnson sent up a package: a surcharge of 10 percent effective on corporations on January 1 and on individuals on April 1, the extension of excise taxes on automobiles and telephone services due to expire on April 1 to the end of 1969, and an acceleration in the collection of corporate income tax payments. They became H.R. 15414.

"Next to peace in Southeast Asia," Johnson later wrote, "I believed the tax surcharge was the most urgent issue facing the country." But he had very little power to influence the Congress. During the first six months of 1968, when the tax bill was under consideration, his presidency, already undermined by years of hemorrhaging, collapsed.

This was one of the most dreadful periods any American President ever faced. In early January HEW Secretary Gardner submitted his resignation. In words that many other officials of the administration could have spoken, Gardner said he did so because Johnson could not unite the country and do what was needed. On January 23 the North Koreans seized the spy ship *Pueblo* and captured its crew. The North Vietnamese and the Vietcong on January 30 launched the massive surprise Tet offensive against virtually all the major cities and towns in South Vietnam, making a mockery of a potential American victory. On March 12 the peace candidate, Senator Eugene McCarthy, polled a stunning 42.4 percent of the vote in the New Hampshire Democratic primary. Four days later Robert F. Kennedy announced his candidacy for President. In a dramatic address on March 31 Johnson withdrew from the presidential race. On April 4 Martin Luther King, Jr., was murdered in Memphis. This was followed immediately by massive rioting in a number of cities, most dramatically, Washington. At this time Califano wrote, "This has been one of the most momentous and shattering weeks in American history." But it was not the end. On June 5 Robert Kennedy was assassinated in Los Angeles.

It was against this backdrop of disintegration that the House considered Johnson's request for the surcharge. The Ways and Means Committee held hearings on January 22 and 23, 1968. Fowler, Schultze, Martin, and Ackley testified strongly, but Mills was not moved. The higher tax would reduce demand and he insisted that the present inflation was cost-push rather than demand-pull. He was annoyed because he found little evidence of an administration effort to reduce expenditures. The senior Republican, John W. Byrnes of Wisconsin, agreed. The Ways and Means Committee summarily stripped the tax increase from H.R. 15414 and passed the bill on February 23 with only the excises and the accelerated collection features. The House approved the truncated measure by voice vote on February 29.

The Senate phase was critical on two counts—the politics and the leadership. Neither the Finance Committee nor the Senate itself was any more willing to enact a tax increase than the House had been. By now a southern Democratic-Republican coalition dominated both chambers. Only liberal Democrats would support such a bill and they were a minority. A tax hike, therefore, must be packaged with a reduction in expenditures on domestic programs, that is, a gutting of the Great Society by opting for guns over butter. The key question then became: how much to gut? For the President, of course, this was an extremely painful choice of evils. Under heavy pressure from Fowler, he reluctantly came around to $4 billion. The southern Democrats, led by Mills in the House and George Smathers of Florida in the Senate, insisted on $6 billion. The Republicans, led by John J. Williams of Delaware, demanded $8 billion.

There was a subtle but unmistakable shift of power in this struggle from the President to Smathers in the Senate and, more important, to Fowler as the spokesman for the administration. Smathers had been in Europe in the fall of 1967 and returned, as he wrote Johnson, convinced that the U.S. "must demonstrate that we have sufficient self-discipline to cut our appropriations and raise our taxes in order to meet the enormous problems of Vietnam, rebellion in the cities, and inflation."

For Fowler the battle was a holy mission. He was convinced that a $25 billion deficit was "perfectly intolerable" because it threatened runaway inflation and the U.S. balance of payments. His job, he said later, was "a backbreaking bonebreaking job which demanded and received every conceivable energy and tactic that I could think of . . . to get the job done." The President called him "one of the most tenacious men he's ever seen," and Fowler did not deny that characterization. He led the testimony, spent endless hours in conference and in lobbying with members of Congress, mediated between the prima donnas, Johnson and Mills, and mobilized an enormous and powerful banking and business lobby to push the bill through.

Senator Russell Long, the chairman of the Finance Committee, held hearings on March 12 and 14, 1968. Only administration witnesses led by Fowler testified. Senator Clinton Anderson of New Mexico announced that he would propose the surtax as an amendment to H.R. 15414 and Smathers supported the move. Asked the administration's reaction, Fowler said, "I would applaud any move. I'm for prompt action."

But the committee rejected the surtax twice. Smathers proposed it alone and it went down to defeat 12 to 5. Williams coupled it with a mandatory $8 billion spending cut, which lost 9 to 8. The Senate committee then started the process of stringing amendments on H.R. 15414 like ornaments on a Christmas tree. They covered industrial development bonds, Aid to Families with Dependent Children, and medicaid. The amended bill was reported out on March 15.

By now the surtax was in desperate trouble. Fowler spent four days on the Hill trying to broker a deal to save the tax, usually with Martin and sometimes also with Charles Zwick, the new Director of the Budget. Fowler and Smathers worked out a strategy for a 10 percent tax increase and a $5 billion expenditure cut. This required Republican support and they worked over Dirksen for votes. "He said he would try . . . ," Fowler wrote Johnson, "but gave me no commitment that he could deliver." Looking forward to the conference, Fowler talked at length to Mills. The chairman had a problem because Ways and Means had no jurisdiction over expenditures, which fell to Chairman Mahon of the Appropriations Committee. He was jealous of the jurisdiction of his subcommittees and did not recognize the importance of the surtax. Nor was Dirksen making much progress with Williams. Fowler thought a 10-5 or 10-6 package ($10 billion tax increase and $5 or $6 billion expenditure cut) might "break this logjam and put us well down the road, but far, far from home."

Fowler's lobbying paid off. Dirksen eventually delivered a phalanx of Republican votes, but the old master exacted his price—$6 billion in spending cuts instead of $5 billion. The Senate debated the bill for a week. Smathers and Williams *together* proposed the crucial 10-6 amendment, which passed 55 to 35 with strong bipartisan support. The telephone and auto excises were stripped away into a separate bill and were quickly passed and signed by the President on April 12. The Senate then hung about a dozen ornamental amendments on the bill. Johnson, in his dramatic withdrawal speech on March 31, pledged that he would sign a bill with the surcharge and "appropriate reductions in the January Budget." In the final Senate roll call on April 2, 1968 H.R. 15414 passed 57 to 31.[7]

Thus, the conference committee received a House bill without the tax and a Senate bill with it. Reflecting the times, the conference became a donnybrook. The brawl dragged on for six weeks and left almost everyone embittered. It was impossible for the public, many members of Congress, and even some of the participants to understand. This was in part because Mills, with conservative Democratic and Republican support, insisted on raising taxes and cutting expenditures not only currently but also into the future. The conflict was also obfuscated by arcane budgetary concepts like the "rescission of unobligated balances" and shorthand like "10-8-4."

At the meeting on April 24, 1968, Mills asserted control over the conference. He declared, Fowler reported, that "the Senate bill was unacceptable and inadequate because it was decisive only on holding back *expenditures* in fiscal 1969 and did not reduce the *upstream authority* to obligate . . . for the fiscal year 1969 and the following." The House, therefore, would take the initiative through its committees.

The Appropriations Committee on May 1 rejected ranking Ohio Republican Frank Bow's motion for a 14-6-6 formula by a vote of 23 to 21, that is, reductions of $14 billion in appropriations and $6 billion each for rescissions and spending. The President said he would accept a $4 billion cut in spending and the Democrats accepted his suggestion.

On May 2, however, Mills moved 14-6-6, the defeated Bow proposal. Califano was convinced that Mills was trying to "torpedo both the tax bill and the Great Society." Rumors spread that Johnson would capitulate at a press conference on May 3. Califano wrote him the evening before, "If you get stuck either with no tax bill or with the provisions . . . Mills is now peddling, . . . the ball game may be over . . . for the rest of the year." He urged the President to come out fighting. "I think we should turn loose everything we have to take the Ways and Means Committee away from Mills." The President heeded this advice and demanded that congressmen "stand up like men." "I think the time has come for all Members of Congress to be responsible and, even in an election year, to bite the bullet and . . . do what ought to be done for their country." He added, "Don't hold the tax bill until you can blackmail someone."

On May 4 the President wrote an open letter to Speaker McCormack, urging him to "do all in your power to secure passage of the necessary tax legislation." His budget of $186 billion was "lean enough" to justify only a $4 billion cut in expenditures. "To accept reductions any deeper . . . is unwise." Barefoot Sanders "stressed to Fowler that under no circumstances should any impression be left with Mills . . . that the President is willing to accept deeper cuts."

Mills backed off. Ways and Means met on May 6 and rejected the Republican-Mills 14-6-6 formula on a party line vote of 15 to 10. It then adopted the tax hike and a $4 billion spending cut, the Appropriation Committee's 10-8-4 formula. The vote was 17 to 6. Mills seems to have gotten Johnson's message—for the time being.

On May 8 the conference reached final agreement under Mills's leadership on a $10 billion surcharge and a $6 billion cut in spending, that is, a 10-8-6 formula. Mills, usually extremely cautious, had taken a big gamble.

It was now $6 billion versus $4 billion, Wilbur Mills versus Lyndon Johnson. Generally speaking, the chairman was in a better political position because he was backed by most of the southern Democrats and the Republicans, who together constituted a majority in both houses, while the President had only the northern Democrats. But there were soft spots for Mills in the House leadership. Speaker McCormack favored $4 billion and was extremely angry with Mills, who, he thought, was trying to blackmail the leadership. The speaker, Sanders reported, said that "since Mills has taken over the leadership of the House, he can get his own Rule out of Committee and get his own votes on the floor for the Conference Report." Majority Leader Carl Albert and whip Hale Boggs were of two minds but said they would vote to follow the President if he asked them. Sanders concluded that "Mills cannot pass the report without active support from the Administration and some liberal Democrats." The chairman did not disagree. He wrote Walter Heller on May 10, "We are still a long way from having votes in the House to pass this conference report."

The President's people were ambivalent. His domestic policy aides headed by Califano urged protection of the Great Society. They were joined by Sanders and Labor Secretary Wirtz. But the Council of Economic Advisers was of two minds. Its members, doubtless, hoped to preserve the Great Society and, after analysis, concluded that a $10 billion tax increase combined with a $6 billion reduction in expenditures was, as Okun wrote, "an overdose of fiscal restraint" that "could weaken the economy excessively, particularly in the first half of 1969." At the same time, the CEA thought passage of the tax hike was critical. "The *financial mess* that would follow failure of the surcharge," Okun wrote the President on May 20, "could *jeopardize our 87-month record prosperity.* It could bring on a recession and slump. Even a mild recession would cost $30 or $40 billion of production and 1½ million jobs." Current economic events accentuated the need for action. Price inflation was at a 17-year record and the bond market was "thoroughly demoralized and close to being disorderly" with extreme jumps in interest rates. The cause, Okun wrote, was *"growing uncertainty and continued delay on the tax bill."* The Treasury, of course, had no doubts. Fowler wrote Johnson on May 9, "I strongly recommend that the Administration accept the bitter with the sweet and work with the House and Senate leadership in securing speedy approval of the Conferees Report." The deterioration of the bond market reinforced his position.

In the lobbying there was no match. *Congressional Quarterly*'s headline read, "Lobbying by Business Key to Passage." The bankers, described by Fowler as "the world's greatest worriers," accepted the surcharge and adored the spending reduction. Nothing can match rising prices and interest rates in energizing bankers to defend the homeland. The American Bankers Association sent the word to its 13,500 member banks to descend upon Congress. Fowler met with the ABA in Puerto Rico to cheer them on, but quickly concluded that it was unnecessary. "I have never seen any group of bankers so keyed up and concerned." In 1963–64, when he was Undersecretary of the Treasury, Fowler had organized a very effective group of 500 prominent businessmen headed by Henry Ford and Stuart Sanders of the Pennsylvania Railroad to lobby for the big tax cut. Now he made a few phone calls and they were back in business. The homebuilders and the U.S. Chamber of Commerce also pitched in.

Many groups—the labor movement, education, the cities, religious organizations—strongly opposed the $6 billion spending reduction and, as Andy Biemiller of AFL-CIO put it, "swallowed hard to accept the $4 billion cut." George Meany visited the President to stiffen his spine and the AFL-CIO executive council denounced the "meat-axe approach to cutting the budget." But these organizations never coalesced into an effective lobby.

On May 21, the day following Okun's memorandum urging the President to accept a cut in spending to get the tax surcharge, Johnson met with Mills, the House leadership, Okun, Fowler, and Zwick. Okun later recalled,

> The President began the meeting by reading my memo. . . . I would say that there was a good deal of emotion, certainly on Wilbur Mills' part, in which he was protesting his allegiance to the President and high regard for him and insisting that all his actions on the surcharge had been entirely misunderstood. . . . Mills made an unqualified promise to the President, which he subsequently broke, that he would make every effort to push that thing through with a four-billion dollar cut on it. . . . He made, appar-

> ently, no effort to get the four-billion dollar cut. In fact, he pushed it
> through with a six-billion dollar cut on it. . . . The President . . . said
> that he would agree to give his full support to the combination of a sur-
> charge and a four-billion dollar cut.

Some of the northern liberals insisted on a vote in the House on a record motion to kill the conference report. The President and Sanders were opposed. If it succeeded, there probably would be no tax increase; if it failed, nothing would have been gained. But the liberals would not be put off on a vote to reduce the cut to $4 billion. Representative James A. Burke of Massachusetts made the motion on May 29 and it was defeated 259 to 137. The majority consisted of 167 Republicans, 63 southern Democrats, and 29 northern Democrats. The minority was made up of 111 northern Democrats, 20 southern Democrats, and 6 Republicans. The hoary conservative coalition was in firm control. The House adopted the conference report on June 20 by a 268 to 150 roll call and the Senate approved it the next day 64 to 16. Johnson signed the Revenue and Expenditure Control Act on June 28, 1968. Since it would have been unseemly for him to celebrate his defeat by Wilbur Mills, no signing ceremony was held.

But Johnson, as Califano put it, had "the last laugh." He did not believe that Congress would actually cut fiscal 1969 appropriations by $6 billion. Thus, he refused to make any reductions himself until Congress had acted. "Congress was unable to cut even $4 billion in spending. . . . Fiscal 1969 ended with a $3.2 billion surplus—and the Great Society programs survived." [8]

It is axiomatic that wars produce inflation, and that, certainly, has been the American experience throughout the nation's history. It was dramatically so in the three wars that occurred earlier in Lyndon Johnson's lifetime. Born in 1908, he was nine when the U.S. entered World War I and thirteen when the postwar inflation ended. While Johnson City was in the remote Texas hill country, politics was the stuff of life and his father, Sam, was a member of the Texas legislature in Austin and a strong supporter of Woodrow Wilson. He took his boy on his campaigns and Lyndon would sit in the gallery in the capitol listening to the debates. He could hardly not have learned that the war had pushed up prices. During World War II and the postwar period inflation was a critical national issue. Johnson sat in the House when he was not in military service and it would have been impossible for him to ignore the question. He was in the Senate and became majority leader during the Korean War, when a host of questions about inflation was thrust upon him.

Yet there is no evidence that Johnson learned anything from these experiences. When he went into Vietnam in 1965 he seemed oblivious to the risk of imposing the cost of the war on an economy close to full employment. His falsification of that cost temporarily confused his economists. But he did not fool Martin and the Federal Reserve. After six months the Council of Economic Advisers figured out the truth and immediately urged a surtax on income taxes. In January 1967, a year and a half into the war, Johnson finally came around. But it was too late because the virus of inflation had infected the wage-price system. The Fed's monetary controls were inadequate, and in the absence of an incomes policy and/or a tax hike, the inflation exploded.

While the President now wanted higher taxes, Congress refused. Johnson tried to blame the Congress, but its leaders had a ready answer. If, Wilbur Mills pointed out, the President had called for an increase in taxes to pay for the war, he could have gotten it easily. As noted earlier, Budget Director Schultze agreed. But Johnson could never get himself, despite the massive military forces and the heavy casualties, to admit that Vietnam was a real war.

Thus, Lyndon Johnson, with Robert McNamara's connivance, was the instigator of the Great Inflation. Once started, it seemed never to stop. During the early years of the Nixon administration prices and wages rose more rapidly than they had under Johnson. With the spike in food prices in 1973 and the first great oil shock of 1974 they surged to a double-digit level. In the latter half of that decade the economy sustained another massive rise in the price of oil. It was not until 1982 that inflation was brought under reasonable control. Johnson can hardly be held responsible for Nixon's failings or for the greed of OPEC. Nor can he or his economists be fairly blamed for failing to foresee that 17-year disaster because there was no precedent.

One may ask what would have happened to prices if Johnson had not entered the war in 1965. Walter Heller, no mean authority, speculated about this question. During 1964 and the first half of 1965, he said, "We were moving under the more or less gentle zephyrs of the 1964 tax cut. We were moving so nicely towards full employment, and with very little price inflation." One of the great tragedies of Vietnam was that it "rudely interrupted" this "great experiment." For certain, if the U.S. had reached full employment, there would have been inflationary pressures. "But instead of having 6 or 7 per cent inflation at the peak, we probably could have held it to around 3 per cent, 3½, just half as much."[9]

15

Turmoil at Home

LYNDON Johnson's presidency played itself out against a backdrop of grave civil unrest. It first appeared in 1964, mounted in intensity during 1965–67, and reached a climax in 1968. Not since the 1850s had a chief executive confronted domestic turmoil on this scale. It caused his presidency to erode for four years and to collapse in the fifth.

There were three sources of this turmoil: opposition to the Vietnam War, black militancy, and student unrest in the universities. While there was some overlap—Martin Luther King, Jr., for example, was both a civil rights leader and a leading spokesman for peace—each of these sources was discrete. All three are treated in this chapter through 1967; the climactic events of 1968 are set forth in Chapter 19.

The first modest signs of dissent from the drift to war in Vietnam appeared during 1964. Two of the nation's leading columnists, Walter Lippmann and James Reston, expressed their concern. In March, Students for a Democratic Society at Yale organized the May 2d Movement, which held a demonstration in New York, attracting about 1000 marchers. SDS then persuaded an equal number of draft-age college students to pledge not to fight in Vietnam. On July 10 a petition initiated by the National Committee for a Sane Nuclear Policy (SANE) signed by 5000 professors was presented to the White House. Hans Morgenthau of the University of Chicago, an authority on international relations who had earlier favored support for South Vietnam, was a signer.[1]

Johnson during 1965 worked hard to keep Congress in line behind the war, particularly the Senate. He sealed off Richard Russell, his mentor and old friend, who thought the war was terrible. Since the Georgian was the respected leader of the southern bloc, he must have carried others from his region with him. Mansfield could hardly be moved intellectually, but he usually made his objections in private. Johnson's biggest problem was J. William Fulbright, the chairman of the Foreign Relations Committee, who had steered the Tonkin Gulf Resolution through the Senate. Shortly, Fulbright became convinced that Johnson and McNamara had lied to him and that the North Vietnamese had not attacked the *Turner Joy*. In 1968 he would hold hearings of his committee which would establish this point. But in 1964–65 he remained silent. George Aiken, the Vermont Republican, and Tom Kuchel, the California Republican, were restive about the war. Frank Church, the Idaho Democrat, became a dove and Johnson roughed him up. At a White House dinner he demanded to know whom Church had consulted on the war. He said Walter Lippmann. "All right, Frank," Johnson snapped, "next time you want a dam in Idaho, you go talk to Walter Lippmann."

In 1965 Douglass Cater, the new aide on domestic affairs, began writing memoranda to the President on Vietnam. On January 25 he wrote that Peter Grose of the *New York Times,* who had just returned from Saigon, was "quite fatalistic" and thought "the next six months may mark the end of the road and urge[d] that we be exploring every opportunity to withdraw with honor." On May 25 Cater summarized a series of Reston columns. The reporter detected a "startling change" in the focus of the administration from domestic issues to the war. The President had thrust himself forward as the sole enemy of Communism. He seemed an "impulsive giant . . . fitful and unpredictable." Reston urged public debate. On June 22 Congressman Jim Scheuer reported "widened unrest among the Congressmen about the situation in Vietnam." On July 10 Cater talked to John Gardner and Walter Heller. They were "concerned that as troubles in Vietnam drag on and deepen, there could be an adverse effect on your leadership." On July 24 Carl Marcy, chief of staff of the Senate Foreign Relations Committee, said that Fulbright, Aiken, Church, and perhaps Russell were concerned that the "U.S. was getting involved in a land war without any support from others." On August 5 Cater wrote that several sources recently in Saigon had told him that "a number of young wire service and network correspondents there are thoroughly sour and poisonous in their reporting."

As these comments suggest, Johnson's effort to conduct the war in secrecy collapsed during 1965. The growing American presence, the rapidly rising number of troops, and the mounting casualty list brought the press and television networks to Vietnam in full force. CBS, NBC, and ABC sent reporters and TV crews to Saigon. "Vietnam," Daniel C. Hallin wrote, "was America's first true televised war." The conflict became a staple on the evening news. Michael Arlen called it "the living-room war." The American people received a crash course on Vietnam and guerrilla warfare and they did not like it at all. In the latter part of 1965 the White House was surprised to receive a large volume of antiwar mail from women. These women, many mothers, were watching the war on television and wanted the President to know that they did not approve.

"The first half of 1965," Tom Wells wrote, "was an electric time for peace activists." On February 8–10 about 300 women, the Mothers' Lobby, descended upon Congress to demand a negotiated settlement and a "dignified withdrawal." On February 13, 3000 people gathered in United Nations Plaza in New York to protest Rolling Thunder. On March 16 Alice Herz, an 82-year-old Quaker and a refugee from Nazi Germany, set herself on fire on a Detroit Street corner. She died a few days later.

On the night of March 24–25, 49 professors and 3000 students in Angell Hall at the University of Michigan invented the teach-in. The university would not allow them to disrupt daytime classes. Throughout the night there were lectures, debates, and discussion groups on Vietnam, all tinged with protest in a framework of reasoned inquiry. At dawn there was a torchlight parade and folksinging. It was a memorable event for the participants and it received national publicity. The following day 2500 participated at Columbia and within a few months 120 colleges had held teach-ins.

On April 17 much the largest crowd yet staged a march on Washington. They picketed the White House and then moved to the Washington Monument to hear speeches by Yale historian Staughton Lynd, Senator Gruening, the independent journalist I. F. Stone, and the civil rights leader Robert Moses, along with folksinging by Judy Collins, Joan Baez, and Phil Ochs. They then marched to the Capitol.

On May 15 there was a 15-hour debate between three academics who favored and three who opposed the war. It was broadcast to 100 colleges and was watched by more than 100,000 people. McGeorge Bundy was scheduled to participate, but Johnson, who opposed his speaking, sent him on a special mission to the Caribbean. Three weeks later he did debate Hans Morgenthau on CBS. On May 21–22 over 20,000 participated in a marathon teach-in at Berkeley.

For reasons unknown, Lyndon Johnson thought he needed a resident intellectual and hired Eric Goldman, the Princeton historian. In February 1965 Johnson's social secretary, Bess Abell, suggested a White House festival of the arts. Goldman and his staff broke the arts into seven categories— painting, sculpture, literature, music, dance, film, and photography—and made lists of the nation's most distinguished artists in each group. Mrs. Johnson was enthusiastic and, after a long delay, the President approved. The date was June 14, the artists were invited, and the program was fixed. As the time narrowed, a number of problems emerged that disturbed the Johnsons. Most important, the poet Robert Lowell, who would read from his verse, announced that he was against the war; the novelist John Hersey would read from his antiwar masterpiece *Hiroshima;* and the critic Dwight

McDonald, who strongly opposed the war, would do a piece on the festival for the *New York Review of Books*. The squabbling at the White House was intense, but Goldman managed to go forward. In fact, Lowell did not come, Hersey spoke out strongly against the war, and McDonald circulated an antiwar petition. After reading the papers the next morning and examining her husband's "dark countenance . . . dour and grim," Lady Bird called it "Black Tuesday."

On June 8 SANE held an antiwar rally at Madison Square Garden. Wayne Morse, the noted pediatrician Benjamin Spock, and Socialist leader Norman Thomas were among those who addressed 18,000 people.

On the anniversary of Hiroshima, August 6, the Assembly of Unrepresented People, a group of radical peace groups, staged a civil disobedience rally in Washington which ended on August 9, the anniversary of Nagasaki. At the close 800 marched to the Capitol and sat in. About 350 were arrested and jailed.

Many of the troops bound for Vietnam embarked from the Oakland Army Terminal. On three days in early August, 200 to 300 demonstrators blocked the railway tracks and were dispersed either by a slow-moving locomotive or by the police.

On October 15–16 the International Days of Protest engaged nearly 100,000 demonstrators in 80 cities and several nations in antiwar activities. In Manhattan a young man ostentatiously burned his draft card. In a number of communities those who favored the war mounted counter-demonstrations. A few days later five men burned their cards in Union Square in New York City before a friendly crowd of 1500.

On November 9 Roger LaPorte, 22 years old, poured gasoline over his body and struck a match in Dag Hammarskjöld Plaza at the United Nations. At Bellevue Hospital he told the aides, "I'm a Catholic Worker. I'm against the war, all wars. I did this as a religious action." A priest gave him last rites and he died.

The radical Vietnam Day Committee on November 20 brought 8000 to a march on Oakland which had a cast of unreality. Allen Ginsberg, the poet of the absurd, wrote the scenario, which included mass calisthenics and singing "Three Blind Mice." But there were violent acts in the streets, clashes with the police, and the vandalism of cars and buildings.

Finally, on November 27 SANE staged a peaceful march on Washington in which 30,000 participated. Dr. Spock, Coretta King, and Norman Thomas were among the speakers at the Washington Monument.

Robert Jay Lifton, the noted psychiatrist, observed that the perception of the Vietnam War changed radically in 1965 "from unpleasant background rumbling (1954–64) to nasty foreground obsession (1965 to 1973)." What did the emergence of protest against the war in 1965 mean? While it made Lyndon Johnson extremely angry, he refrained from saying so publicly and his power as President was only modestly diminished. Nor did the dissent affect his conduct of the war.[2]

Mid-August 1965 was a popular time for high public officials to be on vacation. Edmund G. ("Pat") Brown, the governor of California, was in the Greek Islands. On Thursday, August 12, President Johnson took a long weekend at his ranch on the Pedernales River. He did not want to be disturbed. Both McNamara and Katzenbach were on Martha's Vineyard, an island off Cape Cod.

About 7 p.m. on Wednesday, August 11, California Highway Patrolman Lee W. Minikus was riding his motorcycle just south of the Los Angeles city boundary. A passing black motorist told him that he had just seen a car being driven recklessly. Minikus gave chase and pulled the car over in a black neighborhood near the Watts business district. Marquette Frye, a young black man, was the driver, and his brother, Ronald, was the passenger. Minikus gave Marquette the standard Highway Patrol sobriety test, which he flunked. Minikus radioed for a car to take Marquette to jail and for a tow truck to haul off the car. Since the evening was hot, many people were on the street and a crowd of 25 to 50 gathered. Ronald Frye walked two blocks to his home to tell his mother to come over to claim the car. Another motorcycle policeman, a patrol car, and the tow truck, along with Ronald and his mother, arrived at 7:15. The crowd had swelled to 150 to 300.

Until now Marquette had been cooperative, but his mother scolded him for drinking. He pushed her away, cursed and shouted, and told the officers that they would have to kill him to take him to jail. They tried to subdue him, but he resisted. The crowd became hostile, a patrolman radioed for help, and three more officers arrived. Now Minikus and his partner were struggling with both brothers and Mrs. Frye jumped on the back of an officer and ripped his shirt. A policeman swung at Marquette with his night stick, struck him on the forehead, inflicting a minor cut. By 7:23 other Highway Patrolmen and Los Angeles police officers had arrived. A few minutes later the patrol car left with the brothers.

The crowd had now grown to more than 1000. As the officers were leaving, someone spat on one. They arrested a woman and a man said to be inciting the crowd to violence. All the officers drove off by 7:40. The police car was stoned.

Rumors spread through the area that a pregnant woman had been abused by the police. From 8:15 to midnight a mob stoned autos, dragged white motorists out of their cars and beat them, and menaced a police command post. By 1 a.m. Thursday, the situation seemed under control. The police had made 29 arrests.

On Thursday both black and white leaders preached calm. The Los

Angeles Human Relations Commission held a meeting with neighborhood groups and community leaders. The press, radio, and television provided coverage. At the outset the theme was to persuade residents to remain indoors, and Mrs. Frye called for peace. A black high school boy, however, ran to a microphone to say that rioters would attack nearby white areas that evening. At the close of the meeting black leaders proposed that white officers be withdrawn and that black policemen in civilian clothes and unmarked cars replace them. The police rejected the idea. Rioting resumed and the police set up a perimeter line around the troubled area.

At 5 p.m. Los Angeles Police Chief William H. Parker phoned General Roderic Hill, the commander of the California National Guard in Sacramento, to inform him that troops might be needed. Hill designated a liaison officer in Los Angeles and alerted the 40th Armored Division in Southern California. He also informed Lieutenant Governor Glenn Anderson. An Emergency Control Center was opened at police headquarters at 7:30.

A large crowd at the site of the original incident turned over cars and set them afire. Firemen were stoned and shot at. The first store fire broke out nearby. Shortly before midnight rock-throwing and looting began outside the police perimeter. On Thursday night and continuing until 4 a.m. Friday 500 police officers were unable to restrain mobs that smashed windows with rocks and looted stores.

Friday was the 13th and it was, indeed, a black day. By 8 a.m. many fires had been set and looting was rampant, particularly in the Watts business district. Ambulance drivers and firemen refused to enter the riot area without an armed escort. At 10:50 Chief Parker concluded that the situation was out of control and called the governor's office in Sacramento to ask for 1000 National Guard troops. Lieut. Governor Anderson was reluctant to act in the absence of Governor Brown. He did meet with guard officers and they agreed that 2000 troops should be assembled at armories by 5 p.m. That afternoon the governor was reached by phone in Athens. After a briefing, he ordered the immediate calling of the guard, asked for study of a curfew, and said he would come home as soon as possible.

By this time the Watts Riot, as it came to be called, was a news sensation. The Los Angeles *Times* deployed a small army of reporters and photographers and their material moved out over the wire services. The networks and local TV stations provided massive coverage on the ground and from the air by helicopter. The scenes of a huge city turned into a war zone, of immense looting, and of flames leaping into the sky went out to the nation and to much of the world.

On Friday morning the calls began coming into the White House and Joe Califano handled them. He assumed that the President would oppose sending federal troops into the city and would want to place the responsibility for restoring order upon the state and local authorities. Califano repeatedly called the ranch, but Johnson did not return his calls, "the only time in the years I worked for Lyndon Johnson that this occurred," he later said. The President must have sensed that the Watts Riot was poison for his Great Society and perhaps for his presidency. The white backlash was already evident in Chief Parker's assertion that violence was inevitable "when you keep telling people they are unfairly treated and teach them disrespect for the law."

Early Friday afternoon rioters set systematic fire to two blocks of 103rd Street in Watts, and snipers drove off firemen. By late afternoon gangs had spread the riot 50 or 60 blocks to the north. The first death, a black bystander caught in an exchange of gunfire, occurred between 6:00 and 7:00. Almost no one noticed when Marquette Frye pleaded guilty.

That night the rioting rolled completely out of control, spreading to a much larger area of south central Los Angeles. Fires seemed everywhere. The first contingent of guardsmen, 1336 troops, were in the area at 10 p.m. A second wave of 1000 men joined them at midnight. At midnight Saturday the total on duty was 13,900 guardsmen, 934 Police Department officers, and 719 Sheriff's Office patrolmen. At 11 a.m. on Saturday 100 engine companies were fighting fires, often under sniper fire. That night a fireman was killed when a sheriff's shotgun discharged in a struggle with rioters. Major calls of looting, burning, and shooting were reported every two or three minutes.

The rioting on Saturday morning spread to the maximum extent and continued throughout the day. But the guardsmen gradually established control. They swept the streets and rode on engine companies to stop sniping. The curfew went into effect at 8 p.m. on Saturday; anyone on the street was arrested. Except for the burning of a block of stores on Broadway between 46th and 48th streets, Saturday night was quiet.

On Saturday morning the President had authorized Bill Moyers to put out a statement that the riot was "tragic and shocking" and warning the rioters that their violence would not be rewarded. But he still would not speak to Califano, who was under great pressure from General Creighton Abrams, the Army vice chief of staff. The California National Guard needed food, trucks, tear gas, and ammunition that the Army had available in northern California and Abrams wanted presidential permission to use Air Force planes to haul them south. Anderson called the White House repeatedly to urge bringing down the supplies. Califano talked to McNamara and Katzenbach on Martha's Vineyard. They supported the Abrams request and agreed that regular Army troops should be deployed if the guard was unable to restore order. McNamara also wanted approval to alert forces at Ft. Lewis, Washington, and to send some to the vicinity of Los Angeles. But Califano could not reach Johnson. He got Deputy Attorney General Ramsey Clark to draft the order and proclamation and wired them to the ranch. He also sent a Jetstar to stand by at the Vineyard if McNamara or Katzenbach needed to return to Washington. When Abrams pressed on the supplies,

Califano said, "You've got White House approval." "Do we have presidential approval?" Abrams demanded. Califano repeated, "You've got White House approval." He called Jack Valenti at the ranch to report what he had done. Valenti wrote a "cautious note" for the President, hoping to protect Califano.

Johnson finally phoned at 9:09 p.m. Saturday. He insisted on no federal presence in Los Angeles. "Not one of our people sets foot there until you talk to me." "His voice," Califano wrote, "was heavy with disappointment." Early Sunday morning Johnson called again. He had heard of the airlift and was "deeply distressed, but he sounded more sorrowful than angry." He demanded to know who had authorized the lift. Califano said he had on the recommendations of Abrams, McNamara, Katzenbach, and Anderson. Johnson scolded, "Remember you work for your President."

Then he shifted gears. He wanted an assessment of the situation in Watts. Califano said it was coming under control. Johnson ordered him to issue a statement congratulating the state and city officials, acting under their local responsibility, for restoring order. He also wanted a statement from prominent black leaders condemning the violence.

The President then expressed his real concern: "Negroes will end up pissing in the aisles of the Senate, and making fools of themselves, the way . . . they had after the Civil War and during Reconstruction. . . . Just as the government was moving to help them, the Negroes will once again take unwise actions out of frustration, impatience, and anger." The riots would threaten the gains already made and make it difficult to pass new legislation. "I began to grasp," Califano wrote, "how acutely Johnson feared that the reforms to which he had dedicated his presidency were in mortal danger, not only from those who opposed, but from those he was trying to help." The President told him to get Dick Goodwin to write a White House statement. He phoned back in 30 minutes to hear the draft. Califano told him the Coast Guard was looking for Goodwin, who was sailing off Martha's Vineyard. "We ought to blow up that goddam island!" He then told Califano to instruct Governor Brown to name John McCone the chairman of the state inquiry commission. "An ex-CIA director, conservative, if he says no communist conspiracy and describes the conditions in Watts, we'll be able to help those Negroes out there."

The rioting diminished markedly on Sunday, August 15, but there were a few new fires. Governor Brown lifted the curfew on Tuesday and by the following weekend only 252 guardsmen were still in the area.

After six days of rioting, the inventory of damage to life and property was immense. The entire south central riot area covered 46.5 square miles of Los Angeles County, most of it within the city of Los Angeles. Watts provided only 2.1 square miles. The black population of the county in 1965 was 650,000, of whom two-thirds lived in south central. No one knew how many rioted and estimates ranged from 10,000 to 80,000. A high proportion consisted of young black males, many organized in gangs. The heaviest damage was along major arteries, where stores were burned, smashed, and looted. The casualties were 34 killed and 1,032 injured. Of those who died, one was a fireman, one a deputy sheriff, and one a Long Beach policeman. Of those injured, 90 were Los Angeles policemen, 10 national guardsmen, 23 from other government agencies, and 773 were civilians. Gunshot wounds caused 118 of the injuries.

More than 600 buildings were damaged by burning and looting, over 200 of them totally destroyed by fire. The rioters concentrated on food markets, liquor, furniture, clothing, and department stores, and pawn shops. Stores with signs reading, "A Blood Brother," were spared. Service stations, banks, and car dealerships were hardly damaged. No homes were deliberately burned, and schools, libraries, churches, and public buildings suffered only slight damage. The losses were estimated at over $40 million.

Louis Martin, the deputy chairman of the Democratic National Committee and a politically savvy black, investigated the riot area and held a four-hour session with elected Negro officials. He wrote,

> The most interesting revelation . . . was the fact that State Rep. Ferrell who lives in Watts was threatened by robbers. He reported phone threats and one attempt by rioters to get into his backyard. He and his sons stood an armed watch around the clock. Rep. Ferrell won the district on a racist appeal just four years ago. Up until then the Watts area was represented by a veteran white assemblyman. Earlier the press carried the fact that Councilman Billy Mills had been threatened by rioters. The rioters had no love for "upper class" Negroes.

Watts was hardly the first of the ghetto riots. In 1963 there had been disorders in Chicago and Philadelphia. During 1964 there were disturbances in Chicago, Cleveland, Jacksonville, three New Jersey towns—Elizabeth, Jersey City, and Paterson—New York, Philadelphia, and Rochester. Aside from Watts, 1965 also saw a riot in Bogalusa, Louisiana. But Watts differed from the others in many ways: it was much bigger by any standard of measurement, far more broadly publicized, and more significant by an even wider margin. The others were local events, very important within the community but little noticed elsewhere. Watts was a national event which happened to occur in Los Angeles; in fact, it left its mark on the world.

If this big explosion had occurred in Harlem or in the Chicago Black Belt or in the Philadelphia ghetto the explanation would have been obvious. But Watts? It enjoyed Southern California's much ballyhooed climate. The streets were wide and uncrowded. "We were struck," Martin wrote, "by the neatness of the residential area, well tended little lawns separating hundreds of small one-storey houses which were painted in bright attractive colors." Though public transportation was inadequate, this was not unique to South Central, and Watts was not far from downtown Los Angeles to the north and the centers of industry and employment to the east. Blacks, obviously, were free to vote and to use public accommodations. In 1964 the Urban League had made a survey of the conditions of Negro life in 68 cities and ranked Los Angeles first.

Brown accepted LBJ's suggestion by naming John McCone chairman of his Commission on the Los Angeles Riots, though he tempered McCone's conservatism by appointing a prominent Democrat and distinguished Los Angeles attorney, Warren M. Christopher, as vice chairman. But Johnson proceeded to select his own investigative body chaired by Deputy Attorney General Ramsey Clark, along with Andrew F. Brimmer, a prominent black economist, and Jack T. Conway, a former UAW officer who was now a high-ranking official of the Housing and Home Finance Agency.

The McCone Commission concluded that "there is no reliable evidence of outside leadership or pre-established plans for the rioting." This view was shared by the attorney general, the district attorney, and the police. No radical political organization nor, for that matter, any civil rights group, had anything to do with the riot. It had been started and had grown sponta-neously.

The National Advisory Commission on Civil Disorders later studied a large number of ghetto riots and found that "40 percent involved alleged abusive or discriminatory police actions." The triggering of the Watts Riot fit this pattern. While the McCone Commission stressed that the conduct of the police in this instance was beyond reproach and the facts support that conclusion, this was not the perception in the black community.

In his analysis of the riot Milton Viorst found that policemen were looked upon by residents as "the occupying army of white America, a hos-tile power. . . . They often behaved as savages, as captors without mercy, and they were loathed." The police engaged in random intimidation; they called young black men "niggers" and "boys"; and they stopped and ar-rested whomever they liked. The black officials Martin talked to with one exception "agreed that Police Chief Parker and the police . . . constituted a provocative force in the general unrest which erupted into a riot." Parker bitterly denied these charges and insisted that his officers treated black citi-zens exactly as they did white citizens.

Thus, the trigger of the Watts Riot was the misperception by blacks that the Fryes had been brutalized by the police. But there were deeper reasons for black resentment in South Central and they were exactly the same factors that caused unrest in all the other urban ghettoes: unemploy-ment, particularly among young males, poverty, bad schools, wretched health, rampant crime, drugs, and isolation from the larger community. Added together, they caused rage and it was no surprise that the black hero of the young people of Watts was Malcolm X.

The white community in Los Angeles, the President's task force re-ported, was "deeply shocked" by the riot. The reaction was to "condemn the lawlessness, the impatience, and the destruction. There is a wide feeling that the Negro community lacks gratitude for recent economic and civil rights advances and that its demands will grow." Assistance to the riot areas was seen as a reward for lawlessness. Whites, as well, strongly supported the police. The department received 17,864 letters and telegrams, 99 percent commendatory. "Police Chief Parker," Martin wrote, "seems to be adored like Edgar Hoover by the whites in power." Mayor Sam Yorty, who had earlier attacked him, was "now squarely in his corner."

The President ordered Califano and Lee White of his staff to comb the resources of the federal government for programs that could be started or expanded to address the problems of the ghetto. On September 2 he approved of 49 projects and his task force recommended 35 more. They dealt with manpower training, adult education, business development, legal aid, basic education, and health services. Several years later Sherman M. Mellinkoff, the dean of the UCLA Medical School and a member of the McCone Commission, played a key role in establishing the greatest monument to the Watts Riot, the Martin Luther King, Jr./Drew Medical School in Watts.

King himself was baffled by the riot. He was in Miami on Friday, August 13, en route to Puerto Rico, when he heard the news. Black preachers in Los Angeles asked him to come out. He talked to Bayard Rustin, who thought he could accomplish nothing and might damage himself. King agreed and flew to San Juan. But, on Sunday, as the riot was ending, he decided to go to Los Angeles. Rustin and several other advisers urged him not to do so, but his conscience ruled otherwise. He arrived with Rustin on Tuesday afternoon. He talked with Otis Chandler, the publisher of the *Times,* and Governor Brown. King was awed by the devastation. "You know, Bayard," he said, "I worked to get these people the right to eat hamburgers, and now I've got to do something . . . to help them get the money to buy it." King met with Yorty and Parker and urged a police review board to look into charges of brutality. Parker was enraged and told him there was none in Los Angeles. After the meeting Yorty publicly attacked King and King demanded that Parker be fired.

Rustin was right. King had no reason to come to Los Angeles because he had no power to control events. The trip may have salved his conscience, but it accomplished nothing. Nevertheless, the Watts Riot for Martin King, as for Lyndon Johnson, was a critical turning point.[3]

King and his Southern Christian Leadership Conference had been the locomotive driving the civil rights movement. He compiled a decade of triumph from the Montgomery bus boycott in 1955 to the march from Selma to Montgomery in 1965. It was significant that the first word in the organization's name was "Southern." These victories had been won in the South, where unconstitutional roadblocks to civil rights were widespread, and where black respect for the black clergy prevailed. Here he could also win support—moral, political, and financial—from many northern whites who thought the time had come to end the legal denial of civil rights. King had solidified white backing by insisting on nonviolence.

But by 1965 the situation had changed. There were virtually no constitutional battles left to be won, either in the South or in the North. The dominant residual issue, as Watts had demonstrated, was the northern urban ghetto. Here the problems were exceptionally complex and intractable—poverty, unemployment, housing, crime, health, education, and family—and did not lend themselves to solution by demonstration. Further, the white backlash was growing swiftly and, with it, northern support for civil rights was eroding.

King, like Johnson, had little interest in administration. SCLC, even in the best of times, had been run haphazardly, suffering from a chronic shortage of funds, internal bickering, and sloppy execution, including corruption. Moreover, by 1965 new young black leaders were emerging who were more militant than King and who rejected both him and nonviolence. This was dramatically evident in the Student Nonviolent Coordinating Committee, the Congress of Racial Equality, and, further left, in the Black Muslims with their formidable voice, Malcolm X, as well as in the soon-to-appear Black Panthers.

From Selma in 1965 to his assassination in 1968 King searched vainly for a mission. He made forays into three areas: an attack on a massive northern urban ghetto—Chicago—opposition to the war in Vietnam, and help for the poor. All aroused strong opposition and none was successful.

LBJ, like King, was insatiable. He had gained notable victories in the Civil Rights Act of 1964 and the Voting Rights Act of 1965. Despite waning support and the fact that he did not know what it should deal with, he insisted on another civil rights law in 1966.

In January 1965 Daniel Patrick Moynihan, head of the Office of Policy Planning and Research in the Labor Department, had sent Bill Moyers a memorandum arguing that the disintegration of the Negro family in the urban ghettoes stemmed from the declining status of the black male. This had created a "pathological matriarchal situation." In May, Secretary Wirtz sent the President a more detailed analysis which he called "nine pages of dynamite." In June, Moynihan's study, *The Negro Family: The Case for National Action,* was published. He pointed to the decline in marriages, the rise of illegitimacy, female-headed families, and a dramatic increase in welfare dependency. Moynihan called for a national policy to "strengthen the Negro family so as to enable it to raise and support its members as do other families." His report aroused a firestorm of controversy in the black community and in some liberal white circles.

On June 4 the President delivered a wide-ranging commencement address at Howard University in which he dealt with many black problems, including family breakdown. He promised to call a White House conference in the fall on the theme "To Fulfill These Rights." But the planners were unable to agree upon an agenda and it was deferred until June 1966.

These controversies in 1965, obviously, provided no basis for civil rights legislation. Johnson, therefore, instructed Attorney General Katzenbach to form an interagency task force to draft a bill for 1966, and he drew in Labor, HEW, Defense, OEO, and, significantly, Housing and Home Finance. An idea that emerged was the thorny and explosive question of fair housing, a topic carefully sidestepped in all prior legislation. After extended negotiations between Katzenbach and the White House, the President sent up an omnibus civil rights bill on April 28, 1966.

It was peculiarly lopsided. There were several very specific legal provisions—nondiscrimination in jury selection, authority for the Attorney General to initiate desegregation suits in education and public accommodations, and protection of the security of civil rights workers. Title IV was the blockbuster: a prohibition of discrimination in the sale or rental of *all* housing.

The timing of Title IV was abominable. Watts had been joined by other ghetto riots. Stokely Carmichael, who had taken over SNCC, was bellowing "Black Power!" to enormous coverage in the media. While the bill was being debated during the summer, King was leading demonstrations for open housing in Chicago which were arousing violent opposition. The white backlash was in full tide. In Congress southerners were delighted and Republicans were licking their chops over their prospects in the November elections. In fact, the civil rights leaders had warned Johnson that open housing would arouse fatal opposition. Dirksen declared that Title IV was "absolutely unconstitutional." Senator Sam Ervin of North Carolina, the chairman of the Subcommittee on Constitutional Rights, agreed and added with some satisfaction, "For the first time, we have a bill which proposes that other than Southern oxen are to be gored." A southern Democratic-Republican coalition and a filibuster were inevitable in the Senate.

Thus, the strategy was to start in the House. In the hearings the National Association of Real Estate Boards, representing 83,000 brokers, denounced the bill for abridging "the fundamental right of every person to sell, lease, or rent any part of his real property, or to decline to sell, lease or rent such real property." Between May and August 1966 the House tore Title IV to pieces in both the committee and on the floor. The administration, helpless, caved in on amendment after amendment in the hope of getting a bill, any kind of bill, through. Finally the House passed a measure by a vote of 259 to 157. The mutilated remains of Title IV looked like this: No one could discriminate in the sale, rental, or advertising of a dwelling if he had entered into more than two real estate transactions within the previous twelve months. A broker would be allowed to discriminate with the written consent of the owner. A landlord renting no more than four rooms in his/her own home was exempt, a nod to the famous mythical widow Mrs. Murphy, trying to make ends meet on Social Security and room rents.

Banks were prohibited from imposing discrimination as a condition for making real estate loans.

The Senate never considered this monstrosity. Because Eastland would have killed it in his Judiciary Committee, Mansfield brought it straight to the floor on September 6. The Senate adjourned for lack of a quorum for several days. The leaders then agreed to conduct other business. On September 13 the President pleaded with an unshakable Dirksen to provide the necessary Republican votes. Mansfield called for cloture on September 18. The vote was 52 to 41, 10 votes shy of the necessary two-thirds.

After this defeat the President promised to propose civil rights legislation again in 1967, but he refused to say whether he would include open housing. King said that this catastrophe

> surely heralds darker days for this social era of discontent. The executioners of the 1966 civil rights bill have given valuable assistance to those forces in the Negro communities who counsel violence. Although I will continue to preach with all my might the moral rightness of nonviolence, my words are now bound to fall on more deaf ears.

Larry O'Brien later reflected on "our greatest setback in that session." The President and he had miscalculated politically. They counted on the huge Democratic majorities and Johnson was confident that he could persuade Dirksen to deliver Republican votes for cloture. But the housing and real estate issue went "beyond civil rights." "We were hit with a firestorm from the outset on the Republican side, and, as time went on, the opposition broadened." The President tried "mightily" to move Dirksen, but the minority leader "made a point of announcing his opposition at the outset." Dirksen reflected "the disarray in the House and the cloture vote in the Senate." The Watts Riot did no good. The President was "troubled" and "frustrated."[4]

The sole surviving major city political machine in the U.S. ruled Chicago. "In no other big city in the nation," Len O'Connor wrote, "is Democratic Party control so absolute as in Chicago and in no other city is there so absolute a boss as Richard J. Daley." The mayor could pile up huge majorities for his slates in the city and in Cook County. They had been big enough to squeeze out a victory for Kennedy in Illinois in 1960 and, of course, to carry the state easily for Johnson in 1964. Daley spoke with a powerful voice in Springfield, delivered the entire Illinois Democratic delegation in the House, and was heard loud and clear in the White House. In return for their votes, the machine was said to have 30,000 jobs at its command and provided its supporters with at least 350 in each of the city's 50 wards, pay for those who rounded up voters and for poll watchers on election days, and, in the poorest districts, food, lawyers, and help with the bureaucracy and the police. These services were provided fairly to all ethnic groups, including blacks.

Chicago was called a "city of nations." Nowhere else were ethnic politics played so ubiquitously and by no one so masterfully as Dick Daley. Most of the Irish had come over in the nineteenth century and not many remained in the inner city. But, with the Irish gift for politics, they still sat in the top seats, notably in the mayor's office. The Germans and the Scandinavians did not count because they voted Republican. Only Warsaw had more Poles. There were large concentrations of Czechs, Jews, Italians, Croatians, and Lithuanians. All of the Eastern and Southern Europeans, except the Jews, were Roman Catholic. In fact, in 1960 there were 2.2 million Catholics in Cook and Lake counties, and Chicago was the largest archdiocese in the U.S. You could always tell which ethnic enclave you were in, Chicago *Daily News* columnist Mike Royko wrote, by the "odors in the food stores and the open kitchen windows, the sound of the foreign or familiar language, and by whether a stranger hit you in the head with a rock."

Royko, who knew almost everything about Chicago, caught the essence of its mayor in his 1976 obituary:

> If a man ever reflected a city, it was Richard J. Daley and Chicago.
>
> In some ways, he was this town at its best—strong, hard-driving, working feverishly, pushing, building, driven by ambitions so big they seemed Texas-boastful.
>
> In other ways, he was this city at its worst—arrogant, crude, conniving, ruthless, suspicious, intolerant.
>
> He wasn't graceful, suave, witty, or smooth. But, then, this is not Paris or San Francisco.
>
> He was raucous, sentimental, hot-tempered, practical, simple, devious, big, and powerful. This is, after all, Chicago . . . belly to belly, scowl to scowl, and may the toughest or loudest man win. . . .
>
> Daley was a product of the neighborhoods and he reflected it in many good ways—loyalty to the family, neighbors, old buddies, the corner grocer. You do something for someone, they do something for you. If somebody is sick, you offer the family help. If someone dies, you go to the wake and try to lend comfort. The young don't lip off the old; everybody cuts his grass, takes care of his property, and don't play your TV too loud.
>
> That's the way he liked to live, and that's what he thought most people wanted, and he was right.
>
> But there are other sides to Chicago neighborhoods—suspicion of outsiders, intolerance toward the unconventional, bigotry, and bullying.
>
> That was Daley too. As he proved over and over again, he didn't trust outsiders, whether they were long-hairs against war, black preachers against segregation, reformers against his machine, or community groups against his policies. This was his neighborhood—ward—city—county, and nobody could come in and make noise. He'd call the cops. Which he did.

Blacks were by far the largest ethnic group in Chicago, about 1 million in 1965. They were concentrated in two vast crowded ghettoes—the old Black Belt on the South Side and the former Jewish ghetto on the West Side. The other ethnic groups did not want to mix with them. They wanted to keep their own neighborhoods and to send their children to white schools, that is, they insisted on segregation. No one knew better than Daley that racism was a time bomb waiting to go off that could tear his machine and his beloved city to shreds. In 1965–66 he faced two tough tests.

Title VI of the Civil Rights Act of 1964 required that local school boards disburse federal funds without discrimination based on race. During 1965 Congress enacted the Elementary and Secondary Education Act with a $1 billion appropriation for federal aid to low-income areas. Chicago qualified for a $32 million grant, which the mayor, the board of education, and school superintendent Benjamin C. Willis, who supported the segregation of the schools, were eager to obtain for their underfunded system.

During the summer of 1965 the President imposed enormous pressure on Califano and Francis Keppel, the Commissioner of Education, to obtain pledges from the 5000 southern school districts to desegregate by the time school opened in the fall. "He talked to me several times each day," Califano wrote, "about ideas to spur compliance and gave me the names of politicians, educators, labor and business leaders across the South to call." Johnson made a special effort in Texas. Keppel said, "He damn near drove me crazy." Keppel had a large staff in the field talking to school boards and he kept a daily score card. "We've now got 3,800 of them!" By September only a couple of hundred were left and he "was ready for a nervous breakdown."

In the South the issue was de jure segregation, that is, legally mandated segregation under state law in defiance of both *Brown v. Board of Education* and Title VI of the Civil Rights Act. In September, as Keppel was catching his breath, his office began to receive complaints about de facto segregation in the North. This raised several troubling questions. Did Title VI apply to this type of segregation? If it did, what procedural rules would the agency employ in seeking compliance? What pressures could it bring on school boards to push them into action?

Until August, Anthony Celebrezze had been the Secretary of HEW. A former mayor of Cleveland who knew all about northern big-city segregation, he wanted no trouble before he went onto the bench. John Gardner succeeded him. Assistant Secretary James Quigley had jurisdiction over complaints. Thus, Gardner, Quigley, and Keppel would make the policy at HEW. All opposed segregation on deeply held principle; none showed a concern for political reality or seemed even to be aware of its significance.

Between them, they made a series of critical political mistakes. Quigley had received complaints from Chicago, Gary Orfield wrote, "the scene of the nation's most bitter struggle over school segregation, Boston, the city where the defense of the neighborhood school had made an obscure woman school-board member a dominant figure in local politics, and Chester, the bleak Pennsylvania city where a CORE campaign had produced local violence." HEW chose Chicago because the complaint from Albert A. Raby of the Coordinating Council of Community Organizations was thorough, documented, and brought serious charges. Preliminary investigation suggested that they had substance.

By September Chicago was ready to ask for its grant and there were rumors that Willis intended to use some of the funds in high-income neighborhoods. Keppel, while without authority to withhold at this stage, could defer disbursement. On September 28 the Chicago *Tribune* reported incorrectly that Illinois Superintendent of Public Instruction Ray Page had already approved the Chicago grant. Keppel was concerned that abuse by Willis might embarrass the Johnson administration politically.

He composed a letter to Page:

> Preliminary investigation of certain of the complaints . . . indicates probable noncompliance with the act and the regulation, and brings into serious question the assurance of compliance made by the Chicago school authorities. . . . We believe that these . . . complaints can, with the full cooperation of the Chicago school authorities, be fully investigated in a relatively short time and they can and must be satisfactorily resolved before any new commitments are made of funds.

Gardner approved the letter. Keppel notified Cater, who covered HEW for the White House. He neither disapproved nor informed the President. The letter was hand-delivered to Page in Springfield with a copy to Willis in Chicago on October 1.

To say that outrage was expressed in the Land of Lincoln would be an understatement. Very loud and extremely angry voices filled the airwaves and gained big headlines in the Chicago press—Page, Willis, Congressman Roman Pucinski, Chicago's representative on the House Education and Labor Committee, Senator Dirksen, and, by no means least, Mayor Daley. They delivered the same message: a band of children-hating power-hungry bureaucrats in Washington had conspired to destroy a sacred American principle—local control of the public schools.

The President was shocked. He ordered Califano to investigate, and a memorandum from the Department of Justice pointed out that an ambiguity in the law raised a question about the legality, to say nothing of the political wisdom, of Keppel's letter.

On October 3 the President went to New York to sign the new immigration law and to greet the Pope. The mayor, with Mrs. Daley at his side, was waiting for him in Ambassador Goldberg's luxurious apartment in the Waldorf Towers.

Daley battered Johnson with outrage and, though a devout Catholic, kept the Pope waiting ten minutes. The President offered no defense whatever. He said that he would look into the matter the moment he returned to Washington and that Califano was already lining up Gardner, Wilbur Cohen, Keppel, Katzenbach, and Cater. "Daley," Califano wrote, "was critical to the success of the Great Society. A call to Daley was all that was needed to deliver the fourteen votes of the Illinois Democratic delegation. Johnson and others of us had made many calls to the Mayor and Daley had always come through." The White House meeting, therefore, was a disaster for Keppel. Johnson raked him over the coals and Keppel soon resigned as Commissioner of Education, which he had intended to do anyway.

Johnson sent Cohen to Chicago with instructions to settle the issue immediately. He met with Frank Whiston, the chairman of the school board and a Willis supporter. Since Cohen caved in except for a few meaningless concessions, it took only an hour to reach agreement.

The Chicago disaster ended any hope of using Title VI of the Civil Rights Act to eliminate de facto school segregation for the time being. The city got its $32 million with no questions asked. Other segregated northern school districts received similar treatment. Big-city northern Democrats in the House, led by Pucinski, mounted a campaign against the Office of Education. In the South, Chicago was read as proof that civil rights enforcement could be beaten back with political power. As Orfield concluded, "An earlier hope that HEW would use the administrative discretion provided by the broad injunction of Title VI . . . to prohibit de facto segregation vanished in the first days of October, 1965." Mayor Daley had passed his first test handsomely.[5]

In 1965 King considered four targets for his invasion of the North: Chicago, New York, Philadelphia, and Washington. Adam Clayton Powell, the boss of Harlem, wanted no outside meddling in his town and told King to stay out of New York. Black leadership was weak in Philadelphia and Washington would offend the White House. It had to be Chicago. Bayard Rustin, perhaps the wisest of King's advisers, said, "You don't know what you are talking about. You don't know what Chicago is like. . . . You're going to be wiped out." The Reverend Arthur Brazier of the South Side Woodlawn Organization said, "King decided to come to Chicago because . . . Chicago was unique in that there was one man, one source of power. . . . This wasn't the case in New York or any other city. He thought if Daley could be persuaded of the rightness of open housing and integrated schools that things could be done." King totally misread the mayor. Daley told one of his lieutenants in rage that King was a "dirty sonofabitch, a bastard, a prick. He said, 'King came here to hurt Douglas [the senator was up for reelection in 1966] because Rockefeller gave him dough, that's why he came here, to try to get Douglas beaten. He's a rabble-rouser, a trouble-maker.' "

King was in and out of the city in the summer of 1965 but had no organization. A SCLC meeting with Chicago's Coordinating Council of Community Organizations led to neither a strategy nor an agenda. In January 1966 King rented a $90-a-month cold apartment in the Lawndale ghetto. After the landlord learned who his tenant would be, an army of repairmen arrived to fix it up, much to the glee of the Chicago press. But King stayed in a hotel downtown to keep warm.

Activity finally began on July 10, 1966, with a rally in Soldier Field. King hoped to attract 100,000 people; in fact, 30,000 showed up. He then led a march of 5000 to tape his demands on the door of City Hall.

Tuesday, July 12, was brutally hot and the beaches were closed because the lake was polluted. Although it was illegal, children had long cooled off at fire hydrants by turning on the spray. The fire commissioner, with pressure dropping, ordered them sealed. In the near West Side ghetto at the corner of Roosevelt Road and Throop Street the kids turned the hydrants on and the police shut them off repeatedly. A large crowd gathered. The cops arrested a youngster and rocks began to fly. The officers used their clubs. King, preaching at nearby Shiloh Baptist Church, urged nonviolence to no avail. The water incident quickly turned into a riot: 10 people were injured, 24 were arrested, store windows were smashed, and looting was widespread.

Wednesday evening the riot spread a mile north with fires, stoning of firemen, and looting. There were 11 persons wounded, six of them officers, and there were 35 arrests. On Thursday evening, several miles west, Lawndale and Garfield Park exploded into a major riot which continued until Friday morning. Two persons were killed, one a pregnant fourteen-year-old, 30 were wounded, and 200 were arrested. Daley asked Governor Otto Kerner for the National Guard.

On Friday King went to the mayor's office and they quickly reached an agreement—installation of sprayers on hydrants, access to parks and swimming pools, staying off the streets in riot areas, and an advisory committee on police-community relations. That evening 1500 troops moved into the West Side and stopped the violence. In all, 61 policemen were injured and 533 citizens were arrested.

Mike Royko wrote,

> Now there was a program, and Daley liked it. Give them water. He had a whole lake outside the door. . . . City Hall . . . embarked on a crusade to make Chicago's blacks the wettest in the country. Portable swimming pools were being trucked in. Sprinklers were attached to hydrants, and water was gushing everywhere. One cynical civil rights worker said, "I think they're hoping we'll all grow gills and swim away."

King now turned to housing. On July 31 blacks marched against Halvorsen Realtors in all-white Gage Park. A huge white mob overcame the police, rained bricks, rocks, and bottles on the demonstrators, and over-turned and burned cars. Thirty-one were injured.

On August 2, 500 demonstrators with heavy police protection marched through a tense white crowd to Parker & Finney Realtors in Belmont-Cragin. Almost two dozen whites were arrested.

Two days later 600 demonstrators protected by 1200 policemen started another walk to Halvorsen Realtors, surrounded by many thousands of white protestors. King was hit on the head by a rock. "I have never seen such hostility and hatred anywhere in my life," he said, "even in Selma." There were 30 injuries and 40 arrests. A revisit to Belmont-Cragin on August 7 was more of the same. The demonstrations received enormous coverage in the media, both in Chicago and nationally, fueling the white backlash.

These marches, Alan B. Anderson and George W. Pickering wrote, were designed to "dramatize the dual housing market, expose segregationist realtors, and force the mayor into negotiations of the movement's demands for open housing." But they "provoked or exposed a truly shocking depth of anger, hatred, and potential for violence." With his city being torn apart, Daley agreed to a "summit" at the Episcopal Cathedral of St. James on August 17.

Ben W. Heineman, president of the Chicago & Northwestern Railroad and a notable civic leader, chaired the meetings, which went on for a week and a half. What King now called the Freedom Movement had hastily cobbled together nine housing demands, but the Chicago Real Estate Board paid them only lip service. Daley insisted that the demonstrations stop at once. King refused until he won something in return. On August 19 the mayor got an injunction against the marches. King threatened to stage a demonstration in Cicero on Sunday, August 28. An independent town, Cicero was beyond the reach of the court order and was notorious as the most bigoted and violent locality in the metropolitan area.

The city, the Freedom Movement, and the real estate interests eventually worked out an agreement in principle: Daley would ask for a state open housing law; the Real Estate Board would withdraw its opposition to open housing; the housing authority would try to spread public housing beyond the ghettoes; and so on. King called it "the first step in a thousand-mile journey." But the militants overrode him; they rejected the agreement and insisted on the demonstration in Cicero.

It was a calamity. On September 4, 250 marchers chanting "Black Power!" marched into the town protected by 3000 National Guardsmen, Cook County sheriffs, and state and local police. They faced a raging mob of thousands that pelted them with rocks and bottles and shattered the march.

The consequence of this disaster was that the Freedom Movement was destroyed. King could not even get a vote to ratify the summit agreement. There was no open housing. The agreement, Royko wrote, "was an impressive document, chock full of noble vows and promises. It was also without legal standing and wasn't worth the paper it was printed on." Mayor Daley, who would be overwhelmingly reelected in 1967, had passed his second test. But Lyndon Johnson suffered a double defeat: Congress rejected his open housing bill, and Paul Douglas, one of his staunchest supporters on the Vietnam War in the Senate, went down to defeat.[6]

Lyndon Johnson despised the college students who demonstrated against the war and the draft and loathed the style of the counterculture. He was convinced that their leaders were engaged in an international Communist conspiracy and ordered Director Richard Helms of the Central Intelligence Agency to prove it. He also directed Secretary Rusk to study the dramatic surge in student turmoil around the world in the late sixties. Rusk created a Student Unrest Study Group which prepared a thoughtful report on more than 30 countries. It did not reach Rusk until January 17, 1969, three days before Johnson left the White House. It would have given him small comfort, as would the superficial CIA report.

"The Communist role in student unrest," the State Department study read, "is considerably more often alleged than confirmed." The dominant student New Left was "essentially anti-Communist." Moscow and the Soviet satellites "actually opposed on doctrinal grounds certain major student uprisings, e.g., in France, Belgium, and West Berlin."

If Marxism did not drive worldwide unrest, what did? The proximate causes, the report stated, were rooted in the university, where there was "a growing base of student cynicism with respect to the relevance of social institutions and to the apparent gap between promise and performance."

> Because of the revolution in communications, the ease of travel, and the evolution of society everywhere, student behavior never again will resemble what it was when education was reserved for the elite. The presence in the universities of thousands of lower-and-lower-middle-class students has resulted in an unprecedented demand for relevant instruction. Today's students are a self-conscious group; they communicate effectively with each other outside of any institutional framework, read the same books and savor similar experiences. Increasingly, they have come to recognize what they take to be a community of interests. This view is likely to influence their future political conduct and to shape the demands they make of government.

The peace movement, which became a central feature of American life in the sixties, began a decade earlier in an uneasy coalition of internationalists and radical pacifists. They were deeply concerned about the warlike manner in which the Cold War was waged and by The Bomb. The lead organization, SANE, was soon joined by others, and somewhat later by Students for a Democratic Society, SDS.

SDS traced its orig.ns back to the Progressive era, to the Intercollegiate

Socialist Society with such literary luminaries as Jack London, Upton Sinclair, and William English Walling. After World War II its parent, the League for Industrial Democracy, supported financially by the International Ladies' Garment Workers' Union, along with its appendage, now called the Student League for Industrial Democracy, began to attract a new group of radicals. In 1960 they changed their name to Students for a Democratic Society.

The timing seemed ideal, according to the questionable reasoning of Kirkpatrick Sale, because American universities were now a smoldering "volcano" and students would be "harbingers of a revived left." He laid out four reasons for this development. First, America was moving into crisis with a tattered social fabric, an eroding economy, a corrupt and bureaucratized political system, and the Cold War. Related, second, was a "crisis of belief." Americans no longer trusted their institutions. Young people, third, were moving into positions of power because of their numbers, education, and wealth, which led them to protest. Finally, students were now gathered in enormous numbers in universities, which provided the battlegrounds.

Those SDS members who were intellectuals were influenced by the Columbia sociologist C. Wright Mills, an idiosyncratic leftist from Texas who came to work on a motorcycle and was wholly out of sorts with the America of the fifties; Herbert Marcuse, who tried to marry Marx and Freud; and Paul Goodman, an anarchist who attacked the affluent society and stressed alienation among the young in a book prophetically called *Growing Up Absurd.* According to Todd Gitlin, one of the founders of SDS, members worshipped Marlon Brando as a motorcycling gangster in the film *The Wild One* (1953). "What are you rebelling against?" Brando, snarling, "Whadda ya got?" They quickly picked up the heavy pulse of rock 'n' roll from Elvis Presley.

In July 1962 a disparate group of 59 students gathered for an SDS convention at the UAW camp in Port Huron, Michigan, an almost surreal event. Tom Hayden, who had been editor of the Michigan *Daily,* had composed a 60-page manifesto which the group, after much wrangling, adopted. The Port Huron Statement, despite its length, ambiguities, absurdities, and omissions, became a kind of Declaration of Independence for the youthful American New Left.

Four-fifths of the statement consisted of a denunciation of virtually every significant American institution. It pointed a big finger at two villains: militarism (the Cold War and The Bomb) and racism (with kudos to the civil rights movement). Much of the rest was a statement of Hayden's "social goals and values." He stressed individualism ("human independence"), community ("relationships should involve fraternity and honesty"), and a political system of small group participatory democracy. A "new left" would be the vehicle for reaching these goals, based on students in the universities. They would campaign with "reason, freedom, and love."

Hayden wrote that his generation trusted only three people over 30: Norman Thomas, Wright Mills, and Michael Harrington. "Shortly thereafter," Harrington wrote, "I forfeited that trust." He was an official of the parent LID, and, as a devoted Socialist, abhorred Communism. The SDS delegates were certainly not Communists, but they held the U.S. primarily responsible for the Cold War, made a hero of Castro, and refused to throw an uninvited 17-year-old high school boy out of the Port Huron meeting because he represented a Communist youth organization. Harrington urged the delegates to clean up their act and they refused to heed his arguments. A typical left-wing donnybrook with LID followed. Gitlin wrote, "SDS won, more or less."

In 1963 Gitlin became president of SDS. But it had only a dozen chapters and 1100 members among the 6 million college students in the U.S. It did not seem to be going anywhere. In 1965 it was given an opening when Lyndon Johnson made his military commitment in Vietnam. Although many individual members and several chapters became active in the peace movement, SDS itself maintained an uneasy ambivalence toward the war.[7]

In 1964 the University of California at Berkeley was, if not at the top, extremely close to it among the nation's and the world's institutions of higher learning. Its offerings were exceptionally broad in 15 schools and colleges and 72 departments, supplemented by 58 research organizations. Its faculty of 1467 was distinguished, including nine living Nobel Prize winners, 48 members of the National Academy of Sciences, and one winner of the Pulitzer Prize (poetry). When President Kennedy addressed 92,000 people in Memorial Stadium on March 23, 1962, he noted that his administration was graced with many Berkeley notables. "It is a disturbing fact to me, and it may be to some of you, that the New Frontier owes as much to Berkeley as it does to Harvard University." The library system contained over 3 million volumes and many millions of other published and manuscript materials. A cosmopolitan mega-university, Berkeley had 26,000 students, a very large number of them enrolled in graduate and professional programs, who came from every state in the nation and 90 foreign countries.

Among its many distinctions, the nine-campus University of California system was headed by a president, Clark Kerr, who was widely regarded as preeminent in his field. Born into a Quaker family on a farm in Pennsylvania, Kerr had been educated at Swarthmore and Berkeley (Ph.D. in economics) with a specialty in industrial relations. "His mind," A. H. Raskin wrote, "had extraordinary range and a rare capacity for turning discord into consensus. Kerr ranks among the country's half-dozen most effective peacemakers in the volatile realm of labor-management warfare—a skill that had prompted every President since Harry S. Truman to enlist his help." In 1963 Kerr delivered the Godkin Lectures at Harvard. While his main theme was the significance of what he called the multiversity in a society increasingly dependent on knowledge, he noted that

> undergraduate students are restless. Recent changes in the American university have done them little good—lower teaching loads for the faculty, larger classes, the use of substitute teachers for the regular faculty, the choice of faculty members based on research accomplishments rather than instructional capacity, the fragmentation of knowledge into endless subdivisions. There is an incipient revolt of undergraduate students against the faculty; the revolt that used to be against the faculty *in loco parentis* is now against the faculty *in absentia*.

To put it the way many students did, they were frustrated by the size and bureaucratization of the university. At Berkeley they would use the IBM card caution: "Do not bend, fold, spindle, or mutilate."

Under Kerr, Lewis S. Feuer wrote, "The University of California at Berkeley was probably the freest campus in the country." The American Association of University Professors gave the university its award for academic freedom in 1964. A free speech area was open to everyone. The university refused to punish students convicted of off-campus civil rights disturbances. Compulsory ROTC was abolished. While murder and larceny were frowned upon, anyone could say almost anything pretty much anywhere.

For most of its history the town of Berkeley and the university had been serene, a quiet hillside with a superb view overlooking San Francisco Bay and, not least, a balmy climate. "There is no place in the world," a visiting British professor observed, "where uncomfortable people can feel so comfortable." Around 1960 this began to change. "The gentle sunny surroundings," Feuer wrote, "the relaxed mode of life, the record shops, bookstores, restaurants, and students' apartments, the reputation of the Berkeley police force for its tolerance toward deviants, nonconformists and militants, and the university's free offering of immense cultural riches in lectures, plays, concerts, and books" were irresistible. Nonstudents flooded into Berkeley and "professional students" and their dogs refused to leave. Many hung out in the student union complex, where over coffee they discussed leftist politics, ideology, tactics, and the burdens of life. They constituted a kind of reserve army waiting for the call to the colors.

There were several forays prior to the main battle. In the spring of 1960 a large group from Berkeley disrupted the hearings of the House Un-American Activities Committee in San Francisco's City Hall, leading to a confrontation with the police, including being hosed down the steps and getting arrested. The civil rights struggles in the South in 1963 aroused great sympathy. The novelist James Baldwin, James Forman of CORE, and Malcolm X addressed large crowds. In early 1964 students picketed a grocery chain, the Sheraton-Palace Hotel, car dealers, and the Bank of America in

San Francisco for discrimination against blacks in hiring. Again there were confrontations with the police and many arrests.

Bancroft Way marked the southern boundary of university property. Telegraph Avenue, a major artery to the South, deadended at Bancroft. Directly across the street was a major university entrance. The sidewalk was the property of the city of Berkeley; beyond it a bronze plaque in the brick pavement read: "Property of the Regents of the University of California. Permission to enter or pass over is revocable at any time." It lay in an open strip 26 feet deep. At the rear a row of posts marked the actual entrance. It was not unreasonable for one who did not read the plaque to conclude erroneously that the strip was not university property. It had, in fact, been used by activists for years to distribute leaflets from card tables. Kerr, concerned about the ambiguity and the risk of trouble, had persuaded the regents in 1959 to deed the strip to the city for a public plaza. But, in what Raskin called a "Dostoyevskian" lapse, the university treasurer did not carry out the land cession. "If he had, the whole melancholy chain of events might never have begun."

The university had a rule which forbade political proselytizing on campus. During the spring and summer of 1964 the administrators became concerned about the racket from bongo drums, bike riders in pedestrian areas, leaflet litter, and, more seriously, tables with city permits moving into the strip. In the fall enrollment would rise and there would be a presidential campaign. Thus, the dean of students informed all student organizations that the political proselytizing rule would be enforced on September 21, "including the 26-foot strip of brick walkway."

The student organizations were outraged and formed a United Front. On September 20 they voted to picket, conduct vigils and rallies, and act in civil disobedience if the university held firm. It did. On September 29 the front escalated by setting up unauthorized tables at several places on the campus. The next day those at the tables received citations and were instructed to come to Sproul Hall at 3:00 that afternoon. About 500 marched over and an administrator tried to turn them away. They sat down inside the building.

The United Front now found a voice. Mario Savio, slender and intense, was a brilliant speaker. His grandfather in Italy had been a Fascist, his father in New York a sheet metal worker. Raised as a Catholic, he had attended the church's Manhattan College and had been president of the Fraternity of Christian Doctrine at Queen's College. Now he was a junior in philosophy at Berkeley. He had recently undergone a religious crisis and had abandoned Catholicism. He picked up the concept of alienation from Marx. Savio spent the summer of 1963 helping the poor in Taxco, Mexico, build a laundry. The next summer he was in Mississippi teaching at a Freedom School. In private conversation he stuttered. Before a large audience he spoke with eloquence and command. Now he fired a broad attack on the university and gave the unrest a platform: "The issue is freedom of speech." Thus, the Free Speech Movement.

The next morning, October 1, the tables were back up, three in front of Sproul Hall. Jack Weinberg of CORE was arrested at its table. He went limp (a "limpnick") as the police dragged him to their car. A crowd sat down around the vehicle. Savio removed his shoes and climbed on top. He posed three demands: (1) No suspension of students; (2) Chancellor E. W. Strong must accept "reasonable regulations governing freedom of speech"; and (3) no disciplinary action against anyone setting up tables. Unless these demands were met, Savio threatened "continuous direct action." Charlie Powell, president of the official Associated Students, invited Savio to join him in a talk with the chancellor. They returned in an hour to report that Chancellor Strong refused to yield to pressure, that he would talk only if the demonstration ended.

At 2:30 Savio led 150 demonstrators into Sproul Hall. At 4:00 Jackie Goldberg went into the building to make an appointment with a dean. A policeman told her that, if she tried to enter the office, she would be arrested. She said later, "I just did something very irrational. I just said, 'Well, if you're not going to let us in, we're not going to let you out.' " She told the demonstrators to block the door. Some 400 joined the "pack-in." At 6:00 the police began to lock the doors. The demonstrators tried to push them away and there was a struggle. A girl whose hair was pulled by an officer screamed. Several students dragged a policeman to the floor and took off his boots. Savio bit him in the leg. The students withdrew from the building at 9:00 to join the crowd still at the car.

The next morning, Friday, October 2, some 200 people remained around the police car. Officers from Oakland, Alameda County, Berkeley, and the California Highway Patrol began taking positions at Sproul Hall. By 5:30 there were about 500 officers, including 100 on motorcycles. About 7000 demonstrators and onlookers were in the area.

Kerr met with the United Front leaders to discuss a faculty proposal to break the impasse. After tense negotiations they reached this agreement at 7:20:

1. Demonstrators would "desist" from illegal protest against university regulations.
2. A committee of students, faculty, and the administration would recommend rules of "political behavior and its control."
3. Weinberg would be booked, released on his own recognizance, and the university would not press charges.
4. The "duration of the suspension" of suspended students would be submitted to the faculty's Student Conduct Committee.
5. Student organizations would continue to function in accordance with existing regulations.

Mario Savio addressing the Free Speech Movement at Sproul Plaza at the University of California, Berkeley. October 1, 1964. Lon Wilson, Bancroft Library.

White House aides Joe Califano and Larry O'Brien totting up the huge Great Society gains. August 17, 1965. Yoichi R. Okamoto, LBJ Library Collection.

In Independence, Missouri, LBJ signed Medicare into law, honoring Harry Truman, who started the push for health care. Lady Bird Johnson, Hubert Humphrey, and Bess Truman look on. July 30, 1965. LBJ Library Collection.

LBJ signing the Civil Rights Act, July 2, 1964. Cecil Stoughton, LBJ Library Collection.

LBJ signing the immigration reform law at the Statue of Liberty. October 3, 1965. Frank Wolfe, LBJ Library Collection.

Rachel Carson, whose great book, Silent Spring, *launched environmental concern with chemical pollution. Library of Congress.*

LBJ with his grade school teacher in the schoolhouse he attended in the hill country of Texas. Here he signed the Elementary and Secondary Education Act, April 11, 1965. Yoichi R. Okamoto, LBJ Library Collection.

Secretary Udall with Johnson's strong support created a great many new parks. Here in 1968 Lady Bird Johnson visited the jewel in the crown, Redwood National Park in Northern California. Robert Knudsen, LBJ Library Collection.

LBJ with Senator Edmund Muskie of Maine, the congressional leader on air and water pollution legislation. Yoichi R. Okamoto, LBJ Library Collection.

LBJ backed the arts, including the modern art Hirshhorn Museum on the Mall in Washington, shown nearing completion. Rodin's masterpiece, The Burghers of Calais, is being positioned in the sculpture garden. Library of Congress.

During the Tet offensive in 1968 the Vietcong seized Hué. Here the Marines take the city back in costly and bitter fighting. UPI/Bettmann.

LBJ confers with Vietnam commander General Westmoreland. November 16, 1967. Yoichi R. Okamoto, LBJ Library Collection.

Some of those wounded in Vietnam were returned to the U.S. by air. Library of Congress.

Antiwar protest. Women at the Capitol. January 15, 1968. UPI/Bettmann.

Antiwar protest at the White House, including Coretta King and Dr. Benjamin Spock. May 17, 1967. Robert Knudsen, LBJ Library Collection.

Antiwar protest at the General Logan monument in Chicago's Grant Park during the Democratic convention. August 26, 1968. UPI/Bettmann.

Antiwar protest on the street in Saigon. A Buddhist bonze immolates himself. UPI/ Bettmann.

Secretary McNamara viewing the huge antiwar demonstration at the Pentagon on October 21, 1967, from his office window. UPI/Bettmann.

A troubled President after Tet. LBJ listening to a tape from his son-in-law Chuck Robb, a Marine in Vietnam. Jack Kightlinger, LBJ Library Collection.

The Establishment "Wise Men" who, above, on November 2, 1967, supported LBJ on the war; after Tet on March 26, 1968, the majority urged him to seek peace. Yoichi R. Okamoto (photo above) and Frank Wolfe (photo below), LBJ Library Collection.

Running for the Democratic nomination for President, Senator Eugene McCarthy carried the Wisconsin primary on April 2, 1968. UPI/Bettmann.

Bobby Kennedy won the California primary on June 6, 1968. A few moments later he was assassinated. UPI/Bettmann.

Vice President Humphrey, the Democratic candidate for President, appealed to LBJ for his support and failed to receive it. Yoichi R. Okamoto, LBJ Library Collection.

Republican candidate Richard Nixon and his running mate Spiro Agnew visited LBJ at his ranch on August 10, 1968. Nixon and Johnson agreed on a continuation of the war. Mike Geissinger, LBJ Library Collection.

6. Kerr, already committed, would follow through on deeding the strip to the city.

Savio explained the agreement to the demonstrators and they went home. The police also left. All that remained in the plaza was the battered police car.

Over the weekend the United Front changed its name to the Free Speech Movement. It was now drawing support from the student body, even from the fraternities.

For more than a month FSM engaged in uneasy negotiations with the administration and the faculty over discipline for the violation of rules. FSM demanded protection of speech to the full reach of the First Amendment as administered by civil authorities. The university insisted on its own time, place, and manner rules. Negotiations collapsed on November 9, 1964.

Over Thanksgiving, Strong sent citations to Savio, Jackie and Art Goldberg, and Brian Turner for misconduct during the police car incident. FSM demanded that the charges be dropped and Strong refused. FSM called for a demonstration at Sproul Plaza on December 2. A large crowd, perhaps 5000, gathered. Savio called passionately for civil disobedience by entering the building. Joan Baez sang "We Shall Overcome" as the crowd filed in to participate in what they called a "Free University"—square dancing, watching Laurel and Hardy movies, a Jewish Chanukah service, folk singing led by Baez, a lecture on conflict theory by a sociology professor. The doors were locked at 7:00.

That night Kerr conferred with key regents and the governor. Brown ordered the police to clear the building and arrest the demonstrators for trespass. Over 600 officers from the university, Berkeley, Oakland, Alameda County, and the California Highway Patrol began the arrests at 3:05 a.m. on December 3. It took 12 hours to book 773 persons, who were taken to the county's Santa Rita Prison Farm.

FSM called a strike and pickets patrolled the entrances to the campus. A large crowd gathered in the plaza at noon to hear speeches denouncing the arrests. About 800 professors met in Wheeler Auditorium at 1:00. They criticized the administration, condemned police intervention, and insisted on amnesty for those in jail. FSM demanded that classes be canceled on Friday, December 4, and many were.

Over the weekend Kerr met with the governor, several regents, and members of the faculty. On Sunday he announced that all classes would be canceled on Monday morning. The department heads had drafted a new program. Kerr said he would present it to the students in the Greek Theatre.

Political scientist Robert Scalapino chaired the meeting and only Kerr was scheduled to speak. Savio sat in the press section as 16,000 jammed the theater. Kerr, flanked by the department chairmen, announced that the administration had accepted their terms:

1. The university would be governed by "orderly and lawful procedures."
2. The Senate Committee on Academic Freedom would report the new rules.
3. The chairmen condemned the acts of civil disobedience that had taken place on December 2–3.
4. The cases of persons arrested for such acts were now before the courts. The university would not prosecute them retroactively, but it would impose discipline for any new transgressions.
5. Classes would be held as scheduled.

As Scalapino moved to close the meeting, Savio crossed the stage and two university officers grabbed him. The audience chanted, "Let him speak." Allowed to, Savio announced that there would be a rally in the plaza and asked the crowd to leave. A large number went to the plaza, where Savio urged them to strike classes. Many were not held that afternoon.

Almost 1000 members of the faculty turned out for a meeting of the Academic Senate at Wheeler Auditorium on December 8. Several thousand students gathered outside to listen to the proceedings. Scalapino presented the recommendations of the Committee on Academic Freedom:

1. No discipline for acts prior to December 8.
2. Time, place, and manner rules for political activity presently in effect shall continue.
3. The content of speech or advocacy shall not be regulated by the university.
4. Future discipline shall be handled by a committee of the senate.

The report was adopted by a vote of 824 to 115. The students cheered. Authority seemed to have shifted from the administration to the faculty.

On January 2, 1965, the regents dismissed Chancellor Strong and replaced him with Martin Meyerson, dean of the College of Environmental Design. The FSM disbanded.

The Berkeley uprising, widely covered by the media, was a very important event. It showed, as earlier experiences in Europe and Latin America had already demonstrated, that a university, even a great one, is a fragile institution which can be brought to its knees by a relatively small group of determined students who play the game of confrontation politics skillfully. Its only defense is to call in the police, which inevitably foments violence. That, in turn, undermines the freedom of expression and the civility in human intercourse upon which a university depends. But this is only temporary because a university is virtually indestructible. The sociologist

Nathan Glazer, who was active in these events, wrote in 1968 after several later Berkeley rebellions:

> What about the heart of the university—the teaching of undergraduate and graduate students, the day-to-day research of faculty and graduate students? How are they affected by the student rebellion? The answer is that, up to now, there has been little effect. The structure of the university and its normal activities go on, suffering only minor impact from the events that have made student activism a major political issue in the state, the nation, and now in the world.

Berkeley launched a wave of student unrest that swept through universities both in the U.S. and in Europe. In this country there were serious outbreaks at Columbia, Cornell, San Francisco State, Michigan, Wisconsin, Northwestern, and Boston University. The student demonstrations in Europe were especially important in France and West Germany.

During the summer of 1964 the Republican convention that nominated Goldwater met at the Cow Palace in San Francisco and received Ronald Reagan enthusiastically. He would run for governor of California in 1966, and Pat Brown, who would seek another term, feared that the middle-class backlash from Berkeley would give Reagan a decisive issue. He was right. Reagan capitalized on law and order and attacked Brown, Kerr, and the University of California. He won easily and at the first meeting of the regents after he took office Reagan produced the votes to fire Clark Kerr.

The confrontation at Berkeley was entirely over university rather than national or international issues. Even civil rights was of no consequence. But in time there would be an impact. The tough FSM demonstrators would shortly become stalwarts in the antiwar movement.[8]

At home 1966 was a dismal year for Lyndon Johnson and the Vietnam War. The tension was palpable in Washington, in the White House itself. On February 28 McGeorge Bundy resigned as National Security Adviser to become president of the Ford Foundation. Walt Rostow succeeded him. While Bundy said nothing publicly, there was no doubt that he could no longer stomach Vietnam. A few months later the press secretary, Bill Moyers, quit to become the publisher of *Newsday*. Moyers, Halberstam wrote, had "shown a lack of enthusiasm for the war." Reston called him a war casualty, wounded at the Battle of Credibility Gap. When Walter Heller submitted a memorandum on preparing for the transition at the end of the war, McPherson commented, "I expect Walter Heller's memo will be met by thunderous silence. Maybe I am timid, but I rather hope it will. Oh, what a long war this looks like. A Presidential sign that peace is about to break out, and we have got our problems compounded."

McNamara and McNaughton in the Pentagon became profoundly disillusioned. In McNamara's case there was stress at home. His daughter Kathy opposed the war, defied her parents, and argued with her father. His son Craig, still in prep school, decided that "what we were doing in Vietnam was absolutely wrong." Dean Rusk faced the same problem with his son Richard, who disagreed so intensely with his father's views on Vietnam that he became emotionally scarred. His psychiatrist told him, "You had your father's nervous breakdown." In 1966 Rusk visited an Army hospital in Saigon. The nurse, a captain, "stared long and hard at me with a look of undisguised hatred. . . . From the look on her face she clearly held me responsible for what had happened to those men. I never forgot the look on that nurse's face."

George Ball, melancholy and worn out from interminable meetings at which "would-be Clausewitzes" were "endlessly searching for the elusive keys to victory," resigned on September 30, 1966. He had "never believed for a moment we could win," and had worked on other parts of the world where "vital American interests were genuinely involved." But "the war was a vampire sucking dry the Administration's vitality." He found it "practically impossible to interest the distracted President." "I was depleted—physically, mentally, morally, and financially." The Johnsons gave the Balls a farewell party and they left for a prolonged holiday in Italy. Ball tried to put Vietnam out of his mind, but could not. "What deeply preoccupied me then—and still does [1982]—was how our country could have blundered into the Vietnam mess."

Harry McPherson had "colossal" doubts about U.S. policy in Vietnam. He did a good deal of reading, talked to people who had worked on the civilian side, and had spent two weeks there himself. "I can't think of a worse place in the world to fight a war than in Vietnam." McPherson had developed a sense of "how dense an affair it was; how many strands were running through it, and how unsusceptible it was to the ordinary treatment of major policy commitment, military and political and economic." So he became a " 'dove,' I suppose, in that very unsatisfactory classification." But, "if I behaved like a dove . . . I would have no hope ever of taking part in either decisions or even of having such an effect as a speech writer can have—that I would be aced out of the whole Vietnam thing." He would write a pessimistic memo about the air war and add, "This is the way doves feel about the bombing." He felt terrible about behaving this way and sometimes thought he should quit. But he did not.

Public support for the war dropped sharply during 1966, sinking below 50 percent. This was part of a two-year trend that prevailed from late 1965 to late 1967. This shift in public opinion was quickly reflected in the mood, particularly among Democrats, in Congress.

On January 24 Senator Fulbright announced his opposition to a resumption of the bombing, and Mansfield and Aiken called for an indefinite suspension. Three days later, 15 Democratic senators sent a letter written by Senator Hartke of Indiana to the President endorsing this policy.

Bill Moyers conducted a poll of Democratic members of both houses which was taken between March 19 and June 5, 1966. There were responses from 116 representatives and 25 senators, who were asked to identify the five most important issues to their constituents. In the House Vietnam was first with 82 percent, and inflation, created by the war, was second with 61 percent. No other issue received more than 34 percent. The Senators voted similarly with 76 and 56 percent for the two leaders and no other over 40.

On June 28 Mansfield conducted a "completely free" discussion of Vietnam with Democratic senators and summarized for Johnson the major themes they stressed:

1. There is general support for you among the members in your overwhelming responsibilities as President;
2. The prompt end of the war is seen as most essential and there is confusion and deep concern that we have not yet found the way to end it, either by extension or contraction of the military effort;
3. There is no sentiment among the members for an immediate withdrawal;
4. There is a strong conviction that candidates of the Democratic Party will be hurt by the war.

In July, as Cater put it, "Wayne Morse . . . declared war on his President and is trying to use education legislation as his weapon." Morse said he put "responsibility for the Vietnam War where it belongs—on the doorstep of the White House." Charging that the war had short-changed schoolchildren, he more than doubled the administration appropriations under the Elementary and Secondary Education Act. In mild panic the White House, HEW, the Bureau of the Budget, and the Senate leadership ganged up on the senator's subcommittee to prevent what they called "anarchy." Wilbur Cohen may have been persuasive. Morse asked if the increase was justified on educational grounds. Cohen: "Definitely not."

Morse was not alone in worrying about shifting Great Society funds to Vietnam. Cater was concerned about a sharp cutback in the college loan fund. Mayor Richard Lee of New Haven sent Cater the "cry of an anguished soul" over reductions in school and construction programs. They stood between the "cities and chaos." He had slept in his office for three nights to avoid a riot in his town.

Mansfield did not let up. In October he again urged a formula on Johnson for settling the war: the termination of bombing, a cease-fire, withdrawal of 30,000 troops, and a commitment to deal with the Vietcong.

The February 1966 issue of *Harper's* carried an article by General James M. Gavin, one of the nation's most distinguished soldiers. He recalled the fall of Dienbienphu when General Matthew B. Ridgeway, the chief of staff, asked him to explore a landing in the Hanoi Delta. Gavin said it would bring China into the war and that Hanoi was the worst place for the U.S. to wage a war. Ridgeway agreed and notified President Eisenhower, who said it was "like hitting the tail of the snake rather than the head." Gavin now wanted to stop the bombing, withdraw to enclaves on the coast, and seek peace. Cater asked the President if he wanted to talk to Gavin. Answer: "No."

During the summer McPherson vacationed in Rhode Island and talked to a large number of people, mainly moderate Republicans of means. His conclusions: "*Nobody* I talked to was affirmative about Vietnam." "*Everybody* I talked to at any length expressed the strongest wish for peaceful overtures—for cooperation with the Russians chiefly." These people were of the "well-informed, internationalist middle class, . . . the strongest supporters of every new initiative in foreign affairs since the end of World War II. . . . Their support is vital." Johnson's personality "seems to baffle everybody." He found an enormous mistrust of government outside of Washington. McPherson urged "more talk of peace, peace, peace" with "outright candor."

On August 3 Cater informed Johnson that Secretary Gardner was "worried that the Administration is suffering from a feeling in the nation that the domestic program has lost its momentum." Cater and Moyers agreed. But the President did not want to talk to Gardner.

McPherson learned from a friend at the Israeli Embassy that the National Council of Churches had approached the Synagogue Council of America to join in a statement denouncing the war, which was declined. The National Council, McPherson pointed out, carried great weight. If it attacked the administration on the war, that would "leave us only with the support of the fundamentalists among the Protestants, and that is a bad bed to be in."

The Democratic party and President Johnson suffered a sharp defeat in the midterm elections on November 8, 1966. The Republicans gained 47 seats in the House and 3 in the Senate, along with 8 governors and 677 state legislators. Johnson's control over the House was shattered. He had commanded a 10 to 40 vote majority over the necessary 216 from the 294 Democrats and 140 Republicans. Now the northern Democrats would shrink from 194 to 158, the southern from 100 to 90, while the Republicans would grow from 140 to 187. The Republican-southern Democratic coalition would be back in the saddle. The Democrats, however, hung onto a 64 to 36 majority in the Senate. The GOP won the two most dramatic races: Charles Percy defeated Senator Paul Douglas in Illinois, and Ronald

Reagan swept into the governor's mansion in California over Pat Brown. Many commentators concluded that the Great Society was washed up.

Even Larry O'Brien, now the Postmaster General but still the smartest political observer, was surprised by the size of the Republican victory. He had anticipated a modest swing back after the 1964 landslide, 32 seats in the House, not 47. The political analyst Louis Bean had expected a Democratic decline from 58 percent in 1964 in House voting to 53 or 54 percent in 1966, costing the Democrats about 36 seats. In fact, the Democratic vote fell to 51 percent. Even after the election Richard Scammon and Ben Wattenberg argued that the 1966 decline of 66 seats for both the House and the Senate compared favorably with the Republican loss of 84 in 1922 and the Democratic decline of 77 in 1938. Small comfort.

O'Brien made several swings around the country prior to the election and was surprised and shocked by the impact of the war. "It was," he said, "the beginning of an unraveling of support for the President's Vietnam policy." The congressmen in trouble "felt we should get out of Vietnam, that this was a loser, that it was a bottomless pit, and the President didn't seem to be making a sufficient effort to bring it to a resolution." O'Brien found this sentiment in California, New York, New Jersey, Indiana, even Oklahoma. Mayor Daley "expressed great concern about Vietnam. . . . You wouldn't find a greater hawk than Dick Daley or a more loyal Democrat on the Hill or anywhere else." The mayor personally had no concern, but he worried that Vietnam would be "devastating to the Democratic Party."

In New York O'Brien lunched with the publisher and editors of the *Times*—Harrison Salisbury, Harding Bancroft, Turner Catledge, Clifton Daniel, and the rest of the "top echelon." They spent two hours on Vietnam and a number of them were "distressed and disturbed. . . . It wasn't mean or bitter, but it was clear that these fellows were not at all convinced regarding the policy." He reported to Johnson that he found no "warmth toward the administration."

Despite these disturbing signs for the President, the year was relatively calm on the streets. "For the antiwar movement itself, its putative leaders and its activists," Nancy Zaroulis and Gerald Sullivan wrote, "1966 was an outwardly quiet year." Senator Fulbright held hearings of his Foreign Relations Committee in February on the war, but, despite television coverage, they generated only mild interest. Ball said they were "disappointingly docile."

On February 23 Freedom House gave Johnson an award for his contributions to peace and justice at the Waldorf-Astoria in New York. A crowd of 4000 outside conducted a noisy demonstration. Inside a protester stood on his chair and yelled, "Mr. President, Peace in Vietnam!" He was thrown out.

On March 26 the International Days of Protest staged a hoped for worldwide march for peace. There were said to be 50,000 on New York's streets, fairly large turnouts in San Francisco and Chicago, and smaller numbers in other U.S. cities and abroad.

During the summer and fall the Johnsons were beleaguered. There were rowdy picketers and profane abuse of Lady Bird Johnson at the Metropolitan Opera and the San Francisco Opera House, as well as in New Zealand and Australia. The President, Reston wrote, had to "sneak . . . around the country" to air bases to dodge people asking, "Hey, hey, LBJ, how many boys have you killed today?"

McNamara visited Harvard on November 6, 1966, starting at the Business School, where he had been both a student and a professor. He was greeted cordially. He was then driven across the Charles River to Quincy House. When he emerged and entered a campus police car on Mill Street, a crowd of 800 surrounded the vehicle and rocked it. He jumped out and climbed on top. "O.K., fellas, I'll answer one or two of your questions. . . . We're in a mob and I don't want anyone hurt." He was asked why the administration insisted that the war was the result of aggression by Hanoi after 1957. He said it started in 1954. Then someone asked why the government did not publish the number of South Vietnamese civilians killed. "We don't know." A policeman started climbing onto the car and McNamara pushed him away. "Listen," he said, "I spent four of the happiest years of my life on the Berkeley campus, doing some of the things you're doing here. But there was an important difference. I was tougher and more courteous." Later he said that he feared a loss of life. "I was under tremendous stress and trying to calm the crowd."

Tom Wicker of the *New York Times* had supported the war. During 1966 he covered the protests of the demonstrators and was moved by the mothers who were perfectly willing to go to jail to stop the war. He realized that the peace movement was not just a bunch of "academic lefties." He began listening to their arguments and became convinced that the U.S. had "no business mixing into" that war.

The credibility of the White House and the Defense Department was battered by a sensational series of dispatches from Hanoi written by Harrison Salisbury and published in the *New York Times* between Christmas Day and January 3, 1967. By contrast, according to Melvin Small, they gave the peace movement a "dramatic shot in the arm."

Salisbury was one of the nation's most distinguished reporters, a noted war correspondent, and a Pulitzer Prize winner. He had been trying to get into North Vietnam for a long time and shortly before Christmas learned that a visa was waiting for him in Paris. After picking it up, he flew Air France to Cambodia and the International Control Commission irregular flight from Pnom Penh to Hanoi. He then spent an extremely busy two weeks scouring the country, talking to people at all levels, and examining the impact of the bombing. "One of the (to me) remarkable facts about reporting from Hanoi," he wrote, "was that there was no censorship."

Salisbury observed a "vast gap between the reality of the air war, as seen from the ground in Hanoi, and the bland, vague American communiques with their reiterated assumptions that our bombs were falling precisely upon 'military objectives' . . . with . . . surgical precision." He noted specific houses, schools, churches, pagodas, villages, and other structures of no military value which had been obliterated. Nevertheless, a large, steady flow of supplies moved south by truck and rail. Damage to roads and rail track was quickly repaired. "Strategic air power or even tactical air power was not able to halt the movement of a determined, tough and skillful enemy."

He concluded that the "most important aspect of the war" was the "spirit of the North Vietnamese people and the spirit with which they were fighting the war." It was an "amalgam of patriotism and *élan*." The government had issued rifles to an enormous number of people, including women. "Can you imagine the regime in the South giving guns to all its people?" a party official asked. "They'd never dare."

Premier Pham Van Dong discussed the war with Salisbury in an intense four-and-a-half-hour session. He could not get it through his head that the leading newspaper in the U.S. was *not* controlled by the government. Salisbury assumed that the North Vietnamese had been shaken by the Sino-Soviet split and the launching of the Cultural Revolution in China. He thought, therefore, that this was the time to open secret peace negotiations with the U.S. and the premier left no doubt that his government was prepared to begin talks "immediately and without any preconditions."

Salisbury called Reston as soon as he returned to arrange a meeting with the President and Reston phoned Moyers to set it up. The word came back that Johnson did not want to talk to him. Reston then asked Rostow, who said he would be "delighted" to see him. But, Salisbury said, "I know Walt very well, that it would be *him* telling me what was going on . . . a silly exercise." He wound up with Rusk, who made speeches, and William Bundy, who listened carefully. But nothing came of it.[9]

During 1967 opposition to the war widened and deepened, reaching a climax in Washington in October. Early in the year the peace movement grew significantly, particularly in the churches through Clergy and Laymen Concerned about Vietnam, in the colleges among both professors and students, and in that sector of the black community that was morally offended by the war and was disturbed by a seeming disproportionate number of black casualties in Vietnam.

Clergy and Laymen was predominantly Protestant and had significant influence in the National Council of Churches, but included among its leaders a number of priests and rabbis. William Sloane Coffin, the Yale chaplain and an experienced organizer, was its executive secretary. Martin Luther

King became co-chairman. It stressed political realism, persuasion over confrontation, and a moral commitment to peace. Some of its members were uncomfortable with the dress, hair styles, and language of their peace colleagues from the counterculture. It became the largest peace organization. With Clergy and Laymen, Charles DeBenedetti wrote, "The antiwar movement had enlisted a constituency with direct access to the American center."

The Reverend James R. Adams was the rector of St. Marks Episcopal Church in Washington. The President and his family occasionally attended services there and Harry McPherson was a parishioner and a friend of the rector. The Washington Ad Hoc Viet Nam Draft Committee asked Adams for permission to hold a meeting at the church on the evening of May 7, 1967, in preparation for a lobbying visit to Capitol Hill, and he agreed. About 70 attended, mainly students from New York and Boston universities, but including representatives from SDS, the Progressive Labor Party, the Black United Action Committee, and the Spring Mobilization for Peace, along with agents of the Secret Service.

The agents reported to the President the strong antiwar statements of James Bevel, presently director of the Spring Mobilization. He called Johnson "that cat in the White House." They also noted that Adams was "very sympathetic to this group." Johnson, evidently, complained to his aide.

McPherson wrote the President on May 15 that "this is my day for defense counselling." Jim Adams thought an "urban church should throw open its doors to the community." It had welcomed Young Americans for Freedom, the Young Republicans, the Young Democrats, Women Strike for Peace, Alcoholics Anonymous, and a Library of Congress Chess Club. "Politically it made no sense to let this crowd in the door; but the church, as I long ago learned, marches to a different drummer."

Clergy and Laymen took the lead in the marches against the war by the Spring Mobilization on April 15, 1967. In New York an immense throng, estimated between 100,000 and 400,000, crowded into Central Park. In the Sheep Meadow about 70 young men, mainly from Cornell, burned their draft cards. This was followed by a huge march to Dag Hammarskjöld Plaza at the U.N., where King was the principal speaker. He told David Dellinger that there were more people than had been at the March on Washington. In San Francisco 50,000 paraded up Market Street to Kezar Stadium for a round of speeches. In both cities the demonstrators called for an end to American intervention in Vietnam. On May 18, Dr. Spock, Coretta King, and Bevel went to the White House to present a Spring Mobilization resolution to the President. Neither he nor any significant aide would receive them. In fact, they were kept outside on the sidewalk and Nathaniel Davis (position unknown) accepted the paper.

The political news that reached the White House during 1967 was grim. Congressman Chet Holifield, the California Democrat, received a bill on joint funding simplification. There was "nothing wrong" with it, but the

President ought to "quit sending new ideas to Congress." This was just not the time. The Republicans and the southern Democrats would tear it to pieces. On August 11 Cater talked to Rowland Evans, the columnist, who had been a reliable hawk. Now he was "deeply disturbed." The Republican House leaders Gerald Ford and Melvin Laird have "embarked on a deliberate policy of setting conditions," Cater wrote Johnson, "which you cannot possibly meet." They are laying the groundwork for a "Get Out of Vietnam" policy. Evans saw signs that congressmen who had been on the "hawkish side of the debate are now shifting 180°." Cater had dinner with a group at which Senator Stuart Symington of Missouri "held forth . . . on the necessity to tuck tail and get out of Vietnam." On August 24 McPherson had a "long, dispiriting talk with Joe Tydings," the Maryland Democratic senator, who had supported the war. He now thought it a "political albatross." "People are so frustrated and negative in Maryland," he said, "that any reasonably good Republican could clobber me this year and probably next." On October 24 Cater had his "bi-monthly clash with Reston." The columnist continued to think the war was a disaster and he "lamented the spectacle we were creating throughout the world of an idealistic nation that was coming more and more to rely on pure power." On October 18 the Arizona congressman Morris Udall, the brother of the Secretary of the Interior, wrote the President that he was a "loyal Democrat" who admired Johnson's "exceptional leadership" and accomplishments. "After many months of careful and responsible deliberation, I have concluded that our Vietnam policies are unwise and should be substantially modified. I will express these views in a major address in Tucson next Sunday."

Another chapter in Mike Mansfield's seemingly endless and fruitless endeavor to move Lyndon Johnson arrived on April 29, 1967. He proposed seeking a settlement through China or the U.N. and he again condemned the bombing. He closed with a touching personal note:

> You may recall that when you were the Majority Leader and I was your Deputy sitting next to you, that on occasion I would lean over and tug at the back of your coat to signal that it was either time to close the debate or to sit down. Most of the time, but not all the time, you would do what I was trying to suggest. Since you have been President I have been figuratively tugging at your coat, now and again, and the only purpose has been to be helpful and constructive. . . . One last word—in my opinion, the hour is growing very, very late.

Johnson, Rusk, McNamara, and Rostow, at least, could not appear on a college campus without evoking protest, if not provoking a riot. On May 23 George C. Bedell of the University of North Carolina wrote his old friend Harry McPherson a powerful argument against the war. "I cannot help but feel," he concluded, "that we are headed straight on a course toward WW III. So far as I can tell we have nothing to gain and everything to lose by continuing our present course in Vietnam." On June 9 Under Secretary of Agriculture John S. Schnittker had just returned from a visit to Kansas State University where he had discussed the war with a dozen administrators and professors. Not one supported the Vietnam adventure. All thought it could lead to war with China. They agreed that there was no significant element at the university that backed the war. At the urging of Allard Lowenstein, an activist New York lawyer, the student body presidents and newspaper editors at 200 American universities, including about every significant one, wrote an open letter to the President expressing deep concern about the war and the draft. Prior to publication they asked for a "candid off-the-record discussion of the Vietnam situation" with the President. He refused to see them. Cater suggested Humphrey, William Bundy, or Zbig Brzezinski of the State Department. Johnson wrote, "Not the V.P.—this is a luxury Pres. and V.P. should not have." The students published their letter and their committee met with Bundy. Though he did an "excellent and patient job," Cater wrote, "it did not make any visible converts."

In September, Tip O'Neill, emerging as a Democratic leader in the House and destined to become Speaker, came out against the war. He held Jack Kennedy's old district, part of Boston and Cambridge, that was overwhelmingly working-class ethnic and hawkish. But it had 22 colleges, including Harvard and MIT. Tip had supported Johnson without thinking about the war. But the students in his colleges and his own kids shook him up. He checked widely among military, CIA, and diplomatic people he knew and was shocked by the number who wanted to pull out of Vietnam. He wrote his constituents that his conscience no longer allowed him to support the war. His loss was a big loss to the President.

Walt Rostow, the National Security Adviser, was a prominent Yale graduate. On November 21 the Yale Draft Refusal Committee sent him its statement "because of your personal association with Yale." The committee announced that 303 students and faculty members "would refuse to be drafted into the military so long as the United States continues to fight in Vietnam." The signers consisted of 12 faculty members, 139 undergraduates, and 151 students in graduate and professional schools. The names were published in the *Yale Daily News* and in *The New Journal*, a student magazine.

During 1967 Martin King lent his powerful, though dissonant, voice to the peace movement. Both King and his wife had become increasingly concerned about the war, but he had said nothing publicly. Lowenstein; Carey McWilliams, the editor of the *Nation*; Coffin; and Norman Thomas urged him to take a stand and were talking about him as a third-party candidate for President in 1968. The FBI wiretappers recorded the phone conversations and, presumably, passed them on to the White House. On January 14 King read *Ramparts*, which had an article on the children of Vietnam, showing their burn wounds from American napalm bombs. He froze and at that moment committed himself to trying to end the war.

King delivered his first anti-Vietnam speech in Los Angeles on February 25, 1967, where he joined four peace senators—Ernest Gruening, Mark Hatfield of Oregon, Eugene McCarthy of Minnesota, and George McGovern of South Dakota. A few days later he got into an angry and insulting argument with Whitney Young of the Urban League over the war and Johnson. On March 6 King met with a group of his trusted advisers over whether he should take part in the Spring Mobilization. Only Bevel urged him to do so and King agreed with him. On March 24 he joined Dr. Spock in his first peace walk, leading 5000 people through downtown Chicago to a meeting at the Coliseum. On April 4 King spoke under the auspices of Clergy and Laymen at the Riverside Church in Manhattan on "Beyond Vietnam." This powerful address was probably the most eloquent moral argument made against the war at the time.

There was, he said, an obvious connection between the war and civil rights. The poverty program had held out hope for the poor in the ghettoes, but now the funds to help them were being spent on Vietnam. Young black men who were "crippled by their own society" were being sent to "guarantee liberties in southeast Asia which they had not found in southwest Georgia and east Harlem." King had built his leadership in civil rights on nonviolence. "I could never again raise my voice against the violence of the oppressed in the ghettoes without having first spoken clearly to the greatest purveyor of violence in the world today—my own government." He had been awarded the Nobel Prize for peace. It imposed a duty upon him to work for peace in Vietnam.

King proposed a program for ending the war: stop the bombing in the North and the South; declare a unilateral cease-fire; withdraw militarily from Thailand and Laos; admit the Vietcong to peace negotiations and, ultimately, to participation in the ensuing government; and set a date for removal of all foreign troops.

Despite its eloquence, this address, like everything King did at this time, failed. Friends like Phil Randolph and Bayard Rustin declined to comment for publication. Roy Wilkins and Whitney Young sharply dissociated themselves from King. Neither the NAACP nor the Urban League would sever the connection with Johnson. The speech did not play well in the press. His closest adviser, Stanley Levison, said the text was unbalanced and not clearly formulated.

During the summer of 1967 the black ghettoes in the cities erupted. The Kerner Riot Commission identified 24 disorders in 23 cities, provided profiles of eight, and identified two massive riots—Newark and Detroit.

In Tampa on June 11 a policeman shot a black youth and a riot ensued with the burning of buildings, looting, and several killings. The National Guard was called out. In Cincinnati the next day a similar incident led to a sharp confrontation between blacks and the police. There were 404 arrests and 63 injured people. Again, the guard was brought in to restore order. In Atlanta another police episode led to a confrontation with little evident damage. Northern New Jersey erupted in rioting—Plainfield, New Brunswick, and Newark.

On the evening of July 12 the Newark police arrested a black taxi driver for a traffic violation. A rumor swept the city's immense ghetto that the police had beaten him to death and a large riot broke out with fires, looting, violence, and property destruction. New Jersey's Democratic Governor Richard Hughes branded the action a "criminal insurrection" and he called out the National Guard. The President, who hoped to stay out, nevertheless phoned Hughes and offered to help. By the next day, 15 were dead and 1000 had been arrested. Sniper fire was widespread against both firemen and guardsmen. But Hughes, to Johnson's relief, insisted on handling the situation himself and by July 19 had the city under control. The death toll was 26, 1500 people were injured, and hundreds of homes and stores had been destroyed.

Now the Congress ran wild. Over the President's opposition, a bill passed on July 19 to make a federal crime of crossing a state line to incite or participate in a riot. The rat extermination bill to assist slum-dwellers the administration had proposed and expected to pass easily was defeated in the House 207 to 176. Southern Democrats and Republicans ridiculed Johnson by calling it the "civil rats bill" and suggested that he "buy a lot of cats and turn them loose." He did not get it through until December 4, 1967.

Only a short while after Newark, Detroit burst into the greatest riot of the decade, surpassing even Watts. In the early hours of Sunday, July 23, police raided a black drinking club on the West Side. Again, a rumor spread of police brutality in beating a man and a woman. Massive rioting ensued and Republican Governor George Romney, who had presidential ambitions, called out the National Guard, who were unable to control the city. Before 3 a.m. on Monday, Romney informed the Attorney General that 20 people had been injured and 650 arrested, and there were 150 fires. He suggested sending in federal troops. Clark awakened the President and he ordered the Army put on alert. Romney continued to call Clark with the same message and the latter suspected a political ploy.

The President called in Justice Abe Fortas and they devised a strategy to compel Romney to comply with two federal statutes governing the deployment of troops. Under the first the President would accede to a governor's request if necessary to suppress an insurrection; the second kicked in when violence deprived persons of their constitutional rights and the state was incapable of protecting them. Johnson demanded that Romney comply with both, which he was extremely reluctant to do. The situation, however, was so alarming that at 9:45 a.m. on Monday he phoned Clark to ask for 5000 troops because there was "reasonable doubt" that order could be maintained. Johnson insisted on having the request in writing, but the telegram did not arrive till 12:35 p.m.

The mobilization took effect immediately. Lieut. Gen. John L. Throckmorton was in command at Selfridge Air Force Base 30 miles northeast of Detroit. Some 170 aircraft moved a 2400-man brigade of the 82nd Airborne Division from Fort Bragg, and an equal number from the 101st Airborne at Fort Campbell. The first plane touched down at Selfridge at 4:00 and the others landed at two-and-a-half-minute intervals. One hundred buses leased from the Detroit Bus Company began leaving Selfridge for Detroit at 4 p.m. A civilian team headed by Cyrus Vance, Special Assistant to the Secretary of Defense, and Warren Christopher, Deputy Attorney General, had arrived at Selfridge at 3:00. With Throckmorton they proceeded to police headquarters, where they met Romney, Mayor Cavanaugh, and Police Commissioner Girardon. The latter had 700 state police, 900 local police, and 3000 guardsmen on the streets. Vance told them to commit the reserve of 4000 guardsmen. The local and federal people toured the riot area, which was now quiet. Since Vance considered the Detroit police and the Michigan National Guard "excellent" and in control, he preferred to keep the federal force out of the city. As Califano put it, the President "couldn't stand the thought of American soldiers killing American civilians."

But about 8:30 p.m. the rioting resumed and became worse that night. The paratroopers moved to the fairgrounds. At 10:31 the President signed a proclamation ordering the rioters to disperse, a preliminary before federal troops could enter the city. At 11:00 Vance made a radio-television appeal for law and order. At 11:22 Johnson signed Executive Order 11364 federalizing the Michigan National Guard. General Throckmorton was now in command of all troops. The paratroopers occupied Detroit east of Woodward Avenue and the guard the west.

Federal forces remained in the city for five days. Virtually all rioting ended on Thursday; the paratroopers moved out on Saturday; the curfew was lifted and the National Guard departed on Tuesday, August 1, 1967. The toll was formidable: 40 dead, 2000 injured, 5000 arrested, and 5000 homeless.

President Johnson was badly shaken by the riots and by the nasty political conflict with Governor Romney, which reverberated in the press. On July 27 he addressed the country, opening, "We have endured a week such as no nation should live through: a time of violence and tragedy." He announced the appointment of the National Advisory Commission on Civil Disorders with Governor Otto Kerner of Illinois as chairman.[10]

During the fall of 1967 the smell of confrontation and violence was in the air. According to the recollections of Attorney General Ramsey Clark, this was "the moment that the fever broke in the whole antiwar movement."

Now it became "energized" and that "spelled the beginning of the end for American involvement in the war."

October 16–20 was called Stop the Draft Week and cards were turned in or burned all over the country. The New England Resistance brought 4000 people to a rally on Boston Common on Monday morning to hear antiwar addresses, mainly by clergymen. They then marched to the Unitarian Arlington Street Church where more than a century earlier William Ellery Channing had called for the end of slavery. Here 214 young men submitted their draft cards and 67 others burned theirs with Channing's candlestick.

The University of Wisconsin had a sit-in against the draft in 1966 and a demonstration against the Dow Chemical Company, which made napalm, in February 1967. Now in the week of October 16, Dow recruiters would be interviewing students for jobs. On Monday a handout warned that this would be brought to campus attention on Tuesday and that Dow recruiters in the Commerce Building would be sealed off on Wednesday. The next morning 200 picketers marched in front of the building. On Wednesday they resumed the picketing. But at 10:30 about 100 entered the building, linked arms at the recruiting office, and announced that there would be no more interviews. A large crowd gathered. Chancellor William Sewell had stated that recruiters would be protected. Officials pled with the demonstrators to leave, but they refused. University police and 20 off-duty Madison cops were brought in. After lunch about 30 more city riot police in full regalia arrived. At 1:30 they charged and beat many students, clearing the Commerce Building. A large, angry crowd gathered outside and was attacked with tear gas.

Later in the afternoon 5000 students and 200 professors met in the library mall. They pledged not to give or attend classes until Dow was banned forever. This strike was successful on Thursday and Friday, but it disintegrated the next week. Later Dow recruiters returned, but to a remote building under police protection. Sewell resigned.

The federal government could hardly ignore the events at Madison and on other college campuses. McNamara informed Rostow on December 7 that the CIA had already stopped recruiting in the colleges. The secretary had "advised" Dow to abandon recruiting and believed they had accepted his advice. But he thought it would be wrong for the Department of Defense to stop all visits or even to avoid "sensitive" universities. Instead, he had established a policy based on a "careful, selected basis."

In the East Bay the Stop the Draft Week confrontationists, veterans of Berkeley and the New Left, were tougher and more sophisticated. They had studied the new tactics of the European students and they were perversely inspired by the news that their revolutionary hero, Che Guevara, had been captured and murdered in Bolivia on October 10.

Their objective was to shut down the draft headquarters at the Oakland Armed Forces Examining Station. There was a fairly uneventful sit-in on Monday, October 16, and 124 people, including Joan Baez, were arrested. On October 16 about 2000 demonstrators met at the federal building in San Francisco. A basket circulated through the crowd to collect draft cards. U.S. attorney Cecil Poole, who was black, came out to observe. Dickie Harris, who was also black and a draft resister, approached Poole. "Brother Poole, you head nigger here?" Harris dumped the draft cards on his head. Poole turned about 400 over to the FBI.

The next day, "Bloody Tuesday," 2500 demonstrators closed down the Oakland station for three hours. The police attacked with clubs and Mace and the demonstrators replied with cans, bottles, and smoke bombs. On Friday they came to the scene with French mobile tactics. They had helmets and hard hats, smeared their faces with vaseline against Mace, and spread ball bearings on the streets, effective against cops on horses. Between 4000 and 10,000 demonstrators choked off ten blocks around the induction center. About 2000 police officers chased the fast-moving demonstrators. The latter attacked cars, news racks, parking meters, and trees in pots. They painted CHE IS ALIVE AND WELL IN OAKLAND on sidewalks. By the end of the day, partly inspired by drugs, they exulted over "winning" the battle of the streets.

On October 27 Father Philip Berrigan, a noted crusader for peace, led three others into the Baltimore custom house where the Selective Service cards were kept. They opened drawers and drenched the 1-A files with blood. The press arrived and got photos for the papers and TV, which was the Berrigan idea. The priest and his friends were arrested and sentenced to six years in prison.

On November 14 in New York the Foreign Policy Association celebrated its 50th anniversary with a dinner meeting at the Hilton at which Dean Rusk was the featured speaker. The opportunity to attack the Establishment and the war simultaneously was impossible to resist. About 4000 activists greeted Rusk and the diners with obscenities as the police escorted them into the hotel. Using French and Dutch tactics, the demonstrators stopped traffic with police whistles, sprayed peace slogans on sidewalks, and tossed steer blood, symbolizing the blood spilled in Vietnam, on buildings and cars. Midtown Manhattan was chaos for three hours and there were many confrontations with the police. There were 46 arrests along with the injury of 21 demonstrators and 5 policemen.

The National Mobilization Committee to End the War in Vietnam, an umbrella organization of over 100 centrist and leftist peace groups, planned to bring Stop the Draft Week to a climax with a giant march on the Pentagon on Saturday, October 21. David Dellinger was chairman. Yale-educated, an anarchal (nonviolent) pacifist long associated with A. J. Muste in the Fellowship for Reconciliation, and editor of *Liberation,* he had gone to Hanoi where he talked to Pham Van Dong and Ho Chi Minh. He had arranged for the release of three American prisoners of war. The Reverend James Bevel was national coordinator and Jerry Rubin was Washington project director. An original Yippie, Rubin came out of the Berkeley scene and had run for mayor of the town on a platform of Black Power and the legalization of marijuana. He had appeared before the House Un-American Activities Committee in a Revolutionary War uniform blowing bubbles. Rubin said he wanted to "levitate" the Pentagon and "exorcise" its evil spirits.

Lyndon Johnson was not amused; he was enraged. The vision of a mob of "Communists" descending upon the Pentagon offended him deeply. He ordered the intelligence establishment to track the Mobilization, the Department of Justice to maintain legal coordination under Warren Christopher, and the police and the military to be at the ready with a massive display of force. Dellinger said that the FBI planted agents provocateurs inside the Mobilization.

On October 3 Ramsey Clark met with Paul Nitze of Defense, Lawson Knott of General Services, and their staffs, along with presidential aides Larry Levinson and Matthew Nimetz. They agreed that the leaders of the demonstration must obtain a permit confining its scope, that they would be denied access to the Pentagon itself and other "vital public buildings," and that the prescribed route for the march would be from the Washington Monument to the Lincoln Memorial, across the Memorial Bridge, and into the north Pentagon parking lot.

The Mobilization, according to the FBI, had other ideas. The purpose of the demonstration was to "shut down" the Pentagon. There would be two staging areas, one at the Lincoln Memorial from which the marchers would cross the Memorial Bridge, and the other from the Washington Monument over the 14th Street Bridge. They would join at the south Pentagon lot. The FBI continued: Those wishing to engage in civil disobedience would try to enter the building to sit in halls and doorways, or, if unable to enter, to block the five entrances. The demonstration would continue until Monday. If unable to reach the Pentagon, they would march on the White House. The FBI was convinced that the demonstrators would engage in violence.

The FBI's secret informants did not get it straight. The Mobilization plan was to bring Stop the Draft Week to a head on Friday afternoon, October 20, by having a delegation in Washington for Saturday's demonstration to present a stack of draft cards to the Attorney General. Coffin and Spock led a group of 11 to the Department of Justice at 3:25 with a briefcase they said contained 992 draft cards and copies of others turned in around the country. Clark would not meet with them, but John R. McDonough and an aide did so.

Coffin led off by stating that an increasing number of young men had concluded that the war was illegal and immoral and, "as men of conscience, must refuse to be drafted." Older people, like himself, agreed and supported the resisters. They had counseled the younger men to "evade the draft" and were "aiding and abetting them . . . in such a way as to constitute a deliberate violation of federal law." They did this with full awareness that they could face a five-year prison term and a fine of $10,000.

McDonough said he would report this information to the Attorney General. He asked about the contents of the briefcase and was told of the draft cards. He said he could not accept them, that they must be given to local draft boards. The Mobilization group said they would leave the briefcase with its contents and departed. Two FBI agents took possession of the documents.

When the President was informed, he demanded that Clark prosecute all the "lawbreakers . . . firmly, promptly, and fairly." The next day Clark gave Johnson a report on the contents of the briefcase, said the cards were being referred to Selective Service, and stated that U.S. Attorneys were prepared to prosecute both evaders and aiders and abettors.

The permit issued jointly by the National Park Service, General Services, the D.C. Police, and Arlington County, Virginia, on October 19 was restrictive. The Lincoln Memorial was the sole assembly area. The march would cross Memorial Bridge and proceed by a specified route to only the north parking area.

At 11 a.m. on October 21 the Justice Department expected a crowd of 22,000, the FBI 28,000. These figures excluded those arriving by private car as well as residents of the Washington area. Since the *New York Times* used a figure of 50,000 for the crowd the next day at the Lincoln Memorial, the FBI estimate seems to have been fairly close to the mark.

LBJ mobilized forces adequate to repulse a foreign invasion. The first line consisted of the park police and U.S. marshals. They were backed up by 2000 D.C. policemen together with 1700 National Guard troops. Finally, there were 6000 active Army soldiers, including elements of the 82nd Airborne. There were 2600 in and around the Pentagon, 600 alerted for the White House, 400 for the Capitol, and 2500 in reserve. For good measure there were 45 Secret Service agents in the White House, 30 to 35 in reserve, and 20 in the Executive Office Building, plus 140 White House policemen.

The FBI did not forecast the quality of the oratory at the Lincoln Memorial on Saturday. The 50,000 people who gathered there, including the novelist Norman Mailer, were punished with deadening speeches. "On went the speeches," Mailer wrote. He "had no particular idea of their order or what they said." Dellinger, who spoke for the left wing of the peace movement, made an interesting comment. He declared that this was the end of peaceful protest. Now it would move to "confrontation . . . . This is the beginning of a new stage . . . in which the cutting edge becomes active resistance."

Mailer found the costumes worn by hippies more interesting. Some dressed like Sgt. Pepper's Band or as Arab sheiks or Park Avenue doormen.

Others showed up in western styles—Rogers and Clark, Wyatt Earp, Daniel Boone coonskins. Confederate gray and Union blue uniforms were much in fashion. "There were Martians and Moon-men and a knight unhorsed who stalked about in the weight of real armor."

After the oratory a much smaller group (no reliable estimates of size) gathered haphazardly and lurched their way with several stops across the bridge and into the Pentagon's north parking lot. Most of them just stood around wondering what would happen next. SDS and a group of New York leftists, calling themselves the Revolutionary Contingent, "stormed" the Pentagon itself. Six, in fact, actually entered a side door and were immediately thrown out by U.S. marshals. As darkness fell, there were many confrontations that led to a large number of arrests. Shortly before midnight those who remained were told that the permit was about to expire and that buses were available to take them back to the city. Most left. A few remained and were arrested. The level of violence was not high. In a review of the event, Stephen Pollak wrote Clark, "I would be less than candid if I did not pass along reports that the marshals at the mall entrance, unlike the Military Police, in a few cases used more force than was warranted."

McNamara observed the demonstrators from his office window and found them "terrifying. Christ, yes, I was scared." At the same time he was offended by the disorder and, characteristically, he later told Shapley that the antiwar movement was "under-managed." He said, "They did it all wrong. The way to have done it would have been Ghandi-like. Had they retained their discipline, they would have achieved their ends." Paul Nitze also watched the demonstrators from the Pentagon, knowing that three of his children were among them.

The cost to the government for maintaining order was $1,078,500, of which $641,000 was spent by the Department of Defense. Of the 625 adults arrested, 580 were convicted of violations of federal laws, most for disorderly conduct, but some for simple assault or contempt of court. A few served time, including Mailer, who spent a night in Occaquan Prison. Some said he was either drunk or stoned during the demonstration, and his book, *Armies of the Night,* supports both theories. On Sunday the Johnsons drove around the Lincoln Memorial. LBJ, confusing flower children with antiwar demonstrators, came to see what a hippie looked like. Mrs. Johnson was shocked by the litter.[11]

About the time of the demonstration, Clark Clifford and Walt Rostow met with the President. "Recalling the great comfort he had derived from earlier meetings with several elder statesmen, including Dean Acheson and John McCloy," Clifford wrote, "the President said he wanted to hear from some of the senior statesmen again." He asked Clifford to organize the meeting and he and Rostow drew up a list from which he selected those he wanted. They would meet for dinner with Rusk and McNamara at the State Department on the evening of November 1 and for four hours the next day at the White House with the President. Those who attended were Acheson, General Bradley, Ball, McGeorge Bundy, Arthur Dean, former Treasury Secretary Douglas Dillon, Justice Fortas, former Under Secretary of State Robert Murphy, and several still with the government—Harriman, Lodge, and Taylor. This was the first meeting of what came to be known as the "Wise Men."

The session at State began with upbeat briefings on the war by General Wheeler and Carver of the CIA. The next day each of the Wise Men, according to Clifford, "told the President he should stand firm." Even Ball did not go beyond a narrowing of bombing targets, though Harriman "remained silent during this display of unanimity, looking straight ahead." During the discussion Johnson's daughter Luci brought her five-month-old baby, Patrick, into the room and gave him to his grandfather. He napped quietly in the President's arms as they talked about bombing North Vietnam.

Clifford thought the meeting was "greatly comforting to the President that he had this kind of solid support and that this was the thinking of men who had taken part in this kind of activity for a great many years." [12]

16

Updating the Minimum Wage and Social Security

LYNDON Johnson, despite his eroding presidency and the budgetary squeeze, refused to surrender his Great Society. Califano put it this way:

> There was no child he could not feed; no adult he could not put to work; no disease he could not cure; no toy, food, or medical device he could not make safer; no air or water he could not clean; no discriminatory barrier he could not topple—just as there was no war he could not win and no cease-fire he could not negotiate.

Each year Johnson sent Califano and his aides to the major universities to push the smart professors for new legislative ideas. "The trouble with you Harvard liberals," he said, "is that you think there are no brains in the middle of the country. . . . You don't know a goddam thing about water or power. In Brooklyn you think water comes out of a faucet and electricity out of a socket." Califano usually returned with a stack of suggestions. They would then set up task forces to examine their feasibility and when the State of the Union rolled around in January the message was full of legislative proposals.

But, as time passed, the job grew tougher. When Califano went out to the universities for ideas for 1968, all he found was "criticism of the war." And it was easier to collect suggestions than it was to put bills through Congress. Insofar as even moderately significant legislation was concerned 1966 was not bad unless compared with the 1965 gusher; there was a marked falloff in 1967; and 1968 was pretty much a dry hole. During these years, moreover, there was no fundamental legislative program comparable to the Keynesian tax cut, the Civil Rights Act, federal aid to education, and Medicare.

There were, however, a number of important legislative intiatives in 1966 and 1967: important amendments to the Fair Labor Standards Act and Social Security Act, recounted in this chapter; assistance to the arts and humanities and the establishment of public broadcasting, recounted in chapter 17; and the bold attempt to confront perhaps the nation's most serious problem, urban decay, in the model cities program, recounted in chapter 18.[1]

The mid-sixties was a perfect time to amend the Fair Labor Standards Act both by raising the federal minimum wage and by expanding its coverage to millions of workers still not protected. The northern Democrats had majorities in both houses of Congress, thereby trumping the Republican-southern Democratic coalition which had long blocked such improvements. Economic conditions could hardly have been more favorable. Substantial full employment undermined the traditional argument that the legal minimum caused unemployment. A widely used rule of thumb was that the federal minimum should be half of average hourly earnings in manufacturing. Since these earnings were rising rapidly, this justified a catchup formula for the minimum. Finally, by 1966 consumer prices had taken off on the Great Inflation, thereby eroding the real purchasing power of the FLSA rate, again supporting its increase. But now there was a new counter-argument: the deep concern of the Council of Economic Advisers over inflation and its insistence that no hike should exceed the wage-price guidepost.

President Kennedy had persuaded Congress to enact significant FLSA amendments in 1961. The wage for already covered workers was moved up from $1.00 to $1.15 in 1961 and to $1.25 in 1963, while coverage was extended to 3.6 million new workers. Their minimum would be $1.00 for three years, $1.15 in the fourth, and $1.25 in the fifth year.

On May 18, 1965, President Johnson proposed two amendments to FLSA. He would extend coverage to 4.6 million new workers in construction, laundries and cleaning establishments, hotels, motels, and restaurants, hospitals and nursing homes, logging, taxis, and food processing. At the urging of Secretary of Labor Wirtz, he also suggested increasing the current overtime penalty of time and a half to double-time for hours worked in excess of 48 per week. While there would be problems of administration, Wirtz hoped that "overtime can be reduced . . . [as] an important source of new jobs." On the wage itself the President offered this homily:

> As average wages rise, the minimum wage level should be increased periodically.
>
> The question is not whether the minimum wage should be increased but when and by how much. The Congress should consider carefully the effects of higher minimum wage rates on the incomes of those employed, and also on costs and prices, and on job opportunities—particularly for the flood of teen-agers now entering our labor force.

Thus, Johnson's package without a minimum wage was a horseman without a head. The risk was that someone else would propose the wrong head.

The administration bill and another that would cover farm workers by the minimum wage were referred to the General Labor Subcommittee of which Representative Jimmy Roosevelt of California, a loose cannon eager for labor support, was chairman. He held hearings between May 25 and July 21, 1965. On August 4 the subcommittee by an 8 to 1 vote reported out a "Roosevelt" bill beside which the administration measure was conservative: coverage would be greatly extended to 7.9 million new employees, certain farm workers would have a $1.25 minimum, and the wage for non-farm people would move up in two steps to $1.75.

This bill shook up the Johnson administration. Otto Eckstein, filling in for Ackley as chairman of CEA, was beside himself. The higher minima, he wrote, would directly raise the wages of 6 million workers and of millions more indirectly to preserve differentials. By 1970 labor costs would be 10 percent higher. This would hamper industrialization in the South and economic progress in depressed areas. Roosevelt blithely informed Larry O'Brien that his bill would raise wages only 1.5 percent, well within the guidepost. O'Brien said, "My arithmetic must be off." His calculation came to 12 percent annually. Wirtz informed the President that the coverage extension "may result in killing the entire bill." His fear was that the rogue bill would clear the full committee and carry on the floor. He strongly recommended to Johnson that the measure be stopped at once, but "privately." In October 1965 the Roosevelt bill died in the House Education and Labor Committee.

This farce in the House compelled the White House to get its act together. On December 1, 1965, the President asked Wirtz, Ackley, and Commerce Secretary Connor to recommend "a basis for a realistic bill, with an Administration provision for a minimum wage level, consistent with our guidelines for wage-price stability." This, at least, had the virtue of focusing on the main issue, the minimum wage. But the composition of the group guaranteed that Wirtz, who alone strongly favored a minimum beyond 3.2, would be in the minority. The result was two antagonistic proposals.

Ackley and Connor would impose the 3.2 percent guidepost. They would move the 26 million workers who had been covered before 1961 from the present $1.25 to $1.40 in 1966, $1.50 in 1968, and $1.60 in 1970. The 3.6 million brought under coverage in 1961 would receive $1.35 in 1966, $1.40 in 1968, $1.50 in 1970, and $1.60 in 1972. The 4.6 million who would be covered for the first time in 1966 would advance from $1.25 in that year to $1.40 in 1968, $1.50 in 1970, and $1.60 in 1972.

Wirtz denounced this mechanical linkage to the guidepost. He pointed to the inconsistency with the Council's position in the 1963 Economic Report, which called for "faster increases in wage rates in an industry that

. . . currently pays wage rates exceptionally low compared with those earned elsewhere by labor of similar ability." He also favored compressing the time required to reach the maximum. For those covered prior to 1961, he would grant $1.40 in 1966 and $1.60 in 1967 and for the other groups he would start at $1.25 and $1.35 and move to $1.60 within four years.

The White House through Henry Wilson, who was in charge of congressional relations, firmed up leadership on the Hill. John Dent, a steady Pennsylvania liberal, replaced Jimmy Roosevelt as chairman of the House subcommittee. But the chairman of the parent committee, Adam Clayton Powell, was certain to cause trouble. Wilson persuaded Majority Leader Carl Albert to oversee the progress of the bill.

The difference between Ackley-Connor and Wirtz on the wage remained and Califano got the tough job of reconciling them. Ackley and Connor refused to budge. The former wrote in a memorandum to the White House:

> An excessive rise in the minimum wage will have a serious effect on business' confidence in our non-inflationary protestations. This will be true even for businesses whose wage rates will not be affected by any minimum wage increase so far proposed.
>
> Above-guidepost increases in the minimum wage will benefit some poor workers. But they will injure other workers who are also poor. They will be inflationary. The contribution of minimum wages to poverty reduction is not sufficient to justify raising minimum wages by more than the amounts we have recommended.

Connor echoed these views.

Wirtz was trapped. On February 12, 1966, he wrote two memoranda to the President, one marked "CONFIDENTIAL," the other "PERSONAL." In the first he made a concession, asking for $1.40 in 1966 and $1.60 in 1968. He had argued for 1967 for the second step. "I am persuaded, however, that a 20 cent jump in *one* year—which would be more than in any previous year in the history of the Act—would move it too fast." This might be inflationary and might threaten passage of the bill. In the second memo Wirtz wrote the President that "I want to be sure that you know all the facts":

> My *personal* view is that the $1.60 rate should be adopted for *1967* instead of 1968. I have expressed this view in previous memorandums and have pressed it as strongly as I could in discussions with Califano, Jack Connor, Gardner Ackley, and Charlie Schultze. . . .
>
> My support for the $1.60 in 1967 position has been so strong that the position taken in the accompanying memorandum, supporting the $1.60-in-1968, has to be understood as an acceptance of the result of "negotiations" which I got all out of (in terms of my own convictions) I could.

But this interchange still did not resolve the issue. Califano, who may have expressed the President's view, was ambivalent. On the one hand he felt that the administration must stick to the guidepost, but, as he wrote Johnson, "Running through this, of course is Wirtz' feeling (which I share) that a wage of $1.40 or even $1.60 ($3200) a year) is so low that it is difficult to see how people can live on it." More important, the AFL-CIO refused to accept the Ackley-Connor formula. Meany and Andy Biemiller, the legislative representative, might have gone along, but David Dubinsky of the International Ladies' Garment Workers and Jacob Potofsky of the Amalgamated Clothing Workers refused to do so. Both unions struggled with runaway union shops that fled high northern wages for the low wages of the South. Strong supporters of LBJ, they sought a higher federal minimum to push up southern pay scales. Thus, they insisted on $1.60 in 1967 and the administration refused to go along.

In early March 1966 the sharp pencils at the Council of Economic Advisers, which had lain unused in drawers, came out to devise several alternatives that were submitted to Johnson. He liked this one: $1.40 in 1966, $1.50 in 1967, and $1.60 in 1968. On March 9 Ackley came up with another alternative. The President's favorite would take effect in September of each year. The new idea was to have the 1966 and 1968 increases take effect in *February*. This formula would be lower than the other in payout in the early stages, but would surpass it by 10 cents at the end. Over the whole 24 months, Ackley noted, "it is distinctly lower." Further, he liked higher rates at the end "when we can hope that inflationary pressures will have abated." (Economists, like the rest of us, have never shone as prophets.) In any case, both the Democrats on the committee and the AFL-CIO bought the CEA proposal. The committee members were "highly favorable," Wilson wrote, "with the predictable exception of Mrs. [Edith] Green. If she didn't find some occasion to take exception with what we are doing, the Committee and the House would consider the situation abnormal."

Once the administration, AFL-CIO, and the congressional leadership agreed on the provisions, passage was assured and came swiftly. The Education and Labor Committee adopted an amendment offered by Philip Burton of California to include 700,000 federal employees, expanding new coverage from 7.5 to 8.2 million. The committee reported the bill on March 29. After desultory debate the House adopted it 303 to 93 on May 26, 1966. The Senate Labor and Public Welfare Committee accepted the House bill 15 to 0 on August 23. The Senate approved it 57 to 17 on August 26. The conference quickly resolved minor differences and reported on September 6. The next week the House 260 to 89 and the Senate 55 to 38 accepted the report. President Johnson signed the 1966 amendments to the Fair Labor Standards Act on September 23, 1966.

These improvements were without parallel in the history of the statute both as to amount and coverage. The minimum wages were as follows:

Effective date	Old coverage	Wage New nonfarm coverage	New farm coverage
Pre-1967	$1.25		
Feb. 1, 1967	$1.40	$1.00	$1.00
Feb. 1, 1968	$1.60	$1.15	$1.15
Feb. 1, 1969		$1.30	$1.30
Feb. 1, 1970		$1.45	
Feb. 1, 1971		$1.60	

The Labor Department noted on coverage: "The latest amendments almost fulfill the original act's commitment to eliminate substandard working conditions in interstate commerce." A number of important low wage industries heretofore exempt were now brought within the reach of the statute: hospitals and nursing homes, schools, hotels and restaurants, laundries, food processing, and big farms. Since these industries were large employers of black workers of both sexes, especially in the South, they would be among the main beneficiaries of the 1966 amendments.[2]

When the Social Security Act was passed in 1935 both President Roosevelt and the Congress insisted that the benefits be kept low to protect the solvency of the fund. Thus, in 1940, when the first old-age pensions were paid, the average retired worker received $22.60 per month. While there had been five increases in benefit levels between 1940 and 1965, only three had been across the board and in the aggregate they had failed to compensate beneficiaries even for real losses due to rises in the cost of living. By the midsixties, therefore, everyone concerned with Social Security was convinced of the need for a big boost in benefit levels.

But there was a complication. Between 1961 and 1965 the White House under both Kennedy and Johnson and HEW, particularly its Social Security Administration, were tied up with the passage of Medicare. For the next year Social Security was deeply involved in establishing the health care administration for the elderly. It was, therefore, mid-1966 before the Johnson administration could start thinking seriously about retirement benefit levels and 1967 before a bill could be introduced. By that time the President had lost control over Congress to the southern Democratic-Republican bloc. As a result the bill that would have pranced through the 89th Congress created a donnybrook in the 90th.

This did not dishearten Johnson. When Wilbur Cohen brought in a proposal for a 10 percent increase, the President said, "Come on, Wilbur, you can do better than that." According to Cohen, Johnson reacted with "passionate spontaneity" because he really cared about helping the aged.

This was an opportunity that Cohen had ached for, and during the second half of 1966 he and his team worked furiously to draft a comprehensive improved benefits program. In the summer they determined the most needed changes and worked out the financing. During the fall Cohen devised the specific benefit changes and their funding, which he submitted to the White House in two wide-ranging memoranda on December 15, 1966. They were the basis for the President's program submitted to Congress after the turn of the year.

He submitted a special message on older Americans on January 23. The recommendations for Old Age, Survivors, and Disability Insurance effective July 1, 1967, were as follows:

1. A 20 percent overall increase in benefits.
2. A 59 percent rise for the 2.5 million now at minima to $70 for an individual and $105 for a couple.
3. At least 15 percent for the remaining 20.5 million beneficiaries.
4. An increase in the minimum monthly benefit to those with 25 years of coverage to $100 for an individual and $150 for a couple.
5. Special benefits paid to more than 900,000 persons 72 or older who made little or no contributions would rise from $35 to $50 for individuals and from $52.50 to $75 for a couple.
6. Special benefits for 200,000 who were 72 or over who had never received them before.

Johnson said these payments would cost $4.1 billion in the first year, but he did not say where the money would come from. He estimated that they would lift 1.4 million people out of poverty. He also proposed benefit improvements for welfare recipients under Aid to Families with Dependent Children.

During January Cohen met with Wilbur Mills and other members of Congress to describe the financing. The new benefits would cost about one and a half percent of payrolls. Approximately half could be handled under the present law. The other half would come from an increase in the maximum earnings base from $6600 at present to $7800 in 1968, $9000 in 1971, and $10,800 in 1974 and from a rise in the contribution rate to 4.5 percent in 1969 and 5 percent in 1973. Mills hoped to hold hearings in February. The AFL-CIO strongly supported the legislation. Elizabeth Wickenden, an old friend of both Johnson and Cohen, would coordinate support among the national welfare agencies. The National Council of Senior Citizens and the Senior Citizens Golden Ring Council in New York were happily on board.[3]

Mills introduced the administration bill, H.R. 12080, on February 20, 1967. It went far beyond OASDI to add significant changes in Medicare, medicaid, welfare, and child health. It ran about 200 pages in length and would double in size before Congress was through with it. The Ways and Means hearings continued from March 1 to April 11, 1967, a forum for the testimony of an immense number of witnesses on all these topics.

"Wilbur Mills," Budget Director Schultze wrote Johnson on March 28, "is in no hurry to move it [the bill], since he doesn't want to take up the 6% surcharge soon (and we agree he should not)." Budget, CEA, and Treasury were so concerned about the economy in the first half of 1967 that they urged the use of Social Security as an economic stimulus. They would try to persuade Mills and Russell Long, chairman of the Senate Finance Committee, to split Old Age, Survivors, and Disability benefits from the bill, reduce the average benefit increase from 20 to 12 to 13 percent, and make the new benefits retroactive to January 1, 1967. The lower benefit checks would go out in August. Cohen was not enthusiastic. He said 15 percent might work. Otherwise George Meany would accuse the administration of having "sold out." The proposal died for lack of interest.

The Republicans could hardly permit the Democrats to take full credit for a hefty increase for 24 million oldsters, most of them voters, without being heard from. Their coordinating committee on April 8 denounced the administration bill for imposing "burdens on the weekly paychecks of American workers." They called for an increase in Social Security benefits retroactive to January 1, 1967, and for future automatic increases linked to the cost of living. But the Republicans declined to specify the amounts.

Ways and Means, obviously in no hurry, considered H.R. 12080 for four months and reported it out on August 7. All 23.7 million OASDI beneficiaries would receive a 12.5 percent increase. The minimum monthly benefit would rise from $44 to $50. Financing would come from existing funds supplemented by higher tax rates applied to a larger taxable earnings base.

But Ways and Means did not stress OASDI. Rather, its main fire was directed at administration proposals to increase Aid to Families with Dependent Children welfare benefits. A disproportionate number of recipients were black and the summer of 1967 was a dreadful time in race relations. There had been a series of black riots across the nation, most important, Newark on June 20 and the massive Detroit riot on July 22. In addition, Dr. George A. Wiley, a black militant, had formed the National Welfare Rights Organization, which was organizing black mothers to demand higher AFDC benefits, often by disrupting legislatures. These demonstrations only confirmed Mills and the other conservatives on Ways and Means to punish rather than reward black militants.

They completely rewrote the AFDC program. The states would be required to compel adults and older children not in school to enter the labor market. Attendance at a job training program would become a condition of receiving assistance. Mothers must place their children in day care centers. Fathers must work or take training to qualify for welfare. The committee, concerned about the rapid growth in the size of the program, would impose a "freeze" on numbers to prevent future expansion.

HEW Secretary Gardner issued a stinging attack on these proposals. He said that children would be required "to pay for the real or supposed sins of their parents." Gardner also objected to coercion in job training since most of the people involved were mothers who would have to leave their children at day care centers. Some of the Northern liberals joined him.

But Mills and the House of Representatives ignored Gardner. On August 16 Mills asked the House for a rule on H.R. 12080 that would foreclose amendments and limit debate to four hours. It passed 120 to 7. On August 17 Mills made a stern speech on the floor, saying that his welfare plan would make "taxpayers out of taxeaters." With the freeze he intended to eliminate 400,000 recipients of AFDC by 1972. In a roll call that day the House passed the bill 416 to 3. Though this was supposed to be a Social Security bill, there had been virtually no discussion of OASDI. Further, the Johnson administration had disappeared as a legislative player.

The Senate Finance Committee held hearings between August 22 and September 26, 1967. By this time Wilbur Cohen, usually ebullient and optimistic, was worn out and depressed. After testifying before the committee, he left for Bolivia on September 2, returning on the 14th. In La Paz he stayed at the American embassy and a dinner was given in his honor. He then went to Cochabamba to see his son, Bruce, a recent graduate of Reed College and presently a Peace Corps volunteer.

The Senate hearings became a stage for political theater. Senator Robert Kennedy, now a candidate for President, testified against the House AFDC amendments, which he compared to the medieval poor laws. The House, he said, had vented its frustration by "punishing the poor because they are there and we have been unable to do anything about them." He proposed an *increase* in welfare benefits financed in part by the Social Security tax. Dr. Wiley brought in six welfare mothers, who, instead of testifying, staged a noisy three-hour demonstration against the House bill. When they returned the next day, Chairman Long had the doors barred. He called the women "brood mares" and said, "If they can take the time to march in the street and picket and sit in the hearing room all day, it seems to me they have enough time to get jobs."

After returning from South America, Cohen dedicated himself to persuading Long to restore the administration's OASDI benefits and the taxes to pay for them. By October 17 he thought he had brought Long around "because he wants an increase in benefits, wants to be fiscally responsible in covering the cost and because he wants something to bargain with Wilbur Mills in Conference." Cohen also thought that Republican Senator John Williams of Delaware would go along.

Despite these gleams of hope, the legislative wear and tear had made Cohen despondent. On October 25 he wrote Elizabeth Wickenden:

I have never experienced frustration as I am now. Yes, in the Eisenhower Administration there was a frustration borne more of neglect and apathy. Now the frustration is on a real high level. Everyone wants to do something but can't get enough others to join and get it done. You put your finger on it when you say we are torn apart—but on so many issues. . . . This has been the most difficult legislative happening in my 33 years of experience. I go home each night with the thought in mind that this is the last time! Nobody really appreciates the plight of intermediary in the legislative process. Everyone wants to be the one who takes a position "as a matter of principle." I feel sometimes like I am negotiating a peace settlement between Israel and the Arabs. But then if someone did that I suppose they could claim they made a contribution.

On November 14 the Senate Finance Committee reported H.R. 12080 with amendments. Cohen had won over Long, but he lost Williams. The vote was strictly on party lines, 11 to 6. All the administration benefits were restored: across-the-board 15 percent increase, average benefit boost of 20 percent, and a minimum benefit of $70. The higher costs would be covered primarily by raising the taxable earnings base more rapidly to $10,800 in 1972. The committee significantly modified the House welfare plan by excising the freeze, by eliminating coercive features, and by encouraging the employment of those certified to work by enrolling them in a new Labor Department job training program.

While H.R. 12080 was now over 400 pages long, the Senate showed no mercy by accepting 27 new amendments. OASDI went through as the committee had recommended and the House version of welfare was again liberalized. The Senate adopted the bill on November 22 by a vote of 78 to 6. Four Republicans, including Williams, were in the minority. While Dirksen announced that "a great deal of mischief has been wrought," he, nevertheless, voted aye with his wet forefinger lifted high into the political wind.

Mills, who had the votes, dominated the conference. The across-the-board benefit increase was reduced to 13 percent and the minimum benefit to $55 a month. The House versions of the payroll tax and the earnings base were adopted. More important politically, welfare was restored, as Mills put it, "in substantially the form" in which it passed the House. There would be mandatory training for AFDC recipients and there would be a freeze on their number. The conference committee reported on December 11.

With this report Mills put the President in an escape-proof box. If Johnson promised to veto the bill, there was the probability that he would be overridden and the prospect that he would be blamed for denying 24 million pensioners a substantial improvement in their benefits. If he remained silent, he would have to swallow a number of provisions he strongly opposed and would incur the wrath of liberals, including Bobby Kennedy, as well as labor and blacks.

Gardner and Cohen wrestled with this dilemma all day on December 11. At first they thought that the President should remain silent, but later changed their minds. Both were offended by the reduction in benefits, the freeze, and the requirement that AFDC mothers enroll in training. In addition, Gardner was moved because the welfare changes "are going to be celebrated issues in the liberal community" and would be "perceived as anti-Negro measures by the Negro community." Cohen added to Califano that the bill would be "an excuse for rioting next summer." They both urged the President to come out against the conference report.

Some 19 governors, 11 Democrats and eight Republicans were already on record against the freeze. Liberal Republican Mayor John Lindsay of New York was lining up the big-city mayors against the report. But Daley of Chicago and Barr of Pittsburgh, while agreeing with Lindsay on substance, Califano wrote, "will not oppose it [the report] without some word from the Administration." The AFL-CIO decided that the battle should take place in the Senate and urged a filibuster. George Meany sent telegrams to all the members of Congress. Senator Fred Harris of Oklahoma and Bobby Kennedy demanded a filibuster.

On the afternoon of December 11 Gardner sent Johnson a memorandum recommending "with all the urgency I can express" that he issue a public statement opposing the conference report. If the President did not consider this "feasible," Gardner suggested the following:

> I will not veto a bill that would provide increased social security benefits to 24 million persons, would take one million persons out of poverty, and includes many other important improvements. But the Administration will continue to press strongly for the three improvements in Social Security and the Welfare program which the Senate adopted.

Califano thought it a "mistake" to issue the Gardner statement before the signing ceremony. He thought it unclear. Liberals and labor would say that the failure to veto "indicates that you want the bill to go through." Those who stood with Mills would say "you went out of your way to stir up trouble." Johnson did not issue a statement.

Just before the House vote on December 13 the President called Mills to the White House in a last-ditch effort to change his mind. He thought the chairman was "like a shark in feeding frenzy" determined to punish black welfare mothers. Mills said, "Mr. President, across town from my mother in Arkansas a Negro woman has a baby every year. Every time I go home, my mother complains. That Negro woman's now got eleven children. My proposal would stop this. Let the states pay for more than a small number of children if they want to." When Mills left, Johnson said to Califano: "That's the way most members feel. They're just not willing to say it publicly unless they come from real red neck districts." Later that day the House adopted the conference report by a vote of 390 to 3.

That afternoon, December 13, Senator Muskie called the Senate Campaign Committee together to discuss the filibuster Harris and Kennedy had proposed. Twenty-five senators were present. Mansfield made a powerful statement against a filibuster. As Manatos put it, the majority leader told Harris and Kennedy that they lacked the votes "by the widest of margins." A filibuster would damage the Democratic party, injure the President, and hurt those running in 1968. Bible, Church, McGovern, and Mondale, all up for reelection and the last three stalwart liberals, said they would suffer from a filibuster. Muskie said it would inflame Negro militants and alienate 24 million old people. Clinton Anderson said it would be "suicidal." Sam Ervin said he was reminded of the Aesop fable of the dog with a bone in his mouth who saw his reflection in the stream and, greedy, snapped at the reflected bone, losing the real one he had. With such opposition, there was no filibuster. On December 15 the Senate adopted the conference report by a vote of 62 to 14.

There remained some liberal sentiment in favor of a veto. Meany and Reuther urged Johnson not to sign the bill. But those 24 million OASDI beneficiaries dictated otherwise. He signed the Social Security Amendments of 1967 on January 2, 1968. Since he could hardly have avoided inviting Wilbur Mills, by now an offensive option, there was no ceremony. The President issued a brief and bland statement in San Antonio, which had the virtue of being a long way from Washington.

Of the galling conflict over welfare, Johnson merely said, "My recommendations were not adopted by the Congress. In their place, the Congress substituted certain severe restrictions." He said he had directed Secretary Gardner to work with the states to establish "compassionate safeguards." But Gardner was on the verge of resigning. On the affirmative side Johnson said that he was establishing the Commission on Income Maintenance under Ben W. Heineman, president of the Chicago & Northwestern Railroad, to examine alternatives to the existing welfare system.[4]

The passage of the amendments to the Fair Labor Standards Act on September 22, 1966, and to the Social Security Act on January 2, 1968, reflect the collapse of the Johnson presidency. The dividing line was the congressional elections of November 1966. The 89th Congress had a solid northern Democratic majority; the 90th Congress was dominated by the southern Democratic-Republican coalition, in this case led skillfully, perhaps brilliantly, by Wilbur Mills.

In normal times on the minimum wage business opposition much outweighed labor support. In contrast, OASDI enjoyed strong bipartisan backing, including southern Democrats and the GOP. But the administration made a fatal strategic mistake in joining old-age pensions to other Social Security amendments, particularly Aid to Families with Dependent Children. In the best of times AFDC was unpopular; in the immense white backlash against black militancy in 1967 the program was political leprosy. Mills trapped Johnson by compelling him to accept the punishing welfare amendments as the price for getting the improvements he wanted in Social Security. Johnson was helpless because he had lost control over the Congress.

17

Lyndon Johnson, Patron of the Arts

THE notion of Lyndon Johnson as a latter-day Lorenzo de Medici, patron of the arts, is ludicrous on its face. He was a Texas hill country philistine. There is no evidence that he ever read a poem or a novel of his own choice. His interest in painting seems to have been confined to the noted western artist Peter Hurd for the portrait of Johnson, which he hated. Music, the theater, opera, ballet held no attraction. At the Kennedy White House parties for artists, writers, and musicians he stood about with his hands in his pockets and a sour expression on his face. He had a country boy's healthy suspicion of these artistic types and, with Vietnam, grew to distrust them intensely. He never ceased venting his distaste for the people he called "the Harvards." While he had an insatiable appetite for the media, particularly TV, it was for political news and particularly for coverage of himself. Yet Lyndon Johnson became a noted patron of the arts and the media.[1]

Following World War II the performing arts in America enjoyed a solid expansion as measured by both the number of performances and the size of audiences. This was especially marked for opera, ballet, and off-Broadway and outside New York theater. Broadway and symphony concerts grew more modestly. In many cities this demand led to construction of new or refurbished theaters, concert halls, and opera houses. New York and Los Angeles, the nation's leading cities in the performing arts, moved a step further by joining facilities into a unified performance center.

Lincoln Center for the Performing Arts on Manhattan's West Side above Columbus Circle, fully operating by 1970, was architecturally spectacular, took 13 years to build, and broke all records for cost, $186 million.

This was, Martin Mayer wrote, "a little more than double the entire annual box office income of all the nation's professional symphony orchestras, opera and ballet companies, and repertory theaters put together." Lincoln Center consisted of Avery Fisher Hall, the home of the New York Philharmonic, with 2,836 seats; the New York State Theatre, 2,729 seats, the house for the New York City Opera; the Vivian Beaumont Theatre, 1,060 seats, for repertory; the Metropolitan Opera House, seating 3800; Alice Tully Hall, 1,096 seats, for chamber music; the Juilliard School, including a theater; and a library and museum.

The Los Angeles Music Center was located downtown on a rectangular site with handsome walks, fountains, sculpture, and reflecting pools. Its three units opened between 1963 and 1967. The Dorothy Chandler Pavilion at the south end had 3,250 seats, was the home of the Los Angeles Philharmonic, and was available for opera, ballet, musical comedy, and recitals. The Ahmanson Theatre, with 2100 seats, was at the north end and provided drama, ballet, and musical comedy. The Mark Taper Forum was in between, with a circular theater with 750 seats arranged around a thrust stage.

Washington had never attained standing in the performing arts and many felt that this deficiency in the nation's capital should be remedied. In 1951 President Truman asked the Commission of Fine Arts to investigate ways in which the government could assist the arts. The agency made a comprehensive survey and reported to President Eisenhower on May 15, 1953. Among its recommendations was the establishment of a music center for the performance of opera, symphony, and ballet.

Historically the mainstream Republican party held the view that the arts should be financed by private markets or by private philanthropy, that government must not provide subsidies. Eisenhower, whose main leisure time activities seem to have been golf and bridge, had no interest in the performing arts. Nevertheless, he did not object to the construction of a handsome arts building in Washington as long as the government did not pay for it. On September 2, 1958, therefore, he signed the National Cultural Center Act. The site would be the rise overlooking Roosevelt Island and the Potomac. The National Capital Planning Commission would acquire an additional acre to add to the land already owned by the government. The center would come under the administrative control of the Smithsonian Institution.

A board of trustees was formed with Roger L. Stevens as chairman. The noted architect Edward Durell Stone was chosen and he came up with an original idea quite unlike Lincoln Center and the Los Angeles Music Center. Everything would be housed in one enormous oblong structure, 630' × 300'. Side by side would be a 2800-seat concert hall, a 2300-seat theater for opera, dance, and musical comedy, an 1,150-seat theater for drama and musicals, a 550-seat film theater convertible to a thrust stage for drama and musicals, a pavillion for meetings and band concerts, an art gallery, and eating facilities. The estimated cost was a whopping $66.4 million.

When Kennedy became President, he immediately changed the relationship between the government and the arts. John and Jacqueline Kennedy, their friend William Walton observed, were "susceptible to the comfort of the arts. They couldn't live without them—it [was] woven into the pattern of their lives." The President was deeply interested in literature, paid great attention to architecture, and had some knowledge of painting and sculpture. More important, according to Arthur Schlesinger, was Kennedy's "conviction that the health of the arts was vitally related to the health of society. . . . Excellence was a public necessity, ugliness a national disgrace."

At the inauguration Robert Frost read a poem and the audience by invitation included many of the nation's most distinguished writers, composers, and painters. The Kennedys converted the White House into a national stage for performances and dinners for musicians, artists, and writers. The Presidential Medal of Freedom was rehabilitated and awarded to leading artists. More important, Kennedy started on the development of a national arts policy and enthusiastically backed the National Cultural Center.

He pushed the site overlooking the Potomac. He brought the trustees and the advisory committee to the White House for a concert and urged them to proceed with their important task. He proclaimed November 26 to December 2, 1962, National Cultural Center Week and on November 29 spoke on closed circuit television to groups in 75 cities to back the $30 million campaign Stevens had organized to fund the center. The program ran for two hours, Leonard Bernstein was master of ceremonies, and there were performances by Pablo Casals, Marian Anderson, Van Cliburn, Robert Frost, Frederic March, Danny Kaye, Bob Newhart, and Harry Belafonte.

After the assassination a number of members of Congress introduced bills to rename the National Cultural Center after Kennedy. President Johnson not only embraced this idea enthusiastically, he worked out a critically important funding scheme. The campaign had raised $15.5 million by private subscription. Now the government would match that figure and, in addition, the center would be authorized to borrow a similar amount from the Treasury to be repaid by revenues produced by the underground parking garage. Congress quickly enacted the bill and Johnson signed it on January 23, 1964.

Thus, the project became the John F. Kennedy Center and later the Kennedy Center for the Performing Arts. It was completed in 1971 at a final cost of $71 million. The Kennedy Center immediately joined Lincoln Center and the Los Angeles Music Center as one of the three great architectural monuments to the performing arts in the United States.[2]

While the center was a glittering monument in the nation's capital, the Kennedy administration never removed its eye from the bigger goal: a national policy for the arts. Max Isenbergh, a State Department lawyer who was musical, wrote a discussion paper for an interested group of officials entitled "Issues Bearing upon National Cultural Policy." Secretary of Labor Goldberg, whose wife was an abstract painter, arbitrated the salary dispute between the Metropolitan Opera and the Musicians Union, caused by the fact that the Met was broke. In his award in December 1961 Goldberg added a section written by his assistant, Daniel Patrick Moynihan, recommending "community responsibility" for the performing arts.

Arthur Schlesinger and Pierre Salinger urged Kennedy to bring in August Heckscher as a special consultant to inventory the points at which the government intersected with the arts and to recommend a policy. Heckscher had written the essay on the arts for the Eisenhower Commission on National Goals and was director of the Twentieth Century Fund, which was sponsoring the first serious study of the economics of the arts by the Princeton economists William J. Baumol and William G. Bowen, published as *Performing Arts—The Economic Dilemma*. Heckscher became the two-day-a-week Special Consultant on the Arts and made his report, *The Arts and the National Government*, on May 28, 1963. While Heckscher's report dealt with many topics, its main thrust was to create a National Arts Foundation as "the logical crowning step in a national cultural policy."

President Kennedy sent up a bill to enact Heckscher's recommendations, including the foundation. In December 1963, a month following the assassination, the Senate adopted it by voice vote. But the Rules Committee of the House blocked action. President Johnson sent up the bill again in 1964, a rule was issued, and the House passed it 213 to 135. The Senate reaffirmed its earlier action. Johnson signed the National Council on the Arts and Cultural Development Act on September 3, 1964, a toothless statute. It merely created a 25-member council and gave it a pittance to organize itself. There was neither a granting agency nor a fund to support the arts.

Meantime, a new idea had emerged. The academic disciplines loosely known as the humanities had for years envied the enormous financial support that the federal government had poured into the hard sciences, since 1950 largely through the National Science Foundation. Now the arts seemed on the verge of receiving similar federal largesse. The humanities wanted to come in out of the cold.

The American Council of Learned Societies, the Council of Graduate Schools, and the United Chapters of Phi Beta Kappa joined to form a Commission on the Humanities under the chairmanship of President Barnaby C. Keeney of Brown University. It reported on April 30, 1964, recommending legislation to create a National Humanities Foundation patterned after the National Science Foundation.

In his presidential election swing through New England on September 28, 1964, Johnson spoke at Brown on its 200th anniversary. He said, "I look with the greatest of favor upon the proposal of your own able President Keeney's Commission for a National Foundation for the Humanities." It sounded like a promise and Johnson won the election. In the first week of the 89th Congress in January 1965, 76 bills were introduced to establish a humanities foundation. Thus, the humanities joined the arts; one program became two.

By this time the Democratic chairmen of the House Education and Labor committee and the Senate Labor and Public Welfare Committee were vigorous spokesmen for legislation of this sort. Frank Thompson, Jr., of New Jersey had been the leading champion in the House for years. More recently Claiborne Pell had won a Senate seat from Rhode Island and had persuaded Senator Lister Hill of Alabama, chairman of the parent committee, to create a new Subcommittee on the Arts, which Pell took over.

On March 10, 1965, the President sent his bill to create the National Foundation on the Arts and Humanities to the subcommittee chairmen. The measure was quickly passed by the Senate on June 10. Johnson had to put firm pressure on the Rules Committee to spring the bill out of its clutches. The House adopted several secondary amendments and passed it on September 15. The Senate immediately adopted the House changes and the President signed the statute on September 29, 1965. At a large ceremony Johnson, with characteristic hyperbole, promised a National Theater, a National Opera, a National Ballet, and an American Film Institute, along with many other cultural goodies. "What this bill really does is to bring active support to this great national asset, to make fresher the winds of art in this land of ours." But the White House seemed to have forgotten the humanities.

The administrative system was cumbersome. At the top, theoretically, was the Federal Council on the Arts and Humanities, designed to coordinate the activities of the endowments with other federal agencies. S. Dillon Ripley, the secretary of the Smithsonian Institution, became chairman of this council. But it does not seem to have played a policy role of any consequence.

The two working structures were identical: a National Council on the Arts/Humanities, each with a chairman and 24 members to select projects for support and a National Endowment on the Arts/Humanities to administer the grants. The jurisdictions were broad. The arts program included, but was not limited to, music, dance, drama, sculpture, photography, graphic and craft arts, industrial and fashion design, movies, television, radio, tape recording, and other arts related to them. Humanities included, but was not limited to, languages, linguistics, literature, history, jurisprudence, philosophy, archaeology, the history, criticism, theory, and practice of the arts, and aspects of the social sciences with a humanistic content. Roger Stevens headed both the arts council and endowment. Barnaby Keeney was chosen to chair the humanities council and endowment but was unable to leave

Brown until 1966. Meantime Henry Allen Moe of the Guggenheim Foundation filled the position. The arts council included a number of stars—Leonard Bernstein, Isaac Stern, David Brinkley, Agnes de Mille, Ralph Ellison, and Gregory Peck. The humanities council was manned mainly by academics. Both groups, evidently, were very serious about their undertaking.

Each of the endowments received a basic appropriation of $5 million annually for grants to individuals and groups. In addition, arts got funds for matching grants of $50,000 to each state for the establishment of a state arts program and humanities received an equal amount to match private grants.

Stevens had his council meeting before the legislation was signed. During the first three years the arts endowment, among many others, made the following grants: American Ballet Theatre, an American exhibit at the Venice Biennale, establishment of the American Film Institute, individual choreographers to create new works for dance, production of plays by professional and university theaters, and classical theater for secondary schools (42,000 New Orleans students, for example, saw Arthur Miller's *The Crucible*). Programs were launched in virtually all the states and territories.

A problem that the arts endowment foresaw and inevitably was compelled to confront was occasional attack from the extreme right on the projects it supported for alleged subversion or pornography. This was already evident in the House when the bill was before it. Republican Representative Harold R. Gross of Iowa introduced the "belly dance" amendment by inserting after "dance" the following: "including but not limited to irregular jactitations and/or rythmic contraction and coordinated relaxation of the serrati, obliques, and abdominis recti group of muscles—accompanied by rotary undulations, tilts, and turns timed with and attuned to the titillary and blended tones of synchronous woodwinds." When his amendment was defeated, Gross offered to include baseball, squash, pinochle, and poker as art forms eligible for support. It received the same fate.

The humanities endowment supported less controversial projects: editing and publishing the papers of great Americans; editing and publishing definitive editions of great American writers; archaeological excavations; training programs to improve the quality of the publications of university presses; computer research in the study of foreign languages and in preparing concordances; and assistance to learned societies.

The establishment of the endowments in 1965 was a dramatic new development in American public policy. Never before had the government systematically supported the arts and humanities. The public and the Congress must have concluded that these programs were successful because they endured, throve, and grew over time.[3]

In 1964 Joseph Hirshhorn at 66, having had a heart attack, was feeling the weight of mortality. He had begun to take soundings for the relocation of some of his valuable property that would outlive him.

Hirshhorn had been born in 1900 in Latvia, the twelfth of thirteen children in a Jewish family. His father died when he was a child. His mother then took most of her family to New York between 1905 and 1907, where she worked twelve hours a day, six days a week, in a pocketbook factory for $12.50 a week. "Poverty has a bitter taste," he would say. "We ate garbage." As a child he had no toys.

Hirshhorn dropped out of high school after three months. At 14 he became an office boy on Wall Street. At 17 he went into the Curb Market as a broker and within a year ran $225 up to $168,000. "I'm not an investor," he said. "I'm a speculator." At the end of World War I he lost everything but $4000 and started over. Before the 1929 crash, at 28, he sold out for $4 million.

After World War II Hirshhorn bought land in Blind River, Ontario, and mined for metals. He discovered gold and an enormous uranium deposit at a time when the construction of nuclear weapons and atomic power plants was mushrooming. By the sixties he was said to be worth $140 million. He had a magnificent 24-acre estate in Greenwich, Connecticut, houses in Cap d'Antibes and Beverly Hills, an apartment in New York, two offices in New York and another in Toronto.

Hirshhorn discovered modern art in the twenties and was immediately hooked. He became an obsessed collector. He developed, Abram Lerner wrote, "that inspired greed for art which has dominated so much of his life." In 1945 he came to the ACA Gallery in Manhattan, where Lerner was working, quickly bought four paintings, and left. Lerner had been an artist, was a veteran of the federal arts project, and had studied fine arts at New York University. They became warm friends, shared similar tastes, and Hirshhorn increasingly relied on Lerner's artistic advice. In 1956 Lerner came on board as curator of the Hirshhorn collection and the latter continued to buy furiously. Lerner spent much of his time keeping an inventory of the works, which were variously housed in Greenwich, in an office on 67th Street in Manhattan, in a warehouse on 10th Avenue, or on loan to museums around the world.

By the sixties the collection was immense and had became hard to track, and Hirshhorn and Lerner began to talk about making it publicly available. The former said, "I want my own museum." Lerner agreed. They started with the city they knew best, New York, but could not find a proper location. There were discussions about the Doheny estate in Beverly Hills, but that fell through. The British government offered to build a museum in Regents Park in London. There were soundings from Baltimore, Zurich, Florence, and Jerusalem. More interesting, Governor Nelson Rockefeller of New York, himself a collector of modern art, offered a museum built by the state at the new state university campus in Purchase, only a short drive from Greenwich.

S. Dillon Ripley, who had become secretary of the Smithsonian Institution in February 1964, entered the bidding. An ornithologist, he had been a professor of biology at Yale and director of the Peabody Museum of Natural History. His mother had helped found the Museum of Modern Art and had imbued him with a passion for contemporary works. The Smithsonian was the administrative parent of the federal art museums in Washington— the National Gallery, the Freer Gallery, the National Collection of Fine Arts, and the Renwick Gallery. The notable gap in the nation's capital was a museum of modern art. For Ripley the obvious and efficient solution to this problem was the Hirshhorn collection. He searched the legislation of earlier bequests and found that Congress in 1938 had accepted Andrew Mellon's gift for the National Gallery and his collection of old masters and had also established a $7000 prize for a plan for a modern museum. A competition was held and Eero Saarinen had won, but the Capital Planning Commission had disapproved because it wanted nothing modern on the Mall. Ripley made indirect contact with Hirshhorn through Roger Stevens.

On June 15, 1964, Ripley wrote Hirshhorn of his dream and said that he hoped to "explore the concept" with him. He went to Greenwich to view the art and open discussion. He concluded that he needed help. He informed the President that he hoped to bag Hirshhorn's collection, "valued then at $40 million." That was the kind of art discussion Lyndon Johnson could understand.

Early in 1965 Sam Harris, Hirshhorn's lawyer, with Max Kampelman, a partner in his Washington office, came to see Ripley. The latter asked whether the collector would consider giving his art to the Smithsonian. Harris said, "He would want his name on the museum." "That," Ripley replied, "is simply the identification of a building. . . ." Harris continued, "On the Mall." "I don't see why not." Harris was astonished. "You mean a Hirshhorn Museum on the Mall?" Ripley answered deliberately, "This is 1965 and I think America has grown up."

Ripley was concerned about the competition. He suggested to Abe Fortas, a friend of Hirshhorn's, that a White House luncheon would help. Knowing of Lady Bird Johnson's strong interest in having a Thomas Eakins painting in the mansion's collection, Ripley notified Liz Carpenter, her secretary, that Hirshhorn owned 32 of the painter's works. Ripley wrote Hirshhorn that the collection under Smithsonian guardianship would be assured of independent identity and that it would have more viewers than in any other place in the world, some 12 million annually.

Ripley, Stevens, Hirshhorn, and Harris met to discuss the site. Stevens would have preferred the bank of the Potomac adjacent to his baby, the Kennedy Center. But the others insisted on the Mall at Constitution Avenue and 9th Street.

Ripley was carried away by his enthusiasm. He informed the White House that the collection would be "frightfully important for the cultural growth of Washington." It could do for the city what the Museum of Modern Art had done for New York. "My mother was on the first women's committee of the Museum of Modern Art, when it was four rooms with a police dog as a guard in the Heckscher Building in New York in 1932." He was impressed by the precedents. James Smithson gave his fortune to the United States to establish the Smithsonian Institution. Charles Freer gave his oriental art collection and provided funds for construction of the gallery (cost in 1922 was $2 million, now equivalent to $9.5 million), and an endowment for operation. Andrew Mellon gave his magnificent collection of old masters and $15 million for construction of the National Gallery (current equivalent $45 million) along with an endowment.

Mrs. Johnson held a luncheon for the Hirshhorns at the White House on May 21, 1965. In anticipation, the collector wrote a long letter to the President and his wife on May 17:

> I have had a number of conversations with Dr. Dillon Ripley and Mr. Roger Stevens concerning my art collection. Both of these gentlemen have seen a portion of my collection and have urged that I donate it to the Smithsonian Institution. Their thought is that my collection would be housed in a modern museum to be named the Joseph H. Hirshhorn Museum, which would be erected on the plot of land on Constitution Avenue between 9th and 11th Streets . . . ; that the collection and museum would be maintained, preserved and developed in perpetuity by the Smithsonian Institution under my name; and that the museum would be operated by a Board of Trustees on which I have appropriate representation. . . .
>
> My collection has been built up over . . . more than 40 years and I believe . . . that it is one of the finest collections of modern sculpture and paintings in the world.
>
> I own more than 1,500 pieces of sculpture, produced by such world famous sculptors as Rodin, Bourdelle, Maillol, Manzu, Degas, Daumier, Sir Henry Moore, Lipschitz, Brancusi, Sir Jacob Epstein, Renoir, Picasso, Calder, Giacometti, Marini, Matisse and others. My collection includes 63 works by . . . Moore, generally acknowledged to be the greatest living sculptor. . . . My Giacomettis and Matisses constitute the largest holdings in a single collection in America. Rodin is represented . . . by 16 works, including a major cast of the Burghers of Calais.
>
> [There are] . . . over 4,800 paintings and drawings by scores of American and European artists. I have always sought to encourage young artists—particularly American . . . by purchasing their works. . . . [There is] a thorough representation of the realists, the expressionists, the romantics, and the abstractionists.
>
> . . . the better known painters who are represented: Picasso, Eakins, Hassam, Munch, Bellows, Sloan, Kuhn, Hopper, Sawyer, Wyeth, Beckmann, Marin, Weber, Ben Shahn, Jack Levine, Maurice Prendergast, Dali, Francis Bacon, Larry Rivers, Eilshemius, Kline, de Kooning, Jackson Pollock, Kuniyoshi, Milton Avery, Philip Evergood, Stuart Davis, Feininger, and Hans Hofmann. . . .
>
> I would be pleased to contribute my *entire* collection to the Smithsonian Institution under the conditions mentioned above. In addition to my collection, which is worth many millions of dollars, I would be prepared

to contribute $1 million towards the construction of a museum on the indicated site. . . .

Lady Bird Johnson asked the Hirshhorns to come half an hour early for a tour of the White House. She much admired Eakins and hoped he would put one of the painter's works in the mansion. She had invited Ripley, Stevens, Harris, and Fortas with their wives. At the luncheon Stevens estimated the cost of the museum at $10 million and architect Nathaniel Owings was said already to be at work on the design. Ripley called the gift the greatest to the nation since Andrew Mellon's.

In the middle of the luncheon, Mrs. Johnson wrote, "Lyndon came in, met everybody, thanked Mr. Hirshhorn, and boldly said what I had been wanting to say and couldn't—that it was wonderful that the people of the United States were going to be able to enjoy art works, but that it would be downright selfish if the White House itself didn't get an example." She received the Eakins, a portrait of a little girl, in 1967.

The President, Fortas later recalled, "had a selling job to do and he did it magnificently." He put his arm around Hirshhorn and said, "Joe, you don't need a contract. Just turn the collection over to the Smithsonian and I'll take care of the rest." The collector almost succumbed. "Once the President puts his arm around your shoulder, you're a dead cookie. . . . I knew then there was going to be a deal." But he turned to Harris and said, "What do you think, Sam?" Harris said, "We ought to think about it."

After the President left, Fortas said, "You don't have to worry about this, Joe. Just do as the President says." Harris was angered. "To hell with that, Abe!" Although Johnson had just won a great election victory, Presidents lose power, become ill, or die. "Over my dead body are you going to get this collection without the conditions written into the contract and a statute passed."

The negotiation of the agreement took about a year. Lerner had to prepare a precise inventory of all the works that would be turned over, and Ripley carefully reviewed the Freer and Mellon contracts. During this period Fortas was named to the Supreme Court and Harry McPherson replaced him for the White House.

The agreement was signed on May 17, 1966, by Hirshhorn, Harris, and Ripley. The significant terms were as follows: Congress would enact and the President would approve "no later than ten days after the close of the 90th Congress" [January 1969] legislation providing: The site bounded by Seventh Street, Independence Avenue, Ninth Street, and Madison Drive would be occupied solely by the museum and sculpture garden and the existing structure would be torn down. The new edifice would be called the Joseph H. Hirshhorn Museum and Sculpture Garden, would be free to the public, and would be administered by the Smithsonian. The United States pledged to provide funds for "upkeep, operation, and maintenance." The museum would be administered by a board of trustees of ten members, two ex officio, the Chief Justice of the United States and the secretary of the Smithsonian, and eight named by the President from lists of four nominated by Hirshhorn and four by the Smithsonian.

Hirshhorn and Ripley jointly would select the architects and would approve their plans. The $1 million gift would be used for the acquisition of art. The first director would be chosen by Hirshhorn and approved by Ripley. (Abram Lerner would hold that position.) In the event that the legislation was not enacted in time or the museum was not built within five years thereafter, "this Agreement shall be null and void and the proposed gifts . . . shall not be consummated."

On November 7, 1966, the Congress by resolution accepted the Hirshhorn gift and approved the site on the Mall. The time requirements fixed by the agreement and their potential sanctions put pressure on the Johnson administration. It had to remove two large obstacles before construction could begin. The first was the red-brick Victorian monstrosity called the Armed Forces Museum of Pathology, which McPherson considered "a strong candidate for ugliest-in-Washington." It was at 7th Street and Independence Avenue, smack inside the Hirshhorn site. It had been built in 1887 and for many years had been the headquarters of the Armed Forces Institute of Pathology, a medical library, and a museum. The headquarters had moved to Walter Reed Hospital in 1955 and the library to the Public Health Service in 1956. Only the museum remained on the Mall and it occupied half the building; the remainder was used for offices. Ripley thought the collection almost worthless except for a notable group of microscopes, which many museums would be glad to have. The Bureau of the Budget considered the pathology specimens of "morbid interest only."

But the pathologists refused to move, rejecting several attractive offers the White House made, including three buildings at the Bureau of Standards. They generated a big letter-writing campaign that seriously damped support for the Hirshhorn in the House. The long-range plan was to give them a new museum-laboratory at Walter Reed and they demanded that Congress package it with the art museum. The price for construction was $7.5 million. Due to the budgetary slowdown on construction, McNamara was reluctant to act, but the White House pushed him to ask for an appropriation. In October 1967 the House Appropriations Committee made life more difficult by eliminating the Hirshhorn appropriation. The administration asked for its restoration. McPherson wrote to Budget Director Schultze, "I've talked to the boss about this. He is determined that nothing be left undone that will help us secure the Hirshhorn bequest." The President and Mrs. Johnson talked to Appropriations Committee chairman George Mahon of Texas and he agreed to restore the funds. McPherson's summary: "The arithmetic is that in exchange for a $30 million art collection, we build a $10–12 million gallery and a $7.5 million museum-laboratory at

Walter Reed that we would have in any event constructed in a few years."
He thought the deal a bargain for the government.

The other problem was the constriction of the federal budget resulting
from the Vietnam War and the Great Inflation, which threatened the funds
for the Hirshhorn. Ripley had little trouble lobbying through an appropriation of $803,000 for the architects in the fiscal 1968 budget. The contract
was awarded to Skidmore, Owings and Merrill, with Gordon Bunshaft as
principal architect. His bold and striking design gained the approval of the
Commission of Fine Arts and the National Capital Planning Commission.
The plans were ready for construction in July 1968. But the cost with inflation had now risen to $14,197,000. Hirshhorn agreed to amend the
agreement to defer the date of completion.

The congressional subcommittees, Ripley wrote, are "very nervous
about defending this on the floor" because it would represent a 66 percent
increase in the Smithsonian's budget. It would look "horrendous" in an
"appallingly austere year." He had another idea: the installment plan. Since
construction costs in the first year would be lower than they would become
later, he suggested limiting the fiscal 1969 request to $2 million, "a very
attractive reduction." The Bureau of the Budget approved and he persuaded
Congress to go along.

Ground was broken on January 8, 1969, in a ceremony featuring Chief
Justice Warren, President Johnson, and Dillon Ripley, all very large men,
and Joe Hirshhorn, barely more than five feet tall. The photographs show
that all enjoyed themselves, particularly the donor.

The museum and sculpture garden opened on October 1, 1974. Hirshhorn was now 75. Lyndon Johnson was no longer alive. The dignitaries
present at the ceremony were Lady Bird Johnson, Hubert Humphrey, Senator Fulbright, and Daniel Patrick Moynihan, the ambassador to India. Bunshaft's radical design was encased in a four-story hollow concrete cylinder
sheathed in pink granite. The galleries opened onto a central court. The
museum was set in a garden filled with sculpture. Many considered the
structure stunning and a fitting showplace for modern art. Others were critical because it deviated markedly from the nearby neo-classical National
Gallery and the red brick of the Victorian Smithsonian. Critics called it a
"gargantuan bagel" or the "world's largest doughnut."

The museum opened on a bright and warm autumn day. Only 900 of
the more than 6000 works contributed were on display. It proved an immense success with the public. Within a year it ranked sixth in the nation
in attendance. By 1976 it was drawing 25,000 visitors a day and had passed
the Museum of Modern Art and the Chicago Art Institute, surpassed only
by the Metropolitan, the National Gallery, and the Los Angeles County
Art Museum. Joe Hirshhorn sold his estate in Connecticut and moved to
Washington to be near "his" museum. "The intercession of President Lyn-

don B. Johnson," Abram Lerner wrote, "made Mr. Hirshhorn's choice inevitable." [4]

On October 26, 1967 Chief Justice Warren in his capacity as chairman of the trustees of the National Gallery of Art wrote the President that in 1937 Andrew Mellon had given to the nation his collection and the funds to build the National Gallery. The congressional resolution of acceptance provided that an adjoining area bounded by Fourth Street, Pennsylvania Avenue, Third Street, and North Mall Drive shall be "reserved as a site for future additions to the National Gallery. . . ." The trustees had now decided that this site should be used for a new building to provide for exhibition space, expansion of the gallery's extension program, now serving 3000 communities in all 50 states, and educational and cultural programs. Mellon's son Paul, who was president of the gallery, and Paul's sister, Mrs. Ailsa Mellon Bruce, had just contributed securities and cash "to the value of approximately $20,000,000." With other funds available, this would cover all costs. Legislation had been proposed for Congress to authorize the new building. The Chief Justice asked for the President's support.

Douglas Cater of the White House staff called John Walker, director of the gallery, who said no federal funds would be needed until the building was completed, hopefully in 1972, and they would be for operating expenses. He suggested a small ceremony to express gratitude to the Mellons. But Paul Mellon was abroad.

Thus, the President merely issued a statement on November 6 expressing gratitude on behalf of the nation to the Mellons and urging Congress to authorize the addition. He pointed out that this structure would contribute to the "enrichment and beautification of the Nation's Capital." The architect, I. M. Pei, was widely acclaimed for his neo-classical design. The new wing, in fact, cost $94.4 million, all of it contributed by the Mellons, and opened in July 1978.

Walter Hopps, curator of the National Collection of Fine Arts, said, "Symbolically, I think, it's marvelous that juxtaposed to Mr. Mellon's institution there will be Mr. Hirshhorn's. It is altogether fitting and proper. Both were great; both had the morality of the Great White Shark; and the only thing that differentiates them was their taste and sensibility." [5]

In the 1930s radio was the sole medium of broadcasting and was dominated by three networks—the Red, the Blue—both owned by the National Broadcasting Company—and the Columbia Broadcasting System. During World War II the Federal Communications System ordered NBC to spin off one of its networks in order to increase competition. The Blue Network, the weaker, became the American Broadcasting Company.

Television broadcasting had become technically feasible on the eve of the war and the FCC issued transmission standards in 1941. NBC and CBS immediately established anchor stations in New York. But the war prevented development. In the U.S. in 1944 there were only 7000 receivers for six stations that broadcast four hours a week.

At the end of hostilities the FCC imposed a freeze on the industry to give itself time to study broadcast standards, particularly the use of very high frequency (VHF) as against ultra high frequency (UHF). It selected VHF. Since that part of the spectrum provided only 13 channels and 6 were reserved for noncommercial purposes, only 7 were available. This created a continuing shortage of stations. Nevertheless, the industry developed with phenomenal speed. By 1959 there were 50 million receivers in 86 percent of U.S. homes served by over 500 stations. Since the FCC multiple ownership rule limited an owner to five VHF and two UHF stations, virtually all outlets were owned by persons other than the networks. But almost all the stations became affiliates of one or several of the networks to gain access to national programming.

This system depended upon advertising for its income. The program attracted viewers who did not pay to watch it; the advertiser paid for the program in order to attract an audience for his commercial message. Thus, the bigger the audience, the more the advertiser shelled out to the network and the stations. The network was shaped to reach virtually every receiver in the U.S. and programs were produced to maximize audience size on the ridiculous assumption that everyone had the same tastes and that no part of the audience should be lost because it objected to the show. Thus, the programs became stereotyped and inoffensive—westerns, mysteries, sitcoms, and so on—and were "lowbrow" at best. Since TV was a very effective advertising medium, networks and stations became extremely profitable. Many members of Congress received FCC licenses for stations, Lyndon Johnson among them—he and his wife owned KTBC-TV, the only station in Austin, an affiliate of all three networks.

During the era of radio a number of universities, mainly land-grant institutions in the Midwest and the West, had established educational stations. But they had extremely limited funds, broadcast on very low power, and had difficulty surviving. In 1951, when there were 2200 AM stations, only 37 were educational. FM brought in another 170, which were also weak. They banded together in the National Association of Educational Broadcasters, which looked hopefully to a brighter future in TV. During the FCC freeze NAEB lobbied to reserve channels for noncommercial broadcasting and found a champion in Commissioner Frieda Hennock. In 1951 a financial savior appeared in the Ford Foundation's Fund for Adult Education, which, as part of a comprehensive program to support noncommercial TV, pledged $12 million to provide equipment and programming for stations. The next year the FCC held aside parts of both the VHF and UHF spectrums for educational broadcasting.

The first educational station went on the air in 1953; by 1966 there were 124, mainly VHF, but shifting increasingly to UHF. Of this number, 41 were community stations, 35 were run by universities, 27 by state boards of education, and 21 by school districts. These stations were linked together by National Educational Television, which supplied half the programming—five hours a week of cultural and public affairs shows either produced by NET itself or rented from abroad, largely from the BBC. NET duplicated programs and distributed them by mail. Electronic interconnection, which was far superior, was too expensive for simultaneous nationwide broadcasting, but was used locally in the Northeast, California, and Oklahoma. Despite a total Ford subvention of $120 million, supplemented by governments at all levels, as well as industry and subscriber support, the system was seriously underfunded and its future was in great doubt.[6]

In December 1964 a conference of the National Association of Educational Broadcasters in Washington unanimously proposed a presidential commission to study the financial needs of their system and recommend a national policy. Shortly NAEB leaders met with White House aide Douglas Cater, the HEW leadership—Gardner, Cohen, and Keppel—and FCC Chairman E. William Henry. They agreed on the desirability of a commission, but disagreed over whether it should be appointed by the President or by a private body, a responsibility the Carnegie Corporation was willing to assume. The President, because of his station in Austin, insisted that there should be no conflict of interest, real or apparent. Carnegie won by default.

Gardner handled the selection of the chairman and proposed James Killian, Jr., chairman of the MIT corporation. The secretary wanted the President's approval. While Johnson would have preferred someone else, he did not oppose the choice. In fact, Killian did a masterful job. On October 28, 1965, the Carnegie Corporation announced the members of the Carnegie Commission on Educational Television: Killian, chairman; James B. Conant, former president of Harvard; Lee DuBridge, president of Caltech; Ralph Ellison, the noted black writer; John Hays of the Washington *Post;* David Henry, president of the University of Illinois; Oveta Culp Hobby, president of the Houston *Post;* K. C. Kellam, president of Texas Broadcasting; Edwin Land, president of Polaroid; Joseph McConnell, president of Reynolds Metals; Terry Sanford, former governor of North Carolina; Rudolph Serkin, the famed pianist; and Leonard Woodcock, vice president of the UAW. Carnegie would finance the commission to the tune of $500,000.

The commission's study was comprehensive and thorough. It held 28 days of formal meetings and many others of smaller groups; it heard from 225 individuals and groups; it visited 92 stations in 35 states in addition to 7 foreign systems; and it employed Arthur D. Little, Inc., to prepare the cost estimates. Its report, *Public Broadcasting: A Program for Action,* was published in January 1967 and made a very big splash. Besides its recommendations, the title of the report transformed the discussion from the awkward and obsolete *educational* TV system to the new and exciting prospect for *public* television. Henceforth educational television would be narrowed to "instructional television, directed at students in the classroom." Public television "includes all that is of human interest and importance which is not at the moment appropriate or suitable for support by advertising and which is not arranged for formal instruction."

The commission's vision of the new system differed fundamentally from the network-dominated commercial system. It assumed *diversity* over *uniformity* of tastes. This argued for program production from several sources—a central authority to be called the Corporation for Public Broadcasting, the local stations, and independent producers.

The corporation would play the leading role. To avoid congressional intervention, it should be a federally chartered, nonprofit, nongovernmental institution, but with members appointed by the President. It would be the major recipient of government and private funds, disbursing them to national program production agencies, to local stations both to improve their facilities and to produce programs, and for electronic interconnection.

Interconnection could be used in two distinct ways—networking to transmit a single signal to all stations for simultaneous broadcast, as the commercial networks operated, or distribution of a program from a central point to stations which then had the option of playing it simultaneously or of recording it for later showing at the station's discretion. On the diversity principle the commission anticipated that most programs would be broadcast at different times to fit the individual station's schedule.

A national system so constituted would be expensive. The commission's recommendation for financing was on the European and Canadian examples, an excise tax on television receivers of between 2 and 5 percent. The receipts would be placed in a trust fund upon which the corporation could draw. This would insulate the corporation politically against the annual congressional appropriations process.

Killian engaged Covington & Burling, the noted Washington law firm, to draft a bill. The Carnegie report was circulated widely within the government and received general approval. The key senators, John Pastore of Rhode Island and Warren Magnuson of Washington, were enthusiastic. The educational broadcasters, of course, were ecstatic. The Ford Foundation, now headed by McGeorge Bundy, was a strong supporter. So were the commercial networks, particularly CBS and NBC; ABC went along. In fact, Dr. Frank Stanton, president of CBS, promised a $1 million gift to the new system. He told Cater that he had concluded that the excise tax was the only way to go to get "reasonable insulation from Rooney's world." Thomas Hoving, director of the Metropolitan Museum, formed a citizens' committee to back the report. But Assistant Secretary of the Treasury Stanley Surrey wrote that a tax on receivers would be "more regressive than any excise tax we have or have had, with the exception of the tax on smoking tobacco."

On February 28, 1967, the President sent a special message to Congress in which he endorsed passage of the bill to create the Corporation for Public Broadcasting with a one-year funding of $10.5 million for construction and $9 million for operations. He said nothing about a tax on receivers, but he did establish an internal and secret task force to weigh long-term financing of the system. The only other significant deviation from the Carnegie report was the inclusion of public radio.[7]

Johnson's decision to strip away the Carnegie recommendation for assured financing had a very important permanent result. It meant that the conservatives who dominated Congress in 1967 would control the corporation's funding through the annual appropriations process; in addition, the Republicans among them expected to capture the presidency and perhaps the Congress in 1968. Thus, they felt little concern over a bill that would operate on a shoestring. This guaranteed its passage.

Magnuson, chairman of the Commerce Committee, introduced the bill, and Pastore, chairman of the Subcommittee on Communications, held hearings during April 1967. The administration, the foundations, and both the commercial and educational broadcasters testified in favor. In fact, there was no opposition. The Commerce Committee on May 11 reported it in almost exactly the form in which it had been introduced. The Senate adopted it by voice vote on May 17, 1967.

The House proved only a little more difficult. The Commerce Committee held hearings in July and listened to the same witnesses. It reported a bill amended mainly to assure political neutrality on August 21 by a vote of 15 to 6, all the latter Republicans. The House acted favorably on September 21 by a roll call of 265 to 91.

The conference resolved the differences between the bills in favor of the House on October 18. The House the next day and the Senate on October 26 accepted the report, and the President signed the Public Broadcasting Act on November 7, 1967, at the White House.

Title I extended the life of a 1962 law that subsidized the construction of TV station facilities for three years and increased coverage to public radio. It authorized appropriations of $10.5 million in 1968, $12.5 in 1969, and $15 million in 1970.

Title II created the nonprofit, nongovernmental Corporation for Public Broadcasting to funnel funds to the system, not as a network. The corporation was forbidden to own stations. It would assist stations with their operating costs to produce programs, finance program producers, and establish interconnection. CPB would be governed by a board of 15 directors. Stations were prohibited from editorializing or taking sides in elections. The corporation was banned from interference in the affairs of stations and was directed to adhere to objectivity and balance with controversial programs. CPB received an appropriation of $9 million for 1968 and nothing more for the future.

Johnson waited until after he signed the law before he appointed the internal task force on financing public broadcasting. It consisted of Califano, his assistant James Gaither, Budget Director Zwick, Schultze, Cohen, and Mel White of the Treasury. The task force made a careful study of financial needs on the assumption that funding must be insulated from the political process to the maximum extent possible. It proposed $30 million in 1969, rising swiftly to $135 million in 1973. There would be three possible sources: (1) either a tax on commercial broadcasters or a tax on TV and radio receivers; (2) federal matching of the funds raised by donations from other sources; and (3) general revenues of the Treasury deposited in a trust fund, as with Social Security. The President did not make a choice from these alternatives and made no financing proposal to Congress. By now, 1968, his standing on Capitol Hill, particularly on new taxes, had vanished.

Johnson's final responsibility under the new law was to nominate the board of directors of CPB, which he announced on February 17, 1968. Frank Pace, Jr., became chairman. He had been Director of the Budget and Secretary of the Army under Truman, president of General Dynamics, and chairman of Eisenhower's National Goals Commission. Killian and Hobby came over from the Carnegie Commission. The movie industry supplied Johnson's former aide, Jack Valenti, now of the Motion Picture Producers Association, and Robert S. Benjamin of United Artists. Two were former governors—Joseph D. Hughes of New Jersey and Carl Sanders of Georgia. Milton Eisenhower had just left the presidency of Johns Hopkins and Frank Schooley was from Illinois and NAEB. Michael A. Gammino was a Rhode Island banker, a friend of Pastore; Saul Haas was a Seattle broadcaster and a friend of Magnuson. John D. Rockefeller III had been the main force behind Lincoln Center and Erich Leinsdorf was music director of the Boston Symphony and a friend of LBJ. Roscoe C. Carroll was a black attorney from Los Angeles and Joseph A. Beirne was president of the Communication Workers Union.

This able new board faced formidable difficulties. The recruitment of a staff moved slowly and CPB did not get a president until after Nixon's election. John W. Macy, Jr., former chairman of the Civil Service Commission, took office in February 1969.

The funding problem was crippling. The new system needed a massive infusion of money at the outset to build up station equipment and operating capability, to provide interconnection, and to finance program production. Johnson's task force had anticipated this need and had proposed a hefty increase in the appropriation. But Nixon distrusted public broadcasting and kept its funding very low. When he vetoed the 1973 appropriation, Macy and his top aides resigned. Between 1972 and 1987 the federal government's contribution to public television ranged from a niggardly 16 to 28 percent of its actual expenditures. "The failure to provide adequate funding," Bruce McKay wrote, "invalidated the conditions of the public broadcasting experiment at least as seriously as the denial of [political] insulation."

Interconnection proved difficult, exposed internal division within the system, and consumed more than a year to resolve. CPB, supported by the Ford Foundation, urged creation of a new agency that would, like a network, both produce and distribute programs to its affiliates. But the stations, particularly the large ones, feared centralization of authority in such an agency. Intense and prolonged negotiations led to a compromise settlement. The Public Broadcasting System (PBS) was incorporated in 1969 with authority both to produce and to distribute programs, but the stations received five of the nine seats on its board of directors.

Despite these problems, the remarkable fact about the Public Broadcasting Act of 1967 was that the system it created—CPB, PBS, and National Public Radio—survived and blossomed. In both television and radio the programming sought to fulfill the goals of the Carnegie Commission: service to substantial fragmented audiences with variable tastes along with a stress on public affairs, the arts, and culture to fill the virtual vacuum left by commercial broadcasting. While the initiative to establish this important system had come from the Ford and Carnegie foundations, Lyndon Johnson had responded at once when he received the Carnegie report. It is unfortunate that it did not arrive until 1967 when his control over Congress was so diminished that he could not get adequate funding, in fact, did not even try.[8]

On November 21, 1968, shortly before Johnson left the White House, he and Mrs. Johnson invited the National Council on the Arts to dinner. In introducing the President, Roger Stevens offered this assessment: "President Johnson has done more for the arts than any other President in the history of the United States." Stevens could have added public television and radio. Odd, but true.[9]

18

Model Cities

BY the sixties the large American city had become a bundle of distressing problems—overpopulation, white flight to the suburbs, black ghettoes, unemployment, eroding housing and schools, crime, drugs, transportation bottlenecks, inadequate medical care, and so on, through a long and depressing litany. The universities had begun serious study of urban issues and the Ford Foundation was investing in a pilot program to deal with them in New Haven.

In shaping a study or in devising a policy on the city there are two ways to go. Either one can chip off a discrete problem—such as local or metropolitan government, land use, housing, black ghettoes, or the suburbs—or one can treat the city as an integrated whole in which these problems are interrelated. Historically the literature had concentrated on separate issues and federal policy for a generation had been similarly piecemeal—housing, urban renewal, community facilities, financing, one after the other.

In 1959 scholars at Harvard and MIT formed the Joint Center on Urban Studies to conduct research on city problems. They came from anthropology, architecture, business, city planning, economics, education, engineering, history, law, philosophy, political science, and sociology. Their many studies were published by the Harvard and MIT university presses. The Joint Center soon became the nation's leading source of urban scholarship.

The members of the center encompassed a diversity of views. On the right scholars like Edward C. Banfield and James Q. Wilson argued that the cities would be better off if the federal government retreated to Washington and allowed the local market free rein. The majority committed themselves to the piecemeal approach and worked on their particular specialties. Robert C. Wood, the chairman of MIT's Political Science Department, and Charles M. Haar, of the Harvard Law School, contended that the U.S. was in the midst of an urban crisis which called for a consolidated policy. As Wood put it, "the Cambridge urbanists, except for me and Charlie Haar, were mostly optimists and Pollyannas. They were really convinced that things were getting better in American cities, and so were not policy oriented."

In 1964–65 the Johnson administration, shaping the Great Society, went through a task force population explosion. Bill Moyers and Dick Goodwin established a large number in 1964 and Joe Califano did the same the next year. The labor market for task force members, especially chairmen, flourished. If Lyndon Johnson had prayed that the Lord would provide him with several superb chairmen, He would have sent the White House Robert C. Wood in triplicate.

Wood was born in St. Louis in 1923, but his parents were from the South—Tennessee, Alabama, and Florida. He was raised in Jacksonville and attended its schools. His mother, a school teacher, said that the city's schools functioned in an aura of "savage gentility." He was ready for college at the end of the depression but the family was strapped. Both of his brothers had gone to the University of Florida. "I was lucky," he said, "to get a scholarship at Princeton." He was there two and a half years and then served three with the 76th Infantry Division in the European Theater, completing his hitch with a Bronze Star. After the war he alternated between finishing his education at Princeton and the Littauer School at Harvard and working for the state government in Florida. He received a Ph.D. jointly in political economy and government from Harvard in 1950; by now government was his main interest. He taught briefly at Harvard and then shifted to MIT in 1957. He soon developed a great interest in urban problems.

In 1960 Wood advised John Kennedy and worked on the campaign from a distance. He was more involved in revitalizing the Democratic party in Massachusetts. In 1962 he helped Ted Kennedy in his first campaign for the Senate.

Early in 1964 J. K. Galbraith assembled a group of Cambridge experts, including Wood, to meet with Moyers and Goodwin on ideas for programs. It was, Wood said later, "a very, very good meeting. . . . Moyers was able to convey to that group the impression of an administration that was anxious for ideas and movement on the domestic field side." He had already served on a task force for Robert C. Weaver, the administrator of the Housing and Home Finance Agency. Wood had the impression that the Kennedy-Johnson administrations were moving toward his view that the U.S. faced an urban crisis that demanded an integrated policy.

Kennedy had proposed a severely limited program—the elimination of discrimination in housing, the elevation of HHFA to cabinet status as a department of urban affairs, and the promotion of Weaver to secretary, the first black to become a member of the cabinet. But Kennedy waited almost two years to propose a weak open housing executive order and the House Rules Committee bottled up the urban affairs department, leaving Weaver adrift.

In 1964 Johnson renewed the proposal to create a Department of Housing and Urban Development. In order to help shape the new agency's program, the President appointed a Task Force on Metropolitan and Urban Problems.

Wood was named chairman and he headed a group he called "very high powered people": Mayor J. P. Cavanaugh of Detroit, S. B. Klaman of the Association of Mutual Savings Banks, Ralph McGill of the Atlanta *Constitution,* Paul Ylvisaker of the Ford Foundation, Nathan Glazer, Norman Kennedy, Martin Meyerson, Catherine Bauer Wurster of Berkeley, Raymond Vernon of Harvard, and Karl Menninger of the Menninger Foundation. Menninger would interrupt the discussion periodically to say that everyone ought to go back to living on the farm. Wood wondered whether the White House had gotten the right Menninger brother. It was, Wood said, "a tough . . . report on which to get consensus." Nevertheless, the final result reflected the chairman's viewpoint. He delivered the document—comprehensive, acute, and well written—to the President on November 30, 1964.

The U.S., the task force declared, has been "an urban nation for at least 60 years. . . . Yet we have never fashioned a genuine national response to this . . . urban development." The report was "directed to that end." The prime function of the city was to "ensure options in choice of residence, place of work, meaningful leisure time activities, and effective civic participation." But citizens confronted many barriers in exercising these choices which, in turn, created "anxiety, alienation, and powerlessness." In the preceding 30 years the federal government had piled categorical programs one upon the other to assist cities. But they had not been integrated. The task force, therefore, recommended a number of different new programs, among them, block grants to allow local communities to attack their most pressing needs, rent supplements, strengthening the executive order barring discrimination in housing, support for law enforcement, assistance to city planning, large renewal projects to alter the character of entire neighborhoods, rehabilitation of older dwellings, a national system of development funds, and creation of an urban affairs council in the office of the President.

The impact of this part of the report on the President was clearly evident in his Special Message to the Congress on the Nation's Cities of March 2, 1965. It called for a comprehensive attack on urban problems and urged enactment of a number of the programs the task force had identified.

But there was something else. Leonard Duhl and Antonia Chayes of the National Institute of Mental Health had proposed that the report include a demonstration cities program in three major communities. The task force's final recommendation read as follows:

We believe there is need to accelerate the impact of the varied human development programs by a dramatic demonstration of ongoing and newly conceived urban aids in one or more especially chosen cities. Such a demonstration would involve long-range and short-term planning both for city-wide renewal and a comprehensive program of human services. The city should be of typical size and present typical problems of urbanization.

The selection of the cities could take place through procedures established by the White House. The recipients should be assured of Federal funds sufficient to develop a model program for urban America.

This was the origin of model cities.[1]

Johnson insisted that his task force reports be kept secret, but Mayor Cavanaugh of Detroit showed the demonstration cities proposal to Walter Reuther. Detroit, one of the nation's most racially divided cities, had suffered a massive race riot in 1943 and would soon have another.

Reuther, a man of exuberance and unrestrained rhetoric, embraced the idea enthusiastically. On May 13, 1965, he proposed to Johnson a crash program to build model neighborhoods in the blighted centers of six major cities—Washington, Detroit, Chicago, Philadelphia, Houston, and Los Angeles. They would be "VISIBLE examples of new environments, where new technologies of housing construction and prefabrication, new types of schools, new types of old age centers, recreational facilities and social services" would be erected. Each 700- to 1000-acre neighborhood would contain 15,000 living units housing 50,000 people. "What FDR created for the TVA as a worldwide symbol to combat erosion of the land, President Johnson is asked to initiate to stop erosion of life in urban centers among the lower and middle income population."

The White House sent a copy of Reuther's proposal to Haar. While he found the rhetoric "superfluous" and the details and implementation "obscure," the core idea "should be explored. The creation of entire new neighborhoods to replace decaying areas is a particularly exciting proposal." It would remedy the weaknesses of the current low-income programs. Public housing segregated the poor and the blacks and ignored recreation, education, and social services. Urban renewal displaced the same people and failed to provide them with alternative housing.

Haar preferred *one* carefully worked out model project with attention to relocation and cost. He thought the program should be put in a new agency rather than HHFA to encourage innovation. "It seems a worthwhile, albeit difficult, undertaking."

But demonstration cities had to wait as Johnson concentrated on pushing the bill creating the Department of Housing and Urban Development through Congress. Once that succeeded, he needed to name a secretary. While an expert on housing and an experienced bureaucrat, Weaver had drawbacks. Johnson, according to Kermit Gordon, preferred someone who was "stronger and more decisive and a more effective administrator than Bob Weaver." Moreover, he was unpopular on the Hill, having even alienated Mike Mansfield. But Johnson finally turned to Weaver and immediately ran into trouble with Senator John McClellan of Arkansas, whose committee vote was critical. This led to an involuted Johnsonian maneuver to buy off McClellan with federal funds to build roads in Arkansas. The result was the joint appointment of Weaver as secretary and Wood as under secretary, which was not announced until January 17, 1966. Herbert Kaufman, chairman of the Politics Department at Yale, wrote Wood, "I've thought of many ways to get out of being chairman of a Political Science Department, including suicide, but I never thought of anything that drastic." Haar became Assistant Secretary for Metropolitan Development.

The Watts Riot in August 1965 convinced Johnson to turn to demonstration cities. On September 17 Reuther was in the Oval Office with a dramatic pitch, urging the President to dream and to lead. Johnson was much impressed and promised that he would name a task force.

By mid-October Califano had made most of the selections. Wood, of course, would be chairman and Haar was the only other academic. Reuther, Whitney Young of the Urban League, William Rafsky of the Old Philadelphia Development Corporation, and Edgar Kaiser of Kaiser Industries were also members. Budget Director Schultze worried that Reuther might bust the budget and insisted on adding Kermit Gordon, now at Brookings. The President brought in Ben Heineman of the Chicago & Northwestern Railroad and Senator Ribicoff of Connecticut. The task force received space in the Executive Office Building, a staff, and Harry McPherson as White House liaison. The President, obviously, took this group very seriously. The deadline was December 15, 1965, and Wood, as usual, was on time.

The main thrust of the report was to urge a massive demonstration cities program. Miserly Haar had suggested one city and big spender Reuther had proposed six. Ribicoff strongly urged many more and Johnson, speaking through his task force, made Haar and Reuther look like pikers. The total number was 66—6 with populations over 500,000, 10 between 250,000 and 500,000, and 50 with fewer than 250,000. This big number, Ribicoff stressed, was politically necessary in order to gain the votes of members of Congress who were getting something for their constituents. Thus, all U.S. cities would be invited to compete and a presidential commission would select the winners. Lyle Fitch, a task force staff member, had pointed out that in the space and giant electron accelerator programs the government had successfully stimulated competition with clearly defined objectives and big prizes for winners in the form of federal contracts.

"The objective," the task force wrote, "is to completely eliminate blight in the designated area and to replace it with attractive economic shelter in a neighborhood with amenities essential to a full life." They included schools, hospitals, parks, playgrounds, and community centers. The large cities would each provide 24,000 new or refurbished households to house 50,000 people, the medium-sized 7500 for 25,000, and the small 3000 units for 10,000 people. Each new neighborhood would be integrated by both income and race. While the federal government would provide standards and financing, "the demonstration should establish appropriate mechanisms to foster development of local leadership and widespread citizen participation."

The task force estimated the cost of this program over five years at $2.3 billion. The federal contribution would be 80 percent, approximately $1.9 billion. Local funds would make up the remaining 20 percent. The President and Califano assured Wood that the federal funds, despite the Vietnam War, would be readily available. But this was 1965 when the government was lying to itself about the cost of Vietnam.

The President's insistence on secrecy proved costly in several ways. Since the task force report did not arrive until December 15, 1965, and the President wanted to submit the bill to the new Congress in January 1966, it was written hastily. "Drafted in a week of intensive writing and rewriting," Haar wrote, "the bill was a translation of task force prose into legislativese." Weaver was not consulted until the very end and would not have known what the task force would propose except for a leak. Califano did discuss the report with Labor Secretary Wirtz, who did not think it would work. Wirtz considered it virtually impossible for local officials to be given authority to spend federal funds at their own discretion. Almost all appropriations had to be allocated as Congress specified. Even when administrators had a little discretion, they were under pressure to spend money as Congress intended and as the interest groups expected. But Congress was not consulted at all, leaving the administration open to the charge that it was stuffing something Congress had no hand in preparing down its throat.[2]

On January 26, 1966, the President sent a package of six bills to Congress dealing with urban problems of which demonstration cities was the centerpiece. The next day Wright Patman introduced the measures in the House and Paul Douglas and 15 co-sponsors did so in the Senate. The package was sent to the respective Banking and Currency committees. Demonstration cities was brief and hazy.

"The Congress," it read, "hereby finds and declares that improving the quality of urban life is the most critical urban problem facing the United States." A comprehensive city demonstration program to rebuild a blighted area would be eligible for federal assistance for both planning and reconstruction. The federal government would pay 90 percent of the former and 80 percent of the latter. In each city with a program a federal coordinator would bring all the federal programs together to assist the demonstration. Each plan must provide for relocation of families and businesses displaced. The bill authorized the appropriation of "such sums as may be necessary" to effectuate the program. The statute would terminate on June 30, 1971, that is, be operative for five years.

These were bare bones. In his testimony Weaver fleshed them out. While all cities would be eligible to compete, only 60 to 70 would be chosen. The federal government would provide $12 million for planning and about $2 billion for construction over five years.

Califano had a "great dispute" with Johnson over this bill because it was "so complicated." He wanted to leak it two weeks in advance so that the reporters would have time to understand it, but the President refused because it would antagonize Congress. When Califano held the briefing, an unusually long one, the questions were "too complicated and bad." When finished, he "felt terrible." He had not gotten through. The wire service stories were "abominable." As a result many in Congress and the public never understood what model cities was all about.

The House Subcommittee on Housing of the Banking and Currency Committee heard 75 witnesses between February 28 and March 25, 1966. There was immediate trouble. The *New York Times* reported that the real price tag was double the published estimate. The interest groups that traditionally supported housing were at best ambivalent. The mayors, who were for the bill, had important reservations, particularly over the inadequacy of the funding. Mayor Hugh Addonizio of Newark asked for $10 billion. Cavanaugh of Detroit opposed competition. Lindsay of New York said his five boroughs alone could sop up $2 billion. Daley of Chicago asked for a sharp increase in planning funds. Labor, minority, and consumer groups hardly voiced support. The President, deeply involved in Vietnam, was silent. The Republicans complained about not being consulted or even informed in advance. Weaver was left carrying the ball with no interference. The Democrats on the subcommittee split and the chairman, William A. Barrett of Philadelphia, had no control. On April 6 Weaver informed Larry O'Brien that prospects for enactment were dim. A month later the *Times* proclaimed the bill "dead." The subcommittee, on the other hand, seemed to be moving toward evisceration, including a *total* appropriation of $12 million. The White House appeared to be on another planet.

By the end of May the subcommittee was hopelessly split and, since it was more liberal than its parent, the outlook was, indeed, bleak. Henry Wilson, who worked the Hill for the President, pointed to three fundamental problems: there was no "enthusiasm" among members or the lobbies; representatives were "deeply apprehensive" about racially integrated housing in a time of white backlash; and $2.3 billion was an awful lot of money during a war. Barrett was unenthusiastic and feared "tremendous problems on the House floor." To avoid them, he was working on a deal with the Republicans to cut the appropriation to $12 million for planning alone. Weaver thought the representatives from states without big cities would be interested if the planning appropriation was boosted to $100 million to be split among 400 communities. In many minds demonstration cities was turning into pork barrel.

On June 6, while the President was at his ranch, Califano, O'Brien, Schultze, Weaver, Wood, Haar, Wilson and his assistants, Manatos and Semer, along with McPherson and White House aide Barefoot Sanders held a strategy session. The Barrett idea was quickly rejected as an "emasculation of the bill." "The Administration should fight for its original demonstration cities proposal. . . . Weaver and Wood, as well as O'Brien and his troops are directing their efforts toward getting . . . the bill out of subcommittee and perhaps out of the full committee." The President heartily agreed.

This was followed by a massive lobbying campaign by the administration and a groundswell of support from industry, labor, civil rights, and religious groups. On June 23 an almost intact demonstration cities bill cleared the subcommittee 7 to 3 and the full Banking and Currency Committee on June 28, 1966, by a vote of 18 to 8. The President had gotten the Democrats to toe the line.

Now there was great concern about the House floor and the administration decided to move in the Senate. But there was a problem at the top. The nominal leader, Banking and Currency Chairman John Sparkman, would have nothing to do with demonstration cities. He was a moderate segregationist up for reelection in Alabama under attack from racists. No. 2, Paul Douglas, had the same problem. The Senate's leading champion of civil rights, he was engaged in a desperate struggle for reelection while wearing Chicago's bloodied shirt on his back from the struggle over housing. Douglas would lose. Edmund Muskie of Maine was now next in line and he was of two minds. Demonstration cities was certainly unpopular and his state had no big city. But, having performed brilliantly on pollution, his eye was now on the presidency and this might be a means of building his reputation in the big cities. He was impressed by the actions of the House committees and the President worked him over. He insisted on a number of changes in the bill to soften the language and to build a screen around the desegregation provision. Johnson ordered Califano and O'Brien to fly to Kennebunkport on July 6 to nail Muskie down. The weather was foul and they had to land at Pease Air Force Base in New Hampshire. The commander, expecting the worst, had ordered out the fire trucks and ambulances. But Jane Muskie cheered them up with a splendid lobster stew and they soon had the final language in order.

Now the subcommittee needed one more vote for a majority and a reluctant Thomas McIntyre of New Hampshire was chosen to provide it. He, too, was up for reelection. His state would have few, if any, qualifying cities and Portsmouth Naval Base was scheduled for closing. Since his constituents were proud of their frugality, he wanted a smaller price tag as well as deferral of the closing until after the election. Califano suggested the price: $12 million for planning and $900 million for the first two years; the appropriation for the next three years was deferred. McIntyre proposed the amendment to Muskie's bill, which was adopted. He could now brag to his constituents that *he* had reduced the appropriation. The subcommittee reported the bill favorably 6 to 4. The full committee added $12 million for planning in the second year and accepted Muskie's changes, approving the bill on August 10 by 8 to 6.

Weaver on August 9 sent the White House the Senate head count: 45 for the bill with 9 leaners and 41 against with 4 leaners. Muskie performed with his usual skill as floor leader; John Tower of Texas spoke for the Republicans. He did manage to add an amendment limiting any one state to 15 percent of the planning appropriation. Senator Fulbright made the most powerful speech. Arkansas, he noted, would derive little benefit from demonstration cities because Little Rock was the only town of any size. In the nation this was a summer "filled with strife and violence born of the despair and frustrations of those who seek a better life." Fulbright argued that "something must be done to arrest the human and environmental decay that blights the cities of America." At this time Congress was pouring $58 billion into araments and war and providing $5 billion to go to the moon, "one of the silliest undertakings any great nation ever undertook." Yet there was great opposition to spending $924 million for the cities. The nation's priorities were mixed up. No wonder, Fulbright said, "the people of Europe look upon the United States as the sick man of the world."

On August 9 Tower moved to eliminate all funds from the bill except for $24 million for planning. His amendment was defeated 53 to 27. The Senate then passed the demonstration cities bill by a vote of 53 to 22. The supporters consisted of 39 Democrats and 14 Republicans, the opponents of 13 Republicans and 9 Democrats.

This was a handsome victory for the administration based on the fact that this was still the northern Democratic 89th Congress. The question now was whether the House could be persuaded to accept the Senate bill.

The House subcommittee did so quickly on August 25 by a 9 to 1 vote. The Banking and Currency Committee agreed on September 1 by an easy 23 to 8. The House itself was much tougher. The extreme right wing—Dan Smoot, Billy Hargiss, and Fulton Lewis—conducted a racist campaign against the bill. Smoot broadcast that it was called "Demonstration Cities" because it would pay for Negro demonstrations in the big cities. A head count on September 10 showed the vote, including leaners, ahead 221 to 204, an uncomfortably close margin. Johnson weighed in with a massive lobbying campaign, including telegrams from 22 big businessmen headed by Henry Ford II and David Rockefeller. In the voting on October 14, 1966, a Republican motion to recommit the bill was defeated 175 to 149. The House then adopted it 178 to 141. The majority consisted of 162 Democrats and 16 Republicans, the minority of 60 Democrats and 81 Republicans. The President in the dying 89th Congress was able to hold his northern Democratic majority. There were secondary conflicts that were quickly resolved in conference on October 17. The Senate accepted them the next day 38 to 22 and the House followed on October 20 by 142 to 126.

At the signing ceremony in the East Room on November 3, 1966, the President, despite its official name—Demonstration Cities and Metropolitan Development Act—said that he was signing the "Model Cities" Act. He ordered everyone in the administration thereafter to use that name. He then told Califano, the author of the demonstration cities title, "Don't ever give such a stupid Goddamn name to a bill again." They both smiled.[3]

The timing of model cities could hardly have been worse. It was an extremely complex system which under the best of circumstances would have demanded a lot of time for congressional and public understanding. "The program's first two years," Haar wrote, "centered on struggles to get under way." Even worse, its political birth coincided with the arrival of the hostile 90th Congress and two years later it confronted the election of Richard Nixon, a President who detested model cities.

Weaver chose H. Ralph Taylor as Assistant Secretary for Demonstrations and Intergovernmental Relations on May 24, 1966, six months before the legislation was passed. Taylor had been executive director of the New Haven Redevelopment Agency, the pre-model cities model city, and had also worked for the Agency for International Development in Latin America. He picked Walter Farr, also an AID veteran, to head the Model Cities Administration within HUD. Both were dedicated to the program and got along very well.

Their first responsibility was to select the model cities and move them into the planning stage. Under the statute HUD was authorized to make a grant to a city demonstration agency to cover most of the cost of planning. The agency might be a city, a county, or a new organization created by the local government (usually City Hall) to administer the plan. "The application," HUD announced, "must show in broad and general terms the nature and seriousness of the city's problems and the outlines of what the city proposes to do." If possible, it was to stress innovation.

The standards that the plan must meet were comprehensive and formidable. The program would cover the following: (1) renewal of entire slum neighborhoods both physically and socially; (2) a substantial increase in the supply of standard housing of low and moderate cost; (3) "marked progress" in reducing social and educational disadvantages, ill health, and underemployment; (4) the prospect of being effectuated "reasonably soon"; (5) utilization of private enterprise; (6) relocation of families displaced; (7) integration with existing local development plans; and (8) an input from the residents of the blighted area.

At the outset most cities found it exceedingly difficult to meet these tests because they did not understand them, had no personnel available to devise the plan, or, if they hired consultants, discovered that they did little better. After screening by HUD, the proposals were reviewed by an inter-agency committee composed of representatives from HUD, Poverty, Labor, Justice, and Commerce. Their selections were then reviewed by Taylor, Weaver, and the White House (the President participated directly himself).

By May 1967 HUD had received 193 applications from cities of all sizes in 47 states, the District of Columbia, and Puerto Rico. In this first round 63 cities were chosen on November 16, 1967. In "round one and one-half" in March 1968 there were 12 more winners. In round two on September 6, 1968, Weaver added 33 others. Thus, almost two years were consumed in the preliminary step of city selection.

The process was heavily politicized. The lists of cities Weaver sent to the White House indicated the congressman who represented each town, his party, and whether or not he had voted for the bill. Texas did very well—Houston, San Antonio, Austin, and such other metropoli as Eagle Pass, Texarkana, and Laredo. In fact, Califano received weekly reports from HUD on the Austin application. Johnson wrote on the October 7, 1968, report: "Think moving much too slowly. Speed it up." Senator Muskie's sparsely settled Maine won grants for Portland and Lewiston. Senator Mansfield picked up Butte and Helena, Montana, and Carl Albert got Tulsa, Lawton, and McAlester, Oklahoma. Obscure members of House appropriation sub-committees received grants for such cities as Smithfield, Tennessee, and Pikesville, Kentucky. Mexican-Americans, concerned that blacks would squeeze them out, lobbied for communities with large Spanish-surnamed populations and won in at least Albuquerque and Eagle Pass.

A basic objective was to coordinate all federal programs at the local level to support the model city policy. This proved impossible. HUD's own urban renewal program, its largest, was potentially of great significance. But its officials viewed model cities as a threat by coopting funds intended for physical improvements and spending them on social programs as well as by turning its emphasis from high-value real estate into low-cost housing. Further, urban renewal worked through local agencies insulated against city hall, while model cities went straight to the mayor. There was a similar conflict with the Office of Economic Opportunity, whose community action agencies worked directly with the poor and bypassed city hall. Again, the Labor Department's manpower program flowed through the states and it was legally impossible to divert it to the cities. White House intervention through Califano to persuade these agencies to support model cities brought forth few results. While all offered words of cheer like these from Secretary Wirtz—"I wholeheartedly concur with your letter of September 27, 1968, on the importance of a coordinated Federal response to the Model Cities program"—none would turn over funds or significantly change procedures.

On December 23, 1968, a month and a half after Nixon's election,

HUD announced that the first Comprehensive Development Plan—for Seattle—had been approved. Eight more were accepted before inauguration day, January 20, 1969. While the new President was eager to terminate the program, he met opposition from mayors, governors, members of Congress, and his own HUD secretary, former Michigan Governor George Romney. Funding did not cease until June 30, 1973.[4]

Lyndon Johnson had extremely high hopes for the model cities program. He wrote in his autobiography that it was

> an entirely new way of approaching the problems of the slums. This new approach was based on the proposition that a slum is not merely decaying brick and mortar but also a breeding ground of human failure and despair, where hope is as alien as sunlight and green grass. Along with new buildings to replace the crumbling hovels where slum dwellers wore out their deprived existences, we needed to offer those slum dwellers a genuine opportunity to change their lives—programs to train them for jobs, the means of giving their children a better chance to finish school, a method for putting medical clinics and legal services within their reach. The proposal was an approach to the rebuilding of city neighborhoods in a total way, bringing to bear on a blighted community all the programs that could help in that task.

A noble vision, to be sure.

But, as conservatives never tired of pointing out, it was a mirage. "There was not in 1965, when the second task force did its work," Edward C. Banfield wrote, "the slightest possibility of a federal program being brought into existence which could accomplish any of the various large purposes that Model Cities was supposed to serve." No slums were cleared, no blighted areas were redeemed, low-cost housing was not provided, and there was no flood of new jobs, schools, medical clinics, social centers, and playgrounds in the ghettoes. There was neither enough time nor enough money to accomplish these goals, and the program was unable to overcome the complexities and gridlock inherent in the American system of government.

But there were some unanticipated accomplishments. Rufus P. Browning, Dale Rogers Marshall, and David H. Tabb studied the impact of model cities, along with the poverty program and urban renewal, in ten towns in the San Francisco Bay area. The questions they raised were narrower: Did these programs stimulate local governments to provide services to the poor and increase their ability to organize for the purpose of promoting the responsiveness of these cities? "Respondents were virtually unanimous in perceiving federal social programs as important in shaping both the mobilization and incorporation of minorities, and city government responsiveness. . . . Rather than quieting demands, the programs generated them by providing issues, a staff, and resources for organizing efforts." As a result, blacks and Mexican-Americans won public offices, became influential in city governments, and during the seventies won a growing share of federal funds under the revenue sharing and block grant programs to improve the lives of their constituents. This was hardly Lyndon Johnson's dream, but it resulted in hard gains for the minorities.[5]

19

The Collapse of the Johnson Presidency

JOHN Gardner had been Secretary of Health, Education and Welfare since August 18, 1965. It had been a superb period of his life, a time of enormous accomplishment. Further, "I had developed a great affection for HEW and, really, I loved the place, and I loved many of the people in it and it was mutual in many cases." He had fought "side-by-side with them" on important issues in an atmosphere of "excitement and exhilaration and real combat." He had developed a great admiration for Lyndon Johnson, "as easy man to work with" who gave Gardner "a free hand, . . . a lot of support." Most important, he provided a "positive movement that we all drew on."

In late 1967 and early 1968, however, Gardner had attended several cabinet meetings to discuss Johnson's reelection. "I found to my consternation . . . in early January that I did not think that the President should run for reelection, which put me in a terrible position. . . . Literally every day something was occurring in which I was privy to conversations that should only be participated in by loyal members of the family." The President, Gardner thought, had the right to expect that every member of his cabinet "supports him completely."

A few days later Gardner was in the Oval Office presenting a letter to the President announcing his resignation. Johnson asked why he was leaving. Gardner explained that he could no longer provide total allegiance because he had concluded that Johnson should not run. Again, why? "I . . . don't believe that you can unite the country. I . . . think we're in a terrible passage in our history and that you cannot do what needs to be done."

To Gardner's great surprise, the President said, "I've had the same thought many times." He continued, "I'm going to do what Harry Truman did. I'm going to wait until the end of March."

For both Lyndon and Lady Bird Johnson the departure of John Gardner was a painful loss. He was both an outstanding member of the administration and a treasured friend.

In mid-January Mrs. Johnson gave a luncheon for a large gathering of Women Doers on the topic of Crime in the Streets. After a lunch that was, she wrote, "a little on the sumptuous side," the speeches began. Shortly, Eartha Kitt, a prominent black singer, angrily denounced the Vietnam War. "We send the best of this country off to be shot and maimed. They rebel in the streets. They take pot and they will get high. They don't want to go to school because they are going to be snatched off from their mothers to be shot in Vietnam." She pointed her finger at Lady Bird and said, "You are a mother, too, although you have had daughters and not sons. . . . I have a baby and you send him off to war."

Mrs. Johnson was swept with "a wave of mounting disbelief." Then she took control of herself and closed the meeting. She had seen the reporters' pencils "racing across the pads." Eartha Kitt's outburst had created a brief press sensation.

Mayor Richard Daley of Chicago was a stalwart supporter of LBJ and was generally regarded as a confirmed hawk. Now, Larry O'Brien said, "I was taken aback when Daley expressed concern about Vietnam. He expressed it in human terms, his deep concern about the loss of life, then ultimately in political terms, his wonderment about the ultimate political fallout. . . . It had gotten to him." The fact that his best friend's son had been killed in Vietnam helped turn Daley against the war.

Commander Lloyd M. Bucher had spent 11 years on submarines. In December 1966 he received orders to transfer to secret Operation Clickbeatle, electronic intelligence by small unarmed auxiliaries in the waters of potential enemies. The Navy with Clickbeatle was copying a similar Soviet program, which, however, employed much larger vessels. After extended briefings, Bucher reported to the Bremerton Naval Shipyard on Puget Sound where the ship he would command, the USS *Pueblo,* was being overhauled and fitted with electronic gear. In heavy rain on January 29, 1967, he viewed his ship for the first time. His heart sank.

The *Pueblo* had been built 25 years earlier as a coastal freighter and had been in mothballs for a long time. She would now join two similar ships in the new operation. The *Pueblo* and her sisters may have been the smallest vessels in the Navy—176' long (shorter than some tugs), a 33' beam, displacing a mere 935 tons. A crew of 83 would be stuffed into bunks tiered four high; the galley was miniscule; toilet facilities were very short. The vessel was unseaworthy and needed virtually every kind of repair, plus installation of the electronic gear. She also received two .50 caliber machine guns, but there was no place to install them. The *Pueblo* did not complete sea trials and sail until November 6, 1967. The Pacific crossing required repairs both at Pearl Harbor and at Yokosuka on Tokyo Bay.

The *Pueblo* then labored in heavy seas around Honshu, through the Strait of Tsushima, and up the east coast of Korea. She was now fulfilling her mission by intercepting messages. Late on the afternoon of January 2, 1968, the *Pueblo* was off Wonsan and was observed by a North Korean subchaser, a Soviet built SO1, from 300 yards. The next day two North Korean trawlers inspected the ship from 100 yards.

On January 23 two subchasers and four torpedo boats surrounded and attacked the *Pueblo*. Escape was impossible. The vessel's top speed was about 12 knots, the subchasers 25, and the small boats about 50. Cannon and machine-gun fire killed one seaman and wounded three others. The superstructure was heavily damaged. Bucher was unable to bring his machine guns into the action. The North Koreans boarded the *Pueblo* and forced her into the port of Wonsan, where the crew was imprisoned. Bucher had radioed his predicament and the news sped up the chain of command.

That day, January 23, the President invited Secretary of Defense-designate Clark Clifford to the Tuesday lunch on national security. The news was dreadful and Johnson was weary and depressed. U.S. troops had inadvertently but seriously violated Cambodian neutrality, which demanded a public apology. The day before a B-52 loaded with nuclear weapons had crashed seven miles short of the runway in Greenland and was slowly sinking into the North Atlantic. Denmark was extremely sensitive about nuclear weapons on its territory. The biggest battle of the war in Vietnam was about to begin at Khe Sanh, where 6000 Marines were surrounded. There was talk of another Dienbienphu. Now the seizure of the *Pueblo!* Johnson, paranoid by now, was convinced that it was part of a Communist plot to encircle the U.S. He expected the next blow to fall in Berlin. He was wrong. The surly and ruthlessly independent North Koreans had acted alone. But the U.S. government, concerned about the 82 captive American sailors, had to remain powerless and silent. Rabid hawks denounced the President for failing to retaliate. Trevor Armbrister summarized: "An ill-prepared nation sends an unfit ship with an inexperienced crew on an unsuccessful, perhaps unnecessary mission off the coast of an unfriendly nation."

The real significance of the *Pueblo* incident, Armbrister wrote, was that it "demonstrated—perhaps more shockingly and convincingly than any event in recent years—the real limitations of American power." This is what critics of the Vietnam War, in particular Senators Fulbright, McCarthy, and Robert Kennedy, were saying. Within a week a far bigger demonstration of those limitations would take place.[1]

In July 1967 the North Vietnamese high command reexamined its strategy for a war of attrition to outlast the U.S. The enormous American build-up had changed the prospect from victory to stalemate, which delayed, if it did not threaten, the unification of the country under Hanoi. Thus, they reversed their strategy and called for a "General Offensive and General Uprising." It would be a grand throw of the dice in a massive attack which would, they hoped, generate a revolt of the people of South Vietnam to overthrow their puppet rulers and demoralize the Americans. For the remainder of the year they prepared their forces, North Vietnamese and Vietcong, and poured troops, munitions, and supplies down the Ho Chi Minh Trail.

Military operations started with heavy diversionary attacks around the periphery of South Vietnam intended to suck Westmoreland into a dispersion of his units. In October the North Vietnamese struck at the Marine base at Con Thien near the demilitarized zone, as well as at Loc Ninh and Song Be along the Cambodian border. In November they attacked Dak To in the central highlands. In December they advanced into the Mekong Delta. In January 1968 two crack North Vietnamese divisions moved against the Marines at Khe Sanh in the extreme northwest. From these attacks and many other items of intelligence Westmoreland concluded that a major offensive was in the offing, which he welcomed because of his great superiority in firepower.

Tet was the Vietnamese holiday celebrating the Chinese lunar New Year. It was the most important and sacred day of the year, universally recognized by all religions and social classes and respected in both North and South Vietnam. The northerners had stopped their fire on Tet starting in 1963 and Saigon and the U.S. had done so beginning with 1965. In 1968 they jointly agreed to lay down arms for 36 hours from 1800 on January 28 to 0600 on the 31st. The Year of the Monkey began on January 30.

On January 30–31, 1968, the North Vietnamese and the Vietcong broke the truce with the Tet offensive. It was, Herbert Y. Schandler wrote, "one of the great events of the Vietnam War, a high point in the military action, and, in all likelihood, the only battle of the war that will be long remembered. It has been seen by many as an historic turning point." It had never crossed Westmoreland's mind that the North Vietnamese would attack during Tet. A U.S. Military Academy textbook later stated: "The first thing to understand about Giap's Tet offensive is that it was an allied intelligence failure ranking with Pearl Harbor in 1941 or the Ardennes offensive in 1944. The North Vietnamese gained complete surprise."

The North Vietnamese and the Vietcong launched simultaneous and coordinated attacks against population centers throughout the South—39 of the 44 provincial capitals, 5 of the 6 autonomous cities, and at least 71 of 245 district towns. They aimed primarily at military command installations and centers of civilian authority, intending to shatter morale.

Some 35 battalions, about 4000 men, many in small teams, struck boldly in the Saigon region—Tan San Nhut Air Base, the Presidential Palace, the South Vietnamese Air Force headquarters, government buildings, the radio station, and, most dramatically, the American Embassy.

Nineteen Vietcong commandos reached the compound at 3 a.m.,

blasted a hole in the thick wall, and dashed inside with automatic weapons blazing, killing five Americans in minutes. It took U.S. troops more than six hours to kill the commandos and secure the embassy.

For the first time American television crews based in Saigon had a magnificent opportunity to photograph the raging war in the city itself. Heretofore they had voyaged out to the jungle or to the rice paddies to cover the unseen war. Americans at home, Stanley Karnow wrote, had grown accustomed to a "familiar pattern of images" on their TV screens, "the grueling reality of the struggle—remote, repetitious, monotonous, punctuated periodically by moments of horror." Now, on the January 31 evening news, they witnessed a "drastically different kind of war." "There, on color screens, dead bodies lay amid the rubble and rattle of automatic gunfire as dazed American soldiers and civilians ran back and forth trying to flush out the assailants." The most extraordinary footage was shot on a street corner. The crude, brutal General Nguyen Ngoc Loan, the chief of police, put his pistol to the head of a captured Vietcong and pulled the trigger. NBC showed the event in color on the news and AP photographer Eddie Adams captured it in black and white for the front page of virtually every newspaper in the U.S.

The most bitter battle of Tet took place in Hué, the ancient, beautiful, and cultivated city along the Perfume River on the north coast. Early on the morning of January 31 four powerful columns smashed into the city, overcame the defenders, and ran up the Vietcong flag on the citadel. They carried lists of "cruel tyrants and reactionary elements," rooted people out in house-to-house searches, and shot them, clubbed them to death, or buried them alive. Later about 3000 bodies were recovered in river beds, salt flats, and jungle clearings. The counterattack included South Vietnamese troops, many natives of Hué, who fought well. But the main burden was carried by three U.S. Marine battalions. With heavy artillery and air support they gradually occupied most of the city, pinning the enemy in the citadel. They were not overcome until February 25. By then about 80 percent of the city had been destroyed. The estimated number of soldiers killed: 140 Marines, 400 South Vietnamese, 5000 North Vietnamese and Vietcong. Again, much of the battle for Hué played in American living rooms on TV.

The Tet offensive was broken in eight weeks of bitter fighting which exacted a terrible cost in lives. Clark Clifford reported the number of killed: 3,895 Americans and 4,954 South Vietnamese. It was said that 58,000 of the enemy had also died in battle. While this astronomical figure was hard to believe, Karnow's interviews in the North after the war convinced him that it was "plausible." The Vietcong had been seriously battered and the North Vietnamese had sustained severe losses.

The Battle of Khe Sanh, the largest and bloodiest of the war, overlapped Tet and was fought for a ring of hills in the extreme northwest of South Vietnam between the demilitarized zone and the Laotian border. It was a tribute to Westmoreland's bad judgment. He thought the attacks on the cities to the south were a feint and that Khe Sanh was the main prize. In fact, it was the other way around. President Johnson was equally wrong, but for another reason. He thought the North Vietnamese were trying for a second Dienbienphu and was determined to prevent it. Obsessed, he had a sand table model of the Khe Sanh plateau built in the Situation Room in the basement of the White House. Unable to sleep, he would wander in during the night in his bathrobe to read the messages, to examine aerial photographs, and to get the latest casualty figures. Both sides poured in massive forces and suffered heavy losses. After Westmoreland left his command in June 1968, the Americans, Karnow wrote, conducted "a withdrawal . . . in secret to avoid jarring the American people."

The General Offensive and General Uprising had been a military failure. Giap had surprised the Americans and the South Vietnamese, but he did not defeat them. In fact, the South Vietnamese fought bravely and well to everyone's surprise. Moreover, the people of South Vietnam had not risen against their government. But the North Vietnamese and the Vietcong had not been defeated either. The war dragged on as before, a bitter stalemate. Tet's greatest impact was not on the war, but on the United States, where it was devastating.

Tet stood American public opinion on its head both toward the war and toward President Johnson. The widely held assumption of victory was snuffed out and the hope for an acceptable formula for settlement went with it. Tet made it clear that this would be a long, vicious war, a prospect most Americans could not bear. The views of Walter Cronkite, the CBS news anchor and the most respected of television journalists, were typical. He had supported the President on the war from the start. But after a visit to Vietnam, he made this report on February 27, 1968:

> It seems more certain than ever that the bloody experience of Vietnam is to end in a stalemate. This summer's almost certain standoff will either end in real give-and-take negotiations or terrible escalation; and for every means we have to escalate, the enemy can match us, and that applies to invasion of the North, the use of nuclear weapons, or the mere commitment of one hundred or two hundred or three hundred thousand more American troops to the battle. And with each escalation, the world comes close to the brink of cosmic disaster.
>
> To say that we are closer to victory today is to believe, in the face of the evidence, the optimists who have been wrong in the past. To suggest we are on the edge of defeat is to yield to unreasonable pessimism. To say that we are mired in stalemate seems the only realistic, yet unsatisfactory, conclusion.

White House press secretary George Christian said that when Cronkite made this report "the shock waves rolled through the Government." Bill Bundy thought Cronkite's defection was "an absolute landmark."

The polls dropped like stones in the water. In the six weeks between late January and early March 1968 Johnson's approval rating fell from 48 to 36 percent and those who supported his handling of the war declined from 40 to 26 percent. Over the same period seven major newspapers, including the *Wall Street Journal*, the New York *Post*, and the St. Louis *Post-Dispatch*, along with *Life, Look, Time, Newsweek*, CBS, and NBC came out against Johnson's Vietnam policy. More important, as Doris Kearns pointed out,

> A leader's authority comes from the public's belief in his right and ability to rule, in the willingness of individuals to suspend their own judgment and accept their leader's because they trust him and the system he represents. By 1968 Johnson had lost this trust. The issue was not simply Johnson's loss of popularity; it was his loss of credibility. A majority of people believed he regularly lied to them, and that belief soon spread from matters of personal biography to high matters of state.

A mood of gloom engulfed the President's advisers. On February 27 Joe Califano and Harry McPherson attended a conference on Vietnam in the Secretary of State's private dining room. Those present were McNamara, Clifford—who would succeed him in three days—Rostow, Rusk, Katzenbach, and William Bundy from the State Department. Califano, because of his domestic duties, had not heard a high-level discussion of the war for several years. "It was," he wrote, "the most depressing three hours in my years of public service. . . . McNamara, Katzenbach, and . . . Bundy were beyond pessimism. They sounded a chorus of despair. Rusk appeared exhausted and worn down." As he drove back to the White House with McPherson, Califano wrote, "I was physically shaken. Both of us were completely drained." Califano said, "This is crazy." McPherson agreed. Califano: "It really is all over, isn't it?" McPherson: "You bet it is." McPherson spoke to Deborah Shapley about McNamara at this conference. McPherson had "never heard [McNamara] speak with such terrible emotion." There were tears "in his eyes and in his voice." He condemned "the goddamned Air Force and its goddamned bombing campaign that had dropped more bombs on Vietnam than on Europe in the whole of World War II and we hadn't gotten a goddamned thing for it." McPherson thought that Clifford's gaze was saying, "See where this has gone. Is this where you are going?"

Johnson had long sought to bring his old and trusted friend Clark Clifford into his administration, always without success. In 1967 he drew Clifford into the Vietnam quagmire. Westmoreland wanted more men. Since he already had 525,000, the President was extremely reluctant to provide more. Clifford wrote, "He desperately wanted new commitments from the nations of the region to show the American people we were not carrying the weight of an Asian war entirely on our shoulders." South Korea, in exchange for enormous U.S. aid, had sent 45,000 troops; Australia 5,465; Thailand was committed to 2500; the Philippines, 2000 in noncombat units; and New Zealand, an artillery group of 381. Clifford thought that increasing their levies was "eminently reasonable and achievable."

On July 22, 1967, Clifford and General Maxwell Taylor left on a swing through these nations to persuade their governments to raise their commitments. It was a total failure, including Singapore. "To put it simply, the troop-contributing nations did not want to contribute any more troops. In fact, with the exception of Korea, they made it clear that they resented having had to send any soldiers to Vietnam in the first place." Clifford "jokingly" told Taylor that "more people turned out in New Zealand to demonstrate against our trip than the country had sent to Vietnam." On his return Clifford told Johnson that he was "shocked." Until now a hawk, he tossed away an article of that faith: the domino theory. "On the other hand, I continued to support the [administration's] policy because it seemed to provide the best way out of the war."

In January 1968 the President nominated Clifford to be Secretary of Defense. He was confirmed on January 30, just as the Tet offensive began. McNamara stayed on for another month to prepare the budget. Clifford was "half-private citizen and half-Cabinet member. [He] was free to concentrate almost exclusively on Vietnam."

It was a terrible time. "It is hard to imagine or recreate," Clifford later wrote, "the atmosphere in the sixty days after Tet. The pressure grew so intense that at times I felt the government itself might come apart at its seams. Leadership was fraying at its very center—something very rare in a nation with so stable a governmental structure." His understanding of the war "crumbled—not with a single dramatic revelation, but slowly and unevenly."

At the end of February, General Wheeler returned from Vietnam with a request from Westmoreland, supported by the Chiefs, for 205,179 more men. On February 27, at the meeting Califano and McPherson attended, there was, in Clifford's words, "a fierce discussion" of the proposal with no resolution. Clifford was the challenger. "The American people and world opinion believe we have suffered a major setback. How do we gain support for major programs if we have told people that things are going well? How do we avoid creating the feeling that we are pounding troops down a rat-hole?" He called for a careful review of the troop request. The only immediate decision was that McPherson should draft a major speech for the President for the end of March. The next day Johnson created a task force led by Clifford to review Westmoreland's request.

On March 1, Clifford made a momentous decision. "I had come to the conclusion that my overwhelming priority as Secretary of Defense was to extricate our nation from an endless war." His fundamental problem was to overcome the President's determination to continue the war. This would take time and Johnson would have to swallow in small bites. The Master Manipulator would manipulate the Great Manipulator.

At the first task force meeting on March 2 Clifford pressed Wheeler relentlessly on the troop issue and got these answers:

> Will 205,000 more men do the job? There was no assurance that they would.
> If 205,000 was insufficient, how many more were needed and when? There was no way of knowing.
> Can the enemy respond with a build-up of his own? He could.
> Can bombing stop the war? No.
> Will bombing decrease American casualties? Very little, if at all.
> How long must we keep on carrying the main burden of the war? We do not know when, if ever, the South Vietnamese will be ready to carry the main burden of the war.

These answers shocked Clifford. "The military was utterly unable to provide an acceptable rationale for the troop increase." When he pressed for a plan for victory, he was told that "there was no plan for victory." Clifford was appalled; he had never dreamed that there was no military justification for the war.

With the assistance of Paul Warnke, Assistant Secretary of Defense for International Security and an advocate for ending the war, Clifford drew up a three-point memorandum for the President: (1) 20,000 troops by May 1; (2) a call-up of the reserves; and (3) a deferred decision on the remaining troops depending upon a weekly assessment of the military situation, improved performance by the Saigon government, and a complete review of U.S. political and strategic options.

On March 4 Clifford presented these points to Johnson as a short-run solution. But Treasury Secretary Fowler made a devastating analysis of the impact of calling up the reserves upon the federal budget, inflation, the balance of payments, and the tax increase. In fact, a massive outflow of gold would take place on March 13 with no call-up of reserves. Rusk, surprisingly, proposed a cessation of bombing during the rainy season. This caught Johnson's interest and he directed Rusk to work up a proposal. He also instructed Clifford and Wheeler to discuss the reserve call-up with key senators on defense issues. They met with Richard Russell, John Stennis, Scoop Jackson, and Stuart Symington, all dedicated hawks, who flatly refused support for either the reserves or for more troops. Mansfield told Clifford that the present force in Vietnam was the end of the line. When informed, Johnson realized that no major increase was any longer politically possible.

On Sunday, March 10, the lead story in the *New York Times* was that the administration was torn by a debate over Westmoreland's request for 206,000 more troops. Johnson was furious, certain that it was a treacherous leak. In fact, two brilliant reporters, Neil Sheehan and Hedrick Smith, had pieced it together from scraps and inferences, some supplied by the President himself.

In mid-March the President's political position deteriorated dramatically. Senator Eugene McCarthy of Minnesota sensationally exposed his weakness in the New Hampshire primary, leading Robert Kennedy to announce his candidacy on March 16. Under Johnson's orders, McPherson's latest draft of the speech for the end of the month took a very hard line on the war. In a March 17 extemporaneous address in Minneapolis the President called emotionally for a "total national effort to win the war," which caused an uproar of opposition. "I am shocked," Jim Rowe wrote Johnson, "by the number of calls I have received today in protest against your Minneapolis speech."

Clifford wrote later that the U.S. was in a "crisis that had now almost completely enveloped Washington: a crisis in confidence in the government which—in those pre-Watergate days—was the most serious . . . since the Civil War." Desperately seeking some means of moving Lyndon Johnson to reality, he thought of a second meeting of the Wise Men.

Clifford knew that Dean Acheson had become disillusioned with Vietnam. As Truman's Secretary of State, Acheson had been an original Cold Warrior. Now he was extremely skeptical of military optimism and thought the South Vietnamese "government" a bad joke. Averell Harriman, still in the government, thought the war madness and worked over his old friend Acheson. Acheson's daughter, Mary, had married William Bundy. She told her father that he was "miserable," no longer a hawk and unable to grope his way out of Vietnam. Clifford made a few phone calls which revealed that others among the Wise Men had also changed their views.

On March 19 at the Tuesday lunch he proposed the meeting. At first Johnson was opposed, but Fortas and Rusk urged him to accede and he did. It was scheduled for March 25, six days before the big speech to the nation on Vietnam.

Johnson called a major meeting on March 20 on the issue of the number of troops to send to Westmoreland. But the question that dominated the chaotic discussion was a halt to the bombing. Three positions emerged: continued bombing of the North, backed by Fortas, Bunker, Rostow, Westmoreland, and the Joint Chiefs; cessation of the bombing, supported by Goldberg and Mac Bundy; and stopping the bombing except for the area near the demilitarized zone, for which Rusk and Clifford spoke. In fact, Clifford was for a full halt, but, he wrote, "It was clear that the President was not ready to approve a position that was opposed by Rusk, Bunker, Rostow, and the entire military leadership." Clifford's strategy was to lock in Rusk and push for a cessation in the March 31 speech. But the President closed the meeting by ordering McPherson to "get 'peace' out of the speech. . . . Let's make it troops and war."

Clifford's strategy was now in the hands of the Wise Men, who met for dinner at the State Department on March 25. "It was," Walter Isaacson and Evan Thomas wrote, "possibly the most distinguished dinner party of the American Establishment ever held. The Cold War Knighthood, now bowed and balding but nonetheless formidable, sat down together to dine by candlelight and discuss the Vietnam War. . . ."

They listened carefully to the briefings. Deputy Assistant Secretary of State Philip Habib gave a bleak assessment of the South Vietnamese government and "guessed" it would take five to seven years for it to make any progress. Clifford asked whether he thought a military victory was possible. Answer: "Not under present circumstances." Another question: "What would you do if the decision was yours to make?" Answer: "Stop the bombing and negotiate." Major General William E. DuPuy, who had commanded troops in Vietnam, stressed that Tet had ended in a U.S. victory but that there was still a long way to go. The CIA's George Carver was concerned about the pacification program and expected a long war.

The next day the senior advisers met with the President, who asked Mac Bundy to summarize their views: "Mr. President, there has been a very significant shift in most of our positions since we last met." Now Bundy, Acheson, Ball, Dean, Dillon, and Vance (who was very close to Johnson and, in fact, had questioned the war for the last two years) think the U.S. should "disengage." But Bradley, Taylor, Murphy, and Fortas favored continued support for the military. General Bradley, however, pointed out that he would send only "support troops" and would accept a bombing halt. The President, falsely thinking that the briefers had "poisoned the well," was enraged. More important, he was also deeply shaken.

Clifford's final problem was to turn the speech around. While McPherson was reliably on his side, he took his orders from the President. "The speech," Clifford wrote him, "still locks us into a war that is pictured as being essential to our security."

The critical session took place in Rusk's office on March 28. Clifford pointed to the fundamental problem with the draft: "It is still about war. What the President needs is a speech about peace." Clifford urged a halt to the bombing and, if the North Vietnamese responded, "other steps." To his amazement, neither Rusk nor Rostow "fought back," but neither assented either. Clifford suggested giving the President a choice—one draft on war, the other on peace. Rusk agreed and Rostow was silent.

McPherson worked late on the new version. The next morning he received a call from the President to discuss changes. McPherson grabbed the war speech, but, to his amazement, he soon realized that Johnson was working on the *peace* draft. When finished, he called Clifford and shouted, *"We've won. The President is working on our draft!"*[2]

During 1967 Postmaster General Larry O'Brien was absorbed in shaping a fundamental reorganization of the Post Office. But O'Brien knew that he would soon be drawn into the 1968 presidential campaign. He assumed that Johnson would be the candidate, and, since O'Brien was the pro, he took it for granted that he would manage the President's campaign. He found the prospect painful. "It's nuts and bolts. There's very little, if any glamour attached to it. It's hard, hard work." Years in politics had taught him that all that mattered was victory and you won it by working "harder and longer than the opposition." And you started *early*.

During the summer of 1967 the President asked O'Brien to put together some suggestions for the campaign, both organization and issues. He worked up a "white paper," a 44-page campaign manual, which he submitted to Johnson in September 1967. It touched every base. It listed all the significant jobs and the individuals he considered competent to fill them, voter registration, the primaries, problems in particular states, the issues, possible Republican candidates, answers to likely opposition charges, polling, the media, the black vote, and so on. It was an updated version of what had come to be known in Democratic circles as the O'Brien Manual.

This effort was greeted with deafening silence by the White House, which bothered O'Brien. Meantime, he got about the country to talk to prominent Democrats and was shocked by the fact that Vietnam seemed to have crowded out everything else.

The President did submit the document to his old friend and sometime political adviser Jim Rowe. Early in November O'Brien received a critique from Rowe and gave his answers. A meeting was held shortly which the President attended, but he left early. It was all talk. On November 7, O'Brien, annoyed, wrote Marvin Watson in the White House: "I cannot believe that a campaign can be waged by a committee of viewers. I feel that last Friday evening's meeting following the President's departure was a debacle." There was no response.

In November Senator McCarthy announced that he would enter the presidential primaries in Wisconsin, Nebraska, Oregon, and California and might do the same in New Hampshire and Massachusetts. He said he would directly challenge Johnson on the Vietnam War. Allard Lowenstein had been largely responsible for persuading McCarthy to announce.

Lowenstein, in his late thirties, was a brilliant, tireless New York lawyer with an insatiable appetite for politics. He was about as liberal as one could become and still be accepted by the very tolerant Democratic party. He drew a sharp line at the New Left, which he detested. He had worked on the staffs of a number of notable party liberals—Frank Graham, Adlai Stevenson, Eleanor Roosevelt, and Hubert Humphrey. He had been president of the National Student Association in 1951 just before the CIA took it over, and he must have known about it as it occurred. Afterward he kept in close touch with student activists in universities all over the U.S. By 1967 Lowenstein and those students who opposed the war had turned implacably against Lyndon Johnson. By the summer of 1967 Lowenstein had devised a strategy to deal with the LBJ problem. As Chester, Hodgson, and Page wrote, "it had two mutually necessary wings: he had to fan a 'Dump Johnson' fire in the grassroots, and he had to corral a candidate." In fact, the war fed the flames in the grassroots; Lowenstein concentrated on the candidate.

Bobby Kennedy was the obvious choice, but he thought it hopeless to take on a sitting President by dividing the Democratic party. Lowenstein approached a number of congressional doves and even J. K. Galbraith and General James M. Gavin. A number of the legislators faced tough reelection fights and wanted no more trouble; Galbraith was a Canadian by birth; and the general was a Republican. On October 20 Lowenstein and Gerry Hill, a San Francisco peacenik, had breakfast with McCarthy. He said, "You fellows have been talking about three or four names." He warmed them with a big smile. "I guess you can cut it down to one." Lowenstein had his candidate.

McCarthy was a country boy, born and raised in Watkins, Minnesota ("Population 760 friendly people plus a few grouches"), in the rich green land and clear lakes west of Minneapolis. He did not forget his origins. When a rich Republican he had run against said that he had sold a bull for 10 cents a pound and lost $600, McCarthy said, "The way I figure it, that's 6000 pounds. He should have sold it to a circus and made a fortune." His father was Irish, his mother German, both Roman Catholics. He was a brilliant scholar, an outstanding baseball and hockey player, and a serious student of religion. After the war he taught at St. Thomas College in St. Paul. He got into politics and won a House seat in 1948, moving up to the Senate with the famous Democratic class of 1958.

McCarthy was a loner who treasured his privacy and was an offbeat individualist in the upper house. Perhaps its most intelligent member, he spent much of his time writing—four books and a substantial corpus of poetry. He was not much interested in legislation, was often absent for votes, and most definitely was not a member of the Senate "club." He did not get on particularly with John Kennedy and many speculated over the reason. Perhaps McCarthy explained it with characteristic ambiguity when he said, "I'm twice as liberal as Hubert Humphrey, and twice as intelligent as Stuart Symington, and twice as Catholic as Jack Kennedy." He had no use for the President. Johnson had manipulated him during the 1964 Democratic convention when he announced that he had narrowed the choice to the two Minnesotans, Humphrey and McCarthy, when everyone knew it would be Humphrey. McCarthy deeply resented being used this way.

Now he agreed with Allard Lownstein. He thought the war was a calamity for the U.S. and that Johnson must be replaced. The Pope had urged Catholics to work for peace, and his daughter Mary, who was heavily involved in the peace movement, pleaded with her father not to face history as one who had supported Johnson's war. "There comes a time," the senator said, "when an honorable man simply has to raise the flag."

McCarthy decided to enter the New Hampshire primary, scheduled for March 12, 1968. It seemed like a dumb thing to do. The state was traditionally conservative and Republican. The new electronics industry was providing plenty of jobs under war contracts. The Irish and French-Canadian working class was expected to follow the AFL-CIO in supporting the President. The leading Democrats, Governor John W. King and Senator Thomas J. McIntyre, were stalwarts for Johnson. The first poll showed McCarthy with only 11 percent of the vote. At least his name would be on the ballot; voters would need to write in Johnson's.

But McCarthy's campaign proved a political sensation. While his talent for organization was virtually nonexistent, his mere announcement brought in a flood of money and thousands of volunteers, a few with considerable competence. Even more important, over 10,000 students from as far away as Michigan and Virginia, came to the state to lick envelopes, draw up lists, and, critically, talk to voters in house-to-house canvassing. Two busloads of Yale majors in Romance languages barnstormed in French in Manchester and the northern part of the state. "College students . . . ," Mary McGrory wrote in her column, "have suddenly discovered a use for people over thirty—voting for McCarthy." The boys cut their hair, shaved, and wore neckties; the girls brushed their hair and put on maxi-skirts. McCarthy's diffident style, which turned off audiences that liked a little passion in their politics, had an appeal in restrained New Hampshire. The fact that 60 percent of the state's registered Democrats were Catholic did him no harm. His handling of the war was masterful. He destroyed the arguments for it without attacking the President personally. He even borrowed a pair of skates and played hockey with some semi-pros. He had a terrific finish.

On the night before the primary the President asked John P. Roche, who had been following New Hampshire, "What's Gene going to do?" Roche said, "His name is on the ballot, yours isn't. I can't see how you can keep him under a third." "No," LBJ said, "he'll get 40 percent, at least 40 percent. Every son-of-a-bitch in New Hampshire who's mad at his wife or the postman or anybody is going to vote for Gene McCarthy." Not a bad forecast.

On March 12 Johnson received 29,021 votes, McCarthy, including write-in Republicans, 28,791. Johnson won by a slim 230 votes. The press treated the New Hampshire results as a McCarthy victory and, more important, as a devastating defeat for the President. Larry O'Brien said Johnson needed 60 to 65 percent of the vote to make his performance look respectable. He did not come close.

Bernard Boutin, an active New Hampshire Democrat, had run Johnson's campaign and, despite the fact that he and O'Brien were old friends, had never called him. Thus, O'Brien was not well informed about the primary. Being cut out made him uneasy. Eventually Boutin called. "You probably wonder why I haven't been in regular contact with you." O'Brien said he did wonder. Boutin: "I'm under instruction not to be involved with you on this." O'Brien became upset. He said later, "It did not bother me to the extent that I have been loyal, yet, whether it is the President or others, they distrust me." Despite long association with the Kennedys, "I was not going to do anything but support the guy that I worked for and that was it." Bobby and Teddy understood this, accepted it, and "were not going to consider this some kind of an affront." Yet "there is somebody on the Johnson side saying, 'I don't know about O'Brien.' "

O'Brien busied himself with Massachusetts, for which the filing date was March 5 for the primary on April 30. In January the President had asked him to evaluate the Bay State. He had a poll taken which showed that LBJ could easily defeat McCarthy. But the senator would run a hard campaign and anyone who managed Johnson's had to do the same to win. The President, therefore, needed someone who would stand in for him and be "prepared to organize and campaign vigorously in Massachusetts." O'Brien informed Johnson that he "would be prepared to leave the administration and be the stand-in if that was his desire." The President told him "he didn't feel that he wanted to have [O'Brien] do that." O'Brien went down a list of others, all of whom refused to take on the burden. Finally, Maurice Donahue, president of the state senate, said that he would stand in. O'Brien notified the White House.

There was no answer. On March 5 he told Donohue to stand by while he phoned everyone he could think of in the White House. "I never was able to make the contact; there was no filing." The decision, obviously, had been made by Johnson. As McCarthy wrote, "President Johnson had conceded us Massachusetts and its 72 convention votes."

O'Brien concluded that the White House did not understand the primaries and he sent over a background memorandum on March 6. The system worked for the party that did not have a sitting President. If he was a candidate, however, it created serious problems. In Wisconsin, Nebraska, and Oregon the President's name was mandatory on the ballot unless he certified that he was not running for reelection. In the other 12 primary states he was free to enter his name or not. Johnson had been inconsistent, entering in New Hampshire and staying out in Massachusetts. The only way he could justify not entering, and not very convincingly, was to assert that he was so busy governing the country that he had no time to campaign. "The debacle has occurred," O'Brien concluded, "the game is over. There is no point in discussing stand-ins, primaries from here on out."

He went to Wisconsin at the end of March to assess the primary there. His excuse was an address to 1000 postal employees in Milwaukee. He trooped around the state and talked to knowledgeable people. In his speech

he said kind words about the President and the audience applauded me-
chanically as they supposed they should for the boss. His judgment was
that Wisconsin would be a disaster for Johnson. When he visited the state
headquarters in Milwaukee he found it shut with the lights out. Theodore
White was there about the same date. "Nothing more forlorn, politically,
occurs in my memory of the 1968 campaign than Johnson headquarters
at 800 North Plankinton in downtown Milwaukee. In a barren store-front
headquarters, silent as a funeral parlor, half a dozen people sat at long
tables . . . listlessly turning over papers. No telephones rang."

By contrast, McCarthy's headquarters, O'Brien reported, had a hundred people cheerfully at work under blazing lights. For Johnson the rest of
the state was no better. The President had seen a snippet of the Milwaukee
speech with the audience applauding on TV and phoned O'Brien to say how
pleased he was by the enthusiasm. "So I told him candidly that I was very
concerned about . . . Wisconsin." The applause was meaningless. "I told
him he was going to suffer defeat in the Wisconsin primary." Johnson asked
how bad it would be. O'Brien said it would be "substantial." McCarthy's
campaign was stronger than the one in New Hampshire. On March 25 the
Madison *Capital Times* endorsed him and he packed 18,000 people into the
Dane County Memorial Coliseum. McCarthy got 56 percent of the vote,
LBJ 35, and Kennedy 6 from write-ins.

O'Brien wrote the President on March 27 that he had in the past several days talked to "large numbers of Democratic officials, leaders and
workers around the country." They were "without exception . . . your supporters." They were "fearful of the end result in terms of both the Chicago
convention and the November election, if our present Vietnam posture is
maintained."

On March 28 Johnson had McPherson and Califano to lunch. He
looked long at both of his loyal aides and asked, "What do you think of
my not running for reelection?" Both said he had to be a candidate. But
McPherson added, "I wouldn't run if I were you." Then why should he
enter the race? Johnson asked. "Because you're the only guy who can get
anything done."

On Saturday evening, March 30, Larry and Elva O'Brien were in New
York for a farewell dinner at Toots Shor's for their boy, who was about to
be shipped off to Vietnam. Jimmy Breslin, the columnist, was with them
and they ran into an old friend, Jesse Unruh, the California politico. Unruh
was hot for peace and Bobby Kennedy and expressed very strong opposition
to LBJ, to which O'Brien responded as best he could. Then Unruh made a
terrible mistake, saying, "If you feel that strongly, why isn't your son in
Vietnam?" O'Brien said, "As a matter of fact, this is a goodbye dinner we're
having; he's on his way." The next day Unruh phoned to apologize.

On Sunday afternoon, March 31, O'Brien was at the White House.
Marvin Watson asked him where he would be that evening. O'Brien said

he would be at home. In the early evening he received a call from a presidential aide who informed him that at the end of his televised address the President "is going to announce that he will not seek reelection." "I was," O'Brien said, "absolutely stunned." [3]

Lyndon Johnson had talked about not running for reelection for a long time. Lady Bird had expressed her view as early as the spring of 1964: "She did not want me to be a candidate in 1968." Luci wanted a father who was alive and urged him to quit. As a daughter, Lynda preferred that he not run, but as a citizen, hoped he would do so. In 1965 he began telling aides and friends that he should get out. In early 1967 Governor Connally told him that he did not want to enter the race again for reelection. But if the President needed him on the ticket, he would sign on. "I told him," Johnson wrote, "I felt certain that I would not run and suggested that he base his own decision on that assumption." In November 1967 he asked General Westmoreland whether the soldiers in Vietnam would think that the commander-in-chief who sent them to the battlefield had let them down if he was not a candidate. Answer: "I do not think so." Prior to the State of the Union address in January 1968, LBJ asked his former aide Horace Busby to prepare a brief withdrawal statement. It was supposed to be in his pocket when he delivered the speech. But he "forgot" to put it there. During early 1968 he discussed the question with a large number of other people.

This was all talk and many who knew him did not believe him. He did not make a commitment. An admirer of President Truman, who had faced the same problem in 1952, Johnson attached significance to the end of March. Clark Clifford had worked in the Truman White House. In the fall of 1967 Johnson had asked him to prepare a memorandum on Truman's decision to withdraw, which he did. The President told Clifford, "I may do the same thing as Truman." Clifford did not think he would.

But now in late March 1968 the weight on the President had increased enormously. Tet had turned the war into a catastrophe and Johnson could find no way out. McCarthy was doing splendidly running against him. Johnson was certain that Kennedy would soon join the race. He was losing the early primaries in humiliating fashion and the prospect was no brighter. His ability to move the Congress, as the tax bill proved, had almost vanished. He could hardly leave the secure White House without inciting a riot. The FBI expected serious racial violence in the cities during the summer. What would happen if he went to the Democratic convention in Chicago in August?

Johnson's health gave way under the punishing pressure he endured. In a few entries in Lady Bird Johnson's published diary for March she refers briefly to his condition. March 10 was a "day of deep gloom," March 14 "one of those terrific, pummeling White House days that can stretch and grind and use you," and on March 17 she had a "growing feeling of Prometheus Bound, just as though we were lying there on the rock, exposed to the vultures, and restrained from fighting back." Lyndon was "bone weary," "dead tired," and unable to sleep. "Those sties are coming back on Lyndon's eyes. First one and then the other, red and swollen and painful. . . . His life sounded more and more like the tribulations of Job." Even on March 31, the day of the big speech, "his face was sagging and there was such pain in his eyes as I had not seen since his mother died."

On March 28 the President kept Califano in the Oval Office with one of his long, rambling discourses. Johnson said he wanted to put him into a big job. "But," Califano said, "I have decided to leave next year even if you win." Johnson looked at him "as though [he] were crazy." He wished Califano to continue in his present job and also take over the poverty program now that Shriver was leaving to become ambassador to France. Califano was not interested. "The Italians [Congressman Peter Rodino and Frank Annunzio] are always telling me to put you on the Supreme Court, but I think you'd make a better Attorney General." Califano could make no sense of this. Johnson went on about Gene, Hubert, and Bobby. "The President was slumped in his chair and he looked very tired. He said he knew he was tired because of his eyes. 'They hurt and they always hurt when I'm tired.'"

After Kennedy announced on March 16, Isaacson and Thomas wrote, "Johnson could not sleep. His face was ashen, his eyes sunk and bleary. Folds of flesh hung down from his cheeks. Angry red sties began to pop out along his raw eyelids." Theodore White, who interviewed Johnson on March 26, found him overcome with weariness.

Doris Kearns reported that Johnson dreaded being alone. He needed to be surrounded by people. If they were not available, he had high-tech telephones, three television receivers playing simultaneously, a squawking radio to carry about, and, most important, the AP, UP, and Reuters tickers, "friends tapping at my door for attention. . . . I could stand beside the tickers for hours on end and never get lonely." That took care of the daytime, but the nights were much worse. He was a poor sleeper and was "terrified at lying alone in the dark." He would arise in the middle of the night and, with a small flashlight, pad through the dark halls to the Red Room, in which a portrait of Woodrow Wilson hung.

The Johnson family had a medical history of strokes. As a child, Lyndon would be seated next to his paralyzed grandmother, who sat wizened, speechless, and perfectly still. During the night he had a terrifying dream: He was seated in a straight chair in the middle of an open plain. Stampeding cattle descended upon him. He tried to run away but could not move. He called for help and no one came. Johnson developed a life-long fear of stroke and paralysis.

President Wilson had a real and long history of stroke and suffered a massive seizure in California while campaigning for Senate ratification of the peace treaty and the League of Nations after World War I. Thereafter he lay paralyzed, unable to speak or move. Johnson was frightened because he was certain that he would have such a stroke and suffer the same disability. Now in the dark he walked to Wilson's portrait in the Red Room, which was painted late in his presidency and recorded the great strains of his presidency. Kearns wrote that Johnson "found something soothing in the act of touching Wilson's picture; he could sleep again. He was still Lyndon Johnson and he was still alive and moving; it was Woodrow Wilson who was dead."

Some nights, especially early in 1968, he was unable to sleep for another reason. "I lay awake picturing my boys flying around North Vietnam." He had personally picked their bombing targets that day. "What if one of those targets you picked today triggers off Russia or China? . . . Or suppose one of my boys misses his mark . . . [and] one of his bombs falls on one of those Russian ships in the harbor?" He would picture himself lying on a battlefield in Danang when an American plane was shot down. "I saw it hit the ground, and as soon as it burst into flames, I couldn't stand it any more. I knew that one of my boys must have been killed." He jumped out of bed, put on his robe, and with the flashlight found his way to the Situation Room in the White House basement.

At 3 a.m. the Situation Room, which worked around the clock, buzzed with activity. Five or six professionals from the Pentagon and the CIA monitored the heavy inflow of military messages. As the data changed, they put markings on a giant map on the wall. It was here too that Johnson followed another deployment of "his boys," the Marines in the bloody battle for Khe Sanh.

Lyndon Johnson, Kearns found, had long struggled with paranoia. When the war was young and he expected a quick victory, he toyed with the opposition. In 1965 he said to Fulbright, "Well, Bill, what have you been doing today to damage the Republic? . . . Now you tell your wife I love her and I am sorry you're so damned cranky and grouchy all the time." By early 1968, when the war had become a catastrophe, he would deliver false and poisonous attacks on his presumed enemies—the intellectuals, the big-city press, the TV networks, the liberals, and the Kennedys. "To believe oneself the target of a giant conspiracy," Kearns wrote, "was such a leap into unreason that it could only mean some disintegration of Johnson's thought, that the barriers separating thought and delusion were crumbling."

Samples: "No matter what anyone said, I knew that the people out there loved me. . . . Deep down I knew—I simply knew—that the American people loved me." "The problem is that I was sabotaged. Look what happened whenever I went to make a speech about the war. . . . The St. Louis *Post-Dispatch* or the Boston *Globe* or CBS News would get on me over and over . . . and pretty soon the people began to wonder. . . . They began to think that I might be wrong about the war." "Two or three intellectuals started it all. . . . And it spread . . . until it appeared as if the people were against the war. Then Bobby began taking it up as his cause and with Martin Luther King on his payroll he went around stirring up the Negroes. . . . Then the Communists stepped in. They control the three networks, you know, and the forty major outlets of communication. It's all in the FBI reports."

Johnson had a captive audience for these delusions—the White House staff. "They listened to the President's name-calling," Kearns wrote, "[and] were frightened by what seemed . . . signs of paranoia. . . . [His] voice would become intense and low-keyed. He would laugh inappropriately." He would open a meeting this way: "Why aren't you out there fighting against my enemies?" But none of them dared tell their commander-in-chief that he had delusions.

Despite these difficulties, by the end of March 1968 Clark Clifford prevailed; he turned the President away from the comforting fantasies of his paranoia to face the hard realities of the war. While one cannot pinpoint the exact moment of Johnson's shift, it had to be some time between Wednesday evening, March 27, and Friday morning, March 29. On Wednesday evening Johnson met alone with Mansfield for three and a half hours. He read parts of the speech draft he then had to the senator and it contained nothing about halting the bombing. "I thought," Mansfield said, "it would be a mistake to make the speech because it offered no hope to the people and it only indicated a further involvement." While Johnson mentioned the possibility of stopping the bombing, he clearly had not made that decision. By Friday morning, as McPherson learned, Johnson was working on a "peace" draft of the speech calling for a reduction in the bombing. Perhaps he finally listened to Mansfield.

The Clifford strategy was concerned solely with Vietnam. But Johnson added something himself—withdrawal from the presidential race. By making this change, he gave himself a rationalization for his action on Vietnam.

The speech was scheduled for broadcast at 9 p.m. on Sunday, March 31. The President devoted much time to the address on Friday and Saturday, particularly his renunciation of the presidency, going over it with Horace Busby, his press officer George Christian, and his wife, who read it for the "umpteenth time."

The Johnsons arose early on Sunday to greet Lynda, who had just seen her husband off to Vietnam in California, and then had flown home on a red-eye special. Her mother thought she looked like a "ghost." After breakfast they went for mass to St. Dominic's, which the President found "simple and restful" for prayer. They then stopped at the Humphreys to inform the Vice President of the decision to step aside and to say goodbye before they left for Mexico City. Then back to the speech with Busby. Arthur and Mathilde Krim (he was a motion-picture executive and Democratic wheel) were close friends who were staying at the White House. Johnson read them the renunciation and Krim tried to dissuade him from going through with it. He pointed out that he could no longer unite the country. Again to the speech. At 8:10 p.m. he gave it to his secretary to put on the teleprompter. At 8:40, as he finished dressing, Walt Rostow and Clark Clifford arrived and he showed them the final paragraphs. Rostow was silent. Clifford said, "After what you've been through, you are entitled to make this decision."

They walked to the Oval Office, which was strewn with cameras and cables. The President was surrounded by people he loved—Lady Bird, Luci and her husband, the Krims, the Cliffords, the Rostows, Marvin Watson, and George Christian, who brought in the small White House press corps. Just before he went on the air, Lady Bird walked to him and said, "Remember—pacing and drama." He began to speak at 9:01.

"Tonight," the President opened, "I want to speak to you of peace in Vietnam and Southeast Asia." In order to promote talks, he was "unilaterally" ordering a cessation of bombing of North Vietnam except in the area immediately above the demilitarized zone. He was ready to send his negotiators "to any forum, at any time, to discuss the means of bringing this ugly war to an end." The American team would be headed by Averell Harriman. He called upon Ho Chi Minh to "respond positively, and favorably, to this new step toward peace." Further, the U.S. was "prepared to withdraw our forces from South Vietnam as the other side withdraws its forces to the north, stops the infiltration, and the level of violence thus subsides."

The strength of America, Johnson said, lay in the "unity of our people first. I have put it ahead of any divisive partisanship." Now "there is division in the American house." He called upon Americans to "guard against divisiveness and all its ugly consequences." Thus, "I should not permit the Presidency to become involved in the partisan divisions that are developing in this political year."

The concluding paragraphs, which were all that most Americans paid attention to, were:

> With America's sons in the fields far away, with America's future under challenge right here at home, with our hopes and the world's hopes in the balance every day, I do not believe that I should devote an hour or a day of my time to any personal partisan causes or to any duties other than the awesome duties of this office—the Presidency of your country.
>
> Accordingly, I shall not seek, and I will not accept the nomination of my party for another term as your President.

The President, Theodore White wrote, was "poised, smooth and collected" as he delivered this speech. He seemed utterly different from the man White had interviewed five days earlier. Perhaps it was "inner peace" or "the cosmetician's art."

The peroration was an artfully contrived argument. The President was not leaving because, as he said privately, he was no longer able to unite the country. Rather, he said that he must avoid a partisan race in order to use every moment that remained to him to gain peace in Vietnam.

Clifford, reflecting on the "stunning event I had just witnessed, had two deep regrets." One was that Johnson should have withdrawn earlier and have separated that decision from the war. By putting them together he led many to draw the conclusion that he was being driven out of the White House by Tet (and Bobby Kennedy). His other and more basic regret was that Johnson had made a "grievous error" by failing to inform his closest advisers. "Had I known that the President would be a lame duck with ten months left in office, I would have argued for a full bombing cessation." He might have persuaded Rusk to go along.[4]

The immediate reaction to the President's speech from his friends, Congress, the press, and the public was very favorable, in some quarters euphoric. But it was fleeting. This was because in three critical areas—the war, race, and the presidential campaign—it had no visible impact and that fact became quickly evident.

Hanoi, convinced that Tet had shaken U.S. resolve, had decided on a settlement dialogue prior to the speech. Thus, Ho quickly took up Johnson's offer to meet. An American delegation headed by Harriman and a North Vietnamese under Xuan Thuy, an official of the second rank, sat down in Paris on May 10, 1968. With occasional moments of hope which were quickly dashed, they would sit there for five years listening to each other's endlessly repeated and irreconcilable arguments. The U.S. demanded that the North Vietnamese withdraw from South Vietnam and rejected Vietcong participation in the Saigon government; the North Vietnamese insisted that the U.S. pull out of South Vietnam and that the Vietcong become part of the government of South Vietnam. Neither side would give.

In America the President's speech was widely considered to be the "turning point" in the war. This was a fiction. In fact, the meetings in Paris were window-dressing. The stalemate in the war solidified and the nine months of fighting following the speech were the deadliest. On April 1 Westmoreland ordered his commanders to put "maximum pressure" on the enemy, and that same day Hanoi's high command directed its troops to "intensify" their attacks. There were major Communist offensives in May and August. In the short period between May 5 and 18 alone 1800 Americans were killed, double the rate of Tet, and 18,000 were seriously wounded. The U.S. estimated the enemy killed at over 43,000.

Ronald H. Spector wrote,

> The nine months following LBJ's historic speech saw the fiercest fighting of the war. From January to July 1968 the overall rate of men killed in Vietnam would reach an all time high and would exceed the rate for the Korean War and the Mediterranean and Pacific theaters during World War II. This was truly the bloodiest phase of the Vietnam War. . . .

Even while American forces were experiencing greater success on the battlefield and in the contest for the countryside, American GIs were beginning to show signs of coming apart under the continued strain of fighting a costly stalemated war for objectives that were never clear or compelling. It was during 1968 that the U.S. forces began seriously to encounter the problems related to racial tensions and drug abuse which were to lead to their near disintegration in 1971 and 1972. . . .[5]

In the early months of 1968 Martin Luther King was deeply depressed and he spoke frequently, in public as well as privately, about his imminent death. His Chicago campaign to desegregate the schools and open up housing had failed. His attack on the Vietnam War had gotten nowhere and had earned him widespread denunciation. His Southern Christian Leadership Conference was broke and was deeply divided over his idea to launch a massive poor people's march on Washington in April 1968 for jobs and incomes.

On February 12, 1968, Lincoln's Birthday, Local 1733 of the American Federation of State, County and Municipal Employees struck the city of Memphis for recognition, higher wages, and decent working conditions. It represented 1300 garbage collectors, virtually all black. Mayor Henry Loeb III flatly refused to deal with the union and hired strikebreakers. Many of the sanitationmen attended the Centenary Methodist Church, the pastor of which, James M. Lawson, Jr., mobilized the black community to support the strike. Lawson and King were old and dear friends. On February 23 the police used mace heavily to break up a peaceful march. "To many," Gerold Frank wrote, "it was the moment that a labor dispute became a racial struggle."

Lawson invited King to come to Memphis to speak out for the strikers. Though reluctant, King agreed and addressed a rousing mass meeting of 10,000 packed into Mason Temple. Lawson urged him to return to lead a march of the Memphis poor as the prelude to the march on Washington. King again assented and it was scheduled for 9 a.m. on March 28.

By that hour a huge crowd had gathered at Clayborn Temple. But King's flight was late and it was almost 11:00 before he arrived. A group of black militants, calling themselves the Invaders after a TV program, had penetrated the crowd. They had no aversion to violence. Shortly after the march to City Hall began King heard the shattering of glass. The Invaders were smashing shop windows and looting followed. The police were on the streets in riot gear. A peaceful march degenerated into a pitched battle. For his own safety King was whisked away to a motel. By the end of the day one black youth was dead, 60 had been clubbed, and almost 300 were arrested. Troops patrolled the streets and Loeb imposed a curfew.

This experience left King despondent; he and the black community were blamed for the violence. If this was, indeed, the precursor of the poor people's march on Washington, it was an omen of disaster. "No Memphis," he told his friends, "no Washington." He determined to return for a *peaceful* march on City Hall. It was scheduled for April 5. But he was not certain that he would come back because of his premonition of death.

James Earl Ray, like Lee Harvey Oswald, was a loser, a misfit who never found a niche for himself in American society. He was born and raised in a miserable family that lived in extreme poverty in the worn-out Illinois towns across the Mississippi from St. Louis. He hated school. The teacher's report when he was nine read: "Attitude toward regulations: violates them all. Honesty: needs watching. Appearance: repulsive. Courtesy: seldom if ever polite." He was kicked out for stealing. At the end of World War II he worked in a shoe tannery for a supervisor of German extraction who was an ardent Nazi. Ray hoped to get to Germany.

He enlisted in the Army right after the war and was assigned to the Quartermaster Corps in Nuremberg. His military career, Gerold Frank noted, was not distinguished, and in the end he was discharged "for ineptness and lack of adaptability for military service" and sent home from Germany in the last days of 1948.

In 1955 Ray was arrested for stealing and forging U.S. postal money orders and was sent to Leavenworth. The probation officer wrote: "He is a confirmed criminal and a menace to society when in the free world. . . . Just what motivates him to commit crime is not known."

When he got out of jail Ray became an intinerant thief. In the mid-sixties he was again behind bars in the Missouri State Penitentiary with a twenty-four-year sentence. He was contemptuous of blacks, speaking of Martin "Lucifer" King or Martin Luther "Coon." He made three attempts to escape and was successful in April 1967.

The next year Ray roamed the U.S., Canada, and Mexico, keeping his distance from the police, washing dishes in restaurants, and stealing when he needed money. On March 17, 1968, he filed a change of address card to general delivery in Atlanta. A week later Ray drove his white Mustang into the city. He had a map with King's home, his church, and SCLC headquarters circled. On March 27 Ray was in the Gun Rack in Birmingham asking the clerk about hunting rifles. On the 29th he was in the Long-Lewis Hardware Store in nearby Bessemer, raising similar questions. Later that day he bought a Remington .243 at the Aeromarine Supply Company in Birmingham. The next morning he exchanged it for a more powerful Remington 30.06. The press reported that King would soon be in Memphis.

On March 31 King was astonished and heartened to hear the President announce his withdrawal. He thought this opened the way to the election of a compassionate President who would save the cities and make peace in Vietnam. In his mind this increased the urgency of the poor people's march.

On the evening of April 3 a white Mustang pulled into the New Rebel Motel in the outskirts of Memphis. Eric S. Galt registered and went to Room 34. Ray knew that King was staying at the Lorraine Motel because he read it in the Memphis *Commercial Appeal* and he knew that he was in Room 306 because news photographs showed him entering a door with that number. On that day Ray checked out and rented Room 5B at Mrs. Brewer's rooming house, registering as John Willard. He drove the Mustang to the York Arms Company, where he bought a pair of Bushnell binoculars. He returned to the rooming house and carried the rifle wrapped in a bedspread and the glasses to 5B.

From the window in his room he had an unimpeded view of the Lorraine Motel, 200 feet away. In the bathroom down the hall the view was even better. King's room, like the others, opened onto the balcony. Late that afternoon Ray watched the coming and going of the black leaders in the parking lot and on the balcony.

Around 6:00 King suggested to his friends that they go out to dinner and they began to dress. Gradually activity increased in the courtyard and on the balcony. Ray left his room with his rifle and walked the few steps to the bathroom, latching the hook when he had entered. King finished dressing and went out onto the balcony to greet friends in the courtyard below, leaning against the railing. Ray put his feet in the bathtub and steadied the muzzle of his rifle on the windowsill, taking aim at King. As King started to rise from the railing, Ray fired. The bullet ripped away King's jaw, leaving a gaping hole and dropping him sprawled across the floor of the balcony. He died instantly.

Ray raced out of the rooming house, dropped the rifle in the doorway of a nearby shop, and made a successful getaway. He moved north through the U.S. into Canada and on to London. The FBI, the Royal Canadian Mounted Police, and Scotland Yard tracked him. After a few months a Scotland Yard detective tapped him on the shoulder and he was soon extradited to Memphis. As with Oswald, there was a good deal of speculation about conspiracy. Ray himself talked of "Raoul," a shadowy French-Canadian, who allegedly used him for illicit international operations and provided him with money. Raoul never materialized. At the trial Ray changed his plea to guilty and bargained for a 99-year sentence instead of death. He also signed a stipulation of 55 statements of fact. No. 37 read as follows: "That at approximately 6:01 p.m. April 4, 1968, defendant fired a shot from the second floor bathroom in the rooming house at 422½ S. Main Street and fatally wounded Dr. Martin Luther King, Jr., who was standing on the balcony of the Lorraine Motel." Ray thought that George Wallace would be elected President in 1968 and, as a fellow racist, would pardon him.

The King assassination reverberated around the world with expressions of grief, compassion, and rage, laced with this question: What had brought America to another such calamity? Pope Pius VI expressed his "profound sadness" to the American Catholic hierarchy. There were resolutions of horror in the House of Commons. In Bonn both houses of the West German parliament stood in silent tribute. In Memphis, Mayor Loeb, bowing to public opinion, recognized the sanitationmen's union and accepted a decent contract.

At the King funeral in Atlanta on April 9 the Ebenezer Church was packed with celebrities, and 60,000 to 100,000 others listened to the service outdoors. Attorney General Clark, Jacqueline Kennedy, and most of the presidential candidates were present. Humphrey, Kennedy, McCarthy, and Nixon were there. Wallace was not. Neither was President Johnson. He attended a memorial service at the National Cathedral in Washington on April 6. Johnson did not go to Atlanta because both the Secret Service and the FBI thought it too dangerous. He also canceled his scheduled trip to Hawaii and Saigon.

The black community was enraged. At a meeting of the President with the civil rights leadership on April 5 at the White House, Mayor Richard Hatcher of Gary, Indiana, bitterly attacked racism in American society. The militants, both black and white, who had rejected King's leadership and detested nonviolence now exploited his death. Stokely Carmichael from Cuba issued a call over Radio Havana for "urban guerilla warfare." White America, he charged, specifically Lyndon Johnson and Robert Kennedy, had murdered King. "Now . . . there is no black man who will ask black people not to burn down the cities." He urged blacks to get their guns and take to the streets. Bernardine Dohrn, a white New Left extremist, who later became a leader of the Weathermen, had done legal work for King on open housing in Chicago. In New York, when she heard of his death, she cried. Then she went home to change into her "riot clothes: pants." Dohrn and a friend went to Times Square to rip up signs and trash stores. She said this was the moment for "guerilla warfare."

In fact, a number of large cities, the FBI, and the army had anticipated serious rioting during the summer of 1968, and accounts of their preparations reached the press in early March. After Watts the Los Angeles Police Department had introduced a general staff plan with personnel, intelligence, operations, and logistics divisions. This included a mobile command post, a communications trailer, helicopters, armored cars, and, most important, a Special Weapons and Tactics Team (SWAT), consisting of four-man groups (a rifleman, a spotter, and two officers with shotguns and handguns) to handle snipers. The LAPD planned more than 30 SWAT groups. It wished it could afford a new $35,000, 20-ton tank-like vehicle which carried 20 men and was equipped with a machine gun, tear-gas launchers, a smoke-screen maker, a siren, and chemical fire extinguishers. Chicago, Detroit, Tampa, Washington, Philadelphia, and Newark had less ambitious plans. Army Chief of Staff General Harold K. Johnson told Congress that he had seven brigades (16,000 troops) trained for domestic riot duty with special equipment which could be quickly airlifted anywhere in the U.S.

In 1967 in Detroit and Newark the army had suffered from poor intelligence. To deal with an urban riot, Califano explained, "they have to know where things are. They have to know where the cops are, . . . where they can incarcerate people, . . . where water is, . . . where they can bivouac." Thus, the Army analyzed the major cities to obtain this information. This was, Califano said, "not directed at Communists and subversives; it was directed at keeping order."

On the night of April 4–5 black ghettoes exploded across the nation. Riots broke out in 110 cities and 39 people were killed, most of them black. There were 75,000 soldiers and guardsmen patrolling the streets. Washington took the biggest hit. There were 711 fires, widespread looting, and ten dead, including a white man dragged from his car and stabbed. The President saw the advances made from his speech drain away. "Everything we've gained in the last few days," he said, "we're going to lose tonight." There were 14,000 Army, Marine, and National Guard troops, along with 2800 District police officers on the streets. A good number of FBI and Army intelligence agents dressed as priests and nuns were there gathering intelligence.

Chicago seems to have had the second most serious riot. The night of April 4 was quite calm and schools opened the next day. Absenteeism in ghetto high schools was unusually high and many other students left during the day. Black youths threatened white students and there were several assaults. By noon most high schools in black neighborhoods were closed. White businessmen along West Madison Street shut their stores and went home. That afternoon many shops were damaged, fires were set, and looting began. Vandalism increased on the West Side during the afternoon and the police could not bring it under control. Mayor Daley obtained an executive order from the governor to bring in the National Guard. Madison turned into a sea of fires and snipers. Rioting continued throughout the night. Guard troops were on the streets on April 6, but were unable to cope.

That evening the mayor and governor asked the President for federal troops. Califano brought the proclamation for signature to him in the living quarters. "Johnson's eyes were heavy with fatigue, the jaw sagging," Califano wrote. "Lying on his back in bed, he signaled me to hand him a pen, and signed the papers as he held them up over his head, which he was too exhausted to raise from the pillow."

General George Mather commanded both the federalized Illinois Guard and army troops flown in from Fort Hood, Texas, and Fort Carson, Colorado, landing at O'Hare Field and the Glenview Naval Air Station on the morning of April 7. Daley ordered a curfew for persons under 21 from 7 p.m. to 6 a.m. Calm was restored as the troops spread through the city. The schools reopened on Monday, April 8. They were closed Tuesday as a memorial to Dr. King. On Wednesday the mayor declared the emergency over and lifted the curfew. The army began to withdraw. Chicago suffered over $14 million in property losses and about 3000 persons were arrested.

In the aftermath of the King assassination and the riots, Congress, amazingly, enacted an open housing law, the first such federal statute since Reconstruction. With Johnson's presidency so deeply wounded, it was both a miracle and an ordeal. The northern Democratic and moderate Republican coalition which had passed the Civil Rights Act in 1964 and the Voting Rights Act in 1965 seemed now in disarray. Dirksen, the pivot in defeating cloture for these laws, strongly opposed fair housing and supported cloture in 1966. As a result of the 1966 elections, the House was more conservative. After the 1967 riots white people in the north had no desire to "reward" black radicals and looters.

Johnson had proposed open housing as part of an omnibus civil rights bill in 1966. The House had adopted a modified version, but two cloture votes had failed in the Senate because of the housing provision. The President renewed his request in his civil rights message on February 15, 1967. The House passed it handsomely on August 16, but the Senate loomed once again as an insurmountable barrier.

Enter Clarence M. Mitchell, Jr., the longtime lobbyist for the NAACP and presently the legislative representative for the Leadership Conference on Civil Rights. At the opening of the session no one expected the bill to pass. But Mitchell, according to *Congressional Quarterly*, "refused to accept this prognosis and continued to prod the Administration and Senate liberals until they promised him another big push." Many in Congress went along because they wanted to show the black firebrands what moderates like Mitchell and his NAACP boss, Roy Wilkins, could accomplish.

Debate opened in the Senate on the House bill on January 18, 1968. The big opposition lobby, the National Association of Real Estate Boards, was so convinced that fair housing had no chance that it took a nap. On January 24 the President again urged an omnibus bill—open housing, protection against interference for those exercising their civil rights, enforcement powers for the Equal Employment Opportunity Commission, and reform of jury selection. Only protection of civil rights and jury reform were thought to have any chance.

On February 6 Walter Mondale, the Minnesota Democrat, and Edward W. Brooke, the black Massachusetts Republican, proposed an amendment to the House bill which would exempt only owner-occupied dwellings which housed no more than four families. It would leave 91 percent of the nation's housing covered. Sam Ervin, the North Carolina Democrat, immediately announced a filibuster.

This was Dirksen territory, and, as everyone watched, the old pro rewarded them with another dramatic switch. He urged his colleagues not to look up the speech he made in September 1966 in which he called fair housing unconstitutional. Biology taught that change was always constitutional. "One would be a strange creature indeed in this world of mutation if in the face of reality he did not change his mind." He was worried about ghetto riots and did not want to "worsen the . . . restive condition in the United States." Nor did he want black veterans returning from Vietnam to face discrimination in housing. Perhaps most important, the 1966 elections had added four moderate Republicans to the Senate—Charles Percy of Illinois, Robert Griffin of Michigan, Mark Hatfield of Oregon, and Dirksen's son-in-law, Howard Baker of Tennessee. Baker was said to have urged the switch so that Republicans could appeal to black voters in the 1968 elections.

But it took four roll calls to gather two-thirds of the senators present to end cloture. This required a number of Democratic switches, particularly from small states in the West. On March 4, 1968, the fourth vote required 65 in favor. It was exactly that number, 65 to 32.

As his price for delivering the Republicans for cloture, Dirksen won his own substitute for the Mondale-Brooke amendment. Single-family owner-occupied dwellings sold or rented by the owner rather than by an agent were exempted. This reduced coverage to 80 percent of the nation's housing. It was adopted 83 to 5. The whole bill passed by a vote of 71 to 20 on March 11.

The question before the House was whether to accept the Senate version and avoid conference, where the housing provisions would probably have been weakened. Despite pleas from the President, the Rules Committee, in his words, engaged in "fiddling and piddling." Nixon and Rockefeller, both running for President, joined Johnson in support. On April 9 the Rules Committee reported out the Senate bill. The House went along the next day in a roll call 250 to 172. The President signed it on April 11, 1968.

The new law prohibited the refusal to sell or rent a dwelling because of the buyer's or renter's race, color, religion, or national origin. Brokers and lending institutions were forbidden to discriminate. The sale or rental by a private individual of not more than three houses without use of a broker was exempt from the law.

But the Fair Housing Act of 1968 was an empty gesture. Enforcement was fatally defective. The Department of Housing and Urban Development could only investigate complaints and must turn cases of probable cause over to the Justice Department. HUD had little stomach for enforcement. There was also a debilitating philosophical disagreement over whether Congress intended only to prohibit racial discrimination or sought more broadly to promote racially integrated communities. The real estate industry—builders, realtors, appraisers, insurance companies, banks, mortgage lenders, sellers, and buyers—systematically defied and undermined the statute with virtual impunity. While there were exceptions, most whites and many blacks seemed to prefer to live racially separated and to send their children to segregated neighborhood schools. As a result, while there was a slight movement towards integration, American cities remained overwhelmingly segregated both in their central areas and in their suburbs.[6]

After they watched the President announce his withdrawal on March 31, Larry O'Brien said to his wife, "I have a feeling I won't get to bed this evening without a couple of phone calls." A few minutes later Bobby Kennedy was on the line asking O'Brien to manage his campaign.

Kennedy asked whether he had gotten to him first and O'Brien said he had. Kennedy said, "This is a new ball game. . . . You have discharged your loyalty. . . . We're really going after you. . . . Will you promise me you're really going to seriously think about this now?" O'Brien said he would. Humphrey, who was in Mexico, did not reach him until the following morning and he made an almost identical appeal.

It was a tough call and O'Brien spent a week examining it. He felt badly about leaving the post office before his reorganization plan had been adopted, but felt that he had discharged his obligation to the President. Further, he was the only member of the cabinet with a son in Vietnam and he wanted the war to end.

As between Kennedy and Humphrey, it was pretty much a toss-up. He later said he had asked himself, "Would you feel comfortable with either one of them being President and the answer was yes." "With Hubert, the pluses are pretty obvious. He was bright, intelligent, experienced. The minus might be Hubert had been faulted for not being tough enough. On Bobby the reverse."

He loved Humphrey and admired him greatly. The men and their wives had spent a lot of time together and had become close friends. But the strongest factor was his relationship with the Kennedy family. It went back to 1951. "My memories of Jack, my great regard for him, fondness for him went into the equation. . . . We'd been through a great deal and it had a tremendous effect on my life. So the ultimate decision was that I would go with Bobby."

The following Saturday O'Brien went to see Humphrey to inform him of the decision. The Vice President was deeply disappointed, though, characteristically, low-key, respectful, and understanding. But he wanted something from O'Brien. No one could predict the course of the campaign and at some point it might become critical for the candidates to communicate with each other. He wanted O'Brien to keep the channel open and hoped that Bobby would accept the arrangement. "So we closed out the meeting with our arms around each other and I pretty much staggered out of there."

O'Brien told Kennedy that he was coming on board, which delighted him. He then conveyed Humphrey's desire to keep communications open. "He accepted it with enthusiasm." Kennedy added, "I think he's a terrific guy and there's no fun in running against a guy like Hubert."

O'Brien then went to the President to tender his resignation, which became a long conversation. As it ended, Johnson asked, "Are you going with Bobby?" O'Brien nodded. The President smiled. "I had to feel in his own mind that probably O'Brien, the Kennedy years, what else?" A few minutes after he got to his office Johnson called him to tell him to look at the ticker. "If I missed an adjective describing my regard for you, it's because of the limit of my vocabulary."

Kennedy had spent six tortured months since the fall of 1967 trying to decide whether to seek the nomination. The arguments for doing so were powerful. He hated the war, was convinced that it was tearing the nation apart, and was determined to seek peace. Since Lyndon Johnson stood in the way, he must go. Kennedy had become deeply involved with the under-classes—the crisis of the cities, the misery of the black ghettoes, the dreams of aspiring Chicanos, the difficulties of young people. He was convinced that American democracy could not be fulfilled unless, in Harrington's phrase, the "other America" was brought into the mainstream. Again, in his view, Johnson blocked the road. The recent Kerner Commission report had so argued, and Johnson, annoyed, had pushed it aside.

But every politician learned with his mother's milk that no one in his right mind challenged a sitting President because he always held the winning cards. This is what the knowledgeable people he trusted told him—his brother Teddy, Ted Sorensen, Dick Daley, and many others.

But in early 1968 two events pushed him into the race—Tet, which promised a prolongation of the war, and McCarthy's success in New Hampshire, which both exposed LBJ's weakness and threatened that Mc-Carthy would win without challenge. Like many other experienced politi-cians, Kennedy thought McCarthy was temperamentally unfit to be Presi-dent—among other characteristics, unfocussed and lazy. McCarthy did not disagree.

Thus, on March 15, 1968, in the Senate Caucus Room, where his brother had declared his candidacy, Bobby now made his statement: "I am announcing today my candidacy for the Presidency of the United States. I do not run for the Presidency merely to oppose any man but to propose new policies." With Johnson's withdrawal 15 days later, it became a three-man race—Humphrey, McCarthy, and Kennedy. Humphrey stayed out of the primaries and went after state delegations. Kennedy had no choice but to battle McCarthy in the few remaining primaries—Indiana, Nebraska, Or-egon, and the big prize, California.

At a dinner party in New York a few days after the announcement, Jacqueline Kennedy drew Schlesinger aside. "Do you know what I think will happen to Bobby?" He said no. She said, "The same thing that happened to Jack. . . . There is so much hatred in this country, and more people hate Bobby than hated Jack. . . . I've told Bobby this, but he isn't fatalistic, like me." Romain Gary, the French writer, said to a startled Pierre Salinger, "You know, of course, that your guy will be killed." Bobby was so uninter-ested in assassination that he could not get the name of his brother's assas-sin straight, calling him "Harvey Lee Oswald, whatever his name is."

Indiana was conservative, hawkish, and Republican, expected to go for Nixon in November. It had been a Ku Klux Klan stronghold and the white majority had little interest in blacks. The leading newspaper, the Indianapo-lis *Star,* was extremely right-wing and bashed Kennedy. Governor Roger Branigan was a stand-in for Johnson and brought the entire party establishment to Humphrey. The AFL-CIO, but not the UAW, moved with the governor. O'Brien thought that Bobby should not have entered in Indiana, but came on board too late to prevent it.

Nevertheless, Kennedy ran a strong campaign. He fought hard for the Democratic enclaves—the ethnic pockets in the north, Evansville in the south, the black communities, and college students. In Indiana's heart, Booth Tarkington's small towns, he trimmed his message to stress law and order, dislike for welfare handouts, and opposition to unilateral withdrawal from Vietnam. He barnstormed by rail on a resuscitated Wabash Cannonball. Kennedy carried the primary—42 percent of the vote to 31 for Branigan and 27 for McCarthy. He did surprisingly well in the rural counties. McCarthy seemed to have lost his way in Indiana.

It was a trial run for Nebraska—rural, conservative, very few unionized workers or blacks, Republican. Kennedy did not even want to try, but Sorensen, a cornhusker himself, insisted that he enter and his brother helped set up an organization. Bobby loved the farm families and hit it off with them immediately. In Beatrice the mayor presented him with a deed for an inch of land. Kennedy promised that, if he lost Nebraska, he would settle in Beatrice. "And I'll bring Ethel and all 11 children." (He had only 10; Ethel was expecting.) His solution to the farm problem: buying 26 bottles of milk a day for his kids. Humphrey contested Nebraska, but McCarthy moved early to the West Coast. The tally: Kennedy 52 percent, McCarthy 31, Johnson 5.6, Humphrey 8.4 (write-ins), others 3.5.

Oregon was not Kennedy country. Oregonians were exceptionally self-contained. In the other 49, if you asked someone where he planned to vacation, he would name another state. In Oregon he picked Oregon. They were also well-educated and extremely independent. Thus, they were hazy about national politics and national leaders. There were almost no blacks or Chicanos in the state. The Teamsters was the dominant union and its members remembered Bobby Kennedy as the ruthless prosecutor who put Jimmy Hoffa in jail. The war was probably most unpopular in Oregon. Democratic Senator Wayne Morse and Republican Senator Mark Hatfield were stalwart peaceniks. Gene McCarthy owned the Vietnam issue and Oregonians liked his relaxed style.

Kennedy, in fact, had trouble drawing a crowd. Barnstorming by train, the Southern Pacific Beaver Special, through the Willamette Valley from Portland to Eugene produced only a modest improvement. While he was eager, there were not enough hands to shake. He simply could not reach the urban centers. Results: McCarthy 45 percent, Kennedy 39, Johnson 12, Humphrey 4. This was the first electoral defeat any of the Kennedy brothers had ever suffered. Kennedy learned that McCarthy had the young activists locked up.

Everything turned on California. If Kennedy could carry the Golden State's 174 votes with 190 from his own New York, he would have 28 percent of the 1,312 needed for nomination. Kennedy thought he must have an absolute majority, an extremely difficult goal in a three-man race. Attorney General Tom Lynch headed an administration slate, that is, for Humphrey. But California was Kennedy country, millions of Mexican-Americans, blacks, low-paid and unemployed workers, and students, most of them not politically active. Kennedy said McCarthy got the A students and he had a chance with the rest. The big urban centers in the Bay Area, Los Angeles County, and San Diego were magnets for a charismatic politician campaigning in the streets, often in minority areas.

Kennedy had a strong organization and a number of important local figures, notably Jesse Unruh and Cesar Chavez. But this enormous state demanded a massive and expensive television campaign. Earlier McCarthy had challenged Kennedy to debate and was rejected. Now Kennedy needed the exposure and issued the challenge himself. McCarthy, even more in need of recognition, grabbed the invitation.

The debate was held on the Saturday before the primary in San Francisco with three reporters posing the questions. For most viewers neither candidate landed a heavy blow and the affair was a wash. In the last days Kennedy whipped himself into a frenzy of campaigning almost to the edge of collapse.

On Monday night the Kennedy family took over the sumptuous Malibu beach house of Hollywood director John Frankenheimer. On election day Kennedy slept late and then swam in the Pacific and played with his kids on the beach. On election night Frankenheimer drove them to the Royal Suite of the Ambassador Hotel. The polls closed at 8:00. It turned into something of a cliffhanger and it was late before the decisive results were in: Kennedy won, not by a majority, but by 46 percent to McCarthy's 42; Lynch took the rest.

As midnight approached the huge crowd in the Embassy Room became restive and demanded to see their man. At this time McCarthy had not conceded, but Kennedy's handlers were sure that he had won. At 11:45 he went down in the service elevator, walked through the kitchen shaking hands with cooks and waiters, and then along a narrow corridor to the ballroom. He was greeted by a triumphant crowd. He made a victory speech, brief in deference to the oppressive heat. He was next scheduled for a press conference in the Colonial Room. There were two routes from the ballroom. William Berry, his security man, and Fred Dutton expected him to leave by the swinging doors to the kitchen corridor and started to clear the route. Instead, the assistant maitre d'hôtel, Karl Uecker, led him through a back exit into a dark corridor which led to a well-lit area that opened into the Colonial Room. Berry and Dutton rushed to catch up. At 12:13 a.m. a radio reporter asked him how he would deal with Humphrey and Kennedy started to reply: "It just goes back to the struggle for it. . . ."[7]

Sirhan Sirhan had been born to Bishara and Mary Sirhan, a Palestinian Christian couple, in Old Jerusalem. There were five boys—Adel, Munir,

Sharif, Saidallah, and Sirhan—and one girl—Aida. Bishara beat his children. After the 1948 Israel War for Independence the parents, Sirhan, and two of his brothers as well as his sister migrated to America, settling in Pasadena. The other boys followed later. Bishara hated the U.S. and returned to Palestine after six months.

Sirhan graduated from John Muir High School in Pasadena and spent two years at Pasadena City College. A boy of modest intelligence, he performed poorly. He kept to himself and seemed to have no friends of either sex. Very small, Sirhan had the ambition to become a jockey. He got a job exercising mounts at a horse ranch in Corona, southeast of Los Angeles. But in September 1966 a horse threw him and he was injured, ending his possibility of becoming a jockey. Some thought the fall caused brain damage, but this seems unlikely. In 1968 he appeared to be unemployed.

The notebooks in which Sirhan confided his intimate thoughts leave little doubt that he was disturbed. Several of the psychiatrists who later examined him thought him schizophrenic.

Sirhan was a fanatical Palestinian Arab. He hated Jews and thought the "Zionists" had not only stolen the land from the Palestinians, but had ground them with their heels into the dirt. He believed that the Jews controlled the U.S. and helped those in Israel to suppress the Arabs. While he did not say that Robert Kennedy was a Jew, he was convinced that Kennedy was a tool of the Jews.

The fact that Kennedy was holding his victory celebration at the Ambassador was widely reported by the Los Angeles media. It was a large, prominent hotel on Wilshire Boulevard in the midtown district, easily reached from anywhere in the metropolitan area.

Sirhan's brother had bought an Iver-Johnson .22 caliber eight-shot revolver some time before. Sirhan took it over. When told that it was not much of a gun, he lied by saying he bought it because it was cheap, only $25. He first used it in March 1968 and practiced with it on June 2, two days before the assassination, at the San Gabriel Valley Gun Club.

Sirhan, carrying his Iver-Johnson, was in the crowd in the Ambassador kitchen when Robert Kennedy came very close to him. He fired the first bullet from a distance of one to six inches and it entered the senator's head behind the right ear. It was the killer. But Sirhan, in a frenzy, fired all seven of the remaining bullets. No. 2 passed through Kennedy's coat at the shoulder without entering his body and struck Paul Schrade, a UAW official, in the forehead. No. 3 hit Kennedy in the rear of the right shoulder and was recovered from the sixth cervical vertebra. No. 4 entered the senator's shoulder an inch to the right of No. 3 and struck the ceiling. No. 5 was lodged in Ira Goldstein's left rear buttock. No. 6 passed through Goldstein's left pant leg without penetrating his body and was on its way into Irwin Stroll's left leg. No. 7 struck Irwin Weisel in the left abdomen. No. 8 hit the ceiling and bounced down to strike Elizabeth Evans in the head.

The crowd in the kitchen went into a state of shock, but a number of the men, including Roosevelt Grier, the giant defensive lineman with the Los Angeles Rams, and Rafer Johnson, the Olympic decathlon gold medalist, jumped Sirhan. He fought like a tiger and took some time to subdue. The police then hauled him away.

Kennedy, with his wife at his side, was taken to Central Receiving Hospital 18 blocks distant. Once there, she sent for a priest, Father James Mundell, who gave Kennedy absolution. Father Thomas Peacha, who heard of the assassination on his car radio, drove directly to the hospital and gave the senator extreme unction. The doctors moved him to Good Samaritan Hospital, which had surgical facilities. For a while there were encouraging signs. But at 1:44 a.m. the next morning Robert Kennedy's heart stopped beating. He was with his family—Ethel, two of his sisters, his brother-in-law Steve Smith, his sister-in-law Jackie, and his brother Teddy.

The casket was flown to New York and placed in St. Patrick's Cathedral. At the final mass Edward Kennedy made a moving speech and "The Battle Hymn of the Republic" was sung. The casket was then put on a train which moved slowly to Washington before enormous grieving crowds alongside the track. Bobby Kennedy was then buried in Arlington National Cemetery under a full moon near his beloved brother Jack.

Sirhan Sirhan was provided with outstanding lawyers and psychiatrists, several among them Jews. There was a heated debate over whether he should receive life imprisonment or the death penalty. Evelle Younger, the Los Angeles district attorney, asked Senator Kennedy whether the family wished to express its view on this question. It certainly did and Teddy wrote a letter in longhand. "My brother," he wrote, "was a man of love and sentiment and compassion. He would not have wanted his death to be a cause for the taking of another life. . . . If the kind of man my brother was is pertinent we believe it should be weighed in the balance on the side of compassion, mercy, and God's gift of life itself." Sirhan pleaded guilty to murder and received a sentence of life imprisonment.[8]

On March 16, 1968, Richard Nixon in a hotel room in Portland, Oregon, had watched Kennedy announce for the presidency. When the TV was turned off, he stared at the blank screen, shook his head, and said, "We've just seen some very terrible forces unleashed. Something bad is going to come of this. God knows where this is going to lead." Nixon had no stomach for a campaign against another Kennedy.

His vulnerability to defeat in 1960 was a bitter memory for Nixon. Nevertheless, he was determined to make another run for the presidency and his target year was 1968. He had assumed that John Kennedy would win reelection in 1964 and would leave the political stage in 1968. He positioned himself carefully. He would capture the governorship of California in 1962 to gain national exposure as the chief executive of the nation's most populous state. After his four-year term expired in 1966, he would make his move for the Republican nomination for President in 1968.

But the plan went awry. Pat Brown defeated him by a comfortable 300,000 votes in the 1962 gubernatorial election. As if losing was not bad enough, Nixon capped it with an extraordinary and distasteful press conference. He had refused to concede publicly on election night and had kept an increasingly restive and hostile press corps waiting till the next morning. At that time his press man, Herb Klein, under great pressure from the reporters, insisted that he come down. But Nixon said, "Screw them." Finally, they agreed that Klein would read a brief statement and Nixon would slip out of a back door of the hotel into a waiting car. Klein went down to meet the press.

But, as Jules Witcover described the scene, Nixon appeared suddenly. "He looked his worst. . . . He brusquely interrupted Klein, took the microphone and face flushed, hands jammed into coat pockets, literally spit out the words heard round the political world." This most controlled of politicians now exploded and spewed out the venom of his real feelings. He attacked the press for failing to report what he had said. While he praised Kennedy for his handling of the Cuban missile crisis, which had just occurred, he said he had not been tough enough about the President on his general Cuban policy. He turned back to the press. "As I leave you I want you to know—just think how much you're going to be missing. You won't have Nixon to kick around any more, because, gentlemen, this is my last press conference."

There were two general reactions to this performance. The first was that Nixon was a born loser who could not be elected President. The other was that, even if he had a chance, he had taken himself permanently out of contention. Both were wrong.

Nixon moved from California to a stronger base in New York and became a partner in a law firm which provided him with a large income and gave him the time to execute his plan. It still called for the same target year: 1968. Even though John Kennedy was gone and Lyndon Johnson was President, 1964 remained hopeless. He was pleased that Goldwater was offered to the butcher rather than himself. Meantime, he labored long and hard for four years to unify and strengthen the Republican party and to make himself available for speeches to virtually all the party's candidates and supporters. "Not since the Democrats in 1932," David Broder wrote, "has a party come back so far and so fast as did the Republicans in 1968." Events played into Nixon's hands. The Republicans made large gains in the 1966 elections. Johnson got into trouble over the war and the Democratic party began to splinter.

None of Nixon's rivals for the nomination proved a serious contender. Governor George Romney of Michigan made an early entry and a rapid exit. Governor Rockefeller was much too liberal for most Republicans and seemed uncertain even about running. The most committed candidate, oddly, was Governor Ronald Reagan of California. But he had been in politics less than two years and his extremely conservative views alienated Republican moderates and seemed to assure defeat. Reagan's conservatism, however, was also his strength; he had great appeal to right-wing Republicans, especially in the South.

Nixon recruited a staff consisting mainly of lawyers and advertising men. While they were intellectually feeble, innocent of experience in government, colorless, humorless, and in some cases dishonest, they were fiercely loyal to Nixon.

As was his custom, he worked out what Stephen Ambrose called "his basic all purpose campaign speech," which he used with minor local variations everywhere and which was effective with the conservative audiences he drew. It gave the impression of great conviction on irrelevant issues and he fudged on the important questions, like the war and race. He enjoyed a very large bankroll to finance the campaign, much to the envy of the Democrats.

Nixon did exceptionally well in the primaries. In Republican New Hampshire he received 84,000 votes to Rockefeller's less than 12,000 write-ins and Lyndon Johnson's 29,000. In Wisconsin he got 79 percent to Reagan's 11. He won easily in Indiana and Nebraska. The big test was Oregon, with its many moderate Republicans led by Governor Tom McCall, who was for Rockefeller. Nixon triumphed with 73 percent of the vote to Reagan's 22 and Rockefeller's miserable 4. He skipped California because Reagan was the favorite son. Meantime, Nixon scoured the non-primary states to dredge up commitments for the convention. He seemed to have put his image as a loser behind him.

The 1,333 delegates to the Republican convention gathered in Miami Beach on August 4. That "Wizard of Ooze," Everett Dirksen, was chairman of the platform committee and was faithful to his sobriquet. He promised a "pungent" document which said nothing and he delivered the goods. Example: "We pledge a program for peace in Vietnam—neither peace at any price nor a camouflaged surrender of United States or allied interests—but a positive program that will offer a fair and equitable settlement to all." Dirksen crafted a platform that every candidate could stand on.

Despite his successful campaign, Nixon came to the convention with a razor-thin majority. He had to win on the first ballot or it would drift away. The very conservative Republicans preferred Reagan. Nixon, therefore, had to deal with the southern boss, Senator Strom Thurmond of South Carolina. He had been a Democrat, more properly a Dixiecrat, until 1964, when he switched to Goldwater and the GOP. He controlled his own delegation and could influence several others from the South. Thurmond adored Reagan.

Nixon countered with attractive promises: a big defense program to fight Communism and a slowing of the pace of racial integration. Thurmond came over.

It took 682 votes to win. Nixon barely made it on the first ballot, 692 to Rockefeller's 277, Reagan's 182, and the remainder split among favorite sons. Nixon picked Governor Spiro Agnew of Maryland as his running mate. This was an astonishing choice because Agnew was widely considered incompetent and, perhaps not known at the time, was also a crook. George Ball, who knew his way around, described the selection as "preposterous" and called the governor "a fourth-rate political hack." On the other hand, Theodore White wrote that the Nixon-Agnew ticket would "offer the nation a sober alternative to the leadership of the Democrats."

Nixon was now in an excellent position to carry the South against a northern liberal Democrat, but not against George Wallace. From his obscure base in Montgomery and with his reputation as the nation's most prominent racist, Wallace lusted after the presidency. "George's great weakness," his friend Hamp Graves said, "is running. He's a compulsive runner. We all are in Barbour County." In 1964 he had entered several Democratic primaries and had done very well—Wisconsin 34 percent, Indiana 38, Maryland 43. He could reach into a deep pocket of racism in the white North.

But the Alabama law forbade the governor to succeed himself and his term had expired in 1966. He tried to persuade the legislature to change the law, but failed. He then did the next best thing: He ran his wife, Lurleen. She won and promptly came down with terminal cancer. After several operations she died on May 9, 1968.

Since Wallace nominated himself and his American Independent Party was a paper fiction, he did not need to enter primaries or cultivate delegations. But he had to qualify his name on the ballot in all 50 states, a formidable operation. California alone required 66,000 signatures. He also selected General Curtis LeMay, former head of the Air Force and the nation's leading advocate of the use of nuclear weapons, to run with him. Wallace got on all the ballots and soon was drawing big and enthusiastic crowds to his campaign rallies. Chester, Hodgson, and Page wrote,

> By the eve of the conventions, George Wallace had established certain facts: He would be a national candidate. He would have serious support in the North. "Law 'n' order" was supplanting Vietnam as the prime issue of the campaign. And none of the candidates in the two major parties could any longer afford to ignore the existence of the man from Alabama.[9]

When Johnson renounced the presidency, Hubert Humphrey was stunned because he realized that the goal he had so long yearned for might now be within his grasp. When Kennedy was shot, Humphrey was convinced that he would win the nomination. But his wife restored reality. "Daddy," Muriel said, "the shot that killed Bobby has wounded you, maybe very seriously." "Why," he asked, "do you say that?" "Because people are going to be so sick of politics, so sick of Democrats, that it's just going to be impossible to do anything."

When Humphrey returned from Mexico City, he met with his closest advisers. They assured him that Kennedy would not stampede the Democratic party and that only Humphrey commanded its decisive center. They urged him to announce. He then called all 24 Democratic governors, prominent mayors like Daley of Chicago, James Tate of Philadelphia, and Joseph Alioto of San Francisco, along with George Meany of the AFL-CIO and I. W. Abel of the Steelworkers. Most were very encouraging. At a meeting in New York of wealthy businessmen he won financial support. But in a visit to the White House Johnson told him that he would remain neutral in order to concentrate on ending the war. Humphrey, Albert Eisele wrote, "was not happy at the lack of private encouragement from the man he had served so faithfully."

On April 27 Humphrey shouted to a roaring crowd of 2000 at Washington's Shoreham Hotel that he was their man. His speech was a proper plea for unity, restraint, and civility. But in his bubbly enthusiasm he ad libbed that he also advocated "the politics of joy." In catastrophic 1968 this sounded absurd and he paid for it. His team was quickly out in the field collecting delegates and within a week reported that 1200 of the 1,312 needed to nominate were either in the bag or leaning toward it. An early Harris poll showed Humphrey with 38 percent, Kennedy 27, and McCarthy 25.

Humphrey brought Larry O'Brien on board as both campaign manager and chairman of the Democratic National Committee. While O'Brien recognized that the odds were against them, he thought they had a long shot.

O'Brien was deeply troubled about two problems. The first was that the convention, aside from serving as a showcase for dissent, was convening much too late, the end of August. It had been scheduled a year in advance for LBJ in order to "shorten the period your opposition can achieve center stage. . . . It turned out to be a disaster [for Humphrey] in terms of conducting a campaign." He was also eager to start at once on critically important and expensive TV spots and was constricted by a severe shortage of funds induced by Humphrey's poor showing in the polls following the convention. "You can't avoid the reality," O'Brien noted, "that a down side in the polls has a tremendous effect on your ability to finance a campaign. Political realists have a tendency not to reach into their pocket quickly when it's not a good bet."

The Kennedy assassination undermined McCarthy because much of Kennedy's support shifted to Humphrey and he soon swept beyond the 1,312 needed. McCarthy, uncertain of his desire to be President, became depressed. Humphrey was also discouraged because, as Muriel had predicted, the killing soured the public and particularly his party on the political process.

Wherever he turned Humphrey confronted this fundamental question: Are you your own man on Vietnam or are you speaking for Lyndon Johnson? He tried stonewalling, but that failed. McCarthy, despite his uncertainties, drew large crowds and gained in the polls. The good ship *Humphrey* was stalled in the water and had started to leak. He desperately needed a declaration of independence from LBJ on Vietnam.

On July 25 Humphrey gathered a task force headed by Professor Samuel P. Huntington of Harvard to work out a statement on the war. They agreed that the cornerstone should be an immediate halt in the bombing of North Vietnam. It was worked into a 13-page document called "Vietnam: Toward a Political Settlement and Peace in Vietnam," which Humphrey approved. He was eager to have the President accept it. Johnson had told him to clear policy statements on Vietnam with Rusk. But Humphrey considered this too important and went straight to the Oval Office. Humphrey later recalled,

> The president was very much opposed to it. I . . . went all over it with him. His reaction was, in substance, "Hubert, if you do this, I'll just have to be opposed to it, and say so. Secondly, Hubert, you ought not to do this because we have some things under way [in Paris] now that can lead to very important developments. Thirdly, Hubert, I have two sons-in-law over there, and I consider this proposal to be a direct slap at their safety and at what they are trying to do."

Humphrey, crestfallen, returned to his staff and instructed them to redraft the statement, which proved extremely difficult, really impossible.

Draft No. 11 contained two key changes: Humphrey promised that he would "not do or say anything that might jeopardize the Paris peace talks." Also, while he still called for stopping the bombing, he now added, "when reciprocity is obtained from North Vietnam." He presented these revisions to Johnson at his ranch on August 9, who rejected them out of hand. The President, according to Hymphrey, said,

> You can get a headline from this, Hubert, and it will please you and some of your friends. But if you just let me work for peace, you'll have a better chance for election than by any speech you are going to make. I think I can pull it off. I think I possibly can get negotiations going, and possibly get the beginnings of peace. If I do, that would be the greatest thing that ever happened to this country, and it would be the greatest thing that ever happened to you.

Humphrey read this as a "hint of an imminent breakthrough in the peace negotiations." He did not challenge the President by demanding specific evidence. In fact, on August 9 there were no negotiations. As Johnson would write in his memoirs, "the Paris talks dragged on through the summer. The formal sessions were sterile propaganda exercises. Informal talks during tea breaks and elsewhere were of little more value." In fact, on August 19, with peace nowhere in his mind, the President delivered a very hard-line speech to the Veterans of Foreign Wars in Detroit.

Humphrey came away from the meeting with Johnson with another concern: He was convinced that the President was reconsidering his promise not to run for another term. LBJ was eagerly trying to arrange a summit meeting with Soviet Premier Aleksei Kosygin and had invited Nixon and Agnew to the ranch on August 10, the day after Humphrey's visit. The President had insisted that Humphrey come in secret, but the Republicans came with a large press contingent that gave the friendly meeting wide coverage. Humphrey complained, "That bothered me." If Johnson, in fact, intended to run, his hopes were crushed by a Harris poll as the convention opened that showed all three—Humphrey, McCarthy, and Johnson—tied six points behind Nixon.

Vietnam, of course, was the issue that could split the convention and destroy Humphrey. He did everything he could to bridge the gap between the President and the peace candidates. A week before the convention began, the platform committee met in Washington. Hale Boggs, the House whip, was chairman and a strong Johnson supporter. A hefty majority of its 110 members leaned the same way. While the McCarthy, Kennedy, and McGovern people (Senator George McGovern became a last-minute candidate) had differences, all agreed that the platform plank must call for a halt in the bombing. A score of wordsmiths worked to paper over the differences between the peace candidates, which, more or less, succeeded and then to bridge the gap between them and Johnson, which failed.

On August 20 Soviet troops invaded Czechoslovakia and overthrew the Dubček government. This, of course, strengthened the hard-liners. Johnson sternly ordered Humphrey not to coddle the doves and Boggs gained firmer control over his committee.

By the Friday before the convention opened the peace groups had agreed on their plank. It was read to Humphrey and he accepted it. He read it to Rusk and Rostow and neither saw any problem. That night Johnson showed Boggs a cable from General Abrams saying that a halt in the bombing would have a dire impact upon American troops. The whip's ramrod spine hardly needed further stiffening. Johnson had already decided that he would unalterably oppose the doves' plank. On Monday morning, as the convention was about to open, Marvin Watson came to Humphrey's suite at the Conrad Hilton to inform him that it was unacceptable. Humphrey was astounded, pointing out that it had been cleared with Rusk and Rostow. But, as Johnson said coldly, "It hasn't been cleared with me." The platform committee endorsed Johnson's Vietnam policy by a vote of 65 to 35.

Connally, who headed the Texas delegation, was Johnson's point man to assure that the convention adopted the committee's plank. No one ever accused John Connally of delicacy or even of civility. Further, he would soon desert the Democratic party. He was merciless with Humphrey. He was, O'Brien said, "arrogant" and "abrupt." O'Brien continued, "Any departure from the Johnson Vietnam policy would be considered by him and southerners he claimed he was speaking for as totally unacceptable, and would bring about disruptions in the convention up to and including Connally putting Johnson's name in nomination." O'Brien did not believe the threat.

In Chicago the Democratic convention drama played itself out on two stages—the Chicago Amphitheatre on the South Side where the delegates gathered and on the streets and parks downtown where those who opposed the war battled Mayor Daley's cops. The peace groups differed in viewpoint and style and several had long planned an attack on the convention.

The National Mobilization Committee to End the War in Vietnam was a loose organization which sought to speak for many groups which agreed only on opposition to Lyndon Johnson and his war. During the preceding winter David Dellinger, who headed the Mobe, and several others, particularly Rennie Davis and Tom Hayden, both much to the left of Dellinger, discussed a massive demonstration at the Democratic convention in August. Davis was named coordinator and opened an office in Chicago. But many of the Mobe's constituents, fearing violence, refused to participate and efforts to win support from militant black organizations were fruitless. The organizers assumed that hundreds of thousands would march. In fact, no more than 5000 came to Chicago from other towns.

Jerry Rubin and Abbie Hoffman, prominent hippies, launched a parallel demonstration. They had founded the Yippies, the Youth International Party, which would stage a Festival of Life (Hoffman: "There we were stoned, rolling around the floor. . . . yippie! . . . Somebody says oink and that's it, pig. They would nominate a live pig named Pigasus for President.") They called this the politics of absurdity, which attracted Allen Ginsberg, the poet of the absurd. If Pigasus was elected, they would demand important changes in American society, like the abolition of pay toilets.

In Daley's Chicago any use of public facilities required a permit. Mobe and the Yippies did not hesitate to ask for the moon. Both wanted Soldier Field for the whole convention week, August 23–28, but it was already taken for President Johnson's birthday (born on the 27th, LBJ never showed up). Mobe also wanted two very busy thoroughfares for marches of 150,000 and 200,000 people, along with ten parks for rallies and six for sleeping. The Yippies asked for Grant Park day and night. The city granted none of these requests.

The week before the convention the Yippies gathered in Lincoln Park on the near North Side, where they had to observe an 11 p.m. curfew. The crowds were small. They listened to rock music, heard tributes to the qualifications of Pigasus, and sat on the ground in the lotus position with Ginsberg. He had taken a fling at Eastern mysticism and argued that, if one sounded "om" in this position, tension would go away. If a group "omed," the police would be immobilized. This could come in handy in Chicago. For some reason Ginsberg's theory did not work. There were several mild encounters with the cops, none very serious, which the Yippies invariably lost. Several of them even wound up in jail.

On Monday afternoon, August 26, the scene shifted to Grant Park. Several hundred demonstrators "seized" the huge equestrian statue of Civil War General Jonathan Logan and climbed all over it, draping it with Vietcong and Communist flags. One youth made it to the top of the general's head and sat there. The police attacked, breaking his arm as they dragged him down. Ginsberg was "oming" nearby. Tuesday was quiet as the demonstrators held an "unbirthday" party for the President. Wednesday was climactic both at the Amphitheatre and at Grant Park.

The convention, as David Broder described it, proceeded under wretched conditions:

> The mood of the dissident delegates had been growing increasingly bitter with each passing day. To the inevitable aggravations caused by the overcrowded conditions on the convention floor—movement down the aisles was almost impossible without being bumped, shoved, and pummelled—were added the tightest security regulations ever imposed on a national convention. Delegates had to present special passes for electronic surveillance on entering the Amphitheatre and again when going onto the floor. Packages and purses were opened and searched. Newspapers, in many instances, were confiscated—ostensibly because of fear of fire. Private police employed to keep interlopers off the floor and in the vain effort to unsnarl the aisles often used more force in their work than some delegates thought justified, and there were frequent scuffles. Finally, there were persistent complaints that the dissident-controlled delegations like California and Wisconsin were not being recognized by the pro-Humphrey, pro-Administration convention chairman, House Majority Leader Carl Albert of Oklahoma.

Under these circumstances and with massive police violence taking place in Grant Park, Vietnam came up for debate on Wednesday afternoon. The platform committee language on bombing was as follows: "Stop all bombing of North Vietnam when this action would not endanger the lives of our troops in the field; this action should take into account the response from Hanoi." Since Johnson insisted that the present bombing protected U.S. troops and there was no possibility of a Hanoi response until the stalled Paris negotiations began, there could be no halt to the bombing until some remote and indefinite date in the future. The peace candidates found this totally unacceptable. They insisted on an immediate and unconditional cessation of bombing. The difference was sharp and left Humphrey no room for maneuver. In fact, he had always opposed bombing and in his heart fully agreed with the minority position. But the President demanded that he support the majority and Humphrey caved in.

"For almost three hours," Broder wrote, "many of the party's most distinguished leaders went to the microphone—alternating between advocates of the minority and majority plank, in a debate of rare cogency and emotional power." In the roll call at the end Johnson won 1,567 ¾ to 1,041 ¼. The losers then donned black arm bands and sang the civil rights anthem, "We Shall Overcome." The nominations for President would take place that night.

Meantime, Grant Park and the Democratic headquarters hotel across Michigan Avenue, the Conrad Hilton, had erupted. The Mobe had finally received a permit for a rally at the bandshell between 1 and 4 p.m. McCarthy, concerned about the safety of his followers, urged them not to participate. By mid-afternoon a crowd estimated at 10,000, many from Chicago, had gathered. The police set up lines on three sides and infiltrated the rally with plainclothes officers. The Chicago police had a long and dishonorable history of violence and brutality and their behavior that day was in their classic tradition.

About 3:30 or 4:00 a youth shimmied up the flagpole and lowered the American flag. The cops grabbed him, beat him, and arrested him. The crowd screamed, "Pigs!" They then threw concrete, bricks, sticks, cans, and stones at the attackers. A police line advanced on the crowd, bashing people with their batons. After 20 minutes they fell back. Dellinger then announced that there would be a nonviolent march to the Amphitheatre. As they gathered, the police told them they had no permit and the National Guard blocked the way.

Meantime, about 2000 crowded at the Hilton and screamed obscenities at the cops. There was trouble keeping order and the police feared that Dellinger would move his frustrated marchers to the hotel, which, in fact, was announced shortly after 6:00. The Guard blocked the bridges over the railroad tracks. The crowd attacked and troops responded with tear gas, which the breeze from the lake swept onto Michigan Avenue. When one bridge was left open, the crowd surged across to the Hilton.

As night fell about 4000 demonstrators were encircled by 300 policemen. They taunted the officers, surrounded a police car, and sat down on the avenue. A police line advanced onto those seated and began arresting them to clear the intersection. The cops, tired and angry, beat people indiscriminately, and the intersection, Walker wrote, "fragmented into a collage of violence." Police discipline collapsed. They attacked people with their batons and with mace. They tossed bodies into paddy wagons. By 8:15, after an hour of police violence, they controlled the intersection. Shortly, the National Guard took over the area. Thereafter there was sporadic violence in the Loop. After midnight the police without provocation invaded McCarthy's suite on the 15th floor of the Hilton, which outraged him.

The police reported 192 officers injured, of whom 49 were hospitalized. More than three-fourths of these injuries occurred on Wednesday. A total of 81 vehicles were damaged. It was impossible to count the number of demonstrator injuries. Hospitals reported treating 45 on Wednesday, but that could only be a small fraction of the total. The arrests totaled 668, more than half from the Chicago area. Many newspaper and television reporters were beaten and suffered damage to their equipment.

Nevertheless, the cameras recorded the event and the nation and the world witnessed the sickening violence on television. Among them were Humphrey, who was slightly tear-gassed, McCarthy, and a large number of the delegates at the convention. When Carl Stokes, the black mayor of Cleveland, rose to second Humphrey's nomination, NBC replaced him with the bloody rioting. McCarthy was so angered by police conduct that he refused to go to the Amphitheatre to give his support to Humphrey after his nomination.

Senator Ribicoff went through the motions of nominating McGovern. He looked down at Daley only 20 feet away and said, "With George McGovern we wouldn't have Gestapo tactics on the streets of Chicago." The mayor, purple with rage, shouted an obscenity which could not be heard in the pandemonium.

The balloting began at 11 p.m. and half an hour later Humphrey went over the top with Pennsylvania at 1,317½. O'Brien and others strongly recommended Senator Edmund Muskie of Maine for Vice President and Humphrey accepted him. O'Brien said, "I thought Muskie had a recognition factor that was very favorable. He was ethnic [Polish], which could be helpful. Ed Muskie had a presence that would add significant dimension to the ticket." This was the only good thing that happened to Humphrey that day.

The Democrats left Chicago embittered, deeply divided, and certain that they had already lost the election. While Humphrey in his acceptance speech urged them to take heart, Broder wrote, "he knew and they knew that he emerged from the convention a beaten man." He would say later, "After Chicago, I was like the victim of a hurricane, having to pick up and rebuild but with too little time to do the job." As McCarthy's plane was taking off, the pilot announced over the intercom: "We are leaving Prague." The polls now showed an enormous drop in Humphrey's support and Nixon with a handsome lead. Nixon and Wallace rubbed their hands with anticipation.

During early September Humphrey drew small and often hostile crowds and showed no improvement in his numbers. His campaign was in disarray. When O'Brien proposed an early speech in Boston, Teddy Kennedy told him that it was "premature." O'Brien had the "clear feeling they didn't want him. That was the first cold shower."

As O'Brien viewed the campaign, "there were two overriding problems. One was Vietnam and the second was money." Vietnam was critical because, if patched up, it could bring back the McCarthy and Kennedy supporters, could present a "strong, decisive Hubert Humphrey," and offered a "splendid opportunity to go on the attack" against Nixon and Agnew. In the latter part of September Humphrey decided to make a nationally televised speech on the war on the 25th in Salt Lake City. The trouble was that he set up a drafting committee chaired by Agriculture Secretary Orville Freeman, an ex-Marine and a confirmed hawk. When O'Brien read the proposed speech, he was "appalled."

On the night before the speech about a dozen advisers met with Humphrey in Salt Lake. The two key spokesmen were O'Brien, who demanded a separation from Johnson and a dovish position, and Jim Rowe, LBJ's old friend, who insisted that Humphrey remain loyal to the President. The argument was intense and bitter and dragged on for hours. One of the doves said, "You have an image of not being your own man, not having guts." Humphrey exploded:

> I am sick and tired of hearing this. I am insulted. I have guts. I am my own man. Nobody can question my loyalty to Lyndon Johnson, but nobody can question my ability to be President. I've listened to the Gene McCarthys say that I'm gutless. I'm not going to listen to any more from you people. . . . Give me a pad. I'm going to write this damn speech myself.

Humphrey proceeded to scribble, reading as he went along, and in this process drafted his speech. At 4 a.m. O'Brien got up to leave and he and the Vice President exchanged silent smiles.

Just before Humphrey went on the air, George Ball, who had resigned as U.N. ambassador and was helping Humphrey with the drafting, read the speech to the President. He expected an explosion. Instead, JBJ said, "Well, George, nobody's better than you in explaining things to the press and I know you'll be able to persuade them that this doesn't mark any change in the Vice President's position from the line we've all been following." "I'm sorry, Mr. President," Ball said, "but that's not quite the name of the game." "Well, George," Johnson said, "I know you'll do the best you can."

The key passage in Humphrey's Salt Lake City speech read as follows:

> As President, I would stop the bombing of the North as an acceptable risk for peace because I believe it could lead to success in the negotiations and thereby shorten the war. This would be the best protection for our troops.—In weighing that risk—and before taking action—I would place key importance on evidence—direct or indirect—by deed or word—of Communist willingness to restore the demilitarized zone between North and South Vietnam.
>
> Now if the Government of North Vietnam were to show bad faith, I would reserve the right to resume the bombing.

Was there a difference between the plank in the Democratic platform and the Salt Lake City speech? Ball called the latter "fuzzy" and "pettifogging." O'Brien said the language quoted "is not that exciting . . . with its share of qualifiers." Clark Clifford wrote that Humphrey had made a "cautious proposal . . . not very different from the Administration's bargaining position."

But that was not the public's perception, which read the address as a clean break with Johnson. On the plane ride to a speech in North Carolina there was an enthusiastic wire from Teddy Kennedy. Terry Sanford and the others who greeted them at the airport were, O'Brien said, "just, glowing. . . . There was a big and enthusiastic crowd . . . and, for the first time, no hecklers." Given his own doubt about the language, O'Brien could not understand it. Maybe the power of television. But "it was the turning point."

Now, finally, the Humphrey campaign was on the road. But it was flat broke. This was critical because of TV time. Humphrey's managers did everything they could to get Nixon to debate with Humphrey, or, at least, allow Agnew to debate Muskie. Having been burned badly by Kennedy in 1960, Nixon refused. Both Republican candidates were vulnerable and O'Brien had a group of powerful TV spots (example: a heartbeat slowly crossing the screen with the caption reading, "Spiro Agnew, A Heartbeat from the Presidency"). But the $6 million needed was unavailable.

The oil industry offered Humphrey the money if he promised to keep the depletion allowance. He refused immediately. The textile interests made a similar proposal and received the same answer. "Hubert," O'Brien said, "had a tendency to react from the gut and dismiss from his mind the fact that we're broke, which was admirable." Johnson controlled a private account of $600,000 in the President's Club, which he did not release for the campaign. O'Brien thought that Johnson made this decision because he was upset with the Salt Lake City speech.

In desperation, Humphrey in October asked his old and very rich friend Duane Andreas to invite about a dozen millionaires to lunch at his apartment at the Waldorf in New York. O'Brien presented the problem. Would they *lend* the Humphrey campaign $3 million to put on half their TV spots? Though these moneybags did not expect to be repaid, they agreed to make the loan, and there was limited television coverage in the last three weeks of the campaign.

Now there was other good news. Muskie turned out to be a superb campaigner with very high ratings in the polls. The contrast with Agnew, who was a flop, was dramatic. The Democrats put Humphrey and Muskie on together.

Early on Wallace made important inroads into the hard-hat community in the northern industrial towns. Humphrey, with his strong labor record, attacked him forcefully. More important, the labor movement raised the largest campaign fund in its history for a massive attack on Wallace for being against the working man—125 million pamphlets, 100,000 door-to-door canvassers, 4 million phone calls. It was extremely effective.

By the closing days of the campaign Humphrey had narrowed the race to a couple of points. On the day before the election Harris actually had him ahead of Nixon 43 to 40. Humphrey got last-minute support from several surprising sources. McCarthy on October 28 ended his long silence and endorsed his fellow Minnesotan. On October 31 the President in a television address ordered a halt in the bombing of North Vietnam allegedly because of positive developments in the Paris negotiations. On November 3 Johnson and Humphrey appeared together at the Houston Astrodome as the President endorsed the Vice President and Humphrey proceeded to carry Texas in the election.

But on the most important issue that arose in the closing days of the campaign Johnson did nothing to help Humphrey. Clark Clifford had become deeply concerned about the Johnson-Nixon relationship on July 24, 1968, when the President told him, "I want to sit down with Mr. Nixon. . . . He may prove to be more responsible than the Democrats. . . . The GOP may be of more help to us than the Democrats in the next few months." As already noted, they did "sit down" at the ranch on August 10. Nixon said that as long as the President did not "soften" his position on Vietnam, he would not criticize the administration. Clifford wrote, "I was as appalled as the President was pleased." Nixon's plan was to "offer us his support in return for inflexibility in our negotiating position and thereby freeze poor Hubert out in the cold. . . . Nixon has outmaneuvered the President. . . . Nixon is trying to hang the war so tightly around the Democrats' neck that it can't be loosened."

From the inception of the Paris meetings the North Vietnamese had refused to meet with the South Vietnamese, charging that they were "puppets" of the Americans who had no right to speak for the Vietnamese people. This had prevented any negotiations and had frustrated Harriman and Cyrus Vance, who had recently joined Harriman. On October 11 they asked the Americans whether the U.S. would stop the bombing if they agreed to Saigon's participation in the talks. The next day Henry Kissinger, who had contacts with both the Republicans and the Democrats, informed John Mitchell, Nixon's campaign manager, that there was the probability that Johnson would bring the bombing to a halt before the election. Washington instructed Ambassador Bunker and General Abrams to ask the South Vietnamese government if it would agree to stop the bombing if Hanoi offered to respect the DMZ, to stop shelling cities, and to agree to serious talks with the participation of Saigon. On October 13 Bunker cabled that General Thieu agreed to these terms on the condition that the bombing would resume if Hanoi violated the agreement. Washington accepted this as a commitment. Later Clifford wondered whether Bunker was congenitally optimistic; he knew that Thieu's English, in which the discourse was conducted, was hardly fluent. If Thieu had in fact made an oral agreement, he quickly reversed himself. It soon became evident that the South Vietnamese would not agree to participate in the talks prior to the elections or, for that matter, during the presidency of Lyndon Johnson.

By mid-October, as the presidential race narrowed, Nixon began to fret. Stephen Ambrose put it this way:

> If Johnson could pull off a bombing halt, get Hanoi to a peace table with promises to behave, bring the GVN [Saigon] into the talks, make it appear that a coalition government was about to be formed, and be able to claim that peace and reconciliation were just around the corner, why then Humphrey, already closing fast, would be a sure winner.

Nixon said publicly, "We do not want to play politics with peace." But that is exactly what he proceeded to do by convincing Thieu to refuse to participate in Paris. Clifford called it "a plot—there is no other word for it—to help Nixon win the election by a flagrant interference in the negotiations."

Nixon's agent was Anna Chan Chennault, the Chinese widow of World War II hero General Claire Chennault, who had headed the Flying Tigers. Her credentials for this role were impeccable. She was president of Flying Tiger Airlines, spent a good deal of time in Asia, was active in the China Lobby, was cochair of Republican Women for Nixon, had raised $250,000 for his campaign, and was a friend of Thieu. She was also a buddy of Bui Diem, the South Vietnamese ambassador to Washington.

About July 12, 1968, Nixon and Mitchell met with Chennault and Bui Diem at Nixon's apartment in New York. Nixon directed Chennault to be his channel via Bui Diem to Thieu. Some time later Nixon informed Thieu by this means that, if he refused to send an envoy to Paris, he would get a much better deal for himself and South Vietnam after the election from Nixon than from Humphrey.

It is hard to believe that Thieu could not have worked this out for himself since it was widely assumed that Humphrey, if he won, would drive hard for peace in Vietnam. "The GVN," Ambrose wrote, "was a government without a country or a people. Its sole support was the U.S. government. Its sole raison d'être was the war. For the GVN to agree to peace would be to sign its own death warrant." On November 2 Thieu announced publicly what he had already told the Americans: He would not participate in the Paris talks and he would not negotiate with the Vietcong.

The White House was fully aware of Nixon's plot and the complicity of Anna Chennault and Bui Diem. "The information," Clifford wrote, "had been derived from extremely sensitive intelligence-gathering operations of the FBI, the CIA, and the National Security Agency; these included surveillance of the Ambassador of our ally, and an American citizen with strong political ties to the Republicans." This confirmed the fact that Nixon "went

far beyond the bounds of justifiable political combat." It was "direct interference in the activities of the executive branch and the responsibilities of
the Chief Executive, the only people with authority to negotiate on behalf
of the nation." Nixon had perpetrated "gross, even potentially illegal, interference in the security affairs of the nation by private individuals."

What would Johnson do with this extraordinary story? In reaching his
decision, he conferred with Clifford, Rusk, and Rostow. According to Clifford, there were several peripheral considerations, none important enough
to tip his hand. Clifford wrote,

> Finally, and most important, there was the question of President Johnson's
> feelings about Hubert Humphrey. Throughout the campaign, the President
> treated his Vice President badly, excluding him from National Security
> Council meetings, and threatening to break with him over the platform
> plank on Vietnam. *What mattered to President Johnson at that moment
> was not who would succeed him, but what his place in history would be.*
> [emphasis mine]

Five days before the election Johnson phoned Jim Rowe with Humphrey's campaign in Peoria, Illinois. He told Rowe that he knew about the
Chennault channel from Nixon to Thieu. He said, "I just want Humphrey
to know about it. Tell him about it, and tell him I don't think he ought to
do anything about it. But that's his problem." Rowe's law partner Tommy
Corcoran knew Anna Chennault very well. Rowe asked, "Do you want me
to get Tommy to pull her off?" Johnson said, "It's too late." Rowe informed Humphrey. Shortly, William L. Bundy gave Humphrey the details
of the intercepts and wiretaps that confirmed Chennault's undercover activities. But Humphrey declined to attack Nixon, believing that even Nixon
would not have stooped so low. "Whatever the vice president's instincts,"
Carl Solberg wrote, "they certainly did not include the instinct for the
jugular."

On November 3, two days before the election, the President phoned
Nixon and revealed his knowledge of the Chennault channel. Nixon, Bundy
wrote, "categorically denied any connection or knowledge." This was a
bald-faced lie.

A public denunciation of Nixon for establishing the Chennault connection would, obviously, have come with much greater authority from the
President than from the Vice President. But Johnson kept the story secret.

Clifford thought that Johnson's failure to act denied Humphrey victory
in the election. William Safire, who worked for Nixon on the campaign,
wrote, "When people later wondered why Nixon thought so highly of President Thieu, they did not recall that Nixon probably would not be President
were it not for Thieu. Nixon remembered." "Had the accusation of meddling in the peace talks taken hold," Jules Witcover wrote, "it could have
swung to Humphrey this election that now was a cliff-hanger." There is no

doubt that a Johnson exposure and denunciation of Nixon would have given Humphrey a boost, probably a substantial one. As will be noted shortly, it would have taken very little to put Humphrey over the top.

The fact that Johnson would base so critical a decision on his own place in history reveals a great deal about him. It is, obviously, evidence of his enormous, insatiable ego. Further, it was exceptionally bad judgment even if one makes the ridiculous assumption that the pivot was his own place in history. With the hindsight of history, we now know that Lyndon Johnson is ranked very low among American Presidents. This is in the face of his enormous achievements in domestic affairs. He certainly would not have been esteemed less by historians if he had helped Humphrey defeat Nixon. On the contrary, it would have raised his position.

On November 5, 1968, 73,359,762 citizens voted. Nixon received 31,785,480 votes; Humphrey 31,275,165, Wallace 9,906,473. Nixon got 43.3 percent of the vote, Humphrey 42.6, Wallace 13.5. Of the two-party vote, Nixon got 50.4 percent, Humphrey 49.6. Nixon's victory margin in the popular vote was the lowest in any election since 1912. Nixon, however, won comfortably in the electoral college with 302 votes compared with Humphrey's 191 and Wallace's 46. Nixon won seven states in the South, Wallace five, and Humphrey one (Texas).

Wallace, who seemed very strong early in the campaign, wilted badly at the end. His residual support consisted mainly of white racists, extremists of the right, and super-patriots who wanted to nuke North Vietnam back into the Stone Age.

David Broder concluded that the 1968 election was remarkable because it was so ordinary:

> The central paradox of the 1968 election was that a year of almost unprec- edented violence and turmoil, a year of wild oscillations and extremes pro- duced a terribly conventional result. A year that saw repeated challenges from the nation's political left- and right-wings ended with the country dividing with almost mathematical equality between two candidates of the center. A year that saw more than the usual amount of internal warfare within the major parties and the birth of the most ambitious third party in forty-four years ended in an election which vindicated the two-party sys- tem. A year which posed a constant threat of constitutional crisis ended with an electoral verdict, rendered in the customary way, without recourse to Electoral College bargaining or a contingent election in the House.

Lyndon Johnson, who had been an almost powerless self-proclaimed lame duck for six months, now became a constitutionally powerless lame duck for the last three. The Democratic Kennedy-Johnson interlude had come to an end after only eight years in control of the White House. John- son's war would now become Nixon's war.[10]

IV

CODA

20

Guns or Butter

PERICLES, perhaps the wisest statesman of antiquity, led Athens into a golden age in the years between the close of the Persian War in 449 and the outbreak of the Peloponnesian War in 431 B.C. He greatly extended democracy by granting citizenship to poor males, allowing them to take seats in the legislature, and placing them on juries in the courts. He launched a massive rebuilding program to restore the damage suffered by Athens during the Persian War. The capstone was the Acropolis with its great new structures—the Parthenon, the Propylaea, the Erectheum, and the Odeum. The culture of the city soared to heights matched among city-states only by Renaissance Florence. Architecture, sculpture, painting, drama, literature, music, history, and science flowered. "Few eras in human history," Donald Kagan wrote, "can compare with the greatness achieved by Athens under the leadership of Pericles in the fifth century B.C."

These achievements, as Pericles knew better than anyone, depended upon three interdependent factors: the empire, prosperity, and, above all, peace. Athens possessed by far the largest empire of the Greek world, reaching from Macedonia in the north almost to Crete in the south. It included much of mainland Greece, most of the Aegean Islands, the coast of Asia Minor, and the straits leading into the Black Sea. The greatest navy of its time was its protector.

Athens became wealthy from her empire, which imported her goods and paid tribute to her. A large hoard of gold and silver was deposited in the treasury in the Parthenon.

Peace was the key. Pericles, who had been a commander in the Athenian navy, knew war and much preferred to avoid it. But the Greek world was an unstable system of competing cities which frequently took up arms.

In 433 Corcyra appealed to Athens in its conflict with Corinth, which had brought powerful Sparta to its aid. Pericles engaged in complex negotiations. But neither Athens nor Sparta would make the concessions needed to gain peace. Sparta and the Peloponnesian League voted for war. Proud Pericles, the honor of Athens at stake, went to war in 431 on behalf of Corcyra. Sparta's goal, Kagan wrote, was "the destruction of Athenian power."

Each year as the crops ripened the Spartan army advanced into Attica. The Athenian farmers, their families, and their animals took cover behind the city's walls. The troops destroyed the crops. In this war of attrition which continued for ten years Sparta held the trump cards. The morale of the Athenians was undermined, the treasury was depleted, and the colonies broke away. Worse, ferocious plagues swept the overcrowded city, killing a third of the population, including many soldiers. In 430 the Athenians turned on Pericles for leading them into disaster. They removed him from office and convicted him of embezzlement. In 429 a defeated and saddened Pericles died, evidently a victim of the plague.

In 425 in Athens Sophocles staged his masterpiece, *Oedipus Tyrannus.* While the setting was Thebes and the leading character was the tragic king Oedipus, the Athenians read his name as Pericles.

Finally in 404 the Spartans, now supported by Persia, brought the bitter war to an end as Athens capitulated. She lost her empire and her fleet; the walls were torn down; the treasury was gone; the populace was starving. The Spartans imposed their foreign policy on Athens. They installed a puppet government of oligarchs which destroyed democracy and imposed a reign of terror.

Such was the tragic end of the Periclean dream. Pericles in the twentieth-century phrase had given up butter for guns and had thereby invited disaster. For the Greeks Pericles was an example of what they called hubris, the arrogance that was certain to bring on the destruction of those who dared to rule over others as though they were Gods.[1]

The choice between peace and war goes back to an early stage in human history, but the guns-or-butter metaphor did not emerge until the twentieth century. It was invented, according to William Safire, by Joseph Goebbels, Hitler's propaganda minister, who said, "We can do without butter, but, despite all our love of peace, not without arms. One cannot shoot with butter but with arms." Shortly, Hermann Goering, the head of the German Air Force, said in a radio speech: "Guns will make us powerful; butter will only make us fat." Goering must have spoken from the heart because he was very fat.

In the first phase of the Americanization of the Vietnam War President Johnson insisted that the U.S. could have both guns *and* butter:

> I believe we can do both. We are a country which was built by pioneers who had a rifle in one hand and an ax in the other. We are a nation with the highest GNP, the highest wages, and the most people at work. We can do both. And as long as I am president we will do both.

He repeated this empty promise in his 1966 State of the Union message and the press immediately called it guns and butter. Chairman Wilbur Mills of the House Ways and Means Committee said, "The Administration simply must choose between guns and butter."

This dilemma was the key to the tragedy of Lyndon Johnson's presidency, perhaps the most tragic in the history of that great office. He acted as though he could have both, while everyone, himself included, knew that he could not. Stephen Skowronek wrote,

> The "tragedy of Lyndon Johnson" is a drama without parallel in modern American politics. It is the story of a master politician who self-destructed at the commanding heights, of an over-arching political consensus shattered in a rush of extraordinary achievements, of a superpower that squandered its resources in a remote conflict with people struggling on the fringes of modernity.

Lyndon Johnson generated and shouldered through Congress a formidable bundle of domestic legislation that he called the Great Society. With this very important achievement, he joined two of his illustrious presidential predecessors in the twentieth century—Woodrow Wilson and Franklin Roosevelt. Together they created a significant historical rhythm: a burst of progressive laws occurring approximately a generation apart. Wilson's New Freedom statutes were enacted between 1913 and 1915, Roosevelt's New Deal program between 1933 and 1935, and Johnson's Great Society legislation between 1964 and 1966. They shared several important characteristics: a strong and energetic Democratic President who did not hesitate to lead; large Democratic majorities in both houses of Congress, which followed their President; solid public support; and the guns-or-butter dilemma which eventually led the President to abandon domestic reform and lead the nation into war—Wilson into World War I, Roosevelt into World War II, and Johnson into the Vietnam War.

Measured by legislative output, Johnson's presidency fell into two periods—1964–66 and 1967–68. Although 1964 constituted the second session of the 88th Congress in which the Democratic majorities were modest, the performance was impressive. In November 1964 Johnson won a landslide victory and carried with him very large majorities in both houses. Thus, 1965 was an extraordinarily productive year with the first session of the 89th. The second in 1966 saw a marked fall-off, but remained a strong year. In the second period, reflecting a sharp Republican rebound in Congress in the 1966 elections and the hemorrhaging of the Johnson presidency due mainly to the war, legislative output dropped sharply in 1967 and virtually disappeared in 1968.

On October 24, 1966, Larry O'Brien and Joe Califano submitted a report to the President on the legislative gains of both sessions of the 89th Congress. They reached this conclusion:

In a word, this was a fabulous and remarkable Congress. We say this not because of its unprecedented productivity—but because what was passed has deep meaning and significance for every man, woman and child in this country—and for future generations. A particularly striking feature about the 89th was that its second session was as equally productive as the first.

The report then listed all the bills passed in each session as though each was equal in significance to the others. In the first session of the 89th, 84 were passed of the 87 proposed; in the second session, 97 of the 113 submitted. By this method of counting the second session was even more productive than the first. But the yardstick was seriously defective. Most of the statutes were of very modest importance. A relatively small minority of the laws was significant, and a very small number was of great importance. In 1965, for example, Medicare far outweighed the statute that authorized the legislature of Guam to fix the compensation of its members. Nevertheless, the 89th was in fact a "fabulous and remarkable Congress," as the authors claimed.

The *Congressional Quarterly* in its annual *Almanac* tracked the legislation more comprehensively than O'Brien and Califano. By CQ's rating, 1965 stands alone as the banner year, 1964 is second, 1966 and 1968 are tied for third, and 1967 is last.

Perhaps most significant, CQ also made narrative judgments of the President's legislative performance. It wrote of 1964: "He had great success with Congress." The editors were swept off their feet by 1965, a "legislative grand slam." CQ stated,

It was clear that the first session of the 89th, starting early and working late, had passed more major legislation than most Congresses pass in two sessions. The scope of the legislation was even more impressive than the number of new laws. Measures which, taken alone, would have crowned the achievements of any Congress, were enacted in a seemingly endless stream. . . .

The pace of the session was so breathless as to cause a major revision of the image, widely prevalent in preceding years, of Congress as structurally incapable of swift decision, prone to frustrate demands for progress.

The 1966 session was a big letdown. "With the public increasingly concerned with inflation and the Viet Nam War," CQ wrote, "Congressional Republicans found new Democratic allies in the effort to curb the 'Great Society'—not only its spending programs but almost any measure providing social reform."

CQ summarized the President's performance in the 1st session of the 90th Congress in 1967 as follows:

Mr. Johnson's success in 1967 did not nearly meet his historic accomplishments in getting landmark Great Society legislation through the overwhelmingly Democratic 89th Congress (1965–66). The specter of the war in Viet Nam coupled with the shift to the GOP of 47 House seats and three Senate seats in the 1966 election gave the President a relatively hostile Congress which was intent on holding down Government spending.

Accordingly, the President introduced little in the way of new Great Society programs, preferring instead to improve and expand already enacted programs. Even some of these proposals—notably the antipoverty program, model cities and rent supplements—faced serious trouble. . . .

The President suffered major defeats when the House Ways and Means Committee refused to act on his proposal for a 10-percent surcharge on personal and corporate income tax and when Congress voted the lowest foreign aid bill in 20 years.

By Labor Day the year was notably unproductive. Congress had enacted only six of the 52 bills . . . Mike Mansfield . . . had listed as "must legislation."

CQ on the second session of the 90th Congress in 1968:

Mr. Johnson's success did not nearly meet his historic accomplishments. . . .

In many cases Congress enacted bills requested by the White House only after adding relatively unpalatable provisions or restrictions.

The important income tax surcharge, for example, was approved in conjunction with a limitation on federal expenditures which the President was forced to accept as the price for passage of the tax hike. . . .

The President's spending plans for a variety of health, education and urban welfare programs were cut back considerably by the budget-minded Congress.

This book addresses small numbers and large significance. That is, it deals with only 17 of the bills President Johnson proposed that were enacted which were, in this author's judgment, significant. That term is understood to mean both (a) measures which represented a new policy or an important change in an old policy and (b) statutes which affected very large numbers of Americans. There have been few acts of Congress, even in so productive a period as the Johnson presidency, which can meet both of these tests. For the years 1964–68 there were merely 17, which is less than 1 percent of the 1902 bills, according to CQ, that Johnson proposed to Congress.

These 17 statutes, in turn, break down into two categories: blockbusters and those that are no more than significant. There were six blockbusters, counting both major education and conservation statutes as one, which is justified because the former involved the same principle of federal aid for education and the latter were both concerned with the preservation of the nation's physical heritage. The blockbusters were: the Revenue Act (Keynesian tax cut), Civil Rights Act, Economic Opportunity Act (poverty), and the Wilderness Act and Land and Water Conservation Fund Act, all 1964; and Medicare and the Elementary and Secondary Education and Higher Education Act, both 1965.

President Johnson must share credit with President Kennedy for these statutes because all, excepting poverty, which was only a Kennedy idea, had been drafted and were well on their way through the congressional machinery at the time of the assassination. Had Kennedy lived, there is no doubt that all would have been passed by 1965. Nevertheless, Johnson deserves much of the glory because he quickly endorsed every one (including getting the poverty bill drafted) and brought his legislative experience and skills into play to assure their passage. All were enacted during the first two years of the Johnson presidency, 1964 and 1965.

In addition, there were 11 statutes which, if they did not meet the high test of a blockbuster, were nevertheless significant: the Voting Rights Act, Immigration Act, Water Quality Act, and Clean Air Act amendments and Solid Waste Disposal Act, all 1965; the Fair Labor Standards Act minimum wage amendments and Model Cities Act, 1966; the Air Quality Act and Public Broadcasting Act, 1967; and the Tax surcharge, Social Security Act amendments, and civil rights with open housing, all 1968. Johnson takes the credit for all of this legislation.

If the blockbuster and significant groups are joined, the importance of the first two years of Johnson's presidency becomes dramatic. In 1964 and 1965 the total was ten; in 1966, 1967, and 1968 together it dropped to seven.

These numbers are remarkable. While they look small, they are huge. The likelihood is that a majority of U.S. Presidents did not produce a single blockbuster and many failed even to achieve passage of one significant statute. Clearly, the only President in U.S. history who was on Johnson's level was Franklin Roosevelt. Here Wilbur Cohen, who served under both, on an intuitive "Richter-type scale" of legislative effectiveness with a yardstick of 10, ranked LBJ first at 9.8 and FDR second at 6.7. This can be argued. Despite the fact that Roosevelt was Johnson's great hero, LBJ consciously set out to surpass FDR and he may have succeeded. He certainly was at least FDR's equal.

This legislation in the aggregate thrust the U.S. a giant step forward in the direction of democratization by assisting those who needed help the most. The unemployed found jobs; the elderly gained health care; the young enjoyed greater educational opportunity; blacks and women, among others, overcame discrimination and the former in the Deep South won the right to vote; the poor received hope; discrimination against certain types of immigrants was ended; the national park system was much expanded and great stretches of wilderness were preserved; and the first efforts were made to counter air and water pollution.

For these achievements Lyndon Johnson deserves the lion's share of the credit. He, of course, received great help from others, starting with the critical Kennedy legacy. In the departments Wilbur Cohen on Medicare and Social Security and Stewart Udall on conservation and pollution performed masterfully. Several members of Johnson's White House staff made notable contributions: Larry O'Brien and his assistants, Mike Manatos and Henry Hall Wilson, on congressional relations, Joe Califano on overall domestic policy, Douglass Cater on education. But Lyndon Johnson was at the center of the whirlwind. He relentlessly drove himself, his staff, and the Congress to enact this program. It was a virtuoso performance.

In fact, Johnson did not even stop to catch his breath at the close of the first session of the triumphant 89th Congress. Majority Leader Mansfield, noted for good judgment, recommended a slowdown, taking time for digestion, and concentrating on the administration of the laws that had already been enacted. Many newspapers and magazines sang the same chorus. White House aide Harry McPherson pointed out that congressional investigations would expose much "confusion, duplication, and waste." He recommended that the President beat Congress to the punch by naming Charles Schultze to head an administration investigating commission on the implementation of the new laws. McPherson also suggested a major campaign to explain them to the public.

But Johnson, driven by his need to surpass Roosevelt, would hear none of this sensible advice. There was still room over his fireplace for new coonskins and he intended to get them. The progress of a bill, Doris Kearns wrote, was "the center of Johnson's life, and the ceremony of successful completion was also a personal celebration. . . . The ceremonies were also a public forum in which Johnson bestowed upon the nation his most valued creation—the laws of the Great Society. The ceremony was also a summons to the next series of legislative endeavors." "He adopts programs," Califano wrote, "the way a child eats chocolate-chip cookies." Califano took his son to the hospital after the boy swallowed a full bottle of aspirin. The President tracked him down there and listened to the account. "There ought to be a law," Johnson said, "that makes druggists use safe containers." This led eventually to passage of the Child Safety Act of 1970.

On October 22, 1965, when Congress adjourned, the President wrote a long letter to Mansfield. After thanking the majority leader for playing a major part in "the first session of the 89th Congress [that] will go down in history as the greatest session . . . in the history of our Nation," he pointed to the job left still to be done: "23 major items of legislation, recommended by the Administration, which the Congress did not enact." There was also a batch of budget questions. Johnson sent Califano out to several major universities to dig out legislative ideas and instructed him to establish task forces to flesh them out. For Lyndon Johnson, 1966 would be like 1965, 1967 like 1966, and so on. In his mind, evidently, there were no changes under way in the conditions that he and the Congress would face. He could not have been more wrong.[2]

Lyndon Johnson Americanized the Vietnam War in mid-1965. The conflict would continue until January 27, 1973, almost eight years, when Henry

Kissinger and Le Duc Tho negotiated a cease-fire. This armistice, not a peace treaty, provided for the withdrawal of the few remaining American troops, a prisoner exchange, and related military matters, leaving the fundamental question, the political future of South Vietnam, unresolved. The North Vietnamese gave the answer in the spring of 1975 with a quick offensive that destroyed South Vietnam's military forces and culminated in the capture of Saigon. The seemingly interminable war came to an end because Vietnam was united. Ho Chi Minh was now dead, but his followers had won the war he had started.

Did the United States lose the war? Colonel Harry G. Summers, Jr., called the result "tactical victory, strategic retreat." He wrote, "On the battlefield itself, the Army was unbeatable. . . . Yet, in the end, it was North Vietnam, not the United States, that emerged victorious." Thomas C. Thayer wrote, "The Americans couldn't win in Vietnam but they couldn't lose either as long as they stayed." Stanley Karnow put it this way:

> In human terms at least, the war in Vietnam was a war that nobody won—
> a struggle between victims. Its origins were complex, its lessons disputed,
> its legacy still to be assessed by future generations. But whether a valid
> venture or a misguided endeavor, it was a tragedy of epic dimensions.

That epic tragedy included the costs the Vietnam War imposed on the American people. They were stupendous and are suggested by the following analysis.

The war exacted a terrible human toll on the 3.5 million Americans who served in Vietnam. As of March 1973, some 57,625 U.S. troops had died, 47,205 in combat and 10,420 otherwise. In addition, 153,312 had been wounded or injured and required hospitalization; another 150,341 had been wounded or injured and were not hospitalized. Further, 3,592 were missing and 750 had been captured. Soldiers and marines fighting on the ground suffered 88 percent of combat deaths and 90 percent were enlisted men. Some 12 percent of those who died in combat were black. When the Vietnam Memorial was opened in Washington in November 1982, it listed the names of almost 58,000 men and women who had been killed or were missing in action in Vietnam. Among those not listed were a large number of amputees and paraplegics. About 6,655 persons lost limbs during the war.

The most melancholy cost of the war was that of combat veterans who survived only to suffer from severe, chronic post-traumatic stress disorder (PTSD). The rigorous *National Vietnam Veterans Readjustment Study* made in the late eighties, twenty years after the war, revealed that 36 percent of combat veterans met the full American Psychiatric Association diagnostic criteria for PTSD. When Jonathan Shay published *Achilles in Vietnam* in 1994, there were more than 250,000 of them.

All of these men suffered from severe combat trauma, usually from sniper or mortar fire or from stepping on a land mine. Example from one of Dr. Shay's patients:

> I was walking point. I had seen this NVA soldier at a distance. . . . I stuck my head in the bush and saw this NVA hiding there and told him to come out. He started to move back and I saw he had one of those commando weapons, y'know, with a pistol grip under his thigh, and he brought it up and I was looking straight down the bore. I PULLED THE TRIGGER ON MY M-16 AND NOTHING HAPPENED. He fired and I felt this burning on my cheek. I don't know what I did with the bolt of the 16, but I got it to fire, and I emptied everything I had into him. THEN I SAW BLOOD DRIPPING ON THE BACK OF MY HAND AND *I just went crazy.* I pulled him out into the paddy and carved him up with my knife. . . .
>
> *I lost all my mercy. . . . I just couldn't get enough. . . .* I built up such hate. I couldn't do enough damage. . . .
>
> *Got worse as time went by. I really loved fucking killing, couldn't get enough. For every one that I killed I felt better. Made some of the hurt went away.*

Such experiences often cause PTSD, which clamps its grip on the soldier for the rest of his life. The common symptoms are formidable: loss of memory and perception; constant mobilization for lethal danger with the potential for extreme violence; chronic health problems; expectation of betrayal and exploitation by others; alcohol and drug abuse; despair, isolation, a sense of the meaninglessness of life; and a tendency to suicide.

The cost of PTSD, evidently, has not been estimated, but it must be enormous. The total would have to include at least the following costs over the victim's lifetime: psychiatric care, medical care, hospitalization, and drugs; forfeited income because many of these men are unemployable; incarceration because a disproportionate number are in jail; and welfare support.

The total dollar cost of the Vietnam War was immense and will continue well into the twenty-first century. In 1976 Robert Warren Stevens, using studies then available, divided his global estimate of the cost into four components: (1) the incremental budget cost to the U.S. government during the years the war was fought, that is, excluding defense expenditures that would have been made if there had been no war, estimated at $128.4 billion, (2) budgetary costs, mainly veteran's benefits, incurred since the end of the war that must be paid because it was fought, $304.8 billion, (3) extra-budgetary economic costs imposed by the war on the American economy, $70.7 billion, and (4) indirect economic costs attributable to the war, such as recession, inflation, loss of exports, $378 billion. These four groups of costs add up to the gigantic total of $882 billion.

Was the war worth this immense price in blood and treasure? Admiral

James B. Stockdale, who spoke with special authority, gave the answer. As a naval fighter pilot he had led a group of planes over that part of the Gulf of Tonkin where two U.S. destroyers had allegedly been attacked on August 3, 1964, which gave Lyndon Johnson the pretext for his first giant step into the war, passage of the Tonkin Gulf resolution. Stockdale saw no North Vietnamese boats. He was later shot down, lost a leg, was tortured, and spent over seven years in a prisoner-of-war camp blindfolded. He did not see Vietnam until he returned in 1994. "I was surprised at how junky it looked. God, we were so dumb about it. Did we think of the lives we squandered on this dump?"

Robert Jay Lifton, the noted psychiatrist, celebrated the end of two wars in Times Square. On VE-Day in 1945 he was a medical student who joined a huge throng in a mood of "pure mass joy." When Kissinger announced the standdown in Vietnam in 1973, the square was "seedy, almost deserted." There were "a few Vietnam veterans gathered in anger, some drinking, others apparently on drugs, most simply enraged, screaming at the camera, at the society, about having been deceived by the war and ignored upon coming back."

These veterans were bitter largely because they did not know why they had been sent to Vietnam. Nobody had told them. This was President Johnson's job and he had failed to perform it. This must have been in part caused by his own inconsistency and dishonesty on the record. During the 1964 presidential campaign he repeatedly made the following point: "We don't want our American boys to do the fighting for Asian boys. We don't want to get involved in a nation with 700 million people [China] and get tied down in a land war in Asia."

But in the first half of 1965 Johnson secretly reversed himself and on his own initiative led the United States into that war. He approved Rolling Thunder in February, the marine landing at Danang in March, and the commitment of major ground forces by July. Further, in April, his National Security Action Memorandum No. 328, after approving the troop commitments, stated: "The President desires that . . . premature publicity be avoided by all possible precautions." His intent was that "these movements and changes be understood as being gradual and wholly consistent with existing policy." How could the American people, including those who would serve in the war, understand a new policy that was being withheld from them? David Wise called 328 "one of the most shameful official documents of a shameful time in American history."

Finally, on July 28, the President discussed publicly for the first time the military actions he had already authorized. This was as close as he came to a statement of his war aims in Vietnam. He offered the following arguments in defense of his actions: "Why," he asked, "must young Americans, born into a land exultant with hope and with golden promise, toil and suffer and sometimes die in such a remote place?" Answer: "We have learned at a terrible and brutal cost that retreat does not bring safety and weakness does not bring peace." This is an excellent question and a meaningless response.

Later Johnson says, "Nor would surrender in Viet-Nam bring peace, because we learned from Hitler at Munich that success only feeds the appetite of aggression." In fact, neither South Vietnam nor the U.S. faced the prospect of surrender. The comparison of Ho's North Vietnam to Hitler's Germany is ludicrous. The Nazis commanded enormous military force and, as Johnson put it, North Vietnam was a sixth-rate power.

Ho's goal, the President said, was to "conquer the South, to defeat American power, and to extend the Asiatic dominion of communism." There are two disparate ideas here. Ho's objective, obviously, was to unite Vietnam under his rule. If that required "conquest" of the South and the "defeat of American power," North Vietnam had no alternative but to assume those burdens.

The other idea, extending the "Asiatic dominion of communism," was, of course, the domino theory. If South Vietnam falls, Johnson said, "most of the non-communist nations of Asia cannot, by themselves and alone, resist the growing might and the grasping ambition of communism." Eisenhower had introduced the domino metaphor in 1953 by warning that the loss of Vietnam would lead inexorably to the fall of Malaysia, other parts of Asia, and Indonesia. But it was a metaphor, not a description of reality. North Vietnam had given no sign of either the ambition or the capability to overrun other nations in Southeast Asia. In fact, in the seventies when it had united Vietnam it made no effort to do so. Nor did the other countries fear an invasion by North Vietnam. Neil Sheehan wrote, "There was, in fact, no international Communist conspiracy and no 'Sino-Soviet bloc.' The Communist world of the 1960s was a splintered world. The Chinese and the Soviets had openly despised each other for years." So, too, had the Vietnamese and the Chinese, historic enemies. Sheehan continued, "Guerilla wars could not be spread like bacteria, and countries were not dominoes. They were living entities with national leaders who pursued their own agendas."

Johnson then pointed out that "three Presidents—President Eisenhower, President Kennedy, and your present President—over 11 years have committed themselves and have promised to help defend this small and valiant nation." On its face, this statement was factually correct. But there was a fundamental difference between the Eisenhower and Kennedy policies and the policy Johnson was now implementing. As moderate cold warriors, they had sent equipment, trainers, and advisers to South Vietnam. They had not bombed the North and they certainly had not launched a land war in Asia in defiance of traditional American military doctrine.

Finally, the President left a gaping omission: a strategy for victory. He did not tell the American people how the war would be won or how long it would take. No wonder that thereafter Johnson's aides repeatedly urged him without success to present a credible justification for the war and that the troops in Southeast Asia never knew why they were there.

The absence of meaningful war aims contributed to a massive decline in national morale, which fed both the peace movement and the young men subject to the draft. Draft evasion became the great pastime of the period. Millions of young men went to college or graduate school or got married to avoid service. A great many simply ignored their draft cards and some even burned them. An important haven of escape was the reserves and the National Guard, which Johnson refused to call up. Only 15,000 went to Vietnam and nearly a million remained comfortably at home. A significant group of young men went into exile, particularly in Canada and Sweden. A generation later two prominent politicians were embarrassed by draft evasion—Republican Vice President Dan Quayle and Democratic President Bill Clinton.

The pointlessness of the war undermined the morale of the troops in Vietnam, particularly in the Army. This created rage and mindless killing both of innocent civilians, as at My Lai, and the "fragging" of officers. Drugs and alcohol were widely used and there was racial tension. This came to a head in 1971 with riots among the troops in Vietnam.

One of the great casualties of the war was the credibility of the government, particularly the presidency. Lyndon Johnson had never messed much with the truth and his style—Texas hype, an obsession with secrecy, and a gross misunderstanding of the press—led to massive lying about the war. "There was a certain inevitability," David Wise wrote, "that the term 'credibility gap' should have been born during the Johnson administration." Wise should know because he was White House correspondent for the New York *Herald Tribune* and his dispatch on May 23, 1965, contained probably the first use of the phrase. "It was a case where the man and the times fused." Lying, particularly in wartime, was hardly a new feature of American politics. But, Wise noted, "nothing in our past had matched, in scale and quality, the grand deception of Vietnam." Nixon, who confronted both the war and Watergate, was an even bigger liar than Johnson. Between them they undermined the credibility of American government for at least a generation.

Many of Johnson's supporters recommended that he address his credibility problem. An example is a letter J. K. Galbraith wrote to Califano on December 16, 1966:

> I would strongly urge the President to stamp very hard on this talk about credibility. And he should do it in the only possible way. This is to be particularly unvarnished in not only the good news but the bad. . . .
>
> I would like to urge him to say flatly that we favor the equitable procedure of paying bills by taxation rather than by the inequitable and dangerous levy that is imposed by inflation. And I would also like to urge an

equally flat statement that since personal incomes are now at an all time high, and are partly so in consequence of war spending, we can't justify any argument for cutting back needed civilian expenditures because of the war.

I would urge the President to be equally candid and blunt on the problems that we face on foreign policy and notably on Vietnam. I think the ultimate response would be extremely favorable.

The President did not listen to such advice.

Johnson's deceit, abetted by McNamara, as noted in Chapter 14, launched the Great Inflation. The rapid rise in prices was, in effect, a general sales tax on goods and services paid by Americans and those foreigners who imported our goods. Stevens estimated the inflation of gross national product for 1969–72 at $140 billion. It was much harder on those with fixed incomes than on those whose wages and salaries kept pace with advancing prices.

Perhaps most important, the great meat cleaver of the Vietnam War divided the country in a variety of ways. The conflict bitterly split those who favored it from those who opposed it, the old from the young, the well-educated from those who were poorly educated, most of the country from the South and the Southwest, and, most painfully, families. This did not end with the conclusion of hostilities in 1973; it was much in evidence a generation later. The war was the main cause for the great civil unrest that characterized the late sixties. The U.S. had not known such chaotic and violent division since the sectional conflict of the 1850s that led to the Civil War. The split was deep and venomous within Lyndon Johnson's own Democratic party, particularly at the disastrous Chicago convention in 1968.

One may speculate over what might have been if the country had remained at peace. Economic policy was working superbly in 1965 and it is likely that prosperity would have continued into 1968. In Chicago the Democrats would have renominated the Johnson-Humphrey ticket and it would have won easily. This might have launched a long period of Democratic control of the White House and the Congress. The Great Society would have survived and might have been expanded.

This leads to the guns or butter issue—the Great Society versus the Vietnam War. Johnson tried desperately to have both, but that was impossible. The war squeezed out reform. Arthur Schlesinger wrote in 1966, "The Great Society is now, except for token gestures, dead." This is substantially correct in the sense of further efforts to help the underclass—programs to eliminate poverty, to improve the education of the poor, to raise standards of health care, and to replace the ghettoes with decent housing. The legislative monuments of the Kennedy-Johnson era that primarily benefited the middle class, however, remained in place—tax policy, aid to education, particularly higher education, Medicare, the national parks, wilderness, efforts to improve air and water quality, public broadcasting, and so on. Neither the war nor Nixon undermined these programs. But after 1966 Vietnam and growing Republican strength revived the GOP-southern Democratic coalition which blocked Johnson's efforts to help the underclass, and Nixon later substantially disemboweled these programs. Thus, Lyndon Johnson's great dream of lifting the poor, particularly black people, to a level playing field was destroyed by his own war.[3]

Lyndon Johnson's presidency was a metaphor for a manic-depressive personality: the stunning highs of the Great Society followed by the abysmal lows of the Vietnam War. No other American President has experienced so striking a swing from success to failure. Joe Califano, who certainly was a witness, called his book *The Triumph & Tragedy of Lyndon Johnson*. What manner of man was Johnson that he could spawn such a dramatic transformation?

He was a gigantic bundle of contradictions. Robert McNamara told Califano that he was the "most complicated man he'd ever met" and Califano agreed. The frequent shifts in mood and behavior make one wonder whether he ever established his own identity. What were the main contradictions in his personality?

Johnson possessed a first-class mind, perhaps at the genius level. This included a phenomenal memory and a large vocabulary. George Reedy, who understood him very well, wrote, "The Johnson IQ took a back seat to very few others—perhaps even to none. His mind was magnificent—fast, penetrating, resourceful." Further, "he had the most superbly developed sense of timing in the whole history of American politics." He had an uncanny ability to foresee future events and their impact on particular senators. "He could predict votes other senators did not even know they were going to cast." White House aide Lee White stressed his "single-mindedness." "He keeps his eye on that damned bull's eye all the time." In the debate over the 1957 Civil Rights Act a question of great intricacy under the common law arose—the distinction between civil and criminal contempt. Johnson took a few law books home one evening and the next day, according to Dean Acheson, one of the nation's top lawyers who was helping Johnson with the amendments, was competent to argue the point before any court in the U.S. Intellectually, Acheson said, it was "awe-inspiring." When he became President, Johnson had virtually no understanding of the federal budget. After evening and weekend meetings with Kermit Gordon, his budget director, he attained mastery of the subject.

But much of this intellectual power was piddled away. "He simply *could not see* a concept," Reedy wrote, "without an immediate pragmatic objective." Because of his marginal education and his refusal to read anything not directly related to his job, Johnson was unable to link his brilliance to a broad range of knowledge. Thus, he often perceived only half of a problem. Put another way, he was extremely bright but lacked wisdom.

He was obsessed with politics and cared about almost nothing else—literature, history, art, music, sports. When he was President and threw out the first ball at the Washington Senators opening game, he talked politics with the others in his party and paid no attention to what was taking place on the field.

Johnson cultivated the image of the proud Texan who was a tough, powerful leader. He wore expensive white beaver Stetsons, invoked Davy Crockett and the Alamo, and proudly showed off his handsome ranch on the Pedernales. In fact, he had lived most of his adult life in Washington, bought his clothes from expensive tailors, and moved in the highest social circles. His toughness was only skin deep. In his childhood he had been very insecure and dependent on his strong mother. He dreamed about flight from responsibilities and sometimes did run away. When his parents insisted that he go to college, he fled to California. On the day before the 1964 Atlantic City convention would nominate him for President he informed his wife and his closest aides, including Reedy, that he would not run. Both in 1960 and in 1968 he diddled with the decision to run and never became a serious candidate.

Johnson was extremely funny and was a brilliant mimic. He could split the sides of the people in his audience with his vast store of down-home stories delivered stone-faced in a rich Texas accent. Example: J. K. Galbraith wrote a speech for him. "Ken," Johnson said, "this is a great speech. But I have to tell you that whenever a man makes any kind of economic speech . . . it's like pissing down your leg; it makes you feel warm, but your audience is colder than a Texas norther." Despite this wit, throughout his life Johnson fought spells of deep depression.

No other President except Nixon was so obsessed with secrecy. He did not want anyone to know what he was doing or intended to do until he alone made the announcement. He lectured, threatened, and berated his aides to protect his cocoon of secrecy. Yet he talked incessantly and was an incurable gossip. Smart reporters could sometimes figure out what he was going to do simply by studying what he said. This was eased by the fact that Johnson, though he officially "hated" the press, could not stay away from reporters. According to Charles Mohr of the *New York Times,* this was because he was lonely in the evening, particularly when his wife was away, as she was in early May 1965. Mohr wrote that one week Johnson "walked with the press" every day except Sunday. There were two-hour walks on Wednesday, Thursday, and Friday, on Saturday a walk followed by a long talk on the Truman balcony. On Monday Mohr was off, but there was a twilight walk on Tuesday.

Johnson, as noted above, had great trouble distinguishing between truth and falsehood. But, Reedy pointed out, he could always convince himself that whatever was coming out of his mouth was true. In time, of course, particularly over the war, the reporters and the public became aware of his massive lying and his credibility was destroyed. Some of the lies were whoppers. Example: During the 1964 campaign he repeatedly promised that he would not send American boys to fight and die in Vietnam. He was busy repudiating that pledge even before he was inaugurated on January 20, 1965.

Lyndon Johnson was indissolubly married and was at the same time a womanizer. When someone mentioned John Kennedy's sexual escapades, Johnson would boast that he "had more women by accident than Kennedy had on purpose." Reedy thought this "pure braggadocio. His physical desires were nowhere near those ascribed to JFK and to the extent that he indulged in extra-marital activity, it was usually with girls for whom he had 'fallen.' " Lady Bird Johnson, Reedy wrote, "bore the whole thing with incredible fortitude. Always he came back to her because he needed her. She did have brains; she could be trusted; she would step into the breach at the psychological moment and patch up the gaping wounds he had inflicted." Joe Califano on Mrs. Johnson: "She was a saint. . . . The most extraordinary woman I've ever met, including my own wife and mother."

Johnson loved people in the abstract and treated many who depended upon him outrageously. He was a confirmed New Dealer who unhesitatingly invoked the power of the federal government to help the people at the bottom of the income scale. This, of course, led him to the Great Society. But a streak of cruelty caused him to humiliate his subordinates. Knowing that Hubert Humphrey hated to kill, he demanded that the Vice President shoot a deer at his ranch. He insisted on doing business with his aides in the bathroom while he defecated. He told them that he wanted a "kiss-my-ass-at-high-noon-in-Macy's-window loyalty." An outraged Reedy as witness:

> He was notorious for abusing his staff, for driving people to the verge of exhaustion—and sometimes over the verge; for paying the lowest salaries on Capitol Hill; for publicly humiliating his most loyal aides; for keeping his office in a constant state of turmoil by playing games with reigning male and female favorites. . . .
>
> His manners were atrocious—not just slovenly but frequently *calculated* to give offense. . . . He was a bully who would exercise merciless sarcasm on people who could not fight back but could only take it. Most important, he had no sense of loyalty. . . . To Johnson, loyalty was a one-way street; all take on his part and all give on the part of everyone else—his family, his friends, his supporters. . . .
>
> Occasionally he would demonstrate his gratitude for extraordinary services by a lavish gift—an expensive suit of clothes, an automobile, jewelry for the women on his staff. The gift was always followed by an outpouring of irrelevant abuse.

Califano's ovservation on the effect of LBJ's exploitation upon his aids: "There wasn't a guy on the White House staff who didn't have a hell of a problem with his wife, including me and everybody I knew on that staff. Everybody."

Richard Goodwin and Bill Moyers, after each checked independently with a psychiatrist, became convinced that Johnson was paranoid and, in part for that reason, both left him. Doris Kearns, after interviewing him at length, reached the same conclusion. Douglass Cater said that he drafted many letters of resignation and never sent any of them. Reedy wrote of Johnson's "tantrums" and "rampages," often caused in part by heavy drinking, that were the prelude to "a flood of invective." He speculated unsuccessfully about the causes, "but I cannot avoid the feeling that there were deeper causes which will probably never be known."

Johnson did not vent his rage on Califano. Rather, he refused to talk to him and would give instructions through his secretary. Jack Valenti simply took the President's outbursts. Moyers, according to Califano, "would go out for two hours and just drive around in a car." Harry McPherson spoke of Johnson's "moods." "I suppose," he said, "an analyst would say [he behaved] in some manic depressive way." McPherson's relationship with Johnson became "intense" and he saved his "sanity" by pulling away. He talked to a psychoanalyst friend who said that Johnson was a "clean-tube man." Every once in a while his plumbing got plugged and "he blows everything out: good, bad, fears, rages, all of it. And he has got more to blow out than most people do." McPherson learned to get out of the way when Johnson was about to blow out his tubes.

Thus, if all of Lyndon Johnson's contradictions worked out on the downside, he would have had these characteristics: ignorance of many important matters, a warped over-emphasis on politics, a preoccupation with his own image, a tendency to run away from important decisions, an obsession with secrecy, an addiction to lying, a yen for sex, a cruel streak that caused him to humiliate people who were loyal to him, and a propensity for "moods" and "tantrums" that some called paranoid or manic depressive.

These contradictions, this yin and yang of personality, meant that Johnson was prone to making mistakes of judgment. Reedy devoted a chapter of his memoir to what he called "A Gap of Understanding," that is, Johnson's failure to grasp the role of the press in our society and his mule-like refusal to try to understand.

During his presidency Lyndon Johnson made two momentous decisions. The first was reached on Air Force One on November 22, 1963, immediately after he was sworn in as President: he would push at once for the enactment of Kennedy's domestic program in 1964; he would win election as President in November of that year; and he would announce his own much broader domestic program in 1965. In his mind there was a sharp distinction between government officials who were *elected* and those who were not. He had become an unelected, accidental President. Kennedy had won the office by election and his agenda, therefore, was in Johnson's mind sanctioned. Excepting poverty, all the programs had their legislative origins in the Congress of the late fifties when he had been majority leader in the Senate. He was thoroughly familiar with them and he strongly approved of the tax cut, civil rights, federal aid for education, and Medicare. Now a national figure, he was no longer constrained by Texas conservatism and could act out his own New Deal convictions on the Kennedy program.

The second momentous decision, of course, was to commit American military forces to the war in Vietnam. Here, too, he confronted legitimacy. As an accidental President he could not make that bold commitment. But his landslide victory over Goldwater in November 1964 was a transformation. Reedy, who was working for him at the White House, wrote, "His presidential style changed overnight and it was not a good change." Reedy had been trying to get him to hold a long overdue press conference. Johnson said, "I've been kissing asses all my life and I don't have to kiss them any more. Tell those press bastards of yours that I'll see them when I want to and not before." Reedy thought there would be trouble and that it would not be confined to the press.

Richard Goodwin, who was also in the White House, made an even graver observation. "During 1965, and especially in the period which enveloped the crucial midsummer decision that transformed Vietnam into an American war, I became convinced that the president's always large eccentricities had taken a huge leap into unreason."

These observations lead to the reason for Lyndon Johnson's decision to go into Vietnam: hubris. He was convinced that he headed the world's mightiest military power. With contempt he called North Vietnam a "pissant" sixth-rate or "raggety-ass" fourth-rate nation. With the legitimacy he had won in the election, he need not consult the Congress, or, for that matter, even let Congress or the American people in on his secret. In the Greek sense, this was the arrogance that aroused the anger of the gods and caused them to inflict disaster upon the one who went to war. As with Pericles and Athens, the preference for guns over butter would bring calamity to Lyndon Johnson and to the United States.[4]

Notes

The overwhelming majority of the documents cited in this book are housed in the Lyndon Baines Johnson Library, which is located on the University of Texas campus in Austin. The titles of frequently cited books have been shortened as follows: Irving Bernstein, *Promises Kept* (New York: Oxford Univ. Press, 1991), cited as Bernstein, *Promises Kept;* Joseph A. Califano, Jr., *The Triumph & Tragedy of Lyndon Johnson* (New York: Simon and Schuster, 1991), cited as Califano, *Johnson;* Clark Clifford, *Counsel to the President* (New York: Random House, 1991), cited as Clifford, *Counsel; Congressional Quarterly Almanac,* cited as *CQ Almanac; Economic Report of the President Together with the Annual Report of the Council of Economic Advisers* (Washington: Government Printing Office), cited as *Economic Report of the President;* Lady Bird Johnson, *A White House Diary* (New York: Holt, Rinehart and Winston, 1970), cited as Johnson, *Diary;* Lyndon Baines Johnson, *The Vantage Point* (New York: Holt, Rinehart and Winston, 1971), cited as Johnson, *Vantage Point;* Doris Kearns, *Lyndon Johnson and the American Dream* (New York: Harper and Row, 1976), cited as Kearns, *Johnson; Public Papers of the Presidents of the United States, Lyndon B. Johnson,* cited as *Public Papers, Johnson;* and *Report of the President's Commission on the Assassination of President Kennedy* (Washington: Government Printing Office, 1964), cited as *Warren Commission Report.*

Prologue

1. *Dictionary of American Biography,* Supp. Eight, 205–7. Garner's famous quip is usually bowdlerized as "a pitcher of warm spit." Max Farrand, ed., *The Records of the Federal Convention of 1787* (rev. ed., New Haven: Yale Univ. Press, 1966); Noble E. Cunningham, Jr., "Election of 1800," in A. M. Schlesinger, Jr., F. L. Israel, and W. P. Hansen, eds., *History of American Presidential Elections, 1798–1968* (New York: Chelsea House, 1985), 1: 101–34; John D. Feerick, *From Failing Hands* (New York: Fordham Univ. Press, 1965), ch. 7, app. A; Report of the Twentieth Century Fund Task Force, *The Modern American Vice Presidency* (Princeton: Princeton Univ. Press, 1982), 7.

2. Robert Dallek, *Lone Star Rising* (New York: Oxford Univ. Press, 1991),

576–78; Rowland Evans and Robert Novak, *Lyndon B. Johnson: The Exercise of Power* (New York: New American Library, 1966), chs. 13, 14; George Reedy, *Lyndon B. Johnson: A Memoir* (New York: Andrews and McMeel, 1982), 54, 129; Lawrence F. O'Brien, Oral History Interview, I-6, 11–12, Elizabeth (Liz) Carpenter, Oral History Interview, I-10, Johnson Library; Arthur M. Schlesinger, Jr., *A Thousand Days* (Boston: Houghton Mifflin, 1965), 702–3; Leonard Baker, *The Johnson Eclipse* (New York: Macmillan, 1966), 10, 80.

3. The best treatments of Johnson's vice presidency are Baker, *Johnson Eclipse,* and Evans and Novak, *Exercise of Power,* ch. XV, quote at p. 308. See also Schlesinger, *A Thousand Days,* 703–4; Walter W. Heller, Oral History Interview, 2–5, Johnson Library; Kearns, *Johnson,* 167–68; Reedy, *Johnson,* 24–25, 126; Harry McPherson, *A Political Education* (Boston: Houghton Mifflin, 1972), 191. The camel driver incident is described by two eyewitnesses: George Reedy, Oral History Interview, 11–15, Johnson Library, and Liz Carpenter, *Ruffles and Flourishes* (Garden City: Doubleday, 1970), 41–46.

4. Johnson, *Diary,* 3–5.

Chapter 1. Fifteen Days

1. *Warren Commission Report,* chs. 1, 2; Johnson, *Vantage Point,* ch. 1, quotes at 8, 9, 11, 14; tape recording of the events of Nov. 22, 1963, by Elizabeth Carpenter, Dec. 1963, quotes at 17, 19, 26; Pool Report, Dallas to Washington, Nov. 22, 1963, Johnson to Caroline and John Kennedy, Nov. 22, 1963, all Assassination of John F. Kennedy File, Johnson Library; Jack Valenti, *A Very Human President* (New York: Norton, 1975), ch. 1, quotes on 7, 9, 43; Michael Amrine, *This Awesome Challenge* (New York: Putnam, 1964), ch. 1.

2. Bradley S. Greenberg and Edwin B. Parker, eds., *The Kennedy Assassination and the American Public* (Stanford: Stanford Univ. Press, 1965), 14, 137, 152–59, 219, 235–36; Carpenter tape recording, 23, Jenkins to Johnson, Nov. 24, 29, 1963, Assassination of John F. Kennedy File, Katzenbach to Moyers, Nov. 25, 1963, Moyers Papers, Hatfield to Carpenter, n.d., Appointment file, James H. Rowe, Oral History Interview, II-29, Joseph L. Rauh, Jr., Oral History Interview, I-31, II-23, III-1, 2, all Johnson Library; Johnson, *Vantage Point,* 19–21, 29–30, 31–32, 40–41; Kearns, *Johnson,* 170–71, 177–78; Califano, *Johnson,* 13–14; *Public Papers, Johnson, 1963–1964,* I: 8–10, 12–13, 35, 218–19; Lawrence F. O'Brien, *No Final Victories* (Garden City: Doubleday, 1974), 165; Earl Warren, *The Memoirs of Earl Warren* (Garden City: Doubleday, 1977), 355–59, 358 n.; Bernard Schwartz, *Super Chief* (New York: New York Univ. Press, 1983), 495–96: Amrine, *Awesome Challenge,* 58–60; George Reedy, *Lyndon B. Johnson: A Memoir* (New York: Andrews and McMeel, 1982), 153; *Gallup Poll,* III: 1853, 1857. Walter Heller met with the new President on Saturday evening, November 23. Johnson was anxious about the drop in the stock market on Friday afternoon, about 5 percent. He asked whether he should do something about it. Heller recommended that he remain silent because "no one really knows how to understand the market or influence it." According to Heller, the President said that "the important thing was to create a general sense of confidence and assurance. . . . He felt that would do more for the stock market than anything else, and I agreed." They were right. Heller, Oral History Interview, II-13-14, Johnson Library.

Chapter 2. The Tax Cut

1. For the legislative progress of the tax bill under Kennedy, see Bernstein, *Promises Kept,* 157–59. C. Douglas Dillon, Oral History Interview, 9–11, 13, Kermit Gordon, Oral History Interview, II-6-8, 22–26, III-3, Walter Heller, Oral History Interview, I-22, II-16, Gardner Ackley, Oral History Interview, I-6, Charles L. Schultze, Oral History Interview, I-28; Barr to Desautels, Legislation Report, Nov. 26, 1963, Confidential File, all Johnson Library. Schultze's comment about how hard it was to spend $100 billion in fiscal 1965 was certainly correct. The actual figure in the administrative budget was $96.5 billion, $1.1 billion under Kennedy's 1964 figure. This, as Schultze also pointed out, was because defense expenditures declined $4 billion between 1964 and 1965. *Economic Report of the President, 1966,* 276.

2. Heller, Chronology of Events on Board the Aircraft Carrying the Cabinet Group to Japan on Nov. 22, the Day of President Kennedy's Death, Nov. 23, 1963, Heller, Notes on Meeting with President Johnson, 7:40 p.m., Nov. 23, 1963, Heller Papers, Kennedy Library; Heller, Oral History Interview, I-12-17, II-21-22; Heller to Johnson, Summary Review of the Economic Situation and Pending Issues, Nov. 23, attached to the Administrative History of the Council of Economic Advisers, Notes by Gardner Ackley, Troika Meeting with President Johnson, Monday, Nov. 25, Appointment File, Heller to Johnson, Case for a $101–102 billion Budget, Nov. 25, 1963, GEN-CEA File, all Johnson Library; Gordon, Oral History Interview, III-2-3, 5–7, 12; *Public Papers, Johnson, 1963–1964,* I: 10, 15, 16, 36, 44, 66–67, 84, 86, 90, 113, 177; Johnson, *Vantage Point,* 37; Statement by Senator Harry F. Byrd, Dec. 5, 1963, Byrd Papers, University of Virginia Library, Charlottesville. Dirksen, according to Dillon, took the position that "under no circumstances will the Republicans agree to the Committee's reporting out a bill until they have had a look at the overall budget figures." Johnson had agreed to show him the galley proofs of the budget on either the evening of January 14 or early on the morning of the 15th. Dillon to Johnson, Jan. 21, 1963 [misdated, probably early in January], The Tax Bill, Legislation File, Johnson Library.

3. Barr to Desautels, Nov. 26, Confidential File, Notes on the First Congressional Leadership Breakfast Held by the President on Dec. 3, 1963, Appointment File, O'Brien to Johnson, Jan. 6, 1964, Reports on Legislation, Barr to Manatos, Dec. 17, 1963, Confidential File, Troika Meeting with President Johnson, Monday, Nov. 25, 1963, Appointment File, Barr to Desautels, Jan. 13, Manatos Papers, W. J. Hopkins Memo, Feb. 26, 1964, Legislation File, all Johnson Library; *Public Papers, Johnson, 1963–1964,* I: 9, 21, 37, 69, 115, 158–60, 178–81, 311–14; *Revenue Act of 1964,* Sen. Rep. No. 830, 88th Cong., 2d sess., Rep. of the Committee on Finance (Jan. 28, 1964); *CQ Almanac, 1964,* 518–40; Dillon, Oral History Interview, 8–13, and Heller, Oral History Interview, II-24-25, both Johnson Library.

4. The revenue provisions of the Revenue Act of 1964 are available in the summary section of the already cited Senate Finance Committee's Rep. No. 830. Heller, Oral History Interview, I-18, II-23-25; Heller to Wirtz, March 21, 1964, Records of Secretary of Labor Wirtz, National Archives. Most of the statistics are from the appendices of the *Economic Report of the President* of the late sixties. The profit figures are at p. 3 of the 1966 *Report.* CEA discussion of the need to raise the rate of GNP growth to keep pace with new entrants into the labor force is at p. 40. Walter W. Heller, *New Dimensions of Political Economy* (Cambridge: Harvard

Univ. Press, 1966), 72–73; Arthur M. Okun, "Measuring the Impact of the 1964 Tax Reduction," in Joseph A. Pechman, ed., *Economics for Policymaking, Selected Essays of Arthur M. Okun* (Cambridge: MIT Press, 1983), 405–23.

Chapter 3. The Civil Rights Act of 1964

1. For the background of the civil rights bill under Kennedy, see Bernstein, *Promises Kept*, 102–13; *Gallup Poll*, III: 1827, 1829, 1837–38, 1863.

2. Johnson, *Vantage Point*, 38, 39, 158; George Reedy, Oral History Interview, III-8, XVI-32; Roy Wilkins, Oral History Interview, 23; Hubert H. Humphrey, Oral History Interview, III-13; Paul H. Douglas, Oral History Interview, 6–7; O'Brien to Johnson, Jan. 6, 1964, Assassination of John F. Kennedy file, all Johnson Library; *Public Papers, Johnson, 1963–64*, I: 9; Bruce J. Dierenfield, *Keeper of the Rules: Congressman Howard W. Smith of Virginia* (Charlottesville: Univ. Press of Virginia, 1987), the Albert quote is from the foreword, the Republican crack about arson p. 158. The struggle over the Rules Committee is chronicled in Neil MacNeil, *Forge of Democracy: The House of Representatives* (New York: David McKay, 1963), ch. 15, James A. Robinson, *The House Rules Committee* (Indianapolis: Bobbs-Merrill, 1963), 71–80; William R. MacKaye, *A New Coalition Takes Control: The House Rules Committee Fight of 1961* (Eagleton Institute, No. 29, 1963). Charles and Barbara Whalen, *The Longest Debate* (New York: New American Library, 1985), ch. 3.

3. The texts of H.R. 7152, the congressional reports, and the debates in both houses have been gathered conveniently in U.S. Equal Employment Opportunity Commission, *Legislative History of Titles VII and XI of the Civil Rights Act of 1964*, hereafter cited as *Legislative History*. A play-by-play account of the bill's progress is in Whalen, *Longest Debate*. I have relied heavily on both. From the Whalen the Arends quote is at p. 109, Celler and McCulloch statements at pp. 105–7, Smith quote at p. 111. O'Brien to Johnson, Jan. 21, 1964, Civil Rights Act, Legislation File, Johnson Library. For general works on the sex amendment to Title VII, see Cynthia Harrison, *On Account of Sex* (Berkeley: Univ. of California Press, 1988), 176–82; Hugh Davis Graham, *The Civil Rights Era* (New York: Oxford Univ. Press, 1990), 136–39; and Patricia G. Zelman, *Women, Work, and National Policy, The Kennedy-Johnson Years* (Ann Arbor: UMI Research Press, 1980), ch. 4. *Legislative History*, 2155–76, 3213–28; Emily George, *Martha W. Griffiths* (New York: Lanham, 1982), 149–50; Donald Allen Robinson, "Two Movements in Pursuit of Equal Employment Opportunity," *Signs* (Spring 1979): 415; Whalen, *Longest Debate*, 117; Zelman, *Women, Work, and National Policy*, 62.

4. Whalen, *Longest Debate*, 130, 137, 157–88; Nicholas Katzenbach, Oral History Interview, 8, 20, 21, Johnson Library. For the sketch of Mike Mansfield see *Current Biography, 1952*, 400–02, *1978*, 281–85; Harry McPherson, *A Political Education* (Boston: Houghton Mifflin, 1972), 44–45, 182–85; Joseph A. Califano, Jr., Oral History Interview, *XIX*-16, Johnson Library. Mansfield's appeal to Republicans never ended. Many years later Ronald Reagan, of all people, named him ambassador to Japan. For Hubert Humphrey, see Albert Eisele, *Almost to the Presidency* (Blue Earth, Minn.: Piper, 1972), chs. 1, 4; Whalen, *Longest Debate*, 138; McPherson, *Political Education*, 37–39; Hubert H. Humphery, Oral History Interview, III-9-10, Johnson Library. On the Humphrey quote about kissing Dirksen's

backside, see Carl Solberg, *Hubert Humphrey: A Biography* (New York: Norton, 1984), 224.

5. For the sketch of Richard Russell, see McPherson, *Political Education,* 54–56; Johnson, *Diary,* 42; Reedy, Oral History Interview, V-1, and Douglas, Oral History Interview, 5, both Johnson Library. Burke Marshall, Oral History Interview, 8, 27, Katzenbach, Oral History Interview, 8, 20–21, 168, Emanuel Celler, Oral History Interview, 9, O'Brien to Johnson, June 18, 1964, EX LE File, all Johnson Library. Edwin O. Guthman and Jeffrey Shulman, *Robert Kennedy in His Own Words* (New York: Bantam, 1988), 211–12; Whalen, *Longest Debate,* 130.

6. This section depends heavily upon Whalen, *Longest Debate,* chs. 5–7, quotes at 144–45, 156, 176–77, 194, 203. Graham, *Civil Rights Era,* 144, 149–50. For the sketch of Dirksen, see Neil MacNeil, *Dirksen: Portrait of a Public Man* (New York: World, 1970), 6–8, 216, 219–23; Reedy, Oral History Interview, 10, Johnson Library; Whalen, *Longest Debate,* 153; Humphrey, Oral History Interview, III-8. A rumor floated in 1964 that those two notorious wheeler-dealers, Johnson and Dirksen, had made a secret "payoff" in which the President took a nuclear accelerator away from Wisconsin and awarded it to Illinois in return for the delivery of the Republican votes to close debate on H.R. 7152. There is plausibility to this theory. That is, Johnson eliminated the funding for the Wisconsin accelerator from the 1965 budget in December 1963; a 200-bev. machine was later built in Weston, Illinois, 25 miles from the Argonne National Laboratory; and most of the Republican senators voted for cloture. Dirksen did write a letter to Johnson on December 31, 1963, asking for the Argonne transfer. Donald F. Hornig, the President's new science adviser, answered on January 29, 1964, advising Dirksen that no decision had yet been made. Hornig to Dirksen, Jan. 29, 1964, WHCF, Dirksen file, Johnson Library. But senators are expected to support their constituents. Mike Manatos, who covered the Senate for the White House, was asked if there had been a payoff. "I happen to know," he replied, "that that wasn't the case in this issue." Mike Manatos, Oral History Interview, 20, Johnson Library. In fact, this accelerator location dispute was part of the prolonged conflict over federal support for "Big Science" in which Dirksen played no role. The battle over the Wisconsin accelerator, which had nothing to do with the Civil Rights Act, is traced authoritatively in Daniel S. Greenberg, *The Politics of Pure Science* (New York: New American Library, 1967), chs. 10, 11. The Humphrey statement on quotas is in *Congressional Record,* March 30, 1964, p. 6549; the Margaret Chase Smith quote is from Robinson, "Two Movements," *Signs* (Spring 1979): 148; Udall to Johnson, May 7, Manatos to O'Brien, May 6, 1964, Legislative Background, Civil Rights Act, 1964 File, U.S. Information Agency to Johnson, Foreign Reaction to Senate Passage of the Civil Rights Bill, June 29, 1964, EX LE file, Katzenbach, Oral History Interview, 20, all Johnson Library. The Whalens, p. 188, discuss the origins of the Victor Hugo "quote." While one hesitates to quibble with Everett Dirksen in his shining hour, Hugo did not keep a diary. At other times Dirksen said Disraeli was the author of the famous line. The quote, in fact, is from Hugo's *Histoire d'un crime. Legislative History,* 3003–8, 3017–21, 3129–63; for a discussion of the Motorola case, see Herbert Hill, "The Equal Employment Opportunity Acts of 1964 and 1972," *Industrial Relations Law Journal* (Spring 1977): 12–16; *Congressional Record,* June 10, 1964, pp. 14318–19.

7. O'Brien to Johnson, June 18, July 2, White to Files, Meeting with Negro Leadership following Signing Ceremony, July 6, 1964, all EX LE file, Johnson Library; *Public Papers, Johnson, 1964,* 842–44; *Report of the National Advisory*

Commission on Civil Disorders (New York: Bantam, 1968), 35–37, 229–30; Anthony Lewis and the *New York Times, Portrait of a Decade* (New York: Random House, 1964), 257–61; David J. Garrow, *Bearing the Cross* (New York: Morrow, 1986), 338–39.

Chapter 4. The War on Poverty

1. Fernand Braudel, *Civilization and Capitalism,* vol. II: *The Wheels of Commerce* (New York: Harper & Row, 1982), 506–12; Gertrude Himmelfarb, *The Idea of Poverty: England in the Early Industrial Age* (New York: Vantage, 1985), 307–9, 312, 387–92, 406, 453, 529–31, chs. 12, 14, 19; Lloyd George is quoted by Robert J. Lampman, *Ends and Means of Reducing Income Poverty* (Chicago: Markham, 1971), 7; T. L. Lloyd, *Empire to Welfare State, English History, 1906–1976* (Oxford: Oxford Univ. Press, 1979), chs. 1, 2.

2. Jacob A. Riis, *How the Other Half Lives* (New York: Scribner, 1890). For the literature and art of the Great Depression, see Irving Bernstein, *A Caring Society* (Boston: Houghton Mifflin, 1985), ch. 7. Dorothy Campbell Tompkins, *Poverty in the United States During the Sixties, a Bibliography* (Berkeley: Institute of Governmental Studies, University of California, 1970). For the black migration to the North after 1940 in general, see Bernstein, *Promises Kept,* 17–20; for the Mississippi Delta to Chicago migration, see Nicholas Lemann, *The Promised Land* (New York: Knopf, 1991).

3. John Kenneth Galbraith, *The Affluent Society* (Boston: Houghton Mifflin, 1958), 251, ch. 23; Robert A. Lampman, *The Low Income Population and Economic Growth,* Joint Economic Committee, Study Paper No. 12, 86th Cong., 1st sess. (1959); Conference on Economic Progress, *Poverty and Deprivation in the U.S.* (Washington: 1962); Lemann, *Promised Land,* 118–29; Richard A. Cloward and Lloyd E. Ohlin, *Delinquency and Opportunity* (Glencoe: Free Press, 1960), 211; Oscar Lewis, *The Children of Sanchez* (New York: Random House, 1961), xii, xxiv, xxv–xxvii; Harry M. Caudill, *Night Comes to the Cumberlands* (Boston: Little, Brown, 1962); Michael Harrington, *The Other America* (New York: Macmillan, 1962), 2, 3, 6, 17, 167, 174; Dwight MacDonald's *New Yorker* article is reprinted in J. K. Haddon, L. H. Masotti, and J. C. Larson, eds., *Metropolis in Crisis* (Itasca: Peacock, 1967), 267.

4. Arthur M. Schlesinger, Jr., *A Thousand Days* (Boston: Houghton Mifflin, 1965), 1009–11; Heller to Kennedy, Progress and Poverty, May 1, 1963, Administrative History of the Council of Economic Advisers, Johnson Library; *Economic Report of the President, 1964,* ch. 2, quotes at 57, 59, 77.

5. William Capron and William Cannon gave accounts of their roles in shaping the poverty program in the Federal Government and Urban Poverty, II: 138–58, 169–81, Kennedy Library; Heller to Secy. of Agriculture et al., Nov. 5, 1963, Administrative History of Council, Johnson Library; John F. Bibby and Roger H. Davidson, *On Capitol Hill* (2d ed., Hinsdale: Dryden, 1972), 229–30; Heller, Chronology of Events on Board the Aircraft Carrying the Cabinet Group to Japan on Nov. 22, the Day of President Kennedy's Death, Nov. 23, 1963; Notes on Meeting with President Johnson, 7:40 p.m., Nov. 23, 1963, Heller Papers, Kennedy Library; Johnson, *Vantage Point,* 69–75; Hackett to Heller, 1964 Legislative Programs for Wider Participation in Prosperity, Nov. 6, 1963, in The Federal Government and Urban

Poverty, vol. I, Kennedy Library; James L. Sundquist, *Politics and Policy* (Washington: Brookings, 1968), 137–42, including a summary of the Marris strategies; Charles L. Schultze, Oral History Interview, II-61, Kermit Gordon, Oral History Interview, IV-2-3, 6–9, James L. Sundquist, Oral History Interview, I-23-24, Theodore M. Hesburgh, Oral History Interview, 9, all Johnson Library; *Public Papers, Johnson, 1963–64,* I: 113–14, 184.

6. Sargent Shriver, Oral History Interview, I-1–7, 23–28, 33, 34, 46–48, 70, 71, 85, 87, II-51, IV-45–46, Adam Yarmolinsky, Oral History Interview, I-13, 17–19, III-16, 40, 42–43, Sundquist, Oral History Interview, I-36, 49–50, Schultze Oral History Interview, II-61–62. Administrative History of the Office of Economic Opportunity during the Administration of President Lyndon B. Johnson, 28, 30, Hopkins to Moyers, May 6, 1964, Legislative Background of Economic Opportunity Act File, all Johnson Library. Shriver did not want to be called "czar." He insisted that he was only a "sergeant" and "Look what happened to the czars!" Adam Yarmolinsky, "The Beginnings of OEO," in James L. Sundquist, ed., *On Fighting Poverty* (New York: Basic, 1969), 34–37, 45, 48–49; *Public Papers, Johnson, 1963–64,* I: 376; Yarmolinsky quotes in The Federal Government and Urban Poverty, I: 255, III: 248, 327. Shriver thought that the task force was driven out of the Court of Claims Building by blasting across Pennsylvania Avenue for a new underground headquarters for the President in case of an atomic war. "It made me laugh that in the process of doing that they were blowing down the war against poverty headquarters." Shriver, Oral History Interview, I-79, Johnson Library.

7. The President's poverty message, written by Yarmolinsky, and the bill sent up on March 16, 1964, are in *Poverty,* H.R. Doc. No. 243, 88th Cong., 2d sess.; Christopher Weeks, *Job Corps* (Boston: Little, Brown, 1967), 17–27, 35–36, 76–102. The Wirtz data on youth unemployment are in *Economic Opportunity Act of 1964,* Hearings Before the Committee on Education and Labor, H.R., 88th Cong., 2d sess. (1964), pt. 1, p. 185; Shriver, Oral History Interview, I-8–10 38, II-2–3, III-2, IV-45–46, Yarmolinsky, Oral History Interview, I-16, II-20–21, III-17, Sundquist, Oral History Interview, I-28–29, Schlei, Oral History Interview, I-29, all Johnson Library; A. H. Raskin, "Generalissimo of the War on Poverty," *New York Times Magazine,* Nov. 22, 1964, p. 90.

8. Richard H. Rovere, Oral History Interview, I-10–11, Lampman to Heller, June 10, 1963, which Heller sent to both Kennedy and Johnson, in Administrative History of Council, both Johnson Library; Elinor Graham, "Poverty and the Legislative Process," in Ben B. Seligman, *Poverty as a Public Issue* (New York: Free Press, 1965), Reston quote at 254, 255–56, 270, n. 7; The Federal Government and Urban Poverty, 162, 287, 291, Kennedy Library; *CQ Almanac, 1964,* 208–28, 646–47; Shriver to Johnson, July 16, 1964, Manatos Papers, Johnson Library; *Economic Opportunity Act,* House Hearings, pt. 1, pp. 6, 7, 64–65, 108, 109, 114–15, 146, 184, 185, 309, 314, 631–36, pt. 3, p. 1343; Shriver, Oral History Interview, II-85–92, Yarmolinsky, Oral History Interview, I-15–19, II-10, Schlei, Oral History Interview, I-37, all Johnson Library; Raskin, "Generalissimo," 88, 91; *Economic Opportunity Act of 1964,* H.R. No. 1458, 88th Cong., 2d sess. (June 3, 1964), 11; *Economic Opportunity Act of 1964,* Hearings Before Senate Committee on Labor and Public Welfare, 88th Cong., 2d sess. (1964); *Economic Opportunity Act of 1964,* S. Rep. No. 1218, 88th Cong., 2d sess. (July 21, 1964); *Cong. Record,* July 22, p. 16659, July 23, pp. 16718–27, Aug. 7, 1964, pp. 18574, 18582. For Fitt's role in racial integration of the armed forces, see his memoranda on the National Guard and off-base equal opportunity of Dec. 30, 1963, and May 27, 1964, to Lee

C. White, White Papers, Johnson Library; O'Brien to Johnson, July 31, 1964, For the President, n.d., EX LE file, Johnson Library; Rowland Evans and Robert Novak, *Lyndon B. Johnson: The Exercise of Power* (New York: New American Library, 1966), 432–33; *Public Papers, Johnson, 1963–64,* II: 941. According to Schlei, Yarmolinsky took "a terrific kick in the face" and was "crushed and really let down and puzzled." Schlei, Oral History Interview, I-37. While Yarmolinsky, of course, left the poverty program, he remained in the Johnson administration for two years. He was active in the Johnson presidential campaign in 1964, was sent by McNamara to the Dominican Republic in 1965, and then spent a year working with John McNaughton, the assistant secretary of defense for international security affairs, where he became very unhappy about the Vietnam War. In the fall of 1966 he joined the faculty of the Harvard Law School. Yarmolinsky, Oral History Interview, I-22–31. Harry McPherson probably understood the President as well as anyone could. McPherson said, "He doesn't believe that the end justifies any means; he believes it justifies quite a few means. But he has a curious degree of reserve and feelings of delicacy about some means." Harry McPherson, Oral History Interview, I-16, Johnson Library. On August 7, 1964, the end was to avoid any threat, no matter how remote, to his victory in the election of which the poverty program was an essential part. The means was to remove Yarmolinsky even if it involved "a terrific kick in the face." In delivering that kick, Johnson was restrained by neither reserve nor delicacy.

9. *Public Papers, Johnson, 1963–64,* II: 360–61, 989; Yarmolinsky, Oral History Interview, II-9, III-32, 43–44, Sundquist, Oral History Interview, I-40, Wilbur J. Cohen, Oral History Interview, 9, all Johnson Library. For the Bureau of the Budget's objections to the location of OEO, see Bohen to Task Force, the President's Task Force on Government Organization, Nov. 30, 1966, Task Force on Government Organization file, Johnson Library. For the administrative problems of OEO, see Sar A. Levitan, *The Great Society's Poor Law* (Baltimore: Johns Hopkins Univ. Press, 1969), ch. 2. *Economic Opportunity Act of 1964,* House Hearings, 184.

Chapter 5. Prelude: The 1964 Election

1. Robert D. Novak, *The Agony of the G.O.P., 1964* (New York: Macmillan, 1965), 58; William A. Rusher, *The Rise of the Right* (New York: Morrow, 1984), 94, 98, 117–27, the Sharon Statement is at 90–91; the Goldwater quote is in Richard Rovere, *The Goldwater Caper* (New York: Harcourt, Brace, World, 1963), 11; Lionel Trilling, *The Liberal Imagination* (New York: Doubleday, 1950), ix; Friedrich A. Hayek, *The Road to Serfdom* (Chicago: Univ. of Chicago Press, 1944); Russell Kirk, *The Conservative Mind* (Chicago: Regnery, 1953); Richard Hofstadter, *The Paranoid Style in American Politics and Other Essays* (Chicago: Univ. of Chicago Press, 1965), 29; F. Clifton White, *Suite 3505* (New Rochelle: Arlington House, 1967), 34–36.

2. This sketch is based on Barry Goldwater's autobiography, *With No Apologies* (New York: Morrow, 1979), quotes at 22, 27, 29, 96, 160–63, and Rovere, *Goldwater Caper,* quotes at 4, 8, 22, 40–41, 50–51. The Humphrey quip is from David W. Reinhard, *The Republican Right Since 1945* (Lexington: Univ. of Kentucky Press, 1983), 159–60. Edwin O. Guthman and Jeffrey Shulman, eds., *Robert Kennedy in His Own Words* (New York: Bantam, 1989), 373, 393. According to

Clifton White, Goldwater did not even bother to read Bozell's manuscript of *The Conscience of a Conservative*. White, *Suite 3505*, 204. If one were a new conservative, it must have been fun writing speeches, columns, and books for Goldwater, because the ghost could write whatever he liked. The result was that Goldwater became the "author" of a cornucopia of statements, many of which were both outrageous standing alone and in direct conflict with each other. Many were also very funny. Rovere collected these Goldwaterisms the way others collected incunabula and Monets. His little *Caper* is a treasurehouse of these shockers. History has its ironies. In a sense, Goldwater made Lyndon Johnson, the man who destroyed him in the 1964 election, a national figure. In 1952 the Arizonan defeated Ernest McFarland, the Senate majority leader for reelection, thereby making the job available for Johnson, who used it to vault onto the national stage.

3. White, *Suite 3505*, chs. 4, 12–35, quotes at 85, 280, 407; Novak, *Agony of G.O.P.*, chs. 4–23, quotes at 140, 287; Theodore H. White, *The Making of the President, 1964* (New York: Atheneum, 1965), chs. 3–7, quote at 102–3; Goldwater, *With No Apologies*, chs. 18–21, quotes at 163, 166; Lawrence F. O'Brien, Oral History Interview, IX-2, Johnson Library; John Bartlow Martin, "Election of 1964," in A. M. Schlesinger, Jr., F. L. Israel, and W. P. Hansen, eds., *History of American Presidential Elections* (New York: Chelsea House, 1985), IX: 3584. Drew Pearson is quoted in The Goldwater Candidacy and the Christian Conscience, p. 9, PL 2 File, Johnson Library. Stephen Shadegg, *What Happened to Goldwater?* (New York: Holt, Rinehart and Winston, 1965), 171–72, 188.

4. Adam Smith, *The Wealth of Nations* (New York: Modern Library, 1937), 651, 681, 747; Graham Wallas, *The Great Society* (New York: Macmillan, 1914); Richard N. Goodwin, *Remembering America* (Boston: Little, Brown, 1988), 267–81; *Public Papers, Johnson, 1963–64*, I: 704–7; Kermit Gordon, Oral History Interview, IV-1–2, Johnson Library. For the difficulty, really impossibility, of defining the Great Society, see the essays in Bertram M. Gross, ed., *A Great Society?* (New York: Basic, 1966).

5. Kearns, *Johnson*, 205; Johnson, *Vantage Point*, 92–98; George Reedy, Oral History Interview, IV-21, Lawrence F. O'Brien, Oral History Interview, IX-2, X-25, both Johnson Library; Johnson, *Diary*, 192.

6. Rowland Evans and Robert Novak, *Lyndon B. Johnson: The Exercise of Power* (New York: New American Library, 1966), ch. 20, quote at 436–37; the Henshaw column is attached to Spain to Manatos, July 30, 1964, EX FG 13 04-2 File, Johnson Library; Clifford, *Counsel*, 394–98, quotes at 395, 397; Arthur M. Schlesinger, Jr., *Robert Kennedy and His Times* (Boston: Houghton Mifflin, 1978), ch. 28, quotes at 396–97, 647, 658, 662. Clark Clifford's talking paper without attribution is in Johnson, *Vantage Point*, 576–77, Johnson's account of his confrontation with Kennedy at 98–101.

7. White, *Making of the President, 1964*, chs. 8, 9, quotes at 275–76, 282, 292; Evans and Novak, *Johnson*, ch. 20, quote at 453; Schlesinger, *Robert Kennedy*, ch. 28, quotes at 653, 665; Hubert H. Humphrey, *The Education of a Public Man* (Garden City: Doubleday, 1976), ch. 31, quotes at 299, 301; Albert Eisele, *Almost to the Presidency* (Blue Earth: Piper, 1972), ch. 11, quote at 217; David J. Garrow, *Bearing the Cross* (New York: Morrow, 1986), 345–50; James H. Rowe, Jr., Oral History Interview, 39–42, Joseph L. Rauh, Jr., Oral History Interview, III-7–8, 11–23, Welsh to Johnson, July 27, 1964, PL 2 File, Cater to Johnson, July 21, 1964, Cater Papers, all Johnson Library; Martin, "Election of 1964," in Schlesinger et al., *Presidential Elections*, IX: 3586–88, 3595, 3624; Gerald Pomper, "The Nomination

of Hubert Humphrey for Vice-President," *Journal of Politics* (Aug. 1966): 645, 650, 651, 655. On the FBI role at the convention, see David J. Garrow, *The FBI and Martin Luther King, Jr.* (New York: Norton, 1981); Garrow, *Bearing the Cross,* 347; Schlesinger, *Robert Kennedy, 663–64,* 995 n. 87.

8. White, *Making of the President,* chs. 11, 12, quotes at 320, 330, 347, 356; Shadegg, *What Happened to Goldwater?,* chs. 17–25, quotes at 198–99, 207, 209; Rovere, *Goldwater Caper,* part 2, quotes at 140, 143, 144, 155; White, *Suite 3505,* 413, 415; *Public Papers, Johnson, 1964,* II: 1164; Goodwin, *Remembering America,* 308; Cater to Johnson, Oct. 23, Cater Papers, O'Brien to Johnson, Oct. 4, 9, O'Donnell to Johnson, Oct. 3, Feldman to Moyers, Sept. 10, Landon conversation with Rosenblatt, June 6, Nelson to Jenkins, July 13, Udall to Johnson, July 29, Okun to Heller, Oct. 5, Fowler to Rowe, July 24, Harris Survey, July 13, Biggest Wins, Nov. 4, Van Dyk to Jenkins, Oct. 3, Bailey to Johnson, Oct. 22, The Goldwater Candidacy and the Christian Conscience, Aug. 6, 1964, all PL 2 File, Nelson to Moyers, Oct. 23, Final Week Report, Oct. 29, Finney to Johnson, Oct. 30, Nelson to Johnson, Oct. 29, 1964, all Moyers Papers, James H. Rowe, Jr., Oral History Interview, II-48, all Johnson Library; Humphrey, *Education,* 308. On the Jenkins affair, see White, *Making of the President,* 367–70; Clifford, *Counsel,* 399–402; Bruce Allen Murphy, *Fortas* (New York: Morrow, 1988), 137–38; Shadegg, *What Happened to Goldwater?,* 241–43.

9. White, *Making of the President,* ch. 13; the election returns are in Schlesinger et al., *Presidential Elections,* IX: 3702; *CQ Almanac, 1964,* 1007–8; Cormier to Johnson, Dec. 12, 1964, PL 2 File, Johnson Library; *New York Times,* Oct. 19, 1966.

Chapter 6. Medicare: The Jewel in the Crown

1. *Social Security Bulletin,* Statistical Supp., 1981, pp. 205, 208, 211; Richard Harris, *A Sacred Trust* (New York: New American Library, 1966), 2–3; *Current Biography, 1968,* 96–98; Irving Bernstein, *A Caring Society* (Boston: Houghton Mifflin, 1985, 43–45; Bernstein, *Promises Kept,* ch. 8; Wilbur J. Cohen, Oral History Interview, I-8, 29–33, 44–47, III-1–2, 19, Michael L. Parker, Operating Methods under Wilbur J. Cohen—A Personal View, Administrative History of the Department of Health, Education, and Welfare, vol. I, pt. II, pp. 8–15, Douglass Cater, Oral History Interview, I-25, all Johnson Library; Wilbur Cohen, Oral History, 15, Columbia Univ. Oral History Research Office; Richard N. Goodwin, *Remembering America* (Boston: Little, Brown, 1988), 269; John F. Manley, *The Politics of Finance: The House Committee on Ways and Means* (Boston: Little, Brown, 1970), ch. 4, quotes at 111–12, 151; Nelson Cruikshank, Oral History, 31, 280, Columbia Univ. Oral History Research Office.

2. Manatos to O'Brien, May 20, Manatos Papers, Wilson to O'Brien, Feb. 17, 1964, Wilson Papers, Wilbur Mills, Oral History Interview, 10, Javits to Johnson, Jan. 27, Cohen to Feldman, Jan. 29, 1964, EX LE/IS File, all Johnson Library; *Public Papers, Johnson, 1963–64,* I: 115, 276–77; *Medical Care for the Aged,* H.R., Hearings Before Committee on Ways and Means, 88th Cong., 2d sess. (1964). The main bills are summarized in pt. 1, facing p. 26, Annis testimony, pt. 2, pp. 644, 650–51. Wilbur Cohen, Oral History, 18–19, 20–21, 31–33, Jacob Javits, Oral

History, 7–8, Nelson Cruikshank, Oral History, 302, all Columbia Univ. Oral History Research Office.

3. The 1964 legislative history of Medicare is treated by Harris, *Sacred Trust,* chs. 30, 31; *CQ Almanac, 1964,* 231–39; Sheri I. David, *With Dignity* (Westport: Greenwood, 1985), ch. 7, quote at 120; Peter A. Corning, *The Evolution of Medicare* (Washington: Social Security Administration, Research Report No. 29), 107–12; Theodore R. Marmor, *The Politics of Medicare* (London: Routledge & Kegan Paul, 1970), 58–61. Suggestions Made by Mr. Mills . . ., Jan. 24, Wilson to O'Brien, April 27, July 21, Aug. 13, Medical Care, Sept. 4, 1964, Wilson Papers, Manatos to O'Brien, July 13, 25, 1964, Manatos Papers, O'Brien to Johnson, Jan. 27, Wilson to O'Brien, June 8, Cohen to Celebrezze, July 13, Ribicoff to Johnson, July 20, Manatos to O'Brien, Aug. 14, Moyers to Johnson, Sept. 2, 1964, EX LE/IS File, all Johnson Library; *Social Security: Medical Care for the Aged Amendments,* Hearings, Sen. Committee on Finance, 88th Cong., 2d sess. (Aug. 6–14, 1964), 65, 73–74; *Social Security Amendments of 1964,* Sen. Rep. No. 1513, 88th Cong., 2d sess. (Aug. 20, 1964); *Cong. Record,* Sept. 2, p. 21318, Sept. 3, 1964, p. 21553. The administration covered the Senate-House conference exhaustively, including the following: Cohen to Manatos and Wilson, Sept. 10, O'Brien to Johnson, Sept. 13, Wilson to O'Brien, Sept. 20, Cohen to Gordon et al., Sept. 24, Cohen to O'Brien, Sept. 28, 1964, Wilson Papers, Manatos to O'Brien, Sept. 15, 16, 17, 18, Wilson to O'Brien, Sept. 20, Manatos to Feldman, Oct. 1, 1964, Manatos Papers, Manatos to O'Brien, Sept. 22, O'Brien to Johnson, Sept. 24, Manatos to O'Brien, Dec. 8, 1964, EX LE/IS File, Lawrence F. O'Brien, Oral History Interview, III-49, all Johnson Library; *Public Papers, Johnson, 1963–64,* II: 1200.

4. Of the works on the legislative history of Medicare in 1965, Harris, *Sacred Trust,* chs. 33–40, is especially helpful, Thompson quote at 181 and 198. Others are *CQ Almanac, 1965,* 236–69, 950, 982; David, *With Dignity,* ch. 8; Marmor, *Politics of Medicare,* ch. 4; *Public Papers, Johnson, 1965,* I: 6, 13–14. Cohen, Oral History Interview, III-16, Celebrezze to Johnson, Nov. 15, Cohen to Johnson, n.d., March 2, June 24, O'Brien to Johnson, March 6, 7, April 8, Ackley to Johnson, March 11, Anderson to Johnson, July 1, Cohen to O'Brien, March 16, 17, May 6, 1965, xerox of press clippings of Byrd on Medicare, n.d., EX LE/IS File, all Johnson Library. The question of whether Title VI of the Civil Rights Act applied to Medicare is considered in a packet of documents topped by Celebrezze to Byrd, April 27, 1965, EX LE/IS File, Johnson Library. Manatos to O'Brien, May 13, 19, 20, June 16, 30, July 6, 1965, Manatos Papers, Johnson Library.

5. Report to the President, July 16, Busby to Valenti et al., July 22, Busby to Johnson, July 28, 1965, all EX LE/IS File, Johnson Library; *Public Papers, Johnson, 1965,* II: 811–15; Wilbur J. Cohen and Robert M. Ball, "Social Security Amendments of 1965," *Social Security Bulletin* (Sept. 1965): 1–21.

6. *Public Papers, Johnson, 1965,* II: 788–90; Cohen, Oral History Interview, II-11–13, Cater to Johnson, July 28, Cohen to Cater, July 22, 1965, Cater Papers, Gardner to Johnson, May 29, 1966, is a 10-page report on Medicare along with a 12-page report by Robert Ball, EX LE/IS File, Kermit Gordon, Oral History Interview, IV-16–17, all Johnson Library; Harris, *Sacred Trust,* chs. 37, 40; the account of the meeting with the AMA on July 29, 1965, is at 215–16; Robert M. Ball, "Health Insurance for People Aged 65 and Older: First Steps in Administration," *Social Security Bulletin* (Feb. 1966): 3–13; Arthur E. Hess, "Medicare's Early Months: A Program Round-Up," *Social Security Bulletin* (July 1967): 4–8.

Chapter 7. Breakthrough in Education

1. Theodore C. Sorensen, *Kennedy* (New York: Bantam, 1965), 401; Francis Keppel, Oral History Interview, I-7, Johnson Library; Robert Dallek, *Lone Star Rising* (New York: Oxford Univ. Press, 1991), 43–44, 57, ch. 3, quote at 63; Kearns, *Johnson*, 42; Robert A. Caro, *The Path to Power* (New York: Vintage, 1981), 120, 142.

2. Bernstein, *Promises Kept,* ch. 7, reviews the education programs of the Kennedy administration; there is a sketch of Francis Keppel at 238–39. *Public Papers, Johnson, 1963–64,* I: 706. Hugh Davis Graham describes the Great Society task force program in *The Uncertain Triumph* (Chapel Hill: Univ. of North Carolina Press, 1984), 55–70; Nancy Kegan Smith, Presidential Task Force Operation During the Johnson Administration, June 26, 1978, pp. 3–4, Task Force Issue Paper: Education, n.d., Task Forces on the 1965 Legislative Program: Issue Papers, Moyers Papers, John Gardner, Oral History Interview, I-5–6, 9, all Johnson Library; Stephen K. Bailey and Edith K. Mosher, *ESEA, The Office of Education Administers a Law* (Syracuse: Syracuse Univ. Press, 1968), 40. The sketch of Gardner is based on *Current Biography, 1976,* 153–56. Report of the President's Task Force on Education, Nov. 14, 1964, Wilbur Cohen, Oral History Interview, IV-15, Anthony Celebrezze, Oral History Interview, 16, Kermit Gordon, Oral History Interview, IV-18, Douglass Cater, Oral History Interview, I-13, Cater quote at 80, Brademas quote at 129, all Johnson Library. Eugene Eidenberg and Roy D. Morey, *An Act of Congress* (New York: Norton, 1969), 89, 90, n. 6; Keppel, Oral History Interview, I-8, 13, Johnson Library. For a sophisticated analysis of the child benefit theory see Dean M. Kelley and George R. LaNoue, "The Church-State Settlement in the Federal Aid to Education Act," in Donald A. Gianella, ed., *Religion and the Public Order, 1965* (Chicago: Univ. of Chicago Press, 1966), 110–60, and Statement of George R. LaNoue Before the House Subcommittee on Education, March 18, 1966, attached to Halperin to Cohen, April 13, 1966, LE FA2 File, Johnson Library. *Cochran v. Louisiana State Board of Education,* 281 U.S. 370 (1930), *Everson v. Board of Education,* 330 U.S. 1 (1947). Administrative History of the Department of Health, Education and Welfare, vol. I, pt. II, ch. III, p. 48, Johnson Library; Cater to Johnson, Dec. 19, 26, 1964, Cater Papers, Johnson Library; John Brademas, *The Politics of Education* (Norman: Univ. of Oklahoma Press, 1987), 3–7, 16–17; John Brademas, "The National Politics of Education," in *The Unfinished Journey* (New York: John Day, 1968), 33–52; Valenti to Johnson, Feb. 26, 1965, LE FA2 File, Memorandum to the President, n.d., LE FA2 File, Enforcement of the Principle of Separation of Church and State in the Elementary and Secondary Education Act of 1965, n.d., all Johnson Library; *Public Papers, Johnson, 1965,* I: 1–9, 25–33; Cohen to Moyers, Reaction to President Johnson's Message on Education, Jan. 14, Cater to Johnson, Jan. 14, 26, 1965, Cater Papers, both Johnson Library.

3. The legislative history of ESEA in the House is set forth in Eidenberg and Morey, *An Act of Congress,* ch. 5, and *CQ Almanac, 1965,* 275–93. Keppel, Oral History Interview, I-9, Johnson Library. There is a sketch of Wayne Morse in Bernstein, *Promises Kept,* 230–31. *Higher Education Act of 1965,* Hearings, Sen. Subcommittee on Labor and Public Welfare, 89th Cong., 1st sess. (1965), Pt. I, pp. 297–98; Cater, Oral History Interview, I-16, Cater to Johnson, Jan. 26, Feb. 3, 16, March 2, Perkins to Moyers, Feb. 1, Major Amendments to the Elementary and Secondary Education Act of 1965 Adopted by the General Subcommittee of Educa-

tion in Reporting the Measure to the Full Committee, Feb. 5, O'Hara to Cater, Feb. 26, Judicial Review: An Overview, n.d., Sam (Halperin) to Keppel, n.d., Cohen to Celebrezze, March 23, 1965, all Cater Papers, Johnson Library; O'Brien to Johnson, March 8, Valenti to Johnson, March 23, 24, Wilson to White, March 12, Cater to Johnson, March 26, 30, 1965, all LE FA2 File, Johnson Library; *Elementary and Secondary Education Act of 1965*, H.R. Committee on Education and Labor, Rep. No. 143, 89th Cong., 1st sess. (March 8, 1965); Bunim to White House, April 1, 1965, Manatos Papers, Johnson Library. As Eidenberg and Morey note, Powell was not alone in condemning Edith Green. The Democratic leadership and the White House assumed that she had joined with the Republicans to sabotage the bill. A widely held view was that she was anti-Catholic and the NCWC refused to deal with her. She had been a longtime and active member of the National Council of Churches and now broke off relations with the council.

4. The legislative history of the bill in the Senate is treated by Eidenberg and Morey, *An Act of Congress*, ch. 6, quote at 159, and *CQ Almanac, 1965*, 289–93. Of Wayne Morse, Senator Javits said: "It is one of the tributes to the genius of the chairman's character and one of the ornaments of Congress that when it comes to handling a bill, he yields to no one in delicacy and subtlety and cooperation. His views, very strong views, on other subjects in which he may stand alone are very well known. . . . But when it comes to the need for getting the Senate to back him in a measure in which he is the manager, he has no equal." *Higher Education Act of 1965*, Hearings, Sen. Subcommittee on Education, 89th Cong., 1st sess. (1965), pt. I, p. 95. Cater to Johnson, March 31, April 8, 1965, Cater Papers, Johnson Library; *Public Papers, Johnson, 1965*, I: 412–19.

5. Bailey and Mosher, *ESEA*, ch. III, quotes at 73–76, 88, 89; Graham, *Uncertain Triumph*, 95–97; Cater to Johnson, April 2, with O'Neill to Cater attached, March 31, Cater to Johnson, April 14, 1965, Recommendations of the White House Task Force on Education, June 14, 1965, all Johnson Library. The ill-fated attempt of the Office of Education to desegregate the Chicago school system is treated below at pp. 392–99.

6. The Alanson Willcox memorandum on aid to education under the First Amendment is in *Public School Assistance Act of 1961*, Hearings, Subcommittee on Education, 87th Cong., 1st sess. (1961), 110–38. The significant constitutional challenge under the First Amendment to ESEA was in *Flast v. Cohen*, 389 U.S. 895 (1968). *Notes and Working Papers Concerning the Administration of Programs, Higher Education Act of 1965*, Sen. Subcommittee on Education, 89th Cong., 1st sess. (1967), pt. X. The administration bill is in *Higher Education Act of 1965*, Sen. Hearings, pt. 1, pp. 3–76, followed by a section-by-section analysis, pp. 77–92. *Higher Education Act of 1965*, Hearings, Special Subcommittee on Education, 89th Cong., 1st sess. (1965), 280–85; Office of Education, Higher Education Act of 1965 Fact Sheets, Cater to Moyers, Additional Statistics on Education, Surrey to Cater, April 12, 1965, Wirtz to Cater, Dec. 12, 1964, with Killingsworth attachment, Surrey to Cater, Dec. 14, 1964, Jan. 13, 1965, with attached Summary of Arguments Against a Tax Credit for College Expenses, Surrey to Cater, April 5, 1965, Keppel to Cater, Dec. 18, 1964, with attached Higher Education Loan Program with External Repayments, all Cater Papers, Surrey to Cater, July 15, with attached analysis of the Javits amendment, Dillon to Johnson, Jan. 12, 1965, both FI 5-6-1 File, all Johnson Library.

7. The legislative history of the higher education bill in the House is in *CQ Almanac, 1965*, 294–305; *Higher Education Act of 1965*, House Hearings, 681–

94; Cohen to Cater, July 1, 1965, Cater to Johnson, May 18, July 11, Aug. 25, 1965, with American Bankers Association statement attached, Cater Papers, Manatos to O'Brien, Sept. 20, 1965, with attached Cohen and Willcox memoranda on the Waggoner-Dirksen amendment, Manatos Papers, O'Brien to Johnson, Aug. 6, Jacobsen to Johnson, Aug. 11, 1965, LE FA2 File, all Johnson Library.

8. For the legislative history in the Senate, see *CQ Almanac, 1965,* 302–5. *Public Papers, Johnson, 1965,* II: 763–65, 1102–6; Manatos to O'Brien with attached Cohen and Willcox memoranda, Sept. 20, 1965, Manatos Papers, Johnson Library; Office of Education, *Higher Education Act of 1965* (1965).

9. Keppel, Oral History Interview, I-16, Johnson Library.

Chapter 8. Selma and the Voting Rights Act

1. For the background see Charles E. Fager, *Selma, 1965* (New York: Scribner, 1974), and Stephen L. Longenecker, *Selma's Peacemaker* (Philadelphia: Temple Univ. Press, 1987), quote at 36. *Voting Rights,* H.R., Hearings Before Subcommittee No. 5 of the Judiciary Committee, 89th Cong., 1st sess. (1965), 5–9.

2. David J. Garrow is the authority on these events. See his monographs, *The FBI and Martin Luther King, Jr.* (New York: Norton, 1981) and *Protest at Selma: Martin Luther King, Jr., and the Voting Rights Act of 1965* (New Haven: Yale Univ. Press, 1978), along with his biography of King, *Bearing the Cross* (New York: Morrow, 1986), quotes at 274–76, 354–55, 362.

3. Garrow, *Bearing the Cross,* 278–95, quote at 368; Fager, *Selma,* chs. 1–9, quote at 9–10; Longenecker, *Selma's Peacemaker,* chs. 1–7; Message from Dr. Martin Luther King; White to Johnson, Feb. 3; Notes for Meeting with Martin Luther King and White to Johnson, Feb. 8; Valenti to Johnson, Feb. 9, 1965, M. L. King, Jr., File, Johnson Library; *Public Papers, Johnson, 1965,* 132; Jack Mendelsohn, *The Martyrs* (New York: Harper & Row, 1966), ch. 7, recounts the story of Jimmy Lee Jackson.

4. *CQ Almanac, 1965,* 533–39; *Voting Rights,* Sen., Hearings Before the Committee on the Judiciary, 89th Cong., 1st sess. (1965), pt. 1, pp. 81, 163; *Public Papers, Johnson, 1965,* I: 5; White to Moyers, Dec. 30, 1964, Constitutional Amendment, Jan. 8, Proposal submitted by Joseph Rauh, Feb. 12, Morrisson to Schlei, Meeting with Richard Scammon, Feb. 15, O'Brien to Johnson, March 10, 1965, Issues to be Resolved on the Voting Legislation, n.d., all Legislative Background Voting Rights File, Katzenbach to Johnson, Legislation to Overcome Voter Apathy and Discrimination, n.d., White Papers, White to Johnson, March 4, 1965, M. L. King, Jr., Papers, all Johnson Library.

5. The useful general studies are Garrow, *Protest at Selma,* chs. 2–3, Roy Reid's *New York Times* report at p. 75; Garrow, *Bearing the Cross,* ch. 7; Fager, *Selma, 1965.* Other citations: Johnson, *Vantage Point,* 161–63; the Johnson estimate of Wallace is in Califano, *Johnson,* 56; Burke Marshall, Oral History Interview, 32, Johnson Library; Cook to Josephson, March 10, McPherson to Johnson and Humphrey to Johnson, March 12, White to Johnson, March 13, Wallace to Johnson, March 18, Valenti's Notes, Meeting in the President's Office, March 18, Moyers to Johnson, March 19, McCafferty to Johnson and Johnson to Wallace, March 20, Califano to McNamara et al., Reports Nos. 1–14, March 22–25, 1965, Legislative Background Voting Rights File, Redman Memo, March 20, 1965, FG

135 File, all Johnson Library; Mendelsohn, *Martyrs,* ch. 8, tells the story of James Reeb, ch. 9 of Viola Liuzzo; Wallace quote about Judge Johnson is in Marshall Frady, *Wallace* (New York: New American Library, 1968), 133; *Public Papers, Johnson, 1965,* I: 274–81; Executive Order 11207 is at 3 CFR, 1964–65 COMP., 290; Renata Adler's *New Yorker* piece on the march to Montgomery is in her *Toward a Radical Middle* (New York: Random House, 1969), quote at 22.

6. *CQ Almanac, 1965,* 533–67; *Public Papers, Johnson, 1965,* I: 281–87, II: 840–43; *Voting Rights,* Sen., Judiciary Committee Hearings, 89th Cong., 1st sess. (1965), pts. 1 and 2; *Voting Rights,* H.R., Judiciary Subcommittee No. 5 Hearings; Johnson, *Diary,* 252–53; Mr. Valenti's Notes, Cabinet Meeting, March 14, President's Address Draws Strong Support, Editors' News Service, March 17, Cox to Katzenbach, March 23, White to Johnson, April 8, Katzenbach to Johnson, April 27, 1965, all Legislative Background Voting Rights File, Jones to Watson, March 17, Santaella to White, March 9 and Alexander to White, March 23, Farmer to Johnson, May 7, 1965, all LE HU 2-7 File, O'Brien to Johnson, April 26, 1965, M. L. King, Jr., File, Katzenbach to Johnson, May 21, 1965, Wilson Papers, Manatos to O'Brien, July 26, 1965, Manatos Papers, all Johnson Library; on the Eastland problem, see Hugh Davis Graham, *The Civil Rights Era* (New York: Oxford Univ. Press, 1990), 144–45, and *CQ Almanac, 1965,* 541; *Breedlove v. Suttles,* 302 U.S. 277 (1937); Clarence Mitchell, Oral History Interview, II-7, Johnson Library.

7. Reis to Busby, June 10, 1965, EX FG 135 File, Pollak to Doar et al., June 3, Marer to Pollak, June 11, Pollak to Katzenbach, June 11, Doar to Pollak, July 14, Katzenbach and Macy to Johnson, Aug. 5, 1965, Legislative Background Voting Rights File, McPherson to Johnson, June 17, Macy to Johnson, Nov. 1, Katzenbach to Johnson, Nov. 2, 1965, Macy to Johnson, Jan. 31, Katzenbach to Kintner, May 13, 1966, Macy to Johnson, April 25, 1968, HU 2-7 File, all Johnson Library; *South Carolina v. Katzenbach,* 383 U.S. 301 (1966); *Katzenbach v. Morgan,* 384 U.S. 641 (1966); *U.S. v. Texas,* 252 F. Supp. 234 (W.D. Tex. 1966); *U.S. v. Alabama,* 252 F. Supp. 95 (M.D. Ala. 1966); *Harper v. Virginia State Board of Elections,* 383 U.S. 663 (1966); The Department of Justice During the Administration of President Lyndon B. Johnson, Civil Rights Division, 7, 34, 41–52, Johnson Library.

8. Lee White, Oral History Interview, III-21, Burke Marshall, Oral History Interview, 34–35, Joseph A. Califano, Jr., Oral History Interview, X-1, all Johnson Library.

Chapter 9. Immigration: Righting the National Origins Wrong

1. Daniel J. Kevles, "Annals of Eugenics," *New Yorker* (Oct. 8, 1984): 51, 99–100, 113; Daniel J. Kevles, *In the Name of Eugenics* (New York: Knopf, 1985), chs. 1 and 3; Harry H. Laughlin, *Immigration and Conquest* (New York: Chamber of Commerce of the State of New York, 1939), 6–7, 8–9, 31; *Europe as an Emigrant-Exporting Continent and the United States as an Immigrant-Receiving Nation,* Hearings, H.R., Committee on Immigration and Naturalization, 68th Cong., 1st sess. (1924), 1262, 1294, 1339.

2. There are summary histories of U.S. immigration policy in Vernon M. Briggs, Jr., *Immigration Policy and the American Labor Force* (Baltimore: Johns Hopkins Univ. Press, 1984), chs. 2, 6, quote at 23; Abba Schwartz, *The Open Society* (New York: Morrow, 1968), ch. 6; Laughlin, *Immigration and Conquest,* ch. 3.

See also the introduction to David M. Reimers, *Still the Golden Door: The Third World Comes to America* (New York: Columbia Univ. Press, 1985).

3. *CQ Almanac, 1965,* 459–82, quote at 463; Schwartz, *Open Society,* Rusk quote at 119, others at 31, 117. For Kennedy and immigration see Doris Kearns Goodwin, *The Fitzgeralds and the Kennedys* (New York: Simon & Schuster, 1987), and the revised edition of Kennedy's book published after his death, *A Nation of Immigrants* (New York: Harper & Row, 1964). *Public Papers, Kennedy, 1963,* 594–97; Robert Dallek, *Lone Star Rising* (New York: Oxford Univ. Press, 1991), 169–70; Erich Leinsdorf, *Cadenza: A Musical Career* (Boston: Houghton Mifflin, 1970), 56, 75–79; Feldman quote in Stephen Thomas Wagner, "The Lingering Death of the National Origins Quota System, 1952–1965," (Ph.D. dissertation, Harvard University, 1986), 387; *Public Papers, Johnson, 1963–1964,* 116; *Immigration,* Hearings, H.R., Subcommittee No. 1 of the Committee on the Judiciary, 88th Cong., 2d sess. (1964), 3 vols., Feighan's rough treatment of Schwartz in pt. II, pp. 508, 534–35; Lawrence F. O'Brien, Oral History Interview, II-39-40, Schwartz to O'Donnell with attachments, Jan. 11, and Engel to Johnson, Jan. 17, Schwartz to O'Brien, July 16, Feldman to Valenti, Aug. 12, 1964, EX IM File, Schlei to Johnson, May 7, 1965, Legislative Background Immigration File, Geoghegan to O'Brien, Feb. 14, 18, Wilson to O'Brien, July 11, 1964, Wilson Papers, all Johnson Library.

4. Wagner, "Lingering Death," 419, 438, 439–42, 450; *Public Papers, Johnson, 1965,* 6, 37–39, 1037–40; *Immigration,* Hearings, H.R., 11, 267; *Immigration,* Hearings, Sen., Subcommittee on Immigration and Naturalization, 89th Cong., 1st sess. (1965), 2 vols.; Barber to Valenti, July 8, Schlei to Valenti, July 14, Manatos to O'Brien, Aug. 16, 20, 1965, EX IM File, Basic Provisions of Mr. Feighan's Proposal, n.d., Schlei to Johnson, May 7, Valenti to Johnson, May 8, O'Brien to Johnson, June 16, 17, July 30, Barber to Valenti, June 29, Valenti to Johnson, July 16, Udall to Johnson, Sept. 23, 1965, Legislative Background Immigration File, Valenti to Johnson, July 22, 1965, EX LEX IM File, all Johnson Library; *Report of the Select Commission on Western Hemisphere Immigration* (Jan. 1968), 1–23.

5. The New Immigration Law: Summary of Principal Features, Oct. 6, 1965, Legislative Background Immigration File, Johnson Library; W. S. Bernard, "America's Immigration Policy, Its Evolution and Sociology," *International Migration* 3, no. 4 (1965): 235; D. G. Benn, "The New U.S.A. Immigration Law," *International Migration* 3, no. 3 (1965): 107; Briggs, *Immigration Policy,* 73–82, quote at 82; Reimers, *Golden Door,* 243; *New York Times,* March 22, 1992.

While of little consequence to the passage of the immigration law, the Abba Schwartz affair deserves comment. In March 1966 the Johnson administration abolished the Bureau of Security and Consular Affairs and Rusk offered Schwartz a position as his assistant on refugee matters. Schwartz rejected the offer and left the government. He released the story to the press, which created quite a stir, and in 1968 published *The Open Society.* Aside from being a useful work of scholarship, the book, like the press conference, was an attack on the administration. Excepting a lame backgrounder by Rusk, no one in the administration countered Schwartz. This, of course, encouraged speculation. In his dissertation, for example, S. T. Wagner wrote: "It is quite possible that another deal besides the compromise on Western Hemisphere immigration had been struck to facilitate passage of the reform bill; the Administration may very well have sacrificed Abba Schwartz to appease his most determined Congressional critics" (p. 452). In fact, the administration needed no votes because the bill passed overwhelmingly and a search of both the Kennedy and Johnson Libraries uncovered no support for this theory. The relationship between Schwartz and his superiors in the State Department as well as with the Senate Internal Security Subcommittee was dreadful. In a letter to Charles Mace, a friend and former employee presently with the U.S. Mission in Geneva, Schwartz referred to LBJ as "Daddy Bird," to Dean Rusk as "Deano," to Deputy Undersecretary of State for Administration William J. Crockett as "Crockhead and his gang," and to Deputy Assistant Secretary Michel Cieplinski as "Simple-inski." Schwartz, certainly, was detested by Feighan and the senators on the Internal Security Subcommittee who, doubtless, were pleased to see him go. In fact, Senator Thomas J. Dodd of the subcommittee wrote the President on Jan. 12, 1965, urging that Schwartz be dismissed and that his bureau be abolished. But there are two other possible administration motives that make more sense. The first is that Johnson may have considered Schwartz disloyal. Schwartz made no secret of his commitment to both John and Robert Kennedy and he campaigned for the latter for the Senate in New York in 1964 without White House approval. Given the vendetta between Johnson and Bobby Kennedy, the President could easily have read this as an act of disloyalty. Second, the conduct of Schwartz during the legislative history of the bill aroused concern among its supporters. Dave Brody of the B'nai B'rith Anti-Defamation League, who worked hard for the bill with Larry O'Brien and the Justice Department, told Joe Califano that Schwartz did nothing to get it passed. Henry Hall Wilson of O'Brien's staff was so angered by Schwartz that he gave him "unequivocal instructions" that the bill was "not to be changed by one comma." Relevant documents in the Johnson Library: Dodd to Johnson, Jan. 12, and Rusk to Johnson, Sept. 13, 1965, Confidential File, FG 103-4; Valenti to Johnson, Sept. 1, 1965, Confidential File, FG 105-5; Cieplinski to Valenti, March 18, 1966, FG 105-5; Wilson to O'Brien, July 23, 1965, Wilson Papers; Califano to Johnson, Handwriting File, Box 13. In the Kennedy Library: Schwartz to Mace, May 3, 1966, Schwartz Papers.

Chapter 10. The Environment: From Conservation to Pollution

1. Paul Brooks, *The House of Life, Rachel Carson at Work* (Boston: Houghton Mifflin, 1972), quotes at 16, 293, 306; Frank Graham, Jr., *Since Silent Spring* (Boston: Houghton Mifflin, 1970), E. B. White quote at 19; Rachel Carson, *The Sea Around Us* (New York: Oxford Univ. Press, 1951); Rachel Carson, *Silent Spring* (Boston: Houghton Mifflin, 1962), quotes at 15–16, 103; *Public Papers, Kennedy, 1962*, 655; *Use of Pesticides*, A Report of the President's Science Advisory Committee (May 15, 1963).

2. The sketch of Stewart Udall is based on *Current Biography, 1961*, 464–66, and *Political Profiles: The Kennedy Years*, 511–13. Stewart L. Udall, Oral History Interview, I-30-35, II-5-10, 19, Philip S. Hughes, Oral History Interview, 29, both Johnson Library; *Public Papers, Kennedy, 1961*, 551–52; Johnson, 529–30.

3. Outdoor Recreation Resources Review Commission, *Outdoor Recreation for America* (1962); Land Conservation Fund Proposal, about Jan. 16, Draft Message to Congress, White to Dillon et al., Feb. 8, Udall to Bell, Feb. 12, Bell to White, n.d., Heller to Hughes, Feb. 16, Sasaki to Staats, March 28, Tiller to Hughes, April 4, Sasaki to Andrews, April 5, Sasaki to Hughes, July 12, Lamb to Hughes, Oct. 3,

Bell to Director, Dec. 11, 1962, Sasaki to Staats, Jan. 22, Kennedy to Aspinall, Nov. 4, Udall to Johnson, Nov. 27, 1963, White to Udall, Aug. 3, Udall to Johnson, Aug. 13, Johnson to Rockefeller, Sept. 21, 1964, Udall to Schultze, Jan. 3, 1967, all Legislative Background Land and Water File, Johnson Library; *Public Papers, Kennedy, 1962,* 176–84, 441–43; Edward C. Crafts, Oral History Interview, I-1-3, 9–10, 12–13, Stewart L. Udall, Oral History Interview, I-26, 29, both Johnson Library; *Land Conservation Fund,* H.R., Hearings, Committee on Interior and Insular Affairs, 87th Cong., 2d sess. (1962); *CQ Almanac, 1964,* 474–84, *1965,* 291–99; *Public Papers, Johnson, 1963–1964,* II: 1033–34; Dept. of the Interior, Conservation Yearbook, No. 4, pp. 18–24, No. 5, pp. 40–44; Additions to the National Park System, 1, 14–16, Administrative History of the Department of the Interior, Johnson Library.

4. Sources for the legislative history of the Wilderness Act are Craig W. Allin, *The Politics of Wilderness Preservation* (Westport: Greenwood, 1982), ch. 4, pp. 267–72, and *CQ Almanac, 1964,* 485–92. The Muir quote is from Frederick Frazier Nash, *American Environmentalism, Readings in Conservation History* (3d ed., New York: McGraw-Hill, 1990), 96. The text of the Wilderness Act is App. A in Allin's book. Michael Frome, *Battle for the Wilderness* (New York: Praeger, 1974), 122–26, 137, 148, quotes at 1 and 139; *Public Papers, Kennedy, 1961,* 120; Robert Marshall, *The People's Forests* (New York: Smith and Haas, 1935); the Nov.–Dec. 1992 issue of *Defenders* is devoted to Aldo Leopold; Manatos to Moyers, March 3, Freeman to Aspinall, Sept. 13, 1962, Wilderness Society Memorandum, Feb. 13, O'Brien to Johnson, June 18, Udall to Valenti, July 30, Humphrey to O'Brien, Aug. 4, 1964, all Legislative Background Wilderness Act File, Johnson Library; Zahniser quote in *Wilderness Preservation System,* Hearings, H.R., Subcommittee on Public Lands of the Committee on Interior and Insular Affairs, 88th Cong., 1st sess. (1964), 1205; *Public Papers, Johnson, 1963–1964,* II: 1034.

5. Carson, *Silent Spring,* 39; James M. Fallows, *The Water Lords* (New York: Grossman, 1971), ch. 1, quote at 18; Noel M. Burns, *Erie: The Lake That Survived* (Totown, N.J.: Rowman & Allanheld, 1985), 5, 22–25, 223–25; see also Public Health Service, *Report on Pollution of Lake Erie and Its Tributaries,* pt. 1, *Lake Erie* (July 1965), and International Joint Commission, *Pollution: Lake Erie, Lake Ontario, and the International Section of the St. Lawrence River* (1970). The sketch of Muskie is based on *Current Biography, 1968,* 276–78; *Political Profiles: The Johnson Years,* 447–49; Edmund S. Muskie, *Journeys* (Garden City: Doubleday, 1972), 31; David Nevin, *Muskie of Maine* (New York: Random House, 1972), ch. 5, quotes at 31, 104–5; Theo Lippman, Jr., and D. C. Hansen, *Muskie* (New York: Norton, 1971), ch. 7; Frederic N. Cleaveland and associates, *Congress and Urban Problems* (Washington: Brookings, 1969), 259–60.

6. *CQ Almanac, 1965,* 743–50; *Public Papers, Johnson, 1965,* I: 161–63, II: 1034–35; Task Forces on the Quality of the Environment, Nov. 21, 1966, pp. 3, 4, 5, 7, Dec. 1, 1967, pp. 6–7, 12, Gordon to Wilson, March 6, Cohen to O'Brien, March 18, Hughes to Moyers, April 8, Wilson to O'Brien, Aug. 23, Udall to Califano, Dec. 30, 1965, Califano to Johnson, Jan. 14, Udall to Johnson, May 6, 1966, Legislative Background Water Pollution File, Deutch to Udall, June 30, July 20, 1965, Confidential File LE HE 8-4, Udall to Johnson, Sept. 2, Califano to Johnson, Sept. 8, 1965, EX HE 8-1 File, Gardner to Califano, Dec. 27, 1965, Schultze to Johnson, Jan. 11, Water Pollution Organization, Jan. 11, White to Johnson, Jan. 12, Muskie to Udall, Feb. 7, Califano to Johnson, Feb. 18, 19, 26, 1966, with attach-

ments, EX FG 165.1A File, Lawrence F. O'Brien, Oral History Interview, XIII-2, all Johnson Library. For enforcement of the water program, see David Zwick and Marcy Benstock, *Water Wasteland* (New York: Grossman, 1971), chs. 3, 14; Walter A. Rosenbaum, *The Politics of Environmental Concern* (New York: Praeger, 1973), chs. 5, 6; Clarence Davies III and Barbara S. Davies, *The Politics of Pollution* (Indianapolis: Pegasus, 1975), 27–44, 198–218; Administrative History of the Department of the Interior, 9, 12, 61, Ackley to Califano, Further Report of the Task Force on Pollution Abatement, Dec. 1965, Davies to Director, Nov. 23, 1966, all Johnson Library.

7. The general studies are James A. Krier and Edmund Ursin, *Pollution and Policy* (Berkeley: Univ. of California Press, 1977), quote at 172; Davies and Davies, *Politics of Pollution*, 44–49; John C. Esposito, *Vanishing Air* (New York: Grossman, 1970); and, on the technical side, Charles T. Stewart, Jr., *Air Pollution, Human Health, and Public Policy* (Lexington: Lexington Books, 1979). A. J. Haagen-Smit, "The Air Pollution Problem in Los Angeles," *Engineering and Science* (Dec. 1950): 7–13, and "Chemistry and Physiology of Los Angeles Smog," *Industrial and Engineering Chemistry* (June 1952): 1342–46; Frederic N. Cleaveland and Associates, *Congress and Urban Problems* (Washington: Brookings, 1969), 224–78; James L. Sundquist, *Politics and Policy* (Washington: Brookings, 1968), ch. 8; *Steps Toward Clean Air*, Report of the Special subcommittee on Air and Water Pollution, 88th Cong., 2d sess. (Oct. 1964); *CQ Almanac, 1965*, 780–86; *Public Papers, Johnson, 1965*, I: 163, II: 1066–67; HEW, Office of the Secretary, Background Information Concerning Crankcase Emission (Blowby) Control and Air Pollution, Aug. 7, 1961, Task Force on Air Pollution from Motor Vehicles, Memorandum to the Committee on the Use of Economic Incentives for Pollution Abatement, Aug. 1, 1965, Legislative Background Clean Air File, O'Brien to Califano, Dec. 29, with attachments, particularly Markley to Wilson, Dec. 17, 1965, EX HE 8-1 File, all Johnson Library.

8. Esposito, *Vanishing Air*, 204; *Public Papers, Johnson, 1967*, I: 93–97, II: 1067–70; Califano to Johnson, Jan. 17, Johnson to Watson, Feb. 3, Califano to Johnson, April 20, Gardner to Califano, May 19, Zimmerman to Levinson, May 31, Califano to Johnson, May 31, July 11, Cohen to Johnson, Aug. 17, 1967, all EX HE 8-1 File, Califano to Ackley, Sept. 22, 1966, Legislative Background Clean Air File, Lee to Califano, Dec. 6, 1967, Califano Papers, all Johnson Library.

9. The most important source is Lewis L. Gould, *Lady Bird Johnson and the Environment* (Lawrence: Univ. of Kansas Press, 1988), particularly chs. 7, 8, quotes at 7, 144. Liz Carpenter, Oral History Interview, 4–5, Johnson Library; *Public Papers, Johnson, 1965*, I: 8, 582–84, II: 1074; Liz Carpenter, *Ruffles and Flourishes* (Garden City: Doubleday, 1970), 242; *Beauty for America*, Proceedings of the White House Conference on Natural Beauty, May 24–25, 1965; Elizabeth Brenner Drew, "Lady Bird's Beauty Bill," *Atlantic Monthly* (Dec. 1965): 68–72; Helen Leavitt, *Superhighway-Superhoax* (Garden City: Doubleday, 1970), ch. 2; Califano, *Johnson*, 81–85, Johnson quote at 84; *Highway Beautification*, H.R., Hearings, Subcommittee on Roads, Committee on Public Works, 89th Cong., 1st sess. (1965); Califano to Johnson with attachments, Sept. 12, 1965, Wilson Papers, Lawrence F. O'Brien, Oral History Interview, XII-25, both Johnson Library; *Cong. Record*, Oct. 7, 1965, pp. 26252–55, 26291, 26306, 26321–32; Charles F. Floyd and Peter J. Shedd, *Highway Beautification: The Environmental Movement's Greatest Failure* (Boulder: Westview, 1979), authors' quote at 113, Stafford quote at xiii; Clifton

W. Enfield, "Federal Highway Beautification," in John W. Houck, ed., *Outdoor Advertising, History and Regulation* (Notre Dame: Univ. of Notre Dame Press, 1969), 149–82.

10. Krier and Ursin, *Pollution and Policy,* 252; Task Force on the Quality of the Environment, Oct. 1, 1967, pp. 1–2, Johnson Library. Stewart Udall recounted the conflict with LBJ over the lands set aside in his Oral History Interview, IV, Johnson Library, and the quotes are his. See also the oral histories of Edward C. Crafts, II-7-10, and Califano, V-33-34; *Public Papers, Johnson, 1968–69,* II: 1264, 1369; Johnson, *Vantage Point,* 562–63; Johnson, *Diary,* 772.

Chapter 11. Failure: The Repeal of Right-to-Work

1. Paul Sultan, *Right-to-Work: A Study in Conflict* (Los Angeles: Institute of Industrial Relations, UCLA, 1958); Harry A. Millis and Emily Clark Brown, *From the Wagner Act to Taft-Hartley* (Chicago: Univ. of Chicago Press, 1950), 326–29, 438–40; 61 *Statutes at Large* 136 (1947); Robert Dallek, *Lone Star Rising* (New York: Oxford Univ. Press, 1991), 288.

2. *CQ Almanac, 1965,* 818–31; *Public Papers, Johnson, 1965,* I: 6, 555; Wilson to O'Brien, May 5, Humphrey to O'Brien, July 30, O'Brien to Johnson, Sept. 21, with Biemiller to O'Brien, Sept. 21 attached, Wirtz to Johnson, Sept. 24, 1965, all GEN LE/JL File, Johnson Library; Neil MacNeil, *Dirksen: Portrait of a Public Man* (New York: World, 1970), 264–65; Califano, *Johnson,* Johnson quote on Mansfield at 44.

3. *CQ Almanac, 1966,* 837–40; Califano to Johnson, Nov. 28, with attached Wirtz to Johnson, Nov. 25, 1966, GEN LE/JL File, Lawrence F. O'Brien, Oral History Interview, XIII-19-23, XVIII-6, both Johnson Library.

4. *Public Papers, Johnson, 1965,* I: 121–22, II: 828–29; *CQ Alamanac, 1965,* 613–19.

Chapter 12. Unhinging the State of the Union

1. Joseph A. Califano, Jr., Oral History Interview, I-1-13, XLI-1-2, Johnson Library, covers his background; he discusses the 1966 State of the Union address at length in XXIV, XL, and LVII and more broadly in his book *The Triumph & Tragedy of Lyndon Johnson,* chs. 5–8; Califano interview by author, June 6, 1994; Jack Valenti, *A Very Human President* (New York: Norton, 1975), 84–87; Richard N. Goodwin, *Remembering America* (Boston: Little, Brown, 1988), 423–24; *Public Papers, Johnson, 1966,* I: 3–12. Eric Goldman, the White House historian, had a talent for missing the bus. On July 9, 1966, he sent Johnson a memorandum on the "axiom of American history that wars tend to throw back progressive programs." He pointed to this reaction following every major modern war. "The Civil War was followed by Grantism; World War I by Harding; World War II by the 80th Congress; and the Korean War by Eisenhowerism." Both Woodrow Wilson and FDR took this axiom into account when they asked for declarations of war. Goldman was historically correct and this was a powerful argument *against* going into Viet-

nam in the first place. But that decision had been made a year earlier. Goldman now offered to work up statements on palliatives, such as putting Vietnam "in a larger setting," a Four Freedoms type of declaration, and short remarks answering critics. Johnson approved of his doing so, but nothing came of it. Shortly, Goldman left the White House after a nasty rift with the President and struck back with the academic atom bomb, a critical book. Goldman to Johnson, July 9, 1966, Vietnam Reference File, Johnson Library; Eric F. Goldman, *The Tragedy of Lyndon Johnson* (New York: Knopf, 1969), ch. 17.

Chapter 13. Vietnam: Sliding into the Quagmire

1. The useful general works on Vietnam are Stanley Karnow, *Vietnam, a History* (rev. ed., New York: Penguin, 1991); David Halberstam, *The Best and the Brightest* (New York: Penguin, 1983); Barbara W. Tuchman, *The March of Folly* (London: Abacus, 1985); and George McT. Kahin, *Intervention: How America Became Involved in Vietnam* (New York: Knopf, 1986). Karnow is especially good on the overthrow of the Diem regime. There is an exhaustive history in the *Pentagon Papers*, Gravel Edition (Boston: Beacon, 1971), II: ch. 4, with supporting documents at 727–93. Daniel Ellsberg, *Papers on the War* (New York: Simon and Schuster, 1972), 28; Neil Sheehan, *A Bright and Shining Lie* (New York: Random House, 1988), 174–75, 352, 366; Kennedy quote on Krulak-Mendenhall report in William Conrad Gibbons, *The U.S. Government and the Vietnam War* (Princeton: Princeton Univ. Press, 1986), II: 170–71, Oct. 6, 1963 cable to Lodge at 191, the Lodge quote at 198; Kennedy comment about Mansfield from Karnow, *Vietnam*, 284–85; the Salinger quote from BDM Corporation Study, vol. VI, U.S. Domestic Factors, p. 3-1, Johnson Library; *Public Papers, Kennedy, 1963*, 624, 696; Arthur M. Schlesinger, Jr., *A Thousand Days* (Boston: Houghton Mifflin, 1965), 997; Theodore C. Sorensen, *Kennedy* (New York: Bantam, 1965), 735, 741. On the Halberstam flap: On October 21, 1963, Sulzberger had lunch at the White House and Kennedy told him, "I wish like hell that you'd get Halberstam out of there." The publisher phoned his editors in New York, who said that Halberstam was tired of Vietnam and wanted to come home. They planned to send Hedrick Smith to Saigon to replace him. Sulzberger had dinner with Reston that evening, who said the *Times* could not buckle under that kind of pressure and Sulzberger agreed. Poor Halberstam was stuck in Vietnam. Richard Reeves, *President Kennedy* (New York: Simon and Schuster, 1994), 636–37.

2. Clifford, *Counsel*, 381; Kearns, *Johnson*, 259–60; David Wise, *The Politics of Lying* (New York: Random House, 1973), 19–22; Karnow, *Vietnam*, Johnson quote on "a little pissant country" 411; Halberstam, *Best and Brightest*, Johnson quote on "raggety ass" country at 620; Thomas Powers, *The War at Home* (New York: Grossman, 1973), xvii; George W. Ball, *The Past Has Another Pattern* (New York: Norton, 1982), 336.

3. On the American Establishment: Godfrey Hodgson, *America in Our Time* (Garden City: Doubleday, 1976), ch. 6; Walter Isaacson and Evan Thomas, *The Wise Men* (New York: Simon and Schuster, 1986), 25–32. On McGeorge Bundy: Halberstam, *Best and Brightest*, 56–81 includes all quotes; Milton Viorst, *Hustlers and Heroes* (New York: Simon and Schuster, 1971), 266–82; Schlesinger, *A Thousand Days*, 420–21; Henry L. Stimson and McGeorge Bundy, *On Active Service in*

Peace and War (New York: Harper, 1947). On Robert McNamara: Deborah Shapley, *Promise and Power* (Boston: Little, Brown, 1993), in general; Halberstam, *Best and Brightest*, chs. 12, 13; John M. Logsdon and Alain Dupas, "Was the Race to the Moon Real?" *Scientific American* (June 1944): 37.

4. Tom Wells, *The War Within* (Berkeley: Univ. of California Press, 1994), 9; *Pentagon Papers*, III: ch. 2; Gibbons, *U.S. and Vietnam*, II: chs. 4–5, quote at 302; Karnow, *Vietnam*, ch. 10; John Galloway, *The Gulf of Tonkin Resolution* (Cranbury: Associated Univ. Presses, 1970); Anthony Austin, *The President's War* (Philadelphia: Lippincott, 1971), O'Donnell quote at 30; Eugene D. Windchy, *Tonkin Gulf* (Garden City: Doubleday, 1971); James B. and Sybil B. Stockdale, *In Love and War* (New York: Harper & Row, 1984), 21, 23, 32; *Public Papers, Johnson, 1963–64*, 926–28, 930–32; Wise, *Politics of Lying*, 43, 295. In the present state of knowledge concerning the alleged naval encounter in the Gulf of Tonkin on August 4, 1964, Admiral Stockdale's testimony deserves most credit because he was the only direct witness. Nevertheless, controversy resonates. In a 1991 seminar on Vietnam at the Johnson Library, Tonkin Gulf was a major topic of discussion among 22 prominent members of the Johnson administration. It was published. In addition, Lawrence E. Levinson, who had been an aide to McNamara and who prepared a chronology at the time, wrote a newspaper article on the incident. These authorities agreed, of course, that there had been a North Vietnamese attack on August 2. The disagreement was confined to the alleged event on August 4. Mac Bundy stated that on the morning of that day the President told him, " 'Get me a resolution, because I'm going to make a speech about it tonight. . . .' The two attacks together gave him the opportunity for something which he had perceived as desirable for a long time." Ray Cline, who handled the intercepts for the CIA, said, "You couldn't demonstrate that anything happened on the night of the fourth." Chester Cooper, who was in the Situation Room in the basement of the White House, stated that the "stuff that was coming in . . . was absolutely incomprehensible." General Bruce Palmer, who was with the Joint Chiefs, stated that "*no* second attack ever occurred." These statements support Stockdale. Hanoi, of course, has consistently agreed. Nevertheless, Levinson urges this caution: "Perhaps the most intriguing clues of all are locked in the files of the National Security Agency. These are a series of still highly classified radio-signal intercepts used by the administration officials as the 'clinching proof' that our destroyers were attacked during the evening of Aug. 4." All the efforts of historians to persuade NSA to open its file have failed. Unless they are made available and confirm the contrary, there is no option but to stick with Stockdale. Johnson Library, *The Johnson Years: A Vietnam Round-table*, Ted Gittinger, ed. (Austin: Johnson Library, 1993), 30, 31, 34, 159; Sacramento *Bee*, Aug. 1, 1993.

5. Joseph A. Califano, Jr., Oral History Interview, XVIII-24, Johnson Library; Karnow, *Vietnam*, 418. The evolution of the Working Group report on Vietnam is treated exhaustively in *Pentagon Papers*, III: 210–51, supporting documents at 588–691, quotes at 208, 212, 216, 217, 622. Kahin, *Intervention*, Taylor quote at 237; Ball, *Past*, quote at 388; Shapley, *Promise and Power*, 313; Gibbons, *U.S. and Vietnam*, II: 213, 250–51. Ball sent copies of the Oct. 5, 1964, memo to McGeorge Bundy, McNamara, and Rusk. They were "dead set against the views that I presented and uninterested in the point-by-point discussion I had hoped to provoke." Their main concern was that it might leak. Later Ball said that McNamara was "absolutely horrified. He treated it like a poisonous snake, . . . as next to treason."

Johnson did not see the Ball brief until a month later and only as a result of the intervention of Bill Moyers.

6. Wise, *Politics of Lying*, 48, 295, 344; Charles M. Haar, Oral History Interview, 35–44, Johnson Library; Kai Bird, *The Chairman* (New York: Simon & Schuster, 1992), Johnson quotes at 578, 580, Alsop quote at 580; Halberstam, *Best and Brightest*, 641–42; Bundy to Johnson, Jan. 27, NSF, NSC History, Feb. 7, 9, NSF Memos to President, Wheeler to McNamara, April 6, McCone to Rusk et al., April 2, 1965, NSF, National Security Action Memorandum No. 328, April 6, McNamara to Johnson, July 20, Bundy to Johnson, July 24, 1965, all Johnson Library; *Public Papers, Johnson, 1965*, II: 794–99.

7. Johnson, *Vantage Point*, 153; Thomas C. Thayer, *War Without Fronts* (Boulder: Westview, 1985), xxiii, 3–4, 34, 46, 79, 105; Michael Herr, *Dispatches* (New York: Avon, 1978), 3, 14, 19–20, 38–39, 47, 54, 61–62; Karnow, *Vietnam*, 361, 450–52, 454; Neil Sheehan, *Two Cities: Hanoi and Saigon* (London: Jonathan Cape, 1992), 19; John P. Roche, Oral History Interview, 20, Johnson Library; William C. Westmoreland, *A Soldier Reports* (Garden City: Doubleday, 1976), 83, 144–46; Jonathan Shay, *Achilles in Vietnam* (New York: Atheneum, 1994), 34, 59; *Pentagon Papers*, IV: 136–38, 477–78.

8. This section depends heavily on Shapley, *Promise and Power*, chs. 19, 20, quotes at 407, 408, 425–26, 428–33, 485–86; Johnson, *Vantage Point*, 20; Clifford, *Counsel*, 456–57; Gelb to Clifford, Jan. 15, 1969, *Pentagon Papers*, I: xv–xvi, IV: 424–538; Califano, *Johnson*, 264.

Chapter 14. Launching the Great Inflation

1. Arthur M. Okun, *Inflation: The Problems It Creates and the Policies It Requires* (New York: New York Univ. Press, 1970), 41; David Halberstam, *The Best and the Brightest* (New York: Penguin, 1983), 732–33; Johnson, *Vantage Point*, 438–46; Wilbur Mills, I-21, Gardner Ackley, II-14-15, Walter Heller, II-44, Charles L. Schultze, II-14-19, all Oral History Interviews, Johnson Library; Deborah Shapley, *Promise and Power* (Boston: Little, Brown, 1993), 367–74, quote at 373.

2. Califano provides a graphic account in *Johnson*, ch. 5, quotes at 91, 97, 99–100; a more sedate version is James L. Cochrane, "The Johnson Administration: Moral Suasion Goes to War," in Crauford C. Goodwin, ed., *Exhortation and Controls* (Washington: Brookings, 1975), 215–39. See also *Economic Report of the President, 1962*, 189; Bernstein, *Promises Kept*, 133–37; *Public Papers, Johnson, 1965*, II: 969; Gardney Ackley, Oral History Interview, I-24, Johnson Library.

3. Walter Heller, II-40-41, 44, Kermit Gordon, II-15, Joseph W. Barr, I-22, all Oral History Interviews, Harris to Moyers, Dec. 16, 1965, Confidential File, FG 105-4, Ackley to Johnson, Dec. 17, 1965, EX FG 110 File, all Johnson Library; Robert Warren Stevens, *Vain Hopes, Grim Realities* (New York: New Viewpoints, 1976), 71; Califano, *Johnson*, 106–11; *Public Papers, Johnson, 1965*, II: 1137–38.

4. Stevens, *Vain Hopes*, 77–80; Cochrane, "The Johnson Administration," 252–72; Ackley to Johnson, Aug. 6, 10, 17, 26, Sept. 17, Nov. 8, 1966, EX FG 11-3 File, Ackley to Califano, Aug. 8, 9, 15, 16, Eckstein to Califano, Aug. 23, 1966, Califano Papers, all Johnson Library; *Public Papers, Johnson, 1967*, I: 8.

5. Ackley to Johnson, May 19, June 12, Aug. 8, 1967, Okun to Johnson, Jan.

29, May 22, 1968, EX FG 11-3 File, Ackley to Christian, Oct. 23, 1967, H. H. Fowler et al. to Johnson, Dec. 27, 1968, EX FG 3 File, Califano to the Files, June 9, 1967, Califano Papers, all Johnson Library.

6. *CQ Almanac, 1967,* 643–56; *Public Papers, Johnson, 1967,* I: 8, II: 733–46, 1050; Stevens, *Vain Hopes,* 92; Califano, *Johnson,* 244; Johnson, *Vantage Point,* 449, 450–51; Ackley to Johnson, Feb. 24, May 15, July 22, Aug. 16, Sept. 21, Oct. 27, Dec. 18, Califano to Johnson, June 17, Okun to Johnson, Oct. 27, Fowler et al. to Johnson, July 22, Ackley to McGovern, Sept. 21, 1967, EX FG 11-3 File, CEA, Tax Policy and the Economy, May 23, 1967, Califano Papers, Califano to Johnson, Oct. 7, with attachments, Oct. 16, 1967, LE FI 11-4 File, Charles L. Schultze, Oral History Interview, II-40, all Johnson Library.

7. *Public Papers, Johnson, 1968–1969,* I: 14; Johnson, *Vantage Point,* 451; Califano, Draft for the President, n.d., Califano Papers, Smathers to Johnson, Oct. 2, 1967, LE FI 11-4 File, Fowler to Johnson, March 22, 1968, Confidential File, Henry H. Fowler, Oral History Interview, III-13-18, all Johnson Library; *CQ Almanac, 1968,* 263–78.

8. Fowler to Johnson, April 24, Johnson to McCormack, May 4, Sanders to Johnson, May 9, Okun to Johnson, May 9, 20, American Bankers Assn. telegram, May 27, 1968, Califano Papers, two memos Califano to Johnson, May 2, Zwick to Johnson, May 2, Sanders to Johnson, May 4, two memos Sanders to Johnson, May 9, 17, Mills to Heller, May 10, Fowler to Johnson, May 9, 27, June 10, Califano to Johnson (AFL-CIO telegram), May 13, 1968, all EX LE FI 11-4 File, Okun to Johnson, May 22, 1968, EX FG 11-3 File, Barr to Johnson, May 21, 1968, Confidential File, Arthur M. Okun, Oral History Interview, II-21, all Johnson Library; Califano, *Johnson,* 285, 288.

9. Robert Dallek, *Lone Star Rising* (New York: Oxford Univ. Press, 1991), 46–50; Arthur M. Okun and George L. Perry, eds., *Curing Chronic Inflation* (Washington: Brookings, 1978), 1–2; Walter W. Heller, Oral History Interview, II-40-41, Johnson Library.

Chapter 15. Turmoil at Home

1. William Conrad Gibbons, *The U.S. Government and the Vietnam War* (Princeton: Princeton Univ. Press, 1986), II: 250–51.

2. Nancy Zaroulis and Gerald Sullivan, *Who Spoke Up?* (Garden City: Doubleday, 1984), 1–3, 1965 ch.; Cater to Johnson, Jan. 26, May 25, June 22, July 10, Aug. 5, 1965, Cater Papers, Johnson Library; Tom Wells, *The War Within* (Berkeley: Univ. of California Press, 1994), 35; Daniel C. Hallin, *The "Uncensored War"* (New York: Oxford Univ. Press, 1986), 105; Michael J. Arlen, *Living-Room War* (New York: Viking, 1969); Joseph A. Califano, Jr., Oral History Interview, XVIII-5, Johnson Library. The peace demonstrations are recounted in Charles DeBenedetti and Charles Chatfield, *An American Ordeal* (Syracuse: Syracuse Univ. Press, 1990), chs. 4, 5; Thomas Powers, *The War at Home* (New York: Grossman, 1973), chs. 4, 5; Eric F. Goldman, *The Tragedy of Lyndon Johnson* (New York: Knopf, 1968), ch. 16; Johnson, *Diary,* 286–87; Robert Jay Lifton, *Home from the War* (New York: Simon and Schuster, 1973), 15.

3. *Violence in the City—An End or a Beginning?,* Report by the Governor's Commission on the Los Angeles Riots (Dec. 2, 1965); Report of the President's Task

Force on the Los Angeles Riots, n.d., Califano Papers, Martin to White with attached memorandum, Aug. 23, 1965, White Papers, Johnson Library; Area Redevelopment Administration, *Hard-Core Unemployment and Poverty in Los Angeles* (Washington, D.C., 1965); Califano, *Johnson*, 59–64; *Report of the National Advisory Commission on Civil Disorders* (New York: Bantam, 1968), 120; Milton Viorst, *Fire in the Streets* (New York: Simon and Schuster, 1979), 309, 314–15; Paul Jacobs, *Prelude to Riot* (New York: Random House, 1966), ch. 7; David J. Garrow, *Bearing the Cross* (New York: Morrow, 1986), 439–40.

4. For the trying internal problems of the Southern Christian Leadership Conference, see Garrow, *Bearing the Cross*, 548, 584–87. *The Negro Family: The Case for National Action* (1965); *Public Papers, Johnson, 1965*, II: 635–40; Hugh Davis Graham, *The Civil Rights Era* (New York: Oxford Univ. Press, 1990), 209–10, 258–62; *CQ Almanac, 1966*, 450–72; James L. Sundquist, *Politics and Policy* (Washington: Brookings, 1968), 275–82; Lawrence F. O'Brien, Oral History Interview, XVII-20-24, Johnson Library.

5. Len O'Connor, *CLOUT, Mayor Daley and His City* (Chicago: Regnery, 1975), 37; Leo M. Snowiss, "Chicago and Congress, A Study of Metropolitan Representation" (Ph.D. dissertation, Univ. of Chicago, 1965), ch. 2; Mike Royko, *Boss: Richard J. Daley of Chicago* (New York: New American Library, 1971), 30–31; Mike Royko, *Sez Who? Sez Me* (New York: Dutton, 1982), 95–96; Califano, *Johnson*, 69–70; Francis Keppel, Oral History Interview, 18–19, 23–26, 67–74, Wilbur J. Cohen, Oral History Interview, IV-10-12, both Johnson Library; Gary Orfield, *The Reconstruction of Southern Education* (New York: Wiley-Interscience, 1969), ch. 4, quotes at 172, 206–7.

6. The history of the Chicago Freedom Movement is recounted in James R. Ralph, Jr., *Northern Protest* (Cambridge: Harvard Univ. Press, 1993), 35, 39, and in Alan B. Anderson and George W. Pickering, *Confronting the Color Line* (Athens: Univ. of Georgia Press, 1986), chs. 4–12, quote at 234, the housing agreement is app. II; Garrow, *Bearing the Cross*, chs. 8–9, Rustin quote at 455; and Dempsey J. Travis, *An Autobiography of Black Politics* (Chicago: Urban Research, 1987), I: chs. 16–20. Royko, *Boss*, Brazier and Daley quotes at 149–50, 154–55, 158.

7. Kirkpatrick Sale's *SDS* (New York: Random House, 1973) is the basic study, particularly pp. 17–22, 50–54, 674–77. See also McGhee to Rusk, Report of the Student Unrest Study Group, Jan. 17, 1969, National Security File, Intelligence, Johnson Library; Charles DeBenedetti, "On the Significance of Citizen Peace Activism: America 1961–1975," *Peace and Change* (Summer 1983), 6–20; Irwin Unger, *The Movement: A History of the American New Left, 1959–1972* (New York: Dodd, Mead, 1975), ch. 3; Todd Gitlin, *The Sixties* (New York: Bantam, 1987), chs. 4–7, quote at 125. Massimo Teodori, ed., *The New Left: A Documentary History* (Indianapolis: Bobbs-Merrill, 1969), contains a long selection from the Port Huron Statement, 163–72; Michael Harrington, *Fragments of the Century* (New York: Saturday Review Press, 1973), 132–57, quote at 144. For a sophisticated ideological analysis of the international New Left and the place of SDS within it, see Nigel Young, *An Infantile Disorder? The Crisis and Decline of the New Left* (Boulder: Westview, 1977).

8. Background is from Verne A. Stadtman, ed., *Centennial Record of the University of California* (Berkeley: Univ. of California Press, 1967); *Public Papers, Kennedy, 1962*, 263; A. H. Raskin, "The Berkeley Affair: Mr. Kerr vs. Mr. Savio & Co.," in Michael V. Miller and Susan Gilmore, eds., *Revolution at Berkeley* (New York: Dial, 1965), 81, 85–86; Clark Kerr, *The Uses of the University* (Cambridge:

Harvard Univ. Press, 1963), 103; Lewis S. Feuer, *The Conflict of Generations* (New York: Basic, 1969), 438–39; Max Heirich, *The Beginning: Berkeley 1964* (New York: Columbia Univ. Press, 1968), is a play-by-play account of the conflict; Nathan Glazer, " 'Student Power' in Berkeley," in Daniel Bell and Irving Kristol, eds., *Confrontation: The Student Rebellion and the Universities* (New York: Basic, 1968), 9. There was a great deal of sociological handwringing over two characteristics of the students who participated in the FSM uprising. One was that many were the very bright children of permissive well-to-do parents whose prospects at the university and for careers were very good, and the other was that some were the offspring of Marxian radicals. There is no doubt that both points are correct. One can argue about their significance. The second characteristic is Feuer's theory set forth in the book cited above that all student unrest, including Berkeley, is the eternal struggle of the sons against their fathers, that the sons, unable to punish their real fathers, turn on their surrogate fathers, the university. This is pretty deep stuff for this writer. The philosopher Sidney Hook on p. 132 of the Miller-Gilmore collection described Feuer's theory as "sheer mythology."

9. Wells, *War Within*, Craig McNamara quote at 64, Wicker quote at 85–86, Reston quote at 105; Halberstam, *Best and Brightest*, 761, 777; Shapley, *Promise and Power*, 376–77, 482–83; Jonathan Mirsky, "The War That Will Not End," *New York Review* (Aug. 16, 1990), Rusk quote at 30; Ball, *Past Has Another Pattern*, 424–25; BDM Corporation Study, Domestic Factors, IV: 1.11–13; Fifteen senators to Johnson, Jan. 27, National Security Vietnam File, Manatos to Jones, June 2, Manatos Papers, Moyers to Johnson, June 10 with attachment, McPherson to Califano, July 19, McPherson to Moyers, Aug. 4, Oct. 4, McPherson Papers, Mansfield to Johnson, June 29, Oct. 13, National Security Name File, Cater to Johnson, Jan. 21, 1966 with Gavin attachment, Nov. 29, 1965, with Bean attachment, July 11, 13, 14 (2), 15 with Cohen attachment, July 16, Aug. 4, Sept. 10, 26, Dec. 30, 1966, Cater Papers, Harry McPherson, Oral History Interview, III-7-9, 33, Lawrence F. O'Brien, Oral History Interview, XVI-32, 33–34, 36–37, XIX-7-8, all Johnson Library; Zaroulis and Sullivan, *Who Spoke Up?*, 76; Melvin Small, *Johnson, Nixon, and the Doves* (New Brunswick: Rutgers Univ. Press, 1988), Ball quote at 80, 89–90, 96–97; DeBeneditti and Chatfield, *American Ordeal*, 148–50; Harrison Salisbury, *Behind the Lines—Hanoi* (London: Secker & Warburg, 1967), 69, 93, 137–38, 140, 179; Salisbury, Oral History Interview, 17, 20–23, Johnson Library.

10. Melvin Small, "The Impact of the Antiwar Movement on Lyndon Johnson, 1965–68, A Preliminary Report," *Peace and Change* (Spring 1984): 8; DeBeneditti and Chatfield, *American Ordeal*, 174–75; Johns to Johnson, May 12, McPherson to Johnson, May 15, Davis to Rostow, May 17, Bedell to McPherson, May 23, Schnittker to McPherson, June 9, McPherson to Johnson, Aug. 25, 1967, McPherson Papers, Cater to Johnson, June 20, 21, July 10, Aug. 12, Oct. 4, 1967, Cater Papers, Mansfield to Johnson, April 29, Udall to Johnson, Oct. 18, Lewis to Rostow, Nov. 21, 1967, National Security Vietnam File, Dr. Martin Luther King, Jr., "Beyond Vietnam," April 4, 1967, Clark Papers, Levinson to Johnson with Detroit Riot Chronology attached, July 29, 1967, Califano Papers, all Johnson Library; Tip O'Neill, *Man of the House* (New York: Random House, 1987), 189–201; Zaroulis and Sullivan, *Who Spoke Up?*, 110–14; Garrow, *Bearing the Cross*, 552–58; Commission on Civil Disorders, 40–108; Califano, *Johnson*, 209–23, quote at 214; *Public Papers, Johnson, 1967*, II: 714–33.

11. Clark quote in Small, *Johnson, Nixon*, 10; Zaroulis and Sullivan, *Who Spoke Up?*, 133–35, 137; Sale, *SDS*, 369–74, 377–79; Gitlin, *Sixties*, 249–56; Rostow to Johnson, Dec. 7, 1967, National Security Vietnam File, Clark to Johnson,

Oct. 3, Yeagley to Christopher, Oct. 3, Permit, Oct. 19, Dept. of Defense News Release, Oct. 25, 1967, Christopher Papers, Forces Available in the Area, Oct. 19, Califano to Johnson, Oct. 21, Johnson to Clark, Oct. 21, 1967, Nimetz Papers, McDonough to Clark, Oct. 20, Clark to Johnson, Oct. 21, Brookhart to Kossack, Nov. 8, Dept. of Justice Release, Nov. 13, Pollak to Clark, Nov. 22, 1967, Clark Papers, David Dellinger, Oral History Interview, 1, 7, 13, 35, all Johnson Library; Norman Mailer, *The Armies of the Night* (New York: Signet, 1968), 108, 118; *New York Times,* Oct. 22, 1967; Shapley, *Promise and Power,* 435–36. DeBenedetti used a figure of 100,000 for the crowd at the Lincoln Memorial, "the largest antiwar protest organized to that time in the history of any capital city in a nation at war." He wrote that 35,000 marched on the Pentagon. "A CIA Analysis of the Anti-Vietnam War Movement: October 1967," *Peace and Change* (Spring 1983): 31; Wells, *War Within,* 192, 197, 213.

12. Clifford, *Counsel,* 454–55; Clark Clifford, Oral History Interview, II-25, Johnson Library.

Chapter 16. Updating the Minimum Wage and Social Security

1. Califano, *Johnson,* 176, 253, 338.
2. Bernstein, *Promises Kept,* 198; *Public Papers, Johnson, 1965,* I: 554; *CQ Almanac, 1965,* 858–61, *1966,* 821–30; Wirtz to Johnson, Jan. 30, 1964, EX LE LA File, Wirtz to Johnson, Aug. 4, 1965, LE HE 8-4 File, O'Brien to Johnson, Aug. 3, Eckstein to Johnson, Aug. 4, Wirtz to Califano, Dec. 14, 1965, Wilson to Johnson, Jan. 14, Ackley to Califano, Jan. 31, Feb. 4, Califano to Johnson, Feb. 9, 23, Connor to Johnson, Feb. 12, Ackley to Johnson, March 8, Wilson to Johnson, March 10, 1966, all Legislative Background Minimum Wage File, (2) Wirtz to Johnson, Feb. 12, 1966, Confidential File, all Johnson Library; *Economic Report of the President, 1963,* 86; Susan Kocin, "Basic Provisions of the 1966 FLSA Amendments," *Monthly Labor Review* (March 1967): 2.
3. Saul Waldman, "OASDI Benefits, Prices, and Wages: 1966 Experience," *Social Security Bulletin* (June 1967): 9–12; Wilbur J. Cohen and Robert M. Ball, "Social Security Amendments of 1967: Summary and Legislative History," *Social Security Bulletin* (Feb. 1968): 3–19; Cohen on Johnson cited in Martha Derthick, *Policymaking for Social Security* (Washington: Brookings, 1979), 342. On July 11, 1966, Califano established a cabinet task force on income maintenance chaired by Gardner Ackley. On September 22 Califano instructed Ackley to add both Social Security and welfare to the subjects covered. The task force report recommended a broad restructuring of the Social Security system and limiting increased benefits to 10 percent. The HEW member, presumably Cohen, dissented sharply. For this reason and because the report was couched in general language, it seems to have had no impact on the legislation the administration proposed. But CEA continued to be concerned about the inflationary impact of the very high benefit increases proposed by HEW, but now Johnson ignored the inflation issue. Califano to Ackley, July 11, Sept. 22, 1966, Summary Report of the Task Force on Income Maintenance, n.d., Duesenberry to Califano, Dec. 7, (2) Revised Social Security Proposal, Cohen to Califano, Dec. 15, 1966, Legislative Background Social Security File, all Johnson Library; *Public Papers, Johnson, 1967,* I: 5, 33; Cohen to Cater, Jan. 12, 13, 1967, Cater Papers, Johnson Library.
4. Schultze to Johnson, March 28, 1967, Califano Papers, Levine to Califano

et al., Aug. 11, Cohen to Johnson, Oct. 17, (2) Califano to Johnson, Dec. 11, (2) Manatos to Johnson, Dec. 13, Cohen to Cater et al., Dec. 19, 1967, EX LE WE File, all Johnson Library; *CQ Almanac, 1967,* 892–916; Frances Fox Pliven and Richard A. Cloward, *Regulating the Poor* (New York: Pantheon, 1971), 320–23. The personal material on Wilbur Cohen, including his letter to Elizabeth Wickenden, is from ch. 15 of the unpublished biography of Cohen by Edward Berkowitz, kindly supplied by the author. Califano, *Johnson,* 245–46; *Public Papers, Johnson, 1968,* I: 14–15.

Chapter 17. Lyndon Johnson, Patron of the Arts

1. Harry McPherson wrote, "He had no apparent interests outside government and politics—not the theater, nor books, music, sports, automobiles, handicrafts, stamp collecting, the study of history, anything that would connect with the curiosities and pastimes of private citizens. Breeding cattle did interest him, but that was arcanum to most people." *A Political Education* (Boston: Little, Brown, 1972), 445.

2. William J. Baumol and William G. Bowen, *Performing Arts—The Economic Dilemma* (New York: Twentieth Century Fund, 1966), chs. 3, 4; Mayer quote from *Bricks, Mortar, and the Performing Arts* (New York: Twentieth Century Fund, 1970), 15, 58–63; *National Directory of the Performing Arts and Civic Centers,* 1975 ed.; Gary O. Larson, *The Reluctant Patron* (Philadelphia: Univ. of Pennsylvania Press, 1983), 132–36; Administrative History of the National Endowment for the Arts, I: 3–4; Becker to Campbell, Nov. 17, 1964, Dept. of the Interior, Solicitor to Secretary, Dec. 20, 1965, both Horsky Papers, all Johnson Library; Arthur M. Schlesinger, Jr., *A Thousand Days* (Boston: Houghton Mifflin, 1965), 729–38, quotes at 730–31; *Public Papers, Kennedy, 1961,* 170, 719–20, *1962,* 846–47; *Public Papers, Johnson, 1963–64,* I: 46–47, 218–19.

3. Larson, *Reluctant Patron,* 154–69; Schlesinger, *Thousand Days,* 733–38; August Heckscher, *The Arts and the National Government,* 88th Cong., 1st sess., Sen. Doc. No. 28 (May 28, 1963); Administrative Histories of the National Endowments for the Arts and for the Humanities, Johnson Library; Livingston Biddle, *Our Government and the Arts* (New York: American Council for the Arts, 1988), ch. 2; *CQ Almanac, 1965,* 621–27; *Public Papers, Johnson, 1965,* II: 1022–23.

4. Barry Hyams, *Hirshhorn: Medici from Brooklyn* (New York: Dutton, 1979), particularly chs. 6, 7; Sophy Burnham, "Sound the Hirshhorn!," and Leroy Aaron, "The Collection," POTOMAC, *Washington Post,* March 19, 1967; Abram Lerner, Introduction, *The Hirshhorn Museum and Sculpture Garden* (New York: Abrams, 1974), quotes at 15, 23, groundbreaking photo at 24; Johnson, *Diary,* 275–76, 307; Hirshhorn to Johnson, May 17, Ripley to Goodwin, July 25, Hirshhorn to Johnson, Sept. 21, 1965, Ripley to Johnson, April 12, Agreement dated the 17th of May, McPherson to Johnson, Oct. 5, 1966, Ripley to Johnson, Oct. 10, 1967, GEN FG 999-20 File, McPherson to Johnson, April 14, July 18, 1966, Ripley to Johnson, Oct. 10, 1967, Pierson to Johnson, Oct. 23, McPherson to Schultze, Oct. 25, Hughes to McPherson, Nov. 1, Mahon to Ripley, Nov. 1, 1967, Ripley to McPherson, March 14, 1968, McPherson Papers, all Johnson Library.

5. Warren to Johnson, Oct. 26, Cater to Johnson, Oct. 30, 31, 1967, Cater Papers, Johnson Library; *Public Papers, Johnson, 1967,* II: 993–94; Hyams, *Hirshhorn,* 198–99.

6. Irving Bernstein, *The Economics of Television Film Production and Distribution* (Hollywood: Screen Actors Guild, 1960), chs. 1, 2; John Walker Powell, *Channels of Learning* (Washington: Public Affairs, 1962); John W. Macy, Jr., *To Irrigate a Wasteland* (Berkeley: Univ. of California Press, 1974), ch. 1; Carnegie Commission on Educational Television, *Public Television: A Program for Action* (New York: Bantam, 1967), 105–12; *Ford Foundation Activities in Noncommercial Broadcasting, 1951–1976,* 1–12.

7. Robert M. Pepper, *The Formation of the Public Broadcasting Service* (New York: Arno, 1979), 48–51; *Public Television: A Program for Action,* ch. 3; Cater to Johnson, May 19, June 24, Pifer to Johnson, Oct. 28, 1965, Jennis to Meier, Jan. 30, Surrey to Cater, Feb. 7, Rommell to Cater, Feb. 7, Gardner to Cater, Feb. 10, Hughes to Califano and Cater, Feb. 25, Califano to Johnson, Feb. 27, Cater to Johnson, Feb. 28, 1967, Legislative Background Public Broadcasting File, Cater to Johnson, Jan. 25, 1967, Cater Papers, all Johnson Library; *Public Papers, Johnson, 1967,* I: 250–51.

8. *CQ Almanac, 1967,* 1042–50; *Public Papers, Johnson, 1967,* II: 995–98; Califano to Johnson, Nov. 7, 1967, Gaither to Califano, Jan. 3, 1968, Report of the Task Force on Financing Public Broadcasting, n.d., Gaither Papers, Cater to Johnson, Feb. 16, Zwick to Johnson, March 5, 1968, Legislative Background Public Broadcasting File, all Johnson Library; Bruce McKay, "Financing: Problem or Symptom?," in Douglass Cater and M. J. Nyhan, eds., *The Future of Public Broadcasting* (New York: Praeger, 1976), 148; John Macy's book, *To Irrigate a Wasteland,* is a chamber of financial horrors; Marilyn Lashley, *Public Television* (New York: Greenwood, 1992), 78; Pepper in *Formation of Public Broadcasting Service* traces the negotiations leading to the creation of PBS.

9. Administrative History of the National Endowment for the Arts, Supp. to the History, 6, Johnson Library.

Chapter 18. Model Cities

1. Robert C. Wood, Oral History Interview, 1–11, quotes at 5–6, 8, 11; Report of the Task Force on Metropolitan and Urban Problems, Nov. 30, 1964, quotes at i, 1, 2, 39, Legislative Background Model Cities File, both Johnson Library; *Public Papers, Johnson, 1965,* I: 231–40.

2. Reuther to Johnson, May 13, Haar to Goodwin, June 9, Califano to Johnson, Oct. 9, 13, Meeting of Oct. 15, McPherson to Johnson, Dec. 9, Gordon to Task Force, Dec. 20, 1965, all Legislative Background Model Cities File, Johnson Library; the ordeal of the Weaver appointment as secretary of HUD, convoluted, cruel, and funny, is told by Califano, *Johnson,* 125–30. Wood, Oral History Interview, 3, 18–23, Kermit Gordon, Oral History Interview, IV-13, both Johnson Library; the 1965 task force report is appendix 2 in Charles M. Haar, *Between the Idea and the Reality* (Boston: Little, Brown, 1975), quote at 58; Bernard J. Frieden and Marshall Kaplan, *The Politics of Neglect* (Cambridge: MIT Press, 1975), 36–48; Edward C. Banfield, "Making a New Federal Program: Model Cities, 1964–1968," in Allan P. Sindler, ed., *Policy and Politics in America* (Boston: Little, Brown, 1973), 135–36. Senator Ribicoff, who had plenty of street smarts, was able to attend only the last task force meeting. But he was interviewed by staff member Chester Rapkin. Among Ribicoff's suggestions: "The program could not succeed

unless it involved City Hall, labor, civil rights, employment and the poor. He said if we don't have City Hall we don't have housing, schools and the police, and without these three essential elements success would be severely curtailed. He also feels that the building trades council should be involved directly through the training of people who would initially work on the projects and later be trained to become construction workers. He felt strongly that the poor should be involved even if it costs more and urged that work relief be substituted for subventions wherever possible. He asked us to look into Defense Department contracts with industry which pay for 90 days of training and suggested that we might employ a similar device for slum people. He was concerned about air pollution which he felt was easier to handle than water problems which are essentially state or multi-state oriented. He also proposed that a greater utilization of private funds and capital, particularly from insurance companies and banks, be encouraged by guarantees. I was delighted to see that he felt very strongly about beauty in the cities and urged that whatever reconstruction take place respect a variety of architectural styles and, in fact, the demonstrations themselves could involve architects from all over the world. This was important not only for new construction but also to preserve the traditions of America. . . ." Rapkin to Wood, Nov. 24, 1965, Legislative Background Model Cities File, Johnson Library.

3. Haar, *Idea and Reality*, ch. 3; Joseph A. Califano, Jr., Oral History Interview, 36–37, Weaver to Califano, May 24, Wilson to Johnson, May 30, Califano to Johnson, June 6, Spector to Wilson, Sept. 12, 1966, Legislative Background Model Cities File, Weaver to Califano, Aug. 9, 1966, Manatos Papers, all Johnson Library; Califano, *Johnson*, 133, 135; Fulbright's speech is in the *Cong. Record,* Aug. 19, 1966; *CQ Almanac, 1966,* 210–30.

4. Haar, *Idea and Reality*, quote at 143; Administrative History of the Department of Housing and Urban Development, vol. I, pt. 1, ch. 5; Brief Summary, Comprehensive City Demonstration Programs, Oct. 20, 1966, Legislative Background Model Cities File, Califano to Johnson, July 7, 10, 1967, March 4, 1968, Model Cities Applications, Aug. 16, 1968, Ximinez to Watson, Aug. 17, 1967, Janis to Califano, Sept. 16, 1968, all Califano Papers, Model Cities Program, Farr to Califano, Oct. 7, 1968, Wirtz to Califano, Oct. 7, 1968, Task Force Subject File, all Johnson Library; Frieden and Kaplan, *Politics of Neglect,* 73–87, app. A.

5. Johnson, *Vantage Point,* 330; Banfield, "Making a New Federal Program," 155; Rufus P. Browning, Dale Rogers Marshall, and David H. Tabb, *Protest Is Not Enough* (Berkeley: Univ. of California Press, 1984), 208–14.

Chapter 19. The Collapse of the Johnson Presidency

1. John W. Gardner, II-7-18, Lawrence F. O'Brien, XXI-48, both Oral History Interviews, Johnson Library; Johnson, *Diary,* 620–24; Nancy Zaroulis and Gerald Sullivan, *Who Spoke Up?* (Garden City: Doubleday, 1984), 149–50; Arthur M. Schlesinger, Jr., *Robert Kennedy and His Times* (Boston: Houghton Mifflin, 1978), 825; Clifford, *Counsel,* 465–67; Lloyd M. Bucher, *My Story* (Garden City: Doubleday, 1970); Trevor Armbrister, *A Matter of Accountability* (New York: Coward-McCann, 1970), v, 395.

2. Two useful general works on Tet are Don Oberdorfer, *Tet!* (Garden City: Doubleday, 1971), on the war in Vietnam, and Herbert Y. Schandler, *The Un-*

making of a President (Princeton: Princeton Univ. Press, 1977), on the impact of Tet on Washington, quotes at ix, U.S. Military Academy textbook at 75, Cronkite at 197; Bundy quote in Tom Wells, *The War Within* (Berkeley: Univ. of California Press, 1994), 242. See also Stanley Karnow, *Vietnam: A History* (New York: Penguin, 1991), 536–42, 541, 552–55; Ronald H. Spector, *After Tet* (New York: Free Press, 1993), 117–34; Kearns, *Johnson*, 336–37; Califano, *Johnson*, 262–64; Deborah Shapley, *Promise and Power* (Boston: Little, Brown, 1993), 443–44, 448–52, 476, 485. For the first three months of 1968 in Washington the decisive work is Clifford, *Counsel*, chs. 27, 28. Also: Schlesinger, *Robert Kennedy*, Rowe quote at 866; Walter Isaacson and Evan Thomas, *The Wise Men* (New York: Simon & Schuster, 1986), 681–95, 699.

3. O'Brien, XXI-15-16, 19, 21, 25–26, 32–34, 51–54, 55, 57, John P. Roche, I-60, both Oral History Interviews, O'Brien to Johnson, Mar. 27, 1968, Confidential File, all Johnson Library; Lewis Chester, Godfrey Hodgson, and Bruce Page, *An American Melodrama: The Presidential Campaign of 1968* (New York: Viking, 1969), Act 3, ch. 1; William H. Chafe, *Never Stop Running* (New York: Basic, 1993), 104–8, ch. 4; Theodore H. White, *The Making of the President, 1968* (New York: Atheneum, 1969), ch. 3, quote at 120; Eugene J. McCarthy, *The Year of the People* (Garden City: Doubleday, 1969), 77, ch. 6; Califano, *Johnson*, quote at 266.

4. Johnson, *Vantage Point*, ch. 18; Clifford, *Counsel*, 524–26; Johnson, *Diary*, 633–47; Califano, *Johnson*, 266–69; Isaacson and Thomas, *Wise Men*, 695; White, *Making of President, 1968*, 114, 123; Kearns, *Johnson*, 7, 8, 32, 270–73, 312–17, 342. On March 12, 1968, Bill Moyers told Schlesinger that Johnson was sealed off from reality, that all criticism was written off as personal or political hostility. Moyers used the word "paranoid." Because of his personal debt to Johnson, Moyers said he had taken a long time to reach this conclusion. He thought that "four more years of Johnson would be ruinous for the country." Schlesinger, *Robert Kennedy*, 848. The Johnson-Mansfield conversation on March 27 is in Schandler, *Unmaking a President*, 271–72. The March 31, 1968, speech is in *Public Papers, Johnson, 1968*, I: 469–76.

5. Spector, *After Tet*, xvi-ii, 24–25.

6. The study of the King assassination is Gerold Frank, *An American Death* (Garden City: Doubleday, 1972), quotes at 14, 289, 382. See also David J. Garrow, *Bearing the Cross* (New York: Morrow, 1986), ch. 11, and Stephen B. Oates, *Let the Trumpet Sound* (New York: Norton, 1982), pt. 10. Califano, *Johnson*, ch. 17, quote at 280; Yeagley to Attorney General, April 9, 1968, Report of the Chicago Riot Study Committee, Aug. 1, 1968, for police and military riot preparations, see S.L. to Attorney General with attachment on Los Angeles plan, *New York Times*, March 2, 1968, all Clark Papers, Johnson Library; the Dohrn incident is from Todd Gitlin, *The Sixties* (New York: Bantam, 1987), 306. Joseph A. Califano, Jr., Oral History Interview, LXII-9-14, Johnson Library. *CQ Almanac, 1968*, 152–69, quote at 166; Hugh Davis Graham, *The Civil Rights Era* (New York: Oxford Univ. Press, 1990), 270–73; Elizabeth D. Huttman, ed., *Urban Housing: Segregation of Minorities in Western Europe and the United States* (Durham: Duke Univ. Press, 1991), chs. 14, 19; W. Dennis Keating, *The Suburban Racial Dilemma* (Philadelphia: Temple Univ. Press, 1944), chs. 12, 13; Robert W. Lake, *The New Suburbanites* (New Brunswick: Rutgers Univ. Press, 1981), ch. 10.

7. Schlesinger, *Robert Kennedy*, chs. 37–40, Jacqueline Kennedy quote at 857, RFK on Oswald at 877, Gary quote at 900; Jules Witcover, *85 Days: The Last Campaign of Robert Kennedy* (New York: Putnam, 1969); White, *Making of Presi-*

dent, 1968, ch. 6; Jack Newfield, *Robert Kennedy: A Memoir* (New York: Dutton, 1969); David Halberstam, *The Unfinished Odyssey of Robert Kennedy* (New York: Random House, 1968); Chester et al., *American Melodrama,* Acts 4, 7.

8. Robert Blair Kaiser, *"RFK Must Die!": A History of the Robert Kennedy Assassination and Its Aftermath* (New York: Dutton, 1970). The appendices are particularly interesting—the victims, the trajectories of the eight bullets, Sirhan's notebooks, and Senator Edward Kennedy's plea for mercy.

9. Stephen E. Ambrose, *Nixon* (New York: Simon and Schuster, 1989), II: quote at 133, Nixon watching RFK announce at 145; Jules W. Witcover, *The Resurrection of Richard Nixon* (New York: Putnam, 1970), 14–22; David S. Broder, "Election of 1960," in A. M. Schlesinger, Jr., F. L. Israel, and W. P. Hansen, eds., *History of American Presidential Elections, 1789–1968* (New York: Chelsea, 1985), IX: 3706; Chester et al., *American Melodrama,* Acts 5, 7, 9, Graves quote at 265, on Wallace at 294; White, *Making of the President, 1968,* 149.

10. Albert Eisele, *Almost to the Presidency* (Blue Earth: Piper, 1972), chs. 16–18, quotes at 322, 328, 336, 337, 364, 365; O'Brien, Oral History Interview, XXIII-35-38, 40, 44, 50, 56, 66, XXIV-5, 12, 15, 19–23, 51, 52, Johnson Library; *Public Papers, Johnson, 1968–69,* 896, 903; Johnson, *Vantage Point,* 510; the definitive study of the Chicago convention riot is Daniel Walker, *Rights in Conflict, Convention Week in Chicago, August 25–29, 1968* (New York: Dutton, 1968), quotes at 163, 255; Broder, "Election of 1968," 3705, 3737, 3739; Chester et al., *American Melodrama,* 585; George W. Ball, *The Past Has Another Pattern* (New York: Norton, 1982), 446, 447; Humphrey's Salt Lake City speech is in Schlesinger et al., eds., *Presidential Elections,* IX: 3857–64; Clifford, *Counsel,* 563, 572, 581, 583; Ambrose, *Nixon,* II: 207, 215; James H. Rowe, Jr., Oral History Interview, IV-20-21, Johnson Library; William L. Bundy letter to *New York Times,* June 13, 1991; Carl Solberg, *Hubert Humphrey* (New York: Norton, 1984), ch. 33, quote at 402; William Safire, *Before the Fall* (Garden City: Doubleday, 1975), 88; Witcover, *Resurrection,* 444.

Chapter 20. Guns or Butter

1. Donald Kagan, *Pericles of Athens and the Birth of Greek Democracy* (London: Secker & Warburg, 1990), quotes at 2, 243. In this splendid book Professor Kagan draws many comparisons between Pericles and prominent twentieth-century European and American political leaders. Oddly, Lyndon Johnson is not among them.

2. William Safire, *Safire's New Political Dictionary* (New York: Random House, 1993), 308–9; Richard Goodwin, *Remembering America* (Boston: Little, Brown, 1988), 417–18; Stephen Skowronek, *The Politics Presidents Make* (Cambridge: Belknap, 1993); Lawrence F. O'Brien and Joseph A. Califano, Jr., Final Report to President Lyndon B. Johnson on the 89th Congress, Oct. 24, 1966, Califano Papers, McPherson to Johnson, Nov. 2, 1965, McPherson Papers, Johnson to Mansfield, Oct. 22, 1965, Wilson Papers, all Johnson Library; *CQ Almanac, 1964–1968,* the section in each volume on the Johnson boxscore is the source for the quotes; the Cohen yardstick is in Bernstein, *Promises Kept,* 292–93; Johnson, *Vantage Point,* 324; Kearns, *Johnson,* 249; Califano, *Johnson,* 180.

3. Harry G. Summers, Jr., *On Strategy* (Novato: Presidio, 1982), 1; Thomas C. Thayer, *War Without Fronts* (Boulder: Westview, 1985), 103–13, 257; Stanley Karnow, *Vietnam: A History* (New York: Penguin, 1991), 11; Neil Sheehan, *Two Cities: Hanoi and Saigon* (London: Jonathan Cape, 1992) 35, 59. No one knows the number of Vietnamese casualties. In 1989, when Sheehan was in Hanoi, he was told that 3 million, North and South, combatants and civilians, were thought to have perished. Hundreds of thousands were missing. There, evidently, was no estimate of those maimed. Jonathan Shay, *Achilles in Vietnam* (New York: Atheneum, 1994), quote at 78–79; Robert Warren Stevens, *Vain Hopes, Grim Realities* (New York: New Viewpoints, 1976), especially ch. 14; Stockdale quote, Los Angeles *Times,* Aug. 17, 1994; Robert Jay Lifton, *Home from the War* (New York: Simon and Schuster, 1973), 449–50; for Johnson's pre-1965 statements on Vietnam, see Arthur M. Schlesinger, Jr., *The Bitter Heritage* (Boston: Houghton Mifflin, 1966), 9, 21, 28–29, 50; *Pentagon Papers,* Gravel Edition, III: 702–3; for a comprehensive review of the impact of the war on Americans both at home and in Vietnam, see Myra McPherson, *Long Time Passing* (Garden City: Doubleday, 1984); David Wise, *The Politics of Lying* (New York: Random House, 1973), 22–23, 48, 342. Galbraith to Califano, Dec. 16, 1966, Legislative Background Tax Increase File, Johnson Library. Horace Busby was one of several presidential aides who urged Johnson to explain the war to the American people. In a memorandum on July 21, 1965, as the build-up was getting under way, he pointed out that the reporting of the bombings was all "stark, jarring." The important question was not *what* the U.S. was doing but *"why* it is being done." He recommended showing the American people that it was in their *"self-interest"* to take over South Vietnam. Busby thought the U.S. needed a spokesman like Churchill or Roosevelt. Busby to Johnson, July 21, 1965, Vietnam Reference File, Johnson Library.

4. George Reedy, *Lyndon B. Johnson: A Memoir* (New York: Andrews and McMeel, 1982), x, xiii, 37, 53, 58, 77, 99, 142, 159; Charles Mohr Memorandum, May 5, 1965, Arthur Krock Papers, Princeton University; on Johnson's depression, Robert A. Caro, *The Path to Glory* (New York: Random House, 1981), 136, 147, 172, 196–97, 228; womanizing quote from Robert Dallek, *Lone Star Rising* (New York: Oxford Univ. Press, 1991), 189, and Reedy to author, June 9, 1994; Goodwin, *Remembering America,* ch. 21, quote at 393; Kearns, *Johnson,* ch. 11; Lee C. White, Oral History Interview, I-5, Douglas Cater, Oral History Interview, 28; Harry McPherson, Oral History Interview, III-1, 3, 30–31, Joseph A. Califano, Jr., Oral History Interview, I-37, II-16, IV-46, XXI-14, LVII-15, all Johnson Library; Jack Valenti, *A Very Human President* (New York: Norton, 1975), 97, 251–52n. A brief comment about the word *hubris,* which is used several times in this chapter: It is Greek in origin; is extremely old, having been used 31 times by Homer; is sometimes spelled *hybris;* and was an important concept in ancient Greek politics and literature. Here it receives the meaning that prevails currently in Britain and the U.S.—arrogance combined with contempt for an adversary, leading to the defeat of the one who is excessively arrogant. The Greeks often linked it to the gods, who were insulted by hubris and destroyed the arrogant person or state. They used the word several ways and the core meaning is somewhat different from current usage: an assault on the honor of another, causing shame, anger, and revenge. See. N. R. E. Fisher, *Hybris: A Study in the Values of Honour and Shame in Ancient Greece* (Warminster, Eng.: Aris & Phillips, 1992).

Index